ANNA COMNENA

ANNA COMNENA

ANNA COMNENA

A STUDY

by

GEORGINA BUCKLER

OXFORD
AT THE CLARENDON PRESS

OXFORD
UNIVERSITY PRESS

Great Clarendon Street, Oxford OX2 6DP

Oxford University Press is a department of the University of Oxford.
It furthers the University's objective of excellence in research, scholarship,
and education by publishing worldwide in

Oxford New York

Athens Auckland Bangkok Bogotá Buenos Aires Calcutta
Cape Town Chennai Dar es Salaam Delhi Florence Hong Kong Istanbul
Karachi Kuala Lumpur Madrid Melbourne Mexico City Mumbai
Nairobi Paris São Paulo Singapore Taipei Tokyo Toronto Warsaw

with associated companies in Berlin Ibadan

Oxford is a registered trade mark of Oxford University Press
in the UK and in certain other countries

Published in the United States
by Oxford University Press Inc., New York

© Oxford University Press 1929

British Library Cataloguing in Publication Data

Data available

ISBN 0-19-821471-5

1 3 5 7 9 10 8 6 4 2

Printed in Great Britain
on acid-free paper by
Biddles Ltd., Guildford and King's Lynn

PREFACE

THE *Alexias* affords an insight not only into the career of the Emperor Alexius I and the public events of his time, but also into the mental outlook of his daughter who wrote it. In publishing this study of her moral and intellectual standards, I wish especially to thank three among the many scholars who have kindly helped me: first, Sir W. M. Ramsay, who suggested the idea; secondly, Professor R. M. Dawkins, whose supervision made the work possible; and thirdly, my husband, without whose constant aid and encouragement the writing would never have been carried through.

G. G. B.

OXFORD,
March 1929.

TABLE OF CONTENTS

I. INTRODUCTION

II. ANNA AS A PERSONALITY

III. ANNA AS A CHARACTER

THE THREE THEOLOGICAL VIRTUES:

THE FOUR CARDINAL VIRTUES:

IV. ANNA AND EDUCATION

V. ANNA AS HISTORIAN

VI. ANNA AS WRITER

I. INTRODUCTION

1. GENERAL REMARKS

IT is a well-accepted fact that Byzantine history has never, till within the last forty or fifty years, received at the hand of historians either adequate or just treatment. When Oman wrote his *Byzantine Empire* in 1892 for the *Story of the Nations* series, he thought it necessary to state that he was endeavouring 'to tell the story of Byzantium in the spirit of Finlay and Bury, not in that of Gibbon'. It is indeed to Gibbon's scorn of the Eastern Empire and all its works, as outlined in Chapter XLVIII of his *Decline and Fall*, that most English readers owe their knowledge, or rather ignorance, of that important period covering over a thousand years. He wrote of its annals as a 'tedious and uniform tale of weakness and misery', and for nearly a century even scholars were willing to take those same annals at his valuation. Krumbacher, in his *Geschichte der byzantinischen Litteratur*,[1] says that for a long time literature 'dem Byzantismus meist feindselig gegenüberstand'. Diehl, in his *Études Byzantines*, has traced the growing interest in the subject, with the *Byzantinische Zeitschrift* (started 1892) taking and keeping the lead. But even now, it may fairly be claimed that Byzantine writers have not yet attained to their proper place in the world of letters. To them and to their careful study we owe for one thing the preservation of classical texts, whose dispersal in 1453 has been reckoned as a chief cause of the Renaissance. But for them again the history of much of the Middle Ages would be a blank. Yet many well-educated people would find it hard to enumerate even a few of the historians, grammarians, theologians, and poets of the Eastern Empire.

In the case of the special subject in hand, most Englishmen would be driven to confess that their notion of Anna Comnena was taken from Gibbon or from Scott's *Count Robert of Paris*. No one has yet been found to translate her fifteen books into our language.[2] The Latin version of Migne's *Patrologia Graeca* is often harder, and that in the *Corpus Scriptorum Historiae Byzantinae* always duller, than the Greek original. The only French rendering, done by Cousin, Président de la Cour des Monnaies to Louis XIV, and appreciatively read, it is interesting to note, by Madame de Sévigné, dates from 1675, and is

---

[1] 2nd ed., p. 14.
[2] This want has, since we went to press, been supplied by Dr. Elizabeth Dawes. (*The Alexiad*, Kegan Paul, London, 1928.)

as we might expect full of inaccuracies. In German we have a very much condensed translation in the great Schiller's *Allgemeine Sammlung historischer Mémoires vom 12ᵗᵉⁿ Jahrhundert bis auf die neuesten Zeiten*. Italy has the work of G. Rossi, published in 1849, and Denmark that of Hovgaard, published in 1879–82. But England so far has nothing, not even studies on her and her work such as those of E. Oster[1] and F. Chalandon.[2]

Yet in herself and her times and her writings Anna Comnena is surely one of the most interesting figures known to us. If Sappho excites our admiration as the first woman poet, Anna is the first woman historian. If the First Crusade has a perennial charm for our minds, in her *Alexias* we can compare the only contemporary Greek account of it with those of the Latin Chroniclers. If we once realize that the remarkable dynasty of the Comneni kept the Eastern Empire from dissolution during over 100 years, where else can we get such a detailed picture of its foundation? As Diehl has truly said, in his *Figures Byzantines*, 'Pour la psychologie du personnage l'Alexiade demeure un document de première importance, et d'une façon plus générale c'est un livre absolument remarquable'.[3] Remarkable indeed, when we think of Anna's contemporaries. The 'leaders of the pilgrims', as she calls the Crusading Counts, could only make their mark on the treaty between Alexius and Bohemund, while their names had to be 'written in by the hand of the Bishop of Amalfi dear to God'.[4] Yet at the same period Anna Comnena could quote Homer and the Bible copiously and appositely, draw telling analogies from Greek history true or mythical, and handle terms of theological philosophy with at least perfect assurance. She herself in her Preface makes this claim: 'I desire to expound in this my writing the deeds of my father . . . being not unversed in letters, not unpractised in rhetoric, . . . having well mastered the rules of Aristotle and the dialogues of Plato, and having furnished my mind with the quadrivium of sciences' (i.e. Arithmetic, Geometry, Astronomy, Music). Her military descriptions may show inadequate technical knowledge; possibly, as is suggested by the late Miss A. Gardner in an unpublished paper on 'Anna Comnena and her Surroundings', they may be coloured by Homeric recollections of the Trojan War. Yet Oman, in his *Art of War*,[5] states that she ' has, for a lady, a very fair grasp of things military', and to the ordinary reader her battles are usually vivid and always intel-

---

[1] *Anna Komnena*, Rastatt, 1868–71. [2] *Alexis Iᵉʳ Comnène*, Paris, 1900.
[3] Sér. II, p. 52. [4] XIII. 12, p. 416.
[5] 2nd ed., Vol. I, p. 226 note 1.

ligible; while her explanations as to liquid fire and the cross-bow are among the *loci classici* for the two subjects. Her chrono-logy is not impeccable, but it compares favourably with that of much later writers, even Froissart. We may dismiss many of her statements in religious matters as prejudiced or super-stitious, but it demands some effort even now to wrestle as she does with Hypostasis and Henosis, or with the false doc-trines of Monophysites and Bogomiles. Modern doctors might not consider her competent to act as 'umpire' in their discus-sions over diagnosis and treatment, yet one of them, Dr. H. E. Counsell, has said, in a letter which he has given kind permission to quote, 'The cause of Alexius' death is perfectly evident from the wonderfully graphic account of his daughter'.

Western Europe in Anna's day was torn with fighting and dark with ignorance. When we read the *Alexias* we find our-selves in a pleasant, cultured, and courteous world, where Court ceremonial is stately yet not excessive, where family affection is at least in theory greatly esteemed, and where, though games and sports and banquets have their place and fighting is often unfortunately necessary, yet learning and literature are man's truest and highest interests. It is a world we feel where, if only the wicked would cease from troubling by conspiracies and wars, rest of a very dignified and refined kind might be achieved. The writings of the Fathers form the Empress's chief delight; Nicephorus Bryennius 'my Caesar' is as great in learning as in charm, and Alexius turns with gusto from material strife to spiritual, from fighting Turks or Franks to confuting heretics out of 'the Sacred Books'. Anna scorns as 'barbarians' all other nations but her own; had she not good cause?[1]

2. WRITINGS OF THE COMNENI

WE can now turn to the works which this learned princess has left behind her. First we have a poem, possibly even five, of indifferent merit. Du Cange[2] quotes in full a verse of Nicolas Callicles put, so the Frenchman thought, into the mouth of Anna about a reliquary, but Leo Sternbach states with un-doubted correctness that the poem purports to come from Anna's sister Eudocia, and that the name 'Anna' in the heading in the edition used by Du Cange is due to a confusion arising

[1] Since this was written, a charming little sketch of Anna and her times by Naomi Mitchison has appeared in the *Representative Women* series. (*Anna Comnena*; G. Howe, London, 1928.)

[2] Note on *Alex.* XV. 11, p. 496 c.

from the fact that the elder sister gave the cross to the younger. In editing thirty-three poems of Callicles, Sternbach gives [1] this as I, and in his Appendix to III which we shall discuss later, he says that in the Codex Laurentianus [2] this III is immediately preceded by a poem of Anna Comnena's to the Logos, headed τῆς σοφωτάτης πορφυρογεννήτου καὶ Κομνηνῆς *Ἄννης καισαρί[σσης]* εἰς τὸν Χριστόν. This Sternbach publishes for the first time:

Ὦ πῶς ἄναρχον ὄντα τὴν φύσιν, Λόγε,
ὁ ζωγράφος γράφειν σε τολμᾷ παιδίον,
καὶ τὴν κάτω σύμπηξιν ἐμφαίνων ἅμα
πρὸς τὴν ἄνω πέμπει με σὺν τρόμῳ βλέπειν,
ἐγὼ δὲ φρίττω μὴ σθένουσα προσβλέπειν.
ὦ πῶς ἀμήτωρ ὤν, ἄναρχος τὴν φύσιν,
ὤφθης ἀπάτωρ ἐν χρόνοις τοῖς ἐσχάτοις.
καὶ σὺ τὸ διπλοῦν ἐκπεπληγμένος τόκου,
ζωγράφε, γράφε, μηδὲ διστάσῃς ὅλως·
ἀσυγχύτως σώζει γὰρ ἄμφω τὰς φύσεις.

The play upon words and love of antithesis, shown in the κάτω and ἄνω, and the ἀμήτωρ and ἀπάτωρ, remind us of various passages in the *Alexias*. The idea of trembling before divine mysteries is the same as when Anna asks her mother how she dares read the works of the Fathers, so sublime as to bewilder the mind, adding: 'I indeed tremble, and dare not catch at these matters with the tips of my ears.'[3] And finally the line about the two natures of Christ fits in with the passage about Hypostasis and Henosis in the episode of Nilus.[4] We may reasonably accept the poem as genuine, merely noting that its style is the stereotyped style of Byzantine hymns, and shows the usual indifference of the age to quantity and caesura.[5]

Two seals of Anna Comnena have come down to us, and been published by Gustave Schlumberger. The inscriptions, fairly to be described as doggerel, may be by the princess herself, though neither the words nor the sentiments have anything specially characteristic. The first is merely[6]

Κομνηνοδουκῶν ἐκ γένους σφραγὶς Ἄννης.

[1] Rosprawy Akad. Umiejet. wydzial filol. (Krakow) Ser. II. XXI, 1903, p. 360.
[2] Plut. V, n. 10, s. xiv, f. 177ʳ. See p. 8, note 2, below.
[3] V. 9, p. 147.　　　　　　　　　　　　　[4] X. 1; see pp. 325–29 below.
[5] The following is a rough translation: 'O how does the artist dare to depict as a little boy Thee, O Word, eternal in Thy nature, and while showing the form below sends me to look with trembling on that above, whereas I shudder unable to gaze! O how wast Thou, motherless and eternal in Thy nature, seen fatherless in the latter times! And do thou, O artist, represent in amazement the duality of the child, neither be in doubt at all, for He preserves both natures unconfused.
[6] *Rev. études grecques*, VII, 1894, p. 331, No. 129. For the first word cf. Callicles, Poem XXIII.

The second[1] displays the conventional reverence mentioned above:

> Δι' εὐλάβειαν οὐ φέρει θείους τύπους
> "Αννης Κομνηνῆς ἡ σφραγὶς ἀλλὰ στίχους.

Finally, we find ascribed to Anna without very much evidence an inscription on a reliquary presumably taken to France after 1204 from the Church of St. John the Baptist in Constantinople, and existing in Du Cange's day at Château-dun.[2] This reliquary was a gilded bronze hand containing a wrist-bone of 'The Forerunner', probably much like that still shown at St. Jean du Doigt in Brittany. J. Ebersolt[3] says, 'Cet os avait été détaché par les Byzantins de la main rapportée d'Antioche à Constantinople sous le règne de Constantin VII'. The rest of the hand, the right one according to Du Cange, has a dubious history. Russian pilgrims profess to have seen it in Constantinople in the fourteenth and fifteenth centuries, and it is said to have subsequently found its way to Rhodes, Malta, and Russia,[4] yet according to Du Cange[5] it was given in 1263 to the Abbey of Cîteaux. This is however irrelevant to our subject; the only thing that need now be said is that the case containing this hand bore a verse inscription, to tell how Constantine had rescued it from the barbarians and enshrined it, and how it would for ever protect the Empire. This is a far more ambitious poetical effort than the six lines which, according to Du Cange, were inscribed round the wrist of the gilded hand of bronze covering the fragment now under consideration. These six lines are in the form of a dialogue between the spectator and the reliquary as to what the latter contains.

> Ὁ καρπὸς ὀστοῦν ἡ δὲ χεὶρ χρυσῆ· πόθεν ;—
> ἐκ τῆς ἐρήμου καρπὸς ἐκ Παλαιστίνης.—
> χρυσῆ παλαιστὴ χρυσοδάκτυλος ξένον.—
> ὀστοῦν ὁ καρπὸς ἐκ φυτοῦ τοῦ Προδρόμου,
> τὴν χεῖρα δ' ὠργάνωσε τέχνη καὶ πόθος
> "Αννης ἀνάσσης ἐκγόνου τῆς πορφύρας.

'The wrist (καρπός) is of bone, the hand of gold; whence is it?'—
'It is fruit (καρπός) of the desert from Palestine.'—
'The golden palm (παλαιστή) with fingers of gold is a strange thing.'—
'The wrist is bone from the body of the Forerunner,
But the hand was wrought by the skill and the love
Of the lady Anna, child of the purple.'

---

[1] *Rev. numism.*, 1905, pp. 339–40, No. 254 ; *Sigillographie de l'Emp. byzantin*, p. 641, No. 9 ; = *Anth. Pal.* III (Cougny, 1890) p. 335, No. 271.
[2] *Anth. Pal.* III (Cougny) No. 416, with note on p. 389; = *C. I. G.* 8719.
[3] *Sanctuaires de Byzance*, p. 134.
[4] *Ibid.*, p. 80, note 4.　　　　　　　　[5] *Ibid.*, p. 134, note 10.

The three puns, one on καρπός as both 'wrist' and 'fruit', one on Ἄννη and ἀνάσσης, and one on παλαιστή 'palm of the hand' and Παλαιστίνη, baffle translation, but these same puns and the self-glorification with which the enshrining of the relic is ascribed to the 'art and love of the lady Anna', offspring 'of the purple', are not incongruous with the literary methods of Anna Comnena. Still, at a time when numberless poetasters wrote poems to order in the name of their employers,[1] and in a matter where as we have seen verse inscriptions were a common feature, one is loath to ascribe such a mediocre specimen as this to the pen of a first-rate historian.[2]

Before we turn to her prose we may remark in passing that, in such versifying as she may have done, Anna Comnena had the support, so to speak, of her father and her third brother Isaac. Alexius has left a certain amount of prose such as novels, golden bulls, theological documents, and letters, which we will not consider here.[3] But his two poems of exhortation to his son John merit attention.[4] The first is of 420 lines, the second (unfinished) of 81, and if we feel surprise that Anna never mentions them, we must remember that she hated John and everything to do with him, and may even quite possibly never have seen them. Composing iambics had been since the tenth century an essential part of rhetorical education at Constantinople, and Alexius might well have written these. As to form they are in no way remarkable, and are neither more nor less poetical than other didactic poetry. As to contents they

---

[1] Thus besides the case of No. I of the Poems of Nic. Callicles, of which we have already spoken, we find No. XXIV headed ὡς ἐκ προσώπου Ἀλεξίου τοῦ βασιλέως. (Sternbach, op. cit.)

[2] The same may be said of the seven lines, following in Cod. Laur. after the ten lines quoted on p. 6 above. They are addressed by a woman to Christ as the Bridegroom of Canticles. J. N. Sola (B. Z. XX, pp. 373–83), correcting Krumbacher (G. B. L. p. 278), who took the seventeen lines as one whole, shows that there are two poems, divided by an almost invisible cross and the words 'τῆς αὐτῆς' on the margin of the manuscript. In spite of this heading it may be doubted whether Anna wrote these seven lines, neither words nor ideas being characteristic of her. It is true that ἀντίληψις = 'help' occurs in Al. XIII. 12, p. 410, but this is in a transcribed document; and though ψηλαφῶσα reminds us of Al. V, 6, p. 141, and IX. 10, p. 266, yet whereas the poem has the word in a mystical sense, Anna uses the cognate adjective and noun literally. The religious eroticism is unparalleled elsewhere in her writings. In short, this dull and artificial composition may easily have been fathered on her by an admirer. Sternbach ascribes it to Callicles, and it figures in his collection of the poems as the III mentioned above.

[3] Twenty-seven novels and golden bulls of Alexius and the titles of four more are published by Zachariae von Lingenthal, Jus Gr. Rom., Vol. III; for his letters see H. Hagenmeyer, Kreuzzugsbriefe. We infer from Ekkehard of Urach and Malaterra that many letters of his to Pope Urban II have been lost. There is a Discourse of his 'Against the Armenians' in Anal. Hierosol. Stach. I. 116, ed. A. Papadopulos-Kerameus.

[4] Μοῦσαι Ἀλεξιάδες Κομνηνιάδες, ed. P. Maas, B. Z. XXII, pp. 348–62.

have, in the midst of many conventional maxims concerning kingship, &c. (one at least drawn from the advice of Basil I to his son Leo[1]) an individual flavour, a shrewdness and vigour of judgement, that makes Maas call them 'ein in der byzantinischen Poesie einzigartiges Dokument'. In such matters as allusions, figures of speech, and rhetorical flourishes they are far simpler than the *Alexias*. Another poem ascribed to the Emperor is considered by Maas, even though the age of the manuscript points to a writer of that date, to be too poor in form and matter for the imperial author. It consists of 100 iambic lines of 12 syllables, headed 'Prayer of the Emperor Alexius', and is contained in a manuscript at the Bodleian.[2]

Anna's brother Isaac, the second Sebastocrator, has been established by E. Kurtz[3] as the object of a most laudatory discourse by Theodore Prodromus, in which he is said to excel alike in war, poetry, and philosophy, and to love books. This was long taken as referring to the Emperor Isaac Comnenus, Anna's great-uncle, but it seems impossible to carry her literary ancestry so far back.[4] The third Isaac, Anna's brother, was well known as a writer. In his *Typikon* of the Cosmosoteira Monastery[5] he, its founder, mentions a book composed by him with 'verses heroic, iambic, and popular (πολιτικοῖς), also letters and descriptions.' Two specimens of his verse have come down to us, one headed Περὶ προνοίας ἀπορημάτων, the other a lament of 41 lines written in exile.[6] It is also safe to attribute to him three prose essays on Homer and a paraphrase of Aristeas,[7] and to conclude that he and not his great-uncle was the object of Prodromus' praise.

Before we turn to Anna's greatest work a few words may be said about a prose document which is at least connected with her. E. Kurtz[8] has published the *Prologue* to her Will, written, as he shows, after the death of Alexius in 1118 and before that of Irene in 1123, and therefore older than the *Alexias*. The title is as follows: πρόλογος εἰς τὴν διάταξιν τῆς καισαρίσσης κυρᾶς "Αννης ὡς παρ' ἐκείνης ἐκδοθείς.

---

[1] P. G. 107, col. liii, περὶ τοῦ κρατεῖν τῶν ἡδονῶν. Cf. *Mous. Alex.* I. 161–4.

[2] *Gr. Misc.* 78, ss. xii–xiii.   [3] 'Unedierte Texte' (*B. Z.* XVI, pp 112–7).

[4] Her own uncle Isaac, we may remark, was φιλολογώτατος, V. 9, p. 148, and capable of arguing with heretics (see also II. 1, p. 44), but we have no evidence that he wrote. He was the first Sebastocrator.

[5] Ch. 108, ed. L. Petit; *Bull. inst. arch. russe de C'ple*, XIII. p. 69. On his love of books see *ibid.* XII, pp. 1–33; *B. Z.* XIV, p. 671; *Rev. ét. gr.* XXXIX, 1926, p. 302.

[6] A. Papadopulos-Kerameus, *Hierosol. Bibl.* IV, ss. 55, 106; Kurtz, *Byz.-neugr. Jahrb.* V, 1926, pp. 44–6. In a later generation Alexius II, great-nephew of Anna, wrote an epitaph on his father (*Neos Hell.* XII, 1915).

[7] E. Kurtz, *op. cit.*, p. 106.   [8] *op. cit.*, pp. 93–101.

Kurtz takes the words as proving that she wrote neither the *Prologue* nor the Will now lost, but entrusted them to some one with legal knowledge, possibly Theodore Prodromus, and merely inspired the whole. It is however difficult to believe that both voice and hands are not of Jacob, and the four concluding words of the title can surely be construed to mean nothing but 'as set forth by her'. The style, wording, and ideas are Anna Comnena's own. We find all the familiar characteristics. The very first sentence has a rhetorical question, the first two paragraphs contain Biblical references, and six others follow later. The same phrase occurs which Anna uses about herself in the first chapter of the Preface to the *Alexias*, γραμμάτων οὐκ ἄμοιρος, as well as the curious word ἐξορχεῖσθαι, 'to say in prelude'. The self-praise follows the usual lines: Ἄννα πορφυρογέννητος γραμμάτων οὐκ ἄμοιρος οὐδὲ γραφῶν ἀμελέτητος (cf. ἀμελετήτως ἔχουσα in the *Alexias*) ἀλλὰ πλεῖστά τε τοῖς θείοις λόγοις ἐμμελετήσασα (though as a matter of fact she usually reserves this last claim to her father, mother, and husband) καὶ μηδὲ τῆς θύραθεν[1] παιδείας ἀποληφθεῖσα. She owes her education as well as all else to her parents, whose virtues and achievements are recounted. Alexius as in the larger work sets up endless trophies, the whole world mourns for him, Irene excels in 'virtue' and is its living model, and Anna's pride in her own exemplary filial affection and obedience makes her appeal to Heaven as witness. Her love for her husband, whose noble σειρά (she uses the same word in this connexion in her Preface, perhaps taking it from his own writing)[2] was as remarkable as his other qualities, and her joy in her 'beautiful and highborn children', combine to lead her to the invariable disclaimer of partiality or conceit. She ends with the statement that even the making of her will was due to her mother's wishes. All this seems so like the style and spirit of the *Alexias* that the ordinary reader will be prepared, *pace* Kurtz, to take the document as from Anna's own pen. The only point of difference is the writer's claim, never made in her larger work, that she had longed for τὸν καθαρώτατόν τε καὶ ἄζυγα βίον and had only married the Bryennius, whom she afterwards learnt to love so dearly, at the express bidding of her parents. With this one exception the *Prologue* is too entirely like the *Alexias* for a different authorship to be admissible.

[1] See p. 180 below, especially note 9.
[2] Pref. 3, p. 3; Nic. Bry., Pref., p. 3.

3. SCOPE OF THE *ALEXIAS*

(*a*) PREFACE AND BOOKS I–VII

THIS brings us at last to the work with which her name is almost exclusively associated, and which throws the literary attainments of her father and brother completely into the shade. In length it exceeds the *History* of Thucydides; in interest it falls short only of the very highest.

In considering it, and the moral and intellectual standards of its writer as therein shown, we need scarcely begin with a detailed account of the fifteen books, such as is given in the previously mentioned studies by Oster and Chalandon. Yet something may perhaps be gained from the briefest possible summary, especially as in passing we may point out various topics to be studied later.

The *Alexias* then is a Life of Alexius Comnenus, who was born we believe in 1056,[1] ascended the Byzantine throne in 1081, and certainly died on August 15, 1118. In her Preface Anna strikes the key-note of her history. Having been 'nurtured and born in the purple' she wishes to hand down to posterity her imperial father's great deeds, 'not meet to be delivered over to silence', and in so doing she is only continuing a work begun by her husband, Nicephorus Bryennius Caesar. These two beloved names wake such sad memories that she weeps over their loss and ends her Preface, having introduced into these few pages one quotation from John of Epiphania, one from Polybius, one from Sophocles, two from Euripides, one from Homer, one allusion to the Bible, one to mythology, four to history, seven geographical names, and a great many long and recondite words. Melancholy adorned by learning has at the very outset marked the work for its own.

Book I tells of Alexius from his boyhood till the last months of the troubled reign of the Emperor Nicephorus Botaniates. The chronology at once shows a discrepancy with other sources which we shall discuss in full later: does Anna mean that her father was only fourteen at the time of the 'great campaign against the Persians' headed by Romanus Diogenes in 1070? Rather surprisingly she omits all details as to his ancestors, such as begin her husband's work, and goes straight to the biography. In his first military adventure, when sent by Michael VII against the 'Celt' Urselius in Asia Minor, Alexius displays no less than four of the qualities which his daughter

[1] I. 1, p. 3.

always extols in him: persuasiveness of tongue, preference for devious methods and stratagems, readiness to make friends with any one (even an enemy) who will serve his turn, and clemency to fallen foes. In his second, when as Domestic of the Schools he goes out for Botaniates against Nicephorus Bryennius, the fight at Calaure gives the occasion for the first Anna's numberless battle-pictures, all more conscientious than inspired. It also allows Alexius to show and Anna to praise the wonderful bravery of which we hear so much. In the third contest, where a fresh would-be usurper Basilacius succumbs to his prowess, we are initiated into another secret of Alexius' character, his obedience to his mother.

The story then breaks off to describe the brutal ways in which Robert Guiscard rose to power in Italy, and his impious resolve to cross the Adriatic and attack the Eastern Empire, ostensibly as the champion of the deposed Michael VII. At this point, in speaking of Robert and of his daughter Helena, once betrothed to Anna's own fiancé Constantine Ducas, she shows two of her own deeply rooted qualities, true Byzantine disdain for any race not her own, and jealousy. Two other personal touches may also be noted. First, womanly and imperial modesty prevents Anna from retailing scandal, and to this principle she rigidly adheres throughout her fifteen Books Secondly, the mention of the Pope rouses this daughter of the Orthodox Church to mock at what she considers his vain pretensions to supremacy.

Book II gives a vivid picture of the court intrigues which preceded Alexius' ursurpation (involving not only nobles and favourites but the Empress Maria herself), and his capture of Constantinople by bribing the garrison. Here for the first time we get an insight into the formidable if usually beneficent power of the imperial 'kinsmen', whether blood relations or connexions by marriage. Without the aid of his brother Isaac, his brother-in-law George Palaeologus, and his wife's grandfather John Ducas Caesar, to say nothing of his own vigorous and clever mother Anna Dalassena, Alexius would never have gained the throne. We also see Alexius for the first time practising on another brother-in-law Nicephorus Melissenus his favourite trick of 'keeping in suspense' any one likely to cause trouble. Finally we get a sinister glimpse into the power, venality, and turbulence of armies and fleets.

Book III opens in 1081 with the banishment to a monastery of the deposed Emperor Botaniates. Then follows the rather obscure story of conflict between the two great families of

SCOPE OF THE *ALEXIAS*

Comnenus and Ducas. The quarrel apparently raged round two questions: should Irene Ducas be crowned as well as her husband, and should the ex-Empress Maria remain in the Palace as her virtual rival in power? The Ducas family won on both issues, but in return for this victory they had to let Anna Dalassena replace the Patriarch Cosmas by a creature of her own, Eustratius Garidas. Wonderful pen-portraits of Maria, Alexius, and Irene enliven this part of the Book. Finally, in the Golden Bull appointing Anna Dalassena regent in her son's absence on campaigns, we get the first of the official documents which our historian professes to quote verbatim. It is followed by a long eulogy of her grandmother for purity of morals, open-handedness, and piety, three virtues which the *Alexias* never fails to praise. The Emperor's penance for the sack of the capital on Maundy Thursday by his troops is also instructive in this connexion.

After a digression (prefaced by a long quotation from Psel-lus[1]) on a miraculous escape of her great-uncle the Emperor Isaac Comnenus, Anna turns to the lamentable military and financial condition of the Empire in 1081, and her father's mani-fold efforts to resist Turks on the East and Normans on the West. A second State document, a letter from Alexius to the King (ῥήξ) of Germany, here proposes alliance and intermarriage, while a peace is patched up with the Turks, and Illyria strength-ened against Robert by the dismissal of the disloyal governor of Durazzo. The new one chosen is Alexius' brother-in-law, George Palaeologus, one of Anna's chief authorities.[2] For the ensuing campaign she had not only his reports, but those of a 'Latin envoy from the Bishop of Bari', who accompanied the Norman hosts, so her details at this point are peculiarly vivid, beginning with a fine description of the great storm that wrecked Robert's fleet and barely let him escape with his life to the eastern shore of the Adriatic.

Book IV gives us the siege of Durazzo by the Normans and their puppet, the bogus Michael VII. Alexius summons the Venetian fleet to his aid, and it defeats first Robert's son Bohemund and then Robert himself. In August 1081 the Emperor leaves Constantinople to collect forces, with which he proceeds by way of Thessalonica against the enemy. The Byzantines are severely defeated outside Durazzo, and the Emperor owes his life to his own valour and the miraculous agility of his horse.[3]

---

[1] *Chron.*, Isaac Comn. Byz. T., pp. 221–4 = *Al.* III. 8, pp. 89 sqq.; cf. p. 192 below.
[2] XIV. 7, p. 447.   [3] The question of date is discussed in Ch. 62, below.

Book V opens with the loss of Durazzo to Robert by treason.[1] Then we get the Emperor's drastic methods of raising money in Constantinople by taking Church property in the face of much clerical opposition, and Robert's enforced return to Italy to help the Pope against Alexius' new German ally. The Norman army is left to Bohemund, who captures many towns and twice defeats Alexius in battle,[2] but is finally driven back to Italy by a mutiny among his soldiers due to the Emperor's machinations. Alexius on re-entering Constantinople has the first of his triumphant contests with false doctrine, this time in the person of the neo-Platonic philosopher John Italus, an incident which gives us much insight into Anna's ideals of learning.

Book VI shows us the last Norman forces on imperial soil surrendering to Alexius and his crushing of the insurgent Manichaeans, by an act of treachery which ultimately caused the Patzinak War. For his spoliation of Church property he is obliged not only to justify himself before an assembly but to make handsome restitution.[3] This is followed by the first of the many plots against him, hatched by unnamed 'picked men of the Senate and the leaders of the army', and barely punished by the Emperor, but the story soon returns to Robert Guiscard and his second crossing of the Adriatic. His campaign, chiefly important for having forced Alexius to make disastrous commercial concessions to the Venetian allies, is terminated by death at Cephallenia in the summer of 1085, and this provides Anna with the occasion for a dissertation on the astrology which had foretold it, and for a vivid character sketch of Robert. We are then carried back to 1 December 1083, and the story of Anna's birth, followed in a few years by those of a sister and a brother.

The rest of the Book is occupied first with the Turks, both their domestic quarrels and their struggles with the imperial forces, secondly with the initial Patzinak campaign. In the Turkish War various points of interest may be noted. Sacrilege is punished by demoniac possession; military and naval officers are not distinct but interchangeable; the Empire has never in theory abandoned its claim to a dominion extending from the Straits of Gibraltar to India. Alexius at this juncture blossoms forth as an 'apostle', ever burning to convert heretics and the heathen. As to the Patzinak War of 1086, to which we return

[1] It remains in Norman hands till Robert's death in 1085 (VI. 6, p. 163).
[2] For chronology see Ch. 62, below.
[3] There appear to have been two spoliations and only one restitution. The matter is obscure and is discussed in Chs. 38 and 45 below.

from the Eastern events of 1092, it begins with defeat and disaster, and fresh troops are hurried to the front.

Book VII shows us Alexius fighting in person the next spring (1087). After an eclipse (identified by Chalandon[1] as that of August 1, 1087) he is grievously defeated near Dristra, close to the Danube, being even forced to abandon his sacred banner. Providentially the newly arrived Comans quarrel about booty with their allies the Patzinaks, and Alexius seizes the occasion to come to terms with the latter. This inglorious peace, which Theophylact[2] misrepresents as a triumph for the Empire, is of short duration, and the next campaign brings the loss of 300 of Alexius' beloved young Archontopules. The 500 Flemish horsemen who arrive at this crisis as mercenaries have to be sent at once to Asia Minor, where the Turk Tzachas had made himself an independent sovereign on the West coast, and had beaten the imperial forces on land and sea. John Ducas, Irene's brother, who had been recently successful against the Dalmatians, is dispatched to the Eastern scene of action, and then Anna turns her history back to Thrace and the Patzinaks, who have arrived within twenty leagues of the capital when winter stops the fighting. This Book has several points of minor interest. Over a certain Lake Ozolimne Anna makes a display of somewhat inaccurate learning; for all his defeats Alexius is praised as a second Alexander; twice over we find foreign soldiers of fortune betraying their employers' plans; and the Emperor first shows signs of physical weakness by having ague.[3]

(b) BOOKS VIII–XV

Book VIII reopens the Patzinak campaign early in 1091. Alexius has a success at Choerobacchae, and the joke which he plays on his army, dressing up some of his soldiers like Scythian captives, throws light on the *camaraderie* between the sovereign and his men. An exceptionally severe winter causes another pause; then the Comans reappear and are bribed into alliance, and the Greek victory of Lebunium (April 29, 1091) results in the utter destruction[4] of the whole Patzinak nation. Here we may observe how difficulties of commissariat, and especially

---

[1] *Op. cit.*, p. 106, note.

[2] *P. G.* 126, col. 293–7.

[3] In the summer of 1096 (if we accept Riant's date of January 1097 for Letter 71 in his *Inventaire des lettres historiques des Croisades*; *Arch. de l'Orient latin* I, pp. 136–40.) we find Alexius prevented by *infirmitas maxima* from going to Durazzo to meet the Crusaders. In his later years he was, as is well known, a martyr to gout.

[4] This is filial exaggeration; see Ch. 65, below.

of the water supply, play an important part in eleventh-century warfare. We are also treated by Anna, in her contrasting of Lebunium with Dristra, to a characteristic moral, recalling the old classical teaching as to the inevitable punishment of ὕβρις.

After the fight the Patzinak prisoners are murdered, and, though Anna is careful to exculpate her father, the deed causes a stampede among the Coman allies. Alexius sends their promised rewards after them, and for the time the Empire is freed from all 'Scythians', whether friends or foes. Alexius then returns to Constantinople and is beset by domestic troubles. Two plots, one of two foreign mercenary generals and the other of his own nephew John, now Governor of Durazzo, are discovered and pardoned, and the Book ends with the insubordinate behaviour of the Gabras family, a story which presents several points of interest. First we see that an appointment, even to virtual independence, in a distant town like Trebizond might be considered as hardly better than exile. Secondly, we have a marriage stopped because the bridegroom's father had taken for his *second* wife a cousin of the bride. Thirdly, we find the son of a formidable subject kept as hostage at the imperial court. Fourthly, medieval superstition comes out in the theft of a peculiarly sacred relic on which to swear. As to the whole Book, we may say that it makes us forcibly realize how precarious was Alexius' tenure of empire, when he could not count on loyalty or even respect from his generals, his kinsmen, or the members of his own household.

Book IX takes up the Turkish War from *Book VII*. The three months' siege of Mitylene ends in victory for John Ducas, and the Greek and Turkish leaders make a treaty which both promptly break. Throughout the campaign indeed intrigue and falsehood are rampant on both sides. John's subsequent suppression of revolts in Crete and Cyprus draws forth from Anna two significant remarks. She expresses aristocratic scorn for the Cypriote rebel who 'could not even ride', and notes as something exceptional that Alexius sent to the island as assessor of taxes a man 'not of distinguished birth, but bringing abundant testimony of just dealing and incorruptibility and courtesy'. We also notice how the Emperor, though not present in the field, kept all the military reins in his hands; John Ducas would never have conquered at Mitylene but for his brother-in-law's instructions.

We now go back to Europe, and learn how Alexius in 1093 tried by diplomacy and war to repress the Dalmatians, victorious under Bolcanus over John Comnenus, the Governor of

Durazzo. The Emperor's march is delayed by the conspiracy
of Nicephorus Diogenes, son of the Emperor Romanus Diogenes, an occurrence narrated in a series of peculiarly vivid
pictures. Anna gives us an unwonted wealth of detail about
this youth, his birth in the purple, his ingratitude to Alexius
culminating in two if not three abortive attempts at assassination, the Emperor's vain efforts to win back his affections, and
the final arrest of Diogenes and all his accomplices. Once
more we have Alexius' clemency impressed on us. He fears for
his life at the hands of the infuriated crowd, but he adheres to
his customary methods. The suspicions against the ex-Empress
Maria are hushed up; no severer punishment than prison,
banishment, and confiscation of goods is inflicted on the ringleaders, and for the rest a general amnesty is proclaimed.
The Emperor is free to proceed against the Dalmatians, who
promptly submit.

Book X is in many ways the most remarkable of all. First we
get the Christological controversy between Alexius and the
heretic Nilus; next, the incursions (successfully resisted by the
Emperor in person) of the Comans led by a Greek rebel im-
personating another son of Romanus Diogenes; thirdly, a brief
appearance of Alexius in Nicomedia; and finally the supreme
interest of the First Crusade. Various small incidents may be
noted. In the Coman campaign we get the Emperor's first use
of Sacred Lots as a sort of oracle, we see how the inroads of
barbarians were facilitated by the disloyalty of towns in the
Empire, and on the other hand we find an important fortress
committed to Alexius' former enemy Nicephorus Bryennius,
whose blinding had not incapacitated him from military
usefulness in action as well as in council. At the end of it
we may note the untiring energy of Alexius, who, after
pursuing the retreating foe, crosses in the heat of summer to
superintend fortifications near Nicomedia.

But, as was said above, the climax of the whole work to modern
readers is the coming of the First Crusade to Constantinople,
with the behaviour of the leaders to Alexius and his demands
for homage from them. This will be discussed at length later.
At present three incidents may be singled out for special notice.
One is a naval fight between the imperial fleet and a Count
Prebentzas,[1] a fight memorable to us because in recounting it
Anna minutely describes the Frankish cross-bow, and vigorously
inveighs against the fighting priests of the Latin Church. The
second is the battle outside Constantinople, when the Crusaders

---

[1] His identity will be discussed below, pp. 254 note 6, 465 note 2.

under Godfrey de Bouillon refuse to defer fighting from Holy
Week till after Easter, and the accomplished archer Nicephorus
Bryennius Caesar shoots so as not to kill. The third is the
arrival at the capital of Anna's Prince of Darkness, the great
Bohemund, and whereas in the Illyrian campaign of 1083 he
had figured merely as Robert Guiscard's son and substitute,
here and henceforward he dominates the whole scene, as the
greediest, most unscrupulous, and also the cleverest of all the
Franks. Finally, the oath of homage is taken by the principal
chiefs including Godfrey and Bohemund, and the Book ends
with the departure into Asia Minor of all the Frankish hosts,
followed by Alexius himself.

Book XI carries on the story of the First Crusade. Nicaea is
besieged, and after much fighting the garrison secretly admits
the imperial envoy Butumites. Strong in possession of the
citadel he is able to give commands to the Crusaders, and he
induces all those who have not already done so to swear fealty
to Alexius at Pelecanus.[1] Alexius now speeds the Crusaders on
their way, sending Taticius partly to support them with his
forces, partly to see that captured towns are, according to the
Crusaders' oath, handed back to the Empire. After various
battles the Franks and Greeks reach Antioch and besiege it.
Bohemund now resumes his role of arch-villain, frightening
Taticius home by invented dangers, intriguing with the
Turkish garrison, and finally seizing the town for himself in
violation of his allegiance to Alexius. The finding of the Sacred
Lance[2] gives the Crusaders courage to drive away a relieving
army of Turks. They leave Bohemund installed as governor
at Antioch, and proceed to Jerusalem, where Godfrey is made
king. Anna then returns to tell of her father, whose attempt to
march after the Franks is first delayed and then cut short by
fear of the Turks. Her interest is subsequently focussed on
St. Gilles, Alexius' one friend among the Crusaders, who after
taking Laodicea and other places hands them over to imperial
agents while he besieges Tripoli. But Tancred seizes Laodicea
for himself and his uncle Bohemund; Godfrey dies and is succeeded at Jerusalem by his brother Baldwin; St. Gilles con-
ducts a fresh body of Crusaders from Constantinople Eastwards
across the Halys,[3] meets with disaster, returns to the siege of
Tripoli, and dies. Then the long brewing animosity between

---

[1] On the question of St. Gilles' oath, see Ch. 68 below.
[2] Anna, here at variance with the Latin chroniclers, calls it a 'Nail'. See Ch.
68 below.
[3] Chalandon (*op. cit.*, p. xvii) calls this 'La croisade de 1101'.

Alexius and Bohemund comes to a head, each accusing the other of broken oaths. Their troops fight in Cilicia, and the Pisan fleet attacks the Greek, which gains a victory with new and specially formidable fire-ships.[1] Later on Cantacuzenus besieges Laodicea from the sea in co-operation with a land force. The Book ends with the story, told of other heroes by other writers, of Bohemund's escape from Antioch to Corfu in a coffin on board ship, with a dead cock on his breast to give colour or rather smell to his deception.

These gruesome details agree with the general character of this part of Anna's history, to which the 'barbarous' Crusaders seem to impart a savage flavour. In this Book the new Governor of Smyrna is brutally stabbed by a man accused of theft, and his sailors in revenge sack the town, the captured daughter of the Turk Tzachas is paraded as an exhibit by the Greeks, Crusaders murder Greek priests and laymen who come out in procession to welcome them, storms and liquid fire make naval battles a hideous nightmare, the Greek fleet kills its prisoners, Pisan soldiers rush panic-stricken into the sea and are drowned; in no other single Book do we meet with such concentrated battle and murder and sudden death.

Book XII opens with Bohemund's successful attempts at raising up enemies in Italy against the Empire, while his nephew Tancred wins successes in Cilicia. Alexius, though crippled by gout which only his wife's rubbings can assuage,[2] at this point goes into camp at Thessalonica. Anna's usual praise of her parents is followed by the usual disclaimer of partiality, accompanied by the usual wealth of allusions, quotations, and high-sounding phrases.

We next have a short and rather confused account of Dalmatian affairs, and then Anna turns to the other and greater trials of the Emperor. First we have the plot of the four Anemas brothers, themselves nobles and aided by high military officers, with the rich senator John Solomon as their tool. The convicted ringleaders are with unwonted severity condemned to be blinded after being led in mock procession through the capital. At the last moment Alexius is moved by the prayers of his daughters and wife to grant a reprieve. The eyes of all are spared, but Michael Anemas is imprisoned in a tower

---

[1] *Ibid.*, p. xviii. He believes this incident in Ch. 10 to be referable to 1099, and the aid brought by the Genoese fleet in Ch. 11 to have reached the Crusaders in 1104. See p. 470, note 9, below.

[2] Chalandon (*op. cit.*, p. 274) has a sinister explanation for her presence in camp. See Ch. 37, below.

where the captured rebel Gregory Taronites soon joins him. To him Alexius, possibly because his own sister had married into that family, shows even more than his usual forbearance.

From domestic troubles we pass to external. The Greek admiral-in-chief, Isaac Contostephanus, first fails to take Otranto held by Tancred's mother, and then by his cowardly desertion of his post allows Bohemund to cross with a huge fleet to Durazzo. The reception by Alexius of these sinister tidings gives him a chance to display heroic calm, and the Book ends on this note of pride.

Book XIII, the longest after *Book XV* and *Book I*, describes the great crisis of Alexius' career, his struggle against and treaty with Bohemund. At the start he is delayed five days by the plot of the Aaron brothers, who are finally banished and their mother also. Then the contest with Bohemund begins in earnest. Though hampered by famine and disease, the Norman beleaguers Durazzo for the whole winter, trying against it in succession a penthouse, a mine, and a wooden tower. The garrison holds out, and Alexius thinks he can best help them by stratagem, so he contrives that letters falsely incriminating some of Bohemund's principal men shall fall into the hands of their chief. It is not however till a vigorous new admiral-in-chief is appointed that Bohemund's supplies from Italy are cut off, and he is obliged to sue for peace to the Governor of Durazzo. Several small points in the first half of the Book deserve to be mentioned. Here, as in the Patzinak War, we find Greek generals parading their enemies' heads on spears; the part played by women in Byzantine intrigues may be noted;[1] and finally, in telling us of the deadly effect produced by the Greek archers on their foes, Anna gives a full and very interesting description of Norman armour.

Alexius now summons his enemy to come to him under a safe-conduct, and a long and curious account follows of the minute stipulations made by Bohemund as to hostages, complete silence about the past, and an honourable reception, involving many nice questions of etiquette. Finally the last chapter of the Book covers many pages, and gives the treaty between Alexius and Bohemund at wearisome length. Bohemund renews his oath of fealty, and among the places granted to him for life we find the great bone of contention Antioch, though this concession is mitigated by the Emperor's reserving the right to choose its Patriarch out of the clergy of St. Sophia. The covenant ends with an enumeration of all

[1] Cf. Anna Dalassena in *Book II* and the Empress Maria in *Book IX*.

the holy objects visible and invisible by which Bohemund swore, and of all the signatory witnesses. The wide diplomatic relations of the Byzantine Empire are shown by the presence of a Papal envoy and Hungarian ambassadors.

Book XIV opens with the return to Italy and the death of the discomfited Bohemund. This leaves the stage clear for Alexius, who first deals vicariously but successfully with Asia Minor, and then through Butumites vainly tries to enlist the other Crusaders, especially Baldwin King of Jerusalem, against Tancred firmly established in Antioch. Meanwhile he himself is in the Thracian Chersonese, watching for any dangers to his Empire, whether from sea or land. First a Lombard fleet makes an abortive attack; next a rebel commandant is defeated, captured, and pardoned. Then a treaty is concluded by Alexius with envoys of the vanquished Sultan of Chorassan, but the next year war is resumed and the Emperor handles it in person in spite of gout. The history of his disease follows: Anna ascribes it first to an old accident at polo, next to the interminable standing necessitated by the interviews with garrulous Crusaders, then to anxiety over his Empire, and finally to the literal or figurative poisoning of his 'cup' attempted by some intimate enemy. The incidental pictures of Palace life, the weary courtiers, the patient Emperor, the vigilant Empress, make this passage one of the most admirable in the whole work. The campaign goes on, and finally the victory is such that all Constantinople rejoices. Anna now indulges in a lengthy digression, on the dangers from Scythians, Normans, Turks, and sea-pirates brought on the Empire by her father's predecessors. Next we get an interesting light thrown, first on the sources of her history, secondly on her woes real or imaginary, thirdly on the date at which she wrote this Book, i.e. in 1148 when she was already sixty-four or sixty-five.

She then turns to a threatened Coman invasion, which causes Alexius to hurry to Philippopolis. There while waiting for the foe he converts numberless Paulician heretics. Anna takes this occasion to display, first her orthodox views on doctrine and philosophy; next her acquaintance (not always accurate) with history and geography; thirdly her never-dying admiration for her 'apostolic' father, who may now be said to be at his zenith. The Comans retreat at the bare sound of his approach, and he founds for his converts a new city called after himself.

Book XV, the longest of all, leads us slowly down from the zenith to the nadir. First the Sultan of Iconium, Kilidj Arslan or Saisan, raids Asia Minor seven times and publicly mocks at the Emperor and his gout. When in his wrath Alexius crosses the straits and goes to Nicomedia, fresh sneers at his inactivity arise among his own followers, and Anna, while clinging to her claim of being an impartial historian, has to remind herself and us that discretion is the better part of valour and the mark of a good general. In the end the surpassing ingenuity of his καινὴ παράταξις, first worked out on paper and then put in practice, ensures the success of the Greek arms. The Emperor is able to bring all his booty, prisoners, and refugees safely back from Philomelium to his capital, and on the way thither to extract from the submissive Sultan favourable terms of peace, whereby the old boundaries of Turks and Greeks are restored as they were before the accession in 1067 of the ill-fated Romanus Diogenes. Thus the last campaign of Alexius closes in glory, and though it contains no strikingly dramatic incident, several acts of individual valour among his officers, to say nothing of courtesies exchanged between enemies, throw a sort of sunset glow over the whole. The passage on Turkish archery and tactics is interesting, and we are made vividly to realize the military problems produced by difficulties of getting provisions in a plundered land, by the supreme importance of keeping the horses in good condition, and by the sinister action of deserters. Above all, we feel deep sympathy for any humane general with sick women and dying men among his refugee camp-followers.

Once back in his capital, with a triumphal entry modestly avoided, Alexius turns to philanthropy, and we get a lively picture of the Orphanotropheion which he founds, or rather restores, on a large site encircling the Church of St. Paul. This institution contains orphans and their school, as well as disabled men (especially old soldiers) and infirm women, with attendants of both sexes. In connexion with the school, Anna pauses to deplore the neglect of literary study in favour of mere grammatical analysis, and dwells with complacency on her own excellent education. Next follows the most unpleasant episode in the whole work. A new doctrinal danger arises in the form of the Bogomile heresy, compounded of Paulicianism and Massalianism. The leader Basil is tricked into incriminating himself, and the Senate, Church, and Army all combine with Alexius in condemning him to be burnt in the Hippodrome, a proceeding described by Anna with ghoulish satisfaction. The other Bogomiles are partly converted and released, partly saved by the Emperor from popular lynching and imprisoned for life

After this Anna turns to her father's wonderful achievements in restoring the Empire and his modesty in not wishing them written down, and in conclusion comes one long vivid chapter recounting his last illness and death. This will be discussed at some length later.[1] For the present it is enough to say that if, as Chalandon and Oster believe, all the sentiment expressed is hypocritical and untrue, then this passage should surely rank as one of the masterpieces of fiction. There follows one last outpouring of lamentation over Anna's own 'rivers and streams of misfortunes', and the Book ends with the significant words, 'Let my story have an end, lest writing down my woes I should grow the more bitter'. A traditional ending of the *Alexias* is the epigram included in the supplementary volume of Didot's *Anthologia Palatina*:[2]

Λῆξεν ὅπου βιότοιο ᾿Αλέξιος ὁ Κομνηνὸς
ἔνθα καλὴ θυγάτηρ λῆξεν ᾿Αλεξιάδος.

If this was not composed by Anna herself (and both the sentiment and the Homeric quotation of καλὴ θυγάτηρ[3] are very characteristic), it is none the less a charming conclusion to this unique work.

[1] See pp. 114, 123, 247–9 below.
[2] III (Cougny), p. 335, No. 272.
[3] *Od.* VIII. 320.

II. ANNA AS A PERSONALITY

4. HOPES OF SUCCESSION

BEFORE we consider the characteristics of Anna Comnena as a historian, we shall do well to study her as a woman. The main facts of her life might be gathered at need from other writers, and in her general principles and ideals she is merely the product of her age, but her autobiographical touches supply us with the key to her individual character.

First, as to the ambition which her critics cast in her teeth. The 'bitterness' of which she herself is conscious in the very last word of her work must surely be attributed less to her griefs than to cheated hopes. As a child she had been taught to reckon on being Empress; she never was, and it soured her against her hated brother and successor John. But it is not necessary to assume that she contested the legitimacy of his claim, when once her betrothed, Constantine Ducas, son of the Emperor Michael, had departed this life, probably before she was of marriageable age.[1] She darkly hints at John's treachery[2] and heartlessness[3] as a son, and incompetence as a monarch,[4] but the principle of heredity was too strong in her[5] for her really to think that she and Nicephorus Bryennius had superior rights to the throne. If she disagreed with her husband's emphatic statement[6] that John stood next in the succession as soon as Constantine was dead, would she have referred readers so freely to his book as a supreme authority? If she did indeed conspire against her brother in the first year of his reign, some act of his may have seemed to her to justify his expulsion from the throne that he had been bound to inherit. She is arrogant, bitter, and jealous, she resents the fact that Constantine died and that John was ever born, or a husband, or the father of a son,[7] but she never suggests that he was not the legal διάδοχος,[8]

---

[1] He was still alive in 1094, when she was ten years old (IX. 5–8).

[2] XIV. 4, p. 437.

[3] XV. 11, p. 503. Even Zonaras and John's admirer Nicetas represent him as taking his dying father's ring as a gift or a theft, and then absenting himself from his death-bed and funeral in his desperate desire to make his own position strong.

[4] XIV. 3, p. 433.

[5] II. 2, p. 45. It was 'unjust and unprofitable' for the Emperor Botaniates to put aside the lawful claims of Constantine.

[6] *Hyle*, Pref., p. 10.

[7] XII. 4, p. 356.

[8] In the account of his being crowned (as she had been before) she speaks of the throne as his natural inheritance, which his father would wish to leave him, and in the treaty between Alexius and Bohemund, she takes it as the natural thing for the 'ardently longed for' and 'deeply loved' John to be associated with his father (XIII. 12; so XV. 11, p. 503).

and never hints that Irene preferred her daughter's claims before her son's.

At this point we will deal shortly with this question of hereditary succession, for it closely affects her story. Theoretically in the eleventh and twelfth centuries the senate and army still chose the emperor, while the people had to confirm their choice.[1] The patriarch of Constantinople 'as representing the electors but not the Church', usually crowned the new sovereign with the diadem.[2] In practice however the monarchs had long been able to bequeath their sceptre to sons real and adopted, having usually already associated them with themselves as co-emperors. For one thing, as P. Grenier shows,[3] it was only Constantinople and the adjacent provinces of Thrace and Macedonia that took any interest in the choice of an emperor, and even there the selection of a patriarch was of far greater moment. Yet the being designated as successor by a still reigning emperor did not give a clear title in the face of a military *coup d'état*. Though Botaniates had chosen his sister's son Synadenus[4] to succeed him and also had an ἔγγονος of his own, he yet thinks it prudent to ignore this and send the following message to his formidable opponent Alexius: 'I am now an old and lonely man, possessing neither son nor brother nor any near[5] kinsman, and if thou desirest become thou my adopted son.'

When a new dynasty came in, it was always a case of usurpation backed up by the army. Thus, to take an instance from the *Alexias* itself, it is clear that when the Comneni revolt

---

[1] The *Anon. Syn. Chron.* (*B. G. Med.* VII, pp. 185–7) keeps up this fiction of the 'choice' of an Emperor; John is 'proclaimed at the hands of the subjects'.

[2] N. H. Baynes, *Byz. Emp.*, p. 64. In XII. 5, p. 359, Anna uses the expression βασιλέα χρίσειν of planning to put a usurper on the throne.

[3] *Empire Byzantin*, Vol. II, p. 36.

[4] Anna says προσήκων αὐτῷ κατὰ γένος (II. 2, p. 45). Theodulus Synadenus had married his sister (Scyl. *Hist.*, p. 867 B), and Gelzer assumes that he had made their son his heir; *G. B. L.*, p. 1014.

[5] II. 12, p. 67. The word γνήσιος is one of the many referring to relationship which Anna uses in a non-classical sense, not as 'legitimate', but 'near of kin', cf. XII. 7, p. 365; XIII. 9, p. 401), or even merely ' intimate', with no idea of kinship at all (VI. 4, p. 157; X. 4, p. 278; XIII. 5, p. 390). A similar use of derivatives of γνήσιος, indicating close connexion by blood, occurs twice in the Preface to Niceph. Bryennius' *Hyle*. It might well be that Anna applies 'belonging by race', said of Synadenus with regard to Botaniates (II. 2, p. 45), to a connexion through women, for the imperial 'kinsmen' included, in her loose usage, what we might call 'in-laws'. Similarly the word ἔγγονος in *Al.* II. 5, p. 51, probably means not a 'grandson' of Botaniates, but vaguely a 'kinsman of a younger generation', not near enough to count among the Emperor's γνήσιοι or to have a claim to the succession. It is however possible that though a grandson he was excluded by his youth, as he still needed a παιδαγωγός, and at times of exceptional stress the claim of an adult might outweigh that of a child. See p. 30, below, also p. 492, note 3.

against Botaniates the determining factor in the choice between the two brothers as emperor is the will of the army.[1] Alexius who is the younger is Grand Domestic of the West and his soldiers are at hand, so he is proclaimed in preference to Isaac, the elder, whose troops had presumably stayed behind in the East.[2] Similarly it is reliance on his ἱκανὴ στρατιά that makes Nicephorus Melissenus hope (though vainly) to get half of the Empire.[3]

But it is none the less true that the anarchy of the years 1057 to 1081 had by a revulsion of popular feeling given to the principle of inheritance by the eldest son (a principle born during the eighty odd years of the Isaurian dynasty and grown great during the two centuries, with six generations, of the Macedonian) a fresh chance of establishing itself. We find it prevailing in the twelfth century with more force than ever, and keeping its hold till the Empire fell in 1453. Anna herself considers that the throne belonged 'as a sort of inheritance from his grandfather and father' to Constantine Ducas.[4] Nicetas Acominatus[5] doubtless voiced the popular view when he makes Alexius say that to bequeath his crown (which he himself had won 'by civil slaughters and methods divergent from Christian laws') to a son-in-law instead of to a υἱὸς ἁρμόδιος would be contrary, not only to imperial precedent but also to common sense; it would obviously be wise for a man who had himself been a usurper to lay the foundation of his dynasty as solidly as possible. If John took the signet-ring off the dying Alexius' hand, Nicetas believes it was with the Emperor's consent.[6] The same writer in telling of John's death[7] gives us two interesting facts, first that the Emperor who had himself received the crown ὡς πατρῷος κλῆρος yet passed over his firstborn Isaac for his violent temper, and left the Empire to the second son Manuel, justifying his conduct by the parallels of Isaac, Jacob,

---

[1] II. 7, p. 58. In I. 15, p. 37, Anna makes the interesting statement that 'neither the Greek people (δῆμος) nor the army would have admitted the barbarian Robert to the throne'.

[2] II. 1, p. 43. He had been Duke of Antioch, 1074-9. See Schlumberger, *Sigillographie de l'Empire byzantin*, p. 308. But cf. Chalandon, *op. cit.*, p. 41, note 4.

[3] II. 8, p. 59.   [4] II. 2, p. 45.

[5] *John C.*, 2, p. 4. The views of Nicetas Acom. as to succession rights correspond closely with those of John Cinnamus, who makes the dying John II say (*Hist.* I. 10, p. 14) that Emperors legally bequeathed their thrones ὥσπερ τινὰ κλῆρον πατρῷον usually to their eldest sons. In this instance, however, he chose Manuel the younger son as being (*a*) more suitable, (*b*) predestined by portents, and if neither of his sons had seemed to him fit to reign he would have chosen some one else. In any case his principal subjects had to ratify his choice.

[6] See the less positive account in *Anon. Syn. Chron.*, *loc. cit.*

[7] *John C.*, 12, pp. 29-31.

Moses, and David, whom God had favoured though they were not eldest sons; secondly, that though John's relations and friends ratified his choice, yet some of them felt that their kinship and seniority entitled them to reign instead. This idea that the eldest adult of a house had the right to succeed, (which prevailed in Turkey under the late régime), makes Nicephorus Bryennius[1] feel that the natural and rightful heir to Michael VII was not his young son Constantine but his brother of the same name. When the elder Constantine declined to reign, Alexius according to his son-in-law fully admitted the rights of the younger one to at least co-sovereignty with the Emperor Botaniates and afterwards with himself. Next to Constantine the rightful heir was John, 'marked out for ruling by a double claim' as a Comnenus and a Ducas[2] and thus connected with two former emperors. 'For after the Porphyrogenete had left this life, who had a greater right to rule?' This decided opinion expressed by Nicephorus Bryennius surely disposes of the usually accepted theory that Anna kept all through her father's lifetime that hope to succeed him which could be logically based only on the claims of her first fiancé Constantine. These claims had indeed been so notorious that Botaniates alienated popular sympathy by passing them over in favour of his own brother-in-law whom he hoped to make his successor. On another occasion they served to fill the boy's mother with natural fear for his life at the hands of a usurping emperor ;[3] in the disorders bound to follow the deposition of his stepfather Botaniates,[4] Alexius might well have thought the lawful Ducas heir dangerous and had him killed or at least blinded. Here as in the case of Botaniates' chosen successor Synadenus, and

---

[1] *Hyle*, Pref., p.8. Cf. note 5 on p. 28.

[2] Theodore Prodromus brings forward the same plea in his *Epithalamium* for Anna Comnena's two sons (*P. G.* 133, col. 1400). We are reminded of the union of York and Lancaster in the marriage of Henry VII. It is curious that Anna makes no capital whatever out of her father's relationship to the previous Comnenus Emperor; perhaps Isaac's two years of reign seemed negligibly short. In any case her plea for her father, if put into words, would have been: 'The Empire needed a strong man and got him in Alexius: the usurper may be forgotten in the hero.' But it was undoubtedly the fear lest Ducas claims might be overemphasized which led Alexius, supported by his mother, to have himself crowned first alone, though in the end he had to yield to his connexions by marriage and permit the coronation of Irene Ducas his wife (III. 2). His admission of the seven-year-old Constantine συμβασιλεύειν αὐτῷ was probably due almost as much to his wish to conciliate the Ducas family as to his own sense of justice, or consideration for the ex-Empress (I. 15, p. 36; III. 4, p. 80; VI. 8, p. 167).

[3] III. 1–4. So at an earlier date Anna Dalassena had feared for herself and her children when her husband John Comnenus refused to succeed his brother Isaac on the throne (Nic. Bry. I. 5, p. 19) and the crown passed to another family.

[4] III. 1, p. 71.

in that of the two sons of another deposed Emperor, Romanus Diogenes, Alexius displayed a surprising clemency which his daughter greatly admired. Constantine received from the Emperor not only honour but love,[1] a member of the Synadenus family had a position in the imperial army at Durazzo where he met his death,[2] and the forbearing kindness of Alexius to Leo and Nicephorus Diogenes both in war and peace[3] comes out distinctly in Anna's narrative, being in marked contrast with their harsh treatment by their half-brother Michael VII[4] on the occasion of his coming to power. Yet the serious danger which threatened from the children of previous emperors is shown not only by the whole story of Nicephorus Diogenes' plot and by Anna's grave words[5] about it, but by the fact that an impostor who impersonated his dead brother Constantine (not Leo, as Anna erroneously says[6]) could head an invasion of the Empire by the Comans, who came 'in order forsooth to seat this man on his paternal throne', and could meet with welcome from several of the Emperor's own towns.

Of the precariousness of Alexius' hold upon his power we shall speak later on. Plots are almost as incessant as wars throughout his reign, and his mild treatment of the conspirators seems to point to fear quite as much as to clemency. Usurpation still appeared to malcontents a perfectly natural way of coming to the throne,[7] though a slight colour of hereditary right in the usurper might be desirable. But to Anna, the daughter of just such a usurper, the principle of hereditary succession was already sacrosanct, and she is quite consistent on the subject. Not only to emperors does she ascribe the right of bequest. As a matter of course Robert Guiscard is succeeded by his sons,[8] and St. Gilles at Tripoli first by a nephew and then by a bastard son and that son's son.[9] Under the circumstances she could hardly without stultifying herself have hoped to mount her father's throne in preference to John, and we have no adequate reason for believing that she did so.[10]

---

[1] III. 4; VI. 8; IX. 5–8.
[2] IV. 5, p. 112, and 6, p. 117. It is possible to identify Botaniates' brother-in-law Theodulus Synadenus with Alexius' officer Nicephorus Synadenus, by assuming that either Anna or Scylitzes made a mistake in the first name, as she does about Leo Diogenes (p. 253 below, note 8); or Nicephorus may have been the Συναδηνός τις of II. 2.
[3] IV. 5, p. 112; VII. 2, p. 190, and 3, pp. 195–8; IX. 5–end.   [4] IX. 6, p. 256.
[5] IX. 8, p. 261.   [6] See Du Cange's note on X. 2, p. 271 c.   [7] e.g. XII. 5.
[8] VI. 6, p. 162.   [9] XI. 8, p. 332; XIV. 2, pp. 424 and 428.
[10] Callicles' Poem XX is put into the mouth of John, and hints darkly at 'envy', 'rough paths', 'upraised arms', and the like, which had temporarily impeded his rise to power. But this is too vague to justify Sternbach's note that Irene's 'dolosa consilia' against her son 'manifesto significantur'.

5. HER MARRIAGE

ANNA'S betrothal to Constantine Ducas brought her as we
have seen no solid satisfaction whatever. As to her marriage
with Nicephorus Bryennius which lasted during the greater
part of her life, from 1097 to 1137 at least, we have every reason
to believe that it was happy, and that when the fulsome Theodore Prodromus speaks of the 'black calyx' covering the red and
white rose of her person after her husband's death he alludes
not to external mourning only.[1] In the *Prologue* to her Will, as
we said in our Introduction, Anna depicts herself as having
wished for τὸν καθαρώτατόν τε καὶ ἄζυγα βίον, and having only
married to please her parents. In all probability this is merely
an expression of the conventional prudery which saw special
sanctity in the celibate life,[2] or it may have been a transitory
feeling due to chagrin at the death of Constantine. In any case
we find no trace of it in the *Alexias*, where Nicephorus Bryennius
is not spoken of very often, but always with affection and
respect, as he is also in the *Prologue* just mentioned. By under-
taking to write the life of his father-in-law he may be said to
have been the original cause of his wife's book. Her Preface is
full of him, his learning, charm, and wisdom, his literary achievements, which as his widow she sought to emulate and continue,[3]
his military energy, and untimely death, moving Anna to one of
her most passionate outpourings of grief. One of her sentences
about him is worth quoting in view of the assertion by Nicetas
Acominatus that both Irene and Anna hoped he might succeed
Alexius instead of John; Anna says: 'Alas for the grace that pervaded his limbs, alas for the form not (merely) worthy of a
throne as some say,[4] but even more divine and noble.'[5] But as

---

[1] *Poem on the death of the Princess Theodora*, lines 45–6 (*B. Z.* XVI, p. 88). Anna
frequently mourns over his death and calls it τὸ κορυφαιότατον τῶν κακῶν, greater
even than the loss of her parents (Pref., 4, p. 7; VII. 2, p. 191; XIV. 7, p. 447;
XV. 11, p. 506).

[2] See p. 10 above, and pp. 136, 296 below.

[3] He was 'unable to neglect literature even in the midst of toils and pains'
(Pref. 3, p. 4). His style had 'harmony and grace' (*ibid.*, p. 5). 'He read every book
and pored over every science' and 'gave himself to composition', VII. 2, p. 191.

[4] Eurip., *Aeolus*, Frag. 15, πρῶτον μὲν εἶδος ἄξιον τυραννίδος. The same quotation
occurs in Nic. Bry., IV. 15, p. 96.

[5] Pref. 4, p. 6. Bury (*B. Z.* II, pp. 76–8) changes θειοτέρου καὶ κρείττονος (agreeing
with εἴδους and dependent with it on ὧ) into θειοτέ[ρας μοί]ρας καὶ κρείττονος. This
would be a tempting suggestion but for the fact that in the *Prologue* to her Will Anna
speaks of her husband as ἀνὴρ τῶν ὑφ' ἡλίῳ κρείττων τε καὶ θειότερος, referring to
personality and not to fate. In Zonaras, XVIII. 29, we have the remark that no one
is perfect, θειοτέρας γὰρ τοῦτο μοίρας, which may have suggested the emendation
to Bury's mind. Psellus (*Chron.* Mich. VII, Byz. T., p. 259) says, praising Michael,

this phrase occurs in the middle of one of our writer's most 'purple passages' it seems unnecessary to take it very literally.[1] The next time she mentions Nicephorus (putting aside the references to his History which belong to the question of her sources) it is in connexion with the elder Nicephorus Bryennius, the would-be usurper whom Alexius had conquered at Calaure and who had been blinded.[2] Anna says her husband was τοῦ Βρυεννίου ἐκείνου ἀπόγονος, and the older commentators, Possinus, Du Cange, &c., have taken this word in its classical meaning of 'descendant' not nearer than the second generation, and have seen in the Caesar the grandson of the rebel. J. Seger[3] however has convincingly shown that the son-in-law of Alexius was the son, not the grandson, of Alexius' old enemy, and that Anna's use of ἀπόγονος is as vague as that of Sophocles.[4] The proofs need not be elaborated here, though it may be worth mentioning that Zonaras definitely gives the relationship as that of father and son.[5]

This choice of a son-in-law from a hostile family was probably a piece of diplomacy on the part of Alexius,[6] diplomacy fully justified by the event. In 1097, when the Crusaders are attacking Constantinople, Nicephorus Bryennius has an important command, and distinguishes himself by his magnificent archery; if the men under him shot like Teucer at Troy, he shot like Heracles and his bow was as Apollo's.[7] Later on he is raised to the dignity of Panhypersebastos.[8] In Alexius' last Turkish campaign the Caesar leads the right wing, and

'I have made my history so that any one may know that there is a nature of man absolutely of divine fate (θείας ἄντικρυς μοίρας) and beyond known nature.' But this again is not quite analogous to our text.

[1] In II. 7, p. 57, John Ducas Caesar is said to have μορφὴν τυράννῳ προσήκουσαν. He had actually 'rebelled' against his nephew Michael VII, so was a τύραννος in the technical Byzantine sense. See Ch. 43 below.

[2] VII. 2, p. 191. She ascribes to her husband wisdom (especially in speech), strength and beauty, military powers like Achilles, and great learning. He was 'unique and excelling in all things'.

[3] Byz. Hist. der 10ten u. 11ten Jahrh. I, Nikephoros Bryennios, pp. 14–17. The father of Alexius' enemy also rebelled and was blinded, but in 1057 (Zonaras, XVIII. 2).

[4] In Sophocles' O. C. 534 it refers to a daughter. Anna uses it again for 'son' in XV. 4, p. 471. For her vague terms of relationship see p. 28, note 5 above.

[5] Epit. XVIII. 22. So Theophylact (Ser. II, Ep. 31, P. G. 126, col. 428) addresses the ex-rebel as the συμπένθερος of Alexius (who had formerly defeated him).

[6] See II. 6, p. 57, where we are told that the men of Orestias, the old name for Adrianople, sided with Botaniates against Alexius because the latter had conquered their townsman Bryennius. In Nic. Acom. John C. 2, p. 5 Alexius is made to call his son-in-law rather scornfully 'a Macedonian'. The noble families of Asia Minor looked down on the European ones (Attal. C. S. H. B., p. 288) and the Governors of Eastern Themes took precedence over those of the Western (Const. Porph. de caerim., II. 52, C. S. H. B. vol. I, p. 713).

[7] X. 9, p. 296.   [8] XIII. 11, p. 415.

while guarding himself from blame for 'inexperience or youth', displays great prowess,[1] though on the whole he seems to be a less distinguished warrior than his father, who even as a blinded ex-enemy helps his conqueror Alexius with free-spoken counsel[2] and military service.[3] The great forte of the younger Bryennius was undoubtedly persuasive speech. He exercises it with marked effect on the Emperor's enemies, rebellious Gregory Taronites[4] and stubborn Bohemund,[5] and even on the Manichaean heretics.[6] His influence with his mother-in-law and consequently, whenever she acted as regent for Alexius, with the people of Constantinople is mentioned by Zonaras as the reason why John feared him.[7] He was evidently attractive and popular as well as gifted, and his literary tastes were Anna's own.[8] His μελέτη of the sacred books was due to the instruction of Alexius himself,[9] and was evidently of a thorough nature. He and Anna seem, judging from the *Prologue* to her Will, to have lost as infants one or more of their 'beautiful and high-born children'. Irene's *Typikon*[10] mentions two daughters of Anna's, one unnamed, one called Irene Ducas, both destined to succeed their mother and grandmother in the Patronage (ἐφορεία) of the Cecharitomene Convent. We know that there were also two sons, for Theodore Prodromus has given us an *Epithalamium* on the marriage of both of them.[11] One was called Alexius and the other John, the second name being characteristically paraphrased by the poet as 'the one full of Grace', because Johanan, the Hebrew equivalent of Ioannes, means 'the Grace of God'.

As to Bryennius' career after Alexius' death, we know from Anna that he accompanied John on his Asiatic campaigns[12] and there contracted the illness from which he died, not before 1137 when John went to Antioch. This intimacy tends to prove Nicetas Acominatus correct in saying that Bryennius refused to rebel against his brother-in-law John, whether we do or do not believe this writer's statement that Anna actually did.[13] Such 'slackness as regards grasping at empire' is what we should expect from the author of the *Hyle*, who represents both John

---

[1] XV. 4, p. 473; 5, p. 475; 6, p. 476.
[2] VII. 2, pp. 190, 191.   [3] X. 2, pp. 274 sqq.
[4] XII. 7, p. 365.   [5] XIII. 11, p. 405.
[6] XIV. 8, p. 453.   [7] *Epit.* XVIII. 26.
[8] Nic. Ac. *John C.* 2, p. 4; 3, p. 7. He was λογικῶν μέτοχος παιδεύσεων, an estimate confirmed by Zonaras (XVIII. 26) and Theod. Prodromus (*Epithalamium, P. G.* 133, col. 1401).
[9] XIV. 8, p. 453.   [10] *P. G.* 127, col. 1116.
[11] *P. G.* 133, cols. 1397–1406.   [12] Pref. 3, p. 5.
[13] Nic. Ac. *John C.* 3, pp. 7, 8.

Ducas Caesar and his own father Bryennius as attempting usurpation with great reluctance[1] and seems to admire the John
Comnenus of old days for refusing the crown proffered by his
brother.[2] Possibly some of Anna's 'woes' of which we hear so
much came from her being a firebrand unequally yoked with
a man of peaceful and scholarly phlegm.[3] Even if such differences of temperament are not inconsistent with sincere mutual
affection, they at least prevent uninterrupted harmony.

6. HER SELF-PITY

THE question of these much-heralded 'woes' next claims our
attention. If Anna had no reason to feel that Fate (however
harsh) had been unjust, and if her being passed over for the
throne was only what the birth of her brother and the death of
her fiancé led her to expect, why does she represent herself as
engulfed in troubles 'from her swaddling bands' or at any rate
before she had passed her eighth year? We may begin by mentioning certain subsidiary causes. First there is the factor of self-
pity founded on that vanity which has always figured in the
Greek character, and is indeed not unknown in other nations.
The presupposition is that all the good things in one's life are no
more than one's due, while the evils come from a cruel fate.
Then there is the almost inevitable distortion of view due to
lapse of years. Not many people even if aided by voluminous
diaries remember their childhood as it actually was, and it is
quite possible that distance lent enchantment to Anna's view of
her dead loved ones, and gave her a heightened sense of past
injuries at the hands of men and gods. Still there can be few if
any writers who without any apparent cause have been as
vehement in their cursings of the day when they were born.
Miss Gardner[4] is of opinion that though she loved her parents
and her sisters, and in fact all her family except her brother
John, yet her childhood was made unhappy by dissensions in
the Palace. The Ducas family, the kinsmen of Alexius' wife,
hated and were hated by his masterful mother Anna Dalassena,
who kept her grip on things till far on into the reign.[5] The
ex-Empress Maria, with whom apparently Anna lived, accord-

---

[1] *Hyle*, II. 17, p. 55; III. 5, p. 71.   [2] *Ibid*. I. 4, p. 18.
[3] Nicetas represents her as railing at him for cowardice in declining to try
and unseat John (*John C.* 3, p. 8).
[4] *Op. cit.*   [5] X. 4, p. 279.

ing to the prevailing custom of the day,[1] as the child-betrothed
of her son Constantine, does not seem to have been acceptable
to either the Ducas or the Comnenus party, and was sufficiently
discontented to join (up to a certain point) in the conspiracy
against Alexius of her late husband's half-brother Nicephorus
Diogenes.[2] We get throughout the *Alexias* hints, couched in
obscure language, of plots and intrigues and family quarrels;
possibly a sensitive and clever child was conscious of and
saddened by all this. One other point may be mentioned.
Both Zonaras[3] and Glycas[4] represent Alexius as an unfaithful
husband in his early married life; if this is true, Irene's injuries may well have reacted on her eldest child.

It will, however, be advisable to collect the various passages
in which Anna gives her own autobiography, as we can then
better judge of her true character.

(I) The third sentence of her Preface puts forward her claim
to consideration as her father's biographer. She was 'nurtured
and born in the purple' so that she was familiar with the facts;
she had received an excellent education,[5] and was therefore
capable of narrating them. In the *Prologue* to her Will she
ascribes her educational advantages to her parents' care ; in
this Preface she refers them to Nature, her own zeal for learning,
God above, and ὁ καιρός, a quartet of causes most characteristically chosen. She is careful on all occasions to clear herself
from the charge of bragging or partiality or 'making a parade
of skill in letters', but we feel throughout that in this matter
'qui s'excuse s'accuse'. After this statement of her filial motives
for writing, she passes on in the Preface to her even stronger
conjugal wish, to finish the unfinished work of her husband.
Then the lamentations begin: 'And when I come to this point
I am filled with dizziness in my soul and I wet my eyes with
streams of tears,'[6] mourning over the loss to herself and the

---

[1] III. 1, p. 72. E. Kurtz (*B. Z.* XVI, pp. 87–93) gives a poem of Theodore
Prodromus on the death of Theodora, daughter-in-law of Anna Comnena, in
which Theodora is said to have been brought up by Anna and by Anna's mother
Irene, l. 36 sqq. For the story of Anna's other daughter-in-law he refers to Zonaras,
XVIII. 28. She came to Constantinople in 1118 'um, wie wir in Anbetracht
zahlreicher analogen Fälle hinzufügen können, hier bis zur Erreichung des
heiratsfähigen Alters unter der Obhut ihrer zukünftigen Schwiegermutter erzogen
zu werden'.

[2] IX. 5, p. 255, and 8, p. 261.

[3] *Epit.* XVIII. 24.

[4] *Bibl. Chron.*, Pt. IV, p. 334.

[5] She refers to this again in IX. 10, p. 266, and XV. 7, p. 486; also XV. 11.
More will be said of her education later on.

[6] So in V. 9, p. 148, the memory of her mother's learning is so potent as to
'pierce' her heart, and almost to lead her narrative astray. 'But the chain of
History acts as a restraint.'

world of so great a man as Nicephorus Bryennius. His death was the climax to her woes: 'I truly was conversant with terrible experiences so to speak from the very midst of the swaddling-bands of my imperial birth, and I met with no good fortune, unless any one should think it a good and smiling fortune that my mother and my father were the ruling sovereigns, and that it was the purple from which I sprang up. As for the rest, alas for the surges! alas for the upheavals!' which would move all animate and inanimate things to tears. Compared to her husband's death her previous griefs were as nothing, merely smoke forerunning a terrible fire. But she will not brood over the past; her task is to write about her father, and though the thought of what he was moves her 'to hottest tears, weeping with all the inhabited world', she will delay her start no longer, and so her Preface ends.

(II) In I. 10, p. 23, occurs a rather cryptic sentence. After saying that the foolish betrothal[1] by Michael VII of his son Constantine to Robert Guiscard's daughter was the real cause of the Norman invasion of the Empire, she says she will leave all description of this Constantine for the present: 'I will speak of it in the proper time, whenever I bewail my own misfortunes shortly after the narration of this marriage-contract and the defeat of all the barbarian power.' Constantine in his short life had two 'marriage-contracts' made for him, one with Helena and one with Anna; it would appear that the reference here is to the first one, spoken of in the preceding sentence as τὸ βαρβαρικὸν κῆδος. The question arises, why did she speak of it in the same breath with her 'own misfortunes'? What was the connexion between them? The 'defeat of all the barbarian power' must refer to 1083 and the campaign against Bohemund (for in 1085 Robert, after some naval fighting entailed by his renewed invasion of the Empire, died before his army ever came into action or met with a 'defeat'); yet Anna was not born till December of that same 1083. Probably the sentence may be paraphrased thus: 'I will not speak further of Constantine now; his life and death belong to my own sad history, and before I get to that I must pass from my brief mention of the disastrous contract between him and Helena, to tell of the war which followed therefrom, ending in the destruction of the tyrants from Normandy' (ἡ ἀπώλεια τῶν Νορμανόθεν τυράννων).

(III) In I. 12, pp. 28 sqq., she refers again to the contract

---

[1] Scylitzes (Hist., p. 853 D and 856 A and B) speaks of Michael's neglect in having let the Norman conquer Lombardy and Calabria, but seems to think this marriage-contract a wise measure for getting Robert's aid against the Turks.

between Constantine and Helena and says: 'And when once
more I remember this youth I grow sad in soul and confuse my
arguments: but I cut short my narrative about him, reserving
it all for the proper occasion.' She cannot, however, refrain
from calling him 'a product of the Golden Age', and she adds:
'And I after so many years when I remember this youth am
filled with tears. Yet I hold back my weeping and husband it
for (more) suitable places.' She then repeats the statement that
Constantine was betrothed to Helena, but adds with evident
satisfaction that he was not old enough to consummate the
marriage before his father fell from power, when his betrothed,
whom he had always regarded with horror, was removed from
the scene.[1]

(IV) In III. 1 she dwells on the beauty and charm of Constantine, aged seven, and speaks of him as one of 'my own
people'.[2] It was, she declares, care for him and fear for his life
that made the ex-Empress Maria cling after her second husband's deposition to the shelter of the palace, not any illicit
affection for Alexius as reported by the slander-loving populace.
And she emphasizes her assertions in these words: 'I had certainty in this instance . . . having been brought up with (Constantine)[3] by the Empress from my childhood (till a time) when
I had not yet passed my eighth year. And because she had much
affection for me, she made me a sharer of all her secrets.' A
few lines afterwards she says of Maria: 'I often heard her
herself narrating all that happened to her, and into what fear
she had fallen, especially on behalf of the child, when the
Emperor Nicephorus (Botaniates) laid down his sovereignty.'
Three chapters later[4] Anna tells us how generously, by contrast with the step-father Botaniates, Alexius had treated the
young Constantine; he let him wear what Baynes[5] calls 'the
purple boot the symbol of sovereignty', made him sign all documents after himself and in the same imperial cinnabar, and gave
him a crown and a place in all processions.

(V) VI. 8. These honours were certainly retained by Constantine till the birth of John II if not longer, and for at least
the first four years of Anna's life were shared by her. Her story
of her birth as her parents' eldest-born, 'most honoured child of

---

[1] Chalandon, *op. cit.*, p. 63.
[2] He was her cousin, through her mother, as well as her betrothed.
[3] This seems to be the meaning of συνανατραφεῖσα τῇ βασιλίδι, τῇ βασιλίδι being
dative of agent, and συν implying a companion, here Constantine.
[4] III. 4, pp. 79, 80. Cf. I. 15, p. 36.
[5] *Op. cit.*, p. 32.

the purple and first of the family of Alexius ',[1] is worth transcribing in full.[2]

'So the Emperor' [after a final victory at Castoria over the Normans] 'returns a triumphant conqueror to the metropolis, . . . on Dec. 1 of the 7th indiction' [i.e. December 1, 1083] 'and found the Empress in labour in the apartment assigned of old to empresses in childbed; now the people of long ago had called it The Purple Chamber, whence the name of Born in the Purple has gone out into the inhabited world. And about dawn (it was a Saturday) she gives birth before them to a female child, like, so they said, in all things to its father, and I forsooth was that child. And I have heard my mother the Empress narrating on certain occasions that two days[3] before the arrival of the Emperor into the Palace . . . she was seized with birth-pangs, but making the sign of the cross over her body, she said: "Little child, await awhile the coming of thy father." But her mother the protovestiary, as she told me, reproved her much and said with anger: "Dost thou know if he will come for a month yet? and how wilt thou hold out against such pains?" However, the command of the Empress obtained fulfilment, which even in the womb indicated very plainly my future loyalty to my parents. For after this, when I had advanced in age and arrived at reason, I was whole-heartedly at one and the same time mother-lover and father-lover.[4] And as witnesses of this my disposition I have many persons, nay indeed all who know my affairs. But in addition to these there is the testimony of my many toils and pains on my parents' behalf, and those perils into which I threw myself from love to them, not sparing my honour nor my money nor my life itself: for my love to them so consumed me that I often risked my very soul for them. But I will not speak of this yet. Let my story return again to the things that happened to me from my very birth. For all the wonted ceremonies about the newborn children of emperors were carried out with unusual expense, so it is said, acclamations of course, and gifts and honours bestowed on the leaders of the Senate and of the army, so that they all rejoiced and exulted and sang paeans more than was ever known before, and the blood relations of the Empress in particular did not know what to do for pleasure. And after a few days had past, my parents adorn me like themselves with a crown and an imperial diadem. Now Constantine, son of the previous Emperor Michael Ducas, of whom my story has often made mention, was still reigning conjointly with the Emperor my father, and in deeds of gift he wrote his name in red ink with his, and in processions followed him wearing a tiara and in acclamations was acclaimed

---

[1] XV. 9, p. 490. [2] VI. 8, p. 166.

[3] πρὸ τρίτης ἡμέρας. The familiar Greek idiom; cf. 'He rose again the third day' of our Creed, when we nowadays should say 'second'.

[4] So again in XV. 11, p. 496. In the heading of Alexius' first poem to his son John the Emperor calls himself φιλομήτωρ and his son φιλοπάτωρ, B. Z. XXII. p. 349. Anna says of her father (III. 7, p. 86), τοσοῦτον ἦν φιλομήτωρ. Cf. also I. 8, p. 19.

second. So when I was to be acclaimed the leaders of the acclamations[1] when it was the time to cheer shouted out "Constantine and
Anna" in the same breath. And this indeed was done for a considerable time, as I have often since heard my relations and parents
tell. Perhaps indeed this was a presage of what was to befall me,
both of good fortune and contrariwise of bad.'

Then follows the account of her sister Maria's birth, and of her
parents' prayers for a son rewarded 'in the eleventh indiction',
i.e. between September 1 1087 and August 31 1088, by the birth
of John, an event over which the whole Empire rejoiced or
pretended so to do. Anna has *Schadenfreude* in reflecting that the
baby was ugly and the enthusiasm over him possibly insincere.
But there is, we may repeat, no hint of any sense of injustice in
her concluding words: 'Wishing then to promote this baby to
imperial eminence and to bequeath to him the empire of the
Greeks as his inheritance, they[2] honour him in the Great Church
of God with divine baptism and a crown. Such then was what
happened to me born in the purple, from the very starting-
place of my birth.'

It is worth noting that Anna never expressly says that she was
betrothed to Constantine, though her grief over his loss and her
attitude towards his mother might seem to imply it. For definite
information we must turn to Anna's husband Nicephorus
Bryennius, who says[3] that Alexius proved his constant care for
Constantine by betrothing[4] to him τὴν ἰδίαν θυγατέρα, as well as
by giving him a share in the Empire with all its outward and
visible signs, and thus προμνηστευόμενος αὐτῷ τὰ σκῆπτρα. But
a 'grievous disease' ended the young man's prospects as a
sovereign, and finally 'not long afterwards' his life. We might
assume that Constantine's imperial honours lasted till 1092,
when John's reign as co-Emperor with his father began,[5] but
for two facts. First, Archbishop Theophylact in January 1090[6]
reproaches Alexius for not having yet associated his son with
him in the Empire, which he is less likely to have done if that
exalted place was still occupied by his own former pupil Constantine. Secondly, Zonaras[7] tells us that Alexius deliberately
deprived Constantine of sovereignty, and if we consider this to

[1] Cf. the 'cheer leaders' of American teams.
[2] i.e. the parents.   [3] *Hyle*, Pref., p. 8.
[4] The word συνάπτειν might mean merely an association in imperial honours,
but betrothal seems more probable. Zonaras in telling the story uses the word
μνηστεία (XVIII. 22).
[5] *Neap. Reg. archiv. mon.* V, quoted by Chalandon, *op. cit.* p. 139, note 1.
[6] *P. G.* 126, col. 301. The *Anon. Syn. Chron.* is clearly wrong in saying (p. 177)
that Alexius made John co-Emperor 'as soon as he was born'.
[7] *Epit.*, XVIII. 21.

be the beginning of Anna's mysterious woes 'from without', she herself dates the event for us as 1091, when she had not yet passed her eighth year.[1] If we compare the two passages in which she mentions this fateful 'eighth year', it would appear that the end of her upbringing by the ex-Empress Maria coincided at that time with an outburst of enmity from the ' malice of men'. The whole story is perplexing. Malaterra[2] believes that Botaniates had Constantine castrated, but Chalandon[3] dismisses this as 'invraisemblable, puisqu'Alexis le fiança à sa fille'.[4] It is, however, not impossible that Alexius at first contemplated only a betrothal (in order to appear in the eyes of the people as a supporter of Constantine's hereditary rights) and not a τέλειος γάμος. Anna was a kinswoman of Constantine, whose grandfather, the Emperor Constantine Ducas, was brother to her mother's grandfather John Ducas Caesar, and unless Alexius did later on hope and endeavour to overrule Church laws in her favour, this was probably one of the instances not unknown in medieval history where betrothal was arranged between persons who could never marry.[5] Perhaps her 'mis-

---

[1] XIV. 7, p. 446, and cf. III. 1, p. 72.

[2] *Hist. Sic.* III. 13 (*S. S. Rer. Ital.* V, p. 579).

[3] *Op. cit.*, p. 63, note 1.

[4] Malaterra's obviously untrue statements that Michael VII was deposed because his subjects dreaded his son's marrying one of the formidable Norman race, and that Constantine was 'usque ad exitum vitae exilio relegatus' by Botaniates, make one suspect that 'turpiter eunuchizatus' is equally unreliable.

[5] So Cinnamus tells us that Bela, son of the King of Hungary, was betrothed to the daughter of Manuel I (whose mother's father Ladislaus was brother of Bela's father Geisa), but νόμου συγγενείας ἐμπόδων αὐτῷ γεγονότος, he married Manuel's wife's sister instead; it seems hard to believe he had not known the 'law' all along (*Hist.* V. 5, p. 125, and VI, 11, p. 167). Anna and Constantine as second cousins once removed would have stood to one another in the seventh degree by civil computation, and in the fourth by canon law. Impediments to marriage went up to but did not necessarily include the seventh degree of relationship. The civil computation seemed terribly lax to Peter Damianus, who died in 1072, not long before Anna's birth. He tells of his protest at Ravenna against the jurisconsults who had said: 'Septimam generationem canonica auctoritate praefixam ita debere intelligi, ut numeratis ex uno generis latere quattuor gradibus atque ex alio tribus' (which was exactly the case of Anna and Constantine) 'jure jam matrimonium posse contrahi' (*De parentelae gradibus, P. L.* 145, col. 191). By good fortune we have a novel of Alexius himself on the subject, published as No. 40 in Zachariae von Lingenthal's *Jus Graeco-Romanum*, Vol. III, p. 412, and commented on by the same learned writer in his *Geschichte des gr.-röm. Rechts*, p. 67. He points out that whereas two Patriarchs, John Xiphilinus and Eustratius Garidas, had declared a marriage within the seventh degree unlawful, Alexius issued this πρόσταγμα . . . διοριζόμενον ἀκωλύτως συνάπτεσθαι θείαν καὶ ἀνεψίαν μετὰ θείου καὶ ἀνεψίου κἂν ἔκτου βαθμοῦ συγγένειαν ἐξ ἀγχιστείας ἔχωσι. The Patriarch Nicolas resisted this, and there seems to have been considerable divergence of practice. Leunclavius (*Jus Gr.-Rom.* I. 217, Frankfurt 1596) has among his *Sententiae Synhodales* a decree of the Emperor Manuel I pronouncing invalidity once more and excommunication in the case of marriage within the seventh degree. As Zachariae von Lingenthal gives the date of Alexius' novel as 1092 or 1107, may we not believe

fortunes' began when Constantine was deposed from his imperial position and she simultaneously realized, from protests of Church and people, that her betrothal was a hollow form and that she would never be either Empress or Constantine's wife.[1]

Constantine however remained loyal to Alexius, who according to Anna 'loved him exceedingly like his own son', and in the plot of Nicephorus Diogenes in February 1094, though his mother was implicated, the boy himself was apparently quite innocent.[2] But we cannot fail to notice that on this occasion Anna speaks of him as a landed proprietor able to entertain the Emperor and his suite at his country house, not as her own betrothed. In any case he probably died soon afterwards, before Anna in Zonaras' words was ὡραία γάμου. Certainly in 1097 we find Nicephorus Bryennius already spoken of as the γαμβρός of the Emperor, and as Anna's Caesar.[3]

(VI) Returning to Anna's mysterious sorrows, we next hear of them in the long passage in XIV. 7. After saying that she got the facts about her father's life from eye-witnesses, and was, indeed, present herself 'in most cases', she goes on:

' For my life was not such as is so to speak stay-at-home, revolving under shade and luxury, but from my very swaddling-bands, I swear by my God and His Mother, pains and afflictions and continual misfortunes seized on me, some from without, others from at home. For what I was as to bodily state, I will not say, but let those speak and speak fully who were about the women's apartments. But the external things, and all that befell me before I had passed my eighth

that Alexius issued this novel in 1092 to meet the situation of the betrothal between Anna and Constantine? She was then eight years old (her birthday being in December). Could controversy about her betrothal have been the true beginning of her 'sea of troubles'? We may assume that popular sentiment went against Alexius' decree, or it would not have been opposed by his chief ecclesiastical officer and repealed by his grandson.

The story of Gregory Gabras is a curious instance of the idea that a man and his wife were so much 'one flesh', that relationship by affinity was no less a bar to marriage than consanguinity. Gregory could not marry the daughter of Isaac Comnenus, because his stepmother, the second wife of his father Theodore Gabras, was a first cousin of Isaac's wife. Anna says that 'the Laws and the Canons' forbade such a union (VIII. 9, p. 240). When Bohemund marries one daughter of the French king, and secures another as a bride for his nephew Tancred, we may be sure that there is only one explanation, viz. that the Pope dared not refuse a dispensation to so powerful a prince (XII. 1, p. 346).

[1] Zonaras says Constantine died ἐπὶ τῇ μνηστείᾳ, which seems to imply that he kept his status of betrothed after he had lost that of co-sovereign. But the words might merely mean 'having never been more than betrothed', in which case his betrothal might have terminated with his imperial dignity, and before his death. All we know certainly from Zonaras is that when Anna was nubile her father married her to Niceph. Bryennius (*Epit.* XVIII. 22).

[2] IX. 5–end. Zonaras does not mention Constantine in narrating this conspiracy.

[3] X. 9, p. 295. Du Cange in his note puts Anna's birth three years too late.

year, and all the enemies that the malice of men caused to spring forth against me—this demands the Siren charm of Isocrates, Pindaric eloquence, the rolling periods of Polemon, Homer's Calliope, Sappho's lyre, or any power beyond these. For there is nothing in the way of ills, small or great, near or far, that did not press straightway upon me. And verily the surge prevailed manifestly, and from then even till now, up to the time when I am writing this composition, the sea of misfortunes has been roaring against me, and one after another the waves overtake me.'

She then enumerates the sources of her history, and there follows a difficult passage:

'But I have collected the most and best of these things now that the third after my father[1] is wielding the sceptre, when all flattery and lying have deserted the grandfather himself, and all are flattering the present throne, and towards the departed are showing no adulation, but are narrating the bare facts and stating them as they were. Now I, bitterly lamenting my misfortunes and at this point of time mourning for three sovereigns, my father the Emperor, my lady and mother and Empress, and (woe is me!) my consort the Caesar, keep myself mostly hidden[2] and devote myself to books and to God. And not even the most obscure of people will be allowed to visit me, not to speak of those from whom I could learn what they chanced to have heard from others, nor my father's greatest intimates. For this is the thirtieth year (I swear it by the souls of the most blessed sovereigns), that I have not beheld nor seen nor consorted with any of my father's attendants, and this because many have died, and many are kept away by fear. And in these absurd ways the rulers' [doubtless the hated brother John] 'sentenced me not to be seen, but rather to be hated by the many.'

The only written materials to which she describes herself as having access are 'certain worthless and altogether trifling compositions', which lacked literary skill, but tallied as to fact with her own memories of past conversations, and also with the recollections of the veterans now turned monks who had fought in the struggle that brought her father to the throne in 1081. Why she was allowed to converse with these, monks though they were, when other intercourse was forbidden her and when, as we believe, she was living in the precincts of a very strict nunnery, it is not easy to explain. At any rate, if we consider her seclusion to have been decreed by John in 1118, she was still writing her history in 1148.

[1] i.e. in Greek idiom her nephew Manuel I, who succeeded his father John II in 1143, and reigned till 1180.
[2] ἐγγωνιάζω. Probably used idiomatically for life in a cloister. See pp. 49, 291 note 3, 324 note 5, below.

(VII) In XV. 3, p. 468, we have once more the statement that Anna brought trouble on herself by her devotion to her father. Truth itself, she says, compels her to praise him, and she goes on: 'Let my history be devoted to the substance (φύσει) of truth. For in other respects I showed my loyalty for my father, and also by this' (i.e. my truthful tale) 'I sharpened the spears and whetted the swords of enemies against myself, as all know who have not been ignorant of my affairs.'

(VIII) A most characteristic outburst ends the fifth chapter of this same Book XV. Mention of her brave and talented young brother Andronicus moves her to lament his early death. This in turn makes her question whether sufferers with 'such sensitiveness to ill' as hers would not be happier transformed into stones or birds or trees as in mythological tales. 'For if this were so, easily might the evils that have befallen me have made me a stone.'

(IX) Last but not least, we have the final chapter of the whole work, where Anna is almost as much occupied with her own afflictions as with those of her father. As a loving daughter she is reluctant to recapitulate the many things that devoured her heart, notably his death. Even the remembrance of his modesty which made him shrink from having his biography written moves her to 'lamentations and wailings', but being φιλοπάτωρ τε ἅμα καὶ φιλομήτωρ ἐξ αὐτῶν σπαργάνων, she braces herself to tell the sad tale. As the Emperor's illness gets more and more hopeless the family are subjected to 'turmoil and surge', to 'fear and peril'. Irene weeps floods of tears even while acting as nurse, and the Emperor actually chides her for letting the 'sea of grief' overwhelm her. By so doing however he only 'tears open even more the wound of misfortune' for them all. Anna goes on: 'But I was beside myself and I swear by all-knowing God to my present friends and to the men who shall hereafter light upon this history, that I was no better than mad-men, but was wholly given up to my suffering.' In spite of this she ministers not only to her father but to her mother, who longs to die too. 'The pains of death then encircled us. And then I per-ceived I was out of my mind, for I raved and did not know what I should become or whither I should turn, seeing the Empress plunged into the sea of troubles and the Emperor dying'. Later on Irene says, ' "Let us begin the dirge." So I wailed with her despising all things, and I grieved with her.' The text is here defective, but we can make out that women in the plural, perhaps her mother and sisters, 'tore their clothes lamenting dismally', and that the Empress threw herself on the ground

and smote her head with her hands. When the last moment had
come, Anna says, 'I turned my head, feeling withered and cold,
bending my head to the ground without speaking; then I put
my two hands over my eyes and walking back I wailed.' This
produced a 'great and bitter cry' from the Empress, and sorrow
in 'the whole world' among all those who were not too much
'overpowered with grief' to show it outwardly. As for herself her
'sun set' when her father died, and she can hardly yet believe
that those terrible events were not a dream, for if real how had
she survived them? This brings her back to her old theme,
See if there be any sorrow like unto my sorrow, and the history
ends in a paroxysm of grief. If Alexius was her sun, Irene was
her moon, and she survived both, only to see τὸ κορυφαιότατον
τῶν κακῶν in her husband's death. No form of sorrow had been
spared her, reserved as she was 'for such encirclings of ills'.
Despair came over her and she longed vainly to die or be turned
like Niobe into stone. Yet this was not all, and here we scent
an allusion to Alexius' 'successor on the throne' who, as she tells
us shortly before, had left his father's dying bed and 'pressed
into the Great Palace'. It is nearly certainly to him that his
sister attributes 'the intolerable ills stirred up in the Palace
by men' against her, and though she deprecates bitterness (μὴ
πλέον ἐμπικραινοίμεθα), it is with a vivid sense of her vitriolic
resentment against someone or something that we lay her
pages down.

What then were these terrible woes? What did the malice of
enemies do to her? What does she mean by all these toils and
perils and whetted swords? We can sympathize with her over
the loss of parents and husband,[1] but not with the exaggerated
frenzy into which it throws her; we can pity her for her life
in enforced retirement, but when between the lines we read
her implacable hatred, we feel that in John's place we should
have insisted on the same. Furthermore, even if we take with
a grain of salt Nicetas' well-known story of her brother's great
magnanimity to her after her attempted rebellion,[2] we know
from the *Typikon* of her mother's convent[3] that the widowed
Empress and her daughter and granddaughter were allowed to
live in dignity and ease, administering with well-nigh autocratic power the institution Irene had founded. What then was
the carking sorrow that for nearly threescore years, from her
eighth year to her sixty-fifth, 'engulfed' Anna Comnena? After
eight centuries we cannot tell; we talk a different language

---

[1] Also of children. See the *Prologue* to her Will, lines 64 sqq.
[2] *John C.* 3, p. 8.   [3] *P. G.* 127, cols. 985–1120.

literally and figuratively, and we cannot gauge the depth of feeling beneath her hysterical bombast. One thing is, however, self-evident; if, as experience teaches, great sorrows are dumb (Job being the notable exception that proves the rule), then Anna's were emphatically not great except in her own self-centred, self-satisfied mind.

7. COURT LIFE

THE Byzantine Court of the eleventh century, of which Scott's picture in *Count Robert of Paris* is not wholly a caricature, strikes the reader at the outset by its strange mixture of Pomp and Informality, of Etiquette and what we can only call Casualness. Not only can the eunuch 'attendant on the imperial bedchamber' walk in even when the sovereigns are asleep;[1] access to the august tent is equally open to suspects coming to defend themselves or to their kin, and lampoons may be flung in unperceived.[2] Beggars approach without hindrance to the Empress's door,[3] and as no guards are set at night or portals shut Alexius' murder by Nicephorus Diogenes is only prevented by the presence of a maid-servant fanning away the mosquitoes.[4] 'Frequently', we are told, 'men carried swords under their garments' when approaching the sovereign.[5]

Even military etiquette allows of laxity. Officers not only make pungent jests or criticisms to the Emperor's face;[6] they play what we must describe as practical jokes. Thus Cantacuzenus sends a grotesque pygmy Scythian to lead in before Alexius a gigantic Norman captive, up to whose thigh he barely reached, and 'straightway great laughter arose from all'.[7] Similarly Alexius plays a trick on his brother-in-law, hoping to arouse 'sweet laughter mixed with fear', by dressing up his own soldiers in the clothes of Scythian captives.[8] The Emperor pays visits to the houses of subjects,[9] plays polo and chess with

---

[1] XIII. 1, p. 378; XIV. 5, p. 438; XV. 2, p. 462.
[2] VIII. 8; XIII. 1.   [3] XII. 3, p. 354.
[4] IX. 5, p. 254. Later on Nicephorus tries to kill him coming from the bath (IX. 5, p. 255). Cf. the schemes of other conspirators in XII. 6, p. 361; XIII. 1, p. 377; all based on the certainty of easy approach.
[5] IX. 9, p. 262.
[6] VII. 2, p. 191; IX. 5, p. 254.
[7] XIII. 6, pp. 394, 395. We may note in the Norman army that Robert Guiscard threatens to 'flog' one of his picked soldiers, and the man answers him with considerable insolence (IV. 8, p. 121).
[8] VIII. 2, p. 224.   [9] IX. 5, p. 255; X. 4, p. 280.

his intimates,[1] and invites to a seat at his own table any one whom he specially wishes to honour,[2] though for a subject to presume on kindness or to treat his Emperor as ὁμοδίαιτος is felt to be preposterous. Even on his marches he would summon the ailing and aged among his camp-followers to partake of a 'divine banquet' with him.[3] Finally it gives a curiously democratic and modern touch to the narrative of Alexius' last illness when we read of the Empress sitting up all night on the sick man's bed and holding him up to breathe, or again of the attendants lifting his bed on poles and carrying it about in shifts.[4]

Yet Anna never ceases from impressing on us, in season and out of season, how great her father's dignity both official and personal really was.[5] Not only does he exhaust his ingenuity in inventing for all his supporters high-sounding titles; she dwells with gusto on his clothes, his jewels, and the magnificence of the gilded throne which accompanies him even on campaigns.[6] The 'purple', whether of robe or buskin, figures too often as the symbol of sovereignty[7] to need a series of quotations: we will only refer to one passage where Alexius, overwhelmed by remorse over the sack of Constantinople, scorns even his newly gained 'purple robe and gemmed diadem and golden pearl-decked attire'.[8] Isaac Comnenus the Sebastocrator, when co-Regent with Anna Dalassena in Alexius' absence, is markedly

---

[1] IX. 7, p. 259; XII. 6, p. 360; XIV. 4, p. 434. Similarly John Comnenus in private life did not shun κομψεία σεμνή even with laughter involved (Nic. Ac. John C. 12, p. 32).

[2] II. 1, p. 43, 3, p. 47; X. 9, p. 298; XV. 7, p. 482, and 8, p. 487. So the Persian chief receives the captured Romanus Diogenes as a guest at his board (Nic. Bry. I. 19, p. 32). Cf. the honours of sharing in his καθέδρα καὶ τράπεζα accorded by John II to his brother Isaac (Nic. Ac. John C. 3, p. 7).

[3] XV. 8, p. 488.

[4] XV. 11, p. 499.

[5] She is specially outraged at the impious levity which makes the Turks travesty the Emperor and his gout and his doctors with ribald mockery upon the stage (XV. 1, p. 461).

[6] IX. 9, p. 263.

[7] Anna's bombastic way of describing an accession to the throne is that ' Fortune gives to a man the imperial crown and makes his boots purple' (III. 1, p. 71).

[8] III. 5, p. 81. Even an imperial tent is ἐρυθροβαφής (XIII. 1, p. 376), as well as the largest ever seen (XI. 3, p. 316). Pearls are mentioned again as fastening the imperial garment of Botaniates at the wrist (II. 12, p. 68). But we never hear in Anna's book of a pearl with a name, like the 'Orphan' captured at Manzikert from Romanus Diogenes (Nic. Bry. I. 17, p. 31), and when a treasure is hidden in a thicket, it is not a specially large and brilliant jewel (as in Nic. Bry. I. 24, p. 37), but τὸ ὠμόφορον of the Mother of God (VII. 3, pp. 196, 198). In his first poem to John, Alexius alludes to the pearls and other jewels on the imperial diadem (Mous. Alex. I. 140). Bryennius speaks of 'purple boots' adorned with pearls and jewels (IV. 16, p. 97), and Attaliates of imperial garments heavy with stones and pearls (p. 320).

called an ' ἀπόρφυρος βασιλεύς ',[1] though even minor royalties often wore purple in some form.[2] The imperial diadem is described as follows: 'Like a well-rounded half-globe it confines the head, adorned everywhere with pearls and precious stones, some set in and some hung on, for on each side of the temples strings are suspended with pearls and stones to touch the cheeks. And this is a special feature of the apparel of the Emperor. The crowns of the Sebastocrator and Caesar' (the second and third in the Empire) 'have pearls and stones without the globular top'.[3] Three times Anna tells us that her father (a small man) φοβερὸς προὐκάθητο[4]; indeed, on all occasions where he wishes to make an impression on foes or doubtful friends this sitting on his throne is specially mentioned.[5] His own daughters are in awe of this man, in spite of his εὐπρόσιτον quality[6]; even to save a doomed man's life they dare not disturb him at his public prayers in church, but stand 'timidly outside the doors' till they can attract the Empress's notice and get her to intercede.[7] For the rest, we get from the Alexias a picture of a happy if rather 'precious' family life in the Byzantine palace. Irene reads the

---

[1] V. 2, p. 129.
[2] Beside Alexius' death-bed his womenkind tear their purple raiment and his wife throws off her διάδημα and καλύπτρα (veil), and τὰ κοκκοβαφῆ πέδιλα, assuming instead the black shoes and 'plain dark veil' of mourning (XV. 11, pp. 504, 505). Bryennius (Pref., p. 8) lays the greatest stress on the outward honours that Alexius gave young Constantine Ducas, and Anna considers (III. 4) that the restoration of the boy's ἐρυθρὰ ὑποδήματα, long replaced for him by shameful and ridiculous parti-coloured ones, was an act of wonderful generosity to him and kindness to his mother. The sons of Romanus Diogenes (IX. 6) were cruelly stripped of this outward mark of royalty by their half-brother Michael VII, but for all his affection towards them Alexius does not seem to have given it back.
[3] III. 4, p. 78. This was clearly the ταινία promised to Nicephorus Melissenos together with the rank of Caesar in II. 8, p. 60. Anna describes herself as wearing when a baby a στέφος καὶ βασιλικὸν διάδημα, while the co-Emperor, her betrothed Constantine Ducas, has a τιάρα (III. 4, p. 80; VI. 8, p. 167). Her baby brother John also has a στέφος (VI. 8, p. 168). These three words, ταινία, στέφος, and τιάρα, probably all express the same idea, a crown inferior to the special βασιλικὸν διάδημα properly so-called of III. 4, p. 78. στέφη were worn by the sons of the Emperor Romanus Diogenes during their father's reign (IX. 6, p. 256). A globular crown like the Emperor's is given to Herod in one of the mosaics of St. Mark's at Venice.
[4] VI. 2, p. 154; IX. 9, p. 263; XIV. 3, p. 432.
[5] X. 9, p. 295 (bis), 10, p. 301, 11, p. 304; XI. 3, p. 316; XIII. 6, p. 395; XIV. 4, pp. 435–7; XV. 9, p. 491. We may note that a throne is so important an object as to bear seven different names, περιωπή, κλίνη, σκίμπους, θρόνος, καθέδρα, θῶκος, βῆμα.
[6] III. 1, p. 71. But cf. III. 3, p. 76, Anna predicates this also of Irene (XII. 3, p. 354) and even of Robert Guiscard (VI. 7, p. 165). Thuc. (Hist. VI. 57) describes the tyrant Hippias as πᾶσιν εὐπρόσοδος, and Nic. Acom. says that John II was never δυσπρόσιτος (John C. 12, p. 32). Zonaras has scant admiration for Alexius as a ruler, but admits that he was εὐπρόσιτος and consorted with those round him not σοβαρῶς ἀλλ' ἐκ τοῦ ἴσου σχεδόν (Epit. XVIII. 29). Ord. Vit. (Pt. III, lib. 7, ch. 4) says he was 'amabilis omnibus', and especially 'affabilis militibus' (P. L. 188, col. 519).
[7] XII. 6, p. 363.

Fathers at meals, with her awestruck daughter looking on,[1] and astrology and geometry both seem to have been court topics of conversation.[2] As a lighter touch we may note that she speaks of having stayed with her father in Philippopolis 'on some matter of business', and of having wandered round looking at its old buildings.[3] Certainly she heard and enjoyed hearing her male kinsfolk talk to one another,[4] and the women's apartment was shut off by a curtain only.[5] Of harem-like seclusion there is no trace, least of all perhaps in the long last chapter that describes Alexius' dying illness. Irene and her daughters do the nursing; the Empress gives orders to the servants, and Anna acts as 'umpire' between the disagreeing doctors. Seclusion is a new and unaccustomed hardship laid upon our authoress after her father's death by the unkindness of her mysterious enemies. She says ἐγγωνιάζω τὰ πολλὰ καὶ βιβλίοις καὶ Θεῷ προσανάκειμαι,[6] and from this and Irene's *Typikon* we infer that she spent her retirement in a convent. Her description of herself at sixty-five or thereabouts as 'idly moving a pen at the time of lighting the lamps', and 'slightly nodding over the writing' is not without pathos.[7]

Of the unique grandeur of the Basileus to all Byzantine minds we shall speak later; in no sense was he like ordinary men. Here we are only concerned with outward court ritual. We hear of greetings usual from and to emperors[8] and honours customary for empresses,[9] and the very words breathe the Pomp of Circumstance. The old etymological meaning of the word πομπή is not wholly lost in this book. When Alexius slips unperceived into his capital, so as to escape a triumphal entry, the λαμπρὰ εἰσιτήρια and βασιλικὴ πομπή which he avoids obviously comprised a procession.[10] An even plainer case is where Anna illustrates the fickleness of the mob by saying that one day they honour a man and 'furnish him with an escort' (προπέμπουσι) and the next they cry out for his death.[11]

But a procession is after all only one small concomitant of royalty, and Pomp is usually a figure of speech in Greek as in English. The extravagantly elaborate ritual and outward display over which visitors to the Byzantine court of earlier

[1] V. 9, p. 147.
[2] VI. 7, p. 164; IX. 10, p. 266.
[3] XIV. 8, p. 450.
[4] XIV. 7, p. 447, and elsewhere.
[5] XV. 8, p. 488.
[6] XIV. 7, p. 447. See p. 43, note 2 above, and Ch. 44 below.
[7] XIII. 6, p. 393.
[8] XIII. 10, p. 403; XV. 6, p. 478.
[9] IX. 6, p. 256.
[10] XV. 7, p. 482.
[11] IX. 9, p. 264. We may compare the insulting procession given to the convicted conspirators in XII. 6, when the escort (ἡ πομπή) sings songs of mockery.

days wax eloquent, and which are enshrined in the *Book of Ceremonies* by Constantine VII, play very little part in Anna's story. Such etiquette as she mentions is what would appeal to any one as seemly, i.e. not to come armed into the bathing apartments of a country house,[1] not to sit on equal terms with a sovereign,[2] not to brawl in the presence of royalty.[3] Slaves and vassals and conquered enemies prostrate themselves,[4] the word προσκύνησις being applied, like our 'reverence', to respect paid either to God or man.[5] If the rude turbulence of the Crusaders shocked Anna it would be no less distasteful to courtiers now-a-days.[6]

Quite the most interesting glimpse into twelfth-century etiquette in the *Alexias* is afforded by the demands of Bohemund to the imperial envoys and their replies.[7] If we are inclined to smile at the absurdity of such importance attached to trifles, we need only remember Swift's satires and certain points of modern diplomatic 'protocole' in order to realize that 'plus ça change, plus c'est la même chose'. The passage is worth translating in full. When the envoys try to start with reproaches for his broken faith, Bohemund bursts out with pardonable irritation: 'Enough of words like this, but if anything else is announced to me by the Emperor, that will I hear.' The imperial agents then make various promises of safe-conduct and of money, and Bohemund rejoins:

'Now I know in truth that men have been sent by the Emperor, competent to speak sense and to listen to it. I therefore demand to receive full assurance from you that I shall not be received by the Emperor without honour, but that the nearest of his blood shall come forth six stadia to meet me, and that when I have come to the imperial tent, as soon as I enter the doors he shall himself get up from the imperial seat and receive me with honour. Also that there shall be made to me no reference whatever to the previous contracts, and that I shall not be in any sense put on trial, but that as a free man with perfect immunity I may speak out my desires as much as I wish. Furthermore that the Emperor shall take hold of my hand and place me at the head of his couch, and that when

---

[1] IX. 5, p. 255.
[2] X. 10, pp. 300, 301. Cf. XIV. 6, p. 443, where Irene lets a wounded man sit.
[3] XI. 3, p. 317; VIII. 8, p. 239.
[4] XII. 9, p. 372; XV. 6, p. 478.
[5] II. 5, pp. 51, 52, and 12, p. 66; V. 5, p. 139; XI. 2, p. 316; XIII. 9, p. 401(*bis.*); XV. 2, p. 463, 6, p. 478, and elsewhere. So in *John C.* 3, p. 7 Nicetas Acom. uses the word when the imperial kinsmen get off their horses to salute the Grand Domestic Axuch. The idea conveyed must have greatly changed since the days of the New Testament, for in *Rev.* xix. 10 and xxii. 8, it is said that προσκύνησις is only suitable towards God; see p. 316 below, but cf. Bouquet, *The Real Presence* (1928), pp. 7–8.
[6] XIV. 4.
[7] XIII. 9.

I have entered with two soldiers in coats of arms I shall in no wise bend my knee or my neck in reverence to the Emperor.'

On these vital points the envoys feel bound to offer a compromise, which Bohemund after some resistance accepts, 'making a virtue of necessity'. The Emperor will allow him to bring in two soldiers to the august presence and will take him by the hand to station him 'at the upper end of the imperial couch'. But instead of Alexius' near relations going six stadia to meet him, Bohemund must be content with more distant relations and 'a sufficient distance', while as for the Emperor's getting up from his seat it is quite out of the question, a περιττὴ αἴτησις, and homage must without fail be shown in the bended knee or neck. The matter had clearly tremendous issues, and the psychology lying behind it, which could easily be paralleled even in our own day, ought not to excite our derision.

The actual meeting between the two enemies is thus portrayed: 'So when Bohemund went in, the Emperor extended his hand and grasped his, and after giving the greeting usual with emperors' (we could wish this were more explicitly described) 'he stationed him near the imperial throne.' What happened about the obeisance we do not know.[1]

8. FEELING ABOUT ARISTOCRACY

A FEW words must now be said about the characteristic of aristocratic pride as displayed by Anna. In the first place we should remind ourselves that daughters of reigning sovereigns as writers are rare in all ages. If we laugh at Anna for conceit and pretentiousness is it not fair to ask ourselves: 'Where except in the famous House of Valois can we find her like?'[2] Considering her as a woman, and a woman of noble birth, we at once come up against the quality of feminine and aristocratic αἰδώς which she like all princesses of her day would assume as a virtue if she had it not. She cannot relate unpleasant details or scandal fit only for the vulgar.[3] It would sully her tongue to

---

[1] XIII. 10, p. 403. The expression ἡ συνήθης τοῖς βασιλεῦσι προσαγόρευσις is like in form to the συνήθης τοῖς βασιλεῦσι προσκύνησις of XV. 6, p. 478, where the satraps descend from their horses to salute Alexius, but we perceive that in the first case it is the Emperor who makes the greeting, in the second the Turks do homage to him. We might say that the two τοῖς βασιλεῦσι correspond respectively to a subjective and an objective genitive. Nicephorus Bryennius has this subjective use in Hyle, IV. 2, p. 88 τὴν συνήθη πρεσβεῦσι προσηγορίαν.

[2] Even La Grande Mademoiselle de Montpensier was only a king's niece.

[3] I. 13, p. 31; III. 1, p. 72, and 2, p. 74; XV. 9, p. 490. This marked characteristic of hers sufficiently disproves the absurd story of her coarse abusiveness to her husband (Nic. Acom., John C. 3, p. 8).

expose the Bogomile heresy in full.[1] Even barbarous Latin
names or astrological terms are abhorrent to her and 'defile
the grandeur' of her history or 'obscure' its 'substance'.[2]

This aristocratic sentiment is ingrained in her. The moment
a new character appears on her scene the one point that seems
to preoccupy her is his birth and social position. Hostages,
rebels, courtiers, even enemies—again and again with wearisome iteration she impresses on us that they were 'of the noblest
families', 'notables both by birth and rank', μεγιστᾶνες, ἄριστοι
and so on *ad infinitum*. One is an ἀνὴρ γεννάδας, another ἐκ
γένους λαμπροῦ, others εὐγενεῖς or γενναῖοι, the latter word
being significantly used by Anna both for 'well-born' and for
'courageous'. The mother of Irene Ducas is 'of the first rank
among the Bulgarians',[3] and Irene herself at a crisis behaves in
a manner 'not unworthy of her nobility'.[4] Botaniates chooses
Maria for his wife not only as an ex-Empress but as a high-born
Alan.[5] Courage and military achievements naturally belong to
the upper classes, and the above-mentioned quality τὸ γενναῖον
shines out of their very countenance.[6] Heretics are most dangerous when they lead astray 'a not ignoble band',[7] or when
their teaching sinks deep 'even into the greatest houses'.[8] Godfrey de Bouillon and Hugh of France are justly proud of their
birth;[9] Bohemund's low origin leads him to reckless and base
deeds;[10] Alexius has a right to feel cheated when the well-born
Aspietes proves a coward.[11] The better bred a conspirator is,
and the greater his 'splendour of birth', the more dangerous he
is and yet the more is he entitled to clemency and consideration.[12]
The common herd (and especially, as we shall see later, the
class of slaves) is in Anna's opinion fickle and treacherous and
overbearing,[13] swayed by externals[14] and superstitions;[15] they are
cannon-fodder[16] and deserve Polybius' contemptuous phrase,

[1] XV. 9, p. 490.
[2] VI. 7, p. 165; 14, p. 182; X. 8, p. 289; XIII. 6, p. 393.
[3] II. 6, p. 55.
[4] XV. 2, p. 463; cf. III. 3, p. 76. Nicephorus Bryennius speaks of himself as ὁ
πατρίκιος . . ., μειράκιον ὢν θυμοειδὲς καὶ γενναῖον, *Hyle*, III. 9, p. 75.
[5] III. 2, p. 73.   [6] IX. 6, p. 256.
[7] X. 1, p. 269. The same affected expression οὐκ ἀγεννής is used by Cinnamus,
I. 6, p. 8.
[8] XV. 9, p. 490.
[9] X. 5, p. 285, and 7, p. 288.
[10] X. 5, p. 285, and 11, pp. 301, 303.   [11] XII. 2.
[12] XII. 5 and 6. Insubordination in 'those of higher rank' is only punished with
virtual exile, in XI. 9, p. 334; cf. XI. 7, p. 328. The same idea of the treatment
due to εὐγένεια is found in Nic. Bry. I. 1, p. 16.
[13] I. 2, p. 6, 3, p. 7; II. 4, p. 49; VI. 8, p. 168; XIII. 1, p. 378.
[14] I. 7, p. 17; III. 3, p. 76.
[15] VI. 7, pp. 164, 165.   [16] VII, 3, p. 197.

συρφετώδης ὄχλος, 'crowd composed of sweepings'.[1] The thought of their parents' noble birth is to make the young Archontopules brave.[2] Judged from her sentiments on this subject, Anna might have been a Spartan of ancient days, with the bulk of her father's subjects for Helots.

Of course we must never forget that in her day most of the hard work of the world was done by slaves,[3] and often castrated

---

[1] X. 9, p. 294; Polyb. IV. 75. 5; cf. the ἐδόκει τοῖς ἄφρυσι σύρφαξιν of Nic. Acom. Is. Áng. 3, p. 359.

[2] VII. 7, p. 204.

[3] In view of the statements of P. Boissonnade, in his Le travail dans l'Europe chrétienne au moyen âge (Paris, 1921), it may be well to dwell on this point. Boissonnade first says what no one would deny, that by the fourth century A.D., in consequence of Stoic and Christian ideas and of economic necessity, 'l'esclavage avait disparu presque entièrement, au profit de l'artisanat libre dans les villes et du colonat dans les campagnes' (p. 4), and that its recrudescence during the next three centuries was due to the barbarian invasions (p. 27). But when he says that by the tenth century 'l'établissement du servage' (in the country) 'fut compensé par la disparition de l'esclavage' (p. 55), and twice over claims as the proudest boast of the Eastern Empire that it abolished slavery (pp. 76 and 413) he surely is going against facts. In rural districts Baynes bids us 'distinguish between the free village and the servile village', though the peasants in both were equally 'chained to the land'; he gives no clear dates, but his remarks apparently apply at least to the tenth century and probably to the eleventh and twelfth as well (op. cit., p. 108). Even in the country, then, 'servage' might cover an actual 'esclavage'. But in domestic service, especially in the houses of the great from the Emperor downwards, it is impossible to doubt that slavery continued till the days of Manuel I (1143–80). Anna speaks of slaves as she does of houses, a common object of everyday life. Slaves captured in war, barbarian slaves, bought slaves, fellow-slaves, the slavish mind, occur throughout her pages. To treat people as bought slaves is almost a proverb (XI. 5, p. 321; XIV. 1. p. 421; so in Cinnamus, VI. 8, p. 161). Chalandon, op. cit., p. 16, quotes from Wassiliewsky a story of Basil II, how on returning from a campaign he stopped at the house of a great noble 'qui disposait de 3000 esclaves armés', and how from motives of caution he thought best to carry off so formidable a subject into captivity in the metropolis. Nic. Bry. (II. 26, p. 63) says that a certain Maurice had πλοῦτον πλεῖστον καὶ δούλων πλῆθος, who were also useful in war. So in Alex. XIII. 7, p. 395, the households of the Emperor's sons and son-in-law guard the passes, 'being all eager for battle' (cf. also VII. 7, p. 205). In his second volume, on John and Manuel, Chalandon goes further into the question. On p. 612 he refers to Cinnamus, who in VI. 8, p. 160, says that poverty had driven many free men μισθοῦ τὴν ἐλευθερίαν ἀποδόσθαι, a statement confirmed by a novel of Alexius I (Zachariae v. Lingenthal, Jus Gr.-Rom. Vol. III, pp. 401–7, Nov. 35 A and B), and that Manuel I passed an edict restoring them to their former state. Eustathius of Thessalonica tells us that the same Manuel bought up for the State enemy prisoners, χρήμασι δημοσίοις λυόμενοι, and established them on the land in return for military service (Funeral Oration on Manuel, ch. 18; P. G. 135, col. 984). The Archbishop himself left instructions for all his slaves to be freed after his death; in explanation he says: Ἔστι γὰρ ἡ δουλεία θητεία τις ἄμισθός τε καὶ πολυχρόνιος. The origin of τὸ τοῦ δουλεύειν κακόν is the avarice of men, for God made us all equal and brothers: φύσει ἐλεύθερον ξῶον ἅπας ἄνθρωπος. He will keep his slaves during his lifetime, because he is as kind to them as their own parents (P. G. 136, cols. 1289–90). A sentiment adverse to slavery had indeed begun two generations before. In his above-mentioned Novel 35 Alexius I, though agreeing that 'among men varying fortune admits of masters and slaves' (δεσποτείαν καὶ δουλείαν) and that such things must be, yet is insistent on the idea that all men, of all ranks, are equally Christians and equally the slaves of Christ. Slaves are entitled to have God's blessing on their marriage, for we all hope for one salva-

slaves. The whole class was despised and yet feared, and in spite of its menial position had great power. The career of one Byzantine courtier George Monomachatus is entirely changed by his fear of two 'barbarian slaves, Scythians, of the Emperor' Botaniates,[1] and, what is far more important for our subject, these same two Σθλαβογενεῖς by their hatred and hostility give the Comneni brothers a plausible excuse for revolt.[2] They are παραδυναστεύοντες,[3] and Anna states as an accepted fact not only that they had power to blind enemies[4] but that one of them ventured to covet the throne.[5] This Borilus tried to defend Constantinople by arms against the Comneni, in defiance of his master's orders,[6] and when the latter fell from power he was the first to insult him.[7] Besides these two all-powerful slaves of Botaniates we hear in the course of Anna's history of many other slaves (usually foreign-born) and also of eunuchs, a fact which need not surprise us when we read in Bury the long list of ἀξίαι διὰ βραβείων and ἀξίαι διὰ λόγου reserved for eunuchs in the Byzantine Court.[8] The Great Primicerius Taticius, a σύντροφος of Alexius,[9] was 'not in a free state of birth, for his father had after a foray fallen to the lot of John Comnenus', and he can be taunted by Bohemund as the οἰκέτης of Alexius.[10] A half-breed Turco-Armenian slave tries to assassinate Alexius in the palace

tion, and neither of the two great Sacraments knows δούλων καὶ δεσποτῶν διαφοράν, loc. cit. pp. 403, 406. In practice this must have softened the hardship of the institution, but it is clear that in Anna's day slaves existed and even abounded. N. A. Constantinescu in his paper read before the Congress of Byzantinology at Bukharest (Acad. Roum. Bull., Tome XI, p. 100 note 5) says that they were to be found at Constantinople as late as the fourteenth century, though he considers that already by the eleventh century all serfdom had disappeared in the country, where 'la population domaniale' appears to have been 'parfaitement libre'. He quotes Constantine Porphyrogenitus to prove that even in his day there was 'pas une condition sociale intermédiaire entre la liberté et l'esclavage', and says that the great landowners àll worked their property by means of slaves, paid labourers, and free tenants. According to this critic 'l'attache à la glèbe' was never re-established, but slaves continued to be sold 'sans le domaine', however much theoretical pity the Emperors had for the servile state; the disappearance of serfdom was due to a change in the fiscal system, but 'nous ne savons pas à qui l'attribuer'.

The practice of transporting prisoners of war to found colonies far away from their homes is mentioned by Anna (XIV. 8, p. 451) in the case of John Tzimisces ἐξανδραποδισάμενος the Manichaeans settled them at Philippopolis. Nic. Acom. (John C. 4, p. 11) says that after a victory this method was adopted with some of the prisoners of war; others were enrolled in the Greek army, but the greater part 'captured by the soldiery' were sold.

[1] I. 16, p. 38.
[2] II. 1–4.
[3] II. 2, p. 47.
[4] I. 7, p. 17; cf. I. 6, p. 16; II. 4, p. 48.
[5] II. 4, p. 49.
[6] II. 12, p. 68; cf. II. 11, p. 66.
[7] II. 12, p. 67.
[8] Imperial Administrative System in the Ninth Century (Brit. Acad. Suppl. Papers, 1911, ch. D).
[9] Nic. Bry. IV. 20, p. 99.
[10] IV. 4, p. 109; XI. 9, p. 333.

riding-school;[1] a 'savage Scythian slave' is deputed by the
Aaron brothers to kill the Emperor with a sword,[2] and his
designs are frustrated by his fellow-slave and by an imperial
θεράπων, the eunuch who waits on Alexius' table as he did on
his father's.[3] Such eunuchs had great power. Words spoken by
one to the ex-Empress Eudocia, words which unfortunately for
us Anna leaves to 'newsmongers' to utter, were potent enough
to stop a marriage with the new Emperor Botaniates, either for
herself or for her daughter.[4] The Patriarch Eustratius Garidas
belongs to this class,[5] though castration (unless by a military
conqueror or by a doctor for health reasons), had been made by
the first Canon of the Council of Nicaea a bar to clerical office.[6]
Another eunuch, 'one of the Empress's attendants' becomes the
παιδαγωγός of a young hostage at Court,[7] and may possibly be
the doctor Michael mentioned in Alexius' last illness.[8]   Yet
another, Leo Nicerites, holds important military commands,[9]
and another, Eustathius Cyminianus, is Drungary of the Fleet
and is commissioned to guard the capital.[10] The 'officials employed about the women's apartments' in the Palace play an
important part in the rebellion of Alexius, and can even persuade the Empress Maria to adopt him.[11]   Basil Psyllus the
eunuch is one of the Emperor's immediate attendants, and has
free access to the sleeping-tent of the sovereigns;[12] another of the
same class, also a Basil, is ambassador from Richard of Salerno
to Alexius and has the rank of Nobilissimus.[13] The identification of slaves with their master's family is shown by the fact
that they took their names.[14]

The money value of such human chattels was then, as in the
nineteenth century in America, a check to emancipation. As
we have already seen, Alexius would naturally favour this
humane proceeding,[15] but it was not carried out on a large scale
till the days of his grandson Manuel. It was one of the charges

---

[1] IX. 7, p. 259.   [2] XIII. 1, p. 377.   [3] Ibid., et seq.
[4] III. 2, p. 74.   Scylitzes, p. 864 D, says he was 'a monk renowned for virtue,
called Panagios instead of any other name'.
[5] III. 4, p. 79.
[6] W. Bright, Canons of First Four General Councils, 2nd ed. p. ix.
[7] VIII. 9, p. 241.   [8] XV. 11, p. 501.
[9] VII. 2, p. 193; VIII. 9, p. 242; XIII. 5, p. 390; XV. 2, p. 465.
[10] VI. 10, p. 174; X. 4, p. 279; XI, 10, p. 338; XIII. 1, p. 376.
[11] II. 1, p. 44; cf. XIV. 7, p. 446 of Anna's childhood.
[12] XIII. 1; cf. XIV. 5, p. 438, and XV. 2, p. 462.
[13] XIII. 12, p. 416.
[14] XV. 2, p. 464. We may compare the well-known case in our day of Booker
Washington the ex-slave.
[15] He certainly gave one slave, his own would-be-assassin, his liberty (IX. 7,
p. 260).

of anti-social conduct brought against the Massalian heretics
that they 'gladly receive slaves who run away from their
masters'.[1] Yet these same masters despised those whom they
held in subjection. Twice over Anna implies that τὸ δοῦλον is
not to be trusted either by its masters or by its fellow-servants;[2]
it has a grudge against both, and as in classical Greek τὸ
ἐλευθέριον is a synonym for all that is admirable.[3]

This leads us up to our last point, what a Roman would have
called *Gravitas*. We could hardly get a better summary of the
Byzantine ruler's attitude to life, his ideal of dignity and freedom combined, than in the lines of Alexius to his son John:[4]

$$\pi\rho\acute{\epsilon}\pi\epsilon\iota$$
$$\tau\grave{o}\nu\ \mathring{a}\nu\delta\rho a\ \tau\grave{o}\nu\ \phi\acute{\epsilon}\rho o\nu\tau a\ \tau\grave{\eta}\nu\ \grave{\epsilon}\xi o\upsilon\sigma\acute{\iota}a\nu$$

$$\kappa a\grave{\iota}\ \sigma\epsilon\mu\nu\grave{a}\ \pi\acute{a}\nu\tau a\ \kappa a\grave{\iota}\ \phi\rho o\nu\grave{\eta}\sigma a\iota\ \kappa a\grave{\iota}\ \phi\rho\acute{a}\sigma a\iota$$
$$\grave{\epsilon}\lambda\epsilon\upsilon\theta\acute{\epsilon}\rho a\nu\ \mathring{a}\gamma o\nu\tau a\ \tau\grave{\eta}\nu\ \pi a\rho\rho\eta\sigma\acute{\iota}a\nu.$$

This σεμνότης or ὄγκος is to Anna's aristocratic mind the
supreme virtue of sovereigns. After narrowly escaping assassination Alexius stands unmoved amid his excited subjects, and
when terrible news comes they 'are amazed at his heroic calm';[5]
it would be degrading for him to show or even feel ἐμπάθεια
when an astrologer prophesied his death;[6] he is rarely 'filled
with anger' like other men;[7] he bears 'without a word' the rudeness of the Frankish count,[8] and merely 'got up from his throne'
when Tancred insulted George Palaeologus in his presence.[9]
To be 'more than usual calm' was the Byzantine way of rebuk-
ing insolence. In all his doings an emperor must be majestic:
he must not be 'entangled by blameworthy passions', but must
make decisions 'by the even rule of conscience'; even his edicts
will not pass muster unless 'worthy of the imperial μεγαλοφροσύνη', that untranslatable word, combining the ideas of

---

[1] Fr. Diekamp, *Der Mönch und Presbyter Georgios, B. Z.* IX. p. 23.

[2] II. 4, p. 49; XIII. 1, p. 378. So figuratively of nations in XIV. 7, p. 445. We
may compare her diatribe against the hypocrisy of τὸ ὑπήκοον, meaning 'subjects'
in general (VI. 8, p. 168).

[3] II. 4, p. 51; XIII. 1, p. 376. Cf. Nic. Bry. III. 4, p. 71, where the ἀνελευθερία
of Michael VII makes his subjects revolt; τὸ ἐν χρήμασιν ἐλευθέριον of Alexius is
notable (*ibid.*, II. 22, p. 59).

[4] *Mous. Alex.* I, pp. 156–60.

[5] IX. 7, p. 260; XII. 9, p. 372; XIII. 1, p. 375.

[6] VI. 7, p. 165.

[7] XIII. 7, p. 396; XIV. 2, p. 424, are among the few instances. Nic. Bry. I. 6,
p. 20, praises Alexius as hardly ever moved to anger. Contrast the vehemence of
Bohemund (XIII. 4, p. 389), Nicephorus Diogenes (IX. 5, p. 254, and 6, p. 257)
and others (IX. 8, p. 261; XV. 6, p. 481). Zonaras in his grudging praises of
Alexius says he was not ὀξὺς εἰς θυμόν (XVIII. 29).

[8] X. 10, p. 300.　　　　　　　　　　　　　　　　[9] XI. 3, p. 317.

dignity, justice, and magnanimity.[1] Can we wonder that the Firstborn of the Purple had such sublime contempt for everything not 'noble' in birth and outward behaviour?

9. FEELING ABOUT BEAUTY

IF Anna admired noble birth, hardly less did she admire beauty; like a true Greek she almost makes a god of a handsome face and a well-made form. Her father, mother, grandmother, fiancé, fiancé's mother, and husband are drawn for us to the life, and no friend or even prominent enemy can be mentioned without a personal description.[2] Her portrait of Bohemund[3] has been construed by her critics into an unconscious revelation of her love for him; it is far more reasonable to see in it a reluctant tribute to those external charms which she quite futilely professes to despise,[4] and which she and her contemporaries so highly valued. His beauty is one of the qualities which makes Botaniates choose Synadenus as his successor;[5] for his beauty Alexius cannot help loving the undeserving Nicephorus Diogenes, no less than his worthy brother Leo;[6] it is their 'beauty and strength of body' as much as their 'splendour of race' that moves the Emperor to deliver from captivity in Cairo the Frankish counts whom he had no other reason to like.[7]

A full discussion of this point with reference to the old idea of καλοκάγαθός would lead us too far afield, but it may be worth briefly noting the special points of beauty on which Anna lays stress. A man must be tall[8] (indeed like a Homeric hero he should surpass all others by head and shoulders) and perfectly

---

[1] IX. 6, p. 256; XIII. 1, p. 376. In minor matters we get the respect for εὐσχημοσύνη of the ideal monarch in Nic. Ac. *John C.* 12, p. 31.

[2] Pref. 3 and 4; I. 4, p. 9; III. 1, 2, 3 and 8; VII. 2, p. 191, &c., *ad lib.* So even the heretic Italus in V. 8.

[3] XIII. 10. We may note that she cannot have been in love with Robert, who died before she was two; yet she awards the same unwilling admiration to him as to his son (VI. 7).

[4] I. 7, p. 17; III. 10, p. 94; IX. 6, p. 258.

[5] II. 2, p. 45.

[6] IX. 6, p. 256. So Zonaras says of the husband of Alexius' daughter Theodora, a man not of noble birth, that he was 'in appearance a jewel' (XVIII. 22).

[7] XI. 7, p. 328. The idea that men in important stations should have an outward form to correspond is very well marked in Pref. 4, p. 6; II. 7, p. 57; VI. 7, p. 165.

[8] I. 4, p. 9, 5, p. 11, 7, p. 17, 10, pp. 23, 24; II. 7, p. 57; VI. 7, p. 165; IX. 6, pp. 256, 257; XII. 2, p. 350; XIII. 6, pp. 394, 395; 10, p. 403; XIV. 8, p. 450. Contrast III. 3, p. 77; V. 8, p. 146. Alexius was short, but impressive when seated (III. 3, p. 76; IX. 9, p. 263).

proportioned.[1] In women 'harmony of limbs and parts' is no less essential,[2] and their faces must be neither round nor pointed.[3] Bright eyes with arching brows, fitted to inspire awe as well as admiration, are desirable both in men and women, and many are the references to eyes fixed in thought or cast down in modesty, or again to 'cheerful', 'stern', or 'haughty' glances, as well as to the keen gaze of vigilance,[4] and the 'hot and mad' looks of a truculent controversialist.[5] Incidentally this helps to make us realize the true awfulness to a Byzantine mind of punishment by blinding.

A fair and glowing complexion is repeatedly praised; like the Spaniards of to-day, the dark-skinned Byzantines admired blondes. Golden-red of all shades seems to have been their favourite colour for hair: to be 'ruddy' in locks and skin was considered a beauty.[6] The Byzantines, we may remark, wore their hair longer than our modern men, but shorter than 'barbarians'.[7] When Alexius' helmet falls off, his 'sunny' hair gets into his eyes.[8] The Normans usually wore their hair 'long like women',[9] but Robert Guiscard and Bohemund had theirs cut short, doubtless like their compatriots shown in the Bayeux

---

[1] Robert Guiscard was broad-shouldered, with a good figure, I. 10, p. 24. Bohemund was 'so to speak formed according to the Canon of Polyclitus' (XIII. 10, p. 403; cf. III. 3, p. 76). Leo and Nicephorus Diogenes had height and symmetry and 'the bloom of youth' IX. 6, p. 256; cf. Theocritus, *Idyll* 15, line 85, πρᾶτον ἴουλον ἀπὸ κροτάφων καταβάλλων.

[2] II. 6, p. 55; III. 2, p. 74; 3, p. 76.

[3] III. 2, p. 74, and 3, p. 76. It is curious to note that Psellus mentions as part of the 'unearthly beauty' of the baby Constantine Ducas Porphyrogenitus that his face 'was rounded off into an exact circle'. *Chron.* Mich. VII, Byz. T., p. 264; cf. *Alexias*, I. 10, p. 23, 12, p. 27; III. 2, p. 71.

[4] I. 10, p. 24; III. 2, p. 74, 3, pp. 76, 77, 8, p. 88; IX. 9, p. 263; X. 9, p. 295, and 11, pp. 302, 304; XI. 2, p. 315, and 12, p. 342; XII. 3; XIII. 10, p. 404; XIV. 3, p. 431, 7, p. 449; XV. 9, p. 491. John Comnenus as a baby showed 'secretiveness and keenness' in his dark eyes (VI. 8, p. 168). Constantine Ducas, aged 7, has eyes 'not pale, but like a hawk's, and shining under his eyebrows as though the whites were golden' (III. 1, p. 71). Psellus, in describing him as a little child, says his eyes were γλαυκοί and large and full of 'calm', while his nose was like a vulture! Yet he agrees with Anna that the boy's beauty was more than earthly, οὐκ ἐπίγειον. The word γαλήνη as applied to Constantine's eyes by Psellus may have suggested Anna's comparison of her mother's eyes to a θάλαττα γαληνιῶσα (III. 3, p. 77).

[5] V. 8, p. 145.

[6] I. 10, p. 24; III. 3, p. 77; IX. 6, p. 257; XIII. 10, p. 404. Isaac Comnenus was sallow, and had a scanty beard (III. 3, p. 77). The hated John had a swarthy complexion and a nose 'neither snub nor hooked, but between the two' (VI. 8, p. 168). Cf. the golden hair, pink and white skin and 'sweetly piercing eyes' of the dead child in Callicles, Poem VI.

[7] The ordinary man wore θρὶξ κοσμική; the Bogomile heretics adopted the tonsure so as to counterfeit monastic virtue (XV. 8, p. 486). John Comnenus thought the way his courtiers cut their hair worthy of his personal attention (Nic. Ac. *John C.* 12, p. 31).

[8] IV. 6, p. 117.   [9] Du Cange's note on XIII, 10, 404 B.

Tapestry.[1] In the matter of beards the two races as it were
changed places, the Greeks (and the Venetians) being bearded
and the Normans not.[2] The instances in the *Alexias* of shaving
as a sign of humiliation or mourning need not be quoted; the
last and most dramatic is where as Alexius breathes his last the
newly widowed Empress Irene 'taking a little knife cuts off her
hair to the skin'.[3] It gives, we seem to feel, the death-blow to
that beauty which, by reason of anxiety and devoted nursing,
'wasting had seized' some time back.[4] Even in all her filial
anguish Anna had noted this fact.

Before we leave this question of physical beauty it may be
worth while to transcribe Anna's three most elaborate pen-
pictures, those of the ex-Empress Maria and of her own parents.
Though lengthy they are among her finest and most characteristic passages.[5]

Of Maria she says:

' She was tall in stature like a cypress, and her skin was white as
snow: her face was not absolutely round, and in colour it was a perfect spring flower, nay a rose out and out. But who of mortals could
express the brilliance of her eyes? Her eyebrows were thick and red,
and her glance was sparkling. Apelles and Phidias could not have
done her justice, and her beauty like the Gorgon's head turned beholders into stone with amazement. . . . Such harmony of limbs and
parts, of the whole with the parts, and of these with the whole, none
ever yet beheld in a mortal's body: a living statue, dear to lovers
of beauty.'

The next chapter contains the famous descriptions of Alexius
and Irene:

' Now the outward forms of both the sovereigns Alexius and Irene
were amazing and altogether inimitable, and no painter could paint
them by gazing at some archetype of beauty, nor could a sculptor
mould lifeless substance thus, but even that well-known Canon of
Polyclitus would have seemed to turn into downright clumsiness if
any one had gazed at these living statues, I mean the lately crowned
imperial pair, and then at the works of that same Polyclitus. For
Alexius was not very far exalted above the earth ' [we may note the
apology couched thus in high-flown terms], 'but was drawn out sym-

[1] VI. 7, p. 165; XIII. 10, p. 404.
[2] VIII. 8, p. 239. Cf. the small round beard of the philosopher Italus, a man
of foreign birth (V. 8, p. 146). Bohemund shaved clean (XIII. 10, p. 404). See
Du Cange's note on IV. 2, p. 106 B, though to mock some one εἰς τὸν πώγωνα
may well be 'to his face', 'dans sa barbe'. Robert was only βαθυπώγων to fulfil
a vow, according to Ordericus Vitalis quoted by Du Cange in his note on VI. 7,
p. 165 D. See John Ducas Caesar in II. 6, p. 56.
[3] ἐν χρῷ, XV, 11, p. 505.
[4] XV. 11, p. 501.   [5] III. 2 and 3.

metrically in breadth. So when standing he did not cause such great astonishment in the beholders, but if he sat down on the imperial throne and flashed fierce brilliance from his eyes, he seemed like lightning to send forth irresistible brightness, both from his countenance and from his whole frame. On each side black eyebrows arched, and under them his eye was set, with a glance at once awful and gentle, so that from the gleam of his look, the clearness of his forehead, and the dignity of his countenance with the flush that passed over it, a man derived both fear and encouragement. Then the breadth of his shoulders and the strength of his arms and the expansion of his chest were all on a heroic scale and invariably called the vulgar herd to astonishment and delight. For the personality of the man had beauty and grace and strength and unapproachable dignity.' (ἀπρόσιτος, here used in praise.)

'As for the Empress Irene my mother she was at that time a child and had not yet passed her fifteenth year. For she had shot up like a straight evergreen plant, symmetrically broadened or narrowed throughout her limbs and parts in due proportion. She was lovely to see and lovely to hear, and in truth as an object of hearing and sight she never sated the eye or the ear. For her very countenance distilled the radiance of a moon, but had not been formed in a regular circle as with Assyrian women, nor on the other hand was it long drawn out as with the Scythians, but it departed a little from the exactness of the circle. And the bloom was spread out on her cheeks and presented a rose-bed even to those at a distance. Her eye was sparkling, and with all its charm was terrible in its gaze, so as to draw the eyes of the beholders towards her by her charm and beauty, and yet compel them to shut them with fear, not knowing how to look or how to hide themselves. And I know not whether any Athene was really discovered by the ancient poets and historians, for I hear of her as a myth, spoken of and ridiculed. But if any one had said that this Empress was Athene, manifested in those[1] times in human life, or fallen down from heaven with a celestial gleam and unapproachable[2] radiance, he would not have gone beyond probability. And, what was even more wonderful and not to be found in any other of womankind, on the one hand she restrained the lawless among men, and then when they had been restrained by fear she gave them encouragement, all out of one glance. And her lips were mostly closed and showed her silent, truly a breathing statue of beauty and a living monument of harmony. For the most part her hand acted as charioteer for her speech in perfect harmony, bringing forward the wrist with the arm, and you would have said that ivory had been carved by some craftsman into a framing of fingers and hands. Furthermore the iris of her eyes resembled the calm sea radiating forth its blue in deep-waved serenity. And the white of her eyes all round shone in rivalry with the iris, and they

---

[1] We should say 'these latter' or 'our.' τότε is vaguely used (see p. 492 note 9 below).   [2] ἀπρόσιτος once more.

flashed forth irresistible grace and gave charm unspeakable to her glances. Such in appearance were Irene and Alexius.'

We have now considered Anna's attitude to her family, to her married life, and to her circumstances in general. We have tried to study her sentiments as to externals, birth, beauty, ceremonial, and the like. Summing it up, are we not forced to say somewhat as follows: Anna Comnena spent her youth and middle age in the most sumptuous court in Christendom, where men were striving to maintain classical ideals in the face of barbarians on the East and barbarians on the West. Born in the purple, she associated with her immediate family and the 'kinsmen', and probably with no one else except an occasional learned man. The wonder is, not that she sets so much store by outward advantages, but that she does not set more, indeed that she is not more proud, more conceited, more narrow, more arrogant, than we actually find her to be.

III. ANNA AS A CHARACTER

THE THREE THEOLOGICAL VIRTUES
FAITH
10. RELIGION

IF we turn from externals to the weightier matters of the law, how does Anna stand as to moral ideals? What are the virtues which she admires and the vices which she despises? The field of inquiry is immense. Perhaps we may conveniently bring the subject under two heads and consider how she writes of the three theological virtues, Faith, Hope, and Charity, and of the four cardinal, Temperance, Fortitude, Wisdom, and Justice.

First then as to Faith. What are Anna's ideas on Religion in the generally accepted sense of the word? As her work is full of references to the Divinity that shapes our ends, it is not unreasonable to examine in what way and to what extent she brought her Christian faith into her principles.

At the very outset of her work she strikes, so to speak, a religious note, for it is 'God above' Who has given her her dynastic and educational advantages.[1] From this position she never swerves. God's Providence causes or permits everything that happens, and man must not resist His Will.[2] It makes Alexius Emperor, and gives him victory over his enemies;[3] it preserves him, even by miracles, so that he may fulfil his destined duties, glorifying the Comnenus house and restoring the Greek Empire.[4] All comes from above. Young Constantine Ducas was a 'munificent gift from the hands of God'.[5] It is He Who avenges the injured.[6] It is He Who helps the deserving

[1] Pref. 1, p. 1. Her theology is discussed in Ch. 46.
[2] I. 10, p. 23; cf. VI. 12, p. 178; II. 12, p. 68; III. 9, p. 92; XIV. 7, p. 444; XV. 10, p. 494, and 11, p. 506.
[3] I. 2, p. 6; II. 4, p. 50, and 7, p. 58; VIII. 6, p. 235, and 7, p. 237; XII. 4, p. 357; XV. 3, p. 469. Other leaders also seek victory from God (IV. 5, p. 114; VIII. 4, p. 228; X. 10, p. 301; XI. 3, p. 317; 4, p. 319). The idea of a tribal Deity who supports his own side, one of the oldest and most deep-seated of beliefs, is very noticeable in the *Alexias*.
[4] I. 6, p. 16; cf. III. 8, p. 90; IV. 7, pp. 118, 119, and 8, p. 121; V. 2, p. 129; IX. 7, pp. 258, 260, 8, p. 262, 9, p. 264, 10, p. 265; XII. 5, p. 358, and 6, p. 361; XIII. 1, p. 376. So of other warriors (II. 1, p. 44; X. 8, p. 291). Nic. Bry. (II. 27, p. 64) tells us that in a bad storm Alexius invoked the aid of the Mother of God 'and straightway the sea became calm'. The *Anon. Syn. Chr.* p. 183 *ter* represents Heaven as watching over Alexius.
[5] I. 12, p. 27; cf. VII. 2, p. 191.
[6] I. 16, p. 39.

and His Hand is 'invincible' whether to aid or to overthrow.[1]
We even find σὺν Θεῷ used as a mere phrase, like our 'D.V.';[2]
so is also 'God knows' or 'God is witness'.[3] Into his short letter
to the Comneni brothers Melissenus brings God's name five
times,[4] and the epistle of Alexius to Henry of Germany fairly
reeks with self-complacent piety.[5] Indeed, all diplomatic correspondence paid lip-service to the Powers above. This comes out
very clearly in the treaty between Alexius and Bohemund; the
phraseology has a religious complexion throughout.[6]

Now here it is clear that Anna and her characters show the
tendencies of her times. The same parade of reliance on God
coupled with self-reliance meets us on many pages of contemporary writers. Thus the *Strategicon* of Cecaumenus has the
words: σὺ μὲν τὸ πᾶν εἰς Θεὸν ἀναθοῦ . . . πλὴν καὶ σὺ τὸ καθ᾽ ἑαυτὸν
ποίει καὶ ἀγωνίζου, and we may say that 'ὁ Θεός' is seldom off
this writer's lips.[7] So too Nicephorus Bryennius ascribes to
God's ἐπίνευσις the success of Alexius' usurpation and whole
reign.[8] Turning again to the *Alexias* we find that even the
barbarous Norman, Robert Guiscard, is made to style himself
δοὺξ ἐν Θεῷ,[9] and though God is wroth against him, He yet saves
his men when they invoke His aid.[10] The same is true of the
Crusaders.[11] Prayer can secure material blessings no less than
spiritual,[12] and Alexius earns his daughter's admiration for

---

[1] II. 1, p. 44, and 10, p. 63; IV. 2, p. 105; V. 5, p. 138; VII. 3, p. 197; VIII.
1, p. 222; IX. 3, p. 251, and 10, p. 265; X. 10, p. 301.

[2] II. 2, p. 46, and 4, p. 50; III. 6, p. 84, &c. In XIV. 6, p. 443, in referring to
the past it has more real meaning, 'by God's grace'.

[3] IX. 9, p. 265; XI. 12, p. 342; XII. 1, p. 347; 3, p. 352; XIII. 12, p. 408, &c.
Anna calls on 'my God and His Mother' or on 'The Eye that cannot be deceived'
to attest her truthfulness (XIV. 7, pp. 446–7, and *Prologue* to her Will, line 32).
So Alexius decides that God, not he, must take account of the guilt of Nicephorus
Diogenes (IX. 5, p. 254).

[4] II. 8, p. 59.   [5] III. 10, pp. 93–5.   [6] XIII. 12.

[7] Cec. *Strat.* ed. B. Wassiliewsky, p. 12 and *passim*.

[8] *Hyle*, Pref., p. 12. The right hand from above preserves him (*ibid.* II. 5, p. 43).
Divine Providence wishes him to become great (*ibid.* II. 19, p. 57). On the other
hand John Ducas Caesar is foiled by 'Divinity working against him' (*ibid.* II. 17,
p. 55). So also in his III. 17, p. 80, 19, p. 81; IV. 15, p. 97, of various actions of
Providence. In earlier days Leo (*Tactica*, XIX. 34) had said that no navy can
win without a combination of good sailors and God's favour. God rewards those
who fight for His 'inheritance' (*ibid.* 75).

[9] I. 13, p. 33.

[10] III. 12, pp. 98, 99; IV. 2, p. 105. We may compare the spectators of the great
sea fight in Thuc. *Hist.* VII. 71, 'calling on the gods not to take from them their
hope of deliverance'.

[11] XI. 6, p. 327. Bohemund reckons on the help of ' God and the Cross and the
divine gospels' if he keeps his treaty with Alexius (XIII. 12, p. 415).

[12] So of protection (IX. 7, p. 260); help in battle (X. 10, p. 301); the birth of
a son (VI. 8, p. 167). Gratitude is shown by invoking 'the best blessings' on the
benefactor (X. 4, p. 280). A mother's or wife's prayers are not to be scorned, but

entrusting everything 'to the influence above', and bringing
'God constantly forward'.[1] Oaths are sworn by 'God and His
Mother' or by 'God and all His Saints', or by 'God and the
highest angels',[2] even by the 'unendurable wrath of God', no
less than by the sufferings and cross of Christ.[3] Thanksgivings
to God, accompanied by hymns and even song and dance,
rightly follow success or deliverance,[4] for God not only grants
blessings, but inspires a man with cleverness to win them.[5]
Alexius in his childhood had learnt from his mother (to whom
he is united 'by the grace of Christ'[6]) such a 'fear of God' that
his vicarious sacrilege when his soldiers sacked Constantinople

even more efficacious are those of the clergy, as we shall see on p. 69, or of inter-
ceding Saints. As Alexius drew near to his death, Irene 'made her prayers
more hotly to God on his behalf', and performed 'continuous and unceasing
hymns'; she also paid holy men to pray for him (XV. II, p. 500). For the inter-
cession of Saints we may refer to II. 5, p. 53, and VIII. 3, p. 226, where at a crisis
οἱ εὐσεβεῖς make a πάνδημον pilgrimage 'all night and all day' to a Church of
St. Theodore, and to V. 8, p. 144 for prayer before a holy Image. The idea of
sacred objects as talismans comes out in X. 7, p. 288, where Count Hugh of
France boasts of having 'the golden flag of St. Peter'; in VII. 3, pp. 196–8, where
Alexius bears in his right hand as a standard the veil of the Theotokos, and hides
it in a bush rather than surrender it to a heathen foe; and in XI. 6, p. 327, where
St. Gilles carries the sacred Nail before the crusading armies. So Psellus (Chron.
Basil, II. Byz. T., p. 8) says Basil held a sword in one hand and the 'icon of the
Mother of the Lord' in the other.

For prayers at night, or all night, in the Alexias we may note Anna Dalassena
in church (II. 5, p. 52), the Court attendant who stands 'outside his tent about
the third watch of the night performing the usual hymn-singing' (XIII. 1, p. 378),
the military torchlight procession with 'suitable hymns' before an important
battle (VIII. 5, p. 231), and the 'all-night hymnody' that preceded the drawing
of the Sacred Lots (X. 2, p. 273; XV. 4, p. 471).

[1] V. 4, p. 136; VIII. 5, p. 231; IX. 9, p. 263; XII. 4, p. 357. He twice consults
the Sacred Lots to know the Divine Will (X. 2, p. 273; XV. 4, p. 471). Anna herself refers 'all to God's Providence' and considers that 'Fortune is a divine decree '
(XII. 6, p. 363).

[2] XI. 2, p. 315; XIII. 12, pp. 406, 411; XIV. 7, pp. 446, 447.

[3] XIII. 12, pp. 410, 415.

[4] III. 8, p. 90; VIII. 3, p. 225; XIII. 9, p. 401; XIV. 6, p. 443, and 7, p. 448;
XV. 11, p. 490. With the curiously pagan phrase σῶστρα Θεῷ θύειν we may compare
χαριστήρια θύειν in Nic. Bry. I. 24, p. 37. It is also interesting in this connexion
to read in Nic. Ac. John C. 5, p. 13 and Cinnamus I. 5, p. 7, of the triumph which
John Comnenus, copying Tzimisces of old, accorded after his Asiatic victories
not to himself but to the Theotokos ὡς συστρατηγέτιδι ἀμάχῳ, whom Theodore
Prodromus (P. G. 133, col., 1360), calls the Emperor's συστράτηγον καὶ σύμμαχον
μεγάλην. He seated her image in a car, and walked himself in front carrying a cross.
The same poet wrote a special Ode for this occasion saying that as Constantinople
could not strew her streets with gold and silk garments (as a matter of fact
Nicetas says: ἅπας πέπλος τὰς ἀγυιὰς κατηγλάϊζε χρυσοϋφής τε καὶ περιπόρφυρος, and
C. S. H. B. translates it as tapetes) nor recall Homer from the dead to praise him,
they did their best with 'hymns, paeans, processions, prayers, thanskgivings'.
(P. G. 133, col. 1382.)

[5] XV. 3, p. 470. The idea of God or the angels inspiring Alexius with his new
military παράταξις might easily find its parallel in assertions made during the Great,
War.

[6] III. 6, p. 84.

fills him with terror of 'the divine anger', lest he may be 'altogether accursed of God'.[1]   This leads him to endure grievous penance,[2] and even sixteen years later the feeling of dread remains to haunt his adherents.[3]   In old age he accepts illness as the just reward for his 'multitude of sins'.[4]   This sense of the punishment of heaven falling on human arrogance and presumption, on what Aeschylus called δυσσεβίας ὕβρις τέκος,[5] permeates all religious literature from the earliest times down to our own day and is of course one of the dominant notes of Greek tragedy.   Anna has an interesting passage on the subject, when describing the parlous state into which the Empire had sunk :[6]

For either it was necessary, with God's permission, that the affairs of the Greeks should be in evil case (for I would never make our affairs depend on the motion of the stars), or else the Greek power had come to this condition from the folly of previous rulers.

To a Greek mind folly and impiety were almost identical, yet even man's folly does not always explain his calamity, and the ways of Providence are often inscrutable.[7]   But always an infatuated man who breaks his oaths (sworn, as we saw, before God), or who teaches doctrines contrary to the true faith, is θεοπλήξ or θεοπληγής.[8]   Infidels and heretics are ἄθεοι,[9] and the

---

[1] III. 5, p. 80. For fear of Christ as Judge cf. *Mous. Alex.* I. 123–5, and Callicles, Poem XXIV. 11 put into the mouth of Alexius.

[2] II. 10, p. 64; III. 5, pp. 81, 82.   He purges himself by penance (in the efficacy of which Anna expresses firm belief), so as to 'take hold of the affairs of empire with holy hands'. (The penance consisted of fasting and sleeping on the ground with a hair shirt and a stone pillow. We do not hear of the epiloricum or garment concealing an iron 'thong' inside, such as Alexius himself sent to the Abbey of Monte Cassino; Riant, *Epist. Spuria Alex. ad Rob.*, p. 45) We may note his uneasily defiant justification of church-robbing for military necessity (V. 2, and VI. 3). In a Turk sacrilege is punished by a visitation from heaven (VI. 9, p. 170). This same fear after sacrilege was felt by the Latin hosts in Constantinople, 1204. Riant, *Dépouilles religieuses enlevées à Constantinople*, p. 25.

[3] X. 9, p. 295. So in his poem to John (*Mous. Alex.* I. 124) he speaks of his guilt being judged now, before the Last Judgement.

[4] XIV. 4, p. 437.

[5] *Eum.* 534. Thus at Dristra 'God broke the pride of the Greeks' by a disastrous defeat. At Lebunium they were humble and prayed all night, so God 'unexpectedly granted them victory' over the Patzinaks, who were 'abandoned by divine power' (VIII. 5). The 'wrath of God' (presumably for his broken oaths), and not poor food is the real cause of disease among Bohemund's besieging army at Durazzo (XIII. 2, p. 381, 9, p. 400); it swoops down 'from above' (XIII. 8, p. 399) and at last he himself recognizes the fact (XIII. 11, p. 405).

[6] XIV. 7, p. 444.

[7] So Nic. Bry. (I. 17, p. 31) says that Romanus Diogenes was captured at Manzikert ' Divine Providence ordaining this (οἰκονομησάσης) I know not for what reasons'.

[8] XIV. 2, p. 423; XV. 8, p. 488.

[9] III. 11, p. 95; XI. 2, p. 312; XV. 10, p. 495.

Lord is only mindful of His own.¹ Alexius has carefully studied
the Bible and trained his son-in-law in the same.² He quotes its
words or turns to heaven to justify his actions or beliefs;³ when
he dies, he gives up 'his sacred soul to God'.⁴ Prayers and
hymns, private and public, form an official part of a ruler's life,
and not even his children may interrupt them. As general he
initiates religious ceremonies for his army.⁵ Above all, he helps
holy clergy and monks to continue those devotions which have
peculiar efficacy for the welfare of mankind.⁶ 'Piety towards
God' is, according to his daughter, the key-note of his character,

¹ XV. 10, p. 494.
² XIV. 8, p. 453. Anna's Biblical knowledge will be treated later, in Ch. 29.
³ III. 9, p. 92; VI. 3, p. 156; VII. 2, p. 192; IX. 7, p. 260; XII. 4, p. 357;
XIV. 7, p. 449; XV. 6, p. 477. Cf. XIV. 4, p. 437, where φεῦγε πονηρέ addressed
to the Devil seems an echo of Matt. xvi. 23. When in VII. 2, p. 192, Alexius
preludes a treacherous taking advantage of the Scythian ignorance of eclipses by
the words 'To God I commit the judgement', we see an instance of Byzantine
religiosity at its worst.   ⁴ XV. 11, p. 505.
⁵ III. 8, pp. 87, 88; VIII. 5, p. 231; X. 2, p. 273; XIII. 1, p. 376; XV. 4, p. 471.
After an escape, Alexius and Irene are described as sitting at public prayer 'before
the Mother of God' (XII. 6, p. 363). He 'performed the usual hymn-singing and
made lengthier prayers' to produce the 'usual miracle' at the Blachernae church
without which he dared not start on his campaign (XIII. 1, p. 376). He is present
at the last sacraments and hymns for any of his company that die on a march
(XV. 7, p. 482). Robert Guiscard makes his men spend the night before Durazzo
'conciliating the Deity' by sacrament and prayer (IV. 6, p. 114). The Crusaders
in trouble hold 'night-long prayers' (XI. 6, p. 326), and one of them sallying from
Antioch, 'got off his horse, and prostrating himself three times prayed to God,
calling for assistance. Then all shouted "God is with us" . . . And divine power
in every way assisted the Christians' (XI. 6, p. 327). All armies, Christian or
heathen, are apt before battle to 'call on the Lord of all for pity' (VII. 8, p. 206;
VIII. 5, p. 232). Leo, in his Tactica (XI. 21, XIV. 1 and 2, and XIX. 21), recommends prayers the night before battle and exhortations to the soldiers to do their
duty. Attaliates (pp. 319, 320) praises Botaniates for standing long hours through
a 'hymnody', and at other services for staying to the end, whereas most Emperors
left after the Gospel, to get rid of their cumbrous robes.
⁶ Thus Irene (see note 12, p. 66 above) ' despairing altogether of help from
man', i.e. doctors, not only prayed herself but commissioned monks, hermits,
sick people, and prisoners to pray for the life of Alexius (XV. 11, p. 500) and gave
'rich illuminations' to all the churches. To Anna the life of the clergy consists in
serving God and being 'intent on prayer and antiphonal songs' (XII. 3, p. 351).
For the Church of St. Paul in his Orphanage, Alexius provides an antiphonal
choir of 'singing men and singing women' (XV. 7, p. 485). We may compare
Cinnamus I. 10, p. 14 where John II is said to have planned a pilgrimage to
Palestine to offer a gold lamp-stand; on his death-bed he calls on specially holy
monks to pray that he may live (ibid.). In his Letters to the Abbot of Monte
Cassino (Riant, Epist. Spuria Alex. ad Rob. pp. 42–3) Alexius highly values the
latter's prayers; so too the 'more fervent supplications' of St. Christodulus, in the
Novel assigning Patmos to him (Zach. v. Ling, Jus Gr.-Rom. Vol. III, p. 371).
Leib (Rome, Kiev et Byzance, pp. 94, 214) tells of the monk Cyril praying for the
Emperor and interpreting a dream in his favour. In the Chronicle of Makhairas
ed. Sathas and Miller, p. 22, we find the monk Isaias first inflicting sciatica on
Manuel Butumites, governor of Cyprus under Alexius, as a punishment for kicking
him, and then healing him. Anna credits the clergy with powers of prophecy
(II. 12, p. 68; III. 3, p. 75).

and his best subjects follow him in this.[1] Oaths are not only sworn before God, but actually on the Holy Gospels, or if specially solemn on a specially sacred relic.[2]

The Church as a State institution and the men who held its property and administered its rites come more properly into a later section. Here, as part of the religious life of each individual, we will examine a little more carefully the question of Church ceremonies, and the Saints in whose honour they were performed.

It is obvious that worship, προσκύνησις, in churches and holy places is to Anna one of the most important parts of life, probably (we may remark) the only one of the Crusaders' motives with which she could at all sympathize. The devotions of Anna Dalassena both before and after her son's accession are known to all and a source of pride to her granddaughter.[3] It is natural for travellers to pay their homage to the sanctuaries of the place.[4] Churches are thrown open to the public at the time of the 'daybreak hymn',[5] and hymn-singing forms a part of the regular palace ceremonial.[6] Illuminations and hymns are combined in all worship; the two together are peculiarly acceptable to God.[7]

Special holy days are mentioned. 'Cheese-eating Sunday' corresponds to Quinquagesima, and marks the end of the

[1] X. 3, p. 277. So Nic. Acom. tells us that John II lived a life 'well pleasing to God' (*John C.* 12, p. 31).

[2] The psychology involved reminds us of our own Harold, almost contemporary with Anna, who could not break his oath to William of Normandy, as he had fully intended to do, because he had been tricked into swearing on bones of saints to him unseen. See the interesting 'Considérations préliminaires' in Riant's *Dépouilles religieuses enlevées à Constantinople*. In XIII. 9, p. 402, and 12, p. 415, the 'Crown of thorns and the nails and the lance', all treasures of Constantinople, may have been actually present for Bohemund to swear on; the 'Holy Gospels' certainly were. In XIV. 1, p. 419, the word προτεθέντων is used both of the Gospels and of the Lance. Swearing on relics meets us in II. 5, pp. 53, 54; VIII. 9, p. 242, the ἐγκόλπιος (σταυρός) being usually a reliquary in the shape of a pectoral cross; it is interesting to see that an oath on a large cross was more binding than on a small. Reliquaries figure in contemporary epigrams (see pp. 5–8 above) and constitute some of the presents sent by Alexius to Henry of Germany (III. 10). Nic. Bry. (I. 22, p. 35) tells us that when Anna Dalassena was on trial she produced from her bosom an 'image of the Judge of all' (probably a crucifix), wishing to terrorize the dicasts into doing justice.

[3] II. 5, p. 51; III. 8, p. 89.

[4] II. 5, p. 52; V. 5, p. 139; X. 5, p. 285; XI. 2, p. 316; XIV. 2, p. 428, and elsewhere of the Crusaders. Cecaumenus (*Strat.* p. 78) speaks of the wish 'to worship in the holy temples' as one of the great reasons for going to Constantinople.

[5] II. 5, p. 53.

[6] III. 8, p. 87. In III. 8, p. 90; and VI. 3, p. 157, it is the term used for church worship in general. So Alexius gives to his Orphanage Church choirs to sing antiphonally (XV. 7, p. 485; see p. 69, note 6 above).

[7] VIII. 5, p. 231; XV. 7, p. 485, and 11, p. 500. So Botaniates gave φωτοχυσίαι Attal., p. 319).

'week of preparatory fasting, known as τυροφαγία or the Butter-Week' (which, as a preliminary to real Lent, is still observed in the Greek Church[1]), when 'cheese, butter, milk, eggs, and fish are allowed, but not butcher's meat'.[2] The week before the Butter-Week is Carnival, ἡ ἀπόκρεως,[3] and the Sunday which ends it is Sexagesima.[4] The actual fast starts on the Monday (not, as in the Western Church, on the Wednesday) after Quinquagesima or the Cheese-eating Sunday. Lent as a whole is spoken of as 'the forty days',[5] though with Saturdays and Sundays excluded it stretched itself out from Sexagesima Sunday through eight weeks to Easter Eve.[6]

Maundy Thursday is to Anna 'the great Thursday on which we sacrifice the mystic Passover and also make a feast of it'.[7] It is so holy, from its place near Good Friday in the 'very great and holy week', that even after sixteen years Alexius' followers still dread divine wrath for its desecration by the capture of Constantinople in 1081.[8] Fighting in Holy Week is impious, and should be deferred till 'after the Resurrection Day of the Saviour'.[9] The Patriarch Cosmas celebrates 'holy mysteries' at the feast and before the shrine of St. John the Evangelist.[10] Robert Guiscard and his army take part in 'the undefiled and divine mysteries' (i.e. the Mass) the night before the battle of Durazzo which was fought on St. Luke's Day,[11] and in Alexius' last Asiatic campaign we hear of 'priests called in to sing the final hymns and to impart the sacred elements to the dying', the rites of burial being also scrupulously observed.[12] To commemorate a great deliverance on St. Thecla's Day, September 24, Isaac Comnenus (in the spirit of Philip II with his Escurial) had built a 'beautiful church' in the saint's honour, and here he offered up 'thank-offerings suitable to Christians',

[1] II. 4, p. 51, VIII. 1, p. 221 and *Encycl. Brit.*, 'Lent'.
[2] Sophocles' Dictionary.   [3] VIII. 1, p. 221; XIV. 2, p. 426.
[4] ἡ τῆς ἀπόκρεω κυριακή (VIII. 2, p. 223). Carnival (probably from *caro* and *levare*) has the same sense of leaving off meat, a sense entirely belied by the actual practice during the riotous festivities. On one occasion at this season Alexius gives his troops three days' respite from following him, i.e. from the Friday before Sexagesima to the Monday after it (VIII. 1, p. 221, and 2, p. 224). The attempts of the Western churches to stop private warfare at each week-end do not stand on quite the same footing. See *Encycl. Brit.* 'Truce of God'.
[5] XIV. 2, p. 426. 'Quadragesima' and 'carême' of course contain the same reference to Our Lord's forty days' fast in the wilderness.
[6] The *Encycl. Brit.* points out that when Lent is described as 'the six weeks of the Fast' the Butter Week and Holy Week are omitted.
[7] II. 10, p. 64.   [8] X. 9, p. 295.
[9] *Ibid.* The same name for Easter occurs in XIV. 2, p. 428. Cf. *Encycl. Brit.* loc. cit.
[10] III. 4, p. 79.   [11] IV. 6, p. 114.
[12] XV. 7, p. 482. We hear of no last rites for Alexius himself.

besides taking part in 'holy hymns'.[1] The feasts of 'the great
martyr George', of the 'great martyr Theodore', of the 'chief
apostles', SS. Peter and Paul, of 'Nicolas, greatest of bishops'
in 'midwinter' (December 6), of St. Demetrius, and of the
'falling asleep' (κοίμησις) 'of the blameless Lady, Mother of
God' (better known to us Westerners as the Assumption,
August 15), all figure in Anna's pages, but without any details
as to the rites observed.[2] We read of crowded pilgrimages made
to invoke the aid of St. Theodore in his church not far from
Constantinople,[3] of a very simple ceremonial used in consulting
God by lots,[4] of a procession headed by priests 'clothed in
sacred vestments carrying the Gospel and crosses' coming out
to meet the Crusaders in a small town beyond the river Halys,[5]
of elaborate national thanksgivings after victory,[6] and of a
private service of hymn-singing and long prayers, whereby the
Emperor succeeds in inducing 'the Mother of God in Blachernae' to vouchsafe 'the usual miracle'.[7] On the only two
occasions where Anna describes a religious ceremony at any
length, we may believe that her orthodox and patriotic sympathies were specially stirred. She tells us how in St. Sophia
the philosopher Italus recanted his errors (summarized under
eleven κεφάλαια) 'with his head uncovered and all the people
listening and supplying the curse upon each,[8] and how the army
during the Patzinak War made a desperate appeal to divine aid.[9]
This second passage is worth quoting:

'So when he [the Emperor] could no longer defer the battle, he
called on God as a helper. And as the sun was setting, he himself
first began the invocation to God, arranging a splendid torchlight
procession and singing to Him suitable hymns. . . . Then indeed you

---

[1] III. 8. It is not explained why Anna Dalassena, who bore a grudge against
her brother-in-law for leaving the crown away from the Comnenus family, specially
singled out this church for her 'regular liturgies' and 'continual prayers'.
[2] V. 5, p. 137; IX. 7, p. 259, and 9, p. 265; X. 8, p. 290; XII. 4, p. 356; XV.
11, p. 501; with which last, cf. III. 6, p. 84.
[3] VIII. 3, p. 226. See note 12 on p. 66 above.
[4] Two little tablets or papers, bearing Yes and No respectively, are laid on an
altar. All night 'hymnody' goes on and in the morning a priest or Patriarch takes
up one at random and reads its message aloud (X. 2, p. 273; and XV. 4, p. 471).
[5] XI. 8, p. 331.
[6] VIII. 3, p. 225. See above, p. 67.
[7] XIII. 1, p. 376. For the explanation of this passage see later under Superstition.
Anna doubtless knew that the miracle was familiar to all, so does not describe it.
[8] V. 9, p. 149. Cf. our Commination Service.
[9] VIII. 5, p. 231. It is interesting to compare this with the stirring picture of
the religious ceremony at Athens that preceded the start of the Sicilian expedition
in Thuc. VI. 32. Given the absence of 'libations' and 'sacrifices', Anna's conception
of a great religious service is little different from that of her Attic predecessor, as
shown also in his *Hist.* II. 38; VIII. 70.

might see the sun setting below the horizon, yet the air lighted up, not as though one sun only were shining, but with many other heavenly bodies giving a bright illumination. For all the men fixed lamps and tapers as far as they were able on their own spears and lighted them. And the sounds sent up by the army reached I think as far as the celestial spheres, or rather if truth may be told they were borne up to the Lord God Himself. And from this I feel we ought to infer the Emperor's piety, because he actually did not think fit to make his attacks on the enemy without help from on high. For this man trusted not in men and horses and military devices, but committed everything to the influence above. Now these things went on till the middle of the night.'

The Emperor then takes a little sleep, attacks at daybreak, and wins a splendid victory.

Finally we may note that 'Divine Baptism', called indifferently φώτισμα or βάπτισμα, is conferred as a priceless gift on repentant heretics or Turks;[1] in the case of Anna's infant brother John it synchronizes with his reception of a στέφος.[2] Penance imposed by the Church sets Alexius right with his God.[3]

Such then are Anna's references to ceremonies and sacraments. Of the various saints known to Byzantine hagiography she speaks more often, but usually briefly and without the prefix ἅγιος.[4] St. John the Divine, variously called 'son of thunder', 'hierarch', 'apostle', 'evangelist', and 'theologian' (because he set forth the divinity of 'the Word'), twice gives true prophecies in vision or dream, both times dressed as a priest.[5] St. Demetrius also acts as an oracle through his famous picture at Thessalonica, which speaks cheeringly in a dream to Alexius (who vows if victorious to come on foot to his church there).[6] These are the only saints who take any definite part in the action of the story,[7] but it is pervaded throughout by the writer's great though undefined reverence for Our Lord's 'Heavenly

---

[1] VI. 2, p. 155, 4, p. 157, 9, p. 170, 13, p. 181; XIV. 8, p. 454.
[2] VI. 8, p. 168.   [3] III. 5.
[4] On the other hand the Fathers are 'holy'. V. 9, p. 147; and X. 1, *passim*, where the word πατέρες is only once put in.
[5] II. 7; XII. 4. He has churches in Ephesus and Constantinople (XI. 5, p. 321; XII. 4, p. 355), and his feast occurs in III. 4, p. 79.
[6] V. 5, p. 139. His festival is mentioned in XII. 4, p. 356, and his popularly reputed ownership of a church also associated with the B.V.M. in XII. 6, p. 361. We shall speak later, p. 78, of his wonder-working tomb (II. 8, p. 60).
[7] The 'chiefs', SS. Peter and Paul, are 'guardians of Rome' (I. 12, p. 29; IX. 9, p. 265) and 'the temple of the great apostle Paul' is the centre of Alexius' great Orphanage (XV. 7, pp. 482, 485). Count Hugh carries 'the golden standard of St. Peter from Rome' (X. 7, p. 288). It is by 'God and all His saints' that Bohemund swears to keep the Treaty (XIII. 12, p. 406).

Mother, my Lady'.[1] Five churches among the many dedicated to her appear in the history, three in or near the capital and two elsewhere. That in the Blachernae speeds emperors on campaigns by the 'miracle', of which we shall speak later;[2] from the doors of St. Mary in Chalcopratia Isaac the Sebasto-crator strips off the gold and silver which his imperial brother uses for soldiers' pay and has to make good by a yearly dona-tion.[3] Outside Constantinople the Blessed Virgin, 'spotless', 'super-immaculate', 'Our Lady', 'Mother of God' (terms which all imply a protest against Nestorian and Eutychian heresies), has churches at the Pege monastery in the suburbs of the capital,[4] near Durazzo,[5] and in Sinope.[6] Alexius carries her veil as a flag and hides it in a bush rather than have it captured by the Patzinaks.[7] Anna Dalassena resorts to her as 'mediator' for herself both with God and with the incensed Emperor Botaniates, while her granddaughter invokes God's Heavenly Mother to attest her truthfulness.[8] By tearful, night-long prayers before the picture (εἰκόνισμα) of the Theotokos, in the church built by Cyrus, Praetorian Prefect under Theodosius II, the mother of Michael Psellus had obtained blessings for her son.[9] Finally Alexius dies on August 15, 'the Thursday of that week when is celebrated the falling asleep of our blameless Lady, the Mother of God'.[10] From Anna's first Book to her last the Queen of Heaven, 'the all-holy Mother of the Word that holds all things together',[11] is a reigning sovereign indeed.

Passing to other saints we find in various places churches or monasteries to St. Theodore,[12] to St. Nicolas,[13] to 'the arch-captain Michael',[14] to St. Mark,[15] to the Forty Saints (or Forty Martyrs after whom a lake in Asia Minor is named),[16] to the 'holy martyr Thecla',[17] to St. Andrew,[18] and to the 'great martyr Phocas'.[19] St. Romanus gives his name to one of the

---

[1] XIV. 7, p. 447.
[2] XIII. 1, p. 376. In II. 5 and 6 it is a sheltering-place for noble ladies.
[3] V. 2, p. 129; VI. 3, p. 157.
[4] I. 16, p. 38; and V. 8, p. 145.   [5] IV. 2, p. 105.
[6] VI. 9, p. 170.   [7] VII. 3, pp. 196, 198.
[8] II. 5, p. 53; XIV. 7, pp. 446, 447.
[9] V. 8, p. 144. See Du Cange's note.
[10] XV. 11, p. 501. Anna Dalassena has Our Lord's Transfiguration and the B.V.M.'s 'Dormitio' on her seal (III. 6, p. 84).
[11] II. 6, p. 55.
[12] IV. 6, p. 114; VIII. 3, p. 226.
[13] II. 5, p. 52; IV. 5 and 7; X. 9, p. 294.
[14] IV. 6, p. 116, where Malaterra says 'Nicolas'. See Du Cange's note.
[15] At Venice (VI. 5, p. 161).
[16] II. 5, p. 52; V. 8, p. 145; XV. 4, p. 473.   [17] III. 8, pp. 89, 90.
[18] XIII. 12, p. 415.   [19] VIII. 9, p. 241; X. 9, p. 293.

gates[1] in Constantinople and the holy Elias to a district in
Syria'.[2] A church in Apollonias is said to have been 'built
long ago by the holy Helena in the name of the great Constantine', and one in Cyprus stands 'in the name of the venerable
Cross.'[3] Finally, 'the Great Church in our midst' dedicated to
no saint, but to the Divine or Holy Wisdom, looms large on all
Anna's pages. It would be superfluous to enumerate all her
references to it, but some are rather specially interesting. It was
the scene of the baptism and crowning with a στέφος of John II
as a baby;[4] the Sacred Lots were once drawn there by the
Patriarch, and within its walls Isaac Comnenus assembled 'the
whole body of the church' to listen to his plans for taking
ecclesiastical treasure under military necessity.[5] The heretic
Italus there made his solemn recantation,[6] and its clergy, whom
Anna leaves nameless, had made important contributions to
letters and especially to lexicography.[7]

In passing we may point out that only one convent alluded
to, and that in Italy, has the dedication to the Holy Trinity with
which we in the West are so familiar.[8]

Just one more Saint must be mentioned, familiar to English
readers, and interesting because of a slight obscurity in one
reference. The 'great martyr George' or 'Lord George' has in the
Alexias a monastery attached to the Mangana Palace, churches
at Castoria and near Pelecanus, and a καστέλλιον or πολίχνιον
called after him at Nicaea.[9] His feast is mentioned on one
occasion and his martyrdom at Rama on another.[10] This is
quite simple, but in one passage where Anna is speaking of
Constantinople, we read of 'the plain of the great martyr George
called *the Syceote*'. At first sight we are tempted to see a reference to the thirteenth Region of Constantinople, Sycae now
Galata, and to suppose that some special veneration of St.
George took place there, causing the name to be transferred to
this πεδίον or level place in the capital itself. But from the
evidence collected by Dr. Mordtmann[11] it seems clear that the

---

[1] X. 9, p. 296. Du Cange says that near the Gate stood a church of St. Romanus
built by St. Helena.
[2] XIII. 12, p. 412.   [3] VI. 13, p. 181; IX. 2, p. 249.
[4] VI. 8, p. 168.
[5] V. 2, p. 128; X. 2, p. 273. At the second drawing of lots the army was in
Asia Minor (XV. 4, p. 471).
[6] V. 9, p. 149.   [7] XV. 7, p. 485.
[8] VI. 6, p. 163. We must not omit the 'Treasury (σέκρετον) of [Christ] the
Surety' in Constantinople (VI. 3, p. 157).
[9] III. 4, p. 80; VI. 1, p. 153, 11, p. 176; XI. 2, p. 312.
[10] V. 5, p. 137; XI. 7, p. 328.
[11] *Esquisse topographique de Constantinople*, pp. 21, 22.

πεδίον in question lay between the Porta Charisii (otherwise called the Adrianople Gate) and the church of the Holy Apostles; and though we find in Byzantine literature before Anna[1] no other mention of such a building there, yet the twelfth-century Russian monk Anthony of Novgorod speaks in con-nexion with this part of Constantinople of a monastery of St. George containing the tomb of St. *Theodore* the Syceote. This saint was born in the sixth century at Sykeon on the river Siberis, West of the present Angora,[2] and his name of origin was by a confusion given to the other saint under whose protec-tion his body lay after death.

THE THREE THEOLOGICAL VIRTUES

FAITH

11. SUPERSTITION

IF it is true to say that life in Anna's day had a predominantly religious flavour which it has now lost,[3] at the same time we must admit that much of what was religion to the twelfth-century Byzantine is to us merely superstition. Anna's views on theological dogma will be discussed later, but her attitude to the current beliefs of her day must concern us now. She speaks, though without enthusiasm, of messages from above given in

---

[1] In a metrical paraphrase (not earlier than the end of the thirteenth century) of Nicetas Acominatus, we learn that under Baldwin I (1204–5) a statue of St. George 'Guardian of the Charisian Gate' made miraculous appearances, in conse-quence of which the Emperor had a chapel built to him. Patriarch Constantine in his *Constantiniade* (2nd ed., 1844) states, without giving his reference, that an ancient church of St. George near the Gate of Adrianople was demolished in 1556 to make room for a mosque. (Mordtmann, *loc. cit.*)

[2] W. M. Ramsay, *Hist. Geogr. of Asia Minor*, p. 241.

[3] So Baynes (*Byz. Emp.*, pp. 22, 23) says: 'In the E. Roman Empire the interests and enthusiasms were religious. . . . The Byzantine lived in a world where the supernatural was omnipresent and all-powerful. His holidays were religious festivals . . . his wars were crusades, his emperor the vice-gerent of God, while every startling event in nature was for him a special omen sent for his warning or encouragement.'

So too C. Diehl (*Camb. Med. Hist.* IV, p. 751) says: 'Religion held an essential place in the Byzantine world. . . . From the Emperor down to the meanest of his subjects the Byzantines loved controversies about faith and dogma to distraction. . . . Nevertheless a deep and sincere piety inspired most Byzantine souls.' The whole paragraph is interesting, but too long to quote. To summarize, they 'adored pageants', venerated monks, believed in icons and relics, and 'sought in every event an indication of the Divine Will'. From first to last there entered into their educa-tion and their social life a large element of the Unseen.

dreams or visions.[1] She alludes, as to a well-known fact, to the σύνηθες θαῦμα in the church of the Mother of God in Blachernae,[2]

[1] II. 7; V. 5, p. 139 where the icon of St. Demetrius speaks to Alexius in a dream; XII. 4. In VII. 4, p. 199, she speaks of such an apparition by which the life of her uncle George Palaeologus is saved in war as being either 'a heaven-sent vision' or else 'some other mystery of Providence'. Appearing in dreams is spoken of as calculated to urge a general to fight (VII. 3, p. 193), or merely to alarm an enemy when asleep (XIII. 1, p. 377). The Sultan Saisan comes to a bad end for scorning the warning of a dream (XV. 6).
So in a later reign we find that a later historian, Cinnamus (I. 10, p. 15), trying to conceal the importance which he evidently attached to such matters, makes the dying John Comnenus say of the dream that had assigned the empire to Manuel, his younger son, instead of the elder: 'I know that these things are held mere words by the many, for nothing is so much exposed to the criticism of men as appearances of dreams and oracles (ὀμφαί) of the future.' We feel that both John and his biographer thought the dream had every right to help, as it did, in determining John's choice of his younger son.
[2] XIII. 1, p. 376. It is interesting to see that this passage baffled Du Cange when he wrote his note on it; he was inclined to explain the miracle as some perpetually burning light. But in his later work, Constantinopolis Christiana (Book IV, pp. 84, 85), published in 1680 as Part II of his Historia Byzantina, he gives a quotation in verse from the Liber Virginalis, which, if we assume as he does that 'Lucernam' is an 'error viri in Graecis parum eruditi pro Blacherna', shows beyond all doubt that the 'wonted miracle' was a mysterious unveiling, taking place every Friday, of an icon of the Virgin in the famous church of St. Maria in Blachernae. This church, according to the anonymous Greek author of the Depositio vestis Deiparae in Blachernis was 'as it were the head and metropolis' of all the other churches of the B.V.M. in Constantinople. It was so famous for its 'crebra miracula', especially of healing, that other churches even far off took the name; thus we hear of a St. Maria of Blachernae near Cherson. Its special treasure was the garment (variously called ἐσθής, πάλλιον, ὠμόφορον curtailed into μαφόριον, or πέπλος) of the Virgin, explained by Ebersolt (Sanctuaires de Byzance, p. 46, note 5) as 'le long voile couvrant les épaules que portaient les matrones byzantines', a veil and cloak in one. Every July 2 there was a solemn commemoration of the placing of this precious relic in the church, and we have a ninth-century Canon of Joseph the Hymnographer (P. G. 105, cols. 1004-9) on the subject, making it plain that ἐσθής and μαφόριον are used as synonyms. We may feel sure that it was part at least of this famous relic that Alexius took to the fatal battle of Dristra as a flag and hid in a bush to avoid its capture by his foes (VII. 3, pp. 196, 198), just as on a previous occasion Romanus Lecapenus, 'being in the church of the Blachernae with the patriarch and going into the holy shrine and rendering hymns of supplication to God, took the veil (ὠμόφορον) of the Theotokos and went out armed with sure weapons to keep a tryst with an enemy (Cedrenus, p. 623 c). It is however clear that this garment, which in old days had twice been carried round the walls of Constantinople when the city was in danger (see Du Cange's note on VII. 3, p. 196 D), was at some period divided; Ebersolt (op. cit., p. 133), reminding us that this was an 'usage largement pratiqué par les Byzantins', mentions portions of the veil in reliquaries, and so does Du Cange. Whatever part of it Alexius lost, there was enough left at Constantinople to satisfy the pious fervour of Russian pilgrims almost up to the taking of Constantinople by the Turks (Ebersolt, p. 47, note 1). As to the church of the Blachernae, Paspates (Byzantinai Meletai, pp. 92, 194) dwells on its beauty and fame, and says it was made a Latin church in 1204; he also gives (p. 390) a quaint illustration of all that remains of it: 'quelques pans de mur et un hagiasma', to quote Ebersolt, p. 47. Paspates devotes several pages (pp. 390-5) to its history, and to the ceremonies which took place there. But we will confine ourselves to the 'wonted miracle' in the church, and return to Du Cange's quotation from the Liber Virginalis, which, in lines of fifteen syllables, the third and fourth rhyming roughly with the seventh and eighth, tells us that in

which we know from other sources to have been a weekly miraculous unveiling of an icon of the Virgin Mary; and she tells us that from the coffin of St. Demetrius at Thessalonica,

the 'Lucerna' church of St. Mary at Constantinople there is a representation of the Virgin carrying the Child. She stands 'sindone velata serica', unseen till Friday evening, when:

se expansum et repansum velum sursum recipit

and the Virgin's face and form remain uncovered till the ninth hour of Saturday, when the veil descends again. In all this it is

non libratum arte vatum, nec arte mechanica
non magnete tractum, neque aliqua vi magica

and the miracle recurs every week with the regularity of a clock. Du Cange confirms this by a quotation from Belethus, de Divinis Officiis (ch. li), giving exactly the same account, and Ebersolt (p. 50, note 3) refers to Du Cange. But neither Ebersolt nor Du Cange alludes to the highly interesting passage in Psellus' Λόγος ἐπὶ τῷ ἐν Βλαχέρναις γεγονότι θαύματι, translated into Russian by P. Bezobrazov (Journal of the Ministry of Public Instruction, March, 1889). The editor unfortunately does not give the whole Greek text, which contains a most interesting account of how this Virgin was called on to arbitrate between two parties who claimed a mill; if her covering remained stationary, the monks were to have the mill; if it rose in the air, the mill was to go to their adversary, a general. We are specially informed that this was an extra unveiling, so to speak; not the ordinary miracle of every Friday. In this case the καταπέτασμα shook and floated up, but because it did so later than was expected the matter was referred to the Emperor Michael VII (Ducas), by whose order Psellus wrote out a long and highly technical judgement, 'both a legal record and a panegyric' (to the Virgin), assigning the mill to the strategus, because the Holy Mother had the God-derived power of giving a χρηστήριον. Psellus also says that the world is full of 'traces of unseen feet and hands' and of mysterious voices; colours serve as omens of the future, &c. As Bezobrazov says, he is 'applying to the Christian religion the teaching of Plato about the reflection in the material world of the eternal, of the unchangeable, of Ideas'. This however takes us far from our subject, which is the exact nature of the 'wonted miracle' as described by Psellus. If Ebersolt had read Psellus, he would not have said that this icon was 'sans le médaillon du Christ sur la poitrine' (op. cit., p. 50), for we are specially told that 'the outward form (μορφή) of the Christ-Child changes'. Even the Liber Virginalis says 'Natum gestat'. He is doubtless right in saying that the famous icon was 'dans l'abside de la grande basilique' and not in the circular annex, 'l'église de la Sainte-Châsse', where the sacred Veil was kept, a veil of course wholly distinct from the πέπλος so miraculously withdrawn every week. (For the exact nature of the icon, see p. 316, note 2 below.)

If just when Alexius wished to start on a campaign this weekly miracle abruptly stopped, it is no wonder that he took it as a bad omen.

The passage from Psellus is as follows:

Εἰκών τις αὐτῇ ἐν δεξίᾳ τοῦ νεὼ τοῖς πρὸς ἀνατολὴν εἰσιοῦσιν ἐκκρέματαί τε ἅμα καὶ ἐνήρμοσται ἀκριβῶς, τὴν ἰδέαν ἀμίμητος, τὴν χάριν ἀσύγκριτος, τὴν δύναμιν ἀπαράμιλλος. Καταπέτασμα δὲ αὐτῆς ἐξ ὑφαντικῆς τέχνης ᾐώρηται, ὃ δὴ ὁρμαθὸς εἰκόνων παραλάμβανει τὴν ὕλην πολυτελῶν. Καί ἐστι κατ' ἐκεῖνο μέρος θυσιαστήριον καὶ ἐπιθειάζεται αὐτῇ ὅσα τοῖς τελοῦσι καὶ τελουμένοις νενόμισται, ὕμνοι παντοδαποί, εὐχαὶ ἱλαστήριοι, θυμιά-ματα ἱεροπρεπῆ. Ἐξαίρετον δὲ ταύτῃ τῆς ἑβδομάδος τῶν ἡμερῶν τὸ κατὰ τὴν ἕκτην ἡμέραν τελούμενον μετὰ τὴν τοῦ ἡλίου κατάδυσιν, ἐξίασι δὲ τηνικαῦτα τοῦ νεὼ σύμπαντες, οὐχ ὅσον ἐν δήμοις καὶ πλήθεσιν ἀλλὰ καὶ εἴ τινες θύται καὶ τελεσταί . . . τὸ δὲ πλῆθος ἐστήκασιν ἐν τοῖς προτεμενίσμασι τοῦ νεὼ τῶν προθύρων ἐγγύς . . . ὁ δὲ περὶ τὴν εἰκόνα πέπλος ἀθρόον μετεωρίζεται, ὥσπερ τινὸς αὐτὸν ὑποκινήσαντος πνεύματος καί ἐστι τὸ πρᾶγμα τοῖς μὲν μὴ ἰδοῦσιν ἄπιστον, τοῖς δὲ ἰδοῦσι παράδοξον καὶ τοῦ θείου πνεύματος ἄντικρυς κάθοδος. Συνεξαλλάσσεται δὲ τῷ τελουμένῳ καὶ ἡ μορφὴ τοῦ θεόπαιδος, οἶμαι δεχομένη τὴν ἔμψυχον ἐπιδημίαν αὐτῆς καὶ τὸ ἀφανὲς τῷ φαινομένῳ ἐπισημαίνουσα.

where his famous icon hung,[1] there oozed a miraculous healing unguent.[2] Locusts foreshadow the coming of the Crusaders and a great comet their destruction.[3] The drawing of lots is a legitimate way of ascertaining God's will,[4] and statements are said to be accepted ὥσπερ ἐκ θείας ὀμφῆς.[5] Some men have the gift of prophecy.[6] The sign of the cross makes the foul fiend avaunt,[7] and even delays Anna's own birth three days.[8] The sword of a would-be assassin of Alexius remains miraculously stuck in its sheath.[9]

Did Anna believe all this? She rarely makes any comment on the marvels she relates, and it is not easy to say. In one place, where she is speaking of Alexius' belief in the εὐτυχία of one of his generals, she adds almost apologetically, 'Whatever that is, and whatever is meant by it, for he [the general] had never yet undertaken any action and missed his mark'.[10] In the same way she prefaces her remarks about her father's many trials with the phrase 'as far as Fortune went',[11] and then ascribes the calamities of the Empire, as we saw above, to God's Will or to human folly. She admits the existence of a class of συμβολομάντεις who explained portents,[12] and even her father, though himself believing in 'some natural cause', consults as to the significance

[1] V. 5, p. 139.
[2] II. 8, p. 60. See a reference to this in the autobiography of the Emperor Michael VIII Palaeologus, translated from a Moscow manuscript in C. Chapman's *Michel Paléologue*, p. 175. (His note 3 is erroneous.) We may compare the *Typikon* given by Anna's third brother Isaac to the Cosmosoteira Monastery, where he speaks of two miracles due to his mother Irene's piety; she closed her own eyes in death, and μύρον flowed out of her coffin (ch. 95, *Bull. inst. arch. russe de C'ple*, Vol. XIII, p. 65).
In the *Life of St. Anastasius* (*Archives de l'Or. Lat.* II, p. 426) who lived under Alexius I and John, we are told that this saint, first monk, then crusader, then hermit, heals all who pray at his tomb ἐκ πίστεως.

[3] X. 5, p. 284; XII. 4, p. 355.
[4] X. 2, p. 273; XV. 4, p. 471. In Irene's *Typikon*, ch. 11, new abbesses for her convent were to be so chosen (*P. G.* 127, cols. 1022–1). Oeconomos, *La vie religieuse dans l'Empire byzantin*, p. 226, mentions a method of inquiring into the future on St. John's Eve, which lasted till the third quarter of the twelfth century at Constantinople, and was still in 1918 practised in Crete. The agent was always a young girl who drew out of a bowl of water without looking at them objects which each belonged to some person in the room, while at each extraction a question as to the future was shouted out by the audience. The answer given by the girl was held to refer to the person whose property she was holding at the moment, and was accepted as unerringly correct.

[5] II. 10, p. 62; X. 5, p. 284; XI. 6, p. 326; XV. 8, p. 487. Such an ὀμφή might be accounted responsible for a murder of prisoners (VIII. 6, p. 234).
[6] II. 12, p. 68.   [7] XIV. 4, p. 437.
[8] VI. 8, p. 166.
[9] IX. 7. There is however no marvel quite as incredible as the temple 'not made with hands' of Nic. Bry. II. 26, p. 63.
[10] XIV. 1, p. 420.
[11] XIV. 7, p. 444.   [12] X. 5, p. 284.

of a terrifying comet τοὺς περὶ τὰ τοιαῦτα δεινούς.[1] But surely we may see a faint tinge of contempt in the term; certainly no very robust credulity.[2] She speaks of good and bad omens in the neighing of horses and the fall of the imperial tent or of an imperial statue,[3] very much as people might now, and without exactly committing herself as to her own credence, though she rather surprisingly seems to think such things appeal 'to the more intelligent'. She alludes to ' magic jugglery' and 'potent spells',[4] but this might well be merely rhetorical; more interest in occult powers may be inferred from her statement that an Alexandrian soothsayer divined by the casting of pebbles',[5] which 'was in no way magical but a rational art'. Like all the people of her time she believed in demoniac possession,[6] and in her ascribing of events to the agency of angels or devils she differs little from many writers nowadays. The Devil suggests presumptuous or wicked thoughts,[7] and may, as we saw, be driven away by the sign of the Cross.[8] The angels may attest oaths and suggest military reforms[9] or even fight themselves to help men.[10] Reliance on angelic power to save them from burning was in the case of the Bogomile heretics a sign of their terrible 'delusion'; if they had been orthodox, such a reliance might indeed have been justified by the well-known passage in Psalm xci. 11. The τέρας of stones thrown by no human hand upon their leader Basil's cell, accompanied by a 'sudden earthquake' on a clear starlight night, showed that 'the enraged demons round Satanael' were furious with this man for having revealed their secrets and having raised up 'keen persecution against the error'.[11]

[1] XII. 4, p. 355; cf. p. 357 where he refuses to see a bad omen for his royal self in the fall of a bronze figure called after Constantine. 'Thus,' concludes Anna, 'he committed all things to the supreme Providence of God.'
[2] It is at least worth noticing that she never tells of Alexius' restoration from illness by a θεῖος πέμπλος brought from where it hung before an icon of Christ and laid on his bed, as does Zonaras (XVIII. 25). In Glycas the actual robed and crucified Christ is brought (IV, p. 335).
[3] V. 5, p. 139; VII. 3, p. 194; XII. 4. Cf. Anon. Syn. Chron., p. 187.
[4] I. 3, p. 8; III. 3, p. 76. It is interesting to know that she does not refer, as do Glycas and Zonaras, to popular sayings fulfilled in her father's death.
[5] VI. 7, p. 164.
[6] Epilepsy is due to 'an avenging demon' (VI. 9, p. 170.)
[7] VI. 12, p. 178. In XV. 10 Satanael has seized and darkened the soul of Basil the Bogomile heretic, and 'deceives' him to his destruction.
[8] XIV. 4, p. 437. So Anna Dalassena's appearance is 'revered by angels and formidable even to devils' (III. 8, p. 88).
[9] XIII. 12, p. 411; XV. 3, p. 470. We must note that the monastic life and habit are 'angelic' (III. 1, p. 71).
[10] XIII. 12, p. 407. We may compare the 'Angels of Mons' of the Great War.
[11] This Basil is an 'archsatrap of Satanael', he 'clung with closed teeth to the Devil and embraced his Satanael', a name in the Bogomile theogony which

As to the exact proportion of common sense and superstition
in Anna's mind we are in no position to make a definite
assertion; but indeed there are few of us who would venture
to do so about our own friends, especially if of Celtic extraction.
At any rate she holds her own with her contemporaries, and
even with men of later times, such as Cinnamus, of whose views
we have already spoken as to dreams. The learned Psellus, who
seemed to her and to the world in general the embodiment of
all knowledge, believed in dreams[1] and the virtues of stones,[2]
and discusses gravely whether the demons of whom earth, air,
and water are full, can be male and female, can suffer pain, and
can speak all languages.[3] He did not, it is true, believe in
astrology, though he had studied it; between it and belief in
natural phenomena as prophecies of the future both he and
Glycas draw a somewhat obscure distinction.[4]

On the other hand, the *Strategicon* of Cecaumenus who lived
very shortly before Anna, is most outspoken, condemning

we shall meet later. Basil is δαιμονιώδης and δαιμονιῶν. Anna even believes that
God might conceivably have allowed 'the demons round Basil' to work a miracle
for him (XV. 10, p. 494). So Theophylact (*Comment. on Luke*, ch. 9, 1–6) says:
'Many men have often worked miracles through demons', and again (*Comment.
on John*, ch. 1, 49–51): 'Even demons can simulate miracles φαντασιωδῶς (*P. G.*
123, cols. 813, 1185). Possibly it is to Satanic agency that Anna ascribes the
remarkable fact that when Basil was burnt there was no κνίσσα (XV. 10, p. 494),
a mixture of steam and smell often mentioned in Homeric sacrifice. It was his own
impiety that made the fire leap forward to burn him, and not spare him as it
spared the Three Children in Babylon.

[1] In *B. G. Med.* V, p. 12, in his Funeral Oration on his mother, he says she was
told in a dream to let her son devote himself to learning.

[2] See J. Evans, *Magical Jewels* (Oxford), p. 32. Psellus states as an accepted
fact the medical properties of stones, whether taken internally or worn as amulets.

[3] *De daemonum operatione* (ch. IX. XVII. sqq. *P. G.* 122 and see K. Svoboda's
monograph on 'La démonologie de M. Psellos', Brno, 1927). For his belief in
mysterious voices and the like, see p. 77, note 2 above. Cf. 1 Cor. xiv. 10, 'There
are, it may be, so many kinds of voices in the world and none of them is without
signification.'

[4] Psellus, *Chron.* Mich. V; Theodora; Byz. T. 78, 184; Glycas (I. pp. 26 sqq.).
Zonaras (XIII. 3) believes that the 'art' of astronomers can predict. Psellus, in his
letter to John Longibardus (publ. by Boissonade in *Psellus de operatione daemonum*, &c.,
p. 169) makes the statement that of the sons of Rome οὐδεὶς ἠστρολόγησεν . . . ἢ
γεωμέτρησε πώποτε. Geometry he ascribes to the Chaldaeans and the Egyptians,
but he says nothing of the birthplace of Astrology. Prodromus dedicated to Irene,
wife of the Emperor John's son Andronicus, a poem dealing with the virtues of
the stars and their powers over certain parts of the body, and in the next reign
John Camaterus Archbishop of Bulgaria wrote for Manuel I a poem of 1,351 lines
to describe the influences of the planets according to their 'houses', as well as a
popular poetical exposition of astrology (Krumbacher, *G. B. L.*, pp. 753, 760,
761). It is this idea that the stars or Fate can have power over men 'made in
the likeness of God' against which Glycas passionately exhorts his son (*loc. cit.*).
Plotinus (*Enn.* II. 3, § 1) says the stars can σημαίνειν but not ποιεῖν events. J. Bidez
(*Vie de Porphyre*, ch. III and p. 85) points out that Porphyry, whose learning
Anna praises in XIV. 8, p. 451, believed less and less in astrology as the years
went on.

trust in dreams, 'for many by them have been destroyed',[1]
and in every kind of diviner and enchanter.[2] As to supernatural beings like satyrs and dragons and centaurs, he is
frankly sceptical; God made only two λογικαὶ φύσεις, angels
and men.[3] Yet even he regards a comet as an evil omen of
hostile attack.[4]

Nicetas Acominatus, who survived the taking of Constantinople in 1204, is scornful of the credence given by Isaac
Angelus to λόγια and ὀμφαί and ἡ ἀστρική, and also of all the
superstitions of the vulgar herd, but his words only serve to
prove the prevalence of ἀλλόκοτοι δόξαι in ordinary life, and
we must not forget that when the Latin siege of 1204 came upon
Constantinople, some hooligans broke a statue of Athene in
the Forum of Constantine into fragments, because they fancied
that with her outstretched arm she had summoned the invading
Westerners to the city.[5]

This is the kind of belief that dies hard. We still talk of
omens and luck and more than half believe in them—even in
this twentieth century as much as in all the centuries past.
Shakespeare was probably voicing the opinion of his own day,
rather than trying to express that of Romans in the first century
B.C., when he makes Casca tremble before the 'dreadful
heralds' sent from heaven, and lets Calpurnia say:

> When beggars die, there are no comets seen,
> The heavens themselves blaze forth the death of princes.[6]

Even Cassius, after his famous:

> The fault, dear Brutus, is not in our stars
> But in ourselves that we are underlings—

and his cynical use of natural phenomena to serve his political
ends, is constrained to admit at the last:

> You know that I held Epicurus strong
> And his opinion: now I change my mind
> And partly credit things that do presage.[7]

In judging Anna however we must never forget that in her
the Christian (a devout Christian according to her lights) was
overlaid by the classical student,[8] and even her beliefs were

---

[1] p. 50.   [2] p. 60.   [3] pp. 80 sqq.   [4] p. 66.
[5] Nic. Ac. *Is. Ang.* 3, p. 359.
[6] *Julius Caesar*, Act I, sc. iii, and Act II, sc. ii.
[7] *Ibid.*, Act I, sc. ii and sc. iii; Act V, sc. i. We may compare the effect of
meteors and withering bay-trees on the Welsh captain in *Richard II*, Act II, sc. iv.
[8] τὸ ἑλληνίζειν ἐς ἄκρον ἐσπουδακυῖα (Pref. 1, p. 1).

coloured by the writings of pagan Greeks.[1] Some modern
critics have called Thucydides the master of Anna Comnena.
This would seem too strong a statement, for she never says that
she had studied him. But his tone as regards the supernatural
may still have influenced, even unconsciously, her 'Atticizing'[2]
soul, and made her, as often happens, regard scepticism as a
proof of mental superiority.

In one case where she deals with popular superstition the
accidental likeness to a famous passage in Shakespeare is too
remarkable to be passed over. Robert Guiscard[3] dies in accordance with a prophecy, under circumstances so curiously
resembling the death of Henry IV of England that it seems
worth while to compare the two stories. Anna says of Robert:

'While he was still at Ather, a promontory of Cephallenia, he is
seized by violent fever. Then unable to endure the burning of the
fever he begs for cold water. And when the men round him were
scattered in every direction to look for water, one of the natives says
to them: 'You see that island of Ithaca. In it a great city was built
long ago called Jerusalem, and through age it has fallen in ruins.
In it there is a stream ever giving drinkable and cold water.' And
when Robert heard this he was straightway seized with great fear,
and therefore putting Ather and the city Jerusalem together he
then recognized the death impending over him. For some time
before certain men were prophesying to him the sort of things that

---

[1] It is interesting to compare her attitude towards portents with that of Thucydides and to note the likeness. In his *Hist.* I. 23, he distinctly conveys the impression that the unparalleled horrors of earthquake, drought, and plague, and
the unusual number of eclipses during the Peloponnesian War were not a mere
coincidence, but were somehow due to that War, when also 'traditions which had
often been current before, but rarely verified by fact, were now no longer doubted'.
When Nicias defers his sailing for Athens because of a lunar eclipse the historian
describes him as 'too much under the influence of divination and such like' (*Hist.*
VII. 50), a frame of mind common in Athens where 'soothsayers and prophets' and
others had 'by the influence of religion' raised false hopes of conquering Sicily (*Hist.*
VIII. 1). Yet we feel him to be sympathetic with Brasidas when the latter gives
thirty minae for the service of Athene's temple at Lecythus in the belief that 'the
capture [of the fort] had been effected by some more than human power' (*Hist.* IV.
116). He rehearses without comment, so that we cannot gauge his attitude of
mind, oracular responses from Delphi on which people act (*Hist.* I. 25, 103, 118,
123, 134; II. 102; III. 92) not always to their own advantage. We may trace a
hint of scepticism in his discussion whether the god had foretold λοιμός or λιμός for
Athens (*Hist.* II. 54) and he is not shocked by a suggestion of men working the
oracle for their own ends (*Hist.* V. 16). But his only statements of belief,
or rather unbelief, are given in *Hist.* V. 26, where he calculates the length of the
War, mentions a current prophecy on the subject, and says: 'This was the solitary
instance in which those who put their faith in oracles were justified by the event',
(cf. *Hist.* II. 17); and again in *Hist.* V. 103, where the Athenians speak scornfully
of those who 'when visible grounds of confidence forsake them, have recourse to
the invisible, to prophecies and oracles and the like, which ruin men by the hopes
which they inspire in them'.

[2] Zonaras, XVIII. 26.   [3] VI. 6.

flatterers are wont to tell to chiefs, saying: "As far as Ather itself thou shalt subdue everything; departing thence to Jerusalem thou shalt pay homage to Fate." . . . Finally after six days he dies.'

The parallel in Shakespeare (*King Henry IV*, Part II, Act IV, sc. iv) runs as follows:

K. Hen.   Look, look, here comes my John of Lancaster.
P. John.   Health, peace and happiness to my royal father.
K. Hen.   Thou bring'st me happiness and peace, son John,
             But health, alack, with youthful wings is flown
             From this bare wither'd trunk: upon thy sight
             My worldly business makes a period.

             .   .   .   .

             Doth any name particular belong
             Unto the lodging where I first did swoon?
War.   'Tis call'd Jerusalem, my noble lord.
K. Hen.   Laud be to Heaven! even there my life must end.
             It hath been prophesied to me many years
             I should not die but in Jerusalem,
             Which vainly I supposed the Holy Land;
             But bear me to that chamber: there I'll lie;
             In that Jerusalem shall Harry die.

Prophecies then, even omens, Anna could narrate with tolerance if not credence. But one subject of popular belief makes her burst into indignant contempt, and that is astrology.[1] Her diatribe on the subject is worth quoting in full:

'Touching the death of Robert a certain scholar' [μαθηματικός, probably used in its late narrow meaning of 'astrologer'] 'called Seth[2], greatly pluming himself on his knowledge of the stars, had foretold it after his crossing into Illyria by a prophecy which he put down on a paper and sealed, and entrusted to some of the Emperor's intimates telling them to keep it for a certain time. Then when Robert was dead they open the paper by the man's orders. And the prophecy ran thus: "A great enemy from the West after causing great disturbance will fall suddenly." Then every one wondered at the man's knowledge, for he had risen to the top in this science. And—to turn aside a short time from our story, leaving the history for a little—these are the facts about prophecies.' [The word used, χρησμός, in classical Greek denotes the 'response of an oracle', but here Anna transfers it to prophecies based on astrology.] 'For the invention is comparatively new, and ancient times were unacquainted with this knowledge. For this system of prophecies did not exist in the days of Eudoxus, most learned in astronomy, nor did Plato know this branch, and not even was Manetho the reader of

---

[1] VI. 7, pp. 163–5; cf. XIV 7, p. 444.   [2] For Symeon Seth, see *G.B.L.*, p. 615.

destinies versed in it. But the taking of a horoscope, when making
their predictions, was to them' [here a word is missing, and we may
perhaps supply ἄγνωστος]; 'also the fixing of the centres and watching the whole arrangement [of the stars] and all the other things
which the man who invented this method handed down to his successors and which are intelligible to those who do these follies. But
I some time after this took up this science a little' [possibly in imitation of Psellus] 'not in order that I should practise such a thing
—Heaven forbid !—but so that by judging this foolish science more
accurately I might judge also those who have toiled over it. And
this I write, not for display, but in order to show that under this
Emperor many of the sciences made progress, for he honoured philosophers and philosophy, even though to this study of astrology he
showed himself disapproving, as I imagine because it persuaded the
common herd to turn aside from the purer hopes from above, and
to gape at the stars. This was the cause why the Emperor had this
objection to the study of astrology. Yet even so there was no dearth
of astrologers at that time, but both the aforesaid Seth flourished
just then, and that Egyptian from Alexandria was great in explaining the mysteries of astrology. This man under questions from many
foretold very accurately in several cases, not needing an astrolabe,
but making his predictions by casting pebbles, which indeed was in
no way magical but was a rational art of the Alexandrians. So the
Emperor seeing the young folk flocking to him, because they regarded the man as a prophet, himself twice questioned him and each
time the Alexandrian made a correct answer to the question. Therefore fearing that the harm of many might ensue and all might turn
aside to the folly of astrology, he appointed for the man a residence
at Raedestus, sending him out of the city' [i.e. Constantinople] 'yet
showing much solicitude about him, so that his wants might be
abundantly supplied out of the imperial treasuries.

'And indeed the famous dialectician Eleutherius, another Egyptian, cultivated the elements of this science till he arrived at the
summit of proficiency, not yielding the first rank in any point to
any. And after this the man named Catanances came from Athens
to the capital, eager to excel those before him. When questioned by
some as to when the Emperor was going to die, he predicted his
death as he imagined, but was mistaken in his guess. Now it happened that at that time the wild lion living in the palace had a fever
for four days and then breathed his last, and in this the common
herd thought the prophecy of Catanances was fulfilled. Then some
time passed and again he predicted the Emperor's death and was
mistaken. Nevertheless the Empress Anna his mother did die on
that day which Catanances had pointed out. But the Emperor,
because he had often prophesied about him and always been wrong,
did not care to send him out of the city, partly because the man
was self-convicted [of error] and also lest he himself should seem to
be driving him thence through discomposure. But let us return

again to the point whence we digressed, so that we may not appear star-gazers,[1] obscuring the body of our history by terms of astrology.'

Alexius' real scepticism as to portents from the sky comes out as we have seen in the passage where the comet of April 1106 is described. Yet, while disbelieving himself in any but natural causes, he gets an expert to 'observe the heavenly body'. In a dream it is revealed by St. John the Divine that the comet 'foreshadows the inroad of Celts, while its extinction points to their breaking up at about this spot' (i.e. Thessalonica). Anna's comment merely is :' So much then for the heavenly body that appeared.'[2] Her reasoned conviction on the subject is clearly expressed in a later passage;[3] she thinks scorn to ' make our affairs dependent on the motion of the stars'.

Perhaps her feeling about astrology is partly due to her intense loathing for Manes and all his works. L. Pullan[4] says that Manichaeism started from Persian dualism, but was 'overlaid with Babylonian theories connected with the worship of the stars'. We must admit however that among all the errors of Manichaeans Anna nowhere mentions astrological superstitions, and among her reasons for despising the latter she never adduces any heretical tinge.

THE THREE THEOLOGICAL VIRTUES

12. FAITH AND HOPE

AFTER this attempt to appraise Anna's faith in God, we may as well say a few words about her faith in man. It is so slender as to be almost non-existent, and the same was probably true of all twelfth-century Byzantines. Indeed, like the Red Indian with his curious mixture of suspicion and carelessness, they would have thought a man who trusted his neighbour a fool. A wary incredulity seems to have been their ideal;[5] they

---

[1] This word μετεωρολέσχης is used by Plato (*Rep.* VI. 489) as applied disrespectfully by his imagined 'mutinous sailors' to the 'true helmsman' who studies 'sky and stars and winds'. But the context in the *Alexias* (VI. 7, p. 165) makes it more likely that Anna copied the word from Plut. *Nic.* 23, where it is a term of reproach addressed by ordinary people to 'praters about things in the air', i. e. speculators about astronomical phenomena (Plutarch, *Life of Nicias*, ed. H. A. Holden, p. 118).

[2] XII. 4.   [3] XIV. 7, p. 444.

[4] *Church of the Fathers*, p. 178.

[5] For instance, favourable statements about one's parents will inevitably, so Anna tells us, be put down to partiality or lying unless at once attested by facts (XII. 3, p. 354; XV. 3, p. 468; and cf. the whole Preface).

are the 'canny Scots' of the Middle Ages. When John Ducas
Caesar is told by his grandson that the Comneni are revolting,
he merely boxes the boy's ears for talking nonsense.[1] John Comnenus the Emperor's nephew drives away 'in anger, calling
him a liar and deceiver', the monk who tries to warn him against
the Dalmatian prince.[2] Bohemund smelt a rat, as the saying
is, when Alexius did his best to sow dissension between him and
his most valuable counts; he reflected for six days and then
resolved to ignore the whole matter, 'regulating his treatment
of the men by expediency'.[3] At an earlier date the same spirit
of caution made this chief refuse to eat or even touch with his
finger-tips the food cooked for him in Constantinople by
Alexius' servants, from fear that it might be poisoned.[4] Anna
makes no comment, and it is more than probable that the
Norman's action was the outcome of bitter experience.[5]

The history of the Greek general Manuel Butumites (in
Book XI) throws much light on this subject. After the capitulation of Nicaea he distrusts impartially his turbulent Frankish
allies and the Turkish satraps who have just surrendered. The
latter he sends out of the town in small bodies as fast as he
can, 'lest they should make some evil plot against him' and
'bind and kill his men'. As to the Crusaders, in view of their
large numbers and great lawlessness Butumites 'did not permit
them to enter [Nicaea] all in a body, but opening the gates a
very little he granted entrance to the Celts ten at a time'.

To be betrayed not only by allies but by one's own officers is
a fate against which a sensible chief is always on his guard, and
even the truly loyal subordinate needs to avert suspicion.[6]
Money given for promised military service might well be accepted
and then used against the giver; safe-keeping even in a bishop's
palace may not prove truly safe.[7] If there was one Biblical
maxim which Anna's contemporaries had fully mastered it was:
'Put not your trust in princes nor in any child of man.'

As we should expect, of this mentality Alexius gives the most
striking example. He is always refusing—often unwisely—to
credit some one. He will not believe that young Gregory Gabras
means to run away from court.[8] He 'paid no heed to the insinua-
tions of the multitude' against the two Diogenes, and even when
eye-witnesses revealed the plots of the second brother to him

[1] II. 6, p. 55.   [2] IX. 4, p. 253.
[3] XIII. 4, p. 389.   [4] X. 11, p. 303.
[5] She herself describes Irene as guarding Alexius against 'dangers in banquets'
(XII. 3, p. 352; cf. XIV. 4, p. 437).
[6] XI. 9, pp. 333, 334, 11, p. 340; XII. 7, p. 365.
[7] XIV. 2.   [8] VIII. 9, p. 242.

he 'feigned ignorance'.[1] Suggestions that this Nicephorus had some time back set on an assassin to stab him in the palace riding-school merely made the Emperor angry.[2] When the partial complicity of the ex-Empress Maria in a conspiracy was in question, he refused to accept even the clearest written evidence.[3] When the slave of a later conspirator reveals his master Aaron's plot to compass the death of Alexius, the latter is at first incredulous, suspecting motives of revenge in his informant, and Anna complacently tells us that such chariness of belief was usual with him.[4] She evidently approves of his reluctance to trust his newly sworn liegemen the Crusaders. 'He thought it wise' to go over to Asia Minor to watch their proceedings, and if possible to make conquests by himself so as not necessarily to rely on their oath-keeping; on the other hand their 'immense number' made him afraid to go actually along with them.[5] Later on there is enacted by one of these dreaded Crusaders and Alexius what we might call a very duologue of suspicion at its highest,[6] Greek meeting Greek indeed. Alexius dare not advance against Bohemund because of the traitors in his own camp. Bohemund will not 'venture on the journey to the Emperor' unless he gets hostages and a safe-conduct. Furthermore, he is so much afraid of being entrapped into a position of subservience, that he insists on an oath from the imperial envoys that he will be 'honourably received'. In return the envoys exact assurances as to the safety of those among them who are left as hostages, and everything is sworn on 'the Holy Gospels'.

In an age where East and West, Greeks and Frankish knights, must alike have pleaded guilty to many stabbings and poisonings and other forms of secret violence, it is not surprising that suspicion was everywhere in the air. In Byzantium especially it seems to have been a definite principle always to look below the surface, never to take anything at its face value. And of

---

[1] IX. 5, p. 254, 6, p. 256.

[2] IX. 7, p. 260. Anna would like us to see sheer magnanimity in all this.

[3] IX. 8, p. 261.

[4] XIII. 1, p. 378. Somewhat in the same spirit the second time she tells the story of the liberation from Babylon (i. e. Cairo) of the Frankish counts, she hints at ulterior motives for the generosity first of the Sultan and then of Alexius towards the prisoners. The former may have set them free so as to create a good impression and obviate the suspicion of greed; the latter befriended them largely in the hope that they would do useful propaganda for him against Bohemund's slanders (XII. 1; cf. XI. 7), which slanders were based on the presence of 'barbarian' Scythians in the imperial forces. We may compare the question of black troops in the Great War.

[5] X. 11.

[6] XIII. 8 and 9.

Alexius as the finest exponent of this principle Anna is characteristically proud.

We now come to the second of St. Paul's triad, Hope. Of this we have said enough in connexion with Anna's self-pity and mourning over her lot. Pessimism real or assumed is the perpetual burden of her song. Of course it is never easy for an admiring biographer to avoid being *laudator temporis acti*, at least to the extent of belauding his or her hero's times, but in this case Anna so cordially disliked 'the successor to the throne' that she was bound to think he and his son after him had ruined her great father's Empire.[1] At any rate, be the cause what it may, Anna is no more hopeful or cheerful than the Graiae in the story of Perseus, the three old hags who sat all day moaning that 'new things are always bad'.

THE THREE THEOLOGICAL VIRTUES

CHARITY

13. CHARITY TO CRIMINALS

WHEN we come to Charity we are struck by the much higher level reached by Anna than in the other qualities of Trustfulness and Hope. If we mean tolerance for the views of others, as in our modern phrase charitable judgement, she has none of that, and if we look for real large-heartedness we shall look in vain. But if we use the term Charity to mean clemency and liberality and philanthropy as then understood, we shall find a singularly lofty standard in the *Alexias*.

To begin with the first quality, that of clemency or humanity. Anna believes that God moves hearts to pity so that even criminals may be pardoned.[2] Certainly her picture of her father's forbearance, ἀνεξικακία, towards enemies is very striking, even if we sometimes suspect interested motives of fear or prudence. Not only must we remember the many would-be usurpers whom he allowed to live on in Constantinople; it is quite as true of him as it was of his son John[3] that he never put

---

[1] XIV. 3, p. 433.

[2] XII. 6, p. 363. Towards such criminals the mob shows its innate baseness by outbursts now of savage hatred and now of mercifulness (V. 9, p. 149; IX. 7, p. 260; XII. 6, pp. 362, 363; XV. 9, p. 492, and 10, p. 494). See also p. 52, above.

[3] Nic. Ac. *John* C. 12, p. 32. He claims that his hero never even mutilated any one.

any one to death for a political offence. Sometimes he pretends to be brutal, but he never really is.[1] He pardons rebels and plotters with almost monotonous regularity, and actually sets a slave who has tried to assassinate him free, loaded with 'very great gifts'.[2] He is lenient even to despised astrologers, except when he fears they will lead the people astray,[3] and then banishment with maintenance at the imperial expense is all that he decrees. In the case of one set of conspirators we hear that he waived 'the heavy penalties of the law',[4] and he was evidently glad to let Michael Anemas profit by the quaint archaic custom whereby a criminal who had not yet been led past a certain landmark in the capital known as the Bronze Hands might be reprieved.[5]

This Anemas conspiracy and its punishment has several features of interest. For one thing, it seems to have been specially dangerous, doubtless because the ringleaders were 'such good soldiers'. So Alexius decides on a humiliating mock-procession through the capital for the men, with ignominious shaving as a prelude and blinding as the destined outcome. But when entreated by his wife and daughters he is most happy to remit the sentence, for which there is fortunately just time. The chief cruelty is shown by the σκηνικοί and the ῥαβδοῦχοι who arrange the whole thing and jeer at the victims; the mob runs out to gaze but is 'stirred to weeping and lamentations'. Anna sees the hand of God in her own tender-heartedness and in the

---

[1] I. 3, p. 8; XII. 7, p. 365. In XII. 8, p. 366, his threats to blind his Admiral Isaac Contostephanus were probably merely rhetorical. Even Zonaras (XVIII. 29) says that Alexius was inclined to mercy and slow to punish.

[2] III. 12, p. 97; VI. 4, p. 157; IX. 5–10, especially IX. 7, p. 260; XIII. 1, p. 378; XIV. 3, p. 431. Temporary exile is the usual punishment coupled with confiscation of goods. For restoration to favour, see VIII. 9; XI. 6, p. 326; XII. 5, p. 359, 8, p. 368.

[3] VI. 7. In XIII. 1, p. 377, it is remarkable to read of a severe law against writers of lampoons, but since these must usually have been anonymous (as in the case in question) the punishment cannot have been much oftener exacted than in the case of a truth-telling astrologer.

[4] VI. 4, p. 157.

[5] XII. 6. 'Now the Emperors who had fixed these bronze hands on a certain high watch tower and lofty stone arch had as their purpose to establish this ordinance, that if a man whom the law was condemning to death were the hither side of the Hands, and on his way the tokens of imperial mercy should reach him, he should be delivered from his fate. For the Hands were considered to show that the Emperor embraced these men once more and had not yet let them go from the hands of mercy.' Once they had gone past the Hands they were 'beyond safety' and not even the Emperor could help them. Attaliates (pp. 313, 314) tells us that Botaniates, who was φιλανθρωπότατος (' very humane'), restored a neglected law of Theodosius forbidding Emperors to give summary punishment to any criminal. He read this Novel to the Senate and 'they agreed and were much pleased'. It is interesting to find these practical limitations to the sovereign's theoretically unbounded powers of pardon and punishment.

way the men escorting the procession deliberately slackened
their pace for the messenger of pardon to arrive.[1] Except for
this story, and for that of the Bogomiles which introduces public
executioners (δήμιοι) who perform the burning of Basil,[2] we hear
little from Anna of the way justice was carried out in Constantinople. She does however show that a man on trial was pro-
verbially afraid,[3] and she gives us sinister glimpses of the
extraction of confession from suspects by torture.[4] But on the
whole her code is one of mercy, such indeed as few dared
to show.

Thus to her it is emphatically the duty of a Christian to forgive his enemies, and he should do this even at the risk of
being duped or criticized.[5] So Alexius only puts in chains the
Scythian Neantzes who had betrayed the plans first of his own
countrymen and then of the Greeks and had displayed unparalleled insolence as well,[6] and another deserter, Tatranes
by name, is made into a loyal and devoted subject by the
Emperor's marvellous 'forbearance'.[7] For Anna is anxious we
should think it marvellous. It seems to have been the popular
assumption that blinding must follow rebellion as rendering the
blinded man unfit ever to aspire again.[8] If Urselius is spared
this humiliation and Alexius thus wins golden opinion for
φιλανθρωπία, his reason it is felt may have been that the Frankish

[1] We may compare the way Attaliates praises Botaniates and his 'inexplicable
goodness' in forgiving those who conspire against him, even leaving them their
goods, an act such as none of the Emperors had ever risen to (pp. 294, 314, 318).
[2] XV. 10, p. 494.
[3] III. 5, p. 81. See also the fear of the accused man in XI. 5, p. 323.
[4] IX. 8, p. 261; XII. 6, p. 361; XV. 8, p. 487. In Nic. Bry. III. 26, p. 85, we
read of an exiled man dying 'inhumanly and cruelly tortured'.
[5] IX. 5, p. 254, 10, p. 264. In XII. 7, p. 365, Anna adds to the tale of one such
act of forgiveness the proud comment: ὁποῖος ὁ ἐμὸς βασιλεὺς περὶ τὰ τοιαῦτα. In
view of what has been said of Byzantine suspicion, the passage in XIII. 8, p. 399
('it is better to be deceived than to offend God and transgress divine laws') is of
peculiar interest. In XIV. 3, p. 431, Anna compares her father's much abused
clemency to that of Our Lord. He lets Nicephorus Diogenes keep his estates after
his rebellion (IX. 10, p. 265) and forgives the Empress Maria completely (IX. 8,
p. 261). He restores his nephew John to his governorship at Durazzo after a
venerable Archbishop has accused him of treachery (VIII. 7 and 8). For other
rebels readmitted to favour, see p. 90, note 2 above.
[6] VII. 9; VIII. 4, p. 230.
[7] VII. 10, p. 213. Alexius shows this same ἀνεξικακία as well as generosity with
money when he releases from Turkish captivity the crusading counts who in his
opinion had been hostile and forsworn to himself (XII. 1, p. 347).
[8] I. 3, p. 7; IX. 9. It was so common a proceeding as to have over a dozen
phrases to describe it; see the list in Oster (A. K., Pt. I, p. 23). So Botaniates claims
to blind Bryennius 'for the safety of the many and [Bryennius'] own peace'
(Attal. p. 292). Nicephorus Bryennius remained powerful though blinded (VII. 2,
p. 191; X. 2, p. 274, and 3, p. 276); but Anna seems to think her father-in-law
an exception to all rules. See p. 58 above.

rebel was 'such a man, noble and a positive hero'.[1] Under ordinary circumstances every one would have expected his conqueror to apply the usual treatment. Even court slaves might be powerful enough to inflict this mutilation on an enemy. Alexius' practice was different. When he captures Nicephorus Bryennius he, 'noble man that he was, does not injure (Bryennius') eyes at all. For Comnenus was not a man to proceed after capture against those that had opposed him, but he thought the capture of the enemy sufficient, so that afterwards there followed courtesies (φιλανθρωπίαι) and kindnesses and munificence'.[2] It is the messengers of Botaniates who blind first Bryennius and then Basilacius another ex-rebel,[3] and this fate is ordered for the pseudo-Diogenes pretender[4] not by Alexius but by his mother the Regent. Even in the case of the base and ungrateful archtraitor Nicephorus Diogenes, who was implicated in three attempts on his imperial benefactor's life, Alexius persistently ignores the injury and only reluctantly consents to punish at all. Anna does not feel sure that he was primarily responsible for the man's loss of sight; he certainly did not order torture to extract a confession and he certainly refused to allow other mutilation. Furthermore he did his best not only at the crisis but again later to win the ex-rebel's affection by most generous and complete forgiveness.[5] The very word συμπάθεια acquires in the *Alexias* a new meaning, not 'sympathy' but 'pardon'.[6]

Anna's account of Robert Guiscard's brutality to the Lombard chief whose teeth he extracted and whose eyes he put out[7] and to the captured Venetian and Greek crews whom he cruelly mutilated may be exaggerated, as may the revolting story of Saisan blinded with a candlestick before being strangled, while the savage massacres by the Crusaders sound too pointless to be true.[8] Yet this all serves to prove that in an

[1] I. 3, p. 8. Nic. Bry (II. 28, p. 64) says Alexius showed further kindness to Urselius in his captivity. The same plea of personal distinction deserving respect comes out in the *Alexias*, VI. 9, p. 169, where Philaretus gives wrath at the blinding of his sovereign Romanus Diogenes as an excuse for his own rebellion at Antioch.
[2] I. 6, p. 16.
[3] I. 6, p. 16, and cf. I. 9, p. 22; VII. 2, p. 191.
[4] X. 4, p. 279. [5] IX. 5–10.
[6] *Ibid.*, also XII. 6–7 (six times), and often elsewhere. So he offers Nicephorus Diogenes ἀπάθεια καὶ ἀμνηστία (IX. 7, p. 259). But in III. 6, p. 83, the adjective συμπαθής means 'sympathetic'.
[7] I. 11, p. 27. He and Bohemund blind two traitors among their own Norman counts (V. 5, p. 137).
[8] VI. 5, p. 161; XI. 5, p. 321; XIV. 1, p. 421; XV. 6, p. 480. Usually she does not seem to consider the Turks as cruel as the Crusaders, even though they strangle people with bowstrings (VI. 12, p. 178; XV. 6, p. 481). For the Crusaders, see

age when such things were common she was ahead of her time in the horror with which they inspired her. Only heretics must be prepared to face 'every injury, tortures and chains and sacrifices of the flesh' if they remain obdurate; or again, 'fire and whippings and a myriad deaths'.[1] Yet even to a deposed and exiled heretical bishop 'every kind of care and kindness' is shown by the Emperor's orders.[2] The false teacher Italus must make public recantation of his errors, and a relapse is punished by excommunication, but he is carefully kept by Alexius from popular violence.[3]

In this department of human life two ideas, confused rather than joined, seem to have dictated the procedure. First the heretic was regarded as a focus of religious disease, and as in sericulture the only way is to destroy all infected silkworms, and in a plague to wage war on every rat as potentially dangerous, so the wrong-doer was put to death for the good of the community, lest he should 'communicate his own defilement' to others.[4] And the Basileus as head of the Church and responsible for his subjects' souls was bound to see this done.[5] Secondly, as the sinner's soul was more precious than his body,

---

X. 6, p. 286; XI. 8, p. 331. She clearly feels for the Turks in the cruel killing of their children and friends by some of her father's own soldiers (XIV. 1, p. 420). It is only a low-born impostor who threatens his enemies with crucifixion (I. 15, p. 36). It may be worth noting that the story in XI. 8, p. 331, of the Crusaders massacring the whole Greek population of a town beyond the river Halys, not sparing even the priests who in full vestments had come out to welcome them, receives some slight corroboration from the Life of St. Anastasius (*Arch. de l'Or. lat.* II, p. 426). This monk of German origin, who lived under Alexius I and John II, joined the Crusaders in the λεγόμενος Ἱερὸς πόλεμος but abandoned earthly warfare to return to spiritual, 'seeing in the wars καὶ τοὺς ὀρθοδόξους κακοποιουμένους ὑπὸ τῶν Λατίνων'. In both cases the brutality had a quasi-religious or sectarian basis; to the Latins the Greeks were schismatics, though better than heretics. But see below, p. 94, note 4, and Ch. 47.

    [1] X. 1, p. 270; XV. 8, p. 489.   [2] V. 2, p. 130.

    [3] V. 9, p. 149   Other heretics in X. I, p. 270, are subjected to a 'perpetual curse' on their persons and doctrines. Theophylact (*Comm. on Habakkuk*, II. 10) advocates this as the sole appropriate punishment for false teachers, because the anathema is 'the end and finish of every heretic, namely separation from God', *P. G.* 126, col. 862.

    [4] XV. 8, p. 489.

    [5] A statement made by Alexius during the trial of the Bogomile heretics throws a curious light on Byzantine mentality. He wishes not unnaturally to discriminate between heretics and true Christians; while he condemns the whole number to death he offers them the choice between a pyre with a cross and a pyre without, secretly intending to release those who should choose the former. But the reason alleged is amazing to us: 'For it is better that men really Christians should die rather than that living they should be persecuted as Bogomiles and offend the consciences of the multitude.' This can only mean that by living and being persecuted for heresies they did not share, these men would render their persecutors innocently guilty, so to speak, of calumny and cruelty. When the chief Bogomile has been burnt Alexius will not allow his disciples to meet the same fate from popular fury (XV. 9, p. 491, 10, p. 494); there might conceivably be doubtful cases among them.

the latter was sacrificed to save the former; the pains of death might atone in the eyes of Heaven for the evil deeds of life. On both these theories capital punishment was a logical thing. But a third idea of punishment as neither deterrent nor purificatory but merely retaliatory, comes out in the story of Basil the Bogomile as told by a thirteenth-century writer. He says: 'It was right for him to be destroyed by fire and to have this foretaste of eternal fire, seeing that he had deceived many and had heaped up material for the eternal fire, as wood and hay and stubble.' This quotation from 1 Cor. iii. 12 is followed by an allusion to John xv; Basil was burnt, 'cut off as a rotten tree that does not bear good fruit'.[1]

Euthymius Zigabenus,[2] the monk chosen by Alexius to refute by written arguments all heresies in general and the Bogomiles in particular, adopts this view when he thanks God for preservation from 'the cult of heretics who deliver to destruction the body with the soul'. That is to say, as he explains in speaking of Basil the Bogomile,[3] heretics are shut out of both lives, here and hereafter; they meet first with fire on earth at the hands of righteous men, and then with fire in hell, 'proceeding through the quenchable to the unquenchable'.[4] The soul of the heretic was lost as well as his body. If any one profited at all it was the onlookers who might be saved by the awful example, but that is quite a secondary motive.

The whole question of medieval punishment, especially mutilation and blinding, is most interesting though too big to discuss now. Suffice it to say that Bury considers these barbaric penalties as part of the 'tendency to avoid capital punishment' and of the movement 'in the direction of mildness' after Justinian. He says:[5] 'They were then considered as a humane substitute for death, and the Church approved them because a tongueless or noseless sinner had time to repent.' Baynes[6] does not consider this an adequate explanation, but suggests or implies others that might be given, e.g. the numbers of imperfectly Hellenized barbarians in Constantinople, the 'nervous tension'

---

[1] *Anon. Syn. Chron.*, p. 181.

[2] *Panoplia, P. G.* 130, col. 1360. For this man, see *Al.* XV. 9, p. 490.

[3] *Ibid.*, col. 1332.

[4] It is interesting to find the same point of view in the Latin *Anon. Gesta Francorum*. After describing how the Crusaders spared Greek villages the writer tells with gusto how they burnt a heretical village with its inhabitants (ch. iv).

[5] Introduction to *Camb. Med. Hist.* IV, p. xiii. In App. 11. of Vol. V of Gibbon's *Decline and Fall* he says the *Ecloga* of Leo III, to which in Criminal Law the *Basilica* of Basil I and Leo VI adhered, was meant to be more humane than old Roman Law. The ecclesiastical right of asylum tended also in this direction.

[6] *Op. cit.*, pp. 27, 121–2.

of a populace living in chronic danger, bitterness during the
Iconoclastic struggle, &c. Whatever be the cause, his further
statement is certainly true: 'The most remarkable feature of
Byzantine criminal law is the frequency with which mutilation
was employed as a punishment.' But a later sentence of his
must be at least partly challenged. He says: 'Beside mutilation,
confiscation of property was a frequent form of punishment, but
not so imprisonment, which at least until the twelfth century
was only employed to prevent the escape of the criminal before
trial. Enforced seclusion in a monastery was, however, occasionally practised in the case of State offenders.' This Scholar
would seem to have overlooked several passages in the *Alexias*
invalidating his theory as to imprisonment, and we are obliged
to take up his assertions one by one before leaving this subject.

As to confiscation of goods, he is supported by Anna's stories
of the unnamed conspirators who gave trouble just before
Robert Guiscard's second campaign, of those who sided with
Nicephorus Diogenes, of John Solomon and his fellows, and of
the Manichaean ἀποστάτεις, deserters both from the true faith
and from the army, while as to seclusion in a cloister[1] there
is of course no doubt. This fate befell Leo and Nicephorus
Diogenes and their mother the ex-Empress at the hands of their
half-brother Michael, and from it the more magnanimous
Alexius rescued them, after the reign of Botaniates had inter-
vened.[2] It also befell the deposed Nicephorus Botaniates on
Alexius' accession,[3] just as Botaniates in his day had decreed it
for his predecessor Michael VII.[4]

Now as to the third point. The imprisonment feared by an
imperial tax-gatherer if he arrived 'with empty hands' at the
Treasury may have been a mere preliminary to trial, and the
confinement with chains at Philippopolis decreed for the insubordinate young Gregory Gabras may have been intentionally
as short-lived as the banishment of his two accomplices, who
return to the Emperor's service not long afterwards.[5] But how
can we ignore a statement like this: 'Not having forces enough
to set a guard over so many . . . [Alexius] sent away the ringleaders, Diogenes and Cecaumenus Catacalo, to Caesaropolis
so that they should be imprisoned and chained only, for he did
not design any other punishment for them, though all advised
him to mutilate them.'[6] There seems to be no question of future
judicial proceedings in this case of the Diogenes conspirators,

[1] II. 5, p. 54; V. 3, p. 131; VI. 2, p. 155; VI. 4, p. 157; IX. 8, p. 262; XII.
6, p. 362.   [2] IX. 6, p. 256.   [3] III. 1, pp. 70, 71.   [4] I. 15, p. 36.
[5] II. 6, p. 56; VIII. 9, p. 242; XI. 5, p. 324; XIV. 3, p. 431.
[6] IX. 8, p. 262.

or in that of those concerned in the Anemas plot. John Solomon
was imprisoned at Sozopolis[1] and Michael Anemas, after his
blinding had been remitted, was shut up in a tower near the
Blachernae, σιδηρόδετον ἐπὶ πολὺ ἐν αὐτῷ χρονοτριβήσοντα χρόνον;
there is nothing to suggest that he was ever tried again.[2] His
fellow-inmate of this tower, Gregory Taronites, who throughout
is handled with great gentleness except for being shaven and
paraded through the streets, may well have been there only
on probation, for though he was ἐπὶ πλείονα καιρὸν ἔμφρουρος
he finally received from the mild or prudent Emperor 'pardon
and kindness and gifts and unprecedented honour'.[3] But how
about the pseudo-Diogenes sent after two reprimands to a
distant prison?[4] Still more, what of the obdurate Manichaeans
Cusinus and Pholus? After being confined in 'the porches round
the great Palace'[5] with their fellow-heretic Culeon, they come
before the Emperor. Culeon is converted, but as to the other
two, σιδήρεοι μένοντες, we learn that Alexius, 'throwing them
into the prison called Elephantine and plentifully supplying all
their needs, gave them up to die of their own iniquities alone'.[6]
Surely this is imprisonment not before but after trial. Almost
exactly similar is the story of the Bogomile heretics. They are
first subjected to mild imprisonment coupled with instruction
from selected theologians, and some are converted, but the
obdurate 'died in their heresy, kept in prisons, yet having a
plentiful supply of food and clothing'.[7] This again does not look
like confinement intended to be merely preliminary. Nor does
the last sentence of the whole painful story. After the burning
of the chief Bogomile Basil, to witness which spectacle his followers seem to have been brought out of prison, these remaining
exponents of the heresy are dealt with as follows: 'After this
another very strong prison received these godless men, who were
thrown into it, and lived a long time and died in their impiety.'[8]

It seems clear from these passages that long imprisonments,
even life sentences, were not uncommon in Anna's day,
especially for men convicted of political crimes or theological
errors, though the treatment was not harsh nor the food scanty.[9]

---

[1] XII. 6, p. 362.   [2] XII. 7, p. 364.
[3] XII. 7, p. 365. The fact that Alexius' sister had married a Taronites may help
to explain this. See below p. 276, note 1, also p. 374.   [4] X. 2, p. 272.
[5] Du Cange, in his Notes on 455 c and 494 D, says these porches, τὰ Νούμερα,
were occupied by the palace guards and had prisons off them.
[6] XIV. 9, p. 457.   [7] XV. 9, p. 492.   [8] XV. 10, p. 495.
[9] Only once do we find a complaint of a prison, and that is not a Byzantine but
a Turkish one (XII. 1) 'of the old style', where the captives have a bread-and-water
diet, 'not once seeing the sun'. The way Anna puts it seems to prove that such
treatment of prisoners was exceptional, even among infidels.

14. CHARITY: WAR AND PEACE

ONE side of Charity as affecting human intercourse must now be briefly studied, the all-important question of war and peace as viewed by Anna's eyes. We must state at the outset that war *per se* has for her none of the glamour cast over it by Western chivalry. Peace is to her first and last the aim, the ideal, the greatest blessing that earth can show. A pope is by his office εἰρηνικὸς καὶ τοῦ εἰρηνικοῦ μαθητής.[1] Her mother Irene's beautiful name shows her mission of peace.[2] Peace is invoked upon a friendly state, and pressed upon an enemy.[3] The rashness of young men is partly due to their 'not having tasted the misery of wars', and Anna is on occasion proud of her father for 'peacefully settling matters naturally to be accomplished by war and steel'.[4] He is always more ready for peace than for fighting,[5] and Anna makes a sermon[6] out of this so like Thucydides that one wonders if she was thinking of him: 'It is the mark of bad generals, when things are quiet, of their own action to stir up those around them to war. For peace is the goal of all war.'[7] A word is here left out of the text but the subsequent sense is clear, that it is 'the mark of foolish generals and leaders' to choose war unnecessarily. The Emperor Alexius acted 'entirely contrary to this, and cared exceedingly for living peaceably'; he 'cherished peace' (another lacuna) 'when present and toiled to regain it when lost.' 'And by nature he was peaceful, but this same man when circumstances compelled was most warlike.'[8] Generals who 'rejoice in blood' and who 'ever welcome fighting rather than peace' incur Anna's severe censure,[9] while to win a success 'without bloodshed or combat' is indeed a victory.[10] She says of Bohemund that he 'had never learned

[1] I. 13, p. 32.
[2] XII. 3, p. 354; XV. 11, p. 506.
[3] III. 10, p. 95; XV. 6, p. 478. So Euthymius Zigabenus in his Anathema 14 against the Massalians prays for peace for the Empire. *P.G.* 131, col. 48. We are reminded of the paean on the blessings of peace in Thuc. IV. 62.
[4] VII. 3, p. 195; IX. 10, p. 265; XII. 5, p. 358.
[5] XII. 5, p. 358; XIV. 3, p. 432.
[6] XII. 5, p. 358. In Thuc. II. 61 we read: 'For men who are in prosperity and free to choose, it is great folly to make war.'
[7] Cf. Thuc. I. 120, 124: 'Brave men as soon as they are wronged go to war, and when there is a good opportunity make peace again.' 'By war peace is assured.'
[8] Anna would no doubt have endorsed Thucydides' verdict as to the good and bad effects on the character of peace and war respectively (*Hist.* III. 82).
[9] XI. 1, p. 311.
[10] XI. 5, p. 322 (*bis*), 7, p. 329; XV. 3, p. 467.

to live peaceably',[1] yet she cannot resist putting into his mouth a speech of which the summary might well be 'Peace has her victories no less renowned than war'.[2] An unjust war has no chance of success,[3] and even in a just cause victory is to be sought not only 'through sword-drawing', but by treaties, nay even by 'craft' and 'roguery', in the effort to avoid an appeal to arms.[4]

But if war to Anna is always hideous, never glorious as to Western chivalry, it is doubly so when waged with fellow-Christians, and thus an ἐμφύλιος πόλεμος. Worst of all is civil strife in a Christian community,[5] but even 'barbarians' (if co-religionists[6]) should never be encountered in battle. Robert Guiscard's nobles and his wife Gaita are represented as dissuading him on this ground from attacking Alexius;[7] such fighting is specially horrible in an ecclesiastic[8] or at sacred seasons.[9] When the Crusaders assault Constantinople in Holy Week, the Emperor ἵνα μὴ Χριστιανοὶ κτείνωνται gives orders to shoot wide of the mark, or at the enemy's horses rather than men.[10] It is

[1] XI. 10, p. 337, 11, p. 340. Cf. the stricture of the Corinthians on the Athenians, as 'born neither to have peace themselves nor to allow peace to other men' (Thuc. I. 70).
[2] XI. 4, p. 319. So Polybius (*Hist.* V. 12, 2) says: 'To conquer the enemy by nobility and justice is not less but more useful than successes in arms.'
[3] I. 15, p. 36.
[4] XIII. 4, p. 387. Even Robert Guiscard, according to Anna, tries to throw the blame of the war on his opponent (IV. 5).
[5] II. 11, p. 66, 12, p. 68.
[6] IX. 10, p. 265: 'though Dalmatians they are yet Christians'. In X. 8, p. 291, the Crusaders are begged not to fight with ὁμόπιστοι, and in XIV. 2, p. 422, Alexius claims to have 'cared for them as Christians' and defended them against the Turks.
[7] I. 12, p. 29.
[8] I. 13, p. 32; X. 8, p. 292.
[9] II. 10, p. 64; III. 5, p. 80. In X. 9, pp. 295, 296, Alexius 'felt awe at the sanctity of the day'. History however furnishes several examples of Greek generals who chose holy days for their attacks, hoping to take the enemy by surprise. Leo Diaconus (*C.S.H.B.* pp. 134–8) says Tzimisces attacked the Russians on Good Friday. Attaliates describes how the Greeks attacked the Celt Crispin on 'the Day of Resurrection, the Great Sunday'; they were defeated and Crispin 'condemned the impiety of the Greeks', because on 'the festival of festivals' they went 'against the blood of Christians'; thereby 'mocking the grace of the Resurrection' (p. 124). Cedrenus gives an account of a man seizing an enemy by treachery just after they had celebrated together ἡ κοίμησις of the Virgin (pp. 714–15). To take one more instance, when Cecaumenus Catacalo attacks the Saracens at Pentecost after the priests had performed 'the bloodless sacrifice' and 'he had partaken of the divine mysteries with all his men' he wins an easy victory over drunken and careless Saracens (*ibid.* p. 744 A). A nobler, we are tempted to say more Christian, point of view is found in the Pagan Xenophon, as quoted by T. R. Glover, *From Pericles to Philip* (Camb. 1917, p. 173). For the teaching of the Western Church see *Encycl. Brit.* 'Truce of God'.
[10] X. 9, p. 296. So Nic. Bry. (II. 20, p. 58) says Alexius thought it 'not holy' to kill the men he captured from Urselius the Frank's army, Χριστιανοὺς ὄντας.

indeed 'inhumanity and brutality'[1] when soldiers of the Cross massacre the population of a Christian village, and if Alexius had allied himself with Turks against Christians he would have deserved all Bohemund's bitterness.[2] As it was, the Emperor's mere use of Scythians as mercenaries was twisted by the Norman prince into a proof of his 'ill-will towards Christians', and a reason for raising forces against him.[3] To conclude, we may note that it is in connexion with Bohemund that Anna most clearly gives us her sentiments on the subject.[4] Firstly, the Emperor is prepared to forgive his forsworn liegemen because 'the holy law of the Gospels has commanded Christians to forgive one another everything'; secondly, there is folly as well as wickedness in 'rejoicing over blood of Christians, shed not for their country or on behalf of other Christians',[5] but for a man's own advantage.

Throughout the *Alexias* there is such a distinct leaning to peaceful rather than to warlike methods that it may be worth while to investigate what Anna's Church had to say on the matter. Both theory and practice had varied with changing conditions, but there seems little doubt that in the first three centuries, as Harnack puts it, 'der getaufte Christ wurde eben nicht Soldat'.[6] Cyprian (200-58) described war as wholesale murder, and Lactantius (260-340) said that war, though esteemed lawful for the State, is forbidden to the Christian. As a matter of practice 'conscription though nominally in force was little employed' in the Roman Empire, and 'in the more settled regions exemption could be purchased with little difficulty'.[7] Augustine of Hippo (354-430) was probably the first great teacher to admit that wars could be waged 'by the command of God',[8] and after his day Christian pacifism is chiefly voiced by heretical sects.[9] Yet Basil of Cappadocia (330-79) says, in the thirteenth Canon of his first Canonical Epistle:[10] 'Our fathers did not think that killing in war was murder; but I think it advisable for such as have been guilty of it to forbear communion three years.'[11]

---

[1] XI. 8, p. 331.   [2] XII. 1, pp. 346, 347.
[3] XII. 8, p. 367.
[4] XIII. 8, pp. 399, 400.
[5] In XIII. 12, pp. 406, 411, we find that swearing fealty involves for the vassal war with his lord's enemies and peace with his friends.
[6] *Militia Christi*, p. 49.
[7] M. E. Hirst, *Quakers in Peace and War*, pp. 16, 17.
[8] *De Civ. Dei*, I. 21, *P. L.* 41, col. 35.
[9] Especially Anna's bugbears the Manichaeans, Paulicians, and Bogomiles.
[10] *Ep.* 188, *Can.* 13. *P. G.* 32, col. 681.
[11] The whole question of the attitude of the Church to military service is most

This frame of mind doubtless represented a mere counsel of perfection for Christian laymen, but against fighting clergy the sentiment was strong enough,[1] even in the militant West, to call forth condemnation of the practice from many provincial councils, Gallican and other,[2] as well as from the Emperor Charlemagne. Origen in the third century had logically pleaded[3] that 'since priests are exempted from warfare in order to offer sacrifice with pure hands, Christians have an equal right to exemption, since they all as priests of the One True God offer prayers'. But the popular feeling on the subject, a feeling which in the Great War differentiated England from France, was that it was more un-Christian for priests to fight than for laymen. The seventh Canon of the Council of Chalcedon, A.D. 451, forbade both secular and regular clergy to engage in στρατεία, and even if this word *includes* all forms of public service[4] it certainly does not *exclude* military employment such as the word originally denoted. Charlemagne's Capitulary of 801 put this equally strongly:[5] 'That no priest should thereafter engage in battle. . . . What victory could be hoped for, when the priests at one hour were giving the Body of the Lord to Christians, and at another were with their own wicked hands slaying those very Christians to whom they gave it, or the heathen to whom they ought to have been preaching Christ?' This rule, as

interestingly handled by C. J. Cadoux in his *The Early Church and the World* (1919). C. Neumann in his *Weltstellung des Byz. Reiches* (p. 37) propounds the theory that Islam first gave war the definite consecration of religion and that this inspired the Crusaders.

Riant in his *Inventaires des lettres historiques des Croisades* (*Archives de l'Or. lat.* I (p. 23), says in two notes that whereas Pope John VIII (872–82) had promised 'requies aeternae vitae' to all who died 'pro defensione sanctae Dei ecclesiae' the Eastern Church opposed this. 'En 963 S. Polyeucte força Nicéphore Phocas à rapporter une novelle qui déclarait martyrs les soldats morts en Syrie.' (It would be more accurate to say that Polyeuctus the Patriarch with certain bishops and senators prevented Phocas from passing this decree; they relied on the canon of Basil just quoted (Zonaras, XVI. 25).) The Greeks took less interest in the Holy Places than the Latins, because they had so many relics already at Constantinople. When Alexius in his second letter to the Abbot of Monte Cassino calls the dead Crusaders 'beati' and 'in vitam aeternam transmigrati', Riant (*op. cit.*, p. 170) considers this was merely written to please a Latin prelate.

In the passage in Zonaras, and a parallel passage in Cedrenus, the reference is merely to soldiers killing and killed in war generally; but a war against infidels was doubtless the kind contemplated. So Leo (*Tactica*, XIX. 75) speaks of all Greek admirals as defending God's inheritance.

[1] In *Chron.* Theodora, Byz. T., p. 186, Psellus uses the word Naziraean, which to Anna and other Byzantine writers merely meant 'monk', to denote one of the military monastic orders, whom he heartily disapproves.

[2] See the list in Du Cange's note on X. 8, p. 292 B.

[3] Hirst, *op. cit.*, p. 19.

[4] See W. Bright, *Canons of the First Four General Councils*, p. 169.

[5] Hirst, *op. cit.*, p. 21.

all contemporary histories show us, was generally disregarded
in the West, where fighting priests and even fighting bishops
were a daily phenomenon, down to the time of Froissart or
later.[1] But some imperfectly caught echo of it, perverted almost
into its own opposite, seems to have prompted Anna's diatribe
as follows against the fighting Latin priest on one of the
Crusading ships.[2] 'For concerning the clergy the decisions
arrived at by us and the Latins are not the same.' The Greek
priests are checked from fighting 'by the Canons and the Laws
and the evangelical teaching, but the Latin barbarian will take
in hand divine things, and at the same time putting his shield
on his left arm and setting his spear in rest with the right he
simultaneously distributes the divine Body and Blood, and
glances murderously and becomes a man of blood according to
the Davidic psalm. . . . Our regulations, as I have already said,
were derived from the [lacuna] of Aaron and Moses and our
first Bishop.'[3] This particular Latin priest, a ῥέκτης and a πολέ-
μαρχος rather than a cleric, hurls arrows, stones, and even barley-
loaves against the Greeks 'as if he were doing priest's work and
performing a rite, and making the war into a priestly office'.
This pungent satire is perhaps not unneeded to-day.

Thus even if Anna was wrong in saying there was no rule
against Western clergy fighting she had good warrant for her
opinion. Probably, as Leib suggests,[4] in the case of the Crusading priests 'loin de leur pays et dans des conditions si nou-
velles, plusieurs se jugèrent soustraits aux défenses de l'Église',
though he thinks they were always the exception, not the rule.
In any case, apart from the great soldier of the Cross, Bishop
Adhémar of Le Puy, whom she never mentions, Anna had
cognizance of enough fighting Latin clergy to make her mis-
apprehension natural. One Pope fights in person[5] and another
incites others to do so; at Bohemund's instigation he arms his
own forces and speeds the Norman prince on his way to attack
the Eastern Empire.[6] The Archbishop of Capua may be bribed
to help Alexius;[7] the Bishop of Bari sends one of his followers
with Robert Guiscard's invading army;[8] the Bishop of Pisa is
at the head of the Pisan fleet in the Crusade, and apparently
stirs up his episcopal colleagues in Florence and Genoa to take

---

[1] See Du Cange's note above referred to, and medieval chronicles, passim.
[2] X. 8, pp. 292, 293.
[3] Taken to mean Our Blessed Lord by B. Leib in his Rome, Kiev et Byzance,
p. 255. This is confirmed by XV. 8, p. 488.
[4] Op. cit., p. 256.   [5] I. 13, p. 33.
[6] XII. 8, p. 367.   [7] III. 10, p. 93.
[8] III. 12, p. 99.

part against Alexius,[1] and unspecified 'bishops' are among the
leaders of the crusading hosts.[2] Certainly Anna had little
reason to think that Latin priests saw anything heinous in wielding the sword, and if she moralized over the matter at all it was
to her merely another proof of 'barbarian' inferiority and lack
of true Christian teaching.

15. CHARITY: MILITARY ETHICS

WAR then to Anna was, as the modern phrase tersely puts
it, Hell. Yet war was in fact an every-day occurrence and,
as always, it entailed and was held to excuse many essentially
barbarous acts. Anna's attitude on the subject is interesting.
The sacking of towns and villages, 'slaughters and blindings and
mutilations',[3] are its ordinary incidents, even though they
necessitate penance before God.[4] Troops are reckless and ill-
disciplined; 'much booty' is one of the main objectives of war,
and plunder invariably follows conquest.[5] It is usual to
'dispeople' villages,[6] and captives often meet with scant mercy.
The Scythians would kill their Greek prisoners after Dristra
but for hopes of rich ransom;[7] on a later occasion they actually
put the cruel thought into execution.[8] Even Greeks are not
blameless in this matter. They kill sleeping foes whom they
have entrapped by feigned friendship;[9] they murder prisoners
of war; they retaliate on Turks for broken oaths by killing
'rowers and all' on the pirate-boats they capture;[10] they
massacre 10,000 inhabitants of Smyrna to avenge the murder
of their general;[11] they kill the Pisan sailors whom they have

---

[1] XI. 10, p. 335.   [2] X. 10, p. 299.

[3] I. 2, pp. 6, 7, 14, p. 35; XI. 6, p. 326. In the *Alexias* we get nothing to equal
the barbarity of Basil II, who caused 10,000 Bulgarians to be blinded of one eye.

[4] II. 10, p. 64; III. 5.

[5] I. 12, p. 30; II. 12, p. 68. The men and women round Philomelium, fleeing
from an expected Turkish invasion, are wise to bring away with them 'whatever
goods they can carry' (XI. 6, p. 325). It takes the Crusaders a month to convey
into Antioch all the baggage and booty of the Turkish host (XI. 6, p. 327). Even
in peace time the Manichaean ex-soldiers transported to Philippopolis, true to
their old habits, 'tyrannized over the Christians and seized their goods' (XIV.
8, p. 452).

[6] XV. 4, p. 472. Anna's terse description of the effect of Turkish raids is equally
applicable to all warfare. 'Towns disappeared, lands were ravaged' (XV. 10,
p. 495).

[7] VII. 4, p. 200. We are reminded of Thucydides (*Hist.* I. 30) where the
Corcyraeans put to death nearly all their prisoners.

[8] VII. 9, p. 210.   [9] X. 4, p. 279.

[10] VIII. 6; IX. 1, pp. 247, 248.

[11] Anna calls this 'a pitiful wonder to see' (XI. 5, p. 323).

failed to intimidate by threatening death or slavery;[1] and after
a victory in Asia Minor we hear that they 'did so cruelly treat
the Turks that they even threw their new-born babes into
bubbling cauldrons, while many they slew or captured'.[2] In
this matter Alexius would seem to have been singularly merciful. When he is asked to let the Patzinak prisoners be killed,
so that the imperial soldiers may not lose their sleep by guarding
them,[3] he indignantly refuses, saying: 'Though Scythians, they
are at any rate men, though enemies they are worthy of mercy',
and decrees that they shall only be disarmed. They are however killed in the night by their captors, and Anna surprisingly
suggests a θεία ὀμφή as inspiring the deed. Alexius nevertheless
is with difficulty restrained from punishing the general responsible for it.[4] On a later occasion he gives orders that 2,000
Turks captured by John Ducas at Ephesus are to be dispersed
among the islands, and though he himself goes through Asia
Minor 'slaying many', he carries off his prisoners alive to
Constantinople.[5] Yet we do not find him above parading
enemy heads on spear-points,[6] and the same methods of fright-
fulness are used by his general Cantacuzenus.[7] The Crusaders
do the same at Nicaea,[8] and the inhabitants of Tyre go one
step further and hurl the heads of captives by 'stone-throwing
instruments' into the horror-struck camp of the Frankish
besiegers.[9]

As an instance of the terror a brutal enemy can inspire, Anna,
like Thucydides, gives a dramatic incident where beaten troops
in desperation swim out to a hostile fleet, so as to die by hands
less detested.[10] From a similar motive the Pisans who had landed
in Cyprus for forage,[11] and the Greek forces attacked at Otranto
by Tancred's brother,[12] 'throw themselves recklessly into the
sea'; drowning is better than unknown horrors from captors.
Yet chivalry to captives is not wholly absent, as two instances
show.[13] The Turkish satrap Mahomet gets off his horse to induce
the dismounted Eustathius Camytzes to surrender; on a later

---

[1] XI. 10, p. 336.   [2] XIV. 1, p. 420.
[3] We may compare the difficulties of the Corinthians in guarding their prisoners
on board ship (Thuc., *Hist.* I. 52). Also the unpleasing episode at Agincourt about
which Fluellen exclaims: 'Kill the poys, and the luggage! 'tis expressly against
the law of arms: 'tis as arrant a knavery, mark you now, as can be offered', and
Gower tries lamely to excuse the King (*Henry V*, Act IV, sc. vii).
[4] VIII. 6, pp. 234, 235.   [5] XI. 5, p. 323, 6, pp. 324 and 326.
[6] VIII. 2, p. 223.
[7] XIII. 6, p. 393. See above, p. 20, and below, p. 436, note 3.
[8] XI. 1, p. 311.   [9] XIV. 2, p. 427.
[10] IV. 6, p. 116; Thuc., *Hist.* III. 112.
[11] XI. 10, p. 337.   [12] XII. 8, p. 367.
[13] XIV. 5, p. 440; XV. 6, p. 478.

occasion Alexius tries to prevent a vanquished sultan from prostrating himself, and honours him with a fine horse and with a cloak off his own imperial shoulders. On the whole the Turks as we constantly see compare in this matter not unfavourably with Christians, and Anna is impartial in her judgement of them. It is in them, as it would have been in Greeks, an ἀνδραγάθημα to slay 'all the infantry' (of their opponents) 'except some whom they captured and took to Chorassan for display',[1] and they seem to have treated their prisoners well as a rule.[2]

This brings us to another point in military ethics, the question of plunder in Anna's day. We have said above that it invariably followed conquest, and this is true even in civil wars.[3] On a campaign raids and forayings even in lands theoretically one's own were the only means of getting supplies for soldiers,[4] and though to us it appears like killing the goose that laid the golden eggs,[5] it does not seem to occur to Anna that any other way of handling commissariat was possible. We actually find cases where the food of a friendly country is destroyed, merely to injure the enemy.[6] Alexius himself could not press on to Iconium because the Turks had 'burnt all the fields and plains of Asia, so that neither for men nor horses was there any food at all'.[7] Yet he allows his own men to do the same. Foraying appears as part of the training of the recruits,[8] the full moon being the best time.[9] Franks and Turks and Greeks all put this training into practice. From the nature of the case the Turks were always raiders. Asan sends out 10,000 men to

---

[1] XI. 8, p. 332.

[2] XI. 2, p. 315, and 7, p. 328; XII. 1, p. 346; XIV. 5, p. 439. Where a Turkish prison is 'dreadful' it is one τῶν πάλαι γεγενημένων. See p. 96 above, note 9.

[3] I. 8, p. 20, 9, p. 21; II. 11, p. 66, and 12, p. 67.

[4] VII. 7, p. 205, 8, p. 206; VIII. 1, p. 221; XI. 6, pp. 324, 326; XII. 2, p. 349, 9, p. 370; XV. 4, p. 471. When Turkish vigilance prevents this χορταγωγία the Crusaders are in dreadful straits (XI. 8, p. 331). The same thing happens to Bohemund (XIII. 8, p. 399). The Pisan fleet ravages the Greek islands right and left, and then lands a considerable body of men in Cyprus προνομῆς χάριν (XI. 10, pp. 335–7). With Scythians disorderly plundering is a national 'custom' or vice as well as a necessity (I. 5, p. 12; XII. 8, p. 367). So also with Turks (XV. 2, p. 465), and with the rebel commandant at Acrunus (XIV. 3, p. 431).

[5] Bohemund has famine and disease in his army as a result of his own plundering round Durazzo (XIII. 6, p. 393). This finally makes him sue for peace (XIII. 8).

[6] In XV. 4, p. 473, the Greek troops 'scattered like wild beasts in all directions' on their errand of destruction. So Nic. Bry. (I. 13, p. 27) tells us that Romanus Diogenes at one point contemplated 'burning the plains, so that the enemy may lack food'. Leo's Tactica (XIX. 28) advises against plundering τοὺς ἐπιχωρίους, but specially enjoins (17) pillaging the enemy, and dividing (71) the spoil among the soldiers.

[7] XV. 4, p. 471.

[8] XII. 2, p. 348.

[9] XIV. 5, p. 438.

plunder;[1] Kilidj Arslan 'wasted all Asia, making seven raids';[2] while the chief feature of the Turkish War in XIV. 5 is the *chassé-croisé* of plundering and recapturing booty on both sides. In Alexius' final campaign it is just the same. If the Turks 'scatter for foraging', the Emperor also sends forth 'light-armed men' for the same purpose.[3] His generals are out for rich spoils,[4] and when he himself marches triumphantly home it is with prisoners and booty in the middle of his hollow square.[5]

Non-combatants in those days did not get and doubtless did not expect much consideration. It was 'every man for himself and the devil take the hindmost'. This makes one little episode about plunder in the Coman campaign unique, and justifies quotation in full.[6] The imperial forces had been victorious and had recovered from the Comans much stolen booty.

'However, the Greek host was not allowed by the Emperor to divide this up as usual, but according as it had been lately stolen from the neighbouring lands it was to be given to the inhabitants. So when the royal command had run like a bird into all the country round, each of the men who had been robbed came and recognized his own property and took it. Then beating their breasts and raising suppliant hands to heaven they invoked prosperity on the Emperor, so that one might hear a mixed shouting of men and women going up to the lunar sphere itself.'

As the men robbed were the Emperor's own subjects, it is difficult to understand their extreme gratitude over the restitution. But at least Anna's words make us feel something of the horrors of pillage as then practised.

16. CHARITY TO THE ARMY

WE have now briefly dealt with Anna's ideals of behaviour towards enemies. We will next see how in her opinion Charity should be shown to friends. Baynes[7] has reminded us of the 'subtle influence of a tradition' [in Constantinople] 'which expected from its rulers *philanthropia*,[8] a word which defies

[1] XIV. 1, p. 421.   [2] XV. 1, p. 460.
[3] XV. 2, p. 465, 3, p. 469 and 4, p. 473. All throughout the *Hyle* of Nic. Bry. we read of men going out to plunder, and so being easily assaulted.
[4] XV. 4, p. 470.   [5] XV. 7, p. 481.
[6] X. 4, p. 280.   [7] *Op. cit.*, p. 70.
[8] We must however notice that in the *Alexias* the word has quite a simple meaning of 'kindness', e.g. I. 3, p. 8: 6, p. 16; XII. 6, p. 363 (*bis*); XV. 7, pp.

translation but which sums up the century-long conception of
the Emperor's duty of large humane service to his subjects'
In his coronation oath the Eastern Emperor swore to be
'philanthropic' towards these same subjects, and when we
consider that Alexius, like all the other emperors, was not only
the ruler of his people and the head of his church, but also the
commander-in-chief of his army, we shall readily picture to
ourselves the 'kindnesses' that were expected of him from the
military quarter.

There was indeed a close bond between Alexius as Imperator
and those under him. It is his proud boast that he fights not for
himself 'but for the fame and glory of the Greeks', and has never
hesitated over any sacrifice for the public good.[1] Even before
his accession, when quite a poor man, he had been φιλοδωρότατος
and as a general he had shrunk from no hardships; it was no
wonder that his followers loved him.[2] His soldiers are almost
to him as his children, and he gives vent to bitter groans and
tears over their death, especially in the case of his Grand
Domestic Pacurianus, and of his beloved Archontopules, sons
of his own veterans.[3] 'For it was his custom whenever he won
any battle, to enquire if any of his soldiers had been captured
or had fallen a victim to a hostile hand; and even if he had
routed whole phalanxes and won victory over them, and yet
it had happened that one even of the lowest soldiers had
perished, he reckoned as nought the fact of the victory, but
considered that victory truly a Cadmeian victory, and a loss
instead of a gain.'[4]

This care for his soldiers is a mitigating feature of Robert

---

483 (bis) and 484, and elsewhere. In Attaliates the sense is 'humaneness'. In *Anon.
Syn. Chron.*, p. 181, the term is applied to the love shown by God who humbled
Himself for the human race, a literal use of the two component words, 'love' and
'man'.

[1] XV. 5, p. 474. It was his devotion to the welfare of his Empire that brought
on his fatal illness (XV. 11, pp. 497, 498).

[2] II. 4, p. 50, and 7, p. 58. In VI. 2, p. 155, Alexius gives away to the soldiers
who have served in the Larissa campaign all the property he has just confiscated
from the Manichaeans.

The usefulness of having a generous commander comes out in Leo's *Tactica*,
IV, § 3, quoted by Oman, *Art of War*, I, p. 189. Speaking of officers, he says: 'Their
nobility makes them respected by the soldiery, while their wealth enables them to
win the greatest popularity among their troops by the occasional and judicious gift
of small creature-comforts.' This reminds us of the occasion at Athens when money
'both of the State and of individual soldiers and others', was spent on equipping
the Sicilian expedition, and the trierarchs supplemented the pay of the crews 'out
of their own means' (Thuc. VI. 31).

[3] IV. 8, p. 122; VI. 14, p. 183; VII. 7, p. 204; XIII. 7, p. 395; XIV. 6, p. 443;
XV. 1, p. 461. So John Ducns mourns his subordinate Caspax (XI. 5. p 323).

[4] XIV. 6, p. 443.

Guiscard's character,[1] and the absence of it in Bohemund, who would rather have some of his attendants poisoned than himself,[2] is one of Anna's black marks against him. When the Pisan fleet, 'seized with cowardice', abandon some of their men on the island of Cyprus and make off without them, we read her disgust between the lines,[3] and only the memory that St. Gilles was her father's friend and Tzitas her father's own general keeps her from openly condemning the way they gallop off at Amasea, leaving the Crusading host to destruction by the Turks.[4]

Over and over again we read of the affection, often indeed expressing itself in criticism, felt for Alexius by some faithful attendant who had perhaps served his father before him.[5] Devotion in those days was addressed to a general and not to a country; this feeling survived down to Napoleon and his Old Guard.[6] It could hardly be otherwise when armies were largely composed of mercenaries, serving any side for pay as long as they found a good leader. 'The wandering army' of Bryennius passes easily over to Basilacius,[7] and Alexius' men adhere to him rather than to the Emperor above him, as indeed Botaniates had anticipated with alarm.[8] Ties are lightly formed and lightly abandoned and only an impressive personality in the commander can stem this. Soldiers transfer their allegiance with bewildering frequency, so that generals handle them, especially their important men, with gloves.[9] The deserter, αὐτόμολος, is a most familiar figure throughout the book in all the armies; indeed, it is not unknown for him to change sides twice.[10]

[1] V. 1, p. 125.   [2] X. 11, p. 302.
[3] XI. 10, p. 337.   [4] XI. 8, p. 332.
[5] I. 5, p. 12, and 8, p. 20; IV. 4, p. 109; V. 5, p. 136; VII. 3, p. 195; IX. 5, p. 254, 9, p. 262. Nic. Bry. (II. 6, p. 44) mentions the Theodotus of *Al.* I. 5, as giving Alexius good advice in his first campaign, and saving his life in his own despite.
    The reliance on inherited friendship is very strong (see X. 3, pp. 275, 276, and 4, p. 278). We are reminded of *Iliad* VI, where Diomed and Glaucus stop fighting because of an ancestral bond of hospitality (lines 215-36).
[6] So Tancred refuses to pay homage to Alexius on the score of owing life-long allegiance to his uncle, Bohemund (XI. 3, p. 316).
[7] I. 7, p. 17.
[8] II. 4, p. 49. The phrases ἐπὶ μισθῷ δουλεῦσαι (V. 7, p. 143; cf. VII. 8, p. 208) or θητεῦσαι (VI. 1, p. 153; XI. 2, p. 316), express a tie as of master and servant between a general and his troops.
[9] VI. 1 shows Alexius' eagerness to get men. In VIII. 5, p. 231, in announcing to his army what he wanted done Alexius '*advised* each of the more intelligent, but *commanded* the ruder ones, to do the same'. In XI. 2, p. 316, after a severe reprimand to some officers, 'when he saw they could not even look him in the face for shame, the Emperor changed and made haste to restore their spirits by speeches of a different character'.
[10] So Neantzes in VII chs. 6 and 9.

Yet the system leads at times to a charming personal relation such as existed between the Emperor and many of his younger officers. Just as in Western chivalry pages were brought up in the castles of knights, so Alexius has young men in his Court whom he himself trains in military science, and who owe him special devotion, treating him as 'emperor and general and teacher all at once'.[1] Indeed, The Master's Eye may be a sovereign stimulus to self-control and valour,[2] and the Emperor as commander-in-chief reckons all his officers, whether on land or sea, responsible to him and not to their immediate commanders.[3]

Alexius' labours with and for his army will be taken up in more detail later,[4] but we may say here that his deep and persistent and personal interest in his soldiers, even after their fighting days are over, never fails throughout the story.[5] From first to last he is a Military Emperor, and Anna clearly recognizes the warmth of the tie which bound him and his men together.[6]

17. CHARITY TO FRIENDS

WE have hinted that one of the qualities which endeared Alexius to his soldiers was open-handed Liberality, and we must now think of its application to other spheres of friendly relations. It is probably not a characteristic that specially appeals to us in our day, and the Emperor's lavishness usually seems to us either sheer extravagance or a rather unworthy form of bribe. His principle on the subject is clearly put in his first poem to his son John.[7] He says: ὥστε ἀφθόνως δός, ἀφθόνως δὲ ῥοῦν δέχου. Anna confines her attention, as we will for the present confine ours, to his 'unstinted giving'. His usual donation to friends or suspects or enemies, without which loyalty is not secure and negotiations are liable to crumble to pieces, is

[1] VIII. 9, p. 241; IX. 6, p. 256, and XI. 9, p. 333; XIII. 2, p. 379.
[2] XII. 2, p. 349; XIV. 6, p. 442.
[3] XI. 9, p. 333, where the system leads to virtual espionage, and XIII. 7, p. 395.
[4] See Ch. 57 below.
[5] V. 3, p. 130; IX. 4, p. 251; XIII. 8, p. 398; XV. 3, p. 468, and elsewhere. His readiness to share his men's toil, no matter what the weather, and to reward it handsomely, transpires in X. 5. The almshouse for veterans and care for their orphans in his great Institution tell their own tale (XV. 7).
[6] We will deal with the reverse side of the picture when we consider Disloyalty in the Army (Ch. 57 below).
[7] Mous. Alex. I. 319.

'gifts and honours' unspecified, often coupled with vague promises of more.[1] But sometimes he gives clothes[2] (reminding us
of Gehazi and his changes of raiment), sometimes a fine horse,[3]
and food, often at his own table, on numerous occasions.[4] Not
infrequently some marriage, doubtless involving money-gifts,
is used as a lure, and sometimes 'divine baptism'.[5] He is
generous to possible rivals on the throne; the two ex-Empresses
Eudocia and Maria and their children, the two Diogenes and
Constantine Ducas, are allowed to keep their rank and their
property.[6] Complete amnesty was then as now a way to conciliate opponents, and popular discontent must be met by
lavish gifts.[7] Before his accession his supporters win over the
army, both officers and men, to choose him Emperor, saying:
'He will reward you with great gifts and honours as suits each
man, and not haphazard after the manner of foolish and inexperienced chiefs', an interesting testimony to character indeed![8]
In the anxious first days of his reign he sets himself to secure
allies by systematic bargaining with princes and bishops of all
kinds, including the Pope and the 'king of Germany'.[9] The
last named of these is tempted by a marriage alliance, money,
stuffs, artistic objects, sacred relics and spices, in addition to
dignities for his followers, the whole being enumerated in a
most interesting letter. The general basis and results of these
negotiations are crudely stated by Anna: 'Some at once gave up
their friendship with Robert, while others promised to do so
if they received more.'[10] So in later days, with the Crusaders

---

[1] Every transaction is one of money (I. 2; III. 11, p. 97; IV. 2, p. 105; V. 3,
p. 131: 7, p. 143; VI. 5, pp. 159, 160: 6, p. 163: 9, p. 171: 10, p. 173: 12, p. 179:
13, p. 181; VIII. 4, p. 228; X. 7, p. 289: 11, p. 306; XI. 1, p. 310: 2, *passim*:
3, p. 316: 8, p. 332; XII. 5, p. 357: 7, p. 365; XIII. 4, p. 388: 9, p. 401; XIV.
2, *passim*: 4, p. 434; XV. 6, p. 478). For others besides Alexius using various
bribes (once fifteen mule-loads of gold), see I. 12, pp. 27, 30: 13, p. 31: 15, p. 35:
16, p. 40; II. 5, p. 54: 6, p. 56; VI. 12, p. 177; VIII. 3, p. 226; XI. 2; XII. 5,
p. 360. Thucydides had long before said of the Thracians: 'Nothing could be
done without presents' (*Hist.* II. 97). So Euripides (*Med.* 964) has the famous line:

$$\ldots \pi\epsilon i\theta\epsilon\iota\nu\ \delta\hat{\omega}\rho\alpha\ \kappa\alpha i\ \theta\epsilon o\hat{\upsilon}s\ \lambda\acute{o}\gamma os\cdot$$
$$\chi\rho\upsilon\sigma\grave{o}s\ \delta\epsilon'\ \kappa\rho\epsilon i\sigma\sigma\omega\nu\ \mu\upsilon\rho i\omega\nu\ \lambda\acute{o}\gamma\omega\nu\ \beta\rho o\tau o\hat{\iota}s.$$

[2] XII. 1, p. 347; XIV. 2, p. 428; XV. 7, p. 485, and 9, p. 492.
[3] IX. 7, p. 258; XV. 6, p. 478.
[4] e.g. VIII. 6, p. 235; X. 11, &c. For instances of others using a banquet as
a bribe or lure, see II. 6, p. 56; VIII. 9, p. 241; IX. 3, p. 251; X. 4, p. 279:
7, p. 289.
[5] III. 10, and VI. 5, p. 159; 9, p. 171; 13, p. 181.
[6] III. 4; IX. 5, 6. According to Zonaras, Maria owned a palace and two
convents (XVIII. 21), and Anna represents her with lands in the country apart
from her son's.
[7] XII. 5, p. 357.   [8] II. 7, p. 57.
[9] III. 10.   [10] III. 10, p. 93.

threatening to overwhelm his empire, he buys off his other
enemies with 'honours and gifts'.[1]

It is noteworthy that whereas this giving of money seems to
Anna laudable in her father, the taking of it, in certain quarters
at least, figures in her pages as base venality. The 'race
of Latins' is described as 'loving money and wont to sell for
an obol even what they hold dearest'[2], because some of them
surrender Durazzo for a bribe. For on the whole she does not
share Thucydides' easy tolerance for people who 'will readily
come over to any one that makes an attractive offer',[3] and when
she says of her father and the Counts: 'Thus with money and
words he softened their rude natures',[4] her approval is doubtless
all for him and not for them. When Bohemund first rejects
the imperial bribes as an insult and then accepts them, she
compares him scornfully to a 'sort of polypus'.[5]

To our mind the giver of a bribe is no less dishonoured than
the receiver, and the system is one of recklessness and waste,
especially where as in this case the Emperor was drawing on
state resources. Our criticism is indeed forestalled by Zonaras,
whose *Epitome* was written about the same time as the *Alexias*.
Twice over he inveighs against the evil of an emperor's treating
public money as his own, and spending it according to his own
pleasure.[6] The first time the allusion to this ἄντικρυς τυραννίς
is vague and might refer to any of the rulers subsequent to
Basil II, but the second passage occurs in his summary of
Alexius' character after his death. This Emperor was not personally ἐρασιχρήματος, he tells us, but his wastefulness and
partiality to his own henchmen rendered him unworthy of the
name of βασιλεύς.

But this, needless to say, was not Anna's view. His freedom
in giving, especially to supporters actual or potential, was a part
of the wisdom which marked her father's every action, and its
effect on public finance and public morals does not seem to have
troubled her at all.

---

[1] XIV. 4, p. 434. So the keeping of secret supplies for buying off enemies is
recommended by Alexius to his son John (*Mous. Alex.* I. 322).

[2] VI. 6, p. 163. So Bohemund is made to say to the imperial general: 'Without
money be sure thou canst not take even a castle': he will surrender Laodicea not
because of his oath, but for money (XI. 11, p. 340).

[3] *Hist.* VI. 17, and see his references to suspected venality in generals, in II. 21;
IV. 65; V. 16; VII. 48, 86; VIII. 45.

[4] X. 11, p. 305.   [5] X. 11, pp. 303, 304.

[6] *Epit.* XIII. 3, and XVIII. 29.

18. CHARITY TO THE POOR

THE same spirit of Liberality which made Alexius heap gifts
on friends and foes also induced him sumptuously to endow
his Orphanage and to supply the inmates with 'wine in rivers,
and bread and whatever else men feed on besides bread', on a
scale that reminds his daughter of Our Lord's Miracles of
Feeding.[1] If what seems to her beautiful is to us absurdly
extravagant, that is hardly surprising with a difference of eight
centuries between our viewpoints.[2]

Her mother Irene also has a 'bountiful hand'. On one occasion she restores to the wife of a condemned rebel the house
which had been confiscated from him and assigned to herself,[3] and
above all she gives generously to needy beggars[4] and does 'good
deeds and acts of charity', notably to the clergy, 'those whom she
knew to be serving God and intent on prayer and antiphonal
songs'. 'A liberal hand to the needy' and a keeping open house
for every one, especially one's poor relations and priests and
monks, was great virtue, and was to be seen in the Regent Anna
Dalassena.[5] Even to the present day in Greece indiscriminate
charity is considered a merit, and it is quite startlingly un-
Greek to find Irene urging the able-bodied to work for their
living and not 'go round begging from door to door'.[6] Another
form of charity, which seems to us as pernicious as giving to
beggars, is the bestowal of gifts of every kind (on one occasion
a whole new town with 'corn-lands and vineyards and houses')
on the converts whom Alexius brings over to the true faith.[7]
Anna however sees nothing incongruous in the practice.

But it is chiefly in donations to the Church or the founding
of institutions that generosity was in those days shown and
admired.[8] The passage in XV. 7 about Alexius' great Institution
at Constantinople, a combined orphanage and school and

[1] XV. 7, p. 488. The same generosity to the Orphanage is praised in Alexius
by *Anon. Syn. Chron.*, p. 483.

[2] Attaliates praises Botaniates for his bounty like the Pactolus or Nile (p. 274)
and says Michael VII had handled matters 'meanly, not royally' (p. 301). Scylitzes
says Botaniates was φιλοδωρότατος (p. 867 c). So Ordericus Vitalis (*Hist. Eccl.*,
Pt. III, lib. 7, ch. 4) praises Alexius as ' largus et amabilis omnibus', 'misericors
pauperibus', and 'munerum dator largissimus' *P. L.* 188, col. 519; and Nic. Acom.
commends John's generosity in giving (*John C.* 12, p. 31).

[3] XII. 6, p. 362.

[4] XII. 3, pp. 351, 354. So Prodromus praises Irene as 'most unstinting in gifts', in
his poem on the death of Princess Theodora (line 39, *B. Z.* XVI. p. 88).

[5] III. 8, p. 87. [6] XII. 3, p. 354.

[7] VI. 9, p. 170: 13, p. 181; XIV. 9, p. 456.

[8] At a slightly later date Cinnamus (*Hist.* I. 4, p. 5) in describing Irene of

hospital and almshouse, is too long to translate in full, but too interesting not to be carefully summarized. The very day after his return from his last glorious campaign against the Turks, he turned his attention to the prisoners and refugees whom he had brought back with him. Some of the orphan children were billeted out among his own kinsmen or in monasteries, to be thoroughly trained in sacred and other learning and brought up 'not as slaves but as free'. Others were put in his new or rather restored Orphanage School near the Church of St. Paul 'in the parts near the Acropolis'. Here foreign children as well as natives learnt pure Greek; while 'a teacher presided and children stood round him'. Surrounding this Church, in circles on different levels, were 'dwellings of poor people' and 'refuges for disabled men and women', called by the expressive term πεπηρωμένοι, maimed. They had no plots to till, but each lived in a separate house at the expense of the Emperor, who 'assigned to these brothers' (the name should be noted) any conveniently situated or 'productive' property he chose. Whether Alexius confiscated the lands of others to carry out what his daughter considers as this Christ-like charity, we do not know; in any case he selected ground rich enough to provide wine and bread in profusion, and he and 'those around him' acted as 'diligent stewards and guardians' for an immense number of people who, in the matter of 'goods and income' and men to administer it, are 'like lords'. As Anna expresses it, 'his acts of philanthropy obey the divine command', and he provides not only food but attendance for all who need, thus incurring the double expense of feeding nurses and patients. 'Who could count those eating daily, or the expense of every day and the provision made to each man?' The Emperor it was who made all the arrangements, and 'one of the most distinguished [citizens] presided as steward of this populous city whose name was Orphanotropheion', so called because of the φιλανθρωπία of the Emperor towards orphans as well as old soldiers. She further describes an office (σέκρετα) dealing with the accounts and with the 'inalienable property' awarded by golden bulls to these recipients of charity (τοῖς τρεφομένοις). Finally, she recounts her father's care in providing the Church of St. Paul with clergy, rich illuminations, and choristers (some of whom were women),

Hungary, wife of John II, praises her modesty, virtue, liberality, and piety, and says: 'She passed the whole space of her life in doing good to all who made demands on her for anything, and she built in Constantinople a monastery in the name of the Pantocrator' (really built by John at her desire).

in encouraging deaconesses, and in giving a convent with necessary supplies of food and clothing to the Iberian Nuns who were
in the habit of coming to Constantinople. Of this colossally
costly 'city within the imperial city' Alexius was as justly proud
as Alexander was of Alexandria.

This great institution of the Emperor's was indeed not a
solitary instance of contemporary Byzantine 'philanthropy',
using the word not in Baynes' sense, but in the usual one.
We have many records of such establishments (always attached
to a monastic building) where all the needy were grouped together, the sick, the old, children, poor travellers, and often
the insane. Already before Alexius' day Attaliates, the devoted
servant and biographer of Botaniates, had founded a monastery
and hostelry by his διάταξις, which we still possess with the
inventory of books, furniture, &c.[1] Oeconomos gives a long
account[2] of the *Typikon* in which Pacurianus, Grand Domestic
of the West under Alexius, established an almshouse for old
men and eleven neighbouring hostelries for the poor and
travellers. John II made a hospital with fifty beds and an
almshouse in the Pantocrator (founded by him to please his
Hungarian wife Irene) with a bath establishment adjoining.[3]
His brother Isaac the Sebastocrator founded the monastery of
the Cosmosoteira (where thirty-six sick could be received),
also provided with baths.[4] As for the Cecharitomene Convent
planned by Alexius' wife Irene as a home for pious nuns and
also a refuge for herself and her daughters and granddaughters,
its *Typikon*[5] is one of the most curious documents in existence.
It affords yet another proof that in the twelfth century pious
Byzantines not only created monastic institutions where monks
and nuns could pray for their souls; they also believed in the
practical Christian virtues, and hoped to 'acquire merit' by
hospitals, hostelries, and almshouses.

Finally, the Eastern emperors had an elaborate system of
outdoor relief, preceded by a distribution of counters (σφραγῖδες)
of which great quantities still survive. As an exceptional number of these bear the name of Alexius,[6] perhaps we may conclude that his daughter was right in considering him indeed
φιλοδωρότατος.

---

[1] W. Nissen, *Die Diataxis des Mich. Attal. von 1077*.   [2] *Vie religieuse*, p. 192.
[3] Chalandon, *Jean et Manuel Comnène*, pp. 28–34.
[4] For the *Typikon* see *Bull. inst. arch. russe de C'ple*, Vol. XIII. pp. 17–77.
[5] *P. G.* 127, cols. 985–1120.
[6] G. Schlumberger, 'Monuments numismatiques et sphragistiques', *Revue Archéologique*, Oct. 1880 (p. 7 of offprint).

19. CHARITY TO FAMILY

I. *Married Life and the Position of Women*

ONE more point must now be dealt with, perhaps the most
important of all. We have considered Anna's ideas of
Charity towards enemies and friends, soldiers, and the needy.
We must in conclusion study what she says as to love and
affection in Family Life.

In an age when marriages among the highborn were generally
made (or proposed) to serve some political end of alliance or
dowry or the like,[1] it is interesting to notice that Anna presupposes love between husband and wife. When the Empress
Maria turns against her husband Botaniates it is only because
the even deeper loyalty of a mother to her son's rights is at
stake.[2] When Alexius and his kinsmen do penance for the sack
of Constantinople, their wives voluntarily share in it, φίλανδροι
οὖσαι.[3] The devotion of Irene to her husband,[4] however much it
may please Nicetas Acominatus and his follower Chalandon to
disbelieve in it, is asserted by her daughter so consistently as
scarcely to admit of doubt.[5] The same may be said of Anna's
own married life,[6] even if her husband was originally chosen
so as to appease the partisans of the elder Bryennius, the would-
be Emperor.[7] Yet affection is not all. Marriage and connexion
by marriage are potent political factors in the whole story. Thus,
the wife of Isaac Comnenus was a niece or cousin of the ex-

[1] e.g. I. 10, p. 23: 11, p. 24: 12, pp. 27, 30; VI. 5, p. 159; XII. 1, p. 346. The
Empress Maria is bound to be grateful to John Ducas, who induced the Emperor
Botaniates to marry her rather than another ex-Empress or her daughter (III. 2,
p. 74). Foreign marriages were common, often for reasons of State (II. 6, p. 55;
III. 2, p. 73; 10, p. 94; V. 3, p. 131; VIII. 9; XIII. 12, p. 416). When Anna
shudders at the notion of a marriage between the Sultan's son and herself or one
of her sisters, she writes as a Christian ('God did not permit this'), and also as one
who feared the unknown East (VI. 9, p. 170, 12, pp. 177, 178). We may note the
similar proposal of Tzachas to Constantine Dalassenus (VII. 8, p. 208).
[2] II. 2; III. 4.
[3] III. 5, p. 82. Good wives, according to Nic. Bry. look at themselves in a mirror
μεριμνῶσαι ἀρέσκειν τοῖς σφῶν ἀνδράσιν (*Hyle*, II. 7, p. 45).
[4] The whispers of scandal-mongers as to Alexius' desire to marry Maria (and
therefore to divorce Irene) are scornfully hinted at in III. 2, p. 72. Both Zonaras
(XVIII. 24) and Glycas (IV, p. 334) say that as a young man Alexius was unfaithful to Irene, but that she gradually got a great hold over him.
[5] Especially in XII. 3, and the whole of XV. 11, where her agony over Alexius'
illness and death is described in touching detail. 'It is not possible to say how great
labour she bestowed on him through the whole day and night.' See Ch. 37 below.
[6] In the *Prologue* to her Will she says her soul 'hangs' on her husband and
children (line 69).
[7] II. 6, p. 57. See p. 33 above.

Empress Maria, who had herself in the first place married into the great house of Ducas, the house of Alexius' bride. This constituted strong ties all round, and it was perhaps in the hope of counteracting the hated Ducas influence that Anna Dalassena betrothed her granddaughter (child of the dead Manuel) to the ἔγγονος of the Emperor Botaniates,[1] who in the event proved too young or not sufficiently near (γνήσιος) to have any chance of succeeding the said Emperor.[2] In the same diplomatic spirit she had already married her daughter Theodora to Constantine, son of the former Emperor Romanus Diogenes, intending doubtless to win over yet another powerful ex-imperial family,[3] when the time should come for the prophecies of Eustratius Garidas to be fulfilled and for her son to ascend the throne.[4]

On two subsequent occasions Alexius tried to attach to himself by marriages men of doubtful loyalty. In the case of the ex-Manichaean Traulus united to one of the Empress's waiting-maids, the wife was truer to old ties than to new, and her betrayal of her husband's secrets led to his escape from court and subsequent marriage to 'the daughter of one of the Scythian chiefs', Alexius' most formidable enemies.[5] In the case of Gregory Gabras the betrothal between him and Alexius' daughter, intended as an acceptable substitute for an alliance with Isaac the Sebastocrator's daughter (now rendered canonically impossible by Isaac's second marriage) did not please the youth, who in every sense of the word shrank from it.[6] But as a rule young men and women agreed to these *mariages de convenance* with perfect submission, even when, as in the case of two of Alexius' sons, the connexion chosen was 'barbarian', a Russian princess for one, and a Hungarian for the other,[7] and in the instances where we can judge they seem to have turned out happily.

The importance of women in Anna's day, we may remark, was great enough to compare very favourably even with our own times, certainly greater than in many of the intervening centuries. Of women in the world of letters we shall speak presently. As to the political world Chalandon points out that in the year 1111 there were no less than three widowed princesses reigning in Europe,[8] and we must not forget past precedents in

---

[1] II. 5, p. 51.   [2] II. 12, p. 67.   [3] X. 2, p. 272.
[4] III. 2, p. 75.   [5] VI. 4, pp. 157, 158.
[6] VIII. 9. His affianced bride was Anna's second sister Maria; we find her in at X. 3, p. 276 married to Nicephorus, son of Const. Euphorbenus Catacalo.
[7] B. Leib, *op. cit.*, p. 176.
[8] *Hist. de la domination normande*, p. 313. They were Alaine at Salerno, Constance at Taranto, Adelaide in Sicily.

the great power wielded by a Pulcheria, an Irene, a Theophano, and a Zoe. It is for the wrongs of his daughter quite as much as for those of the deposed Emperor Michael that Robert Guiscard professes to go to war.[1] When Alexius leaves Constantinople his Regent is not his brother but his mother.[2] This same Anna Dalassena bears the surname of her maternal family not her paternal,[3] and a like testimony to the importance of women is given us by the names of Anna's own children, not one of whom bore the name of Bryennius.[4]

Women lead a free enough life. They ride openly on horseback to church, and converse with doorkeepers, imperial messengers, and others, though the younger women at least 'wrap a shrouding veil round the face'.[5] Empresses consort with young nobles and have power to protect their favourites.[6] Irene and her daughters associate with learned men;[7] during Alexius' illness they co-operate with the doctors and give orders to the attendants.[8] There is a γυναικωνῖτις, but at one point at least it is only separated from the main palace by a curtain.[9] As we said in speaking of Anna's early and middle life, seclusion was unknown to princesses.

Some women even fight, though Anna deprecates this as unwomanly; to their presence in a camp however she has no objection,[10] and it is quite fitting that a soldier's widow with sons at the front should shelter a general in distress.[11] When Alexius wishes to suppress the Manichaeans he imprisons their wives.[12] If any of the first colonists of his new Alexiopolis should have no lineal descendants, the Emperor decrees that their wives shall inherit the property instead of its reverting to the crown.[13]

Yet on the whole Anna has a poor opinion of women, probably with the same unconscious exaltation of herself by contrast

---

[1] Bks. I, IV, *passim*. So Alexius punishes the pseudo-Diogenes for insulting his sister Theodora by his pretence of being her dead husband (X. 2, p. 272).

[2] III. 6–8; X. 4, p. 279.

[3] This was Charon (Nic. Bry. I. 2, p. 17).

[4] Prodromus' *Epithalamium*, P. G. 133, cols. 1397–1406, and Irene's *Typikon*, ch. 80, P. G. 127, col. 1116, show us that one was Comnenus and three Ducas. Similarly Anna Comnena is called by Prodromus πορφυρογέννητος καισάρισσα κυρὰ Ἄννα ἡ Δούκαινα (poem mentioned in P. G. 133, col. 1017), and 'a shoot of the Ducas stem' (poem on the death of Princess Theodora, line 43).

[5] II. 5, pp. 51–3.   [6] II. 1, pp. 44, 45.
[7] V. 9, p. 147.   [8] XV. 11.
[9] II. 1, p. 44; XV. 8, p. 488.

[10] I. 15, p. 35; IV. 6, p. 116; VI. 5, p. 161; 6, p. 162; VII. 3, p. 196, and 6, p. 203; XII. 3. Irene on a march shares her husband's tent (IX. 5, p. 254). The mother of Tancred is σταθηρὰ τὴν γνώμην as well as στρατιῶτις; she outwits the imperial admiral and her troops defeat him, but she does not fight in person (XII. 8).

[11] VII. 4, p. 200.   [12] VI. 2, p. 155, 4, p. 157.
[13] XIV. 9, p. 456.

that made some of our cleverest women anti-suffragists. Women are good enough as semi-professional mourners, indeed their liability to tears and other emotion is an attribute of their sex,[1] and they can help their menkind as fellow-penitents.[2] But when it comes to serious matters, such as regency, she fears that her father may be blamed 'for entrusting the government of the Empire ὡς γυναικωνίτιδι', and she justifies his choice by the unique 'virtue and sense and activity' of her grandmother.[3] Women are leaky vessels and cannot even keep their husbands' secrets.[4] In speaking of the Empress Irene's fears at a time of danger Anna expresses her feelings on the whole matter in a passage worth translating :[5]

'The Emperor straightway enjoined on the Empress a return to Byzantium. She was terrified, but kept her fear in the recesses of her heart, and showed it neither in words nor in gestures. For she was manly and staunch in mind, like that woman sung of by Solomon in Proverbs, and showed no womanly and cowardly feelings, such as we mostly see women experiencing when they hear something alarming. Their very colour accuses their soul of cowardice, and frequently they wail dolefully when ills are impending over them as it were near at hand. But that queen, though she was afraid, was afraid for the Emperor lest he should suffer anything strange; only secondarily was she frightened about herself. Therefore at that crisis she had no feelings unworthy of her nobility, but she departed unwillingly from the Emperor, often turning back towards him and frequently looking at him ; nevertheless she braced and as it were coerced herself, and so with difficulty parted from the Emperor.'

[1] So τὸ τῶν γυναικῶν φιλοπενθές in IV. 4, p. 109; I. 14, p. 34; XV. 2, p. 463; 10, p. 495. To call a warrior a 'woman' is the deadliest form of contempt (XV. 6, p. 480). Cf. XV. 11, p. 501, of a woman admired for playing the man. Nic. Bry. tells us how the Persian king to shame soldiers who had 'run away from danger' dressed them in female attire. (*Hyle*, I. 8, p. 22.)

[2] III. 5, p. 82.

[3] III. 7, pp. 85, 87; IV. 4, p. 109. Nic. Bry. (I. 5, p. 19) describes Anna Dalassena as δεινή τις καὶ λέγειν καὶ πράττειν. Yet Alexius tells John (*Mous. Alex.* I. 133–9) that even a woman or child may be fortunate in her or his reigning, but only a man and an able man can reign with dignity (σεμνῶς).

This contempt for women was of course a Greek tradition, *vide* the famous sentence in Pericles' Funeral Oration: 'To a woman not to show more weakness than is natural to her sex is great glory, and not to be talked about for good or for evil among men' (Thuc. II. 45). When civil war broke out at Corcyra 'the women joined vigorously in the fray, hurling tiles from the housetops, and showing amid the uproar a fortitude beyond their sex' (*ibid.* III. 74). Thucydides also tells us of a time when 'the whole Argive people, the citizens themselves, their wives and their slaves' (significant combination!) 'set to work upon the wall' (V. 82).

[4] VI. 4, p. 157, and XV. 6, p. 481, where a 'nurse' is equally indiscreet.

[5] XV. 2, p. 463.

Already in an earlier passage Anna has given us what we may believe to be her conception of the Ideal Woman, embodied in this mother of hers.[1] She went into camp with her husband, but reluctantly.

'For her nature was like this: she did not at all wish for publicity [οὐ πάνυ τι δημοσιεύεσθαι ἤθελεν] but for the most part was a stay-at-home, and did her own works, I mean the reading of books of the Blessed Men' [i.e. Saints] 'and the paying heed to herself, and good deeds and acts of charity to men, especially to those whom from their appearance and their life she knew to be serving God, and to be intent on prayer and antiphonal songs. And when she had to make herself public, for some urgent need as Empress, she was filled with modesty and straightway blossomed out in a blush on her cheeks. The wise Theano[2] on one occasion, when her fore-arm had been bared and some one said to her jestingly, "Beautiful is the forearm", replied, "But not public". So the Empress my mother, image of dignity, resting-place (καταγώγιον) of holiness, not only did not love to make her forearm and her glance public, but did not even wish that her voice should be sent forth into unfamiliar ears. Such a great and wonderful portent of modesty was she. But since, as they say, "not even the gods fight against Necessity", she was compelled on the Emperor's frequent campaigns to go with him. For on the one hand her innate modesty tended to keep her inside the Palace, and on the other hand her devotion to the Emperor and burning love to him drove her all reluctant out of the Palace for various reasons, and first because the disease of the feet which had attacked him required the greatest care.'

Then follows an account of his gout and how the Empress rubbed him.

'Furthermore there was a second, and very important reason for the Empress to travel with the Emperor, that many traitors kept on arising on all sides, so that he needed great watchfulness and a truly many-eyed strength.[3] . . . Was it not then right that the sovereign threatened by such great ills should be guarded by a thousand eyes? . . . Whom then did it beseem to be present as the Emperor's helper rather than her his wonted counsellor? Who better than she would watch the Emperor, and menace those scheming against him, sharp in seeing what was advantageous for him, sharper in perceiving the machinations of his enemies? Wherefore my mother was to my lord

[1] XII. 3. So in the last chapter of the whole book (XV. 11) if Alexius is the φωστήρ of the world, Irene, 'in great fact and name the Peace of East and West', is an 'all-shining λύχνος'. The contemporary poet-doctor Callicles calls Irene ὁ λαμπτήρ (see Du Cange's note on XV. 11, p. 496 c).
[2] The pupil, possibly also the wife, of Pythagoras.
[3] Cf. XV. 1, p. 462. Chalandon (Alexis 1er, p. 274) believes that Alexius only took Irene on campaigns because she was too disloyal and too formidable to leave behind. We shall discuss this later in Ch. 37.

and father everything at all times, at night an unsleeping eye, by
day a supreme guardian, to the dangers of the banquet a good antidote, and against harm in food[1] a salutary medicine. These causes
therefore put on one side the innate modesty of that woman, and
she learnt to endure the gaze of masculine eyes. Yet not even then
did she forget her innate decorum, but by her glance and her silence
and her careful behaviour she managed to remain even more unknown' [i.e. than at home] 'to most people, and only this fact, that
an Empress was accompanying the army, was made plain by the
litter borne on mules and the imperial curtain upon it. In all other
ways the sacred body was concealed, except that some very great
care seemed to be taking charge of (διέξαγοι) the Emperor's ail-
ments, and that an unwearied watch over the Emperor was per-
ceived by all, and an unsleeping eye which was never closed to
what went on.'

Anna then says that 'all of us who were devoted to him' helped
in guarding him, and hints at slanderous reasons given for the
Empress's presence in camp, a matter which need not delay
us now.

She nexts hastens to assure us that Irene took no part in the
actual fighting, which would have written her down as a
Tomyris or other barbarian woman.

'In other fashion was she armed, not with the spear of Athene or
the leather cap of Hades; nay, her buckler and shield and sword for
standing nobly against misfortunes and the catastrophes of life . . .
were her energy in action and her firm resistance against passions
and her unfeigned faith, as Solomon says. Thus my mother armed
herself against such wars, though in other respects she was most
peaceful, as her name [Irene] implies. . . . So taking all the coin she
possessed of gold or other quality, and some others of her goods,
she departs from the city. And for the rest in going through the
streets she extended a bountiful hand to all the beggars and to those
in rough garments or naked, and none who begged went empty
away. And when she reached the tent assigned her, she did not
straightway turn to repose remaining inside it, but throwing it open
she afforded free entrance to suppliants, for to such she was very
accessible and allowed herself to be seen and heard. And not only
did she give the poor a share of her goods, but she also gave them
good advice. And all that she saw to be vigorous in body but lazy
in their way of life, she urged to works and action that they might
thence gain their livelihood, and not, after giving up effort through
carelessness, go round begging from door to door. And no times or
seasons restrained the Empress from this activity. So then David
appears "mingling his drink with weeping", but this empress was
seen mixing her eating and drinking with pity every day.'

[1] Cf. XIV. 5, p. 437.

The combination described by Anna of supremely feminine αἰδώς (the word occurs four times in the passage) and no less feminine soft-heartedness, with the virile qualities of watchfulness, sharpness, activity, steadfast faith, and good counsel, is eminently characteristic of her point of view. This her ideal was never reached but by two sovereign ladies, her mother and her grandmother,[1] to whom Anna would dearly like to have made a third; as to her mother, she reiterates her sentiments in the closing chapter of her book, when dealing with Irene's last hours as an Empress. This is what she says:

'Always in former perils also the Empress had a manly mind, but especially on this occasion did she play the man. Though deeply moved by the feeling of grief, she stood like an Olympic victor wrestling against those keenest pains. For she was pierced in soul and troubled in heart by the sight of the Emperor's state, yet she braced herself and stood firm against trials. And though she received mortal wounds and the pain of them entered into her marrow, yet she resisted. However, her tears flowed down in floods, and wasting came to the beauty of her face, and her life seemed to hang by her nostrils' (ἐν ῥισὶν ἀπηώρητο τὴν ψυχήν, as we might say 'was hovering on her lips').[2]

The contrast between masculine sense and feminine sensibility could not be more forcibly expressed, and the passage justifies our assertion that Anna had on the whole a poor opinion of her own sex.

Yet women play a great part in her story. To say nothing of intriguing women like the Empress Maria[3] or ambitious women like the Empress Eudocia[4] or of Anna's immediate relations, we have constant references to 'women and children' accompanying men even under arduous circumstances of marching and war.[5] Care for their wives and children is an argument by which Palaeologus wins the fleet over to Alexius' side; it ranks with the Venetians only next in importance to

---

[1] In III. 6 and 7 Anna Dalassena is just such another Virtuous Woman, pious, open-handed, fond of priests, yearning for the conventual life, yet a wise, zealous, and indefatigable ruler.

[2] XV. 11, p. 501. In the *Prologue* to Anna's Will, line 69, we get the phrase ἐξήρτημαι τῆς ψυχῆς (on husband and children).

[3] II. 1–4; III. 1–4; IX. 8. We may remember the mother of the Aaron conspirators exiled like them (XIII. 1, p. 378). This fate befell Anna Dalassena under Romanus Diogenes (Nic. Bry. I. 22, p. 35, and II. 1, p. 40).

[4] III. 2, p. 74.

[5] VII. 3, p. 196; VIII. 5, p. 233; IX. 1, p. 247; X. 4, p. 280; 5, p. 284; XI. 3, p. 318; 6, p. 325; XV. 4, p. 473. We may contrast the old Greek way of sending women away into safety from a besieged town (Thuc. IV. 123).

their loyalty to the Emperor;[1] the way to make men in a
town happy is to send for their wives and children and settle
them there; while wrath over the treatment of a sister may
turn a man into a rebel.[2] On a march the Emperor will halt
his whole army if some refugee woman is in childbirth.[3]
Honours to his womenkind are held out as a bait to a Turkish
sultan, though as a matter of fact the only honour that befalls
one of these princesses is to be paraded as a prisoner in the
Greek army, to show the world that her home has really been
captured.[4]

In the great Orphanotropheion Alexius ordains that men and
women shall live side by side, each in a separate house, and
the nursing of the sick is done by both sexes, men waiting on
men and women on women; he also 'made the work of the
deaconesses his care', besides appointing women singers as well
as men for the church in the institution.[5]

Certainly the Byzantine woman, as depicted in Anna's pages,
had no right to complain of neglect at the hands of the other
sex, even though to our special writer Woman is emphatically
The Lesser Man.

II. Kinsmen

The importance of women comes out in Anna's pages nowhere more plainly than in the respect paid throughout to
Mothers. In their conspiracy the Comneni brothers rely implicitly on the sympathy, good counsel, and discretion of their
mother Anna Dalassena, whose proceedings during the eventful
period are narrated quite as circumstantially as theirs.[6] In the
first instance the effect of her tears on Romanus Diogenes had
kept Alexius as a boy from fighting,[7] just as later on Alexius
himself checked the military ardour of Constantine Ducas out of
consideration for the latter's mother Maria.[8] To please his own
mother, 'whom he so dearly loved' and by whose 'admonitions
he directed his conduct', Alexius till he marries has a monk in

[1] II. 11, p. 65; VI. 5, p. 161. So σπλάγχνα πατρικά are a good excuse for doubtful
conduct in a man (VIII. 9, p. 241).
[2] VI. 4, pp. 157, 158; VI. 12, p. 180.   [3] XV. 7, p. 481.
[4] XI. 2, p. 313, 5, p. 322.
[5] XV. 7. We may compare the extraordinarily interesting provision made in
the *Typikon* of the Pantocrator Monastery not only for a male staff and male sick
but also for female patients and assistants and helpers of all sorts, including
a woman doctor (Oeconomos, *Vie religieuse*, pp. 195–6).
[6] II, *passim*.
[7] I. 1, p. 3. See the fuller account in Nic. Bry. I. 12.   [8] IX. 5, p. 255.

his military tent.[1] At the crisis of his fortunes, before Botaniates
has formally surrendered, Alexius and Isaac hesitate whether
to press on, or to go and 'pay the accustomed obeisance' to
their 'mothers', Maria the forceful mother-in-law of Alexius
and of George Palaeologus being here included.[2] The 'ever-
ready wrath of the mother of the Comneni' against the Ducas
family[3] tried in vain to hinder Irene's coronation, but succeeded in ousting Irene's champion Cosmas from the Patriarchate. From the moment of his accession, Alexius treated
Anna Dalassena as his κοινωνός no less than his brother Isaac;[4]
she is his 'queen, nurse and conductress in all things',[5] even in
the 'things troubling his conscience'; he has her called δέσποινα,
and to her in a lengthy Golden Bull he commits the regency
during his absence with practically unlimited financial and
administrative powers.[6] After the contemplated treachery of
his nephew John Comnenus has been foiled, Alexius begs the
culprit's father Isaac the Sebastocrator to 'go and tell our
mother of our affairs',[7] and later on we hear of her having a
criminal blinded in Constantinople.[8] Her rule according to
Zonaras and Glycas was oppressive and unpopular, but Alexius
in Anna's eyes remained to the end her docile son and servant.[9]
'In all that befell him he did not perform even any chance
action without her counsel,[10] but had her as a colleague and also
partner in his plans, not only time and again coming to her in
secret and making known to her his administration of affairs,
but also in various ways demonstrating publicly that without
her brain and judgement the affairs of the Empire would
perish.'[11] The Golden Bull of her regency itself begins with

---

[1] I. 8, p. 19; III. 5, p. 80; 7, p. 86; cf. VI. 8, p. 167; XV. 11, p. 496. Alexius
in the heading of his first poem to John (B. Z. XXII, p. 349) calls himself φιλομήτωρ
and his son φιλοπάτωρ. Nic. Bry. (I. 12, p. 26) says that Alexius 'was, if any man
was, war-lover and mother-lover'; he did not even resent her thinking him too
callow for the command against Urselius (ibid. II. 20, p. 57).

[2] II. 12, p. 66; cf. II. 6, p. 54. George Palaeologus pays this obeisance to the
father whom he means to fight (II. 11, p. 66).

[3] III. 2, p. 72. She first hated Constantine X Ducas, who accepted the crown
in 1059 from Isaac Comnenus when her own husband John refused it (Nic. Bry.
I. 4, p. 18). This offer and refusal are not mentioned by Psellus, Attaliates, or
Scylitzes.

[4] III. 2, p. 73.　　　　　　　　　　　　[5] III. 5, p. 81, 6, p. 83.

[6] III. 2, p. 75, 6, pp. 82-5.

[7] VIII. 8, p. 239.　　　　　　　　　　　[8] X. 4, p. 279.

[9] Zonaras (XVIII. 21, 24) and Glycas (IV, p. 334) say that Alexius finally
resented his mother having all the real 'management of affairs' (though she never
shared in the 'cheers'), but was 'in awe of his mother' and let her go on ruling;
she however retired voluntarily into a convent. Zonaras says that τὰ πρὸς κάκωσιν
of the subjects were popularly attributed to Anna Dalassena and not to her son.

[10] So Theophylact (παιδ. βασ., II. 30) tells Constantine Ducas that God will aid
him if he obeys his mother, P. G. 126, col. 285.　　　[11] III. 6, p. 82.

the words: 'There is no safeguard equivalent to or stronger than a sympathetic mother who loves her child',[1] and lays special emphasis on the efficacy of her prayers.[2]

Other mothers too occupy important if not always equally honourable places on Anna's stage. The Empress Eudocia is formidable enough for her step-son Michael VII to banish her on his accession.[3] Later on she intrigues to regain the crown for herself or her daughter Zoe, by the expedient of a marriage with the Emperor Botaniates.[4] The love of the Empress Maria for her 'only child' Constantine Ducas affects the course of events more than once.[5] In short, if there was a fixed principle in medieval Byzantine ethics, it was the French sentiment of duty to 'ma mère'.[6]

It is therefore interesting to find Anna, though full of reverence for her mother, still laying special stress on her devoted admiration for her father. She loved both parents, obeyed them, and suffered on their behalf,[7] but her father is from the nature of the case her hero and her idol.[8] Looking at the matter from the other side we hear nothing from Anna of her father's feelings towards his children, though twice over we are informed that he loved other young men as though they were his own sons.[9] Of the loving pride over John which rings through Alexius' poems to him, we naturally get no hint from the jealous Anna, who, we may remark, never mentions her own children throughout the book.

[1] III. 6, p. 83.
[2] Cf. the 'fervent prayer' by which the mother of Michael Psellus gained wisdom from above for her son (V. 8, p. 144). Nic. Bry. (II. 20, p. 57) says that Alexius started out against Urselius, ἐφοδιασθεὶς ταῖς εὐχαῖς of his mother. The *Prologue* to Anna's Will asks: τί . . . μητρὸς εὐχῆς μακαριώτατον ἄλλο ; (line 56.)
[3] IX. 6, p. 256. [4] III. 2, p. 74. [5] III. 1; IX. 5, p. 255.
[6] When John Comnenus, anxious over his precarious new throne, fails to attend his father's funeral, one of his biographers tries to exculpate him not primarily from impiety to his father but from disobedience to his mother (Nic. Ac. *John C.* 2, p. 6). In the *Alexias* Nicephorus Palaeologus and his son George quarrel openly (II. 11, p. 66).
[7] In XII. 3 she praises first Alexius and then Irene, deprecating in both instances the accusation of boasting or untruth. In V. 8, p. 148, the memory of Irene's learning makes her almost forget her duties as historian. She even showed her εὔνοια to her mother by obedience before her own birth (VI. 8) and Irene relied on her as an oracle (XV. 11, pp. 497, 504). In XV. 3, p. 468, we hear that she had suffered for her εὔνοια to her father. She was φιλομήτωρ καὶ φιλοπάτωρ (VI. 8, p. 167; XV. 11, p. 496), as she shows by her outburst of grief in her last chapter (XV. 11, p. 505 to end). In the *Prologue* to her Will she says she married to please her parents and contrasts herself complacently with spoilt children; but how indeed could she refuse obedience to parents 'so great and so grand in virtue, of whom the world was not worthy'? Even the making of her will was done by her mother's wishes (lines 47–58, 85–7)
[8] Pref., *passim*.
[9] Constantine Ducas (IX. 5, p. 255) and the two Diogenes (IX. 6, p. 256).

Before we leave the matter of family affection, something must be added about the 'kinsmen' who figure so often in Anna's story. Their power for good and evil is one of the most remarkable features of the time, and no Highland clan ever clung closer together[1] (with all the implied privileges of family criticism and quarrelling, combined with mutual helpfulness) than did the imperial συγγένεια at Constantinople. This word should by rights mean kinsmen in race, but Anna usually makes it include both blood-relations and connexions by marriage,[2] the two classes that keep on appearing in her pages as οἱ ἐξ αἵματος καὶ ἀγχιστείας προσήκοντες συγγενεῖς. Many different degrees of relationship play their parts in the story, and each must be shortly considered.[3]

First we have the older generation. Mothers-in-law in those days seem to have lived up to their proverbial reputation as personages that counted. Maria, Irene's mother, uses her

---

[1] The success of one member of a house reflects glory on the whole (II. 7, p. 58; cf. Thuc. VI. 16). Anna Dalassena's 'hearth' acts as a 'common resting-place to the poor of her own family' (III. 8, p. 87). So Attaliates says Michael V was a fool to ill-treat his kinsmen and deprive himself συγγενικῆς βοηθείας (p. 12) and he thinks it ὥσπερ εἰκός when Constantine Monomachus gives a relation λαμπρὰν τύχην (p. 22).

It is in Anna's eyes one of the pathetic features of the Empress Maria's lot, part of the λύπη of living in a foreign land, that she has no 'body of kinsmen round her' (II. 2, p. 46; III. 1, p. 71, 2, p. 73). This loneliness had evoked the sympathy of John Ducas Caesar in days past, and the Comneni brothers offer to supply by their devotion the lack of relations born. Her whole story reminds one of Medea, whose sorrows primarily came from leaving her country for a foreign husband, and were doubled by her having no kin to share them (See Eurip. Med. 34, 328, 440-2, 649, 798-801, and especially 253-8, where her words:

ἐγὼ δ' ἔρημος ἄπολις οὖσ' ὑβρίζομαι
. . . .
οὐ μητέρ', οὐκ ἀδελφόν, οὐχὶ συγγενῆ
μεθορμίσασθαι τῆσδ' ἔχουσα συμφορᾶς

may well have been in Anna's mind when she dwells in Maria's case on τὸ ἐπ' ἀλλοτρίας εἶναι, μὴ συγγενῆ, μὴ συνήθη, μηδένα τὸ παράπαν ὁμόχθονα κεκτημένην (III. 1, p. 71).

[2] II. 7, p. 57 : 8, p. 59 : 12, p. 67; VII. 3, p. 195; VIII. 1, p. 221 : 2, p. 224; XV. 6. p. 477. So we may stretch προσήκων κατὰ γένος (II. 2, p. 45) into meaning a 'brother-in-law or nephew' (Scylitzes, p. 867 B).

[3] In VII. 2, p. 192, Anna adduces as a proof of her husband's veracity in his History the axiom that 'he would not have lied' about either his father or his father-in-law, 'seeing that he was connected by marriage with the one and a blood-relation of the other'. One secondary proof of the importance attached to kinship is in the practice of adoption, so as if need be to secure the desired relation artificially. The Empress Maria adopts Alexius 'according to the form long in use in such a case' (II. 1, p. 44). Du Cange (note, ad loc.) says that such adoptions were usually made into a solemn religious ceremony. Botaniates offers to make Alexius his θετὸς υἱός (II. 12, p. 67). In time past Romanus Diogenes had adopted as a brother, 'because it seemed good to both', the Nicephorus Bryennius who was afterwards blinded (X. 3, p. 275). Anna tells us that the transaction was of common occurrence (X. 3, p. 276); it evidently involved the next generation in the ties of friendship thus made.

powerful tongue 'threatening most dreadful things' to win over
to Alexius' side her other son-in-law George Palaeologus.[1]
Much later her acquaintance with Euthymius Zigabenus is one
of the things that commends this learned monk to the Emperor.[2]
Even an elderly grandfather-in-law is an influential person:
John Ducas Caesar, obviously actuated by family sentiment for
Irene, is of material assistance to Alexius in his usurpation.[3] In
the early days of the new reign he figures as a sort of Grand
Old Man of the Ducas House, balancing their great antagonist
the imperious Mother of the Comneni; the friction between
the families (ended apparently by some sort of bargain) finds
its highest expression in the two.[4] It is significant, by the bye,
that the Ducas family are those who rejoice most when Irene
is blessed with children; barrenness in her would have meant
loss of power for her kin.[5]

Next we have brothers and sisters. Anna bursts into wailing
over the untimely death of her favourite brother Andronicus,[6]
and describes her sisters as sharing in the loving watch at their
father's death-bed.[7] One of them, her 'best-loved' Maria, is
'the resting-place of all virtue'.[8] Only 'the successor to the
throne' has no good word from her pen. On the whole we see
that 'a brotherly disposition' is to her as now the synonym for
friendliness.[9] Isaac and Alexius loved one another like Orestes
and Pylades;[10] the elder brother helped the younger in every
conceivable way and waived in his favour his own claims to the
throne.[11] He takes charge of the capital in Alexius' absence,[12]
raises money even by unpopular methods[13] for his wars, and
aids him in his struggles with heretics and rebels.[14] Only in the
affair of his own son John, whom he defends with bitter words
against his brothers Adrian and the Emperor,[15] and in the
obscure episode of Gregory Gabras,[16] do we see any hint of

---

[1] II. 6, p. 54.   [2] XV. 9, p. 490.   [3] II. 6–end; III. 1–4.
[4] III. 1 and 2. But see Krumbacher, *G. B. L.*, p. 1013, for his rebellion against
his nephew, Michael VII, ending in his own enforced retirement in a monastery.
Another nephew of his, Constantius Porphyrogenitus (called by other writers
Constantine), died for Alexius at Durazzo (IV. 5 and 6, and *v.* Du Cange's note
on IV. 6, p. 116 D).
[5] VI. 8, p. 167.   [6] XV. 5, pp. 475–6.   [7] XV. 11, *passim.*
[8] *Ibid.*, p. 504; VI. 8, p. 167. The sister of Bohemund (Anna's doubt whether
she was sister or sister-in-law is settled for us by Albert of Aix) greatly helps her
brother's cause by valour and cunning (XII. 8).
[9] X. 3, p. 275. Cf. the description given by Nicetas of John's generosity to his
brother Isaac who had been his prime supporter in 1118, but later on had tried
to stir up external enemies against him. John gladly forgives him, 'for a strong
thing is affection interwoven with kinship' (*John C.*, 2, p. 5; 9, p. 21).
[10] II. 1, p. 44.   [11] II, *passim.*
[12] IV. 4, p. 109.   [13] V. 2.
[14] V. 9; XII. 6, p. 361; XV. 8.   [15] VIII. 8.   [16] VIII. 9.

wavering loyalty in Isaac. He and Adrian[1] and the other brother Nicephorus were honoured with all the titles that Alexius' fertile brain could invent,[2] in striking contrast to the harshness of Michael VII to his Diogenes half-brothers.[3] Respect for his sister Theodora made Alexius imprison the man who impersonated her husband,[4] while wrath over the ill-treatment of his four sisters causes the Manichaean Traulus to revolt, and with him go 'all those who belonged to him ἐκ συγγενείας'. The wrongs of his daughter Helen, if authentic, would have seemed even in Anna's eyes an excuse for Robert Guiscard's invasion.[5]

Next to these in importance come brothers-in-law.[6] Michael Taronites, married to the eldest Comnena, proves ungrateful for Alexius' kindness and is disgraced and exiled after the Diogenes conspiracy.[7] But George Palaeologus, husband of Irene's sister Anna, though by no means always in harmony with the imperial will,[8] may be said to be Anna's second hero from the very days of her father's revolt; proof would be merely tedious. Whether in the capital or at Durazzo or at Castoria or in the Patzinak War or at Pelecanus with the Crusaders, he is always in the foreground. While he and the Ducas family are helping on the revolt (largely, as they say plainly, for the sake of their kinswoman Irene[9]), another brother-in-law Nicephorus Melissenus, married to Alexius' sister, is a dangerous rival,[10] but is turned by judicious bestowal of honours into a loyal supporter.[11] In the suspected plot of the Emperor's nephew John, this Melissenus, with the other 'kinsmen of blood and connexion' ('and no stranger' adds Anna), is present at the angry scene between the three brothers.[12] The Empress's brothers Michael Ducas and John Ducas are no less useful as generals.[13]

---

[1] Adrian succeeds Pacurianus as Grand Domestic (VIII. 4, p. 229).
[2] III. 4.   [3] IX. 6, p. 256.   [4] X. 2, p. 272.
[5] I. 12; VI. 4, pp. 157, 158. Cf. the way the relations of Elchanes and Bolcanus follow them in their attitude towards Alexius (VI. 13, p. 181; IX. 10, p. 265).
[6] Marriage makes two parties 'take over each other's concerns as kinsmen' (III. 10, p. 94).
[7] III. 4, p. 78; IX. 6 and 8. Yet his cousin the rebellious Gregory Taronites appears to reap benefit from Michael's connexion with the imperial house by meeting with exceptional kindness from the Emperor (XII. 7).
[8] III. 2, p. 72; IV. 5, p. 112 (bis); VI. 7, p. 166; VIII. 2, pp. 223, 225.
[9] III. 2, p. 72. They insist on her coronation (ibid., p. 75).   [10] II. 8–11.
[11] III. 4, p. 78; IV. 6, p. 115; V. 5, p. 139; VII. 3, 4. He, like George Palaeologus, is jealous of the Emperor's prowess in VIII. 2 and 3, p. 225, but continues none the less to be one of his trusted commanders (VIII. 3, p. 227, 4, p. 229; 6, p. 235; X. 2, p. 273).
[12] VIII. 8.
[13] II. 7, p. 57; V. 7, pp. 141, 142; VII. 3, pp. 196–8; VIII. 4, p. 229; IX. 1 and 2; XI. 5. Michael, phalangarch in the Larissa campaign (V. 7, p. 141), is said

In the next generation we get the nephews John and Alexius Comnenus. Considering them on their merits, we may say that John proves of little value, but his brother Alexius is in every way worthy of the trust reposed in him.[1] Another imperial nephew, John Taronites, is the Emperor's loyal subject and outspoken critic.[2] In her husband's brother-in-law Marianus Maurocatacalo Anna gives us a fine example of a truly dashing officer, whose prowess she greatly admires, and a first cousin of hers called simply Nicephorus also displays warlike daring. But when she comes to her own nephew, the Emperor Manuel, she shows that there is no love lost between them.[3]

If we turn from the duties to the privileges and dignities of kinship whether through blood or marriage we cannot remind ourselves too often how enormously important they were. The Comneni brothers may associate freely with Maria, because Isaac has married her niece or cousin, and Alexius' wife is the kinswoman of her first husband.[4] Hostages are more honourable if they are the kin of those who give them;[5] to be received by a sovereign's 'nearest relations' is a testimony to high rank.[6] It is therefore an almost hopeless sign of 'folly' to make attacks by letter on the 'kinsmen and connexions' of the imperial family, and a man guilty of this is best reasoned with by some relation of his own 'sharing in the same blood'.[7]

Honours are freely given to the Emperor's kin; marvellous new titles,[8] offices of dignity, military commands, governorships, their name is Legion. First Irene's brother John Ducas, and then successively Alexius' nephews, John and Alexius the sons of Isaac, hold the vitally important post of Durazzo. John Taronites another nephew of the Emperor's is made eparch of Constantinople.[9] One brother of the Emperor's is Great

to have loved the Emperor 'exceedingly' (VII. 3, p. 198). In II. 6, p. 55, John carries the news of the Comnenus revolt to his grandfather, who boxes his ears as a liar. On the other hand, it is interesting to see that the Emperor's brother Adrian wishes to save the rebel Nicephorus Diogenes because he is his brother-in-law (Adrian having married Nicephorus' half-sister), and the same tie makes the ex-Empress Maria take at least a small part in the conspiracy (IX. 5, p. 255, 7, p. 259). We have already seen that Botaniates hoped to be succeeded by his brother-in-law or nephew Synadenus (II. 2, p. 45; Scyl., p. 867 B).

[1] VIII. 7 and 8; IX. 4; XII. 4, 8 and 9; XIII. 3. Cf. Camytzes' useful nephew in XIV. 5, p. 440.
[2] X. 2, p. 273; XII. 7; XIII. 1, p. 376, where see Du Cange's note.
[3] X. 3, p. 277 : 8, passim; XIII. 7, p. 395 : 8, p. 398; XIV. 3, p. 433 : 7, p. 447; XV. 4, p. 473.
[4] II. 1, p. 44, and 3, p. 48. This also gives Maria an excuse for remaining in the Palace with Alexius, her connexion as well as adopted son (III. 1, p. 71).
[5] IX. 4, p. 252, and 10, p. 265.
[6] XIII. 9.   [7] XII. 7, pp. 364, 365.
[8] III. 4.   [9] XIII. 1, p. 376.

Domestic of the West, another Great Drungary of the Fleet; one brother-in-law is Protostrator, another, George Palaeologus, is, so to speak, the sovereign's right-hand man. Even relationship too vague to be defined entitles a man to a post of distinction.[1] We find honourable mention of the imperial sons-in-law, Nicephorus Catacalo, husband of Anna's sister Maria,[2] and above all Nicephorus Bryennius, 'my Caesar', of whose career we have already spoken. Of Alexius' sons only one, Andronicus, plays any military role at all in his Biography.[3] John is only twice mentioned by name, except officially in the treaty between Alexius and Bohemund. Otherwise during his father's lifetime he is only 'a male baby', 'one of the Porphyrogenetes', or 'the successor to the throne'; though when he has become Emperor Anna represents him as waging active wars.[4]

As we read her history, where military and other promotion seems to depend almost exclusively on closeness of relationship to the ruler, a state of things which she takes completely for granted, we find ourselves marvelling that so many of the 'imperial kinsmen' proved such good soldiers. It was a clear case of 'more by luck than good guidance'. Seldom is any qualification but the blood royal in some shape or form needed for any post of honour or of its accompanying danger, and those who possess that cling together like some swarm of bees. The 'kinsmen' on both sides go with the Emperor as a matter of course to the front, and stand near him in battle;[5] when rebellion threatens they form a crescent-shaped bodyguard on each side of the throne and by their loyalty prevent any attempt at assassination.[6] In the examining of frustrated conspirators, or parleyings with foreign enemies, they support the Emperor by their presence.[7] They share in his penance;[8] they are equally

---

[1] So Constantine Dalassenus is first governor of Sinope, then Thalassocrator, then general (VI. 9, p. 170; VII. 8, p. 206; VIII. 5, p. 232; IX. 1, 3), and Rhodomerus has a military command (VIII. 4, p. 229; XI. 2, pp. 314–16).

[2] X. 3, pp. 276, 277. Through him his father has many important commands.

[3] XV. 5, p. 475.

[4] Pref. 3, p. 3; VI. 8, p. 167; XII. 4, p. 356; XIII. 7, p. 395, 12, *passim*; XV. 11, p. 503.

[5] VII. 3, p. 195; VIII 3, p. 227; IX. 5, p. 253; XIII. 1, p. 376; XV. 2, p. 463.

[6] IX. 9. On the other hand it is significant to see Anna singling out for praise her maternal uncle John Ducas, on the ground that 'The Emperor knew him to be . . . not at all disinclined to disobey his orders' (VII. 8, p. 209, and IX. 1, p. 247). The story of the abortive ἀποστασία of Alexius' nephew John Comnenus (VIII. 7, 8) gives point to this peculiar form of eulogy. A brother-in-law of Alexius is involved in the conspiracy of Niceph. Diogenes (IX. 6, p. 258, and 8, p. 262), and a certain Constantinus Exazenus Ducas in that of the Anemas brothers (XII. 5); he is restored to favour in XII. 8, p. 368; XIII. 1, p. 376.

[7] XII. 6, p. 361; XV. 6, p. 477. In XI. 3, pp. 316, 317, George Palaeologus draws on himself insults by this.   [8] III. 5.

responsible with him for the care of his veterans' children,[1] and they join in his recreations.[2] It is from various kinsmen at the palace, especially uncles on both sides, that Anna has learnt much of her history.[3] It is the 'band of encircling kinsmen' who try to make the distracted Empress take care of herself when Alexius is dying.[4] On the other hand, they remonstrate with him when he seems to them blameable.[5] They check his righteous indignation[6], and he is bound to tell them his plans.[7] When they try to dissuade him from fighting, only the Sacred Lots give him the courage to ignore their wishes.[8] When Nicephorus Diogenes was blinded it was quite possibly due to high-handed action on their part, merely authorized by Alexius.[9] They shrink from no boldness towards their sovereign lord, and their peculiar position gives them much of his power with none of his responsibility.[10]

We might with ease trace the same potency of the blood-tie for good and evil among the 'barbarians' of Anna's history, but it hardly seems worth while. Enough has been said to show that her world was still in the stage where marriages and blood-relationship brought about or resolved quarrels high and low. If the 'sister's son to Barnabas' occasioned by one act of his a lifelong severance between two apostles, it is hardly strange that men and women less saintly and more mundane were swayed by family feeling even beyond the considerations of justice or reason. In this point of her mentality at any rate Anna is a woman of her time.

[1] XV. 7, p. 482.   [2] XII. 6, p. 360.
[3] VI. 8, p. 167; XIV. 7, pp. 447, 448.   [4] XV. 11, p. 501.
[5] I. 3, p. 8; VII. 3, p. 197.   [6] VIII. 6, p. 235.
[7] V. 5, p. 139; VIII. 1, p. 221; X. 2, p. 273, and 9, p. 295.
[8] X. 2, p. 273. To please them he goes to Anchialus (X. 2, p. 274).
[9] IX. 9.
[10] It is striking to find that one of the recommendations of the widowed Maria as a wife for the Emperor Botaniates was that, being of foreign birth, 'she had no crowd of kinsmen about her, by whom the Emperor might be troubled' (III. 2, p. 73). Cecaumenus (λόγ. νουθ. pp. 98–9) draws the same moral from the story of Michael IV, who 'became hated . . . through the misdeeds of his relations'.

THE FOUR CARDINAL VIRTUES

20. TEMPERANCE

WHEN we turn to the Four Cardinal Virtues ordinarily so called we are at once struck with important differences between Anna's standard and ours. Our views on Temperance may be identical with hers, but her Wisdom seems to us mostly Cunning, and of Justice in the broad sense she knows nothing, while her profound conviction that Discretion is the better part of Valour makes her Fortitude appear to us a sadly emasculated thing.

Let us take first the one quality in which her standard on the whole resembles ours, Temperance.[1] Throughout her book she shows a fine scorn for self-indulgence or weaknesses of the flesh, and there is not one coarse or sensual passage.[2] Among her father's excellences was his δίαιτα μηδὲ ἀπαλή, ἀλλὰ πάνυ σω-φρονεστάτη καὶ λιτὴ καὶ ὅλως γυμνική τε καὶ στρατιωτική.[3] His was no life of inglorious ease. He allowed himself no ῥαστώνη,[4] even after severe labours. He kept his body absolutely under control, giving it when young little recreation, and only resorting to sports as exercise when his doctors recommended this for the gout.[5] Anna speaks with admiring awe of her grandmother's σωφροσύνη, and her drastic reforms in the Court, where 'lawless passions' had long held sway; she says proudly that as a consequence one might have thought the Palace a monastery.[6] This great lady's son had the same high standard; he is 'altogether like a priest both in virtue and in learning'[7] and is well qualified to 'regulate the morals' of a young protégé.[8] In choosing homes for the orphans whom he wishes to educate he draws on three sources, his own kinsmen, the heads of monasteries, and 'all those of virtuous life'.[9] It grieves his daughter

[1] She had perhaps partly formed her ideals on classical models. Her master Plato classes together σωφροσύνη, ἀνδρεία, ἐλευθεριότης and μεγαλοπρέπεια (Rep. III. 402).
[2] In III. 1, p. 72 : 2, p. 74, she expresses her loathing for scandal. Cf. XV. 9. p. 490. [3] XV. 11, p. 498. [4] V. 4, p. 135; 5, p. 137.
[5] XIV. 7, p. 449. We may compare the contemptuous account of the old Emperor Botaniates given in Anon. Syn. Chron. (p. 172). He amused himself μίμοις καὶ κιθάραις καὶ γελωτοποιοῖς καὶ τραπέζαις ἀβροδιαίτοις. Anna is most zealous to prove that her father's illness did not come from luxurious living (XIV. 4, p. 433).
[6] III. 8, p. 87. [7] VI. 13, p. 181.
[8] VIII. 9, p. 241. [9] XV. 7, p. 482.

to think that debauchery (ἔργα ἀθέμιτα) was one sad result of the general neglect of education after his death.[1] One of Irene's sources of strength was her 'firm resistance against passions'.[2] Even in barbarians chastity deserves respect,[3] while impurity earns due punishment from heaven.[4] The only severe words which Anna has to say against the Turks are due to her (probably erroneous) notion that they 'yield to Dionysus and Eros', and are 'most passionate in every sort of sensuality'.[5] Drunkenness and gluttony are deplorable, however common, as are also insolence, rudeness, swearing, or any other lack of self-control.[6] One of Anna Dalassena's beneficial reforms in the palace is fixed hours for meals.[7]

We may remark in passing that food and drink, both in metaphor and in fact, play almost as large a part in Anna's story as they do in the Homeric poems, or for that matter the Bible. Banquets are one of the recognized pleasures of life, and it is consistent with this that butlers and cooks are not infrequently mentioned,[8] and are even taken on campaigns. The commissariat of a medieval army was one of its great difficulties,[9] and lack of all food or merely of food 'permitted to Christians' may be a more potent conqueror than the enemies' troops.[10]

---

[1] XV. 7, p. 486.
[2] XII. 3, p. 353. So Prodromus (B.Z. XVI. p. 88) calls Irene 'mistress of her passions, not of the world only'.
[3] X. ii, p. 305; XI. 6, p. 327.   [4] XI. 6, p. 326.
[5] X. 5, p. 284; XV. 1, p. 460.
[6] V.5, p. 138; VIII. 6, p. 235; IX. 3, p. 251; XI. 3, p. 317; XII. 2, p. 349. In X. 2, p. 272, there is a curious reference to 'epicures after they have reached satiety', and in X. 4, p. 279, the drunken Comans are vividly described. Constantine VIII was πολυβορώτατος (Psellus, Chron., Const. VIII. Byz. T., p. 24).
[7] III. 8, p. 87. Theophylact (παιδ. βασ. II, 24) tells his pupil Constantine Ducas it is a good rule not to eat before sweating (P. G. 126, col. 284). The Typikon of Irene (P. G. 127) contains minute rules as to the diet of the nuns. They are to have two meals, ἄριστον and δεῖπνον, consisting of nothing more than wine and vegetables and bread. No food may ever be eaten between meals, for fear the nuns should share the fate of Eve (cols. 1064–72). The Mélanges offerts à M. Gustave Schlumberger, Paris, 1924, has in its first volume an article on 'Les Calendriers de régime à l'usage des Byzantins' by Dr. E. Jeanselme. There are six preserved, of which the most important is by a certain Hierophilus (eleventh or twelfth century) who 'se conforme pour ce qui concerne le régime, variable suivant les saisons, à des règles traditionnelles', possibly older even than Hippocrates. The whole is founded on the theory of the body's four humours. (See p. 216, note 8, below.)
[8] II. 3, p. 47; IV. 1, p. 104; VIII. 4, p. 228; 9, p. 242; X. 11, p. 302; XV. 6, p. 476.
[9] XI. 1, p. 309, and 2, p. 312; 4, p. 319; 6, p. 326; 7, p. 330; 10, p. 337; XIII. 7, p. 397, and 8, p. 398. The Crusaders carry with them sacks of barley loaves to eat, hard and solid enough to serve as missiles (X. 8, p. 293).
[10] IV. 3, p. 108; XIII. 2, p. 381, and 8, p. 399. In I. 10, p. 22, 'certain qualities of food' are said to be 'the origins of fevers' (see V. 5, p. 138; XI. 9, p. 333). The constant anxiety about δαψιλεῖς πανηγύρεις, literally 'plentiful markets', runs

On three occasions we hear of the Emperor's ἄριστον,[1] while his heroic courtesy to the Crusaders and his zeal to convert the Manichaeans are shown by remaining long hours ἄσιτος.[2] Fasting is a very real penance;[3] the deposed Botaniates in his monastic seclusion says, 'Only abstinence from meat annoys me'.[4] Above all, 'clear drinking-water ever flowing' is the primary need in such hot latitudes whether at home or in camp,[5] and the slaking of thirst in battle gives rise to two of Anna's most graphic pictures.[6] 'Lack of food and drink' makes soldiers forget their discipline.[7] The giving of food is an important part of 'care', whether to one's master, or to protégés, or to enemies.[8] At Alexius' death-bed his daughters ply him with suitable food in suitable vessels while the kinsmen try to force the heart-broken Irene to eat.[9] The 'pleasures of the table' was no empty phrase to twelfth-century Byzantines.[10]

Other pleasures make their appearance from time to time. Anna alludes to throwing dice of the ordinary kind, and to

through the whole story of the Crusade. The last sentence of X. 9 will serve as an example. Like the Latin *mercatum* and *commeatus*, the word gradually came to mean merely 'supplies', elsewhere called τὰ ζωαρκῆ (VII. 6, p. 203; X. 5, p. 285; 9, p. 298; 10, p. 299), or τὰ χρειώδη ὅσα εἰς τροφὴν (XII. 9, p. 371). In the *Strategicon* of Cecaumenus, p. 33, we get the phrase ποιῆσαι πανήγυριν πωλεῖν τε καὶ ἀγοράζειν, where 'market' is the meaning. We may compare the ἀγορὰν παρέχειν of Thuc. VI. 44, 50. In the case of a beleaguered town, besiegers and besieged might suffer equally from famine. The habit of reckless plundering, of which we have already spoken, was of course at the root of the difficulty. The taking of mules loaded with provisions into the very heart of the besieged Laodicea was one of Bohemund's most successful acts of bravery (XI. 11, p. 340). Later on his army suffered from having to eat millet (XIII. 2, p. 380).

[1] XII. 9, p. 372; XIII. 1, p. 377; XV. 2, p. 463; so of Irene, V. 9, p. 147.
[2] XIV. 4, p. 436, and 8, p. 454. So in Nic. Bry. (II. 6, p. 44) a keen general goes without food.
[3] III. 5, p. 82.
[4] III. 1, p. 71. Du Cange in his note points out that Basilian monks always abstained from meat, but this is apparently now confined to Fast Days. Prof. A. H. Sayce has authorized me to relate his experience at Orchomenus in Boeotia. After the forty days of the Advent Fast he encountered thirteen meat courses in a monastery, and the Hegoumenos ate twice of each. In Irene's *Typikon* the fasts are severe. On the first and last day of Lent no food is eaten at all. Meat is never allowed, and fish only at festivals, *loc. cit.*
[5] II. 8, p. 60; VI. 6, p. 162; IX. 5, p. 255; XV. 1, p. 462. So St. Gilles' first step towards besieging Tripoli is to cut off its water-supply from Lebanon (XI. 7, p. 329). Regel publishes in his *Fontes Rerum Byzantinarum*, pp. 126-31 (Oratio VII) a letter from Eustathius of Thessalonica begging Manuel I to make an aqueduct for Constantinople, which was suffering from lack of water. Cinnamus (VI. 8, p. 160) tells us that he did so.
[6] VIII. 5, p. 233; XV. 4, p. 472.   [7] I. 11, p. 26.
[8] XI. 12, p. 341; XII. 1, p. 347; XV. 7, p. 482; 9, p. 492.
[9] XV. 11.
[10] It is interesting to find Theophylact, Archbishop of Achrida, sending his ex-pupil Constantine Ducas fish 'from our lake' (Ser. II, Ep. 64, *P. G.* 126, col. 481).

ὀστρακίνδα, a game of chance where a potsherd with one white and one black face was thrown like a die ;[1] also to the use of ψῆφοι or pebbles in a kind of divination which she terms 'in no way magical, but a rational art of the Alexandrians' ;[2] also to chess as serving 'to sweeten the brine that was in him from his many cares',[3] and to draughts.[4] She speaks of fishing[5] and falconry.[6] Children's games, in which she once tells us young Constantine Ducas excelled, are three times mentioned without further explanation, and there is one reference to 'quail fights and other more disgraceful pastimes', as fashionable during the century before her father's accession.[7] But in view of the well-known importance of the horse in peace and war all through the Middle Ages, it is not surprising that of all amusements riding in its various forms figures the oftenest in the *Alexias*. The upper classes, both men and women, rarely condescend to go on foot, and show exceptional deference by dismounting.[8] The most usual phrases for methods of progression bear reference to the turning or pulling in or letting out a horse's rein, and a fine horse was as much a treasured possession then as now.[9] To ride well is no less 'a science proper to gentle blood' to Anna[10]

[1] I. 3, p. 7; VI. 5, p. 158; IX. 9, p. 264.

[2] VI. 7, p. 164.

[3] XII. 6, p. 360. See p. 216, note 8, below.

[4] XV. 7, p. 486. This is coupled with 'other ἔργα ἀθέμιτα.' So in Psellus, *Chron.*, Const. VIII, Byz. T., p. 24, we find a scornful allusion to Constantine's passion for draughts and dice, which made him neglect the Empire and even his own meals.

[5] XIII. 12, p. 406; XV. 8, p. 487.

[6] VII. 9, p. 210.

[7] (a) III. 1, p. 71; IX. 2, p. 249; XV. 3, p. 466; (b) V. 8, p. 144 (cf. below, p. 166).

[8] II. 5, pp. 51, 52; 7, p. 58; V. 5, p. 139; IX. 1, p. 245; XI. 6, p. 327; XIV. 5, p. 440; XV. 6, p. 478. We find one horse in the *Alexias* with a name, Sguritzes (IV. 7, p. 119). Du Cange (note, *ad loc.*) says this means 'dark', 'Subfuscus'; it is the name of a eunuch of the Empress Zoe's, 'one of those nearest to her' (Cedrenus, p. 741 C.).

[9] I. 5, p. 13; IV. 6, sqq. (where we find a good rider lying down flat on his horse); VII. 7, p. 205: 9, p. 212; IX. 7, p. 258; X. 7, p. 289; XIV. 2, p. 429, with Du Cange's note; XV. 6, p. 478. For miraculous horses, see IV. 8, p. 121; VII. 4, p. 199. In XIII. 5, p. 391, panic makes soldiers get on each other's horses by mistake. See also Ch. 58 below.

[10] She has contempt for a Cypriot rebel who 'did not even know how to mount a horse, but if he chanced to have mounted and wished then to ride forth, he suffered from confusion and shaking' (IX. 2, p. 249). Nicephorus Diogenes gains popular admiration by his proficiency in riding and other forms of sport (IX. 6, p. 257). Anna's brother-in-law, the son of Euphorbenus Catacalo, rides as well as a Norman (X. 3, p. 277). Alexius (*Mous. Alex.* II. 64) says John's riding would astonish the Celt (another tribute to Western horsemanship), and Anna rhapsodizes over that of her favourite brother Andronicus, XV. 5, p. 475. Theophylact claims for his pupil Constantine Ducas the power to ride well (παιδ. βασ., I. 4; *P. G.* 126, col. 257). Prodromus in his *Epithalamium* says Anna's two sons had learnt to ride, play polo, hunt, and set phalanxes in array. In his poem complaining of Providence he cites the having Arab or Thessalian horses as one of the unfair advantages of the vulgar rich (*P.G.* 133, cols. 1336, 1402, and cf. 1293). Anna speaks of 'horses

than to Spenser,[1] and in the case of Franks, men are nothing without their horses.[2] Throughout the pages of the *Alexias*, hunting on horseback which often involved the use of arrows,[3] some game like polo,[4] and what we might call 'hacking'[5] are the recreation of all nobles. The Comneni brothers 'frequently turned to the chase, when no great anxiety about public affairs overflowed them'.[6] Horse-racing had not yet ceased to be a popular pastime; indeed it is at such a gathering that Alexius catches the cold which finally ends in his death.[7] He seems to have been by nature a sportsman, but as Emperor his attitude towards amusements of all kinds is clearly stated by his daughter in a memorable passage.[8] He devoted himself to his imperial duties, 'only occasionally refreshing his body by hunting and recreations. For among other things he was a philosopher in this, the bridling of his body and making it more docile to himself. For he delivered it up to toils in the fullest

---

of noble race from Damascus and Edessa and Arabia itself', bought for the Greek army (XIV. 2, p. 429). One proof of the popularity of this Arab strain is that the medieval Greek word for 'horse' (φαρί) comes from the Arabic.

[1] *Faerie Queene*, Bk. II, Canto IV. 1, and cf. Bk. II, Canto III. 46. When Shakespeare's 'young Harry' displays his skill in riding, it is

> As if an angel dropp'd down from the clouds . . .
> To witch the world with noble horsemanship.
>   (*Henry IV*, Pt. I, Act IV, Sc. i.)

We may compare the contempt of the army for the poor riding of John the eunuch in Nic. Bry. IV. 32, p. 104.

[2] V. 4, p. 133 : 6, p. 140; XIII. 8, p. 398.

[3] VI. 10, p. 174; IX. 5, p. 255; X. 9, p. 296; XII. 9, p. 372.

[4] IX. 6, p. 257; 7, p. 259; XIV. 4, p. 434; 7, p. 449. See p. 133, note 10, above.   [5] IX. 6, p. 257; XV. 2, p. 466.

[6] III. 3, p. 77. Their uncle the Emperor Isaac loved riding to hunt cranes or hares, or to throw the spear at bears or boars (Psellus, *Chron.*, Is. Comn., Byz. T., p. 224). It was an advantage to live in the outskirts of Constantinople, so as to be nearer the country for hunting (Nic. Bry. I. 1, p. 17). John Ducas Caesar was a great hunter (*Hyle*, I. 18, p. 31, and II. 2, p. 41), as was his nephew Constantine, brother of Michael VII (Psellus, *Chron.*, Mich. VII, Byz. T., p. 265). In *Hyle*, II. 28, p. 65, a convalescent is ordered by his doctors to go out hare-hunting. Theophylact says that Constantine Ducas loved to hunt wild animals and to shoot them from horseback (παιδ. βασ., I. 4, *P. G.* 126, col. 257). Anna tells us of an occasion when Alexius' soldiers were forbidden to use their horses 'either for hunting or for rides', so as to keep them fresh for 'cavalry charges' later (XV. 2, p. 466).

[7] IV. 2, p. 105; VI. 10, p. 174; XIV. 8, p. 450; XV. 11, p. 496. Attaliates (p. 10) says Michael IV held an ἀγῶνα ἱππικόν τε καὶ πεζικόν. Benjamin of Tudela speaks of games every Christmas in the Hippodrome, and the *Knytlinga Saga* describes such games during the visit of Sigurd King of Norway to Constantinople in 1110. Riant (*Expéditions et pèlerinages des Scandinaves*, p. 199) says Alexius gave his guest a choice between the games and a sum of money. In *Hyle*, IV. 32, p. 104, Alexius gets up races as a farewell to the troops he is handing over to another general. A Vienna MS. (ed. by S. Papadimitriu in *Serta Borysthenica*) gives us a description, by a Logothete of the Course, of horse-racing in 1168.

[8] XIV. 7, p. 449.

measure, and then again recalled it from toils; but even the
recreation of this man was a second toil, a reading and examining of books, and attention to the command: "Search the
Scriptures". But hunting and the game of polo were of secondary, nay third-rate importance to my father, while he was yet
a younger man' and had no gout. Afterwards, by doctors'
orders, 'he gave himself to gymnastics and riding and other
sports', so as to get rid of the uraemia 'by continual rides'.[1]
In his hard life there was indeed little time for sport, little
even for the bath which was one of the great luxuries of
the age, a solemn performance hardly to be prepared for under
a week.[2]

There is no mention of any attendance by the Emperor or
his Court at any theatrical performance,[3] though the allusions
to stage matters in the *Alexias* are numberless. Such words as
ἐκτραγῳδεῖν, δρᾶμα with all its derivatives especially δραματουρ-
γεῖν, σκηνή, ὑποκρίνεσθαι, κωμῳδεῖν, occur so often that even
a bare list of references would be of formidable length. They
are nearly always used figuratively and in a derogatory sense,
but their constant recurrence shows what an important feature
of daily life the theatre must have been.[4] Anna puts into
' τραγικός ' the same tinge of contempt that we are apt to imply
in 'theatrical',[5] and ἐκτραγῳδεῖν is no more respectfully used;
δρᾶμα comes to mean a rather low trick,[6] and the phrase σκηνὴν
περιτιθέναι or ῥίπτειν implies the setting up or the tearing down
of a false pretence.[7] If ὑποκριτής has not quite acquired its present sinister meaning, both it and its cognate verb come very
near to it. And significantly enough the one play mentioned is
a farce acted by the Turks to jeer at Alexius' supposed malinger-
ing, while the only time we hear of actual σκηνικοί they are the
cruel instruments of mockery towards convicted plotters, for
whom they devise every kind of horrible insult.[8] Anna may

[1] See p. 216, note 8, below.
[2] VI. 10, p. 174; VIII. 1, p. 221; IX. 5, p. 255; X. 4, p. 279; XII. 1, p. 347:
3, p. 350. Baths as a part of medical treatment are mentioned in XII. 8 and 9.
[3] All dramatic performances had ceased; *G.B.L.* p. 644. 'The theatre built
of old by great Constantine' means the Hippodrome (VI. 10, p. 174).
[4] In Psellus (*Chron.*, Const. VIII, Byz. T., p. 23) we learn that this Emperor,
worthy father of the pleasure-loving Zoe, ἐμεμήνει περί τε τὰ θέατρα καὶ ἱπποδρομίας.
[5] XIII. 3, p. 382. So the θεατρικὴ παρασκευή, from which Alexius shrinks on
his victorious return to Constantinople, probably does not mean any *literal*
'theatrical display' (XV. 7, p. 482).
[6] XI. 2, p. 314; XIII. 1, pp. 377, 378; XIV. 2, p. 427.
[7] I. 12, p. 29; XII. 8, p. 366; XV. 6, p. 480. In XV. 8, p. 488, a real screen is
thrown down. The figure comes from throwing down the back-wall (σκηνή) of
a stage and revealing the actors concealed behind it.
[8] XII. 6; XV. 1, p. 461.

quote from the Attic dramatists[1] and allude to their choruses, but she seems to have but a low opinion of the art for which they laboured.[2]

Turning back to more serious matters and taking temperance in its broadest sense, we must remember that the Christian ideal of personal purity had led by Anna's day to preference (in theory at least) for the celibate and especially the cloistered, sometimes called the 'higher' or 'angelic' life. The shelter of a cloister sought willingly or unwillingly by men fallen from high estate, was also the fit resting-place of widowed princesses. It was a φροντιστήριον, a place for holy 'reflection'.[3] But furthermore there was, as we saw in connexion with Anna's marriage, a real or assumed conviction that it was better never to marry at all.[4] The stricter the celibacy, the greater the sanctity. The ascetic life of the Patriarch Cosmas, worthy of the hermits of old,[5] is much in his favour; and as we have already seen the prayers of monks are specially efficacious. For we must never forget that the lower clergy, who were married, lived like artisans and were treated as such: 'les moines seuls comptaient pour quelque chose'.[6] It was therefore all the more to be deplored that the monastic morals of the time had sunk very low; the fact that the strict rules of Irene's *Typikon* were necessary would prove this, even without contemporary letters and edicts. This however belongs to the region of historic fact; the point now at issue is Anna's standard as to what we so narrowly term morals.[7] We may state at the outset that in a woman ἀρετή has for her almost the same restricted sense as our term 'Virtue'. Sometimes it is used more broadly, as when the princess Maria is called the 'resting-place of all virtue',[8] but usually it means Chastity above all.[9] When Cinnamus

[1] Pref. 1, p. 1; 4, p. 8; I. 2, p. 5; 8, p. 19.
[2] XV. 9, p. 491. We may note that J. B. Eriau has written a book on *Pourquoi les pères de l'Église ont condamné le théâtre de leurs temps* (Paris, 1914, 2 vol.), on which the review in *B. Z.* XXIII, p. 422 makes this comment 'hauptsächlich wegen der unsittlichen mimischen Aufführungen'. Cecaumenus (*Strat.* p. 49) recommends generosity to all πλὴν μὴ εἰς μίμους. Cf. λόγ. νουθ. p. 94.
[3] e.g. VI. 3, p. 156; XV. 7, p. 485.
[4] See p. 32 above and Ch. 45 below. [5] II. 12, p. 68.
[6] Le Barbier, *St. Christodule et la réforme des couvents grecs*, p. 10.
[7] We may note that it is one of her gravest charges against the Bogomile heretics that their leader had 'certain female disciples, women of bad character and altogether vile' (XV. 8, p. 487). Cf. XV. 9, p. 490.
[8] XV. 11, p. 504. So in the *Prologue* to Anna's Will Irene is a 'living type of virtue', but also 'shines with virtues' (in the plural); later on ἀρετή is predicated of both Anna's parents and of her husband, lines 25–30, 57, 62. Anna Dalassena also in the *Alexias* has ἀρετή (virtue in general) and νοῦς (III. 7, p. 85).
[9] In III. 7, p. 86, 8, pp. 87, 88, the word seems to apply to Anna Dalassena's austere morals, also called her σωφροσύνη. In Cec. *Strat.*, p. 43, the well-born

wishes to praise the Hungarian wife of John II, he describes her as σωφρονεστάτην τε εἴπερ τινὰ καὶ ἀρετῆς ἐς τὰ μάλιστα μεταποιουμένην.[1] Even in a man ἀρετή has a special flavour of being unspotted from the world, and as such is rather curiously contrasted by Anna with wisdom. The Patriarch Cosmas is 'a rule and type of virtue'; he has practised 'every form of self-denial', he is indeed so 'reverend and full of sanctity' as to be credited with prophetic powers; yet Anna Dalassena is able to get rid of him by persuading people of his 'simplicity and unworldliness', and inducing them to bring about his resignation. His successor Eustratius Garidas 'makes a show of virtue', but in matters of the intellect lets himself be lamentably deluded by the heretic Italus.[2] Again, Bishop Leo of Chalcedon was 'not one of the very wise and learned (λόγιοι), but one who cultivated virtue and whose nature was austere and stern'.[3] Alexius, as we have already said, was 'altogether like a priest both in ἀρετή and in λόγος'.[4] So it is interesting to find him impressing on his son John that empire over himself is more to be esteemed than empire over his subjects,[5] and saying with more moral than poetic fervour:

$$ἕν, ἕν τὸ σῷζον· ἀρετή· ταύτης ἔχου.[6]$$

With this sentiment his daughter would certainly have agreed.

THE FOUR CARDINAL VIRTUES

21. FORTITUDE AND WISDOM

BETWEEN Temperance and the other three virtues which we shall be forced to consider together there is a link in twin qualities which Anna rates highly, and which presuppose a body kept under and brought into subjection. These are Vigilance and Energy. An 'unsleeping eye', the power to 'watch and be sober', a readiness 'when the crisis calls', come under

---

wife is συνέσει καὶ ἀρετῇ κεκοσμημένη, but not sufficiently so to resist the seductions of a young male guest. The writer's cynical moral is: Never trust your wife or your daughter with any man; keep them shut up and never have a woman for enemy or friend (pp. 42–3, 51, 61).

[1] *Hist.* I. 4, p. 5.
[2] III. 2, p. 75; V. 9, p. 148. So the heretic Nilus was 'clever in making a show of virtue' (ἀρετὴν ὑποκρίνεσθαι as of Garidas), and this virtue and his 'austere nature' gained him followers. But his ignorance and want of general education led him into gross theological errors (X. 1).
[3] V. 2, p. 129; cf. also VII. 4, p. 199.   [4] VI. 13, p. 181.
[5] *Mous. Alex.* I. 400.   [6] *Ibid.* 1. 254.

the first head.¹ The second head comprises the untiring self-denying δραστηριότης ('activity') which Anna so often praises even in an enemy,² and the almost untranslatable word σπουδή, to which perhaps 'zeal' comes nearest. This term of praise or its derivatives occurs with positively wearisome frequency throughout the book, just as it does in the *Hyle* of Nicephorus Bryennius.³ It is applied to eagerness in learning or teaching,⁴ determination to achieve an object by fair means or foul,⁵ military persistence,⁶ or mere haste of movement.⁷ It may even denote some quite insignificant ambition, such as Robert's decision to observe his racial customs in the wearing of a beard for a vow.⁸ σπουδὴ κενόσπουδος is a sort of proverb for lost labour.⁹ The guardian of another's interests should be σπουδεργός, just as it is a compliment to call a man ὀμβριμοεργός or θερμουργός,¹⁰ but σπούδασμα has a tinge of contempt in it, like our 'the rage'.¹¹ Since σπουδή figures as one of the chief virtues all through the *Alexias*, it is appropriate that Anna should use it of herself in the Preface, that Alexius should claim it for himself in the first Book, and that it should be predicated of all around him, especially his wife,¹² during his dying illness in the last.

Before we entirely leave Vigilance and Energy and pass on to Courage and Wisdom, we must not forget the kindred and characteristically Byzantine ideal of Sharpness, ὀξύτης. The word occurs so often on Anna's pages that a fair-sized essay might be written on it alone. Almost her first words about her father's prowess are, 'He was sharp in detecting what was

---

¹ III. 9, p. 92; IV. 4, p. 109; X. 5, p. 283; XII. 3, and 4, p. 356; 9, p. 371; XIII. 5, p. 389; 7, p. 397; XIV. 1, p. 421; 5, p. 437; 7, p. 444; XV. 1, p. 462; 6, p. 477. The phrase ἐγρηγορέναι διὰ παντός occurs in X. 4, p. 281; 7, p. 288; XII. 8, pp. 366, 368; XIII. 1, p. 376; XIV. 3, p. 429; XV. 2, p. 465. Cf. I. 1, p. 4.

² e.g. III. 2, p. 73 (*bis*): 7, p. 85; IV. 1, p. 104; VIII. 4, p. 229; IX. 3, p. 250; XII. 3, p. 353; XIII. 4, p. 386; XIV. 7, p. 444.

³ Cf. also *Mous. Alex.* I. 204, 401, and Cecaumenus, *Strat.* p. 19.

⁴ V. 8 and 9; XIV. 8, pp. 451, 453; XV. 7, p. 485·(*bis*); 8, p. 487.

⁵ e.g. II. 1, p. 44; VI. 2, p. 154; 4, p. 158; VIII. 7, p. 237; IX. 6, p. 256; 7, p. 258; 8, p. 261; 10, p. 265; X. 5, p. 285; 11, pp. 301, 304, 305; XI. 2, p. 316; 6, p. 324.

⁶ e.g. IV. 5, p. 112; V. 3, p. 132; 5, p. 138; VI. 5, p. 159; 6, p. 162; VII. 8, p. 206 (*bis*); 10, p. 215; VIII. 3, p. 226; IX. 3, p. 250; 5, p. 253; XI. 1, p. 310; XIV. 2, p. 426; 4, p. 435; XV. 5, p. 475.

⁷ XI. 10, p. 338; XII. 1, p. 348; 6, p. 364; XV. 1, p. 461; 6, p. 479.

⁸ VI. 7, p. 165.

⁹ XI. 9, p. 334; XIV. 3, p. 433; XV. 3, p. 465.

¹⁰ II. 11, p. 5; V. 5, p. 137; VIII. 1, p. 221; 2, p. 223; XV. 7, p. 483.

¹¹ XV. 7, p. 486. So Nic. Acom. uses the word of Irene's intrigues against her son (*John* C. 2, p. 4).

¹² Pref. 1, p. 1; I. 2, p. 6; XV. 11, p. 499.

needed and sharper still in carrying it out'.[1] A keenness of sight and hand, a presence of mind, γοργότης γνώμης,[2] and good judgement resulting in swift action, such is the full force of the word. Sometimes ὀξύς is coupled with that essentially Greek epithet which gave the scholastic St. Thomas in medieval Greek his title of ἀγχίνους instead of Aquinas. The Comneni brothers are ὀξεῖς καὶ ἀγχίνοι; Alexius especially is for ever showing quick-wittedness described in various terms.[3] Robert Guiscard has the same two qualities; Eumathius Philocales combines quickness with good sense.[4] Another laudatory epithet of the same class in the Alexias is κρυψίνους,[5] which we may note is used in a derogatory sense of Alexius by Nicetas Acominatus.[6] The possession of ὀξύτης νοῦ may enable a student to rise superior to blindness and other handicaps,[7] and gives the very desirable power of forecasting the future.[8] As we might expect, in an object of Anna's dislike or fear τὸ ὀξύ or ὀξύρροπον acquires a sinister complexion;[9] thus her brother John showed by his eyes 'as far as a baby can, his secretiveness and sharpness'.[10] Once the Greek fleet attacks ὀξέως καὶ ἀσυντάκτως, distinct blame being conveyed.[11] But otherwise Anna's standard throughout is that of Thucydides, who in praising the Athenians in general and Themistocles in particular says: 'They are equally quick [ὀξεῖς] in the conception and in the execution of every new plan.'[12] 'From his own native acuteness . . . he was the ablest judge of the course to be pursued in a sudden emergency and

---

[1] I. 1, p. 4; II. 1, p. 45; 3, p. 47; III. 5, p. 81; 7, p. 86; IV. 6, pp. 115, 117; 7, p. 119; X. 1, p. 269; XI. 11, p. 339.
In IV. 6, p. 114, the statement that Alexius' plans were ποικιλώτερά τε καὶ ὀξύτερα than those of Rob. Guiscard hardly seems borne out by his severe defeat. Nic. Bry. (I. 6, p. 20) says Alexius was ὀξύτατος καὶ δραστηριώτατος, and yet kind and sweet-tempered.

[2] IV. 6, p. 117; VII. 2, p. 192. The adverb γοργῶς has the same sense, passim. (See p. 495, note 13, below.)

[3] II. 2, p. 46; III. 8, p. 88; VII. 6, p. 203; 10, p. 214; VIII. 1, pp. 221, 223; 2, p. 224; 5, p. 233; IX. 1, p. 246; 9, p. 262; X. 7, p. 289. In II. 4, p. 51, the populace admire Alexius' dash (ὁρμή) καὶ ἀγχίνοια so much that they make a song about him. Slowness may be fatal (VII. 3, p. 198; IX. 2, p. 249). The word ὀξύς had a variable meaning in older Greek. Thus Iamblichus uses it in De Comm. Math. Sci. to mean 'clever' and in the Protrepticus to mean 'hasty' in temper. For admiration of cleverness we may quote Gul. Apul., de Rebus Normannorum, Bk. IV, line 82, who says of Alexius 'Astuta ratione vigens'.

[4] VI. 7, p. 165; XIV. 1, p. 421.   [5] II. 10, p. 62.
[6] John C. 2, p. 5.
[7] V. 8, p. 144; IX. 10, p. 266.
[8] Cf. V. 7, p. 142; VI. 14, p. 184; X. 10, p. 299; XII. 5, p. 358.
[9] VIII. 2, p. 223; 5, p. 231; 9, p. 240; IX. 6, p. 257; 9, p. 263; X. 5, p. 286: 11, p. 304; XI. 3, p. 317. She seems to shudder at the ingenious τέχνη, whereby Bohemund had himself conveyed from the port of Antioch to Corfu in a coffin (XI. 12).
[10] VI. 8, p. 168.   [11] XI, 10, p. 336.   [12] Hist. I. 70.

could best divine what was likely to happen in the remotest future. . . . In a word Themistocles . . . was of all men the best able to extemporize the right thing to be done.'[1] Of just this kind of mind Alexius was according to his daughter a perfect example. His special cleverness perhaps lies in his power, as we might say, of sizing up a situation or a character,[2] a power gained by 'not taking superficial views nor shutting his eyes to the truth',[3] and enabling him to think quickly of the best thing to do. He won as many victories ὀξύ τι στοχασάμενος as he did by might.[4] And in this matter as in all others Irene was his help-meet, 'sharp in seeing what was advantageous to the Emperor, sharper in perceiving the machinations of his enemies'.[5]

Anna is always much impressed by inventiveness. Several times she praises her father for some 'novelty' in one of his various fields of activity.[6] The first of these passages occurs in her solitary reference to that statecraft about which so many Byzantine manuals were written. It is just after her father's accession, when he had created a number of new offices and titles, and she says:

'And if any one should erect sovereignty into a kind of science (ἐπιστήμη) and lofty philosophy, as being the art of arts and science of sciences, he would marvel at my father for making new the things under his sovereignty, both the offices and the names, like some scientist and master builder. Yet we must remember that those who preside over the sciences of speech invented such matters of names for clearness' sake, but this arch-professor of kingship Alexius had ordained everything for the benefit of the empire, making frequent changes both in the order of affairs and in the calling of names.'[7]

This rather obscure sentence seems almost an apology for her father's display, in so serious a matter as statecraft, of the 'newness' which she so greatly admires in him elsewhere. She speaks with reverential awe of his wonderful new line of battle,[8] of his devices for defending a town καινοπρεπέστερον, as well as of his siege-engines after a wholly original pattern,[9] of the alarming fire-ships which he built such as the Pisans had

---

[1] *Hist.* I. 138. Nic. Bry. (III. 2, p. 69) says his father was δεινὸς ὑπαισθέσθαι τὸ μέλλον καὶ προφυλάξασθαι, στρατηγῆσαί τε κατ' ἐχθρῶν δοκιμώτατος.

[2] V. 7, p. 143; VI. 10, p. 173; VII. 6, p. 203; VIII. 1, pp. 221, 223; 2, p. 224; 5, p. 232; X. 11, p. 302; XI. 11, p. 339. In all these passages we have Anna's favourite ὁποῖος ἐκεῖνος.

[3] IX. 6, p. 256; X. 11, p. 302. For his resourcefulness, expressed in various ways, see also IV. 6, p. 115; VII. 10, p. 214; X. 10, p. 299.

[4] XV. 3, p. 467.   [5] XII. 3, p. 352.

[6] So Cecaumenus (*Strat.* p. 13) gives as a vital maxim in war: νέα σοφίσου.

[7] III. 4, p. 79.   [8] Especially XV. 7, p. 481.

[9] III. 9, p. 92; XI. 2, p. 312.

never seen,[1] and of his (to her) ingenious and surprising way of handling the Bogomile heresy.[2]

It has been often pointed out that the Byzantines admired Cleverness more than Courage, outwitting your enemy more than overcoming him by force of arms. This finds full expression in the *Alexias* and is indeed such a striking part of Anna Comnena's psychology that it must be dealt with rather fully. She does admire Valour, sheer physical courage (except in a hated Bogomile heretic, as in XV. 10), but she admires Discretion more. Her generals, friends or foes, all show bravery and fortitude;[3] her father does not differ from the barbarous Robert Guiscard and Bohemund in being φιλοκινδυνότατος (he is also μεγαλοκίνδυνός τε καὶ πυκνοκίνδυνος),[4] and he is for ever σφαδάζων to fight, so that he has to be restrained from rashness by his followers. He once states as an axiom that a noble death is better than ignominy, ' τοῦτο γὰρ ἴδιον μεγαλοψυχίας '.[5] Furthermore in every battle there is at least one single combat vividly portrayed, and a certain chief gets a high position entirely owing to the Emperor's recollection of his personal prowess fourteen years before.[6] But all the time she agrees with her uncle Michael Ducas that while the 'common herd' may expose their life in battle, an emperor must not. It is not cowardice that restrains him, but duty; for his death 'brings world-wide peril', and if saved he may 'fight another day and win'. On one occasion a leader 'reckons it a victory not to expose himself to danger for no necessity'.[7] Indeed any general or admiral, far less precious than an emperor, may be pardoned for not facing superior forces or wind and enemies together, because 'not even Heracles can fight, they say, against two'.[8]

[1] XI. 10.   [2] XV. 10, p. 495. It was καινοπραγία τις καὶ τόλμη παράδοξος.

[3] e.g. Pref. 3, pp. 3, 5; I. 1, pp. 3, 4; 4, p. 9; 5, p. 10; 10, p. 23; 13, p. 33; 14, p. 34; XIII. 9, p. 400; XIV. 5, p. 440. When fleets retreat they should blush for it (XIV. 3, p. 430). A rebel is contemptuously dismissed by Anna as 'very cowardly towards every form of war' (XII. 5, p. 360). Cowardice is 'ignoble' (XIV. 5, p. 439), and Pacurianus dreads being suspected of it (VI. 14, p. 183). Robert Guiscard is brave, though violent and wrathful (IV. 8, p. 121).

[4] I. 1, p. 3; IV. 3, p. 107; 8, p. 121; V. 4, p. 133; 5, p. 137; VI. 11, p. 176; VII. 3, p. 195; XI. 5, p. 321; XIII. 4, p. 386; 8, p. 398; XV. 3, p. 467.

[5] I. 5, p. 12; II. 4, p. 50; VII. 3; X. 4, p. 280; cf. Thuc. *Hist.* II. 42 of men 'minded to resist and suffer, rather than to fly and save their lives'. Once Anna's Caesar yearns to fight, but restrains 'his raging spirit' (XV. 5, p. 475).

[6] XII. 2, p. 350; cf. IV. 6, p. 117.

[7] V. 3, p. 133; 4, pp. 134, 135, 136; VII. 3, pp. 197, 212. So of the King of Germany (V. 3, p. 133; cf. Theophylact, παιδ. βασ. II. 22, *P. G.* 126, col. 281) and 2 Sam. XVIII. 3.

[8] I. 6, p. 15; II. 9, p. 61; III. 9, p. 92; 11, pp. 95, 96; V. 4, p. 133; VI. p. 153; 10, p. 172; 12, p. 176; 13, pp. 181, 184; VII. 4, p. 199; IX. 5, p. 253; X. 3, p. 275; XI. 1, p. 310; 6, p. 325; 7, p. 329; XII. 8, p. 369; 9, p. 369; XIII. 7, p. 396; 8, p. 399; XIV. 2, p. 427; 5, p. 440.

It is the combination of ἀνδρεία καὶ σύνεσις (the two qualities being usually alternatives) that makes a man the best chief; he should have 'cleverness, strength, and daring'.[1] Anna has unvarying praise for the resourceful man who is ἀκαταπτόητος, ἀκατάπληκτος, ἀκλόνητος, ἀκατάσειστος and the like, qualities which argue the calm steadfast mind so dear to her aristocratic temper.[2] This is the very antipode of that insolent ὕβρις or ὑπεροψία or φρύαγμα which has its head turned by success, and draws down on itself ἔκτισις.[3]

The greatest merit may be marred by blowing one's own trumpet or even letting others blow it;[4] it is a sign of vulgarity, just as a 'lawless deed' of daring is 'worthy of a barbarian soul',[5] and bravery may be dimmed by ῥᾳδιουργία.[6] When the 'crazy Latin who dared to sit down on the Emperor's seat' dies at Dorylaeum, we feel that he is punished not only for reckless disregard of Alexius' wise counsel, but for that never-to-be-forgotten act of insolence.[7] It is almost equally foolish to scorn advice, to be elated by success, or to cherish forlorn hopes, three flaws in the sweet reasonableness which was part of Anna's military ideal. She, like Cecaumenus in the *Strategicon*, con-

---

[1] II. 4, p. 50; V. 1, p. 127 (VIII. 2, p. 225; XI. 7, p. 329; XII. 9, p. 372). In V. 1, p. 126, Alexius and Robert Guiscard are said to be γνώμῃ καὶ ἀνδρίᾳ κατάλληλοι, rivals.

[2] In view of the fact that Alexius hardly passes a year of his adult life without conducting some war, Anna may reasonably be proud of his dogged endurance. He was 'the same whether in victories or in defeats' (VII. 9, p. 213; cf. XIV. 7, p. 499). He would hardly rest even in his beloved Constantinople (I. 3, p. 8; X. 5; XIV. 1, p. 419; 3, p. 350; and cf. VII. 11, p. 217 with VIII. 1, p. 221) or enjoy ordinary recreations (V. 4, p. 135; XIV. 4, p. 433), or take necessary sleep (II. 7, p. 58; VII. 10, p. 214; VIII. 5, p. 231; X. 5; XIII. 8, p. 398), and at crises his calm intrepidity 'causes wonder to all' (X. 9, p. 295; XIII. 1, p. 375). When Irene is 'vexed and grieved' at criticism of him he laughs, δεινὸς ὢν περὶ τὰ τοιαῦτα (XV. 3, p. 466). Other passages bearing on this point are: III. 12, p. 99; IV. 1, p. 103; V. 4, pp. 134, 135; VI. 5, p. 159; IX. 5, p. 254; XIII. 8, p. 398. In V. 3, p. 133, Anna couples τόλμη καὶ γενναιότης γνώμης. See p. 454 below, also p. 304 on the sinister aspect persistence assumes for Anna in the case of heretics.

[3] I. 1, p. 3; III. 12, p. 98; V. 6, p. 141; 8, p. 146; VI. 5, p. 160; VIII. 5, pp. 233, 234; X. 9, p. 295; XIII. 2, p. 381. Alexius dreaded any public triumph (XV. 7, p. 482). In XIV. 2, p. 423, the ὕβρις of Tancred leads him to absurd boasting. Cf. Thuc. III. 39, 'Too swift and sudden success is apt to make cities insolent' (εἰς ὕβριν τρέπειν); also Thuc. III. 82; IV. 17.

[4] VII. 3, p. 198; XV. 3, p. 468; 11, p. 496. Cf. Pref. 1, p. 1. The boasting of the two sons of Romanus Diogenes ends in the death of one (VII. 3, pp. 195, 196). So the Latin priest dies boasting (X. 8). The ideas and phraseology of XV. 3, p. 468, remind one strikingly of Psellus' Funeral Oration on his mother, *B. G. Med.* V, p. 11, and of Nicephorus Bryennius' words about his father, *Hyle* IV. 15, p. 96.

[5] VII. 9, p. 211.

[6] VII. 8, p. 209. τὸ θαρρεῖν however is commendable on one's own side (XIII. 3, p. 382), and even ῥᾳδιουργία 'when the καιρός presents itself' (*ibid.* 4, p. 387). [7] X. 10; XI. 3, p. 317.

siders that a general's supreme duty is to save his men and
avoid risks,[1] and though his valiant example may at times spur
his soldiers on to courage, he is at liberty to flee when his men
do.[2] She would entirely have endorsed the sentiment of Polybius,[3] that Rashness is a great fault in a general. Indeed she
says it was her uncle Isaac's only blemish as a warrior.[4] Her
father on the other hand 'had Reason for his captain, and was
neither carried out of himself by passion, nor swept away by
desires'.[5] From the very outset of her story she takes as much
pride in his 'tricks and devices' as in his valour, and proclaims
with infinite satisfaction: 'If ever any one was inventive and
good at devising paths out of tangles, my father was that man.'[6]
If there is no path open but retreat, his captain Reason permits
that. He has no blame for his general Taticius when he lets
himself be frightened away from Antioch, partly by dread of
his crusading allies, partly from dislike of sharing their hardships; very shortly afterwards we find this general holding
another important command.[7]

In short the Byzantines in such matters were full of inconsistencies between theory and practice. In theory every one of
noble birth was brave and fought to the death, regardless of
self; in practice they were cautious and cunning, and could
always find excuses for the most inglorious actions. We may
end this part of the subject with Anna's Confession of Faith on
the subject.

'I think it is courage (ἀνδρεία) when a man gains a victory with
wise counsel; for passion in the soul and energy (δραστήριον) without
reflection come under condemnation, and it is rashness instead of

[1] III. 11, p. 96 (see Cec. *Strat.* pp. 9, 10, 16, but contrast p. 54); VI. 10,
p. 172; 13, p. 180; XI. 11, p. 338. In I. 6, p. 15, a wise retreat shows τὸ ἀνδρεῖον
καὶ εὔψυχον. This idea of discretion as the better part of valour for outnumbered
forces runs all through Thucydides, e.g. *Hist.* VII. 11, and VIII. 79. He says in
VIII. 27 that there is no dishonour in such a retreat, but 'the deepest dishonour
under any circumstances in a defeat'.
[2] VII. 10, p. 215; XIII. 5, p. 390; XIV. 2, p. 427.
[3] *Hist.* III. 81, 9.
[4] III. 3, p. 78. Youth is deplorably rash (VIII. 7, p. 237). So are the Varangian
Guard (IV. 6, p. 116). Alexius sends two generals with one body of Crusaders,
chiefly 'to restrain them as far as possible from senseless dashes' (XI. 8, p. 331).
[5] XIII. 4, p. 386. See Ch. 57 below.
[6] I. 2, p. 5. See Ch. 60 below.
[7] XI. 4, p. 319; 10, p. 335. It is interesting to find Leo (*Tactica*, XIX. 35)
saying openly: 'Few in the crisis of battle prefer death to inglorious flight, whether
among barbarians or Greeks.' He also (66) forbids fighting unless with a force
equal to or greater than the enemy's. Cf. Alexius' advice to his new recruits
(III. 11, p. 95). Yet Anna's anxiety in XI. 6 by throwing the blame on the
Crusaders to explain away her father's failure to follow their perilous path, seems
to show she was ashamed of it. See p. 462 below.

bravery (θράσος ἀντὶ θάρσους). For we are brave in fighting people whom we are competent to fight, and rash when we are not competent. Thus whenever a danger hangs over us, so as to attack us face to face from ' [lacuna in text], ' then we take up the war some other way and strive to conquer the enemy without fighting. Now the highest valour is the wisdom of generals in gaining a victory without fighting. . . . For I have always thought the best plan was to devise something crafty and general-like (πανοῦργον¹ καὶ στρατηγικόν) whenever the army is not adequate against the strength of the enemy. . . . For Victory is one, but the ways by which it accrues to the generals are diverse and varied in nature. . . . Now my father the Emperor sometimes conquered his enemies by might, sometimes by using thought, and on some occasions had some brilliant inspiration (ὀξύ) in the actual battles and by daring straightway gained the day. Sometimes he made use of a strategic trick, sometimes he fought with his hands, and thus he often set up many trophies in a way least expected. For the man was a lover of dangers if any one was . . . but sometimes with bared head he stripped to encounter them . . . sometimes he pretended to yield and enacted a terrified man, as occasion served and events suggested.'

With a comparison of her father to a caltrop, 'for these, however you throw them, will stand upright for you', and one of her stereotyped protestations that truth and not filial partiality compels her to praise so splendid a person as her father, she turns back to her history.²

Certainly if the Byzantines did not aspire to be harmless as doves, they set immense store by being wise as serpents. Sharpness and Caution were even more highly esteemed than Courage, and Fortitude was but the handmaid of Wisdom.³

In connexion with Fortitude one point that must strike an Anglo-Saxon is the open way in which Anna's characters give vent to their emotions.⁴ This is of course a Homeric trait and one still to be observed in Latin countries, but it is specially noticeable in the *Alexias*, because it seems to us so inconsistent with the 'unshaken' quality and the 'dignity' on which as we have seen she lays so much stress. Anna at one place represents her

¹ Cf. XIII. 4, p. 387, where she asserts that on occasion a general must be ready πρὸς πανουργίαν.
² XV. 3. See p. 517 below.
³ The constantly recurring phrase τὴν ἑαυτῶν σωτηρίαν πραγματεύεσθαι gives the key to much of Byzantine behaviour (IV. 6, p. 116; VI. 1, p. 153; IX. 5, p. 255; XIII. 8, p. 399; 12, p. 412; XIV. 5, p. 440 (bis); XV. 8, p. 487 and cf. IX. 2, p. 249). The contrasting words such as τῆς ἑαυτῶν ζωῆς ἀφειδήσαντες are significantly rarer (II. 7, p. 58; VII. 3, p. 197; X. 3, p. 277; XI. 7, p. 329; 8, p. 331).
⁴ The embracing of one man by another is of course a mere matter of national custom (I. 3, p. 8; 11, p. 25; II. 6, p. 57; 11, p. 65; VIII. 6, p. 235; 8, p. 238). Yet in X. 9, p. 293, 'embraced him effusively' has a ring of contempt for Latin exuberance.

father as sitting or standing unmoved by hunger or fatigue or
pain or exasperation all through the endless verbosities of the
Crusaders, and enduring all as the due punishment of his sins.[1]
Or again she swears to the truth of her history 'by the Emperor's
perils on behalf of the welfare of the Greeks, and by the
struggles and misfortunes which he endured on behalf of the
Christians',[2] and says that the tension of cares and unceasing
devotion to noble causes helped to bring about his heroically
borne illness and his death.[3] Yet this model of Fortitude weeps
and groans in sorrow or repentance or sympathy, and on one
occasion at least Anna feels it necessary to impress on us that
this did *not* show 'weakness of soul'.[4] It is not only women who
perform 'the duties of kinship' by mourning and shrieking,
though tears in theory are womanish;[5] men in pain are expected to howl and roar like lions,[6] they become 'frantic with
grief' in suffering or fear,[7] they groan and weep with sympathy
or rail with uncontrollable anger,[8] and every battle-field re-
sounds to heaven with shouts and yells,[9] to which even the
Emperor contributes.[10] Indeed to shout the war-cry (ἐννάλιον)
is a regular order given by a general,[11] as a means of terrifying
the enemy.[12] Barbarians according to Anna have a peculiarly
hideous battle-cry, and even howl all night round an enemy's
camp like dogs or wolves.[13] But everyone shouts or cries or

---

[1] XIV. 4, p. 437.

[2] XIV. 7, p. 445; XV. 10, p. 495.

[3] This is the doctor's verdict in XV. 11, p. 498. So 'endless hardship' and
'frequent campaigns' killed her husband Nicephorus Bryennius (Pref. 3, p. 5).

[4] III. 5, p. 82; IX. 10, p. 265; XII. 1, p. 347. We have already spoken of his
tears over his fallen soldiers (p. 106 above). In Nic. Bry. I. 12, p. 26; II. 26, p. 63,
Alexius weeps 'founts of tears' in sympathy with his mother over his brother
Manuel's death, and is 'filled with tears and groans' over the deserted state of his
grandfather's home at Castamon.

[5] I. 14, p. 34; VI. 6, p. 162; XV. 2, p. 463: 10, p. 495. Irene throughout
Alexius' last illness is 'deeply moved by the feeling of grief'. She weeps floods of
tears, 'wails continuously', and beats her breast. After his death she is distracted
with grief, and excitedly strips off all her insignia of sovereignty (XV. 11). Anna
Dalassena mourns bitterly over her son Manuel (I. 1, p. 3). The mother of Michael
Psellus prays over her son's future with 'hot tears' (V. 8, p. 144).

[6] I. 3, p. 7.

[7] I. 6, p. 16; III. 12, p. 98; IX. 10, p. 265.

[8] I. 3, p. 8; VIII. 8, p. 239; IX. 7, p. 259.

[9] I. 5, p. 12 (*bis*); 6, p. 15; 8, p. 19; VI. 1, p. 153; 11, p. 176; 14, p. 183;
VII. 11, p. 216; IX, 1, p. 247; X. 9, p. 297; XI. 2, pp. 313, 314; XIII. 3, p. 386.
In the sack of Constantinople the shouts and cries were such that 'a man might
have said an earthquake was occurring' (III. 5, p. 81); cf. the last fight in Syracuse
Harbour in Thuc. VII. 71.

[10] V. 4, p. 134; VIII. 5, p. 233.

[11] V. 5, p. 139; VI. 14, p. 183; VII. 1, p. 189.

[12] XI. 4, p. 319.

[13] VII. 11, p. 216; XV. 5, pp. 474, 475; 6, p. 476. So Thucydides speaks scornfully of 'barbarian cries' (IV. 126).

wails aloud to express his feelings, and tears his hair or beats his breast or wrings his hands or smites his thigh in joy or fear or sorrow.[1] A distracted general dies of 'the intolerable affliction' of his son's death, 'after beating his breast for three nights and days with a sling-stone'.[2] After unpardonable violence in debate, the repentant tears of John Italus were 'his only trait worthy of a philosopher'.[3] Alexius restrains the crowd 'by shaking his head and waving his hand and shouting frequent admonitions'.[4] The birth of children to the sovereign calls for 'paeans' of joy real or pretended;[5] so, with dancing and hymn-singing added, does a national victory,[6] while disloyal subjects welcome their emperor's enemies with shouts.[7] The choice of an emperor is appropriately called ἀνάρρησις[8] or ἀναγόρευσις,[9] and cheers (εὐφημίαι) in sign of devotion are among the most important of imperial prerogatives.[10] After a conspiracy has been discovered the suspects shield themselves by shouting out their desire to retain their emperor on the throne, and their gratitude for his amnesty.[11]

A good specimen of the contemporary attitude towards emotion is given in XV. 10, when Anna is describing the ravages of the Turks. We have all the stock phrases: 'swords and spears were sharpened', there were 'battles and wars and slaughters.' Besides being plundered the land was 'defiled by blood of Christians'. Of the survivors some were carried away captives and 'wailed over their sufferings'. Others were seized with 'trembling' and hid themselves 'deeply groaning', while they 'bewailed one a son, one a daughter', or wept and 'dropped hot tears like women', over some other kinsman. The lot of no

[1] I. 15, p. 36; IX. 5, p. 254; 7, p. 260; X. 4, p. 280; 9, p. 295; XI. 12, p. 341; XIV. 1, p. 420; XV. 11, p. 506. In Nic. Bry. I. 5, p. 19, Anna Dalassena tries to get her way with her husband 'by tears and groans'; cf. also his I. 12, p. 26: 25, p. 38.
[2] VII. 6, p. 204.
[3] V. 8, p. 146, reading μόνον οὐκ ἀφιλόσοφον.
[4] IX. 8, p. 260. Public oratory has moved far from 'the decorum of the Bema', first violated by Cleon, Plut. Nic. 8 (ed. Sintenis, Vit. III. p. 10).
[5] VI. 8, pp. 167, 168.   [6] VIII. 3, p. 225.   [7] X. 3, p. 274.
[8] e.g. II. 7, p. 57; VI. 14, p. 183, and often elsewhere.
[9] II. 8, p. 59.
[10] II. 7, 8 and 11; III. 2, p. 73; IV. 2, p. 106; VI. 8, p. 167; XI. 2, p. 314; XII. 8, pp. 267, 268; XIV. 6, p. 444. In V. 3, p. 133, εὐφημία is used for the acknowledgement of a man as duke, and in II. 8, p. 60, of a Caesar. In sound a prayer might be mistaken for it (VII. 8, p. 206).
[11] IX. 9, p. 264. The somewhat analogous description of the enthusiasm of Constantinople over Alexius' victory as reported by Camytzes is worth quoting: 'The inhabitants of Constantinople became one voice and one lip and cheered (ἀνευφήμουν) and hymned the Emperor, and worshipped him (ἐξεθείαζον) and blessed him for his generalship, and knew not how to restrain their pleasure over him' (XIV. 7, p. 448).

one, dead or alive, captive or refugee, was ἄδακρυς οὐδ᾽ ἀστέ-
νακτος. It is an interesting instance of how Anna as we might
say piles on the agony, especially as it does not agree very well
with the picture given elsewhere in the book of conditions in
Asia Minor under the Turks, who seem on the whole to have
been ruthless in their ravages but merciful to the persons of the
conquered. As for Anna herself, she cannot mention a painful
subject or touch on a sad chord of memory without 'dizziness',
'streams of tears', 'hottest tears', the sensation of a burning fire
and a piercing sword in her soul, and a longing to break into
'mourning and lamentation'.[1] Yet she can always so to speak
check the flow by thinking of her duty as a historian; she can
reserve her grief to 'the appropriate time', or in other words
'husband it for the suitable passages'.[2] Sometimes in connexion
with her father she is conscious of a double task, first as biographer and secondly as chief mourner over his death and her
other woes.[3] All through her long account of his last illness,[4]
there is an undertone or burden of wailing. She is anxious for
us to realize that though it did not unfit her for wise judgement and practical service her grief was intense, as great as her
mother's and greater even than that of her sisters.[5] And however
genuine her emotion may have been, her parade of it cannot
fail to jar on a twentieth-century reader.

Turning back from Fortitude to Wisdom we find other things
that jar on us. False excuses in a secretary seem to Anna worthy
of a solemn pun,[6] and Alexius' pretence of showing 'much
honour' to his brother Isaac, simply because he feels himself
sure of the crown, is a legitimate way of 'consoling his brother
by dissimulation about the sovereignty'.[7] Later on he is be-
lauded as a κρυψίνους, a man who can ἐπισκιάσαι things at will.[8]
Again, his daughter feels only pride in his use of superior astronomical knowledge to play a trick on the ignorant Patzinaks,
who it must be admitted were on their side trying to cheat
him.[9] The proverb which she twice quotes about enemies,
'The crab never learned to walk straight',[10] would appear to

[1] Pref. 4; IV. 8, p. 121; VII. 2, p. 191; XIV. 3, p. 431; XV. 5, p. 475; 11,
pp. 496, 506, 507. [2] I. 10, p. 23; 12, p. 27; IV. 8, p. 121.
[3] XV. 11, pp. 495, 496. [4] XV. 11.
[5] She speaks feelingly of the general sorrow: 'those [masculine] whose voices
were not overpowered with grief wailed, beat their breasts and lamenting dismally
sent their voices up to heaven . . . weeping over their benefactor' (XV. 11, p. 506).
[6] II. 8, p. 60.
[7] II. 7, p. 58. Cf. μεθ᾽ ὁσίου προσχήματος to a heretic in XV. 8, p. 487.
[8] III. 10, p. 63.
[9] VII. 2, pp. 192, 193. Cf. the deceitful peace overtures of the Dalmatians in
IX. 4, p. 252. [10] VI. 4, p. 158; IX. 1, p. 247.

a dispassionate reader unpleasantly appropriate to the great
Alexius, and we find ourselves positively pleased when he and
his generals are outwitted by the even more unscrupulous
Bohemund.[1]

Before we leave the subject of Wisdom it may be interesting
to spend a few moments on a form of it to which Anna attaches
great importance. This is the Wisdom that comes from experience, and Anna, who was by no means young when she wrote,
values it highly. The words πεῖρα, ἐμπειρία, πολυπειρία occur
again and again as terms of approval.[2] They are used of her
husband,[3] of generals and admirals and soldiers without number,[4] once of doctors in the specialized sense which corresponds
with our word 'empiric',[5] but above all of Alexius, whose
experience is recognized even by his enemies.[6] The Varangian
Guard at Durazzo suffer from ἀπειρία and over-zeal, and in the
same passage 'birth and military experience' are coupled together as the two great military requisites.[7] The idea of πεῖρα
runs into that of skill, skill in strategy,[8] skill in mechanics or
shipbuilding,[9] skill in dialectics;[10] while στρατιωτικαί or πολεμι-
καὶ ἐμπειρίαι may be translated 'military arts'.[11] Thus, 'much
experience of Latin customs' is a good equipment for a diplo-
mat,[12] and one of the great advantages gained by study of
'sublime writers' is ἡ ἀπὸ τούτων ἐμπειρία.[13]

[1] XI. 4 and 12.
[2] e.g. I. 4, p. 10; and repeatedly elsewhere. This respect for experience runs
through Thucydides; it was the great advantage which the Athenians had over
the other Greeks. Similarly Polybius shows the superiority of ἐμπειρία μεθοδική
over inexperience (Hist. I. 84, 6), and Nic. Bry. I. 10, p. 24, contrasts the ἀπειροπόλεμος Greek general with the ἐμπειροπολέμοις Turks; cf. Al. I. 4, p. 10, and XI.
8, p. 331.
[3] Pref. 4, p. 6; cf. XV. 5, p. 475.
[4] I. 1, p. 4; 5, p. 10; 11, p. 24; III. 6, p. 84; 7, p. 85; 12, p. 97; IV. 1,
p. 103; 4, p. 109; 5, p. 112 (bis); V. 5, p. 137; VII. 3, p. 195; VIII. 2, p. 224;
X. 2, p. 274; 10, p. 298; XI. 2, p. 314; 5, p. 323; XII. 8, p. 368; XIV. 5, p. 441;
XV. 3, p. 469; 5, 474; 6, p. 478.
[5] IV. 4, p. 110.
[6] I. 1, p. 4; 7, p. 18; III. 9, p. 92; IV. 5, p. 113; V. 1, p. 126; VII. 10, p. 214;
X. 3, p. 275, and 9, p. 297; XV. 3, pp. 469, 470.
[7] IV. 6, p. 116; cf. V. 1, p. 126. The population of Constantinople being ἀνάλκιδες
καὶ ἀπειροπόλεμοι are terrified of the Crusaders (X. 9, p. 295). Lack of military
experience may prove fatal (X. 6, p. 286; XII. 8, p. 367; cf. III. 11, p. 95). The
rebel Rhapsomathes is so ἀπειροπόλεμος as not to be able to ride (IX. 2, p. 249).
John Comnenus is defeated through inexperience and rashness (IX. 4, p. 252).
Alexius as a young Emperor shuns the reproach of being ἀπειροπόλεμος καὶ
ἀνεπιστήμων ἀρχηγός. (V. 1. p. 127.) The Turk Tzachas had in his youth been
taken prisoner 'deceived by inexperience'. (VII. 8, p. 208.) Aspietes is called
ἀπειροπόλεμος, but we should rather describe him as a good soldier who had
deteriorated (XII. 2, p. 349).
[8] XIV. 3, p. 429.
[9] VII. 8, p. 205; XI. 1, p. 311.
[10] V. 8, p. 146.
[11] XI. 6, p. 325; 10, p. 338.
[12] XIII. 9, p. 400.
[13] XV. 7, p. 486.

This reverence for experience is connected with the feeling towards Old Age which the Byzantines had inherited from the Greeks. As Mahaffy has pointed out in his *Social Life in Greece*, the Greeks with their love for beauty could not help shuddering at the physical effects of advancing years. Yet in theory Old Age was venerable in classical times from its wisdom, as the words γερουσία and *senatus* show. Anna expresses this idea when she says: 'Age has something to say wiser than the young.'[1] Anna herself was at least sixty-five when she completed her book,[2] and we know that in her day people rarely lived over sixty,[3] so that she was quite one of the elders. It is interesting to compare her views with those of her father, who also lived longer than the average. In his poems to John he exalts πεῖρα, saying:[4] 'Follow old men who bring counsel, in whom is experience of many things, whose teacher is Time.' At the same time, if there be found a *young* man who is wise, his advice is not to be despised, for the combination is τεράστιόν τι καὶ Θεοῦ δῶρον μέγα.[5] John must have been just such a wonder, for though he was a youth yet among his fine qualities his father mentions proficiency in war, a merit usually associated with maturity and experience.[6]

THE FOUR CARDINAL VIRTUES
22. JUSTICE

AS far as Justice in the narrowest sense of the word is concerned, Anna's standard is much the same as our own. The qualities of 'just dealing' and 'contempt for money' are valuable in every judge everywhere; they are probably no less rare in the East now than they were in her day. When she ascribes them to the official whom Alexius sends to restore financial order in Cyprus, she also speaks of his ταπεινοφροσύνη, the essentially New Testament characteristic of 'lowliness', in this instance an amiable and not overbearing manner.[7] In his first poem to his

[1] III. 7, p. 86. So Thucydides considers the youth of Alcibiades to have been, in his attaining influence at Athens, a handicap only counteracted by his noble birth (*Hist.* V. 43). Cecaumenus (*Strat.* p. 46) advises his reader to avoid the young, and also any of the old who think and do τὰ νεωτέρων.
[2] XIV. 7, p. 447, gives us the date of writing as 'the 30th year' after the death of Alexius, fixed for us by other sources as 1118, and we know Anna was born December 1, 1083 (VI. 8, p. 166).
[3] *Mous. Alex.* I. 202.   [4] *Ibid.* I. 72.   [5] *Ibid.* I. 83.
[6] *Ibid.*, II. 61. Nic. Bry. (I. 1, p. 16), says that the first Manuel Comnenus managed affairs ἐπιστημόνως λίαν καὶ νεανικῶς, another instance of the wisdom of age coupled with the ardour of youth.
[7] IX. 2, p. 250.

son John, Alexius himself lays the greatest stress on justice and
probity in governors; all who neglect these should be put to
death without mercy.[1] So it is satisfactory to learn that in his
daughter's eyes at least this Emperor was the embodiment of
justice.[2] At a late period of his reign she says:[3] 'After having
entered the palace and offered thanksgivings to God and the
Mother of God' [for victory] 'he turned to his usual ways. For
having settled the external wars and beaten off the seditions of
rebels he turned to law-courts and laws. For as either occasion
presented itself he was the finest dispenser of peace or war.'
He was not above having his enactments criticized by a trusted
secretary, a man 'versed in Greek laws', so anxious was he to
decree things 'worthy of imperial $\mu\epsilon\gamma\alpha\lambda o\phi\rho o\sigma\acute{\upsilon}\nu\eta$'.[4]   His clemency to criminals was, as we have seen, a marked feature of
his character as depicted by his daughter, but the details of his
legal and financial administration are not now relevant. It is
the Byzantine conception of Justice and Honour as a whole
that here concerns us.

To begin with, oath-breaking is significantly regarded as a
heinous crime.[5] The religious sanction given to oaths, by calling
God and saints and angels to witness, a sanction vitally necessary in that age of mutual suspicion, was of course largely
responsible for this point of view. When Alexius writes to
Henry the German, he three times emphasizes the need for the
King to take an oath in a proper and binding manner, and
the vicarious swearing of his 'faithful Albert' is not enough.[6]
Throughout the book the solemn paraphernalia of oaths and
pledges and hostages would seem to tell the same tale. No
one trusts his neighbour's bare word. The Comans give oaths
and $\pi\acute{\iota}\sigma\tau\epsilon\iota\varsigma$ to their successive allies, and this is done by or
expected from other warriors also;[7] hostages usually of noble
birth are given or promised either independently or in exchange
by Greeks to Turks,[8] by Turks to Greeks,[9] by Dalmatians to

---

[1] *Mous. Alex.* I. 372 sqq.
[2] Only once does she accuse her father of unjust or at least hasty behaviour to
a subordinate (XIII. 7, p. 396).
[3] XIV. 7, pp. 448, 449.
[4] XIII. 1, p. 376. We possess twenty-seven of these enactments (collected by
Zachariae von Lingenthal in his *Jus Gr.-Rom.*) with the titles of four more. See
p. 8, note 3, above.
[5] Hence the $\phi\rho\iota\kappa\alpha\lambda\acute{\epsilon}o\iota$ $\acute{o}\rho\kappa o\iota$ of XIII. 12, p. 411, and the $\acute{o}\mu\acute{o}\sigma\alpha\iota$ $\tau\grave{\alpha}$ $\phi\rho\iota\kappa\omega\delta\acute{\epsilon}\sigma\tau\alpha\tau\alpha$
of XIII. 12, p. 410; XV. 8, p. 489; cf. Attal. pp. 11, 15 and Cec. *Strat.* p. 74.
[6] III. 10, p. 94. The 'compact' comes in again in V. 3, p. 130.
[7] I. 9, p. 22; 13, p. 32; VII. 6, p. 202; VIII. 4, p. 228; X. 2, p. 272; XI. 2,
p. 315.
[8] I. 2, p. 5; IX. 1, p. 247.   [9] IX. 1, p. 247.

Greeks, by Normans to Greeks and by Greeks to Normans,[1] even by doubtfully loyal subjects or allies to their lord.[2] Barbarians as might be expected break their oaths, and Greeks themselves when they wish to be believed have to 'swear by God', preferably on an object of acknowledged sanctity too large to be overlooked.[3] Even an Emperor's word of honour had to be confirmed by a written document, if possible a golden bull 'in red letters and with a golden seal', which would create a valid πίστις καὶ ὁμολογία for many years to come.[4] The Turk Tzachas asks the Greek general for a 'contract in writing as is the custom with Greeks and also with us barbarians'.[5]

Even in friendly relations men are not trusted overmuch. An official going to take up a post gives πίστεις τῆς δουλείας,[6] and on the other hand Alexius' brother-in-law George Palaeologus will not leave such a post without seeing the imperial seal-ring which ensures his safety from treachery.[7]

This brings us to the idea of a safe-conduct. The Norman count Bryennius,[8] compelled by his disloyal troops to surrender Castoria, 'utterly refused to go over to the Emperor, but swore never to bear arms against him, if only he would give him men to escort him safely as far as the boundary of the Greeks, and thus let him go to his own land. And the Emperor very readily granted his request.' We have here two features of warfare known even to this day, parole on the one side and a safe conduct on the other. Later on the Comans get an escort back to their own land, and in return give hostages in confirmation of their promise not to plunder.[9] The Turks who surrender at Smyrna bargain for the right to 'depart home immune from harm'.[10] The Emir Tzachas is to go free in consideration of leaving Mitylene unmolested; he violates his part of the compact, so the Greek general does his.[11] In this particular case there is a curious use of casuistry. The argument of the Greek subordinate to his superior, in begging leave to attack the perjured Turk, is not 'an eye for an eye', in which there would have been rough justice; it is as follows: 'Thou truly didst swear, but I was not present. Do thou keep inviolate the pledges which thou hast given, but I who was not present and

---

[1] IX. 4, 5, and 10; XII. 4, p. 356; XIII. 9, 10.
[2] I. 16, p. 38; VIII. 6, p. 235.
[3] II. 2, p. 46; 5, p. 53; VII. 4, p. 199; VIII. 9, p. 242. So promises and oaths are as it were contrasted in IX. 6, p. 257.
[4] II. 8, p. 60; III. 2, p. 73; 4, p. 79; VII. 6, p. 202; IX. 8, p. 261. See also p. 236 below.
[5] VII. 8, p. 208.   [6] I. 16, p. 39.   [7] IV. 5, p. 112.
[8] VI. 1, p. 154.   [9] VIII. 6, p. 235.   [10] XI. 5, p. 322.
[11] IX. 1, pp. 247, 248.

did not swear and know nothing of your mutual agreements will make ready for the battle against Tzachas.' He receives the desired permission. Later on Bohemund's visit to Alexius on the one side and that of the hostages from the imperial camp to him on the other, are carefully guarded by a safe-conduct.[1] The proud 'barbarian' declines to be reproached for his own past breaches of contract, to which his opponent piously ascribes all the misfortunes of the Norman army, but he will see to it that faith is kept with himself.[2] In the end a solemn treaty is signed and sworn,[3] terminating the hostility of twenty-seven years.

Now the mentality displayed in much of this is different enough from our own to need comment. Of course we must never forget that, as Sudermann taught us in *Die Ehre*, conceptions of Honour differ so entirely in different countries and at different times that it becomes almost impossible to give a definite meaning to so Protean a word. Still the Byzantines were Christians, and we have a right to feel shocked when we see them worshipping the Father of Lies almost equally with the Spirit of Truth. Thus in Anna's pages oath-breaking pure and simple may bring down the judgement of heaven, but any form of deceiving an opponent is a sign of superior brains. It is easy enough to persuade any one that some ostensible friend will betray him if it suits his interest; the dupe is conscious that he would act in that way himself, as all around him do.[4] The thought of such a proceeding moves Anna not to disgust but to 'laughter';[5] such fickle characters are merely put on one side as 'unprofitable to the state', as well as frequently unsuccessful.[6] No one is surprised at any man or army or city changing sides; and Constantinople, Durazzo, Nicaea, and Antioch are all treacherously surrendered. It is fully expected that every one will be swayed by the crudest self-interest, into which the right and wrong of the case hardly enter.[7]

Springing from this same motive of self-interest we find, as

---

[1] Once before this a question of a safe-conduct had come up between Bohemund and Alexius, who thus desires to shield the carriers of his bogus incriminating letters from the wrath of the Norman prince (XIII. 4, p. 389).

[2] XIII. 8–11; XIV. 1, p. 419.   [3] XIII. 12.

[4] I. 2, pp. 5, 7; V. 1, p. 125; and VI. 6, p. 163. For the attitude of mind we may compare Thuc. V. 43.

[5] I. 15, p. 37. Similarly she seems amused with the cleverness by which Theodore Gabras gets his way by a well-calculated parade of paternal affections (VIII. 9, p. 241).

[6] I. 16, p. 39.

[7] II. 4, p. 50. In IV. 6, pp. 117, 118, the Dalmatian troops openly wait to see which side is winning and to espouse that.

another indication of the standard of honour, a startling readiness to betray one's associates. Not only are deserters almost an indispensable help in war; not only do rovers carry news from one camp to another;[1] a man's plans are often not safe with his closest friend, if that friend has anything to gain by disclosing them. Thus Adrian Comnenus by persuasion urges, and an official by torture induces, Nicephorus Diogenes to gain his own pardon by betraying his fellow conspirators; in fact he does this not once but twice, his second plot having been revealed by one of his friends.[2] The scheme of Gregory Gabras to escape is told by him to several confidants, and made known to the Emperor by one of them. This is the court butler, who seems to have acted as the Emperor's detective, being sent on a later occasion to the front, with instructions to write back confidential letters about the campaign and the general conducting it. It is curious to see that in course of time, as often happens, the Emperor gets suspicious of his own spy and keeps him in practical banishment.[3] In two subsequent conspiracies the terror of the leaders and the disloyalty of a slave respectively put Alexius in possession of all the names;[4] and finally Diblatius the Bogomile confesses under torture the secrets of his leader.[5] Every one is looking out for himself and it is better to trust no one.

The fact that a man has sued for peace or sworn a treaty does not do away with the advisability of preparing an army against him, or stirring up for him the hatred of others. An emperor may instruct his envoys to agree to terms which he has no intention of fulfilling,[7] for the end justifies the means and 'every sort of trick'.[8] To genuine allies lying is in theory base; Anna tells us that her father harangued his soldiers in

[1] VII. 2, p. 190; 8, p. 208; IX. 4, p. 253; 9, pp. 210–12; XIII. 8, p. 399; XV. 1, p. 460; 4, p. 470; 6, pp. 476, 477. The story of the Turks Saisan and Masout and Pucheas is a sort of kaleidoscope of treachery, ὁποῖα εἴωθεν ὡς ἐπίπαν γίνεσθαι, as Anna adds cynically (XV. 6, p. 479).

[2] IX. 7, p. 259, to 8, p. 262, and 10, p. 266.

[3] VIII. 9, p. 242; XI. 9, pp. 333, 334.

[4] XII. 6, p. 361, after a nameless informer had given the first hint, XIII. 1, p. 378.

[5] XV. 8, p. 487.

[6] VI. 10, p. 171; cf. VII. 2, p. 192; VIII. 4, p. 228; 5, p. 230. Thus Alexius fears his so-called friends the Crusaders, and intrigues against them with the common enemy the Turk (XI. 1, 2).

[7] VI. 12, p. 178; cf. X. 11, p. 304, of his pretended consent to a request.

[8] VII. 8, p. 206; XIII. 4. Butumites' lie to Baldwin is only regrettable because it is not believed (XIV. 2, p. 427). Alexius successfully hoodwinks the Crusaders as to the capture of Nicaea (XI. 2, p. 314). So in I. 2 and 3, Alexius deceives the men of Amasea 'because he had not sufficient forces to stand up against such numbers'. See also X. 4.

the field on its iniquity and was scrupulous to avoid even the appearance of so great an evil.[1] Yet this does not prevent the Greeks and the Crusaders from so freely intriguing against each other that they may be said to vie in duplicity. The end of their uneasy partnership is described in a passage worth quoting as showing what allies could suspect, rightly or wrongly, about one another: 'Now Bohemund' [who had previously gone behind the backs of his Crusading comrades and the Greeks to gain Antioch, and 'was keeping the plan secret'], 'not wishing to hand over Antioch to Taticius according to the oaths previously given to the Emperor, but coveting it for himself, plots an evil plot by which he might induce him to depart, though reluctantly. Therefore going to him he says: "I wish to reveal to thee a secret, being solicitous for thy safety. A report brought to the ears of the Counts has troubled their minds, namely that the Emperor has persuaded the Sultan to dispatch against us the troops coming from Chorassan. And thinking this true the Counts are conspiring against thy life." Taticius, moved by fear as well as by the famine then prevalent, immediately leads his troops away.'[2] Potential or actual enemies, especially heretics, may legitimately be inveigled into a man's power and kept there by any method.[3] Even when the actors are 'barbarians' this makes distasteful reading,[4] but when it comes to a Thirteenth Apostle we feel positive disgust, and are thankful that in this respect at least the old order has changed.[5]

In short, it is not unfair to say that though Anna's history is saturated with the notion of *noblesse oblige*, we do not find it 'obliging' any one to the simple everyday virtues of truth and uprightness. In a somewhat free application of the familiar line we may say of the twelfth-century Byzantines that their Honour rooted in Dishonour stood.

[1] VIII. 6, p. 235.   [2] XI. 4, p. 319.
[3] VI. 2, pp. 154, 155; 10, pp. 174, 175; VII. 2, pp. 192, 193; X. 4; XV. 8–10.
[4] The Turks act thus in VI. 12, p. 179; IX. 3, p. 251; XV. 6, p. 480. We may compare the way the Duke of Brittany lured the Connétable Olivier de Clisson by pretended hospitality and then 'fettered him with three bolts of iron' (Berners' translation of Froissart, Vol. II, Ch. 83).
[5] The question of Stratagem in War is more fully dealt with in Ch. 60 below.

23. IDEALS OF OTHER WRITERS

SUCH then are the general lines of Anna's character, as unconsciously delineated by herself. Her standard of affection and kindness is high, her piety is real, her views on self-restraint are so sound that not one impure statement or suggestion finds a place in her whole book. She has Faith in God, but little Faith in man, and no Hope. She hates cruelty, counts peace and forgiveness as Christian duties, and has Charity for all but heretics and her brother John. Temperance is her watchword, and she admires Justice, but Fortitude and Wisdom are inextricably mixed in her mind with cunning and guile, while of honour in our sense of the word she has no conception. Now in all this she was the product of her age, as a cursory glance at contemporary writers will show.

We need not dwell long on her predecessor Michael Psellus, whose 'sharpness of mind' she so greatly admires, and who was 'famous as having arrived at the summit of all wisdom'.[1] It is well known how, as Rambaud[2] points out, he flattered the four emperors whose minister he was, and then held them up to obloquy in his *Chronography*. Like Anna, he admires ἀγχίνοια and ὀξύτης beyond all other qualities,[3] while in his religious attitude he is less free from superstition than she is. He showed practical esteem for the 'angelic' life by going, though only temporarily, into a monastery. (As Rambaud says, in those days 'on entrait au couvent, on en sortait'.) Finally, if we take a pleasanter side of his character, his devotion to his mother (to say nothing of his other family affections) was as great as the parent-loving Anna herself could have wished.[4] But the form of his *Chronography*, rather resembling gossipy memoirs than a real biography, is so different from that of the *Alexias* that we can hardly expect much similarity in detail.

It would be interesting to compare Anna's ethical standard with that of each of her contemporaries individually. But space does not allow of this, and we must spend on the matter only a few words. Attaliates, who held office under Romanus Diogenes, admires much the same qualities as Anna:

---

[1] V. 8, p. 144. [2] *Rev. Hist.* III. pp. 241–82.
[3] *Chron.*, Mich. IV, Const. IX, Is. Comn., Mich. VII, Byz. T., pp. 47 (*bis*), 164, 209, 265.
[4] E. Renauld, *Étude de la langue et du style de Michel Psellos*, p. 430. For his monastic life see *Rev. Hist.* III. pp. 252, 267.

wisdom, piety, generosity, and clemency. His heroes show on
the one hand energy in suppressing enemies and rebels, and
on the other λόγων σπουδάσματα. His mob is turbulent and
foolish and sacrilegious;[1] his noble ladies are marked by αἰδώς,
his noble lords by bounty and justice. And above all every
event that happens is due to God's satisfaction or displeasure
with the mortals concerned.[2] 'Nemesis from the Divinity' comes
as a punishment and a call to repentance: 'for the true and
blameless faith of us Christians, when we chance to fall away
from virtues, is rather an accusation and a condemnation.'[3]
His morality is exalted and stern indeed.

Scylitzes, about 1018–79, and his copyist Cedrenus, at the
beginning of the next century, are not quite as high-minded.
Cedrenus calls the seizing and blinding of a man by treachery
'a sweet and wonderful thing';[4] Scylitzes narrates without comment the death under torture of a man accused of peculation.[5]
But the broad lines of conduct are the same; lavish giving by
superiors is to be commended, though too often met by ingratitude from inferiors, virtue is contrasted with learning, over-
confidence is always punished.

A certain family likeness may probably be traced in all
Byzantine morality, but there is one eleventh-century writer
whose sentiments so closely resemble Anna's that we almost feel
she must have read him. This is the Cecaumenus (or more
probably two of the name), whose *Strategicon*, from which we
have already quoted several times, was apparently written between 1071 and 1078, while its supplement, the λόγος νουθετη-
τικός, is believed by its editor[6] to have been addressed in 1081
to no less a person than Alexius. A short summary of the points
of agreement between Cecaumenus and Anna may be permitted here. They are fully in accord in referring everything
to God's Providence, yet teaching that He helps those who not
only fear Him but help themselves. Both are overflowing with
Biblical allusions and attach great importance to prayer and
study of sacred books;[7] both preach justice, courage, kindness,
clemency, courtesy, and moderation. Both give the same picture of an unstable, almost anarchical, state of public affairs,

---

[1] They rush into the streets at any excitement, make a noise like an angry sea,
and even plunder churches (pp. 10, 14, 15).

[2] On p. 293 he makes Botaniates say the judgement of heaven, i. e. his own success,
proves the wickedness of his opponent Bryennius.

[3] p. 197.   [4] p. 714 A.

[5] pp. 867 D–868 A.   [6] B. Wassiliewsky. Petrograd, 1896.

[7] Cecaumenus was ἄμοιρος λόγου (p. 75), but enjoined Bible study (pp. 19,
83).

where even the strong ties of blood are not unbreakable and no man can trust even his friends or his wife and daughter ;[1] while honour towards enemies is unknown. Both admire filial reverence, and enjoin liberality to monks, kindness and respect to inferiors and even barbarians, and justice to all.[2] Envy may be averted by humility, and Peace is better than War, whose aim and goal it is. In war a general should never be careless or overtrustful, he should show craft in concealing his strength and vigilance in the use of scouts, and he should above all seek not to lose men in fight. Much may be done by diplomacy and bribes, and rash daring or self-confidence ($\H{\upsilon}\beta\rho\iota\varsigma$) is hardly less to be deprecated than cowardice. We only wish that Anna had given us as complete a list of things to be avoided as does her predecessor, i.e. the foolish young, bad friends, fresh mushrooms, borrowers, drink, bloodshed, superstition, nearly all doctors, and any parade of learning.

Another comparison deserves special care, that between Anna and her husband Nicephorus Bryennius, on whose history we know she drew. In the *Alexias* and the *Hyle* there are not only likenesses of word and phrase and even of whole passages; we also note the same general point of view. As usual every event is referred to Providence,[3] yet Bryennius' characters show a most mundane reliance on such things as advantageous marriages[4] and bribes of all kinds.[5] 'Excess of virtue' ($\mathring{\alpha}\rho\epsilon\tau\mathring{\eta}$) makes an emperor neglect his own worldly interests, but this same $\kappa\alpha\theta\alpha\rho\acute{o}\tau\eta\varsigma$ fits him to be a bishop.[6] Men are praised on the one hand for being merciful and kindly, on the other for being $\mathring{\alpha}\gamma\chi\acute{\iota}\nu o\upsilon\varsigma$ and $\beta\alpha\theta\upsilon\gamma\nu\acute{\omega}\mu\omega\nu$ (what we should call 'cunning'), for possessing noble birth and the valour that goes with it, for showing $\sigma\pi o\upsilon\delta\acute{\eta}$ and giving proof of Experience. Woman, the weaker vessel, occasionally displays the fine qualities of men. War entails war-cries and deserters and plundering; an enemy may be craftily seized at a banquet, but the lives of fellow Christians should be spared. Kinsmen play an important part and a general argues as to his plans with his followers. The

---

[1] Cecaumenus might almost be said to have taken as a motto *Micah*, vii. 5: 'Trust ye not in a friend, put ye not confidence in a guide: keep the doors of thy mouth from her that lieth in thy bosom.'

[2] $\mathring{\alpha}\nu\theta\rho\omega\pi o\acute{\iota}$ (or $\lambda o\gamma\iota\kappa o\acute{\iota}$) $\epsilon\mathring{\iota}\sigma\iota\nu$ $\mathring{\omega}\varsigma$ $\kappa\alpha\acute{\iota}$ $\sigma\upsilon$, in *Strat.* pp. 7, 12; cf. in Anna VIII. 6, p. 234. So in Alexius' Novel 35, about slaves.

[3] *Hyle*, II. 5, p. 43; III. 11, p. 77; 17, p. 80; 19, p. 81; 21, p. 82; IV. 15, p. 97.
[4] *Ibid.* III. 6, p. 72. [5] *Ibid.* III. 10, p. 77; 16, p. 79, etc.
[6] *Ibid.* III. 20, p. 82; 24, p. 84. We have already seen that as to ambition Bryennius and his wife did not agree (*Hyle*, I. 3, p. 18; II. 17, p. 55; III. 5, p. 71; and see the story of Anna's conspiracy against John and Bryennius' apathy in Nic. Acom. *John C.* 3, pp. 7, 8).

bravest heroes weep and groan and 'roar like lions' with emotion. These points recur so often that it seems useless to give references. Except that the *Hyle* is on the whole written in easier Greek, it would be hard to tell whether any passage came from it or from the *Alexias*, so wholly alike is the spirit displayed.

As to the two other chroniclers whose lives and writings were more or less contemporary with Anna, John Zonaras (whose life Krumbacher believes to have extended 'vom Ausgange des 11. bis etwa in die Mitte des 12. Jahrhunderts'), and Michael Glycas (who according to the same writer 'wurde im ersten Drittel des 12. Jahrhunderts geboren und lebte bis gegen das Ende des Jahrhunderts'),[1] much the same may be said. Zonaras like Anna ascribes the Greek defeat by the Patzinaks to their vainglory, and their subsequent victory to their humbled frame of mind, ταπεινωθείσης τῆς στρατιᾶς καὶ τὸ πᾶν τῆς θείας ἐξαρτώσης ῥοπῆς.[2] Monasteries are good refuges for the sad or the infirm.[3] Generosity in giving, whether to friends or the needy or conquered enemies, is admirable in a monarch;[4] so is consideration for the sick and aged.[5] Popular sayings about future events are chronicled with at least partial belief.[6] An emperor should be approachable to all, but should show special honour to those who live ἐναρέτως. He must be moderate, reasonable, slow to anger, merciful, and temperate, but to these virtues of a private man he should add justice, adherence to the laws, and impartiality. Zonaras considers that Alexius did not rise to this imperial ideal;[7] Anna would have entirely accepted the ideal, and denied that her father fell short of it. The theory of the two writers is identical, even if in this instance they differ as to its application. Glycas[8] like Zonaras blames Alexius for arbitrariness in government, but he admires his philanthropy and, again like Zonaras, he represents the people as *fearing* his death, an incidental touch that seems to prove his popularity and confirm Anna's statements on the subject. We may note that Glycas and Zonaras tell, as she does not, of many catastrophes in the reign, such as earthquakes, fires, and ruinous storms of wind and rain. Possibly her silence was due to her filial desire not to darken her picture unnecessarily.

The writings of Alexius himself have already been mentioned

---

[1] *G. B. L.*, pp. 371, 380.   [2] *Epit.* XVIII. 23.
[3] *Ibid.* 21, 22, 24.   [4] *Ibid.* 24, 27.   [5] *Ibid.* 27.
[6] *Ibid.* 28, where there are three such recorded; Anna only records the two about Robert's death (VI. 6 and 7), but Glycas follows Zonaras in this matter.
[7] *Epit.* XVIII. 29.   [8] *Bibl. Chron.* III. pp. 333–5.

in several connexions. His poems have been quoted when the sentiments agreed with Anna's; his novels deal with special incidents and are hardly relevant here. As to his letters to the Abbot of Monte Cassino,[1] the most striking feature, apart from their execrable Latin, is the constant reference to the prayers of the Abbot for the Emperor, entreated by him as indubitably efficacious and rewarded with munificent gifts (as from a humble sinner to a great saint) of money and other objects.[2] If Anna honoured monks and approved of generosity towards them, she was certainly following in her father's footsteps.

It is therefore instructive to see how two of the Emperor's clerical subordinates regarded him. Archbishop Theophylact of Achrida praises him fulsomely for his suavity, temperance, prudence, and moderation, as well as for his achievements in war; he speaks slightingly of his attitude towards learning.[3] On the other hand he belauds Constantine Ducas' ἀγχίνουν and μνημονικόν,[4] his sense, dignity, and philosophic intelligence, while the Empress Maria is extolled to the skies for generosity, philanthropy, hospitality, learning, piety, and concern over her son's education, qualities which combine to make her 'the dove of the Lord, beautiful and perfect'.[5] In the second part of his book written to the young prince, he holds up a very high standard of kingship, i.e. virtue, self-discipline, love of work, piety, hatred of flattery, devotion to the State, military vigour, wise choice of associates (especially learned and educated men), and above all clemency (τὸ φιλάνθρωπον). He should only use the sword ἀναγκαίως καὶ βιαζόμενος; if otherwise he is a 'Tyrant' and not an 'Emperor'. He should surpass all his subjects in virtue and wisdom, and should remember the maxim: λόγοι τιμῶσί σε, τίμα καὶ σὺ τοὺς λόγους. Then he may hope to have God

---

[1] Three are given by P. Riant in his *Epistula Spuria Alexii Comneni ad Robertum* (pp. 41–5); the last two of these are also published as Epistles V and XI in Hagenmeyer's *Kreuzzugsbriefe*.

[2] For the parade of humility we may compare the 'Nil boni habeo in me . . . super omnes homines pecco' in the third letter with the words put by Anna into her father's mouth in XIV. 4, p. 437, ἀξίως πάσχω· εὐλόγως μοι ταῦτα γίνεται διὰ τὴν τῶν ἐμῶν ἁμαρτιῶν πληθύν. Also the account in Nic. Acom. (*John C.* 2, pp. 5, 6) of the dying Alexius turning his eyes τοῖς ψυχαγωγοῖς ἀγγέλοις, and holding up his hands τὸ θεῖον ἐξιλεούμενος ἐφ' οἷς που καὶ παρεσφάλη τοῦ δέοντος. In the first letter Alexius sends a *pallium triacontasimum* (i.e. adorned with thirty stripes of gold and purple) for the altar of the Abbot, and in the third he sends an *epiloricum*, a garment gilded outside but concealing an iron *lorica* or corslet of thongs such as gave to St. Dominic, after fifteen years of such a penance, his name of *loricatus*.

[3] Λόγος εἰς . . . Ἀλέξιον (*P. G.* 126, cols. 288–305).

[4] Παιδ. βασ. I. 5 (*P. G.* 126, col. 257). For the combination, cf. Psellus on Const. IX, *Chron.*, Byz. T., p. 164.

[5] Παιδ. βασ. I. 7–13 (*P. G.* 126, cols. 260–5).

as βασιλείας συλλήπτορα.[1] In all this Anna would have con-
curred, with the mental note that her father fulfilled all the
requirements.

Euthymius Zigabenus is of course principally concerned with
Alexius as the theologically minded sovereign who ordered the
compiling of the treatise against heresies, known as the *Panoply
of Dogma*. He therefore lays the greatest stress on his piety and
his love of true doctrine. Yet he is also not a little impressed
by his military resourcefulness and his 'myriad trophies' in war.
Like Anna, he greatly admires his inventive mind, his ἀγχίνοια,
and his skill in 'answers'. But noblest of all is his zeal against
heresy, sharpened by study of 'the divinely inspired writings'.[2]

The later writers who in part cover the same historical ground
as Anna, are John Cinnamus, born shortly after 1143, Nicetas
Acominatus, whose birth is put by Krumbacher[3] 'um die Mitte
des 12. Jahrhunderts' and who certainly outlived the Latin
capture of Constantinople in 1204, and the anonymous writer
of the *Synopsis Chronike*,[4] which is brought down from the Creation to 1261. These do not really concern us, but it is interesting
to note briefly how persistently the same point of view as to
essential matters of life and ethics survived in the Byzantine
Empire.

In reading Cinnamus' account of wars, we might fancy ourselves back in the *Alexias*, so universally accepted as part of the
natural course of events is the existence of deserters and be-
trayers of plans, and of mercenaries who change sides. Feigned
flights and crafty attempts to detach one enemy from another
are as admirable in a man[5] as ἀρετή and pious liberality in
a woman, while the prayers of monks on his behalf and his own
generous gifts at holy shrines should bring success to a monarch,
especially one who converts the heathen to Christianity. Like
Anna he despises barbarians *per se*.

Nicetas like Anna shows us the prominence in court life of
the kinsmen and especially of the mother, though women are
not as a rule highly esteemed. Nobility, open-handedness
especially to the Church, mildness, clemency, military prowess,
and the strenuous self-discipline that prefers a tent to a palace
and drives away luxury and obscene talk like a λύμη, these are

---

[1] Παιδ. βασ. II. 1–5, 12, 16, 21, 22, 25–8, 30 (*P. G.* 126, cols. 268 sqq.).

[2] Three poems of Euth. Zig. published by C. Neumann in *Gr. Geschichtschr. des 12.
Jahrh.*, and Pref. to *Panoplia Dogmatica* (*P. G.* 130, cols. 20–9).

[3] *Op. cit.*, p. 281.

[4] Ed. by C. Sathas in *Bibl. gr. med.* VII, 1894.

[5] He thinks it foolish to call flight cowardice if it is successful; the only object
is to win, and all means are equally good. He protests against the new-fangled
notion of Honour brought in by Manuel Comnenus from Western Chivalry.

all predicated of his heroes, especially John II.[1] John shows
φιλοδωρία to his favourite Axuch and φιλανθρωπία to his troublesome sister Anna; he pardons his rebellious brother Isaac, not
nursing secret grudges ὁποῖα οἱ ἐν ἀρχαῖς φιλοῦσι τεχνάζεσθαι,[2] a
cynical view of sovereigns not to be paralleled in the *Alexias*.
Pious rulers wish to make pilgrimages, shrink from war 'with
Christians', and never resist the will of God, to whom all success
must be ascribed.[3] Dreams and prophecies and oracular sayings
have their importance;[4] a crown passes to a son, especially the
eldest son, ὡς πατρῷος κλῆρος,[5] and fealty is sworn on the Sacred
Books.[6] It is a similar environment to Anna's similarly described, and whereas she has her wonderful father for a subject,
Nicetas has the equally wonderful John, about whom, as
'approved' by all and the κορωνίς or climax of his house, he
allows himself the satisfaction of saying πᾶσαν ἀρετῆς ἰδέαν μετιὼν
οὐκ ἀνίει.

The Anonymous Chronicler writes on the same lines, though
much more fully, and like Anna he holds Alexius as a hero. In
contrast with his slothful predecessor Botaniates, who cheapened
all honours by reckless bestowal and let himself be ruled by
slaves, Alexius appears as energetic, pious, ready to confess
wrongdoing,[7] liberal to monks and nuns and the children in
his Orphanage,[8] learned and valiant against false doctrine,[9]
endowed with σωφροσύνη and wisdom.[10] Irene is a prudent
administrator and has reached a high pitch of ἀρετή; she is to
the poor rather a mother than an empress.[11] So, too, the Emperor devotes himself without stint to his empire and is loved
by all for his father-like beneficence; God gave him many
victories, especially over the 'God-hated' Patzinaks, and by
crushing all rebellions He showed the world 'by the events
themselves that his sovereignty was guarded and guided from
above'.[12] He was gifted with high thoughts and zeal (σπουδή),
and he met every crisis with appropriate action. He made
friends of enemies by his κρυψίνοια, and though he did usurp
the throne and take Church-treasure, his subsequent behaviour
entitled him in both these matters to praise rather than blame.[13]

---

[1] *John C., passim.*   [2] *Ibid.* 3, p. 8; 9, p. 22.
[3] *Ibid.* 11, p. 26: 12, pp. 28, 29.
[4] *Ibid.* 5, p. 12; 11, pp. 27, 28; 12, p. 30.
[5] *Ibid.* 12, pp. 29, 31.   [6] *Ibid.* 12, p. 31.
[7] e.g. in his Golden Bull περὶ τῶν ἱερῶν inserted in *Anon. Syn. Chron.* p. 173.
He has a σεβασμία ψυχή, ibid., p. 177.
[8] *Anon. Syn. Chron. ibid.*
[9] His pretended discipleship to Basil the Bogomile is a βουλὴ συνετὴ καὶ θαυμασία,
ibid. p. 179.   [10] *Ibid.* p. 183.
[11] *Ibid.* p. 182.   [12] *Ibid.* p. 183.   [13] *Ibid.* pp. 185–6.

In short he was 'great in counsel and great in deed', and he ruled for thirty-seven years θεοφιλῶς τε καὶ εὐλαβῶς. He died as a monk and was buried in the Philanthropos monastery which he himself had built.[1] Even Anna could not have written a more sustained encomium on the great Alexius, and even she could hardly have dismissed more lightly the rumour (λόγος) about Irene's ambitions of a crown for her daughter as opposed to her son, and about the Emperor's death-bed duplicity in making both parties think he favoured their claims.[2]

Only one other writer need detain us, and that merely because he lived and wrote in Anna's own day. This is Theodore Prodromus, the needy poet, who addressed poems to every possible member or hanger-on of the imperial family, in the effort to earn a scanty livelihood. Under the circumstances we need not give much heed to his principles or sentiments; no Vicar of Bray was ever more determined to worship the rising sun, and his conventional epithets of praise are too wearisome to enumerate. We will only say that in his verses Alexius shows εὐνομία in peace, prowess in war, gentleness, constancy, &c. Irene has a 'bountiful hand', and displays piety, pity, and 'every other virtue'. Anna, we hear, practised ἀρετή with vigour, and thought it the appurtenance of character, not of birth; John is a paragon of every virtue.[3] This exhibition of cupboard love in the *Graeculus esuriens* is hardly less pathetic than comic, but it teaches us little about the moral standard of the day.[4]

We have however examined enough material to enable us to repeat our former assertion that in the main features of her outlook on life Anna is the product of her age. But two qualities are peculiar to herself. The first is her pride of birth combined with intellect, the second is her filial devotion. We have spoken of her birth and her life in a palace, we have dealt with her affection for her father as far as it illustrates her moral character. We must now consider that intellect on which she so greatly plumed herself, how it faced her environment in twelfth-century Byzantium, and above all how far it enabled her to draw a faithful picture of her times.

[1] *Ibid.* p. 186.
[2] *Ibid.* p. 187. Curiously enough τὸ κρυψίνουν, previously used (p. 184) in praise of Alexius, here conveys blame, if indeed he deserved the epithet.
[3] See a selection of the poems in *P. G.* 133.
[4] The same is true of the works of the other court poet Nicolas Callicles, edited for us by Leo Sternbach. Their subjects, religious or funereal or purely laudatory, prevent the writer from giving any real expression of his opinions, though VII, on the death of a princely child, is full of feeling and charm. John Comnenus appears throughout in a favourable light (XVI, XX, XXV, XXX).

IV. ANNA AND EDUCATION

24. REFERENCES IN *ALEXIAS* I–VIII

IT is important to know exactly what Anna says about education and learning, and we must examine *seriatim* the passages where she deals with them. In the famous opening of her Preface (to which we have so often to refer) she gives this explanation of her resolution to write: 'I, Anna, daughter of the Emperor Alexius and the Empress Irene, nurtured and born in the purple,[1] not unversed in letters, but having bestowed special pains on the study of Greek (τὸ ἑλληνίζειν ἐς ἄκρον ἐσπουδακυῖα) and being not unpractised in rhetoric, and having well studied the Aristotelian system (τὰς 'Αριστοτελικὰς τέχνας, literally the 'arts' or 'rules') and the dialogues of Plato, and having fortified my mind with the *quadrivium* of sciences[2]— for these things must be told, and there is no bragging in the matter, how many gifts Nature and my zeal for knowledge have bestowed on me, and the God above apportioned and favourable opportunities contributed—I wish through this my writing to recount those deeds of my father which do not deserve to be abandoned to silence.'[3]   We may note that in Anna's eyes sex is no bar to her writing her father's Life and continuing her husband's History. She may be thought partial or unfilial, as the case may be, but it never occurs to her that others may doubt her competence;[4] and we should all be prepared to admit that her range of study is impressive. Among the teachers with whose methods she was familiar she refers to 'those who preside over the λογικαὶ ἐπιστῆμαι.' These seem here to mean grammar and logic, for she speaks of their professors as inventing names for clearness' sake.[5]   Later on she describes Bishop Leo of

---

[1] Cf. XV. 9, p. 490, where she speaks of herself as a 'historian and a woman and the most honoured child of the purple, first of the children of Alexius', these being, in her opinion, her three distinguishing characteristics.

[2] The *quadrivium* was Arithmetic, Geometry, Astronomy, and Music; the *trivium* was Grammar (including study of the classics), Rhetoric, and Dialectic which comprised the logic of Porphyry. This division of the 'seven liberal arts' was first made by Boethius (*ob.* 524) (*Camb. Med. Hist.*, V, p. 765). We may compare the late tenth-century grouping of learning of the Moslem Brethren of Sincerity. Their 'philosophic studies' comprised 'propaedeutics' (Arithmetic, Geometry, Astronomy, and Music), Logic, Physics, and Theology (*Camb. Med. Hist.*, IV, p. 292).

[3] Pref. 1, pp. 1, 2.   [4] Pref. 2, p. 2, and 3, p. 5.

[5] III. 4, p. 79.

Chalcedon as unacquainted with the laws either of Economics (οἰκονομίας) or of the Church, a man who in his 'ignorance' could not state his case with cogency, 'as he was entirely without training in argument' (λογικῆς μαθήσεως ἀμέτοχος).[1] This remark leads on naturally to Anna's next handling of educational matters, which takes up the better part of two chapters (Book V, Chapters 8 and 9), and is of very great interest for our purpose.

First of all, she gives a graphic picture of the state of learning at her father's accession.[2] After describing the early days of Italus the philosopher, she says:

'Then he came to the city of Constantine, a city not deficient in all education and art of learning (τέχνης λογικῆς). For though from the reign of Basil, born in the purple' [i.e. Basil II, Emperor 963–1025] 'till the rule of Monomachus' [i.e. Constantine IX, Emperor 1042–54] 'learning had been neglected by the many, yet its flame had never died out; so it blazed forth again and sprang up, and came to be an object of interest to students in the times of the Emperor Alexius. For before this most men lived in luxury and sport, engrossed because of this luxury in quail fights and other more disgraceful pastimes, and making learning and all art-training (παίδευσις τεχνική) of secondary account. Such then was the condition in which Italus found people here, and he associated with masters who were both uncultured and rude by nature, of whom there were several at that time in the imperial city. So after getting some instruction in letters (παιδεία λογική)[3] from them, he finally resorted to the famous Michael Psellus, who had little intercourse with wise teachers, but by natural cleverness and sharpness of mind[4] . . . had arrived at the summit of all wisdom, and become renowned for wisdom in those times, having mastered the learning of the Hellenes and Chaldaeans. To him then Italus resorted, but because he could not, in his uneducated[5] and barbaric fashion, tolerate teachers at all even in learning, he was unable to go to the bottom of philosophy: for he was full of conceit and barbaric folly, thinking that even before he began learning he was superior to all, so that from the very start he opposed Psellus himself. So having plunged deep into dialectics he made daily disturbances in public meetings, concocting sophistical contentions, and always putting forward something and again producing an argument to support it. This man

[1] V. 2.
[2] This is borne out by other writers, though naturally Psellus, who flourished before this date, puts the beginning of the revival earlier. For the year of his death see Krumbacher, G. B. L., pp. 433, 434.
[3] The heretic Nilus suffered from total lack of this (X. 1, p. 269); παίδευσις λογική was imparted in Alexius' orphanage (XV. 7, p. 485).
[4] Aided by his mother's prayers.
[5] The reproach of ἀπαιδευσία is three times applied to him (V. 8, p. 144; 9, p. 148 (bis).

then was chosen as friend by the then Emperor Michael Ducas[1] and his brothers, and although they thought him of secondary importance to Psellus, yet they clung to him and joined in his wordy warfare; for the Ducases, both the Emperor's brothers and the Emperor Michael himself, were fond of learning.'

After an interlude of rather sinister diplomatic activity at Durazzo, Italus succeeded Psellus, who had become a monk and left Constantinople, as Chief of the Philosophers,[2]

'and he was zealous to expound the Aristotelian and Platonic books. And by reputation he was very learned, specially skilled, if ever any one was, in investigating the most difficult Peripatetic doctrine, and dialectics even more. But to the other arts of letters (τέχναι τῶν λόγων) he was not at all adapted, for he was imperfect in the art of Grammar, and had not tasted of Rhetoric's nectar: not from thence was his speech (λόγος) fashioned and polished into beauty.'

His barbaric manner[3] in speaking, with frowns and 'asperity', is then portrayed, and Anna goes on:

'His written composition was full of dialectical sallies, and his tongue was loaded with arguments, and even more when he discoursed in conversation than in his writings. For he was so powerful in discussions and so unerring that his antagonist was automatically brought to silence[4] and reduced to helplessness. For on both sides of the question he would dig a trench, and cast his opponent into a pit of perplexities. So skilled was the man in Dialectics, and thus did he smother his opponents by continual questionings, confusing and perturbing their minds. And whatever merit (ἀρετή) he gained from his learning (λόγος), his temper (θυμός) dissolved and obliterated it,'

a statement which we can well believe, as he used to strike his opponent in the face and then weep with bitter remorse. A personal description of him follows, and the Greek princess adds:

'In speech he was what might be expected from one who, having come as a boy from Latin peoples into our land, had learnt Greek thoroughly, but was not at all pure in pronunciation, bringing out his syllables clipped. Indeed most people could not fail to notice that his way of speaking was not clear, and that he dropped the ends of his words, and by those tolerably versed in rhetoric he was seen to be a barbarian. And from the same cause his written com-

---

[1] Emperor 1071–8.
[2] On this definite rank in the Palace see Du Cange's note on V. 8, p. 145 c.
[3] He was ἀμουσότατος (V. 8, p. 146) and had an ἦθος ἀπαίδευτον καὶ βαρβαρικόν. He would κωμῳδεῖν on most unsuitable occasions (V. 9, p. 148).
[4] Later we hear again that 'he did not even allow the rival disputant to exhaust his arguments', but would 'close', literally 'sew up', his mouth (like Alexius with the three chief Manichaeans, XIV. 9, p. 455).

positions were indeed filled in every direction with dialectical passages, yet he could not wholly escape the evil of incoherence, nor solecisms scattered here and there. This man then was put at the head of all the philosophical teaching, and the youths swarmed round him, for he explained to them the teachings of Proclus and Plato and the two philosophers Porphyry and Iamblichus, and especially he expounded to those who desired it the principles of Aristotle, and his treatise[1] which offers the use as it were of an Instrument of Reasoning, because he was specially proud of this, and had worked at it specially hard. Yet he was not able at all to help those wishing to learn, seeing that he had his temper and the general unruliness of his disposition to hinder him. For look, I beg you, at his disciples, John Solomon and men like Iasites and Serblias, and others who were very zealous in learning, most of whom I myself have seen later coming to the Palace. They knew nothing accurately, but set forth their dialectics in disorderly fashion, and with confused transposing of the parts, not understanding anything soundly, but putting forward the theory of Ideas, and even in a veiled way Transmigration of Souls, and other such strange doctrines resembling these.'

Then follows an interesting glimpse into the intellectual standard of the Court under Alexius I.

'For who with any share of learning ($\lambda \acute{o} \gamma o v$) was not admitted, when that sacred couple, I mean my parents the Emperor and Empress, were toiling all night and day at inquiry into the divine words ($\lambda \acute{o} \gamma \omega v$)? But I will digress a little, for the rules of rhetoric permit me. I remember my mother the Empress, with the midday meal[2] set before her, holding a book in her hands and scrutinizing the words of the holy doctrinal Fathers, and especially Maximus the philosopher and martyr.[3] For she was not so much occupied in scientific investigations as in dogmas, wishing to cull true wisdom. And wonder often came over me, and wondering I would sometimes say to her: "How hast thou voluntarily looked up at so great a height? I myself tremble and do not dare to catch at these matters even with the tips of my ears. For the entirely speculative and intellectual character of the man gives as it were vertigo to those who read him." But she smiling said: "Commendable is this timidity, I know, and even I myself do not approach these books without awe. But yet I cannot be torn from them. Thou therefore wait a little, and having first looked into other books thou wilt savour the sweetness of these." '

This tender recollection almost makes Anna break down, but

---

[1] 'Aristotle's Logical Writings collected under the name of $\tau \grave{o} \; \acute{o} \rho \gamma a v o v$' (Liddell and Scott.)

[2] $\acute{a} \rho \iota \sigma \tau o v$ may be either breakfast or 'luncheon'.

[3] A monk, usually called the Confessor, who opposed Monothelitism and died in exile from his sufferings (fl. circ. 580–662; see p. 180 below).

she returns to Italus and his disciples. His teaching according to her 'stirred up the mass of ignorant people to insurrections and made not a few of his intimate pupils into rebels, and I might mention many if time had not taken away my memory. But these things' [i. e. the early events of Italus' life] 'happened before my father was raised up to the summit of empire. So when he found life here[1] deficient in all education and art of learning (τεχνὴ λογικὴ), with learning (λόγος) driven far away, he himself was eager to foment such sparks of it as there were hidden under ashes, and did not rest in urging towards study (μάθησις) all who were inclined to its branches (τὰ μαθήματα); for there were only a few of such men, and they had stopped short at the portals of Aristotle. But he gave orders that the study of the divine books should rank above Hellenic culture (Ἑλληνικὴ παιδεία).'

The rest of the chapter is taken up with the trial of Italus for false doctrines. As Oeconomos has pointed out, and as we shall see later, he really incurred odium as a neo-Platonist philosopher rather than as a heretic. At present we will only consider a few of the many curious points in this long passage.

First we note the constant recurrence of the word λόγος and its derivatives. It soon becomes obvious that the meaning is not uniform, but may be 'word', 'argument', 'speech', 'history', 'letters' or 'learning', with the last meaning predominating.[2] In a later passage τέχνη τις λογικὴ ('a rational art') is applied to divination by casting pebbles, which is carefully distinguished from Magic.[3] Alexius is described as 'most priestly in virtue and λόγος', and 'apostolic in will and λόγος',[4] in connexion with his conversion of Moslems; here the stress is probably laid on his oratory, rather than on his learning in general.[5] But later on we are told that 'in all his deeds and his words (λόγοις) he had Reason (λόγον) for his captain'.[6] When Anna is passionately championing her father against criticism, she asserts that he did not neglect τοὺς λόγους but combined them and arms,

[1] i.e. in Constantinople.
[2] In other places it means 'rumour' (I. 12, p. 28; VI. 7, p. 165; XI. 4, p. 319) or 'scientific principle' (XI. 2, p. 312; XIV. 4, p. 433) or 'discussion' or parleying (X. 6, p. 286; XI. 5, p. 322; 7, p. 330). In Cinnamus, *Hist.* I. 10, p. 15, from 'rumour' the meaning has almost come to be 'nonsense'.
[3] VI. 7, p. 164.   [4] VI. 13, p 181.
[5] So Bohemund's inferiority to Alexius alone καὶ τύχῃ καὶ λόγοις should probably be rendered 'in position and eloquence', as his oratorical powers have just been eulogized (XIII. 10, p. 404).
[6] VII. 3, p. 197; XIII. 4, p. 386. So λόγος means 'reason' in X. 7, p. 287. Sometimes it may mean either 'reason' or 'speech'.

conquering barbarians by the latter and heretics by the former.[1]
Here the two senses of 'learning' and 'convincing arguments'
are hard to disentangle. Again, when we hear that the Emperor
'conquered in didactic discourse (λόγοις) those who busied
themselves about λόγον',[2] the word may mean 'learning'[3] or
'oratory', but probably the latter. It is indeed safe to say that
of all exhibitions of learning and all fruits of education, persuasive and eloquent speech was the most admired in Anna's
day. Argument is tried on enemies in the field, on formidable
visitors like the Crusaders, on conspirators or heretics at home,
on soldiers in camp; and whether it is her father[4] or her husband[5] that is in question, Anna's supreme pride is in their
oratory. She admires a powerful voice even in an enemy[6] and
is furiously indignant when her father is called 'The Lisper'.[7]
To be 'dread in speech' is almost as fine as to be 'dread in
action',[8] and the power to soften all hearts or get one's way by
'honeyed words' is a great asset.[9]

An interesting and neat definition of eloquence is given in connexion with Anna Dalassena. 'She was truly a most persuasive
orator; she was neither garrulous and one who lengthily pro-
tracted her speeches (τοὺς λόγους), nor did the inspiration of her
discourse (τοῦ λόγου) quickly desert her, ἀλλ' ἐπικαίρως ἀρξαμένη εἰς
τὰ καιριώτατα πάλιν κατέληγε.'[10] Many a modern auditor can sympathize with Alexius' acute suffering under the reverse of such

---

[1] XIV. 8, p. 453. [2] XV. 8, p. 487.
[3] In the trial of the Bogomile heretics Alexius called for aid on ὁπόσοι λόγου
μετεῖχον, here doubtless ecclesiastical learning *par excellence* (XV. 9, p. 491). Bishop
Leo of Chalcedon was 'not one of the very wise and λογίων' (V. 2, p. 129).
[4] I. 2, p. 5; III. 3, p. 76; VI. 10, p. 173. He is represented as making speeches,
long or short, to convert or persuade people in IX. 5–9 X. 1 and 11; XIV. 3;
XV. 9. After keeping his word to his Coman allies about booty 'he made a discourse of considerable length to all his men about lying' (VIII. 6, p. 235). He
harangues the Crusaders with good advice (X. 10, p. 301, and 11, p. 305) and
his rebel subjects in IX. 9. He talks the Persian envoys round with 'clever explanations' (XIV. 3, p. 342). It is curious to find Alexius himself decrying λόγος in
his first poem to John (*Mous. Alex.* I. 91) as opposed to deeds, οὐδὲν γὰρ οὐδὲν ῥᾳδιώ-
τερον λόγου.
[5] Pref. 3, pp. 3 and 5; XII. 7, p. 365; XIII. 11, p. 405; XIV. 8, p. 453. This
talent was inherited from his father (VII. 2, p. 191; X. 3, p. 276).
[6] I. 7, p. 17; 10, p. 24; VI. 7, p. 165. [7] I. 8, p. 19.
[8] IX. 4, p. 251; cf. II. 1, p. 44; IX. 9, p. 263. Nic. Acom. says Irene
loved Bryennius as εἰπεῖν ἱκανώτατον καὶ οὐκ ἐλάττονα διαπράξασθαι (*John C.* 2,
p. 4).
[9] II. 3, p. 47: 6, p. 56; VI. 10, p. 173. Cantacuzenus appeals 'cleverly' and
successfully to his troops' fears (XIII. 5, p. 391). So Nic. Bry. (II. 21, p. 59) says
that Alexius was 'sweet in words if ever any one was'. This is what Anna says of
Constantine Ducas, aged seven (III. 1, p. 71), and of Nicephorus Diogenes (IX. 6,
p. 257; cf. VII. 6, p. 202; VIII. 8, p. 238; 9, p. 241; IX. 2, p. 249; 9, p. 259;
XI. 3, p. 316.
[10] III. 7, p. 86.

conciseness in the case of the loquacious Crusaders.[1] Speech is to
Anna powerful for good or evil. We find the sentiment expressed
once[2] and implied very frequently that 'speech (ὁ λόγος) often
gains victories that war cannot'. For this reason Alexius tries
to keep his army from all communication with the enemy host
of Bohemund,[3] to whom individually Anna pays this tribute:
'His discourses (ὁμιλίαι) were precise, and he gave answers
affording no handle anywhere.'[4] The gift of the gab, if we
may use the term, was never more esteemed than at Byzantium
800 odd years ago.[5] One effect of this may be noticed here in
passing. As the power of ὁ λόγος, both spoken and written, was
the true aim of all education, it is not surprising to find (though
Anna later on deplores the fact) great stress laid by the thinkers
of her day on grammar and dialectics, as much indeed as on
the subject-matter of the books from which they were learnt.

At present we will consider some other points in the story of
Italus. First of all, teachers are in Anna's eyes essential, and
those who try to do without them like Italus[6] are crazy with
conceit. Next we infer that to arrive 'at the summit of wisdom'
is equivalent to mastering 'the learning of the Hellenes and
Chaldaeans': men must go 'to the depth of philosophy' and
study Aristotle, Plato, and the neo-Platonists such as Proclus,
Porphyry, and Iamblichus. A first-rate teacher must have the
ancillary graces of correct grammar, polished utterance, and
'the nectar of Rhetoric'. To prefer luxury or sport to study is
disgraceful, and all men of letters should be welcome at court,
but 'the divine words', including the works of the Fathers, are
the crown and summit of learning.[7] Alexius, while fanning into
a flame all smouldering sparks of intellectuality among his

[1] XIV. 4. Garrulity is blamed in the conspirator John Solomon (XII. 5, p. 360)
and also in all 'Latins' (X. 9, p. 294), yet we never find Anna sharing Thucydides'
dread of over-clever oratory and of one who 'elaborates a sophistical speech' to
deceive (*Hist.* III. 38; VI. 17; VII. 48; VIII. 68).
[2] XI. 4, p. 319.   [3] XIII. 4, p. 386.   [4] XIII. 10, p. 404.
[5] Cf. the curious statement in Cecaumenus (*Strat.* p. 42) that a man who sees
others wronged and does not speak is a devil (διάβολος). Yet a man must guard his
tongue (*ibid.* p. 61). To Nic. Bry. the fact that Michael VII was βραδύγλωσσος is
one of his worst defects (II. 14, p. 51). The highest praise is that given to Botaniates
by Attaliates (p. 321): he knew when to speak and when to be silent. Callicles
(Poem VI. 21) says of a dead boy that his speech was 'as a sweet shower, as dew
from heaven'.
[6] V. 8, p. 144. So Nilus in X. 1, p. 269. This was a handicap even to the great
Psellus (V. 8, p. 144). Cf. his words about himself οὔτε διδασκάλοις ἀξιολόγοις
περιτυχών (*Chron.*, Const. IX, Byz. T., p. 107). Absence of training vitiated the
arguments of Bishop Leo (*Al.* V. 2, p. 130).
[7] Ordericus Vitalis (*Hist. Eccl.*,.Pt. III, Lib. 7, Ch. 4) makes this the climax of
his eulogy on Alexius, that he was 'divinae legis cultor devotissimus' (*P. L.* 188,
col. 519).

subjects, esteemed theological study above all else,[1] as did his wife Irene.

Before we leave this matter we may note the curious fact that the whole passage about the sparks and the fanning, as well as the statement that certain men had 'stopped short at the portals of Aristotle', is taken from Psellus' biography of Romanus III (Argyrus).[2] The text of both authors shall be given. Psellus, after saying that Romanus 'thought he knew many times as much as he really did', and had only a superficial veneer τῶν λόγων, continues:

εἴ που σπινθῆρές τινες σοφίας ὑπὸ σποδιᾷ παρεκρύπτοντο ἀνεχώννυε καὶ πᾶν γένος κατέλεγε, φιλοσόφους φημὶ καὶ ῥήτορας καὶ τοὺς ὅσοι περὶ τὰ μαθήματα ἐσπουδάκασιν ἢ μᾶλλον σπουδάσαι ᾠήθησαν. βραχεῖς γὰρ ὁ τηνικαῦτα χρόνος λογίους παρέτρεφε, καὶ τούτους μέχρι τῶν Ἀριστοτελικῶν ἑστηκότας προθύρων.

Anna's words about her father are as follows:

εἴ που σπινθῆρές τινες ἦσαν τούτου [sc. τοῦ λόγου] ὑπὸ σποδιᾷ κρυπτόμενοι, ἀναχωννύειν ἠπείγετο καὶ [τοὺς] ὅσοι περὶ τὰ μαθήματα ἐπιρρεπῶς εἶχον (ἦσαν γάρ τινες καὶ οὗτοι βραχεῖς, καὶ οὗτοι μέχρι τῶν Ἀριστοτελικῶν ἑστηκότες προθύρων).[3] . . .

K. Dieter[4] makes use of another passage where Anna inserts phrases from Psellus into her totally irrelevant context,[5] to discredit a rather important statement of hers wrapped up in these phrases. It might be legitimate to do the same here, except that Anna's words agree with everything else that she tells us about her father, and that two emperors may well have 'fomented' sparks of learning. But in any case it is interesting to note that both Psellus and Anna seem to regard standing at the portals of Aristotle as a low grade of knowledge, beyond which the real φιλόσοφοι had to pass, and to consider the study of 'Aristotelian books' as preliminary to that of Plato and his followers. What chiefly concerns us here however is that to Anna Manner is hardly less vital than Matter, and her veneration for the externals, grammar and good pronunciation and 'the nectar of Rhetoric', may account for the elaborate speeches put by her into the mouths of her characters.[6]

---

[1] So in XIV. 7, p. 449, we learn that Alexius' chief recreation was 'the reading and examining of books', and especially searching the Scriptures, and in XV. 9, p. 490, that he commissioned Euthymius Zigabenus to write against heresies. Anna only claims this knowledge for herself in the *Prologue* to her Will, line 13.

[2] Psellus, *Chron.*, Romanus III, Byz. T., p. 26. This Emperor, the first husband of Zoe, reigned 1028–34.

[3] V. 9, p. 148.   [4] *B. Z.* III, pp. 386–90.

[5] VII. 2, p. 190, compared with *Chron.*, Basil II, Byz. T., p. 12.

[6] This is especially wearisome in XIII. 9.

One other interesting thing comes out of the story of Italus, namely that Anna believed in the moral power of education as given by professors. In this instance it has an evil effect, 'stirring up the mass of ignorant people to insurrections and making not a few of his intimate pupils into rebels'. One of them, John Solomon, figures as the leader of a conspiracy in Book XII, and Anna professes to have forgotten the names of many others.[1] We could wish that she had explained how the study of Aristotle and the neo-Platonists could possibly make men τυράννους, unless the strange spectacle of a dialectician shouting and frowning and hitting out and weeping set a bad example of violence to his hearers. In a later passage[2] Anna speaks approvingly of a man who 'had his tongue free, and was not muzzled in censuring what was low,[3] but was as the Stagirite commands the dialectician to be'. But the 'barbaric' methods of Italus jar on her taste as on ours.

In Book VI we have another reference to Alexius' encouragement of learning.[4] His daughter says that 'under the Emperor many of the sciences (ἐπιστημῶν) made progress, for he honoured philosophers and philosophy herself'. But he discouraged Astrology[5] and his daughter considers he was perfectly right. Books VII and VIII are full of Patzinaks and Comans and other troubles foreign and domestic, and Learning is put on one side.

[1] Chs. 5 and 6. Among his pupils who do not occur in her pages elsewhere, but may have been some of the 'rebels' indicated, are 'certain men like Iasites and Serblias'. Iasites may be the undesirable husband of her sister Eudocia. See Du Cange's notes on V. 9, p. 147 A, and XV. 11, p. 502 A. This Constantine Iasites took part in a Council about Image Worship under the Patriarch Nicolas, who held office 1084–1111 (*P. G.* 127, col. 973, Novel 22 of Alexius). A John Serblias is the recipient of a letter from Archbishop Theophylact of Achrida (Ser. I, Ep. 8, *P. G.* 126, col. 321). His foible seems to have been undue haste and negligence (ἀμέλεια), but there is no hint of rebellion, except in so far as he was evidently in touch with Gregory Taronites, the mysteriously pardoned rebel of the *Alexias* (XII. 7) to whom three of Theophylact's other Epistles are addressed. The one to Serblias concludes with the prayer: 'May the Lord preserve thee from every snare of the Devil and from negligence towards good works.' Serblias does not appear in the dictionaries either of Pape or of Pauly-Wissowa. We may note that one pupil of Italus, during the Trial, of which we have a full Report, claimed to have learnt from his master no heresies, but only τὰ τῆς λογικῆς πραγματείας and was consequently acquitted ('Trial of Italus' (*Bull. inst. arch. russe de Constantinople*, Vol. II, p. 64, ed. Th. Ouspensky).   [2] XIII. 1, p. 376.
[3] Reading ἀναισχυντίας not ἀναισχυντίαις as in *C. S. H. B.* See p. 204 below.
[4] VI. 7, p. 164. Theophylact in his Address (*P. G.* 126, cols. 288, 305) implores Alexius to promote ἡ σοφιστική, because 'a most imperial rule of custom . . . throws open the Palace τοῖς ἑκάστοτε σοφισταῖς', and not to be ἀφιλολογώτερος than preceding emperors. This implied reproach agrees with Zonaras, XVIII. 29; even Zigabenus only praises Alexius for interest in Theology, not in other learning (Pref. to *Pan. Dogm.*, *P.G.* 130, col. 21, and see Neumann, *Gr. Geschichtschreiber*, pp. 33–5).
[5] See pp. 84 sqq. above.

25. REFERENCES IN *ALEXIAS* IX–XV

IN Book IX, at the end of the story of Nicephorus Diogenes, we have an allusion to one of the sciences in which Anna considers herself 'not altogether untrained'. This is geometry, and the passage is remarkable.[1] Diogenes had been blinded after the failure of his conspiracy, and, 'being frantic with grief and shunning residence in the metropolis, was set on dwelling on his own estates, altogether immersed in the books of the ancients, which others read aloud to him. For being deprived of light he used the eyes of others for reading. And this man was so great in natural powers that though he could not see he easily apprehended things hard for the seeing to interpret. He thereupon went through a complete education (πᾶσα παιδεία) and even, most wonderful of all, far-famed geometry,[2] and meeting one of the philosophers' [or 'learned men' in general] 'he ordered him to furnish the figures to him in solids. Then by the touch of his hands he had apprehension of all the theorems and figures of geometry, like the famous Didymus[3] who by sharpness of intellect even without eyes came to the summit of music and geometry.' She diverges at this point to the heresy of Didymus, and then resumes: 'Every one therefore who hears these things wonders, but I have seen the man [Diogenes] and marvelled at him and heard him speaking about such matters. And I myself, being not altogether untrained in such things, perceived that he had an accurate knowledge of the theorems. But even though he occupied himself with learning (περὶ λόγους) yet he did not desist from his ancient grudge against the Emperor.'

Though Anna thus speaks of geometry as a palace topic, it is not a science which engages much of her thoughts. Indeed there are only two other allusions to it, one figurative to a 'centre' and a 'circle',[4] and one where she uses πόρισμα not with her usual sense of 'treasure' but in its technical meaning

---

[1] IX. 10, p. 266.

[2] This science was popularly supposed to have been invented or greatly furthered by the Egyptians (Iamblichus, *de comm. math. sci.*, Ch. 21, ed. N. Festa, p. 66; Proclus *in I Euclidis librum*, ed. G. Friedlein, p. 64). Psellus, in his letter to John Longibardus, says a man who is neither Chaldaean nor Egyptian has nothing to do with geometry; no Roman ever 'was an astrologer or geometrician'; they were all soldiers (Psellus, *de operatione daemonum, &c.*, p. 169).

[3] See p. 304, note 9 below.

[4] VI. 3, p. 156. In VI. 7, p. 164, she speaks contemptuously of 'fixing of centres' in astrology.

of 'corollary' or 'consequence'.[1] She does however refer to applied science when she speaks of falling bodies gaining momentum,[2] and of centres of gravity,[3] and also in a long passage[4] describing Bohemund's construction of a siege-tower. This turret overtopped the walls of besieged Durazzo by five or six cubits, and was furnished with wooden gangways to be let down on to the battlements so that the besiegers might pass in. The calculations needed in its construction cause her to comment on the ὀπτικὴ ἐπιστήμη or κατάληψις ἀπὸ τῶν διοπτρῶν that 'the barbarians' must have possessed. This 'apprehension' would seem to be a matter of fairly simple trigonometry, involving the use of an optical instrument (διόπτρα) for measuring distances and heights, such as Polybius[5] mentions as used in signalling. She modestly admits that others have 'greater skill in mechanics',[6] so she can give herself up to wholly uncritical and admiring descriptions of her father's operations in digging a trench and building a fort,[7] or of his entirely original siege-engines that caused 'wonder to all',[8] or of the map that he drew, doubtless with proper instruments, for one of his admirals.[9] But she is not personally interested in such matters, and it is more profitable for us to return to her views on education in the Humanities.

As we might expect from the claims made in her Preface, Anna makes frequent references to Aristotle or his teaching (nine in all) and eleven to Plato and his followers near or remote.[10] We will deal with these later. She also speaks of 'The Porch'[11] and often brings in the characteristic Stoic word ἡ οἰκουμένη, in which, as Bury has pointed out,[12] the Stoics showed their feeling that the whole world was 'a man's true fatherland'. It is but fair to say that Anna's cosmopolitanism of outlook is confined to this one word, which serves on occasions to enhance Alexius' greatness. The whole world weeps with her over his death, for he was the Light of it.[13] So, too,

---

[1] XIII. 6, p. 394. Contrast X. 5, p. 285; XII. 8, p. 367. It is interesting to note that Iamblichus (*de comm. math. sci.*, Ch. 23, p. 70) and Proclus (*in I Euclidis librum*, p. 65) both say that Pythagoras first put geometry εἰς σχῆμα παιδείας ἐλευθέρου.

[2] VII. 11, p. 217.   [3] XII. 4, p. 355.   [4] XIII. 3, p. 3.
[5] *Hist.* X. 46, 1.   [6] XI. 1, p. 311.   [7] X. 5, p. 282.
[8] XI. 2, p. 312.   [9] XIII. 7, p. 396.
[10] It is curious that she never mentions Plotinus.
[11] VIII. 6, p. 236; X. 2, p. 271; XIV. 8, p. 453.
[12] *Hellenistic Age*, p. 26.
[13] Pref. 4, p. 8; XV. 11, pp. 505, 506. The same general sorrow over his death, with the same words ζημία and οἰκουμένη, occurs in the *Prologue* to Anna's Will, lines 27–8. All the world knows how many Manichaeans he converted (*Al.* XIV. 9, p. 456). He washes off 'much brine of the world' in X. 2, p. 271. In I. 13, p. 31,

'the world' believed that Bohemund was truly dead, and 'the world' never saw ingenious daring such as his.[1] Anna's use of the word is purely rhetorical, without any philosophic implication whatever.

One thing is certain. Anna has a wholesome respect both for Authority and for Thoroughness in matters of the mind. Intellectual shallowness and conceit are (theoretically at least) distasteful to her. She has sovereign contempt for the 'empty-headed' conspirator John Solomon[2] (himself as we have seen a disciple of Italus),[3] who 'thought he had come to the summit of Aristotelian and Platonic learning ($\mu\alpha\theta\dot\eta\mu\alpha\tau\alpha$)', and who was inflated by vanity in spite of his failure to attain 'philosophic knowledge' ($\epsilon\ddot\iota\delta\eta\sigma\iota\varsigma$ $\phi\iota\lambda\dot\sigma\sigma\phi\sigma\varsigma$). In her mournful retrospect over her life in Book XIV, Ch. 7, one of her grievances is that she has no written material about her father except 'worthless and altogether trifling compositions', which she further damns with faint praise as 'simple in diction and artless and adhering to truth, not displaying any affectation ($\tau\iota$ $\kappa\sigma\mu\psi\dot\sigma\nu$)[4] or trailing along in rhetorical bombast'. If Oster is right in thinking she had access to the state archives with all her father's enactments and letters, she could not fairly complain of lacking the (to her) finest literary models, and the sentence may be untrue self-pity. But at least we discover what her standard of good writing was; it must err neither on the side of bombast nor on that of the simplicity which results in 'worthless and trifling compositions'.

But of all Anna's references to Education, much the most interesting is the long one in XV. 7. Here she gives an account of the teaching imparted to the Orphans whom Alexius wished to befriend. Those in private families or monasteries were brought up 'not as slaves but as free', and were 'thought worthy' of every kind of education, $\pi\alpha\nu\tau\sigma\dot\iota\alpha\varsigma$ $\pi\alpha\iota\delta\epsilon\dot\iota\alpha\varsigma$, and particularly of thorough grounding in 'the sacred writings'. The children in the imperial orphanage itself received the '$\dot\epsilon\gamma\kappa\dot\upsilon\kappa\lambda\iota\sigma\varsigma$ $\pi\alpha\iota\delta\epsilon\dot\iota\alpha$'

the Pope is said to claim presidency over the whole world, and in VI. 3, p. 157, we are told that 'the world' was enslaved by barbarians. For the faint trace of cosmopolitan feeling, when Alexius refuses to kill Patzinak prisoners, saying, 'Though Scythians they are at any rate men', we may compare the argument of Themistius quoted by Bury (*op. cit*, p. 29) that barbarians should not be destroyed, because they are part of the dominion of an Emperor who is 'sovran of all the human race'. Eustathius Archbishop of Thessalonica, sublimating the Stoic idea by Christian teaching, was so enlightened as to say that all men have God for their Maker, and He hears the prayers of Barbarians as well as Greeks. (*In. S. Quadr. or.* IV. 37–8. *P. G.* 135, col. 708).

[1] XI. 12, p. 341. The name Porphyrogenete has gone out 'into the world' (VI. 8, p. 166).

[2] XII. 5, p. 359.   [3] V. 9, p. 147.   [4] Cf. III. 6, p. 83.

which, Liddell and Scott tell us, 'every free-born youth in Greece went through before applying to professional studies'. In Plutarch's *Alexander*[1] τὰ ἐγκύκλια means school-learning in general, and Anna probably used the word with the same wide meaning.[2] At the end of the chapter she gives a more detailed account of the school, and this time she dwells, with scant approval, on the grammatical part of the curriculum. We will translate her words in full: 'On the right of the great shrine' [the Church of St. Paul] 'stood a school of Grammar (τῶν γραμματικῶν) for orphan children collected from every race, in which a teacher presided, and the children stood round him, some excited over grammatical questions, and others writing down the so-called σχέδη.[3] And there one might see a Latin being trained, and a Scythian learning Hellenic Greek, and a Byzantine ('Ρωμαῖος) handling the writings of the Hellenes, and an uneducated Hellene learning his own language correctly. Of such a nature were Alexius' efforts as to education in letters'[4] (λογικὴ παίδευσις). Then follows a criticism on Anna's part which causes Krumbacher to say with doubtful justice that she was wedded to 'Altertümelei', and had absurdly exalted notions about elementary education.[5] She says: 'Now the art of the σχέδος' [i.e. analysis] 'is an invention of the moderns and of the generation in our days. I pass over some Styliani and the men called Longibardus[6] and all who used their art for the collecting of names' [possibly in the technical sense of 'nouns'] 'of all sorts and the Attici and those who formed part of the sacred register of the Great Church in our midst' [i.e. St. Sophia], 'whose names I omit. But now not even of secondary consideration is the study of these sublime poets and prose-writers too, or the experience learnt from them: draughts are the rage and other wicked practices (πεττεία δὲ τὸ σπούδασμα καὶ ἄλλα τὰ ἔργα ἀθέμιτα). And this I say, grieved for the complete neglect

[1] Ch. 7, *Vit.* III. p. 285.
[2] Fr. Fuchs (*Die höheren Schulen v. K'pel im Mittelalter, Byz. Arch.* 1926, p. 45), rather scornfully says that 'as always Anna archaizes' in including under ἐ. π. 'die Gesamtheit der ἐπιστῆμαι'. If so, she would merely be following Plutarch and Quintilian instead of the Fathers, who (like most Byzantines after them) used the phrase as equal to 'preliminary education'. But it is difficult to extract a grandiose meaning, or indeed any very precise meaning at all, from the word ἐγκύκλιος as she brings it in twice in XV. 7. See p. 180 below.
[3] σχέδος is explained by Sophocles in his Dictionary as a tablet on which was written a passage for grammatical analysis, 'the analysis comprising inflection, etymology and definition'. More will be said on this later in Ch. 27.
[4] This seems a better rendering than the 'logica institutio' of C. S. H. B.
[5] G. B. L., p. 592. He is of course right in saying that the parsing and analysis done in nineteenth (if not also twentieth) century schools might well be called Schedography.
[6] This will be commented on later, Ch. 27.

of general education (παίδευσις ἐγκύκλιος). For this inflames my
soul, because I have spent much time on these same things'
[i.e. Schedography], 'and when I was freed from childish study
of them and arrived at Rhetoric and took hold of Philosophy,
and in the midst of the various branches of science (μεταξὺ
τῶν ἐπιστημῶν) turned eagerly to poets and prose-writers and
thereby polished off the roughnesses of my speech, then with
Rhetoric's aid I condemned the manifold complication of this
Schedography.' Shortly afterwards Anna tells us how her father
gave the task of writing a 'Panoply of Dogma' against heresy
to the monk Zigabenus, 'who had arrived at the summit of
Grammar, and was not unmindful of Rhetoric, and understood
dogma like no one else'.[1]

Finally, in the account of Alexius' last illness[2] we have two
definite claims made by Anna to superior knowledge. At one
place when the medical authorities differed as to treatment she
says: 'I myself was present by command of the Empress in
order to be umpire at the conversations of the doctors, and
I heard what was said, and I for my part agreed with the words
of Callicles, but the vote of the majority conquered.' Then
again her mother the Empress Irene 'often gazed at me and
awaited my oracular response (τὸν ἐμὸν τρίπουν), as was her
custom in critical events at other times, in expectation of what
I should pour forth (ἀποφοιβάσαιμι) to her'. This of course
implies an identification of the writer with the Pythia at
Delphi. It is therefore all the more striking to find her 'despising philosophy and learning' and giving herself up to the
humblest offices of a nurse.

26. GENERAL EDUCATION OF THE DAY

WE have now reviewed all Anna's references to Education,
and know with certainty what she considers her special
advantages and attainments to have been. The next step in
studying her personality is to discover, first whether her estimate of herself agrees with that pronounced by those who knew
her, and secondly whether her education was exceptional for
her day.

As to the former point we have testimonies to her learning from
Theodore Prodromus, Zonaras, and Nicetas. The first calls her

---

[1] XV. 9, p. 490.   [2] XV. 11.

'wise Anna, absolute intellect, home of the Graces',[1] and again
'Fourth Grace' and 'Tenth Muse', who reckoned knowledge the
adornment of an imperial soul as purple of an imperial body,
who sought truth and followed philosophy πᾶσι πάσας ὑπεράρασα
τοῖς καλοῖς, one who was γενναιότερόν τε ὁμοῦ φρονήσασα καὶ βασι-
λικώτερον.[2] Zonaras is hardly less laudatory : (Bryennius') 'wife
pursued education in letters (τῆς ἐν λόγοις παιδείας) not less if
not more than himself, and had a tongue that talked Attic
accurately, and a mind most keen (ὀξύτατον) towards the height
of speculations. And this had come to her by keenness of
natural powers and by industry (σπουδή), for she had engrossed
herself in books and learned men and associated with them in
no dilettante fashion (οὐ παρέργως).'[3] Even the hostile Nicetas
says of her : ἥτις δὴ τῆς τῶν ἐπιστημῶν πασῶν ἐπόχου φιλοσοφίας
ἐδείκνυτο μέλημα καὶ πρὸς πᾶσαν ἐρρύθμιστο μάθησιν.[4]

From these three criticisms we infer it was in her love for
Philosophy and 'speculation'[5] that she was a rara avis, and this
brings us to our second point. Diehl has stated that a taste
for the classics was seldom so universal at any period as at
Constantinople under the Comneni. He even believes Anna to
have studied Latin, but it is impossible to infer this from her
writings, and she writes as if the language needed an inter-
preter.[6] Knowledge of Latin is claimed as a great acquirement
for himself, his fellow student John Mauropus, and the Emperor
Romanus III by Michael Psellus,[7] who as we have seen was
Anna's ideal of the learned man, yet even he never quotes a
Latin author. He himself tells us[8] that by the age of twenty-five
he was versed in Rhetoric, Philosophy, Geometry, Music, Law,
Astronomy, Medicine, Physics, Occult Sciences, and Plato : on
many of these he wrote. We know that he gave instruction to
Michael VII, about whose love and facility for learning he is so
rhapsodical as to throw Anna's mild praises into the shade.[9]

---

[1] Poem on the death of Theodora, line 44, B. Z. XVI, p. 88.
[2] Epithalamium (P. G. 133, col. 1401) on the two sons of Anna and Bryennius.
Prodromus wrote a poem of 118 lines to Anna asking her help, presumably as
patroness of literature, but only the beginning and the end are published in
Notices et Extraits, Vol. VIII. Pt. II, p. 175.
[3] Epit. XVIII. 26.   [4] Nic. Ac. John C. 3, p. 7.
[5] In 1146 John Tzetzes wrote a letter to her invoking her aid against the heretic
Tzurichus (G. Hart, Suppl., Vol. 12 (1881) of Jahrb. für class. Philol., pp. 45–6).
[6] V. 8, p. 145.
[7] B. G. Med. V. 148 and 492 ; Chron., Rom. III, Byz. T., p. 26.
[8] In Chron., Const. IX, Byz. T., pp. 107 sqq.
[9] Chron., Mich. VII, Byz. T., pp. 260, 261 ; Al. V. 8, p. 145. Zonaras mentions
Michael's interest instilled by Psellus in grammar, metres, dialectics, history, and
'philosophical speculations', but deplores all this as 'childish practices' in an
emperor (Epit. XVIII. 16). Theophylact (P. G. 126, col. 260) adopts the same tone.

Finally, Anna's statement that he had mastered the learning of
the Chaldaeans is confirmed by his *Commentary on the Chaldaean
Oracles*, and short *Summary of the Doctrines of the Chaldaeans*.[1]

We have seen that the term ἐγκύκλιος παιδεία (of which
Renauld strangely says 'c'était comme le second degré de l'enseignement'[2] when we should rather say 'premier') was an
accepted one, though not of very precise signification. Psellus
says of Bishop John of Euchaita: 'Having first learnt ἐγκύκλιον
παιδείαν, and come furthermore to the summit of the art of
grammar, thus he lays hold on the greater[3] sciences (τῶν
μειζόνων μαθημάτων ἀντιλαμβάνεται).'[4] Psellus himself, we may
remark, received his general education at Constantinople.[5] A
definition of the ἐγκύκλια μαθήματα is given by Tzetzes as taken
from Porphyry's Lives of the Philosophers[6]: it is the circle that
comprises all the sciences (μαθήματα), i. e. Grammar, Rhetoric,
and Philosophy, and the four Arts of Arithmetic, Music, Geometry, and Astronomy. The expression however is used in
Byzantine writings rather loosely, and usually with a less comprehensive meaning than that given to it by Tzetzes. Thus the
great Maximus, who was born in Constantinople in 580 and
went to the School there, studied 'Grammar and the rest of the
ἐγκύκλιος παίδευσις', and then arrived at the 'summit of Rhetoric
and the art of speech'.[7] The monk Cosmas in 710 professed to
have τὴν ἐγκύκλιον ὥσπερ θεμέλιον,[8] and also to have studied
Rhetoric, Dialectic, Ethics in Aristotle and Plato (we note
Anna's order again), Physical Science, Arithmetic, Geometry,
Music, Astronomy, and finally τὰ τῆς θεολογίας μυστήρια. Theodore of Studium, born in 759, was handed over to a γραμματιστής
to learn τὴν προπαιδείαν (apparently a synonym for παιδεία
ἐγκύκλιος). In his case it included Grammar, the Greek language, Rhetoric and Philosophy, in fact all parts of παιδεία ἡ
θύραθεν, profane learning as opposed to sacred.[9] About a cen-

---

[1] Both in *P. G.* 122.   [2] *Étude de Psellos*, p. 406.
[3] Cecaumenus (*Strat.* pp. 46, 75) was ἄμοιρος λόγου and without 'Hellenic education', but he said all children ought to learn λογικὰ καὶ θεωρητικὰ μαθήματα.
[4] *B. G. Med.* V, p. 147.   [5] *B. G. Med.* V, pp. 14, 91.
[6] *Chil.* 11, 532, in Porph , *Opuscula Selecta*, p. 15, ed. A. Nauck.
[7] *P. G.* 90, col. 69.
[8] *P. G.* 94, col. 441. We find τὰ ἐγκύκλια used of the education of John the
Hymnographer, born 783 (*P. G.* 105, col. 944).
[9] Fritz Schemmel, *Die Hochschule von K'pel vom 5. bis 9. Jahrh.*, p. 11. θύραθεν
has this meaning in the description of Bishop Eustratius of Nicaea and his acquirements (XIV. 8, p. 453) as well as in the *Prologue* to Anna's Will about herself,
line 14. When opposed to οἱ καθ' ἡμᾶς, as in Zonaras XVIII. 25, λόγοι οἱ θύραθεν
regularly mean 'die antike Bildung' in contrast to 'die christliche Theologie';
Fuchs, *op. cit.* p. 39, notes 2 and 4. Cf. *Al.* Pref. 4, p. 6. In Cinnamus (VI. 2, p. 147)
we get three distinct branches, παιδ. ἐγκ., μαθήματα τὰ ἐκτός, δόγματα τὰ θεῖα.

tury later Leo, Archbishop of Thessalonica and the teacher of
Philosophy at Constantinople, learnt and taught Poetry and
Geometry as well as his own subject. He was specially devoted
to the works of Aristotle, which the Church had decided were
suitable for Christian education.[1] Shortly before his day Constantine (afterwards St. Cyril) went in 841 from Salonica to
Constantinople at the age of fourteen and studied the same
subjects as Cosmas, minus Physical Science and plus Homer.[2]

This last study reminds us once more of Psellus who knew the
whole *Iliad* by heart at fourteen,[3] and in whose day Education
as a whole revived from its sleep of nearly a century. Basil II,
the great soldier-emperor, had 'utterly despised' learned men,
so Psellus tells us, and though he adds a statement that in spite
of this philosophers and rhetoricians abounded in his reign,[4] yet
Anna was fully justified in saying that from the middle of the
tenth century to the middle of the eleventh 'learning had been
neglected by many'.[5] The educational careers which we have
just enumerated were those of the scholarly few. What was
considered sufficient for average young nobles in those days is
interestingly set forth by Nicephorus Bryennius.[6] Basil II, to
whom the two Comneni Isaac and John had been entrusted by
their dying father, gave them παιδαγωγούς and παιδοτρίβας, to
train their character and teach them the arts of war, i. e. to make
proper use of armour and shield, to 'brandish a spear and ride
well and shoot an arrow at a mark', but above all to understand tactics and encampments and ambushes. They lived in
the Studium monastery for the double purpose of imbibing virtue
from the holy monks, and of getting out easily into the country
for hunting and drill. So Theodore Prodromus[7] seems to sum
up the εὐανάγωγος ἀγωγή of Anna's two sons as riding, polo,
hunting, and military science. Can we wonder if Psellus tells
us that the young men in his day preferred the theatre, money,
and dress to study?[8] It is one of the merits rightly to be
credited to Anna Dalassena that she provided her two youngest
sons (doubtless after doing so for her elder ones) with ἐγκύκλιος
παίδευσις at the hands of suitable teachers.[9]

---

[1] See Krumbacher, *G. B. L.*, pp. 430, 722.   [2] *Camb. Med. Hist.* IV, p. 218.
[3] i. e. in 1032.   He probably lived 1018–78.
[4] *Chron.*, Basil II, Byz. T., p. 15. Basil reigned 963–1025.   [5] V. 8, p. 144.
[6] *Hyle*, I. 1, pp. 16, 17. On the other hand, Renauld (*Étude de Psellos*, p. 408),
after stating that when Constantine Monomachus came to the throne education
consisted in 'la lecture mal comprise de quelques œuvres d'Aristote et de Platon',
points out that if any learning had been preserved at all it was due to the aristocracy.
[7] *Epithalamium* (*P. G.* 133, col. 1402).
[8] Psellus, *De operatione daemonum, etc.*, p. 143.   [9] Nic. Bry. I. 6, p. 21.

One of the latest writers on Byzantine Education is Fritz Schemmel,[1] to whom we have just referred in a note, and it may be well briefly to summarize his statements. The School (*Hochschule* as he calls it) founded by Constantine the Great was moved by Constantius to the Capitol from the στοὰ βασιλική. Julian was educated in the School, which later on seems to have been moved back to the Stoa by Justinian. In 425 Theodosius II established in the School ten Greek grammarians and ten Latin, five Greek sophists and three Latin, two jurists and one philosopher. Till Justinian these teachers were almost all heathen, and parents arranged for their small children to receive their first education from the clergy. After Justinian the School is not mentioned. We hear in the eighth century at Constantinople of a small seminary for twelve boys who studied 'church doctrines', and we know that the Studium cloister had a Boys' School; but under Michael III (842–67) his uncle and virtual sovereign Bardas found it advisable to start a new State School in the Magnaura (part of the great Palace), where the Philosophy was in the hands of the Archbishop Leo who had already been teaching it in the Church of the Forty Martyrs. Similarly under Constantine Monomachus (1042–54) a new School of Law was required and attendance at it made compulsory for all would-be lawyers and judges, as well as a new Faculty of Philosophy for studying Theology and the Classics.[2] Even if the Orphanage School of Alexius I was a revival and not an entirely new foundation as Anna represents it, it would seem to have filled a great need. In the various State Schools the Emperors chose the teachers, paid the salaries, and assumed the right of visiting the schools, where, so Schemmel tells us, they would ask questions and invite good scholars to dine. There is still extant a portrait[3] of Michael Psellus as Hypatos

---

[1] (a) *Die Hochschule von K'pel vom 5. bis 9. Jahrh.*, Berlin, 1912. See p. 180, note 9, above. (b) *Die Schulen von K'pel im 12. bis 15. Jahrh.*, Philolog. Wochenschrift, February 21, 1925. More recently in the *Byz. Archiv* Fr. Fuchs has published the work mentioned above on p. 177, note 2. In his Preface he dwells on the fact that there were always 'zwei Träger des höheren Schulwesens . . . das Kaisertum und das Patriarchat', till finally the State offices of Chief of the Philosophers (head of the γυμνάσιον, as Psellus calls it) and νομοφύλαξ (head of the διδασκαλεῖον νόμων) were both absorbed by the Patriarchate and held by clergy of St. Sophia. The Imperial University and the Patriarch Schools were long distinct and even antagonistic.

[2] C. Neumann, quoting from the Novel of Constantine Monomachus given in the works of John Mauropus, says that before this law-students had had to go to Rome or Beyrout (*Weltstellung des byz. Reichs*, p. 67). This 'monde universitaire' was, according to N. Jorga (paper read before the Congress of Byzantinology at Bukharest, *Acad. Roum. Bull.*, Tome XI, p. 155), 'créé contre l'enseignement du clergé'.

[3] Reproduced in Νέος Ἑλληνομνήμων XII (1915), p. 241.

of Philosophy standing to deliver a lecture before the seated
Michael VII. As we shall see later, his successor Italus was
deposed for heresy.

Side by side with the State Schools there were what we might
call the Church Schools. We have already spoken of two, but
there were others under the Patriarch,[1] the principal one being
attached to the Church of the Holy Apostles. The education
was divided into two parts, higher in a central atrium, elementary in halls around. The subjects taught were Grammar
(i. e. Dialectics, Metre, &c.), Arithmetic, Singing, Rhetoric,
Philosophy, and Medicine, and the Patriarch superintended
daily. All this came to an end after the Latin conquest of
Constantinople in 1204.[2]

For any detailed information as to Schools we look in vain
to the *Alexias*. Even Anna's facts as to the learning imparted
in her father's Orphanage serve chiefly to exalt him as a Mae-
cenas, and to bring into prominence her own educational
superiority. She never tells us precisely what teaching it was
that Psellus and Italus and Nilus had missed. Her account of
the upbringing of her fiancé Constantine Ducas is regrettably
short. She merely says that at seven years old he was, besides
being marvellously beautiful, 'sweet not in words' (or 'learning',
ἐν λόγοις) 'only, but also unequalled in all the varied movements
and turns of games'.[3] Strangely enough we learn little more
about his education from the παιδεία βασιλική of his tutor Theophylact, afterwards Archbishop of Bulgaria. He tells the young
man he is proud to be his teacher, and he credits him with
sense, dignity, quickness in learning, and tenacity in remembering, saying that his intelligence is οἷον φιλόσοφον. He also
praises his learned mother Maria for having provided her son
with instructors to train his tongue, form his mind, and teach
him history. But as to his actual pursuits, we only hear of
riding, wielding a spear, hunting wild animals, and shooting
from horseback. It is true that in Part II he exhorts the young
man to excel in 'wisdom', to 'honour letters', and to frequent
the society of learned and educated men, but as to what the
boy really studied we know nothing.[4] In the next generation
Anna's nephew, the Emperor Manuel, is praised by his admiring subjects, Eustathius and Cinnamus and Prodromus, for his
many-sided proficiency in Church Dogma, War, Philosophy,

[1] Psellus, *Ep.* 162, *B. G. Med.* V. p. 420.
[2] For a library in a monastery see ch. 106 of the *Typikon* of Is. Comnenus; *Bull.
inst. arch. russe de C'ple*, Vol. XIII, pp. 17-77.
[3] III. 1, p. 71.
[4] *P. G.* 126, cols. 253-85.

and Medicine.[1] But as emperors were supposed to be models in learning as in all else, this really tells us little. One interesting light on the facilities for acquiring knowledge at Constantinople in the early twelfth century is thrown by the last of the three writers just named. Prodromus like Anna claims to have studied Grammar, Rhetoric, Aristotle, and Plato, and he has mastered Homer, but his constant cry is that the barbarous Greek of the streets and market prevails over classical speech, and no one cares for learning; also that only the rich can have libraries, while the poor *littérateurs* have to cling to affluent patrons or starve.[2]

When all is put together, we really know very little about the education of the average Byzantine man, but about that of the Byzantine woman we know still less. Psellus' mother was not, like Theoctista mother of Theodore of Studium, an educated woman, though so determined for her son to be a man of letters; but in the next generation his daughter Styliane loved learning, while not neglecting γυναικῶν ἔργα.[3] It does not seem to have been difficult for women to study, but those who wished to do so were doubtless rare. In the first half of the fifth century Eudocia (formerly Athenais), wife of the Emperor Theodosius II, being the daughter of an Athenian professor, studied Rhetoric, Literature, Philosophy, Astronomy, and Geometry with professors from the Constantinople School and also wrote verses, to say nothing of making a public speech to the Senate at Antioch.[4] The same Emperor's sister, Pulcheria, was also a learned woman. Most appropriately in this reign the School at Constantinople was furnished with its complement of professors; it was soon to be without a rival, when Justinian had ruined the School of Athens,[5] and the Arabs had destroyed those of Tyre, Antioch, and Alexandria. In the reign of Leo I, 457–74, we find a sovereign who declared his preference for spending money on teachers rather than on soldiers; his imperial daughter received instruction from the learned Dioscorius.[6] Damascius, a Syrian who lived under Justinian, dedicated his *Life of Isidore* to their joint pupil Theodora, learned in Philosophy, Mathematics, Poetry, and Letters.[7] Then we get a long gap, and the next learned woman is Cassia or Cassiana or Kasia the nun, born about 810, that γυνή τις τῶν Εὐπατριδῶν σοφὴ καὶ παρθένος to whom

[1] C. Neumann, *Gr. Geschichtschreiber im 12. Jahrh.*, pp. 48, 101, etc.
[2] *P. G.* 133, cols. 1291 sqq., 1313 sqq., 1419–22. [3] *B. G. Med.* V, p. 65.
[4] Diehl, *Figures Byzantines*, Sér. I, pp. 25–49, and Fritz Schemmel, *Die Hochschule von K'pel vom 5. bis 9. Jahrh.*, p. 5.
[5] Schemmel, *op. cit.* pp. 8, 12. [6] *Ibid.* p. 6.
[7] *Problèmes et solutions touchant les premiers principes*, trans. A. Chaignet, p. vii. Demo, the female critic of Homer, is assigned to the second half of the fifth century; *G. B. L.* p. 530.

verbal tradition as quoted by Theodore Prodromus[1] ascribed the original first four poems of the Canon of the Great Sabbath. These verses were afterwards changed for four by Bishop Marcus of Otranto because οἱ ὕστερον judged it ἀνάξιον . . . γυναικείοις συμμίξαι λόγοις τὰ . . . μουσουργήματα of the great Cosmas who had written poems 5–8. This would seem to argue a not very high esteem for 'feminine words', but it is possible that the incongruity so keenly felt depended on the solemn sanctity of a hymn. When at a much later date Nicetas Acominatus says his History must be simply worded, so as to please workmen and soldiers and women, it is doubtful which of the two aspects of the case he wishes to emphasize, the illiteracy of women or their love of study.[2] Shortly before Anna was born, the Empress of the day was Eudocia Macrembolitissa, wife first of Constantine X and then of Romanus Diogenes. Till quite recently she was credited with what Krumbacher calls a 'mythologisch-antiquarisches Sammelwerk' known as Ἰωνιά, but this is now put as late as the sixteenth century.[3] She may well however have written the instructive treatises and the poem on Ariadne's hair mentioned as hers by Rambaud.[4] The next Empress, Maria, is praised by Theophylact for love of learning (φιλομαθές) and pursuit of τὰ θεῖα λόγια, as well as for providing her son with tutors, but he gives no further details.[5] In the following century (1147) John Tzetzes dedicated a book on the *Iliad* to John's wife, the Hungarian Irene, as ὁμηρικωτάτη.[6]

One more fact closes the meagre result of inquiries on the subject: neither in the Patriarch's School nor in Alexius' Orphanage School do we find any mention of girl pupils.

There is a small point which deserves a little further study. Anna we may repeat gives no evidence of understanding Latin. Indeed her attitude to all foreign tongues is that of a haughty Greek towards a world of barbarians. Half-breeds of course speak two languages, and men who know Latin or even Scythian may find such knowledge useful on occasions.[7] But her

[1] *Commentary on Canon of the Great Sabbath* (P. G. 133, col. 1235–8). See *Anth. Gr. Carm. Christ.* by Christ and Paranikas, where another poem 'On the woman a sinner' is ascribed to Cassia, and also (in the first four poems of Canon XIII of Cosmas) several verses which spoil the acrostic and clearly do not belong (pp. 104, 196).   [2] Pref. I, p. 3.   [3] *G. B. L.*, p. 578.

[4] Article on Psellus, *Rev. Hist.* III, p. 273.

[5] Παιδ. βασ., I, 12, 13 (P. G. 126, col. 265).

[6] G. Hart, Suppl., Vol. 12 (1881) of *Jahrb. für class. Philol.*, p. 22.

[7] V. 8, p. 145; VII. 9, p. 211; VIII. 5, p. 232; X. 5, p. 285: 8, p. 291, and 10, p. 301; XI. 2, p. 315; XIV. 2, p. 424; XV. 5, p. 475. In XIII. 9, p. 400, we read of a Greek 'acquainted with the Celtic tongue', apparently Norman-French, and of two of his companions who have had 'much experience of Latin customs', one of them (Marinus) having spent his life at Naples.

noble husband cannot understand the Crusaders,[1] and she herself feels that the insertion of any 'barbaric' names (which she
cannot pronounce διὰ τὸ ἄναρθρον)[2] must 'defile the grandeur of
the history' and break up its 'body'.[3] Italus' pronunciation of
Greek was 'what might be expected from one who had come
from Latin people', and he also made 'solecisms' in writing.[4]
In Alexius' Orphanage School one great object was to turn
these 'children collected from every race' into Ῥωμαῖοι as soon
as might be. So every one, whether Latin or Scythian or Hellene,
was to be seen ἑλληνίζων to the best of his ability. The idea
which Oster[5] reads into the passage, that each child made a
careful study of his own native language, is contrary to the
conceptions of any Byzantine of that day, and would have found
scant approval from Anna herself.[6]

The exceedingly bad Latin in Alexius' letters to the Abbot
of Monte Cassino[7] has been a puzzle to critics. Even if he
could not write Latin, was there no one at Constantinople that
could? Riant[8] believes that the original Greek chrysobulls
were accompanied by rough Latin translations, made by some
Greek at Constantinople for the benefit of those who acted as
envoys. These rough notes he suggests may have been fastened
to the outer covering of the chrysobulls, and filed away instead
of the originals by mistake. In any case we need not credit the
Emperor with the grammatical and other errors, as we feel sure
he personally had no acquaintance with this despised barbarian
tongue, any more than his learned daughter. Already by the
middle of the tenth century Constantine Porphyrogenitus could
speak of the replacement of the Latin language by Greek.[9] This
process, which found its counterpart in the gradual forgetting
of Greek by the Westerners, so that Neumann[10] believes the
Chronicle of Theophanes early in the ninth century to have
been the last Greek work read by both the Greek and the
Roman public, had begun many centuries before with Justinian's
Novels: in Anna's day it was complete. 'East and West could

---

[1] X. 9, p. 397.
[2] X. 10, p. 300.
[3] VI. 14, p. 182; X. 8, p. 289; XIII. 6, p. 393. Cf. VI. 7, p. 165.
[4] V. 8, p. 146. We may note that the German Luitprand, who visited Constantinople in 949, tries to embellish his Latin with Greek after the manner of
Cicero.
[5] A. K., Part I, p. 41.
[6] XV. 7, p. 485.
[7] Preserved in the Register of Petrus Diaconus in the Archives of Monte
Cassino.
[8] *Inventaire des lettres historiques des croisades* (*Archives de l'Orient latin*, I, p. 140).
[9] de Them., Introduction (C. S. H. B., Vol. III, p. 13).
[10] *Weltstellung des Byz. Reiches vor den Kreuzzügen*, p. 15.

come to no understanding, because quite literally they could not understand one another.'[1]

27. ALLUSIONS IN *ALEXIAS* XV

BEFORE we proceed to consider the evidence of Anna's learning in various other spheres we will deal with some remaining questions of literary education. First of all, to whom does she allude in her diatribe against Schedography? She speaks of Stylianus, Longibardus, and Atticus as well-known men of learning (especially in lexicography), and couples with these names the clergy of St. Sophia as a whole.[2]

We will begin with Schedography itself. Psellus claims to have restored this study to the world of education,[3] which may account for Anna's thinking it 'an invention of the moderns'. Renauld[4] reminds us that in any case γραμματική for the Byzantines 's'occupait en particulier de l'interprétation philologique, littéraire, mythologique, critique, historique, des auteurs anciens, d'abord des poètes . . . ensuite des prosateurs'. From this to 'grammatical analysis' of selected passages on tablets there is but one step: only in Anna's opinion it was a step downhill, as it put the literary contents of the masterpieces studied, with all that might be learnt from them, in the second place instead of the first. Still, the masterpieces were not wholly forgotten, so she would have us think, till after her father's death.

On this passage Krumbacher has, as always, useful information to give.[5] He says that various schedographic lexicons and alphabetical glossaries exist, and a treatise by Moschopulos (who lived 1283–1328) περὶ σχεδῶν was printed as early as 1545. But when he translates Anna's words πεττεία δὲ τὸ σπούδασμα as meaning that Schedography was 'ein Brettspiel' he

---

[1] Baynes, *Byz. Empire*, p. 95. Even the learned Photius knew no Latin; *G.B.L.* p. 516. We may note that, doubtless as a mark of special learning, the rector of Constantine Monomachus' new Faculty of Philosophy had to know Latin as well as Greek (C. Neumann, *Weltstellung, &c.*, p. 67). Mileto in Calabria must have been a great exception to all rules. Leib (*Rome, Kiev et Byzance*, p. 128) says Latin, Greek, and Arabic were all official languages there, while the Court spoke Norman-French.

[2] XV. 7, p. 485; see p. 177 above.

[3] *Ep. to Psephas* (*B. G. Med.* V). Christophorus Mytilenaeus, quoted by Fuchs (*op. cit.* p. 44), says in one of his poems that when Encyclic Wisdom builds her house . . . Schedography is taught. This poet flourished about 1035; Krumbacher (*G. B. L.* p. 737) puts him roughly at 1000–50, while Psellus' dates are later, 1018–79.

[4] *Op. cit.* p. 407.   [5] *G.B.L.* p. 591.

seems to go completely off the track. If we take them thus
there is no sense to be made of her next phrase καὶ ἄλλα τὰ ἔργα
ἀθέμιτα. In our translation given above, 'now...draughts are the
rage and other wicked practices', we are supported by the
C. S. H. B., 'calculorum vero lusus studium est et reliqua occu-
patio nefaria'.

About the individual grammarians whom she mentions we
have little information. First as to Stylianus. The name was
clearly not uncommon. Psellus had a daughter Styliane on
whom he wrote a Funeral Oration, and two men named Stylianus are mentioned by Krumbacher. One of them was the
ninth-century theologian who was Archbishop of Neocaesarea
and wrote a treatise, now lost, against Photius.[1] Nothing
leads us to believe he was a grammarian. The other was a
Protoasecretis about whom at an uncertain date an epigram
was written by one Symeon.[2] The epigram is still unpublished,
but a copy made from the manuscript in Rome[3] contains no
word as to any literary attainments of the recipient, though it
credits him with an ἐλεύθερον φρόνημα.[4] Zonaras tells us of two
more of the name, one the father-in-law of Leo VI for whom
the new title of Basileopater was coined, and the other a 'proto-
pope' of the Palace under Nicephorus Phocas.[5] These two may
be excluded. Or is it perhaps possible to assume that this is
one of Anna's inaccuracies, and that she meant Syrianus? This
name was borne by one of the two senior *Grammatici Graeci* connected with the Capitol School at Constantinople in 425,[6] and
also, unless we identify the two, by the head of the neo-Platonic
School at Athens in the fifth century, who wrote commentaries
on Aristotle, and on the τέχνη ῥητορική of Hermogenes of Tarsus.[7] The suggestion is at least plausible.

With Longibardus we come to rather firmer ground. In the
Vatican and in Paris there are manuscripts of Λογγιβάρδου τοῦ
σοφοῦ παρεκβόλαιον τῆς σχεδογραφίας, which Krumbacher[8]
thinks was composed in the eleventh century. A Florentine

[1] G. B. L. pp. 77, 78. A. Papadopulos Kerameus quotes Pope John VIII as
writing to Stylianus about this document: τὸ δὲ σὸν χειρόγραφον ὃ πεποίηκας εἰ καὶ
πολὺν χρόνον καὶ πολλάκις ὑφ' ἡμῶν ἐζήτηται ὅμως οὐδαμοῦ τοῦτο ἀνευρεῖν δεδυνήμεθα
(B. Z. VIII, p. 653).
[2] G. B. L. p. 785.
[3] Cod. Barb. gr. I. 74, fol. 1.
[4] line 13. There was of course nothing to hinder a Protoasecretis from being
literary; Psellus in his day occupied such a post.
[5] Epit. XVI. 12 and 24.
[6] Cod. Theod. VI. tit. 21.
[7] See Smith's Dict. of Greek and Rom. Biog., and also Renauld, op. cit. p. 411,
note 1.
[8] Op. cit. p. 591.

manuscript bearing much the same title has been published by
N. Festa in the *Byzantinische Zeitschrift*,[1] and in his article, called
Note preliminari su Longibardos, he says: 'Che altro è questo[2] se
non un saggio di quel genere scolastico che i bizantini designa-
rono col nome di schedografia?' though he explains that the
proper schedography was short and in catechetical form, and
the work in question is neither. In the fifth volume of his
Bibliotheca Graeca medii aevi, Sathas gives us after his Prologue
a list of the works of Psellus contained in the Paris Codex 1182.
Two are addressed to John Longibardus (apparently a Roman
by birth), one being an ἐπαινετικός,[3] the other headed "Εἰς
Λογγίβαρδον Ἰωάννην καταναγκάζοντα αὐτὸν εἰς τὸ ἑρμηνεῦσαι
τάχιον τὰ μαθήματα".[4] Possibly this was Anna's learned
grammarian, though Geometry seems to have been his predi-
lection, and Psellus rebukes him as unaware of the greatness
of knowledge or the patience needed to attain it,[5] and so
better fitted to be a soldier. The editor Boissonade however believes that the man in question was no less a person
than John Italus, Psellus' scholar and opponent. Du Cange[6]
points out that Italians as a whole were much given to grammatical study, but here it is more than likely that 'the wise
Lombard' was an appellation meant to hide a definite identity.
Anna herself speaks of τοὺς λεγομένους Λογγιβάρδους. Behind this
nom de plume, if it was one, we are not likely ever to penetrate
with certainty, though if it conceals John Italus[7] there was
every reason why Anna should not wish openly to praise her
father's great heretical antagonist.

The last name, Atticus, may of course be similarly interpreted
as 'a writer of Attic Greek' (though there is here no qualifying
'so-called'), but in Pape-Benseler's Dictionary we find an Atticus who was a παιδοτρίβης.[8] He was presumably the same as the
fifth-century Patriarch of Constantinople, and so would have
a place also among the learned clergy of St. Sophia to whom

---

[1] XVI, pp. 431–53.
[2] The title in his manuscript has περὶ συντάξεως instead of τῆς σχεδογραφίας,
as in Paris and Rome.
[3] No. 56, φ 50.
[4] No. 87, φ 101*. This has been published by J. F. Boissonade in his *Psellus
de operatione daemonum, etc.*, pp. 164 sqq.
[5] He says οὔπω ἔγνωκας ὁποῖον τῶν μαθημάτων τὸ μεγεθὸς καὶ ἡλίκον τὸ ὕψος καὶ ὅτι
οὐ διὰ ῥᾳδίας ἡ πρὸς ἐκεῖνα ἄνοδος, and advises him to leave Geometry and 'all other
Music' and devote himself to Arms (pp. 166, 169).
[6] Note on XV. 7, p. 485 c.
[7] Fuchs identifies Psellus' correspondent with John Italus, but adds in a note:
'Wer der Longobardos ist, der die Schrift über die Schedographie verfasste, bleibt
fraglich' (*op. cit.* p. 34).
[8] He refers to Socr., *H. Eccl.* VIII. 27.

Anna next refers. As Krumbacher points out, 'nicht weniger als vier Metropoliten treten im 12. Jahrhundert in den Dienst der profanen Litteratur',[1] and two of them, Michael Acominatus probably, and Eustathius Bishop of Thessalonica certainly, began their clerical career in Constantinople. Of Eustathius Krumbacher says:[2] 'Anfänglich bekleidete er die Stelle eines Diakons an der Sophienkirche[3] und wirkte ausserdem als öffentlicher Lehrer der Beredsamkeit.' Two of the Patriarchs between 824 and 1111 bore the nickname of Grammaticus, and an earlier one that of Scholasticus; while one of the duties connected with the office was to superintend what Schemmel calls the Patriarchenschulen.[4] In the ninth century there was even, according to N. Jorga, 'un essai de donner à l'Église des patriarches sortis du monde universitaire créé, contre l'enseignement du clergé, par l'école de Bardas'.[5]

Theodore Prodromus (who elsewhere[6] complains of the coldness to him of St. Sophia) addresses one of his many Eulogies to John Hieromnemon or Agapetus (who held the See of Constantinople from 1111 to 1134), and 'borrows from the Ecclesiastical Muse' a prayer that he may be preserved.[7] This prelate, when chosen Patriarch, was another of the many learned deacons of Constantinople, part of the body whose aid Alexius invoked in combating heretics.

Besides these, Oeconomos[8] tells us that under Manuel I there were two deacons in the Church of St. Sophia famed for sacred and profane learning, Michael of Thessalonica[9] and Nicephorus Basilaces, the latter of whom 'connaissait bien l'antiquité et avait étudié notamment Platon et Marc Aurèle'. It is not

---

[1] Op. cit. p. 17.

[2] Op. cit. p. 536. In the Preface to Fontes rerum Byzantinarum W. Regel points out that Eustathius' 'Orationes' are really our best materials for Byzantine history in the second half of the twelfth century.

[3] So also did Theophylact, Archbishop of Bulgaria and tutor of Constantine Ducas. Fuchs says that the Deacons of the Great Church were primarily expounders of (1) the Gospels, (2) the Old Testament, especially the Psalter, (3) St. Paul's Epistles—but also imparted profane learning (op. cit. pp. 35 sqq.).

[4] We know this was actually done by the learned John Camaterus at the end of the twelfth century, 1199–1206 (Schemmel, Die Schulen, etc.).

[5] Op. cit. p. 155. See above, p. 182, note 2.

[6] In his farewell poem to Byzantium, of which the opening lines are given in P. G. 133, col. 1010, and the substance in Notices et Extraits, Vol. VIII. Pt. II, p. 209.

[7] Ibid. p. 151, a letter referred to by J. G. La Porte du Theil, from MS. CCCV in Vatican. Zonaras, XVIII. 25, does not give John's name, but says of him when he succeeded Nicolas that he was λόγοις ἐντεθραμμένον τοῖς τε θύραθεν καὶ τοῖς καθ' ἡμᾶς; cf. p. 180, note 9.

[8] Vie religieuse, pp. 30, 32 and notes.

[9] According to C. Neumann he was Professor of Evangelical Exegesis (Gr. Geschichtschreiber, p. 74).

surprising that the learned refuter of heresies, the monk Euthymius Zigabenus, was according to Anna known to those of the 'ecclesiastical register',[1] to which term in the passage about Schedography she adds τῆς μεγάλης ἐκκλησίας. The clergy of St. Sophia were not the whole of the 'ecclesiastical register', but they were a most important part. If Anna does not mention the most distinguished of them all, the great Patriarch Photius[2] whose Λέξεων συναγωγή would have made him a perfect instance of 'those who toiled over the collection of all sorts of names', it is a deliberate omission. His political career earned him the hatred temporary or lasting of two emperors, and his reputation was far from savoury among writers of the court circle. Like Italus he could only be praised by Anna in a cryptic fashion if at all.

28. PLAGIARY IN GENERAL

WE now come to the big topic of the results of Anna's education, in the general knowledge which she shows in her writings. Did she really understand her own numerous allusions, and when she quotes does she do so accurately? Had she more than a bowing acquaintance with her authorities?

This brings in the interesting question about which E. Stemplinger has written a whole book,[3] the question of plagiarism. He is dealing with Classical times, but he is careful to point out how many of the same principles and practices were maintained by the Byzantines. One fundamental difference between Western and Eastern medieval Europe lay in the obvious fact that the former studied Roman writers, and the latter Greek. Stemplinger even asserts that Nicephorus Bryennius devoted himself specially to Xenophon, and Anna Comnena to Thucydides and Polybius. Homer was 'die Bibel der Alten', and for the Constantinople Library copies were made of Plato, Aristotle, Demosthenes, Isocrates, and Thucydides. In the schools, after Reading and Listening, came first Paraphrase and then μίμησις of Style.[4] For according to the experts[5] there were four styles, each appropriate to the matter in hand, each exemplified by some great writer. All material was public property, like

---

[1] XV. 9, p. 490.
[2] He held office as Patriarch 858–67 and 878–86 under the Emperors Michael III and Basil I.
[3] *Das Plagiat in der gr. Lit.*, Leipzig, 1912. See also *G.B.L.* p. 746.
[4] pp. 115 sqq.   [5] Demetrios, περὶ ἑρμηνείας.

light and air, and all imitation was legitimate, if it was not mechanical, or done with deliberate intent to deceive. The older historians for instance put their own names in their first sentence, but seldom mentioned their sources; so the Byzantine writers copy whole passages verbally without acknowledgement.[1] Down to the age of Aristotle it was etiquette never to speak of contemporaries by name and never to give exact references. There was nothing unusual in saying 'I heard' instead of 'I read' (Aristotle and Aristides permitted this) or in inventing authorities, like Plato with his Solon and the Egyptian priest. Writers copied from themselves, or from the collections of extracts which all literary men made for their own use.[2] From Alexandrian days onwards we have books of Proverbs, and of stereotyped forms for beginnings and endings, for eulogies and descriptions, &c.[3] As for the sentiments, Aristotle taught that men liked to hear 'allgemeine Gedanken',[4] and the λόγοι βασιλικοί and λόγοι ἐπιτάφιοι of medieval times go right back to Pindar and Thucydides. Yet a sense of the necessary unity of style[5] prevented Classical writers from inserting patches

---

[1] Nic. Bryennius copies frequently in this way from Psellus, e.g. his I. 1, p. 28 = *Chron.*, Rom. Diog., Byz. T., p. 250, a feigned flight to lure an enemy on being the subject. So also do Zonaras and Scylitzes, as well as Anna herself in at least three instances. See note 2 on p. 557 of Renauld's *Étude de Psellos*.

In Pref. 2 of the *Alexias* we have two textual but unacknowledged quotations. One is from the Introduction to the fragment of history left by Johannes Epiphaniensis (ed. Dindorf, *Hist. gr. min.* I, p. 376), ἀλλ' ὡς ἂν μὴ πρᾶγμα . . . ἀποσβέννυται σκότῳ, which is copied verbatim by Anna except that she puts ἀμάρτυρον for ἀδιαβόητον. The other, ὅταν γάρ τις . . . ὀκνητέον, is compressed from Polyb. I. 14. If this shocks our literary morality, we must remember that almost in our own day we have John Wesley writing in the Preface to his *Christian Library of Practical Divinity* (1750):—'I have been obliged not only to omit the far greatest part of several eminent authors, but also to add what was needful, either to clear their sense or to correct their mistakes. . . . I apprehend myself to be at full liberty so to do. I therefore take no author for better for worse.' Having carried out this method of procedure, he then felt he could be responsible for everything contained in the *Library*.

[2] *Das Plagiat*, pp. 218–21. Nicholas Callicles has two closely parallel passages in two poems on similar subjects, VII. 1–5 and XXII. 29–33. Stemplinger says Strabo is seldom quoted by name, because he served so largely as an *Exzerptenwerk*.

[3] So Nic. Bry. copies a sentence of his description of Alexius (I. 6, p. 20) almost verbatim from Psellus' description of John Ducas Caesar (*Chron.*, Mich. VII, Byz. T. pp. 265–6).

[4] *Das Plagiat*, p. 229.

[5] A sense of stylistic unity even in Byzantine times is shown in the Preface of Zonaras' *Epitome*. After giving his reasons for writing a history he forestalls criticisms on his style in this: 'Borrowing (ἐρανισάμενος) my histories from many books, in many particulars I should use the composition (συνθήκαις) and phrases of those writers: and in whatever I shall imitate or paraphrase (παρῳδήσω ἢ παραφράσω) I shall change the form of my language to correspond with the character of those others, lest my composition should seem to be inharmonious (ἀσύμφωνος) with itself.' Most writers Classical or Byzantine did the opposite, and changed the language of their authorities to correspond with their own.

from other works into their own as the Byzantines freely did; the ancients modified their quotations to suit their own work. Thus Hermogenes forbade inserting a verse citation into a prose work: it had to be turned into prose. All this worked against verbal accuracy, which was further impaired by quoting from memory, or at second and third hand;[1] we can thus readily understand why Anna Comnena has lapses. Speeches, Dialogues, and Letters in historical compositions did not as a rule even pretend to be authentic. Finally we may mention the cases where an author's words were deliberately changed for polemical purposes, and others where 'Kryptomnesie' was at work; under this head we may put several of Anna's faulty Biblical allusions.

In short, Stemplinger's 'Schlusswort' as to Classical Literature applies equally well to Byzantine. Verbal quotations were the exception, 'freie Uebertragung' the rule, for the principle prevailed 'dass es ein geistiges Eigentum im absoluten Sinne nicht gibt'.

29. THE BIBLE

HAVING thus glanced at the general notions prevalent in Anna's day as to the ethics of quotation, we will consider her application of those notions. And first we will take up her knowledge of the Bible, always remembering that the Eastern Church has never restricted the reading of the Bible by the laity, as has the Church of Rome.

In the short *Prologue* to her Will we find seven Biblical quotations or allusions, all apposite except the statement that Jacob was 'blessed by his father for obedience to his *father*', a strange version of the story in *Genesis* xxvii. As a matter of fact this can be explained away as a *lapsus calami* in the only known manuscript of the *Prologue*,[2] where either from dittography or

---

[1] *Das Plagiat*, pp. 242, 248. Aristotle, Plato, Pliny, and the Scholiasts all made mistakes from this cause. Learning by heart was of course one great form of education, from Classical times down to the invention of printing and even beyond.

[2] This is Codex Barocc. 131 in the Bodleian Library, where the handwriting is very small, illegible, and full of contractions. If the lost original from which the writer copied was at all like it, he might easily indeed have written καὶ Ἰακὼβ εὐλογούμενος ὑπὸ τοῦ πατρὸς διὰ τὴν πρὸς τὸν πατέρα εὐπείθειαν instead of πρὸς τὴν μητέρα, as the definite article in each case is one letter with accents, and the noun is three letters of which the two last, ρ and α, are identical in the two words, while μ might easily be mistaken for π, the τ being wholly omitted in both. Furthermore, the words immediately preceding are: "ἐπερρώννυέ ⟨με⟩ πρὸς τὴν ὑπακοὴν" (to her

mere carelessness a second 'father' has been written instead of 'mother'. Psellus[1] tells us that his mother used to soothe him to sleep with stories, not of myths or bogies, but about Isaac led to the slaughter through obedience to his *father*, and about 'Jacob meeting with paternal praise because he acted according to the suggestions of his *mother*'. The antithesis between Father and Mother is not only demanded in the *Prologue* by the balance of the sentence in question, but seems implied in the following one, τί γὰρ εὐλογίας πατρὸς τιμιώτερον, τί δὲ μητρὸς εὐχῆς μακαριώτερον;

One word more about the *Prologue*. In it she lays claims to 'divine learning'; in the *Alexias* she seems to regard such learning as it were from the outside,[2] but she gives proof of it on every page.

In the fifteen books of the *Alexias* Anna has two references to the Apocrypha, forty to the Old Testament (of which thirteen are to the Psalms),[3] and forty-five to the New. Out of all these, twelve are distinct quotations, introduced by, 'as the apostolic saying is', 'like the words of David's lyre', and so forth; seventeen are allusions to Biblical personages, Ham the son of Noah,[4] Aaron and Moses, Herod,[5] the Son of Thunder, David, Zedekiah, Saul, Solomon, Job, the Three Children, the Maccabees, Mary Magdalene, and Our Lord Himself.[6] The rest all come into Anna's composition as naturally as into that of any educated person nowadays.[7] 'Sevenfold into the bosom', 'fearing lest a tumult be made', 'carried about by every wind',

---

parents in marrying) "Ἰσαὰκ σφαττόμενος πειθοῖ τῇ πρὸς τὸν πατέρα", and it is notorious how frequently a phrase is repeated by error. In the manuscript the πρὸς τὸν πατέρα referring to Jacob is in the same line as the πρὸς τὸν πατέρα referring to Isaac, and may well be held to present a mere example of dittography.

[1] *Funeral Oration on his Mother* (B. G. Med. V, p. 17).

[2] V. 9, p. 147.

[3] C. Diehl (*Manuel de l'art byzantin*, p. 379) says that the Byzantines, with their taste for 'spéculations religieuses et théologiques' always loved the Psalms, and were encouraged in this by the monks: 'Saint Basile n'avait-il pas dit que les Psaumes contenaient la théologie tout entière?'

[4] Drunken Noah appears in Cec., *Strat.* p. 5.

[5] The fury of Herod was one of the *loci communes* of medieval and even later literature. An old carol gives one instance: 'Herod the kynge, In his ragynge.' Another will occur to every reader in Hamlet's address to the players, where he says of tearing a passion to tatters that 'it out-herods Herod' (Act III, Sc. ii).

[6] We might add the Hagarenes and Ishmaelites, terms which Anna commonly applies to Moslems in general, because of the Bible story tracing the descent of the Arabian desert tribes from Ishmael, son of Hagar. We shall speak later of her references to Ashtoreth the Sidonian goddess.

[7] Her husband's History is by no means so soaked as hers in Biblical knowledge, but all Byzantine writers possess it to some degree. Nicolas Callicles her contemporary has more allusions to the Scriptures than even she herself; he draws from a wider field than hers, including the Book of Revelation.

'watch and be sober', 'zeal not according to knowledge'. Such is the phraseology that meets us at every turn, and as a rule it is applied correctly. That being so, it seems invidious to point out certain inaccuracies, but as they illustrate Anna's literary standard, this must be done.

First of all there are a number of very loose quotations, true to the spirit, but not the letter. Over and over again Anna speaks of people sent empty away, but she always uses the word ἀποπέμπειν,[1] whereas in the *Magnificat* the verb is ἐξαποστέλλειν. Flying soldiers 'give their backs to the enemies to strike', whereas Isaiah gave his εἰς μάστιγας; the 'lot' of the righteous is κλῆρος in the Psalms, κληρονομία in the *Alexias*; in another place the same idea of 'nets' and a 'pit' is expressed by different words from the original.[2] Her demoniac 'lay' and St. Mark's 'wallowed', both foaming.[3] The Crusaders are seized χαρᾷ καὶ φρίκῃ, just as the Women at the Sepulchre departed μετὰ φόβου καὶ χαρᾶς.[4] Sometimes the phrase is like a far-away echo of some Biblical passage, as when domestic enemies are thought worse than those from outside[5] or when Alexius bids the Devil avaunt.[6] In these cases we can only say that the Bible suggested to Anna a thought, which she expresses in a somewhat similar form of words. Again we need not quarrel with her for sentences compounded from various parts of the Bible, inextricably mixed.[7] But there are passages where she is evidently trying to quote, and quotes wrong. It is of course a small matter when she gives the locust and the cankerworm of Joel in the reverse order from the prophet's,[8] or when in saying: 'And the like once happened to Saul, for God rending rent his kingdom,' she takes this Hebraism (retained by the *Septuagint*) from God's words to Solomon and applies it to the incident of Saul and Samuel's mantle.[9] But when she states that Greek priests might not fight, she makes this extraordinary quotation as being an εὐαγγελικὸν δόγμα, "μὴ θίξῃς, μὴ γρύξῃς, μὴ ἅψῃ· ἱερωμένος γὰρ εἶ". The second verb γρύξῃς ('grumble') is clearly a mistake for γεύσῃς; we should then have the 'Touch not, taste not, handle

---

[1] So Nic. Bry. (III. 4, p. 71) has κενὸς ἀπεπέμπετο.
[2] I. 6, p. 15, cf. *Is.* l. 6; III. 10, p. 93, cf. *Ps.* cxxv. 3; XV. 6, p. 480, cf. *Ps.* lvii. 6.
[3] VI. 9, p. 170; cf. *Mark* ix. 20.
[4] XI. 6, p. 327; cf. *Matt.* xxviii. So Attal. p. 19, has χαρᾷ καὶ φόβῳ συνεχόμενοι.
[5] XIII. 8, p. 399; cf. *Ps.* lv. 12–14, and *Matt.* x. 36.
[6] XIV. 4, p. 437; cf. *Matt.* xvi. 23.
[7] Thus XI. 6, p. 326 is made up from *Joel* ii. 12, 13; *Matt.* xi. 21; *Jonah* III. and *Dan.* ix. 3. Again, XII. 3, p. 353, is drawn from *Wisdom* v but tinged by 2 *Cor.* vi. 6, 7, while XIV. 7, p. 449, is a combination of *Gen.* iii. 15 and *Gen.* xlix. 17.
[8] I. 14, p. 35; cf. *Joel* i. 4.
[9] III. 5, p. 80, really taken from 1 *Kings* xi. 11, not 1 *Sam.* xv. 28.

not' of St. Paul,[1] and a glance at the Epistle will show that St. Paul gave the phrase as an instance of men's absurd ordinances, whereas Anna takes it seriously as a rule of life. Again in one of her eulogies on her father, she says that nothing separated him from the love of *Christians*, neither pains nor pleasures, &c. No one can fail to see in this a confused memory of St. Paul's magnificent: 'Who shall separate us from the love of *Christ*? shall tribulation, or distress,' &c.[2] The change of the word 'Christ' into 'Christians' shows that Anna had entirely misunderstood the passage; St. Paul was extolling the love of Christ for us, Anna twists the phrase into praise of her father's large-heartedness. Furthermore in describing Alexius' munificence to his orphanage, she brings in Our Lord's feedings of the multitude, but gives the numbers as 7,000 and 5,000, instead of 5,000 and 4,000. The ἑπτακισχιλίων may be either simply a mistake for τετρακισχιλίων, or a confusion from τοὺς ἑπτὰ ἄρτους τῶν τετρακισχιλίων.[3] In the same passage she says that Alexius appointed in the Church 'singing men and singing women like Solomon'. This is quite incorrect, as Solomon merely confirmed his father David's arrangements for music performed by male Levites, and women-singers when mentioned in the Bible have no connexion with religious worship at all.[4]

On the whole, we may say that these are small and few errors, but the investigation seems to show that she did not verify her references.

One other thing remains to be said on this subject. In the account of the trial of the Bogomiles she says: " κάμινοι . . . ἑπταπλασίως κατὰ τὸν μελῳδὸν ἀνήπτοντο ". There is a passage in the book of Daniel very similar to this,[5] but as that book is in prose, why does she use the word μελῳδός? A short examination of the *Anthologia Graeca carminum Christianorum*[6] will show that the Three Children of Babylon figured in all Greek religious poetry. Thus, in the eighth-century Triodion on the Wednesday in Holy Week, written by the great hymno-

---

[1] X. 8, p. 292; cf. *Col.* ii. 21.
[2] XII. 3, p. 352; cf. *Rom.* viii. 35.
[3] XV. 7, p. 483; cf. *Matt.* xvi. 10.
[4] XV. 7, p. 485; cf. 1 *Chron.* xv. 16–28, also chapters xvi and xxv; 2 *Chron.* vii, 6 and viii. 14; 2 *Sam.* xix. 35; *Ezra* ii. 65; *Neh.* vii. 67; *Eccles.* ii. 8. The words used by Anna are ᾄδοντες καὶ ᾄδουσαι. After Josiah's death he is mourned by professional mourners of both sexes, οἱ ἄρχοντες καὶ αἱ ἄρχουσαι θρῆνον (2 *Chron.* xxxv. 25; cf. 1 *Esdras* i. 32), where the A.V. misleadingly gives 'the singing men and the singing women'. A ψάλλουσα, or female singer to the harp, is mentioned as a dangerous siren in *Ecclus.* ix. 4. For women in religious cults we may compare the αὐλητρίς and ὀλολύκτρια κοινή at Pergamon (Dittenberger, *Sylloge*, 3rd ed., No. 982).
[5] XV. 9, p. 492; cf. *Dan.* iii. 19.
[6] Christ and Paranikas (Teubner, 1871).

grapher Cosmas (who, except for Romanus and John Damascene, is the only μελῳδός mentioned by Suidas),[1] we read:

ἑπταπλασίως κάμινος ἐξεκαύθη ποτὲ
ἐν ᾗ παῖδες οὐκ ἐφλέχθησαν.

In the same Anthology there are twenty-seven other references to the story, many of them dwelling on the piety[2] which entitled the youths to deliverance, and to the heavenly dew by which the fire was extinguished. It was the absence of such miraculous aid that proved to Anna (or so she says) the criminality of the Bogomiles. Her words about the Three at Babylon, that the fire enfolded them 'like some golden bed', may contain a reference to the hymn where John Damascene compares the Virgin's womb, often called by other writers a χρυσῆ κιβωτός,[3] to a κάμινος in which God re-created the whole world 'as He saved the three children'.[4]

30. HOMER AND OTHER POETS

NEXT in order of importance comes Anna's familiarity with Homer, who was to her ὁ ποιητής as much as Shakespeare is to us 'The Bard',[5] and from whom the very name of her work was copied, an *Alexiad* in imitation of an *Iliad*. Oster has given us a list of her Homeric quotations, but it is not complete, and he also omits to say where they are to be found in the *Iliad* and the *Odyssey*.[6] There are, as a matter of fact, besides the stereotyped Homeric phrases such as πολύτροπος, βυσσοδο-μεύειν, 'loosing the stern-cables', &c., sixty-six references in the *Alexias* to the *Iliad* and the *Odyssey* (not forty-four as Oster has it), of which two are composite, forty-seven belong to the *Iliad*, seven to the *Odyssey*, and ten to both. These last ten are the question 'Who and whence art thou?', the comparison

---

[1] p. 189, and see Du Cange's note on *Al.* XV. 9, p. 492 A; *G. B. L.* p. 675.
[2] *Anth.*, pp. 168, 207, 235, &c.
[3] *Ibid.*, pp. 147, 240.
[4] *Ibid.*, p. 234. Cf. also p. 168, where Cosmas says that the Virgin's womb, unconsumed by the fire of Divinity which entered into it, is comparable to the δροσοβόλος κάμινος which did not burn "οὓς ἐδέξατο νέους."
[5] She uses 'Homer's Calliope' or Homer's muse' or 'all the Homeric muses' as a periphrase for his Epic Poetry (VII. 11, p. 215; X. 2, p. 271; XII. 3, p. 353; XIV. 7, p. 446; cf. Psellus, *Chron.*, Const. IX, Byz. T., p. 168). The use of ὁ ποιητής for Homer is found in Polybius, and down to Psellus. By 'the poet' Plato means either Homer or Hesiod, whereas Thucydides when he means Homer says 'the poets' or 'the ancients'. Rambaud says of Psellus (*Rev. Hist.* III, p. 265), 'Il fait d'Homère une sorte de prophète biblique', a kind of unconscious Christian.
[6] *A. K.*, Pt. III.

of the countless Crusaders to leaves and flowers in their season,[1] the description of Alexias as a young man 'with his first beard, as they say',[2] the three passages where she speaks of blaming the blameless,[3] the twice-used epithet Ἀρηΐφιλος,[4] the statement that Homer condescended to speak of the Boeotians and of 'certain barbarous islands',[5] and the phrase ἄχθος ἀρούρης, of which we shall speak later.[6] The two composite citations are such as our investigation into Byzantine methods of quoting might have led us to expect. The words in question ἄφωνος ἔκειτο occur twice,[7] the first time followed by χαμᾶζε κατὰ τὸν ποιητήν. But χαμᾶζε in Homer is only used with verbs of motion (the sentence most like ours is χαμᾶζε κάππεσεν)[8] and the word ἄφωνος is not found in him at all. The nearest Homeric passages are ὁ δ' ἐπὶ χθονὶ κεῖτο ταννυσθείς[9] and ὁ δ' ἄρ' ἄπνευστος καὶ ἄναυδος κεῖτ' ὀλιγηπελέων,[10] and these can hardly be said to be near at all, though probably the second one is really the source of Anna's phrase. The first time she says ἄφωνος ἐκεῖτο she continues φωνὴ δ' οὐρανὸν ἧκε, which again has a Homeric ring, but is not Homer. We find αὐτὴ δ' οὐρανὸν ἷκεν (or ἧκε or ἵκει)[11] and we also have φωνὴ δέ οἱ αἰθέρ' ἵκανεν,[12] and Anna seems to have made a judicious mixture of the two.[13]

On the whole however she quotes Homer (sometimes introducing his words with a phrase like καθ' Ὅμηρον, but rather more often not) with greater verbal accuracy than the Bible. Miss Gardner, as we have seen, suggests that her descriptions of real battles were coloured by deep-seated memories of the Siege

---

[1] II. 6, p. 56; cf. Il. xxi. 150; Od. i. 170; X. 10, p. 299; cf. Il. ii. 468; Od. ix. 51.

[2] I. 1, p. 4; cf. Il. xxiv. 348; Od. x. 279.

[3] Pref. 2, p. 2; V. 1, p. 127; XII. 3, p. 353; cf. Il. xi. 654; xiii. 775; Od. xx. 135.

[4] II. 7, p. 58; V. 4, p. 133. Applied to Menelaus thirteen times in the Iliad and once in the Odyssey.

[5] X. 8, p. 289; cf. Il. ii. 494 sqq.; Od. x, passim.

[6] XIV. 2, p. 423; cf. Il. xviii. 104; Od. xx. 379.

[7] X. 9, p. 297; XV. 4, p. 473.

[8] Il. xv. 537-8.   [9] Il. xx. 483.

[10] Od. v. 456-7. In X. 8, p. 292, we get the actual words ἄναυδος . . . ἔκειτο, but so far separated that they can hardly count as a quotation.

[11] Il. ii. 153; xii. 338; xiv. 60.

[12] Il. xv. 686.

[13] So ἀπέπεμπεν ὀϊστούς (X. 9, p. 296) seems an echo of ἐκχεύατ' ὀϊστούς (Od. xxiv. 178), and ἔκθορε is used for the Homeric ἔκφυγε in X. 9, p. 297; cf. Il. v. 18; xi. 376; xvi. 480, οὐχ ἅλιον βέλος ἔκθορε χειρός instead of οὐχ ἅλιον βέλος ἔκφυγε χειρός. This may be due to a faint memory of a somewhat similar passage, where, as a matter of fact, ἐκ ἔθορε occurs two lines before (Il. xv. 573, 575). There is one curious misreading in XI. 1, p. 310, where Anna says: ὁ ἥλιος ἐπὶ κνέφας ἦλθε, which can only mean 'The sun went into twilight', ἐπὶ being a preposition; in Il. xi. 194, 209; xvii. 455, the phrase is (εἰς ὅ κε) δύῃ τ' ἠέλιος καὶ ἐπὶ κνέφας ἱερὸν ἔλθῃ '(until) the sun sets and holy twilight comes on', ἐπί being a prefix to ἔλθῃ.

of Troy.[1] Certainly the more forcibly does she wish to portray
valour, the more Homeric she becomes. Her husband stands
out among his contemporaries as did Achilles whom 'Homer
hymned'; Turkish tactics are once actually contrasted with
those of the *Iliad*;[2] her praise of skill rather than violence
reminds her that Homer's charioteers excel one another 'by
art';[3] her heroes follow their prototypes by 'remembering their
fierce prowess',[4] and the Crusading hosts are not restrained by
Homer's 'nine shouting heralds', being recalcitrant alike to
Alexius' messengers and to Alexius himself.[5] The one great
mistake she makes is in putting into the mouth of Odysseus
words really spoken to Telemachus first by Eumaeus the swine-
herd and then by Penelope.[6] When she applies ἄχθος ἀρούρης
in an almost complimentary way to Tancred's great bulk, it
does not necessarily prove ignorance of the fact that Homer
uses it in a contemptuous sense as 'a burden of the earth'.[7]

Taking it all round, her familiarity with the text and matter
of Homer is such as a modern reader may well envy;[8] his
characters are household words, and allusions to them need
no explanation. The dream in which a false Nestor appeared
to Agamemnon, the valour of Achilles, the archery of Teucer
and the two Ajaxes, all serve the turn of her history. Often
her quotations are subtle in their reference. Thus in describing the marvellous shooting of her husband she says,
'For not like those Homeric Greeks did he draw the string
to his breast and fit the iron [head] to the bow, showing in
their fashion the prowess of hunters, but as it were some
Heracles. . . .' This refers to Pandarus aiming at Menelaus, and
her phrase 'the prowess of hunters' (surprising in the middle of
a battle) is explained by the fact that the bow of this archer
was made of the horns of an ibex which he himself had hunted
and shot.[9]

Before we leave the Homeric field, we may remark how rich
Anna's writings are in allusions to Greek mythology, part trace-

---

[1] See p. 4 above.   [2] VII. 2, p. 191; XV. 3, p. 469.
[3] XV. 3, p. 467.
[4] I. 5, p. 12; VII. 7, p. 204; XII. 8, p. 368; XII. 5, p. 391. Cf. *Il.* VI. 112
and elsewhere. We may remark that she never interprets Homer allegorically, or
with neo-Platonic preconceptions, as did Porphyry, Iamblichus, and many others.
[5] X. 10, p. 300.
[6] II. 11, p. 66; cf. *Od.* xvi. 23; xvii. 41.
[7] XIV. 2, p. 423; cf. *Il.* xviii. 104; *Od.* XX. 379.
[8] Her husband quotes Homer less frequently. He and his wife both apply *Il.* v.
801, of a man 'small but warlike', to a general, he to Manuel Butumites (*Hyle*, II.
27, p. 63) she to Pacurianus (II. 4, p. 50).
[9] X. 9, p. 296; cf. *Il.* iv. 105–11, 123.

able to Homer and part not. It would be tedious to give
references, but the list itself is noteworthy. She speaks of Zeus,
Athene, Aphrodite, Hades, Ares, Apollo, Eros, Himeros, and
Dionysus among the gods; of other superhuman beings and
demigods such as the Gorgons, Giants, Muses and Fates,
Typhon, Adonis, Asclepius, and of Heracles as the typical
strong man;[1] of fabled men and women like Hector, Paris,
Menelaus and Agamemnon, Achilles and Patroclus, the Ajaxes,
Teucer, 'Neleus' son', Odysseus and Penelope, the Argonauts,
Admetus and Alcestis, Orestes and Pylades, Palamedes, Orpheus, Midas, Atreus, Niobe; of the stories about Pegasus, or
the Golden Age, or the Dragon's Teeth,[2] or the Erymanthian
Boar; of metamorphoses into stones and birds and trees. The
illustrations are always apt, and easily comprehensible except
in the case of one passage, where, if she blunders, it is to an
extent hardly believable of so highly educated a writer. In
speaking of Durazzo, Anna says[3] that 'in later times', i.e. after
the wars between Pyrrhus and Rome, the walls were 'rebuilt
by Amphion and Zethus', and she adds that this is proved by
inscriptions in the town. We can only suppose either that a
word of comparison such as ὡς has dropped out of the text, or
that the real builders wishing to remain unknown concealed
their identity behind the mythical builders of Thebes, as the
prototypes of all architects. But it is a puzzling passage. One
other place may be mentioned, where she makes a distinction,
intelligible but unfamiliar to us, between the Pallas qualities
and the Athene qualities of the great goddess.[4] She says
that Robert Guiscard's warlike wife Gaita was Pallas[5] (the
brandisher of a spear) rather than Athene, this being, so she
implies, the name of the deity in her character of goddess of
wisdom and of women's work, especially spinning.

[1] In X. 9, p. 296, she alludes to the legend that Apollo gave to Heracles a bow
and arrows, which were afterwards rendered deadly by the Hydra's blood.

[2] She three times speaks of a Cadmeian, i.e. empty, victory: XIV. 6, p. 443:
9, p. 455; XV. 3, p. 467. This may refer either to the sowing of the Dragon's
Teeth by Cadmus at Thebes, or to the story of Eteocles and Polynices, who killed
one another there in single combat. The same phrase occurs in Nic. Acom., *Man.
Comn.*, Bk. II. 1, p. 50.

[3] III. 12, p. 99. We must note that the same tradition is preserved by Gul.
Apul., *Rer. Norm.* IV. 241. He says of Durazzo:

> Destructam spatio post composuere minori
> Zethus et Amphion.

Heuzey (*Mission de Macédoine*, p. 352) attributes Anna's statement to confused
tradition and to a possible 'lecture fautive de quelques marbres antiques', but he
believes her to have really committed 'cet étrange anachronisme', which to our
mind is incredible.

[4] IV. 6, p. 116.　　　　　　　　　　　　[5] From πάλλειν.

As to other poetic literature, the store of references is not
large, curiously small indeed in view of the importance attached
by her to the study 'of the sublime poets'.[1] She quotes Sophocles
only once[2] and Euripides five times,[3] neither of them by name;
while the one reference to Comedy is ushered in by τουτὸ δὴ τὸ
τοῦ Ἀριστοφάνους.[4] The fourth of the Euripidean citations needs
a word of comment. It is the well-known Σπάρταν ἔλαχες, ταύταν
κόσμει, brought in[5] as showing the motive behind the contented
resignation of Leo Diogenes, son of the Emperor Romanus IV,
under the rule of Alexius. But she gives the words not as we
find them in Stobaeus[6] but with two changes, Σπάρταν for
Σπάρτην and ταύταν for κείνην. It is more than likely that she
got the phrase second hand from Plutarch, who uses it thus
twice.[7] At any rate she quotes it in the correct sense of 'Thou
hast Sparta for thy lot, make the most of it', whereas our own
Burke[8] mistranslates κόσμει as 'adorn', so that on this point the
twelfth-century Byzantine princess was better informed than
the eighteenth-century Irishman.

One other reference in the *Alexias* to Tragedy does not seem
to admit of perfect verification. When in enunciating such an
accepted sentiment as the superior wisdom of old age she says
ὡς ἡ τραγῳδία φησίν[9], she is apparently not quoting any particular line, though her phrase τι λέξαι τῶν νέων σοφώτερον may
well be an echo of Athene's words to the Chorus in the
Eumenides of Aeschylus:[10]

γεραίτερα γὰρ εἶ
καὶ τῷ μὲν εἶ σὺ κάρτ' ἐμοῦ σοφωτέρα.

As regards other poetry, one of her quotations is not quite

[1] XV. 7, p. 486.
[2] Psellus speaks of ὁ τραγῳδός once meaning Euripides (*Chron.*, Mich. VII, Ch. 9,
Byz. T., p. 263). Anna uses κατὰ τὴν τραγῳδίαν both of Sophocles (*Ajax* 646 in
Pref. I, p. 1) and of Euripides (*Hec.* 518 in Pref. 4, p. 8; Frag. 969 in I. 2, p. 5;
Orestes 2 in XV. 11, p. 506).
[3] (*a*) *Aeolus*, Frag. 15, in Pref. 4, p. 6, where it is introduced by ὥς τινες λέγουσιν;
the same passage is quoted in Nic. Bry. IV. 15, p. 96. (*b*) *Hec.* 518 in Pref. 4, p. 8.
(*c*) Frag. 969 in I. 2, p. 5. (*d*) *Telephus*, Frag. 722, in IX. 6, p. 257, introduced
by κατὰ τὸν εἰπόντα. (*e*) *Orestes* 2 in XV. 11, p. 506.
[4] *Clouds* 192 in I. 8, p. 19.
[5] IX. 6, p. 257.   [6] xxxix. 10.
[7] *Mor.* 472 E and *Mor.* 602 B just as Anna has it (ed. Bernardakis, III. pp. 228,
558; but see Dindorf's note on Eur. *Telephus*, Frag. 722). Psellus quotes the same
phrase with ταύτην in his letter to John Longibardus when advising him as a Roman
to forego 'geometry and all other music' and adhere to the profession of arms
(Psellus, *De operatione daemonum*, &c., p. 168). It was a favourite quotation with
Cicero (*Att.* i. 20. 3, and iv. 6. 2). See translation in Lewis and Short, *Latin Dict.*,
s.v. *Sparta*.
[8] *Reflections on the Revolution in France* (1790).
[9] III. 7, p. 86.   [10] Lines 848–9.

happy, for she says Sappho where she means Alcaeus[1] in giving the quotation 'Shame prevents me'.[2] But this is a pardonable confusion in view of the fact that the line in question, ἀλλά με κωλύει αἴδως, though not written by Sappho was yet addressed to her, and provoked a retort from her, as Aristotle[3] tells us.[4] The allusion in the *Alexias* to the 'Gardens of Adonis'[5] as a type of evanescent pleasures is quite apposite; we know from Theocritus[6] and Euripides that these 'gardens', consisting of forced flowers which died almost immediately, were a special feature of the demigod's festival.[7] In conclusion, the reference to Pindar's Fragment[8] contrasting the slowness of a foot-soldier with the speed of a 'Lydian chariot'[9] doubtless came into her hands through Plutarch.[10]

31. PROSE WRITERS

FROM Poetry we will turn to Prose. Beginning with Fiction we find Anna alluding to Aesop's Fable of the ass putting on the lion's skin.[11] This presents no difficulty, but in another passage we read a statement twice repeated, that some one drew on a fox's skin.[12] The first time this phrase describes how Nicephorus Diogenes falsely smiled on the Emperor he hoped to kill, the second time how he concealed his lion-like violence under a cloak of humility, ταπεινοφροσύνη.[13] In the line where Aristophanes contrasts lions and foxes[14] the latter stand as a symbol of cowardice, but in all other literature, ancient and modern (Aesop's Fables, *Reineke Fuchs*, and the like), cunning is their accepted characteristic. These words of Anna's seem to be a composite recollection, not of the Aesop's Fable just mentioned, where an ass draws on a lion's skin and is detected by the fox, but partly of St. Peter's exhortation that his readers

---

[1] Frag. 19, in Bergk, *Anth. Lyr. Gr.* ed. Hiller, p. 185.
[2] XV. 9, p. 490.   [3] *Rhet.* I. 9, p. 1367.
[4] Frag. 23, in Bergk, *op. cit.*, p. 197. Anna speaks of the Sapphic Lyre in XIV. 7, p. 446.   [5] XIV. 9, p. 456.
[6] *Idyll* 15, line 113 (*Adoniazusae*)

    ἀπαλοὶ κᾶποι πεφυλαγμένοι ἐν ταλαρίσκοις
    ἀργυρέοις.

[7] *Melan.* Frag. 518. Plutarch seems to allude to this in *Nic.* 13.
[8] Plutarch is our authority for the Pindaric authorship. Elsewhere Anna speaks of 'Pindaric μεγαλοφωνία' (XIV. 7, p. 446).   [9] VI. 14, p. 185.
[10] *Nic.* 1, and *Mor.* 65 B.
[11] XV. 8, p. 488.   [12] IX. 5, p. 254, and 6, p. 257.
[13] ταπεινοφροσύνην μὲν ὡς ἀλωπεκῆν ποτε περιβαλλόμενος ἔστιν οὗ καὶ τὸ θυμοειδὲς καθάπερ λέων ἐμφαίνων ποτε.
[14] *Pax* 1189, οἴκοι μὲν λέοντες ἐν μάχῃ δ' ἀλώπεκες.

should be 'clothed with ταπεινοφροσύνη' largely because their adversary the Devil is 'as a roaring lion',[1] and chiefly of the maxim in Plutarch, "Οπου ἡ λεοντῇ μὴ ἐφικνεῖται, προσραπτέον ἐκεῖ τὴν ἀλωπεκῆν'.[2]

One instance of a confused quotation from memory occurs in Anna's handling of those philosophers of whom she talks so glibly. In the case of Aristotle, out of the nine allusions already mentioned five merely bring him in as a teacher of τέχναι and a writer of books, especially of the Organon,[3] with his 'portals' lower down in the ascent of learning than those of Plato,[4] though his philosophy is once called ἡ δεινοτάτη περιπατητική.[5] One is a mere reference to the famous Mean[6] and argues no special study. But two are accurate renderings of Aristotle, one without acknowledgement,[7] while the remaining one is the mixed quotation of which we spoke. Anna says[8] of John Taronites the new Prefect of Constantinople, once an intimate 'under-secretary' to Alexius and then a great legal expert, that he was given to 'extolling the decrees of the Emperor, whenever he decreed things worthy of the imperial

[1] 1 Pet. v. 5, 8.   [2] Lys. 7.
[3] Pref. I, p. 1; V. 8, p. 148; 9, p. 148; XII. 5, p. 359. John Solomon, one of Italus' pupils, 'thought he had come to the summit of Aristotelian and Platonic learning, but had not well attained the knowledge of philosophy'. He turned into a rebel (V. 9, pp. 147, 148; XII. 5, p. 359).
[4] V. 8, p. 145; 9, p. 147, and the usual order of 'Aristotle and Plato', Pref. 1, p. 1. Psellus has the same order in Chron., Rom. III, Byz. T., p. 26, and in his Summary of the Chaldaean Doctrines (P. G. 122, col. 1153), and in speaking of his own education (Chron., Const. IX, Byz. T., p. 108). He puts forth purely Platonic doctrines in his Discourse on the Blachernae Miracle (Journ. of Min. of P. Instr., March 1889). Furthermore, in B. G. Med. IV. Prol. p. li, note 3, we have a treatise (not published before) Ἑρμηνεία περὶ δόγματος, where Psellus says of Aristotle as compared to Plato: ἀνθρωπικώτερον τὰ πολλὰ τῶν θεολογικῶν δογμάτων ἥπτετο ... καὶ οὔτε θεολογοῦντος γνοίης ὅ φησιν, οὔτε φυσιολογοῦντος ὅτι βούλεται. Farther on we read, οὐδεὶς ἂν τῶν πάντων ἀνθρώπων διαμιλλήσαιτο Πλάτωνι, except Greg. Nazianzen. Rambaud declares Psellus made of Plato 'un père de l'Église', unwittingly a precursor of Christianity (Rev. Hist. III. p. 265). Prodromus says that when a man wishes to appear learned he professes to love Plato and always carries one of his works (Vatican MS. CCCV; see Notices et Extraits, VIII. Pt. II. p. 103). He himself studied the philosophy of Aristotle and the ὑψηλολογία of Plato (P. G. 133, col. 1297, and cf. col. 1420). Chalandon states that Platonic studies never wholly ceased at Constantinople, and that even Psellus learnt his enthusiasm for Plato from his master John of Byzantium (op. cit. p. 316). Porphyry (in a lost work) and the Turk Farabi both wrote 'to establish the agreement between the doctrines of Aristotle and Plato'. (Camb. Med. Hist. IV, p. 296. See also Smith's Class. Dict., sub Porphyrius.) Photius esteemed Plato less than Aristotle, G. B. L., p. 516.
[5] V. 8, p. 145.   [6] X. 11, p. 303.
[7] XIV. 7, p. 445, ὡς πού τις ἔφη φιλόσοφος, κράτιστον προτιμᾶν τὴν ἀλήθειαν; cf. X. 10, p. 305; Eth. Nic. I. 4, p. 1096, ἀμφοῖν γὰρ ὄντοιν φίλοιν ὅσιον προτιμᾶν τὴν ἀλήθειαν. XIII. 4, p. 386, σπάνις γὰρ προσηγορίας κατὰ τὸν Σταγειρίτην πολλὰς φιλίας διέλυσε; Eth. Nic. VIII. 6, p. 1157, εἴρηται " πολλὰς δὴ φιλίας ἀπροσηγορία διέλυσεν", an equivalent for 'out of sight, out of mind'.
[8] XIII. 1, p. 376.

magnanimity (μεγαλοφροσύνη), having a free (ἐλευθέρα) tongue
and not being muzzled in his censure of what was low (οὐκ ἐπὶ
ψόγῳ ἀναισχυντίας στομούμενος),[1] but the sort of man the Stagirite prescribes that a dialectician (διαλεκτικός) should be'.[2] Now
in the first place the word διαλεκτικός is invariably used by
Aristotle in a slightly derogatory sense, to denote a man who
reasons from merely probable premisses.[3] Thus he contrasts
διαλεκτικῶς πρὸς δόξαν with κατ᾽ ἀλήθειαν,[4] herein differing from
Plato, who treats the Dialectician as the true philosopher.[5]
Secondly Aristotle never says in so many words that any one
ought to have a 'free tongue', though he uses the word ἐλεύθερος
in a laudatory sense of a man who is his own and not another's,
and of philosophy as μόνη ἐλευθέρα οὖσα τῶν ἐπιστημῶν.[6] He
also points out that tyrants love bad men, because they love
flattery, and this no man having a free spirit (φρόνημα ἐλεύθερον) will give them.[7] But the occurrence in Anna's sentence
of the words μεγαλοφροσύνη and ψόγος, together with the sentiment expressed, inclines one to see in it an echo of the passage
in Aristotle on the Magnanimous Man.[8] The duty of the
μεγαλόψυχος is: 'To be concerned about truth rather than about
opinion, and to speak and act openly (φανερῶς); παρρησιαστὴς[9]
γὰρ διὰ τὸ καταφρονεῖν.' He does not talk much about people
'for it concerns him neither that he should be praised, nor that
others should be censured (ψέγωνται), nor again is he given to
praising (ἐπαινετικός). διόπερ οὐδὲ κακολόγος, &c.' It would
seem that faint memories of Aristotelian and Platonic catch-
words, and a certain similarity both of sound and of sentiment,

---

[1] C. S. H. B. reads ἀναισχυντίαις, takes στομοῦν = 'to equip the mouth' (as in
Eur. I. T. 287), and translates 'nam libera utebatur lingua, non ita quidem, ut
impudentia semper convicia in ore haberet'.
[2] For the sentiment we may compare the παιδεία βασιλικὴ of Theophylact,
II. 15, P. G. 126, col. 277, where he says of an Emperor's faithful friend that 'he
will be severe in words that he may be sweet in deeds'.
[3] I wish to acknowledge with gratitude the help as to this matter given me by
Mr. W. D. Ross.
[4] Top. I, p. 105.
[5] Dialectics are a gift of the gods and the end of learning (Rep., VII. 532 sqq.;
Soph. 253; Phil. 17 and 57).
[6] Metaphysics, I, p. 982.
[7] Pol. V. 11, p. 1314. In Plato, Rep. IX. 576, tyrants are said never to taste
ἐλευθερίας καὶ φιλίας ἀληθοῦς, because they are always ruling over or being ruled by
some one else. The contrast between the Tyrant and the ideal Ruler, especially
in their attitude to flatterers and true friends, is drawn for young Constantine
Ducas by Archbishop Theophylact in his παιδ. βασ. (P. G. 126, cols. 265–85).
[8] Eth. Nic. IV. 8, p. 1124.
[9] Cecaumenus (λόγ. νουθ., p. 101) has this advice to offer to an Emperor: get
a good friend καὶ δὸς αὐτῷ παρρησίαν ἐλέγχειν σε καθεκάστην ἐφ᾽ οἷς ἐλάθησας
καὶ ἔπραξας παραλόγοις. This was apparently just what John Taronites did for
Alexius.

have produced a hybrid quotation, as in the case of her reference to *Romans* viii above.

As to her study of Plato of which she boasts in her Preface,[1] we have little evidence in her book. She mentions his Dialogues or Books twice[2] and his μαθήματα once,[3] and she points out that he never knew or taught the Astrology which she despises.[4] She has three allusions to the Academy, once with Plato's name preceding,[5] and she speaks of 'Proclus and Plato and the two philosophers Porphyry and Iamblichus'.[6] But she has little to say of the Platonic or neo-Platonic teaching, merely making brief references, without explanation, to 'Ideas' and 'Metempsychosis',[7] and bringing in the ἑνὰς ἢ τὸ ἕν as well as the writings of Porphyry into her diatribe against the Dualism of the Manichaeans.[8] We may also mention here a few places where she uses Platonic phrases, θῶπες λόγοι,[9] or the δεύτερος πλοῦς,[10] or describes a man in battle as καθάπερ θηρίον εἰς ἑαυτὸν συστρεφό-μενος.[11] Other references to philosophers are very scanty. She alludes three times cursorily to 'the Porch', and once to the female Pythagorean ἡ φιλόσοφος Θεανώ, as a type not of learning but of modesty.[12] This exhausts the list.

As to the historians, we have already[13] stated that Stemplinger believes Anna to have studied Polybius closely. He gives no proof, and the likenesses between the two writers are not salient, always excepting the passage in Pref. 2, p. 3, which is copied loosely from Polybius, *Hist.* I. 14. The same cannot be said about Thucydides, the other classical writer whose History the German critics consider to have greatly influenced the *Alexias*. Curiously enough, Anna does not explicitly acknowledge any debt to Thucydides; she never quotes him or mentions him by name, whereas her husband couples him with Demosthenes as a type of literary skill.[14] Yet her likenesses to him are both fundamental and superficial. Her whole way of telling a story, with causes enumerated and sententious dicta interspersed, is like his; so too is her detailed description of

---

[1] Pref. I, p. 1.   [2] *Ibid.*, and V. 8, p. 145.
[3] XII. 5, p. 359.   [4] VI. 7, p. 164.
[5] VIII. 6, p. 236; X. 2, p. 271; XIV. 8, p. 453.
[6] V. 9, p. 147.   [7] V. 9, pp. 147 and 149.
[8] XIV. 8, p. 451. See later in Ch. 54.
[9] IX. 9, p. 264; cf. Plato, *Theaet.* 175 E.
[10] XI. 8, p. 331; XV. 6, p. 479; cf. Plato, *Phaedo*, 99, also in Aristotle, *Eth. Nic.* II. 9, p. 1109.
[11] X. 8, p. 293; XIII. 3, p. 381. Cf. Plato, *Rep.* i. 336, where the active form συστρέφειν is followed by " ἑαυτὸν ὥσπερ θηρίον ".
[12] VIII. 6, p. 236; X. 2, p. 271; XII. 3, p. 351; XIV. 8, p. 453.
[13] See p. 191 above.   [14] *Hyle*, Pref., p. 13.

the tactical dispositions, moves, and so forth in every battle. Like him she crowds her pages with names of people and places; like him she puts into the mouths of her characters 'sentiments proper to the occasion'.[1] She cannot however be said to draw upon his facts to any appreciable extent, nor upon his vocabulary as much as she does in the case of the later historian Plutarch.[2] One instance where she might have quoted from Thucydides and did as a matter of fact quote from Plutarch is worth mentioning. Pericles[3] before war breaks out reminds the Athenians that they have 'uncoined gold and silver in the form of private and public offerings, sacred vessels used in processions and games, the Persian spoil, and other things of the like nature. . . . There were also at their disposal considerable treasures in various temples. If they were reduced to the last extremity they could even take off the plates of gold with which the image of the goddess was overlaid. . . . They might use this treasure in self-defence, but they were bound to replace all that they had taken' (χρησαμένους τε ἐπὶ σωτηρίᾳ ἔφη χρῆναι μὴ ἐλάσσω ἀντικαταστῆσαι πάλιν). This might well have been in Anna's mind when she justified her father's taking Church property for his soldiers' pay, first by the State necessities, secondly by his intention (afterwards executed) to make restoration.[4] But her actual words, τὰ ἀφαιρεθέντα εἰς δέον ἀνήλωτο κατὰ τὸν Περικλέα ἐκεῖνον,[5] are a clear quotation from Plutarch's Pericles,[6] where after describing how Pericles first went to quell a revolt in Euboea and then bribed the Lacedaemonians to leave Attica, he says: "τοῦ δὲ Περικλέους ἐν τῷ τῆς στρατηγίας ἀπολογισμῷ δέκα ταλάντων ἀνάλωμα γράψαντος, ἀνηλωμένων εἰς τὸ δέον, ὁ δῆμος ἀπεδέξατο", &c. We must note that here the ten talents seem to have come from the public treasury, and that there is no mention of temples. Still the similarity of language shows plainly which was Anna's source.

When she alludes to the oratory of Aeschines, Demosthenes, Isocrates or Polemon,[7] we need not conclude that she had read their works. Her phrases 'the ringing sound (ἠχώ) of Demosthenes', 'the Siren-charm of Isocrates', the 'rolling periods'

---

[1] Thuc., *Hist.* I. 22.
[2] For Thucydides see p. 493, note 15, and for Plutarch see Ch. 72, below. Tzetzes, born about 1110, speaks of owning a copy of Plutarch; *G. B. L.* p. 526.
[3] Thuc., *Hist.* II. 13.   [4] V. 2 and VI. 3.
[5] VI. 3, p. 156.   [6] Ch. 23.
[7] II. 6, p. 56; VI. 10, p. 175; VIII. 6, p. 236; X. 2, p. 271; XIV. 7, p. 446. Polemon is doubtless the second-century rhetorician of whose works only two funeral orations have come down to us, and whose style Smith's *Classical Dictionary* describes as 'imposing rather than pleasing'. 'Ροῖζος in Attic Greek means a whistling or a rushing, but Sophocles' Dictionary explains it as a rolling of the letter ρ.

(ῥοῖζος) of Polemon are merely rhetorical flourishes, as conventional as the regularly recurring epithets in Homer.

She is familiar with the fact that public speakers in Greece were forced to time themselves by the water-clock,[1] and as to other points of Greek history her statements are usually accurate. She speaks of Pericles and (as we have just seen) of his persuasive power over the Athenian people,[2] of rich Croesus,[3] of Alexander the Great, of his flute-player Timotheus and of his calling cities after himself,[4] of Lysimachus and Demetrius Poliorcetes,[5] and of the Olympic Games.[6] She twice alludes to the strength of 'Babylonian walls' (doubtless with a recollection of their siege by Cyrus), and their far-famed height and thickness;[7] and she tells us that chess was imported from Assyria.[8] She knows by repute the excellence of Persian shooting in old days as well as in her own, and says that Gades was the birthplace of the battering ram.[9] She considers it the 'summit of all wisdom' for a man to have 'mastered the learning of the Hellenes and Chaldaeans'.[10]

Yet one or two patent inaccuracies serve to show that in history also Anna quoted from memory.[11] Thus she ascribes to Alcibiades the trick really practised by Themistocles, when he kept the Spartans amused while the walls of Athens were being built apace. She tells us that the Paeanian (i.e. Demosthenes, of the Attic deme Paeania) 'mentions this fine trick somewhere in his speeches'. Demosthenes does indeed refer to the story,[12] but gives the name correctly as Themistocles, so that this is clearly an involuntary misquotation of Anna's. She may perhaps have confused this incident of the walls with the occasion when Alcibiades did play a mean trick on the Spartan envoys, causing them to contradict themselves and appear liars.[13]

Again, she is wrong in saying that the Sacred Company was invented by the Spartans;[14] in reality it was invented *against* the Spartans by the Thebans.[15] Then her account of the self-

---

[1] XIV. 4, p. 435.   [2] VI. 3, p. 156.   [3] II. 4, p. 51.
[4] Pref. 4, p. 6; VII. 5, p. 201; IX. 5, p. 253; XV. 7, p. 485 (cf. Nic. Bry. II. 27, p. 63).
[5] VII. 5, p. 201; XII. 9, p. 370.   [6] XV. 11, p. 501.
[7] XIII. 8, p. 398; XIV. 2, p. 423. Her further reference to 'the great Assyrian Ninus' in the second passage is historical to her, though not to us.
[8] XII. 6, p. 360.
[9] XIII. 3, p. 382; 8, p. 398. It is a curious coincidence that ram-fights, such as Anna describes in the first of these passages, are still encouraged in Spain.
[10] V. 8, p. 144; cf. XIV. 8, p. 451. We shall deal with the Chaldaeans in speaking of Anna's theology, also with her ignorance as to Islam; pp. 331, 350, below.
[11] VI. 10, p. 174; cf. Thuc. I. 90.
[12] c. Lept. 20, 73.   [13] Thuc. V. 45.
[14] VII. 7, p. 204.   [15] Plut. Pelop. 18.

mutilation which Zopyrus the Persian carried out in order to assist his master agrees neither with Herodotus nor with Ctesias; the former makes the man live in the reign of Darius I (521–485) and the latter in that of his son and successor Xerxes (485–465), while she dates it as ἐπὶ Κύρου who died in 529 B.C.[1] From Ctesias she gets another allusion and gives it correctly. When exclaiming against the very idea of her mother fighting, she says Irene had no wish to resemble 'Tomyris and Sparethra the Massagete'.[2] The first of these was the queen of the Massagetae whose kingdom Cyrus invaded, and who herself fought in the battle where he was killed.[3] But Sparethra is little known to fame. She was the wife of Amorges, king of the Sacae, a Scythian tribe near the Caspian and as such liable to be confused with the Massagetae. Her husband was captured by Cyrus, whereupon she raised an immense army, partly of women, and fought till Amorges was released. This story does not occur in Herodotus or Xenophon, but only in the *Persica* of Ctesias.[4]

When describing Philippopolis[5] she makes two mistakes, first in saying that it was on the site of the ancient Crenides,[6] which Strabo and Appian tell us was really true of Philippi, and secondly in ascribing its foundation to ὁ Ῥωμαῖος Φίλιππος, the Emperor who reigned 244–9, instead of to Philip of Macedon, son of Amyntas.[7] Another mistake in connexion with the house of Macedon may be either an error in the text or a proof of ignorance in the writer. Anna says that Alexander the Great might boast of Alexandria in Egypt, and of Bucephala in the land of the Medes, and both these descriptions will pass. But she goes on 'or of Lysimachia κατ' Αἰθιοπίαν'. There was no such place in Ethiopia, and what she certainly meant, or should have meant, was κατ' Αἰτωλίαν where there was a Lysimachia called after Alexander's general, though not actually founded by him.[8]

She knows something of Roman'history, and brings in Pyrrhus,[9] Aemilius, Scipio, and Hannibal.[10] To the later story of Rome she never alludes: no Western emperor (except Philip, as above) or writer or even theologian figures in her pages.

---

[1] X. 4, pp. 277, 278; Herod. III. 154–8. Ctesias, *Persica*, Frag. 29, 22, ed. C. Müller in *Herodotus*, p. 50, Didot, 1844. See Grote's *Hist. of Greece* (ed. of 1888), iii, pp. 445–6 and note.   [2] XII. 3, p. 353.   [3] Herod. I. 205 sqq.
[4] C. Müller gives it as Frag. 29. 3, *op. cit.* p. 46.
[5] XIV. 8, p. 450.
[6] Her name Trimontium is however a correct alternative for Philippopolis, according to Pliny (*Nat. Hist.* IV. 41).
[7] Amm. Marc. 26. 10, § 4, says it was formerly Eumolpias.
[8] XV. 7, p. 485.   [9] III. 12, p. 99.
[10] I. 1, p. 4; cf. Nic. Bry. II. 3, p. 42. There is here an interesting instance of

32. ART AND SCIENCE

SUCH then was Anna's equipment for writing a literary composition; she is well read and quotes appositely, if not with invariable correctness. Before we deal with the much more serious question of her qualifications for producing a valuable History, we will consider her intellectual standards in art, in the physical sciences, and in medicine.

In art we get references to Apelles and Phidias and the Canon of Polyclitus, also to Thericles the Corinthian potter.[1] She frequently talks of marble or bronze statues, sometimes as the highest type of beauty or dignity.[2] She alludes to one εἰκών of St. Demetrius and one εἰκόνισμα of the Theotokos, both presumably pictures.[3] She dwells on the architecture and the marble floor and walls of the famous Purple Chamber,[4] and seems proud of the στῆλαι that foreigners went to gaze at in the streets of Constantinople, as well as of the groups of statuary near the Palace.[5] She deplores the neglect of 'all art training' in the early part of the eleventh century.[6] But on the whole the information given by her as to artistic matters is extremely scanty. She describes the gilded animal-heads in bronze and iron prefixed to Alexius' new ships as vehicles for liquid fire,[7] and she has seen 'ivory carved by a craftsman'.[8] Her enthusiasm however seems only roused by the *objets d'art* sent from Alexius to Henry of Germany.[9] She dilates not only on the 'hundred pieces of purple' but on the articles of 'wrought silver,

how Anna used her husband's work, but did not always improve on it. He compares the youthful Alexius following his elder brother to war, to Scipio Aemilianus Africanus Minor, who as we know at the age of seventeen accompanied his father L. Aemilius Paulus in his campaign against Perseus King of Macedonia. Anna takes the two names Aemilius and Scipio and adds a third, Hannibal, comparing her youthful father to all three. But whereas Scipio and Hannibal began their military careers in their teens, Aemilius did not figure as a public character at all till he was over thirty, and was at least sixty-one when he conquered Perseus.

[1] III. 2, p. 74; 3, p. 76; X. 8, p. 293; XII. 4, p. 357; XIII. 10, p. 404.
[2] III. 2, p. 74; 3, pp. 76, 77; XII. 3, p. 351; 4, p. 357; XIII. 2, pp. 379, 380; XIV. 4, p. 436. It should be noted that these are probably all secular. L. Bréhier, in his paper read before the Congress of Byzantinology at Bukharest (*Acad. Roum. Bull.*, Tome XI. p. 56), says that all through Byzantine history 'la statuaire religieuse est tolérée, mais elle n'en est pas moins un art spécifiquement païen, et comme tel suspect'. Statues in churches though never actually forbidden were so rare in the Eastern Church as to excite the surprise of the Russian pilgrims in Constantinople in the fourteenth and fifteenth centuries when they happened to find any. See farther, Ch. 48 below.

[3] V. 5, p. 139; 8, p. 144.
[4] VII. 2, p. 190.
[5] III. 1, p. 72; VI. 11, p. 174; VII. 2, p. 190.
[6] V. 8, p. 144.
[7] XI. 10, p. 335.
[8] III. 3, p. 77.
[9] III. 10, p. 94.

and coin of Romanus of the ancient standard,' on 'a gold (σταυρὸς) ἐγκόλπιος[1] with pearls, a box inlaid with gold having within it relics of various saints, a small sardonyx vase, a crystal drinking-vessel, and a "fulmen" bound with gold', the last-named object being the conventional representation of a thunderbolt frequently found as an ornament on statues and coins of Zeus or his syncretistic equivalents.[2]

We now come to Anna's few definite allusions to any form of Music. Her attitude on the subject seems to have been decidedly Philistine, if we may judge from the passage where Alexius shows special kindness to the sick and aged refugees marching along with him, by providing them with a 'divine banquet', where 'no organs or flutes or drums or any annoying music' are heard.[3] Flutes inspire to action[4] and a procession needs 'all sorts of musical instruments and cymbals',[5] to say nothing of singing as an outward expression of piety or emotion in general.[6] But otherwise all the music in her pages is martial. The army moves to the sound of the flute,[7] and is roused by a drum.[8] Trumpets sound for signal or for war-cry[9] (ἐνδόσιμον or ἐννάλιον), and a battle only begins ἀπερισαλπίγκτως when a surprise is planned.[10] 'Trumpets and drums' terrify a city into surrender, and 'with trumpets and horns' the Emperor is proclaimed there.[11] 'The recall' is sounded by drum or by trumpet.[12] The war-cry is not only played but shouted,[13] and must usually have failed to be in any sense musical. Yet that is virtually all the Music which we can extract from Anna's pages. Even ecclesiastical music, which must have had so large a part in her religious life, meets with scant attention. The singing of the regular Church Canons receives one incidental allusion:[14] hymns are frequently coupled with prayers as a part of devo-

---

[1] Doubtless a reliquary in the form of a pectoral cross.
[2] See A. B. Cook's *Zeus*, Vol. II, pp. 722–806.
[3] XV. 7, p. 482.
[4] Pref. 4, p. 6, and IX. 5, p. 253. In XIV. 1, p. 421, 'flutes and lyres' appear to be the usual feature of city life.
[5] IV. 1, p. 104.
[6] Anna twice expresses her wish to sing a μονῳδία, XV. 5, p. 475, and 11, p. 496.
[7] XV. 7, p. 481, like the Spartans in Thuc. V. 70.
[8] VII. 9, p. 210.
[9] I. 5, p. 11 : 13, p. 33; VII. 2, p. 190, and often elsewhere. We do not however find silence proclaimed by a trumpet to let prayers begin, as in Thuc. VI, p. 32. The word ἐνδόσιμον, literally 'key-note', is often used by Anna for orders in general, whether taken or given (II. 4, p. 49; VI. 10, p. 175; X. 2, p. 273, and 4, p. 278; XI. 1, p. 311. Cf. Nic. Acom. *John C.* 3, p. 8). Sometimes it is best translated 'hint'.
[10] VII. 9, p. 211.   [11] XI. 2, pp. 313, 314.
[12] XIV. 5, p. 440; XV. 7, p. 481. Sometimes the phrase τὸ ἀνακλητικὸν ἠχῆσαι is used without specifying the instrument (VIII. 5, p. 232; XV. 6, p. 477).
[13] XV. 5, p. 474.   [14] XV. 9, p. 492.

tion, and one of Alexius' gifts to the Church in his Orphanage
is antiphonal music, performed by choirs both of men and
women.[1] But the only form of vocal expression in which Anna
displays any real interest is the popular or topical song, composed and sung to celebrate current events. It is known as an
ἀσμάτιον or παρῴδιον, and on one occasion at least is sung antiphonally.[2] Otherwise both Art and Music seem to leave the
writer cold.

So in quite another line do the beauties of nature. Her
references to roses[3] are purely conventional, introduced to
praise a fine complexion, just as cypresses to her are merely
objects of unusual height.[4] Beech and oak are mentioned, but
δρῦς seems as a rule to mean any timber-tree,[5] and χαμαίδρυον
(properly germander) any shrub.[6] We read of vines and wheat
as the usual objects of cultivation,[7] especially by 'the commoner
sort'.[8] Barley and millet are brought in, though the latter is
considered 'improper food' for human beings.[9] Anna once
speaks of rosin (δάκρυον εὔκαυστον) as collected from 'pines and
certain other such evergreen trees', and blown through 'pipes
of reed' in the device known as liquid fire.[10]

This want of interest in natural objects is all the more curious
because to the larger physical phenomena, such as come under
physical science or geography, she pays a good deal of attention. Thus she puts clearly and simply the prevalent scientific
notions of her day. Her mother preferred theological study to
φυσικαὶ συζητήσεις[11] and her daughter doubtless did the same.
Yet she speaks of an eclipse, which one of her father's 'under-
secretaries' had accurately predicted, in language that could
hardly be bettered.[12] 'The sun's light failed, so that the whole

---

[1] XV. 7, p. 485. Hymns have been dealt with in Ch. 10 above.
[2] II. 4, p. 51; VIII. 5, p. 233; XII. 6, p. 362.
[3] III. 1, p. 71; 2, p. 74, and 3, p. 77.
[4] III. 2, p. 74; XV. 6, p. 476.
[5] I. 6, p. 16; III. 8, p. 90; VI. 14, p. 183; XIV. 5, p. 440, and 8, p. 452.
[6] V. 5, p. 140; VII. 3, p. 198; X. 4, p. 279.
[7] X. 5, p. 284. In V. 6, p. 141, Bohemund refreshes himself by eating grapes,
and in XI. 11, p. 340, vines outside a besieged city are cleared away to allow of
mounted sallies.
[8] XIV. 9, p. 456; XV. 7, p. 483.
[9] VI. 14, p. 182; VII. 3, p. 195; VIII. 3, p. 226; and XIII. 2, p. 381. In the
passage in VIII. 3, p. 226, Tzachas tried to win over the Emperor's mercenaries,
'fawning on them with substantial promises if only they would leave the Emperor
and come over to him ὁπηνίκα τὰς κριθὰς καταλάβοι'. 'Getting the barley' may be
used for storing crops in general, or αἱ κριθαί may be a colloquial term for 'spoils',
like 'getting the beans' in American slang.   [10] XIII. 3, p. 383.
[11] V. 9, p. 147. This would include the various branches of mathematics, in
which, as we saw in Ch. 25, Anna took little interest.
[12] VII. 2, p. 193. This eclipse serves to date the Patzinak War. See Chalandon,
op. cit. p. 105, note 1.

disc was obscured by the passing before it of the moon.' She twice mentions the familiar phenomenon that in winter the sun rises to our view at a point south of its summer rising-point; this she expresses as a going or bending of the sun 'to southerly circles', after the autumn equinox.[1] She has good authority for saying that a certain night in midwinter was 'shining with its full moon at that time more than in spring'.[2] She alludes to the signs of the Zodiac and other solar matters. Thus, a statue at Constantinople is blown down by a violent wind 'with the sun at the time passing through Taurus', and this agrees with the date of April 14 furnished from another source.[3] She speaks of Capricorn, of the Vernal and of the Autumnal Equinox,[4] and her statement about the 'season of summer, when the sun had passed Cancer and was hastening to Leo, when, they say, is the rising of the dog-star',[5] is one of the data for determining when Robert Guiscard landed in Illyria. We must however note in passing a slight looseness of usage as to the terms for the seasons,[6] a feature of her vocabulary which meets us in other places. We perceive that she holds the doctrine of revolving spheres, first stated by Anaximander, and often mentioned by Aristotle. Her phrase 'the lunar sphere'[7] shows her belief that 'the earth was supposed to be the centre of a series of concentric spheres or globes revolving round it, one appropriated to the stars, another to the moon, another to the sun'.[8] When she speaks of a great comet she discusses its exact nature, whether a δοκίς or an ἀκοντίας,[9] and though Alexius is sufficiently enlightened to believe that 'such things are dependent on some natural cause', yet in order to be on the safe side he resorts to experts for observation and explanation of the portent. A 'sudden earthquake' with stones falling from heaven on a clear night of moon and stars is so remarkable as to be at least a plausible proof of a heretic's guilt.[10] Anna speaks of earthquakes as if

---

[1] I. 16, p. 37; XV. 3, p. 468.

[2] X. 8, p. 290. Lockyer, in his *Elementary Lessons in Astronomy*, p. 171, says: 'In winter, when the sun is lowest the moon is highest, and so in winter we get more moonlight than in summer.'

[3] XII. 4, p. 357, and Du Cange's Note.

[4] I. 16, p. 37; VIII. 3, p. 226; XV. 3, p. 468.

[5] III. 12, p. 98. The *Encycl. Brit.* says the Greeks found that the heliacal rising of the dog-star occurred as the sun entered Leo, i. e. about twenty-three days after the summer solstice of June 21. But heliacal risings vary. See Ch. 62 below.

[6] It is hard to reconcile her use of φθινόπωρον in VII. 2, p. 190, with that in XIV. 8, p. 449.

[7] X. 4, p. 280.   [8] Liddell and Scott, sub v. σφαῖρα.

[9] XII. 4, p. 55. *C. S. H. B.* translates 'trabalium vel iacularium', which we may roughly render 'meteor or shooting star'.

[10] XV. 8, pp. 489, 490.

familiar with them,[1] though curiously enough she omits from
her story the great one in her father's reign chronicled by
Zonaras and Glycas.[2] She twice records snowstorms 'out of
season', one on September 24, accompanied by thunder and
lightning, swollen streams, and tempestuous winds;[3] one in
August, with violent land-breezes from the mountains stirring
up the sea and causing shipwrecks.[4] The winter after Alexius'
success at Choerobacchae against the Patzinaks was very severe
and marked by such an unheard-of fall of snow as to block up
houses.[5] Throughout the *Alexias* storms and winds and waves
play a considerable part.[6]

Her geographical knowledge gives her evident satisfaction.
She loves to trace the course of rivers,[7] and to give their local
names, even if with an apology for 'barbarizing'.[8] She speaks
glibly of the variable currents in the straits between Boeotia
and Euboea, of the situation of Sicily, and the respective distances from one another, and position with regard to winds, of
points on the Italian and Illyrian shores.[9] She brings in a whole
string of names in Asia Minor in order to impress the reader
with the extent of her husband's campaigning.[10] As a rule her
geographical knowledge is accurate, though a few errors may
be pointed out. Thus she wrongly places Peristhlaba Magna
on the Danube, instead of sixty miles to the South;[11] she apparently turns two lakes situated beyond that river into one of

[1] III. 5, p. 81.
[2] *Epit.* XVIII. 22; *Bibl. Chron.*, IV. p. 333.
[3] III. 8, p. 90. She never attempts, like Cecaumenus (*Strat.* p. 83), to explain
thunder and lightning; she merely records them.
[4] III. 12, p. 98. We may contrast her description of the sea-battle with the
Count of Provence: 'Although it was midwinter, yet there was a complete calm'
(X. 8, p. 290).
[5] VIII. 3, p. 226.
[6] e.g. III. 12; VI. 6, p. 163; X. 7, p. 288; XI. 10 and 11. A wind brings on
Alexius' last illness (XV. 11, p. 496). In storms we usually hear of a κλύδων, but
once of a τρικυμία μεγάλη, the 'third wave' (XI. 10, p. 337), which was said to be
the largest and is so used by Plato.
[7] Vardar, I. 8, p. 18; Danube, VII. 2, p. 192; Drymon (now Black Drin),
XII. 9, p. 371; Maeander, XIV. 1, p. 422; Scamander and others, XIV. 5, p. 439;
Maritza, XIV. 8, p. 450.
[8] I. 8, p. 18; VII. 11, p. 215; XIV. 5, p. 439. So of a ford, VIII. 4, p. 230;
a range of mountains, IX. 1, p. 245; and of towns or fortresses or a κλείσουρα in
VIII. 3, p. 227: 9, p. 241; XIII. 5, p. 391: 12, pp. 413, 414; XIV. 2, p. 427;
XV. 1, p. 462; 2, p. 464.
[9] I. 16, p. 37; II. 3, p. 48; VI. 5, p. 159; XI. 2, p. 312; XII. 8, p. 368. Similarly
her term of ὁ μακρὸς αἰγιαλός is most appropriate to so long a promontory as the
Thracian Chersonese (XIV. 2, p. 427). Alexius makes a map of the Adriatic for
one of his admirals (XIII. 7), specially considering the winds.
[10] Pref. 3, p. 5.
[11] VII. 3, p. 194. She is evidently confusing it with the other Peristhlaba near
the river's mouth.

greatly exaggerated size.[1] She fancifully prolongs the Haemus
Mountains across the Adriatic to the Hercynian Forest,[2] and
she puts Mopsuestia on the Saron (or Sarus) River and not on
the Pyramus.[3] The various problems connected with her references to Durazzo will be considered later, but we may say here
that she seems to think Crusaders who 'crossed the straits of
Lombardy' would naturally go 'through the parts of Hungary'
on their way to Constantinople,[4] and she is very hazy as to the
interior of Asia Minor.[5] Indeed her description even of parts of
Bithynia which she had probably herself visited is not at all clear,
and it is confusing that, while she generally uses ἀνατολή to
mean simply the East, she has it at least twice in the modern
Greek sense of Anatolia or Asia Minor.[6] But on the whole she
makes surprisingly few geographical mistakes, and if we have
difficulty in identifying, for instance, Calaure and the other
Thracian localities of the campaign against Bryennius in
Book I, or the hill Lebunium in Book VIII, this comes from
her and her first readers' familiarity with the spots, making
accurate descriptions superfluous.[7]

To natural history she chiefly refers in figures of speech. A
polypus is like a ship with oars or like a grasping man.[8] Men dig
like moles, and enemies are driven back by fire as a swarm of
bees by smoke.[9] Invaders are compared to insect-pests,[10] which
also appear in the actual form of locusts devouring vines and
sparing wheat, though even here Anna's interest is in the symbolic interpretation.[11] The way rams butt against one another

---

[1] VII. 5, p. 200, with Du Cange's note.

[2] XIV. 8, p. 451, 452.

[3] XII. 2, p. 349. Both rivers flow 'from the mountains of Taurus' down 'into the
Syrian sea', but it was over the Pyramus that Constantine constructed the magnificent bridge of Mopsuestia.

[4] X. 5, p. 285.

[5] In XIV. 5, p. 439 the passage reads as if the Turk 'passed through Adramyttium and Chliara' on the way from Cyzicus to Parium, whereas from Cyzicus
Adramyttium lies South-West and Chliara very nearly due South, while Parium is
West on the Sea of Marmora. Perhaps this is merely awkwardness of construction,
the phrase 'having passed through Adramyttium and Chliara' referring to Monolycus' march after he left Parium and Abydus. But in XIV. 6, p. 443, she evidently
places Acrocus near Philadelphia, when it is in fact near Cotiaeum far to the
North-East. The geography in XV. 4 is also hard to follow.

[6] XI. 10, pp. 335, 337. Possibly also XII. 2, p. 350.

[7] It is difficult to see why Chalandon (op. cit., p. 133, and Camb. Med. Hist.
IV, p. 330) makes Lebunium a river, when Anna distinctly speaks of it as a hill
(VIII. 4, p. 230; 5, p. 232). Zonaras (XVIII. 23) does not mention any sites of
battles in the campaign.

[8] X. 8, p. 290, and 11, p. 304. In the sense of some one holding on tenaciously
it is used by Nic. Acom. in John C. 2, p. 6. The Anon. Syn. Chr., p. 179, uses it of
some one clouding matters, as with sepia.

[9] XIII. 3, pp. 382, 383.

[10] I. 14, p. 35.

[11] X. 5, p. 284.

in fight serves but to explain how a battering-ram is used in a siege,[1] and when mice eat bread or turn into lions, it is to give a warning in a dream.[2] Horses and oxen only come into her pages as usual means of transport. She speaks of calling out 'a serpent lurking in a hole' by means of 'the secret spells of enchanters' (ἐπῳδῶν ἴυγξιν ἀπορρήτοις), and this may be a version of the often-recorded fact that snakes can be attracted by music.[3] But on the whole, of any careful observation of Nature the *Alexias* shows no trace.

In the sphere of Medicine Anna is much more at home, or at least displays much more familiarity. We shall leave to the last her detailed picture of Alexius' illness and death, and for the present we will consider her *obiter dicta* on the subject. Some illnesses she lays at the door of χυμῶν σηπέδονες (literally 'putrefactions of the juices'),[4] some at that of 'irregularities and badness of climate',[5] coupled with anxiety. There are "σπερματικοὶ λόγοι" (best rendered 'hereditary' or 'germ-containing causes', of course with none of the specific meaning which we now give to the word 'germ'), of disease,[6] and 'luxurious living' tends to produce gout.[7] She herself in her youth had caused anxiety by her 'bodily state' to those about the women's apartment,[8] but she seems to have grown up robust, to the extent of travelling with her father.[9] She speaks of gangrene eating its way through the body,[10] of swollen intestines as a prelude of death,[11] of child-

---

[1] XIII. 3, p. 381. [2] XV. 6, p. 479.

[3] XV. 8, p. 486. Her use of the word ἴυγξ deserves a longer discussion than it can get here. Proclus speaks of οἱ ἰυγγικοὶ θεοί (in *I Euclidis librum*, p. 91), and Psellus gives ἴυγγες an important place in the Chaldaean cosmogony (*Summary of the Chaldaean doctrines*, P. G. 122, col. 1149). Liddell and Scott derive the word from ἰύζειν, 'to cry out', and though its acquired meaning of 'spell' came from the belief that if bound to a wheel a wryneck as it turned round 'drew men's hearts along with it', yet the connotation of *sound* may still in Anna's day have been latent in the name, as it clearly is in ἐπῳδῶν.

[4] I. 10, p. 22; cf. Polyb. *Hist.* I. 81. 7, where this is used figuratively of the soul.

[5] Pref. 3, p. 5; I. 10, p. 22; cf. Nic. Bry. II, 28, p. 65. Herod, II, 77 says that diseases are produced by changes of seasons.

[6] XIV. 4, p. 433. This phrase occurs in Plutarch and also in the neo-Platonic philosophers like Iamblichus and Nicomachus Gerasenus and Plotinus (*Enn.* III. 1, § 7). In XIV. 4, p. 437, Anna speaks of a 'cause not antecedent only but inherent' of her father's illness (προκαταρκτικός and συνεκτικός).

[7] XIV. 4, p. 433. [8] XIV. 7, p. 446.

[9] XIV. 7, 446, and 8, p. 450.

[10] IV. 1, p. 105. In Polyb., *Hist.* I. 81, 6, 7, though the word is not 'gangrene' but τὰ ἕλκη, the vivid picture of the poison eating its way through the body may well have given Anna the notion of using the same metaphor as the classical historian. In him the idea is of brutality, in her of greed; in both the evil force never desists till it destroys the whole.

[11] Pref. 3, pp. 5, 6, where perforation of the bowel seems to be the danger feared, and XV. 11, p. 500.

birth pangs and swaddling-bands,[1] of fever and pleurisy,[2] and
a quartan ague.[3] A man loses his sight 'by disease'.[4] Epilepsy,
where a man 'lay foaming', is of course due to demoniacal
possession,[5] as is madness, $\lambda\alpha\mu\pi\rho\grave{\alpha}$ $\mu\epsilon\lambda\alpha\gamma\chi o\lambda\acute{\iota}a$,[6] but she is aware
that 'intestinal disease' comes from improper food, and that
worry of mind aggravates a bad physical state.[7] If she speaks
of the 'humours' of the body as determining health or disease,
she does but follow the physiologists of her day; and if she
believes that in gout the 'sediments', unless removed by some
detergent draught, tend to become dispersed throughout the
whole system, she does but state a commonplace of Medicine.[8]
On the whole her diagnosis of illness is far less vague than that
of many a nineteenth-century novelist, and the 'deadly sickness'
of which St. Gilles dies[9] is almost her only indefinite description.

[1] Pref. 4, p. 6; VI. 8, p. 166; XIV. 7, p. 446; XV. 11, p. 496.

[2] VI. 6, p. 162; 7, p. 165. The two combined made the Emperor Isaac so ill
that he abdicated, according to Psellus (*Chron.*, Is. Comm., Byz. T., p. 225) and
Nic. Bry. I. 4, p. 18.

[3] VII. 9, pp. 212, 213. The shivering and teeth-chattering may in this case
have been due to malaria, complicated by septic wounds.

[4] IX. 10, p. 266.   [5] VI. 9, p. 170.

[6] XIV. 9, p. 457; XV. 8, p. 488.

[7] Pref. 3, p. 5; XIII. 2, p. 381; 8, p. 399; XV. 11, pp. 497, 498.

[8] She speaks in XIV. 4, p. 434 of the Emperor's pains in the affected parts
drawing the 'humours' ($\acute{\rho}\epsilon\acute{\upsilon}\mu\alpha\tau\alpha$) to themselves, and then of the $\acute{\rho}\epsilon\acute{\upsilon}\mu\alpha$ attacking
him and 'bringing great pain'. He rode (XIV. 7, p. 449) 'in order that part of
the flowing down matter' ($\acute{\upsilon}\lambda\eta$, the 'sediments' or 'deposits', chiefly of urate of
soda, of which the *Encycl. Brit.* speaks under *Gout*) 'might be carried off'. (The
same article says: 'Regular but moderate exercise in the form of walking or riding
. . . is of great advantage'.) Then the 'humour' settles in one of his shoulders and
the consultant (XV. 9, p. 497) fears that 'if it is not purged by cathartics it will
hereafter flow into one of the vital parts or into the heart itself'. (The same
article says: 'The administration of some simple laxative will be of service, as well
as the free use of alkaline diuretics.') When Anna uses $\acute{\upsilon}\lambda\eta$ as practically synonymous with $\acute{\rho}\epsilon\acute{\upsilon}\mu\alpha$, this is consistent with ancient and medieval physiology. The
same article says: 'Galen regarded Gout as an unnatural accumulation of humours
in a part', the humours being of course 'the different kinds of moistures in man's
body', of which the four primary were phlegm, blood, yellow bile, and black bile,
on whose 'right proportion and mixture' health as well as character depended
(*Encycl. Brit.*, under *Humour* and *Medicine*). See p. 131, note 7 above. Anna's fear
that the 'remedy with pepper' had done more harm than good (XV. 11, p. 499), at
a further stage of her father's illness is based on her shrewd opinion that the drug had
'diffused the sediments, $\tau\grave{\alpha}s$ $\acute{\upsilon}\lambda\alpha s$, and could not get the better of them, but drove
them into the cavities of the arteries'. Dr. Eliz. Dawes (see p. 3, n. 2, above)
suggested in conversation that when Alexius played chess 'on awaking in the early
morning' in order to 'sweeten the brine that was in him from his many cares'
(XII. 6, p. 360) this describes a hygienically sound attempt to dissipate the uric
acid by recreation. The above quoted *Encycl. Brit.* article on *Gout* gives the advice
in such cases of a famous French doctor: 'Fatiguez la bête et reposez la tête.'

[9] XI. 8, p. 332. Three fatal illnesses mentioned by Nicephorus Bryennius do not
come into Anna's pages. (He also speaks of a violent nose bleeding, II. 6, p. 45.)
The *Hyle* tells us that Alexius' brother Manuel died of a disease of the ears (I. 12,
pp. 25, 26), Constantine Ducas, son of the Caesar, of a sharp attack of pain,
probably appendicitis (II. 17, p. 55), and Andronicus his other son of dropsy, over
which doctors laboured in vain (III. 1, p. 68).

In war she speaks of wounds and sometimes of bandaging,[1] and one wounded general at least is attended by 'one of the ἐμπείρων ', doubtless part of the Ambulance Corps described by Leo in his *Tactica* as accompanying every army, and consisting of a doctor and a surgeon and six or eight bearers.[2] But her panacea for weary soldiers, after they have cleansed away dust and gore and other traces of κακοπάθεια, is Rest, which is mentioned repeatedly in her pages,[3] and which, as we have seen above, Alexius in his strenuousness denied himself,[4] though he secured it for his men 'so as not to seem harsh and thoughtless'.[5]

She does not speak much of drugs, though she realizes the danger of poison administered in food, and speaks of the 'salutary medicine' that may be given as an antidote.[6] Twice she alludes to smearing a cup with some sweet like honey (the medicinal reputation of which among the ancients is attested by the *Encyclopaedia Britannica*), not in order to make a bitter draught more palatable,[7] but with distinct curative aim. The first time, where the sense is probably literal, she says this was done 'in order that most of the harm should disappear' (literally 'slip through', διολισθαίνειν) ;[8] the second time its object was 'that the demoniac [i.e. Basil the Bogomile] should vomit forth his madness' (literally 'black humour', μελαγχολία).[9] In Alexius' last illness we hear of a 'remedy with pepper'[10] (which to her

---

[1] IV. 4, p. 110; 6, p. 117; 8, p. 122; V. 1, p. 125; VII. 9, p. 212; XII. 2, p. 350, with which cf. IV. 6, p. 117; XIV. 6, p. 443,. So in *Hyle*, IV. 38, p. 107. John II died of a poisoned wound (Nic. Acom. *John C.* 11, p. 27), but Anna never speaks of such.

[2] IV. 4, p. 110; Oman, *Art of War*, I, p. 192. It is noteworthy that in XV. 7, p. 482, men dying on the march are attended not by doctors but by priests. Zonaras (XVIII. 27) says that in Alexius' army the old men rode on beasts of burden, and the sick were carried on men's shields; if this is true it is curious that Anna omitted to mention such a proof of her father's kindness.

[3] Pref. 3, p. 5; I. 3, p. 8; 7, p. 18; III. 12, p. 99; IV. 2, p. 107; V. 1, pp. 125, 126; 3, p. 133; VII. 8, p. 210; 11, p. 217; VIII. 6, p. 234; X. 4, p. 278; 5, pp. 282, 283; 11, p. 302; XI. 2, p. 315; 6, p. 327; 7, p. 329; XV. 2, p. 465; 4, p. 472. So we get ῥαστώνης χάριν as a motive: II. 8, p. 61; IX. 5, p. 255; XII. 3, p. 354.

[4] III. 2, p. 73; V. 4, p. 135; VIII. 1, p. 221; XII. 3, p. 350; XIV. 1, p. 419; 4, p. 433; though in IX. 5, p. 255, he consents ἀνακτήσασθαι ἑαυτὸν τῆς ὁδοιπορίας. Rest indeed often acts as a snare to an army or an individual (I. 6, p. 16; 11, p. 26; VIII. 1, p. 222; XIII. 6, p. 394, and 7, p. 395).   [5] VIII. 1, p. 221.

[6] X. 11, pp. 302, 303; XI. 2, p. 315; XII. 3, p. 352. In XV. 8, p. 487, she speaks of 'carrying the whole drug' to some one who is being deceived; in modern slang we might use the same metaphor and say 'giving a complete dope'.

[7] As in Lucretius, *De Rer. Nat.* I. 936–41. Honey in Plato (*Phil.* 61) is a synonym for pleasure, and is to be mixed with the 'sober draught' of water.

[8] XIV. 4, p. 437. This passage seems to be a darkly worded insinuation that her brother John tried to poison their father.

[9] XV. 8, p. 488. μελαγχολία also occurs in XIV. 9, p. 457, in the same sense.

[10] Cecaumenus (*Strat.* p. 53) recommends pepper for the liver and advises phlebotomy three times a year; but for the rest, he tells people to cure themselves by fasting and warmth and repose, without doctors or poultices or potions.

thinking only aggravated the disease), essence of roses used to revive him from fainting, and oil with which, when the case was clearly hopeless, the doctors 'anointed the Emperor's head, for it seemed to them wise'. A purgative is suggested, but not administered; later on phlebotomy and cautery are tried.[1] But on the whole Anna's conception of Hygiene is the sound one of Prevention rather than Cure. A 'well-tempered climate' should be sought, and a man should not lightly expose himself to extremes of heat or cold, or to bad weather; it is only Alexius' devotion to duty that makes him violate this rule.[2] On the other hand 'medical wisdom' recommends regular exercise to improve the circulation and combat incipient disease, and a reputable doctor, 'using the rule of his craft', will attack the most urgent symptom first.[3] Bad smells, especially from dead bodies, are dangerous to health.[4] Heat and dust, with the consequent thirst, are the greatest enemies of fighting men;[5] sun in the eyes is hardly less of a handicap.[6] Her maxims are all a case of glorified common sense.

For this reason her attitude towards doctors is interesting. She has not the horror of them expressed by Cecaumenus, with his 'Pray that thou fall not into the hands of a doctor, however learned', and his sinister suggestions that they deliberately foster disease for money.[7] Nor does she scorn them utterly, like Theo-

---

[1] XV. 11. It is remarkable that there is no trace in the *Alexias* of any use of amulets or of magic formulae, such as J. Evans (*op. cit.* p. 122) mentions in the West as traceable to 'Byzantine sources'.

[2] I. 11, p. 26; X. 4, p. 281, and 5, p. 283; XII. 3, p. 352; XIV. 8, p. 454; cf. Nic. Bry. II. 28, p. 65. In II. 8, pp. 60, 61, τὸ ἐπιτερπὲς καὶ εὔκρατον of a spot consists in having trees and in being 'blown on by every wind'. A 'well-mixed' air, not too hot and not too cold, is often praised by Byzantine writers. Theophylact, παιδ. βασ., I. 3 (*P. G.* 126, col. 256), claims this merit for Constantinople, just as Herodotus extolled Hellas for her fairly tempered seasons, III. 106. When Alexius is dying he craves cool air (XV. 11, p. 503; cf. Glycas, IV, p. 335).

[3] XIV. 4, p. 435; 7, p. 449. One wonders what illness Isaac Comnenus feigned when the doctors advised hare-hunting as a remedy (Nic. Bry. II. 28, p. 65).

[4] III. 12, p. 99; VII. 5, p. 201; VIII. 6, p. 235; XI. 12, p. 341; XIII. 10, p. 402. So Cecaumenus (*Strat.* p. 11) advises not to keep an army long in one place: γίνεται γὰρ ὀσμὴ καὶ ἐξ αὐτῆς ἀρρωστίαι. We can recall the ghastly description by Thucydides of the intolerable stenches in the quarries of Syracuse, with the Athenian prisoners dying by scores (*Hist.* VII. 87).

[5] XI. 7, p. 329; cf. Thuc. IV. 35. In IV. 3, p. 108, naval plans are upset by the drying up of rivers in summer heat. Dust and arrows darken the air at Larissa (V. 6, p. 141), as at Pylos in the famous description of Thucydides (*Hist.* IV. 34), so similar as to rouse the wonder whether Anna was not thinking of it. The picture in VIII. 5, p. 233 of the battle where Alexius presses the neighbouring peasants into the service of the army as water-carriers is one of the most vivid in the whole book. We read of ἀνυδρία from summer heat round Lopadium (XV. 1, p. 462).

[6] IX. 1.

[7] *Strat.* p. 53. Psellus speaks contemptuously of the trust of Romanus III in ἰατρικαὶ τέχναι (*Chron.*, Rom. III, Byz. T., p. 40). It is curious to find Proclus (*in I Euclidis librum*, p. 38) saying that Hippocrates makes plain the usefulness

dore Prodromus,[1] but she considers herself quite as capable of being an 'umpire' between medical men who disagree as Psellus must have claimed to be when he controverted a diagnosis of 'the first of the doctors'.[2] Her attitude towards the 'sons of Asclepius' during her father's last illness is distinctly patronizing. She is more than half contemptuous over their apathy and confusedness as to diagnosis, their false optimism intended to buoy up the family, and their retreat from the bedside when things come to their worst. All along she rates their efforts as far less effective than those of his own family who 'toiled' over him.[3] She tells us at great length how she undertook such humble but essential tasks as giving easily swallowed food, feeling the pulse, and counting the respiration.[4]

This brings in the question of nursing, and it is interesting to see that the system prevailed then which continued down to the nineteenth century, and still lingers on in many places; the sick were nursed not by professionals, but by amateurs and friends.[5] The fact that charitable institutions were not specialized, but received within one containing wall the sick, the old, and orphans, made such a plan of nursing easier; the many people going about in good health could all take a hand. Thus in Alexius' Orphanage, besides a school for children and an almshouse for old or poor people, there was a department for those 'incapacitated in their limbs or in their whole bodies', by blindness or lameness or 'some other ill'. Anna says: 'I have seen an old woman waited on by a young one, and a blind man led by a seeing one, and a footless man having feet not his own but another's, and a handless man led by the hands of other men, and babes tended by strange mothers, and paralytics served by able-bodied mortals.' In short, Alexius 'gave assistants to each incapacitated person',[6] though the era of the trained nurse was not yet.

of τῆς ἀστρολογίας for Medicine, but we must remember that he means by Astrology the scientific study of the heavens, as does Iamblichus.

[1] *Notices et Extraits*, VIII. Pt. II, p. 104. Prodromus excepts from his general condemnation of doctors as charlatans Nicolas Callicles and a Michael Lizix, who also may have been one of those who attended Alexius, being identical, if so, either with Anna's Michael Pantechnes or with her 'Michael the eunuch'.

[2] XV. 11, p. 497; Psellus, *Chron.*, Is. Comn., Byz. T., p. 226.

[3] Anna is like Prodromus in admiring Nicolas Callicles (XV. 11, pp. 496, 497). She seems to describe him as a consultant, whereas Michael Pantechnes was apparently the regular physician (see p. 278 below), and not free from jealousy of the greater men called in.

[4] XV. 11.

[5] In the public hospitals in Siena at least as late as 1903 the sick patients were nursed by the convalescents.

[6] XV. 7. In the hospital attached to the Pantocrator Monastery the work was

One passage on the treatment of sickness[1] is worth translating. Alexius was marching back from Philomelium to Constantinople, with the centre of his hollow square containing
prisoners, refugees of all ages and both sexes, and booty.

'And whereas many of the women were with child, and many men
were afflicted with diseases, whenever any woman was drawing near
her delivery, then a trumpet sounding by the Emperor's order made
them all halt, and straightway the whole host stood still on that spot.
And as soon as he heard that the woman was delivered, another
unusual call proclaiming a move on was sounded and urged advance
upon all. Or if any one died, the same thing again took place, and
the Emperor was present with the dying man, and priests were called
in to sing the final hymns and to impart the sacred elements to the
dying. And when all the rites for the departing had been duly performed, not until the dead man had been put in a coffin and buried,
not till then was it permitted for the battle-array to move a step.'

Such was Alexius' treatment of others, and in his own illness
we feel that, however drastic such methods as cautery and
bleeding may seem to us, he had every care that contemporary
science could dictate.[2] It is tempting to go into the matter at
length, so vividly and interestingly is it handled, but such a proceeding is out of place here. Suffice it to say that his symptoms,
to quote Dr. Counsell once more,[3] were 'gout, then renal disease
with thickened arteries, a big heart, hypertrophy (that is the
cause of the weight he feels in his chest). Then you get either
oedema of his lungs or water in his pleural cavities (the symptoms would be much the same to an ordinary observer), and
this would give all the symptoms of "air-hunger" from which
he suffered. Then he gets all the troubles which arise from an
enlarged heart which is beginning to fail and getting dilated,
dropsy, ascites . . . with uraemic symptoms, the ulcerated palate
and swollen tongue. Quite probably his swoonings may have
been slight uraemic convulsions, but they may have been really
only faints from the failing heart.'

It is hardly necessary to point out the truly remarkable

---

done by ten men doctors and one woman, twelve male assistants and four female,
eight supplementary male helpers and two female, eight men servants and two
female, with two pathologists and three surgeons to do the diagnosis in a consulting-
room with eight assistants, the pay of the whole staff being carefully prescribed.
This was an unusually elaborate institution (see Oeconomos, *Vie religieuse*). The
Cosmosoteira Monastery had a hospital with eight attendants and one doctor for
thirty-six patients. See review of the *Typikon* in *B. Z.* VIII. p. 574.

[1] XV. 7, pp. 481, 482.

[2] XII. 3, pp. 351, 353; XIV. 5, p. 438; 7, p. 449; XV. 1, pp. 460, 462; 11.

[3] See p. 5 above. Gout was a favourite topic of Byzantine epigrammatists;
G. B. L. pp. 711, 737.

feature of the last chapter of the *Alexias*, namely that a death-bed of 1118 should be made so real to us of 1928, and by a woman not a doctor. It is indeed startlingly modern to find Anna discussing whether heredity, or loose living, or an accident, or over-exertion of mind and body, or poison,[1] or a cold,[2] had caused her father's gout; and to read of Irene's skilful massage[3] and his own attempts to cure himself by exercise whenever the pain allowed him.[4] We come across such human touches as 'we could not believe' (Callicles in his diagnosis) 'because we did not wish to do so'; or 'the Empress . . . learning from [Alexius] what he was suffering, felt as if hers were the pains'; or again that the doctors 'dissembled over the crisis . . . and suggested hopes that did not appear sound.' We can almost see the poor Emperor, naturally a strong man ('indeed he was altogether unused to drinking medicine'), fighting against the 'halter' of oppressed breathing, and demanding almost angrily to know the cause.[5] 'In his distress he found one refreshment, that of motion,' as many an asthmatic patient has found to-day, and the Empress gets his attendants to carry him about on a litter, in the attempt to soothe his restlessness. Round his bed stand his devoted daughters plying him with liquid food and sprinkling him with rosewater. His wife forgoes food and sleep, and with tears streaming down her face holds the patient up to relieve his breathing. 'Every doctor was summoned' by her in her desperation, and when they fail she resorts no less desperately to prayer, her own and that of others, though curiously enough there is no mention of calling in priests or procuring the last rites for the dying man. Finally Irene is so utterly unable to control her grief as to call forth from Alexius 'valiant and manly exhortations though his last'. Just so do patients and their families behave to-day, and there is no new thing under the sun.

[1] XIV. 4, pp. 433–7; XV. 11, p. 498.
[2] XV. 11, p. 496.
[3] XII. 3, p. 351; XV. 1, p. 462. Yet this seems to have been a source of mockery alike to Greek and Turk (XII. 3, p. 353; XIII. 1, p. 377; XV. 1, p. 461; 3, p. 466).
[4] XII. 9, p. 372; XIV. 7, p. 449.
[5] We are reminded of Tennyson's *Northern Farmer, Old Style*.

V. ANNA AS HISTORIAN

33. BYZANTINE IDEAL OF HISTORIOGRAPHY

WE have now dealt at some length with Anna Comnena as an educated woman. It remains to consider her as a historian, and in order to do that we must begin with her own ideal of Historiography.

We have already said that classical writers approved stereotyped forms for beginnings and endings, and nowhere is this truer than in the Prologues of historical works. Over and over again historians try to impress on the reader in a stately introduction their sense that Truth is their ideal and that such composition must not be lightly and unadvisedly taken in hand. Herodotus writes his history in order that the deeds of men may not be effaced by time nor remain unsung.[1] Thucydides, after deploring the carelessness of men in searching for facts and weighing evidence, and their taste for tales that 'please the ear' rather than tell the truth, says: 'I have described nothing but what I either saw myself or learned from others of whom I made the most careful and particular inquiry. The task was a laborious one . . . and very likely the strictly historical character of my narrative may be disappointing to the ear.'[2] Polybius does indeed begin by stating[3] that the advantages derived from writing and studying history are too well known to need recounting, but very shortly afterwards[4] we find him elaborating the theme that the duty of an historian is to be impartial, in a passage which Anna copies without acknowledgement.[5] Again later he defines the province of poets as being to move their readers, but that of historians to instruct them through the truth.[6] Diodorus Siculus occupies his first two chapters with a lengthy defence of his profession, reminding us of the first two of Anna's Preface.[7] Dionysius of Halicarnassus lays down as the two inevitable preoccupations of a historian, first the choice of a worthy subject, secondly the skilful

---

[1] *Hist.* I, Pref.
[2] *Hist.* I. 22. So nearly one thousand years later John of Epiphania (*Hist. Gr. min.* I, p. 376) writes as a duty, because he was an eyewitness of the war with Persia.
[3] *Hist.* I. 1, 1–3, and again in 35. 9, 10; III. 31; V. 75. 5, 6; XII. 7.
[4] *Hist.* I. 14.   [5] Pref. 2, p. 3; cf. p. 205 above.
[6] *Hist.* II. 56. 11, 12.
[7] To show how conventional much of this is we may note that whereas he speaks of History making Time 'the guardian of whatever it transmits to those who come after' (*Bibl.* I. 2, 5), Anna, with equal meaning or non-meaning, describes History as a 'strong bulwark against the stream of Time' (Pref. I, p. 1).

treatment of it,[1] and this passage would almost seem to have been in Anna's mind when she dwells on her father's excellences and the care with which she has handled them.[2] From Dionysius we also gather that the Proems of histories were always supposed to express concern both over the instruction of the ἐπιγιγνόμενοι (truth in history being to him 'the beginning of learning and wisdom'[3]) and also over ensuring that the memorials of great men should not 'perish with their bodies'; Anna's Proem does this to a marked degree. She is careful in her choice of a starting-point, 'where the narrative will be plainer and more historical',[4] just as Polybius dwells on the importance of selecting an ἀρχή known to all without dispute,[5] and Diodorus feels that readers despise History not based on admitted dates,[6] while Plutarch is at pains to establish as on a map the boundary-line where legend ends and history begins.[7] In theory at least Greek historians pursued the Truth, the Whole Truth, and Nothing but the Truth, and when Isocrates says that the aim of history is not objective truth but profit to the readers, he speaks as a rhetorician, not as a serious critic.[8]

These protestations of veracity and of pursuing a lofty aim can be paralleled far and wide in the Byzantine historians. We have seen how Anna fills her Preface with them.[9] Her husband, in his, gives a similar account of his objects. He has written partly to please the Empress Irene, and partly because his own feeling towards Alexius was too deep for him to 'pass over his deeds in silence, so that they would perish in the abyss of forgetfulness'; but he is composing neither a History nor an Encomium, only providing a ὕλη ἱστορίας for later biographers.[10]

Long before Bryennius' day Theophanes, who wrote in the second decade of the ninth century, had told his readers in the Preface to his *Chronography*, that he reluctantly undertook to continue the work of a friend in spite of his consciousness of ἀμάθεια καὶ τὸ στενὸν τοῦ λόγου. It involved 'searching out and examining many books' of old historiographers and logographers and putting events 'in their own places in regular order'. (Chronology is his obsession.) He hopes to provide for his readers οὐ μικρὰν ὠφέλειαν and begs their prayers and indul-

[1] *Antiq. Rom.* I. 1; also *ad Pomp.* 3, 2 (ed. Jacoby, Vol. I, p. 2, and *Opusc.* ed. Usener, Vol. II, p. 232).   [2] Pref., *passim.*   [3] *Antiq. Rom.* I. 2.
[4] Pref. 4, p. 8.   [5] *Hist.* I. 5.
[6] *Bibl.* IV. 1.   [7] *Thes.* 1.
[8] E. Stemplinger, *op. cit.* p. 149.
[9] Cf. also I. 10, p. 23; III. 1, p. 72; 2, p. 74; 8, pp. 90, 91.
[10] *Hyle*, Pref. p. 13. Psellus, we may note, begins his *Chronography* not with a Preface but with a long descriptive Title.

gence in return, φίλον γὰρ τῷ Θεῷ τὸ κατὰ δύναμιν. In later days, slightly before Bryennius and Anna wrote, Michael Attaliates produced his History. After a laudatory address to the Emperor Botaniates he opens his narrative with the assertion that History is χρήσιμον εἰς τὰ μάλιστα τῷ βίῳ; the lives of the good and the bad alike teach lessons. He himself is busy with military and legal affairs, but he feels bound to write 'so that things worthy of record (λόγου) may not, through the passing of time, be buried in the depths of oblivion, but may have an undying memorial'.[1] He aims at setting forth as far as he can the causes of events, and in fact does so on all occasions. Later on[2] he explains that he does not wish to resemble the servant who hid his lord's talent, but desires in his writing first to preserve the memory of Botaniates, secondly to spur on posterity by that emperor's example.

Coming down to Anna's contemporaries, we find that Zonaras in his Preface defends himself against the sneers of those who consider the pursuit of letters a πάρεργον. He has chosen to employ on it his exile from public affairs, partly to atone for his past misdeeds, partly to please his friends by writing an ἔργον κοινωφελές. (He himself regards a great deal of history as 'most necessary' to be learnt.) They urged him to avoid on the one hand the long descriptions of wars and localities, and the various discussions and orations in which many historians aim at displaying their own learning, and only succeed in wearying their readers; and on the other hand the undue brevity which omits deeds 'worthy to be sung', with all that shows the 'character and nature and intentions' of the persons portrayed. Other writers again make their composition unreadable by ἰδιωτικαῖς λέξεσιν ἢ καὶ βαρβάροις ἐνίοτε. So Zonaras' friends beg from him a σύντομον ἱστορίαν, setting forth only τὰ καιριώτερα of all that has happened, and at length his inertia yields to their importunity, largely because he fears that Satan may find some mischief still for idle hands to do. He invites the reader's indulgence towards imperfections, as he has no adequate supply of books, and furthermore authorities often disagree, so that to enumerate every one of the contrary opinions would be tedious.

Cedrenus[3] at the outset gives an elaborate account of his motives in writing:

[1] Hist., opening paragraph, p. 8. None of the Byzantines seem to share the lofty sentiment of Sir Thos. Browne in his Urne Buriall about men dead and gone: 'The greater part must be content to be as though they had not been, to be found in the register of God, not in the record of man.'   [2] p. 322.
[3] pp. 1, 2. He wrote under Alexius I, and brings his work down to 1057, copying Scylitzes (who we may note carries his history to 1079) textually.

'Many men before us, lovers of God and lovers of history, have laboured at the epitomizing of history. . . . But they failed in accuracy. . . . For each put forward his own subject, one for instance the praise of an emperor, one the blame of a patriarch, another the eulogy of a friend. . . . I, having gone through the books of these men, collected suitable material, adding also what I had learnt unwritten from men of old.'

He left his work 'to posterity as a delicate food', first to act as a reminder to those who have read the books of other historians, because neglect brings oblivion 'obscuring and confounding the memory of deeds', secondly to be a ὁδηγός to those who have not read them.[1]

Glycas, who as is usual in such a work begins his chronicle with the creation of the world, prefaces it by saying he means to indite a 'short writing', adding: 'for I know that if a discourse is extended to great length it greatly burdens the hearing'.[2] He also implies that whereas the aim of other chroniclers is to win honour for themselves, he is only thinking of the instruction of his son, addressed as 'my dearest child'.

Cinnamus, also under Manuel I, follows the old models when he begins: 'In no wise was the task of history held inglorious by the wise men of old. Nay, it fell to the lot of most of them actually to gain honour thereby . . . and because all things that occurred in course of time were in danger of being again lost from sight, they handed them down to the coming age by engraving them in books as on imperishable pillars.' Though Cinnamus is conscious of not having enough knowledge or leisure for his task, yet 'not on that account must the affairs which came about in our age be altogether passed over in silence'.[3]

Similarly Nicetas Acominatus, who saw the fall of Constantinople in 1204, has his clear theory of history-writing. 'I thought it not right to pass by in silence things worthy to be remembered and set forth, so great in number and so important. Therefore through this my writing I put them down plainly for those who come after.' He thinks it right that History should pillory vice, and its τέλος σκοπιμώτατον is Truth, but the language must be

---

[1] So the sixth-century John of Epiphania (see p. 225, note 2, above) says he will begin with a brief outline of the facts, to be a reminder to those who know and a starting-point of information for those who do not.

[2] Bibl. Chron. I, p. 1, written under Manuel I (1143–80). He may be thinking of Zonaras and the latter's lengthy eighteen books (from which he himself freely borrowed), written in spite of the author's professed dread of verbosity.

[3] Hist. I. 1, pp. 1, 2.

simple (more so than is popular with historians) because it has to appeal to workmen and soldiers and women.[1]

The family likeness between all these preambles speaks for itself. The Byzantine who began to write a history or a chronicle[2] felt that he was entering on a solemn and exalted task, a duty owed to the dead, and still more a service to be rendered to the living. So it behoved him to be lucid and interesting and instructive, but above all truthful.[3] Whatever lapses from the truth Byzantine historians may have made in practice, in theory it was their one and only goal. The seventeenth-century French writers, of whom it has been said[4] that 'their purpose was most commonly political or moral instruction, and the presentment of historic fact was always quite subsidiary', would have shocked Anna Comnena[5] quite as much as they do the history student of to-day.

34. ORAL AND WRITTEN SOURCES

IN this pursuit of truth it was customary for classical authors to appeal, when their personal knowledge ended, to eyewitnesses or to common opinion,[6] and this fashion was faithfully copied by the Byzantines. Thus at one point Nicephorus Bryennius says: 'All know these things and the circumstances lie on the lips of all.'[7] Cinnamus says he will deal only briefly with affairs that he neither saw himself, nor learnt with certainty.[8] Attaliates will write simply, as suits history, and confine himself to things he himself saw.[9] Nicetas Acominatus will rely, as to everything that happened before his time, on what he had

---

[1] *Hist.* Pref. 1, pp. 2 and 3.

[2] In regard to this special point of truthfulness it has not seemed necessary sharply to divide the Byzantine historians, as Krumbacher does, into the two classes —Geschichtschreiber and Chronisten; the generalizations above given apply to both.

[3] Just as Tacitus professed to write *sine ira et studio*, so we get protestations of impartial truthfulness down to the very end of Byzantine historiography. See the Prefaces to George Acropolites, John Cantacuzenus, and George Phrantzes in Krumbacher, *G. B. L.* p. 287, note 1, p. 298, note 2, and p. 307, note 1.

[4] In a paper read before the Modern Language Association at Oxford by the Hon. Alice Bruce.

[5] She explicitly scorns people who allow prejudice to blind them and who 'judge matters by preference and not as they are' (III. 1, p. 72, and 2, p. 75).

[6] So Thucydides, above. Polybius, *Hist.* IV. 2. 2, 3, attaches great importance to having 'assisted at some events ourselves, and heard others from those who saw them'.

[7] *Hyle*, Pref. p. 7.

[8] *Hist.* I. 8, p. 11.

[9] *Hist.* (beginning), p. 8.

learnt from eyewitnesses.[1] Anna goes upon the same lines. She
has got her information from 'those who saw the facts', whose
sons and grandchildren are alive as she writes,[2] or from her
parents,[3] or from her uncles (especially George Palaeologus),[4]
and other 'actual soldiers' or 'older men' who took part,[5] or
from her father-in-law Bryennius, or from the Empress Maria,[6]
or from the ex-enemy Peter Aluph, or a 'Latin envoy sent by
the Bishop of Bari to Robert' Guiscard and consequently present at his Durazzo campaign,[7] or even from the ferrymen who
had picked up news that came straight from the front.[8] At
every turn she tries to impress upon us that her knowledge is
either taken from her own recollections or gained at first hand
from others who participated in the events.[9]

Of the written sources of the *Alexias* we must now speak
briefly. Anna herself refers to the unfinished though already
published[10] ὕλη ἱστορίας of her husband Nicephorus Bryennius
Caesar, begun at the command of his mother-in-law as a means
of preserving Alexius' great deeds from oblivion. As it ter-
minates before the abdication of Nicephorus Botaniates, it
affords material only for Anna's first two books, and not even
for the whole of these. Still it has considerable importance for
us, not merely as the 'Onlie Begetter', according to Anna, of her
own work,[11] but as giving her a model for its general lines. Thus
she tells us[12] that it is in imitation of Bryennius that she altogether omits τὰ παιδικά of her father, and in its descriptions,
form of narrative, and above all (as we saw before) its sentiments, the *Alexias* so far resembles the *Hyle* that, but for its far
more difficult and stilted Greek, the wife's work might come
from the husband's hand. On five occasions[13] she explicitly
advises her readers to consult her husband's writings as fuller

---

[1] *Hist.*, Pref. 1, p. 4. We may compare the statements all through the *Gesta
Dei per Francos* of Anna's Western contemporary, Guibert de Nogent, that the author
has scrupulously tried to get at the truth, especially from eyewitnesses.
[2] Pref. 2, p. 3; cf. XIV. 9, p. 456. For X. 8 she probably drew on her Maurocatacalo brother-in-law.
[3] VI. 8, p. 166; VII. 3, p. 198; XIII. 8, p. 398; XIV. 7, pp. 447, 448. So
Nic. Bry. (II. 6, p. 44) quotes Alexius' words.   [4] XIV. 7, pp. 447, 448.
[5] III. 9, p. 91; VII. 3, p. 198; VIII. 2, p. 225; IX. 1, p. 245.
[6] I. 6, p. 16; III. 1, p. 72.
[7] III. 12, p. 99; IV. 6, p. 117. This Latin envoy has been held to be the
source on which William of Apulia drew for his *Poema de rebus Normannorum*. See
Krumbacher, *G. B. L.* p. 275.
[8] XIV. 7, p. 447.   [9] XIV. 7, pp. 446, 448.
[10] J. Seger (*op. cit.* p. 33), points out that it was customary to publish each part
of a work as it was written. Thus Attaliates (p. 322) promises a second part to his
work, a promise which he never fulfilled.
[11] Pref. 3.   [12] *Ibid.*
[13] I. 1, p. 4; I. 4, p. 9; II. 1, p. 43; VII. 2, p. 191; X. 2, p. 271.

than her own, though curiously enough she is inaccurate in stating their scope, saying[1] that his book begins with Romanus Diogenes, whereas the first reign described is actually the earlier one of Isaac Comnenus. The opening of the second chapter of her first Book is a free version of Book II, Chapter 21 of the *Hyle*, and even more closely copied are the three speeches put into her father's mouth in the same episode. Similarly Bryennius' fourth Book is the quarry from which her accounts of the elder Bryennius and of Basilacius are hewn.[3] For later events we feel sure Anna must have used her husband's recollections, especially as to the many scenes in which he played a part.[3] It is therefore almost inconceivable that she should have disagreed *in toto* with Bryennius' view about John's right of succession[4] and yet should never mention the fact. We may remark that she alludes to ἄλλα τινὰ συγγράμματα of his μνήμης καὶ λόγου ἄξια,[5] now lost. On the whole we may apply to the reign of Alexius the lament over the dearth of contemporary historians which Bury utters as to the lives of John II and of Manuel I,[6] and conclude that, like Cinnamus and Nicetas, Anna had to rely on sources 'almost exclusively oral'.

For Byzantine events before her day we know that she took extracts verbatim from the *Chronography* of Psellus[7], and she may have read the works of Attaliates and Scylitzes and Leo Diaconus, possibly even an early issue, so to speak, of Zonaras; but her references to past events are too infrequent to need special notice here. For Alexius' Patzinak Wars she is our sole authority, and we cannot trace her sources. In the First Crusade she narrates on the whole the same facts as the Latin chroniclers,[8] but from too utterly different a point of view to

---

[1] Pref. 3, p. 4.

[2] J. Seger (*op. cit.* p. 57) considers that Bryennius cannot wholly be trusted where his personal prejudices are concerned. He also believes that he wrote the adulatory earlier part, especially the Preface, while Alexius was alive, and changed his tone in Books III and IV after the Emperor's death (pp. 32, 33).

[3] Notably the episode of Godfrey de Bouillon at Constantinople (X. 9).

[4] *Hyle*, Pref., p. 10; cf. p. 27 note 6, above.   [5] Pref. 3, p. 4.

[6] J. B. Bury, reviewing F. Chalandon's *Jean II et Manuel I* (*B. Z.* XXII, p. 195).

[7] Thus III. 8, p. 89 = *Chron.*, Is. Comn., Byz. T., pp. 221 sqq.; V. 9, p. 148 = *Chron.*, Rom. III, Byz. T., p. 26; VII. 2, p. 190 = *Chron.*, Basil II, Byz. T., p. 12. Her phrase in Pref. 1, p. 1, οὐ περιαυτολογία τὸ πρᾶγμα occurs in Psellus' Funeral Oration on his mother. *B. G. Med.* V. p. 11.

[8] She probably got facts from Taticius, for after he left Antioch her story of the Crusade is meagre and far from accurate. Thus she calls Peter the Hermit a bishop, possibly confusing him with the Legate Bishop Adhémar of Le Puy, or with the Provençal priest Peter Bartholomew, said by the Latin Chroniclers to have found the sacred object, which she calls a 'Nail' and not a 'Lance'. Also she makes Godfrey de Bouillon be captured by the Turks (which he never was) at the battle of Rama, which took place a year after his death (XI. 4, 6, 7). For her chronology in the matter of the Pisan fleet see p. 470, note 9, below.

make any mutual influencing possible, even if she could by
any miracle have seen their writings and read their 'barbarous'
language. In her theological passages she owes much to her
father's chosen champion of orthodoxy, the monk Euthymius
Zigabenus, but she may also quite possibly have studied the
Conciliar Decrees for herself.

An elaborate defence of her whole method of writing history
occurs in XIV. 7, and the assertions which she makes of her
truthfulness are worth studying:

'Following the facts themselves and neither adding on my own
account nor taking away, I both speak and write what has happened. And the proof is at hand, for I do not take back my composition to 10,000 years ago, but there are some who survive to the
present day, and who knew my father and who tell me the facts
about him, by whom no small part of the history has been here
contributed, with some telling and remembering one thing and some
another, as each chanced to do, and all agreeing. And in most cases
I too was present with my father and accompanied my mother. . . .
Some things then . . . I know of myself' [we may believe that her
memories dated at least from the Crusaders' coming to Constantinople when she was 13] 'and the things that happened in the wars
I got from those who fought beside my father (for I questioned them
in various ways about these matters), and also from certain ferrymen who brought us news. But above all I often listened face to face
to the Emperor and George Palaeologus when they discoursed about
these things.'

She then hints in veiled language at the tyranny which had
kept her for the last thirty years from consorting with any who
were attached to her father or could have given her information; we are therefore bound to conclude that her first-hand
evidence was all collected before her father's death, whereas
her history was not written for three decades afterwards, when
'the third after' Alexius was reigning, i.e. Manuel (1143-80).
In her retirement she could only go for fresh materials to 'certain worthless and altogether trifling compositions', and to aged
monks who had been laymen and fighters in the far-off days
before her father's accession. The information from these two
sources, when carefully weighed, proved to tally with what
Anna had often heard from her father and from her paternal
and maternal uncles. 'From all which things the whole body
of the truth is woven together.'

At the end of the same Book XIV she asserts that 'among
men now alive there are many witnesses' to the Emperor's
dealings with the Manichaeans, and his ordinances for the new

town of Alexiopolis. As always, she deprecates the charge of filial partiality and shrinks from the very idea of being 'convicted of falsehood'.[1]

Once more before she closes her story she makes the claim which is as it were the keynote of her history, that she is both φιλαλήθης and φιλοπάτωρ.[2] Not because she loves her father does she praise him, but because 'the nature of the facts'[3] and his astounding merits compel her. She appeals for confirmation to 'all that have not been ignorant of our affairs'. Truth has been her supreme aim in writing, and this has brought on her the hatred of her enemies. 'Verily,' she sums up, 'I would not betray Truth under the form of History.'

With this ideal before her, it is natural that we should find her attempting to weigh evidence and get at real truth. We may assert almost positively that she never deliberately falsifies facts, and does her best to be impartial to friend and foe in praise or blame.[4] She had prejudices, racial, social, and personal, but if she deceives us it is only when she herself is deceived. Thus, in discussing her father's share in the blinding of Nicephorus Diogenes, she says: 'God alone may know: I at any rate have not been able hitherto to find out for certain.'[5] Again, 'God alone knows' why the Sultan of Cairo released the crusading counts, and she tries to assess his probable motives.[6] She studies astrology a little, not in order to practise it, but 'so as by more accurately judging this foolish thing to judge those who have toiled over it'.[7] We have already spoken of the cautious and sceptical spirit which made it hard for Byzantines to take anything at its face value. This in Alexius led to surprisingly enlightened views as to portents and omens,[8] and the same feeling inspires Anna with at least the rudiments of historical criticism. Abel Lefranc[9] claims for Guibert, Abbot of Nogent, the place of pioneer in this field, and certainly the frank contempt shown in his *De pignoribus sanctorum* for relics (even for a tooth of Our Lord's) and bogus miracles and trust in the Ordeal, as well as for the absurd and never verified histories of saints told by monks whose ignorance and vice he

---

[1] XIV. 9, p. 456. Cf. XII. 3, p. 354, and the whole tone of the Preface.
[2] XV. 3. She draws a sharp distinction between historians and writers of panegyrics (III. 8, pp. 87, 91). The latter she despises and suspects of suppressing inconvenient facts (III. 8, p. 88; V. 1, p. 126). See p. 245 below.
[3] This phrase occurs in the same connexion in VII. 3, p. 198.
[4] This is what she claims in the quotation from Polybius, Pref. 2, p. 3.
[5] IX. 9, p. 265.   [6] XII. 1, pp. 346, 347.
[7] VI. 7, p. 164.
[8] XII. 4, pp. 355 and 357; see pp. 85–86 above.
[9] *Études d'hist. du moyen âge dédiées à Gabriel Monod*, ed. E. Lavisse, Paris, 1896.

lashes, is startlingly modern to our ears. But all the time, right across Europe, a Byzantine princess was cautiously refusing to commit herself as to visions[1] or prophetic inspiration,[2] speaking with scarcely veiled contempt of the 'experts' who explained portents,[3] weighing testimony, scrutinizing motives, and in short trying as far as in her lay to retrieve Truth from the bottom of its proverbial well.

35. DOCUMENTS AND ENVOYS

IN this connexion it is interesting to learn how Anna herself tells us she treated documentary evidence. Before transcribing the Golden Bull as to her grandmother's Regency, she says :[4] 'Since it is right for the writer of history not to transmit in the gross ($\pi\alpha\chi\upsilon\mu\epsilon\rho\hat{\omega}s$) the deeds and the decrees of good men, but delicately to delineate the deeds as far as possible, and on the other hand set forth the enactments, I myself will follow this path, and will set forth the contents of the aforesaid Golden Bull, only omitting the artificialities of the scribe.' This sound principle of history-writing, that facts may be summarized but *pièces justificatives* must be given in full, strikes us all the more because, as Stemplinger has pointed out, even Thucydides (like all the writers of antiquity) 'stilisierte' the $\psi\eta\phi\acute{\iota}\sigma\mu\alpha\tau\alpha$ and other archives of which he made use.

In regard to the official documents which she quotes in full or to which she alludes, Oster and Chalandon believe Anna to have had direct access to the State archives.[5] Oster reasons that not only must she have possessed the copies made by her husband for continuing his work, but researches into the past must have been permitted by her brother John as a good vent for her dangerous energy. The argument is not altogether convincing, but is at least plausible. The longest of these documents is Bohemund's treaty with Alexius,[6] filling many pages and concluding with a long list of signatory witnesses. The

---

[1] II. 7, pp. 58, 59; VII. 4, p. 199.   [2] II. 12, p. 68.
[3] X. 5, p. 284; XII. 4, p. 355.   [4] III. 6, p. 83.
[5] Fr. Dölger (Corpus der Gr. Urkunden des Mittelalters, Reihe A, Abt. 1) says in his Introduction to *Regesten der Kaiserurkunden* that Anna is almost alone among her contemporaries in quoting documents verbatim, and he believes with the two critics just cited that like Constantine Porphyrogenitus she had through her birth unusual opportunities for consulting the imperial archives. We may remark that where we know her sources (e.g. her husband's History) we find her faithful to them, and this inclines us on doubtful points to give credence to her rather than to any more or less contemporary writer with whom she disagrees.
[6] XIII. 12.

next in length are the letter[1] to the King of Germany and the above-mentioned Golden Bull[2] appointing Anna Dalassena Regent. Other letters and rescripts merely mentioned[3] or given textually are too numerous to quote.[4] Anna may also well have seen the ordinance now lost concerning Alexius' gifts to his Orphanage, and the acts of the Assemblies condemning Leo of Chalcedon, Italus, Nilus, and Basil the Bogomile.

Documents of all sorts are mentioned. Golden bulls may, as we saw, confer Regency or assign property,[5] make a contract or treaty,[6] or grant a safe conduct or pardon.[7] (In the case of a treaty each side of course keeps a copy of the provisions, the one as a Golden Bull, the other as a 'written oath'.[8]) The material used as sealing-wax was gold,[9] and every important person had his or her distinctive seal.[10] The signing of State documents was a jealously guarded prerogative of empire. There was a special inkstand with its pen,[11] and the ink was of cinnabar, producing 'red letters'.[12] The document would be prepared by a secretary,[13] but the right of signature belonged only to the Emperor and co-Emperor[14] or their regent,[15] though according to Bury[16] the $\chi\alpha\rho\tau o\upsilon\lambda\acute\alpha\rho\iota o\varsigma$ $\tauo\hat\upsilon$ $\kappa\alpha\nu\iota\kappa\lambda\epsilon\acuteio\upsilon$[17] used in practice to sign for them, and Du Cange cites an instance where a Logothete signed imperial documents concerning the public taxes.[18]

The trust in written promises rather than verbal was, as we

---

[1] III. 10.　　　　　　　　　　　　　　　　[2] III. 6.

[3] III. 9, p. 92 ; 10, p. 93 ; IV. 2, p. 105 ; VI. 5, pp. 161–2 ; XI. 7, p. 329 ; XII. 2, p. 348, etc.

[4] V. 5, p. 138 ; VI. 12, p. 177 ; VIII. 7, p. 237 ; IX. 3, p. 250 ; X. 7, p. 288 ; XI. 9, pp. 332, 333. Of these letters obviously very few make any pretension to authenticity; they are like what Stemplinger calls the 'Maskenreden' or fictitious speeches put into the mouths of their characters by classical and later writers, including Anna herself. The communications to or from Greek or 'barbarian' in the *Alexias* bear the stamp of only one personality, that of the writer; she would probably never have thought that any reader would take them literally, so that the question of veracity did not arise. See above, Ch. 28.

[5] III. 6, p. 83 ; XIV. 9, p. 456 ; XV. 7, p. 485.

[6] IV. 2, p. 105 ; VII. 6, p. 202 ; XI. 2, p. 313 ; XIII. 12, p. 416.

[7] III. 12, p. 97 ; VI. 4, p. 158.

[8] XIII. 12, p. 416.　　　　　　　　　　　　[9] III. 4, p. 79.

[10] In III. 6, p. 84, Anna Dalassena's seal is said to bear the Transfiguration of Our Lord and the Dormitio of the B.V.M.

[11] II. 10, p. 62.

[12] III. 4, pp. 79, 80 ; XIII. 12, pp. 407, 416.

[13] II. 8, p. 60.　　　　　　[14] III. 4, p. 80.　　　　　　[15] III. 6.

[16] *Imperial Administrative System in the Ninth Century.* Ch. C. VII. (4).

[17] The inkstand was shaped like a dog; see Du Cange's notes on II. 10, p. 62 D, and XI. 10, p. 338 A. In XI. 10, p. 338, we find Eustathius Cymineanus, a eunuch holding $\dot\eta$ $\tauo\hat\upsilon$ $\kappa\alpha\nu\iota\kappa\lambda\epsilon\acuteio\upsilon$ $\dot\alpha\xi\acutei\alpha$, made Great Drungary of the Fleet. Cf. Alexius' Novel 22 in *P. G.* 126, col. 972.

[18] Note on III. 1, p. 70 A.

have already seen, a characteristic mark of the Byzantine caution, but the same spirit prevails to-day. 'Get it in writing' is the maxim of business now as then. So the people of Nicaea will do nothing without 'written promises' from Alexius;[1] a γραμμάτιον has to carry the imperial reprieve to the sentenced conspirator Anemas,[2] and a document once written by a sovereign has such power that it can be used against himself.[3] Even the casting of Sacred Lots is done by rolls (πύκτια) or papers[4] (χαρτία) on which Yes or No is written. The language of documents was so far stereotyped that Bohemund expresses his desire to 'keep the proper phrase of those who make contracts in writing';[5] we can judge of such ἰδιότης by the bombast of the three principal state papers in the *Alexias*.[6] Writing out passages for analysis was part of the education given in the imperial Orphanage,[7] and the Emperor himself not only knew how to write, when the Western counts did not,[8] but could draw a map[9] and work out military plans on parchment.[10] The monasteries had written inventories (βρέβια) of their possessions, kept accurately enough to constitute a legal record.[11] On the whole however it must be confessed that though as we know in other ways the Byzantine archives were very rich in lists, tax-returns, and registers of all sorts, yet except for casual references to the military or the senatorial or the ecclesiastical register Anna Comnena shows little cognizance of the fact. At the same time she makes us feel what intimate and vital service was rendered to a sovereign by his 'secretaries'. They form part of his household, they draw up his documents,[12] they take down (possibly

---

[1] XI. 1, p. 310, and 2, p. 313. See other instances on p. 151 above.
[2] XII. 6, p. 364.   [3] VI. 9, p. 170.
[4] X. 2, p. 273; XV. 4, p. 471.   [5] XIII. 12, p. 407.
[6] III. 6, even though Anna here professes to have removed τὰς κομψείας; III. 10, and XIII. 12.
[7] XV. 7, p. 485. Writing was sometimes put to a bad use, as in the case of the lampoons thrown into Alexius' tent in the face of severe penalties. It is curious to read of 'a soldier's wallet' filled with papers of the sort (XIII. 1).
[8] XIII. 12, p. 416.
[9] XIII. 7, p. 396.   [10] XV. 3, p. 469.
[11] VI. 3, p. 156.
[12] The words used are ὑπογραφεύς, ὑπογραμματεύς, and νοτάριος (II. 8, p. 60; III. 8, p. 88; XIII. 12, p. 416, and elsewhere). Cinnamus (I. 8, p. 10) speaks of a man who had been ὑπογραμματεύς to the Emperor 'from a child'. Nic. Acom. tells of one who grew rich ἐκ τοῦ τάσσειν φόρους (*John C.* 3, p. 7). So Eustathius of Thessalonica speaks affectionately of a συνδιάκονος as ἐμὸν θρέμμα καὶ ἀγαθὸς ὑπογραμματεύς (*P. G.* 136, col. 1300). In VII. 2, p. 192, the 'under-secretary' Nicolas predicts an eclipse. Another, 'one of the nobles taken into Alexius' household from childhood', is a great legal expert and his master's invaluable critic; he becomes prefect of Constantinople (XIII. 1, p. 376). A third rose to be Logothete τῶν σεκρέτων (see Du Cange's note on IX. 8, p. 261 A), i.e. Grand Treasurer, most important of all the Logothetes.

in shorthand) the confessions of his enemies.[1] The Emperor was dependent on them at every turn.

One other small point remains to be noted. In the very large correspondence carried on by the Emperor we cannot fail to be impressed with the importance not only of the 'secretaries' who actually conducted it, but also of the messengers who carried the letters to their destination.[2] On rare occasions they are trusted to speak their own words and to act as pleni-potentiaries, especially if akin to the person addressed;[3] usually they are provided with papers.[4] Even from and to besieged towns letters are carried,[5] and generals threaten their enemies or their Emperor in writing.[6] Letters to deceive or persuade, letters of accusation or sharp remonstrance or mere informa-tion, letters to collect mercenaries or give orders to officers and allies, indeed letters of any and every kind appear in every phase of the story.[7] At one point Alexius demands ἀπόρρητα γράμματα as a kind of secret service information from two of his young officers about their commander at the front,[8] and in his dealings with his troublesome nephew John Com-nenus he carries to a fine point the diplomatic trick of sending letters to say one thing and an envoy to say another.[9] 'Letters and friendly greetings' between his army and the Normans

---

[1] IX. 8, p. 261; XV. 8, p. 488.

[2] We may remember the passage in Thucydides: 'Nicias, fearing lest his messen-gers, either from inability to speak or from want of intelligence, or because they desired to please the people, might not tell the whole truth, wrote a letter' (*Hist.* VII. 8). Theophylact (Ser. I, Ep. 11, *P. G.* 126, col. 324) alludes feelingly to the difficulty of finding reliable messengers. 'For many men are ready (πρόχειροι) to accept letters, but to carry them and deliver them to him to whom they were written, they are slothful and as it were handless' (ἄχειρες).

[3] When the wounded Eustathius Camytzes brings to Irene the tidings of her husband's victory the proceeding is so informal that he does not wait to change his clothes, and she lets him sit in her presence to tell his tale. He bears no letter, but makes a speech next day in the Forum of Constantine to spread the good news (XIV. 6; cf. XII. 7, p. 364).

[4] Even the imperial envoy Butumites carries not only verbal messages but 'imperial letters' (XIV. 2, p. 424), and a messenger important enough to have his name mentioned takes a letter as well as 'sufficient money' to 'Babylon', i.e. Cairo, for ransoming the counts (XI. 7, p. 328; XII. 1, p. 346. We are assuming that these two passages tell one story, not two, and that Bardales and Nicetas Panucomites are one and the same man).

[5] IV. 1, p. 103; 8, p. 122; V. 5, pp. 137, 138; XI. 2, pp. 313; XIII. 8, p. 399. In X. 4, p. 278, a letter is shot in, tied to an arrow.

[6] XII. 2, p. 348; 7, p. 364.

[7] VI. 9, p. 170; VIII. 3, p. 226; 7, *passim*; IX. 4, p. 252; XI. 3, p. 316; 7, p. 329; 8, p. 332, 9, *passim*; XII. 1, p. 346; 3, p. 350; 4, p. 356; 7, p. 364; 8, p. 366; XIII. 1, p. 376; 8, p. 399; XIV. 5, pp. 438, 439; XV. 2, p. 465.

[8] XI. 9, p. 333. In XIII. 7 Lantulph writes openly to Alexius complaining of his chief Isaac Contostephanus, and this breach of discipline is favourably taken.

[9] VIII. 7, pp. 237, 238.

with whom they are at war are one of the dangers he dreads, and at the same crisis he himself writes bogus incriminating letters.[1]

Some at least of these missives were carried by special runners, like the Scythian 'with winged feet, as the saying is' who announced to the Emperor the landing of Bohemund in Illyria.[2] The γραμματοκομισταί in charge of the bogus letters just referred to have to be guarded against injury,[3] doubtless a necessary precaution in that treacherous age. Even the story of Bellerophon finds its counterpart in that of George, son of Decanus, though imprisonment and not death is the fate he carries for himself in the letter.[4] In theory of course the person of envoys, even more than of mere letter-carriers, is sacred; they are received with honour and the task is almost invariably entrusted to men of distinction.[5] Anna's horror against the Pope for mutilating the German envoys would be entirely justified if the story had been true.[6] When her father on a flimsy pretext seizes the 150 Patzinaks who have come to treat about peace no reader will be otherwise than pleased that they escape after all.[7] When it is a question of getting an oath from a person at a distance, specially important messengers are sent.[8] A 'Latin envoy sent by the Bishop of Bari' accompanies Guiscard's army, while ambassadors in our sense of the term appear as witnesses to the treaty between Alexius and Bohemund, coming from the Pope, the Hungarians (whom Anna calls Dacians), and an Italian prince.[9] Envoys to remonstrate or persuade figure in delicate negotiations; yet even plenipotentiaries, capable of 'adding to the words' lies

---

[1] XIII. 4.

[2] XII. 9, p. 372. In III. 12, p. 97, we hear of a ταχυδρόμος, in VIII. 8, p. 238, of a γραμματοκομιστὴς δρομαῖος.

[3] XIII. 4, p. 389.

[4] VIII. 9, p. 242.

[5] I. 15, p. 35; 16, p. 39; IV. 2, p. 107; VI. 12, p. 178; cf. V. 5, p. 139. Count Hugh of Vermandois sends to John Comnenus at Durazzo twenty-four envoys, 'clothed in golden armour with greaves and all,' headed by a Count and an apparently important deserter (X. 7, p. 288). In VII. 6, p. 202, the envoy Synesius seems to be given power of independent action, while the Coman πρέσβεις are generously treated. Shortly afterwards the Emperor himself has to send πρέσβεις to sue for peace (ibid. p. 203). Cf. Bohemund to Duke Alexius in XIII. 8, p. 399, where neither letters nor envoys are expressly mentioned. In XIV. 3, p. 432, we see an attempt to overawe the Turkish envoys, but no violence is shown.

[6] I. 13, p. 31.

[7] VII. 2, p. 193.

[8] III. 10 and V. 3, p. 130; XI. 8, p. 332; XIII. 12, p. 411; XIV. 2.

[9] III. 12, p. 99; XIII. 12, p. 416, and see Du Cange's note on 'Ρισκάρδος Σινίσκαρδος. The word πρέσβεις is used of the Venetian delegates who treat with Alexius (IV. 2, p. 105).

of their own invention, receive detailed instructions from the Emperor beforehand.[1] He was his own Foreign Minister quite as much as his own Commander-in-Chief.

Enough has now been said to show how important in Anna's eyes was the written word. Her father, one feels, must have been always receiving or issuing letters, or causing his secretaries to draw up multifarious documents, and from her babyhood her whole conception of a historian must have been permeated with the maxim, 'Litera scripta manet'. What she in her turn writes she intends to last for ever.

36. SUBJECT—THE BASILEUS

WE have said that classical historians laid great stress on the choice of a worthy subject. In this as in other particulars Anna does not forget her models. It may be said that her two exceptional advantages as a historian are, first that she has no rival whom she wishes to controvert[2] but only a respected husband to supplement, secondly that she has a dearly-loved central figure for her story, dominating and giving connected interest to the whole. It is difficult for us to appreciate, however often we try to grasp it, the attitude of veneration, almost of worship, in which the Byzantines stood to their $\beta \alpha \sigma \iota \lambda \epsilon \acute{\upsilon} s$. Diehl has pointed out[3] the triple root of this feeling. From the Roman Empire he had inherited the role of Imperator, 'that is, both the supreme war-lord and the unimpeachable legislator', from the East he had acquired the prerogatives of the autocrat to whom subjects bow down as slaves, and through the Church he had come to be regarded as 'the elect of God, His vicar in earth'.[4]

In the truest sense of the word Divinity did hedge a king in the Byzantine mind. He is the $\beta \alpha \sigma \iota \lambda \epsilon \acute{\upsilon} s$ while every other

---

[1] XI. 8, p. 332; XIV. 2, p. 427. Inasmuch as Alexius usually prefers diplomacy to arms, it is strange to find his daughter treating 'mildly sending envoys' instead of fighting as a childish playing at war (IX. 2, p. 249). But the general in question is not her father.

[2] e.g. as Polybius does Phylarchus.

[3] *Camb. Med. Hist.* IV, p. 726. Cf. Cec. *Strat.* p. 74: 'The Emperor enthroned at Constantinople always wins.'

[4] We find Attaliates in his address to Botaniates (before his History opens) making for that Emperor very much the same claims that Anna did for her father; he is $\beta \alpha \sigma \iota \lambda \iota \kappa \acute{\omega} \tau \epsilon \rho o s$ than his predecessors; he has conquered enemies and rebels; his zeal for learning is incomparable; above all he reigns as God's chosen.

monarch is rightfully only ῥήξ.[1] When the arrogant Turkish emir calls himself Emperor, uses 'the insignia belonging to emperors', dwells at Smyrna 'as though an imperial residence', and actually aspires to the Empire,[2] his presumption is so preposterous and incredible that Alexius can easily persuade the Sultan of Nicaea that a Turkish and not the Greek throne is all he can really be coveting.[3] Nothing in the world was as godlike in Byzantine eyes as the Emperor of the 'Romaioi'. He was head of Church and State; he summoned Councils and only by his authority could their edicts be carried out; he made and unmade Patriarchs and was himself the great champion of Orthodoxy. In short, he was as truly a *Roi Soleil*[4] as any Louis XIV, and in writing his biography his daughter was writing the history of the time. The Emperor is the mightiest sovereign in the world and his realm the one true Empire,[5] the only fitting theme for her story. All the world acknowledges his greatness; he 'is not one of ordinary mortals'.[6] Never in the story of the Crusade does she express the slightest surprise, or even satisfaction, when the Counts take the oath of homage to the Emperor; it is merely as it should be with 'barbarians'.[7]

All this helps us to realize the seriousness, almost the awe, with which she undertook her task and contemplated her subject.[8] C. Neumann points out that to turn from Byzantine writers of the twelfth century to their contemporary chroniclers in the West is to turn, in all such matters as narration, order, character-drawing, and political science, from civilization to barbarism indeed.[9] May it not well be that pride in their noble

---

[1] I. 13, p. 30, &c.; XI. 7, p. 329. Note the one exception, due according to Neumann (*Weltstellung*, &c., ch. II, p. 28) to a convention even older than the days of John Tzimisces, that βασιλεύς is used of the Bulgarian monarch (VII. 3, p. 194; XII. 9, p. 371). The Latin chroniclers call the French king Rex Regum, but to Anna it is sheer madness for his brother to style himself βασιλεύς τῶν βασιλέων (X. 7, p. 288).

[2] IX. 1, p. 245.

[3] IX. 3, p. 250. When the pseudo-Diogenes claims the throne he goes into battle 'clothed in purple and attired like an emperor', and it is this insolence that brings on him a personal assault by one of the young Greek officers (X. 3, p. 277).

[4] XV. 11, p. 505. So Alexius is the sun and Irene the moon in the second poem published by C. Neumann (*Gr. Geschichtschreiber im 12. Jahrh.*) from the Vatican MS. of the *Panoplia* of Euthymius Zigabenus (lines 25, 27).

[5] To marry the Sultan's son would have been 'to share a kingdom sadder than any poverty' (VI. 12, p. 178).

[6] This is admitted by Robert Guiscard in IV. 5, p. 113; V. 3, p. 132, and the Sultan of Chorassan in XIV. 3, p. 432. In the same spirit Nic. Bry. fills the Preface to his *Hyle* with protestations of his own unworthiness to write either a history or an encomium of so great a hero as Alexius. [7] X. 7 and sqq.

[8] She will insert nothing unworthy of such a theme and such a writer (I. 13, p. 31; III. 2, p. 72; VI. 7, p. 165; XV. 9, p. 490).

[9] *Gr. Geschichtschreiber im 12. Jahrh.*, p. 3.

subject, pride in themselves as the true 'Ρωμαῖοι,[1] lay at the
root of this superiority? In the case of Alexius' biography this
pride was double distilled. He has in fact the distinction of
being the founder of the first truly Greek dynasty, and in his
daughter's eyes he is the great restorer of the 'Roman' Empire.[2]
Two passages in her work give as it were her confession of
faith, her fixed point of view. After describing the great extent
of the Roman sovereignty in old days, and its shrinkage before
the accession of her father who 'widened the circle' once more,
she concludes:[3] 'And he would have restored the Empire to its
former prosperity, if the continual struggles and frequent toils
and dangers . . . (for the Emperor was μεγαλοκίνδυνός τε καὶ
πυκνοκίνδυνος) had not hindered him in his desire.' This is
always the burden of her song; his achievements would have
been still more marvellous if he had had a fair chance, and even
as it was men might wonder whether the great deeds of his
reign were facts or figments of a dream.[4] The second passage
is in the same strain. 'The greatness of the subject oppresses'
her; her desire is twofold, to write history and to present, as he
had never let it be presented in his lifetime, the pathetic picture
of her father's trials.[5] She has an imperial as well as a filial
duty to perform.

This brings us to the consideration of a small but important
side-issue. How far did Anna, with the parade of emotion of
which we have already spoken, approve of pathos in the writing
of history? In theory she abjured it altogether, and would
have accepted the distinction drawn by Archbishop Eustathius[6]
between ἱστορία and συγγραφή, history and narrative, both
equally truthful but such that the second calls for pathos and
the pointing of morals, while the first must set forth the causes
and motives of events and actions, must give descriptions, display learning, and please the ear, and yet must throughout be
written ἀπαθῶς. Thus whenever Anna finds herself specially
moved she recalls herself with some ostentation to the straight
and narrow path of her history. She may wish to weep as a
woman, but as a historian she wipes away her tears and pulls
herself together from τοῦ πάθους, when she perceives that she is
being 'carried away from the task' before her.[7] She checks her

---

[1] The word 'Ρωμαῖοι is translated 'Greek' throughout this essay, never 'Roman',
except in inverted commas.
[2] In I. 6, p. 16, she says: 'God preserved Comnenus for greater honour like some
precious possession (χρῆμα τίμιον), wishing through him to restore the Empire of
the Greeks.' See p. 256 below.   [3] VI. 11, p. 176.
[4] XV. 10, p. 497.   [5] XV. 11, pp. 495, 496.
[6] De Thess. urbe capta, P. G. 136, cols. 9 sqq.
[7] Pref. 4, p. 7. For τὸ προκείμενον cf. III. 8, p. 91; XV. 11, p. 497.

weeping so that she may not 'confuse the history by mixing with historical narratives laments' of her own.[1] 'The law of history'[2] conquers the πάθος which inclines her to wail over her dead brother Andronicus; she feels however bound to 'go beyond the rules (δεσμοί) of history' and to relate the tragic circumstances of her father's death.[3] Similarly, when she descants on her mother's theological learning, she knows that the 'law of rhetoric' permits it, but the 'rule of history' cuts her short.[4] In another place she calls as witnesses 'all who are minded to unveil the truth without πάθος '.[5] But the best statement of her theories on the subject occurs in the story of the campaign against Robert Guiscard and may be given in full. After narrating her father's wonderful escape at Durazzo, she says:[6]

'But in the midst of my writing I have forgotten, partly from the nature of history, partly from the wonderfulness of the facts, that I am describing the successes (κατορθώματα) of a father. For because I do not wish to make my history suspect I often hurry over my father's acts, neither exaggerating them nor adding sentiment (πάθος). But would that I were free from this filial sentiment (πάθος πατρικόν) and at liberty, so that as it were grasping the abundant material I might show what familiarity my loosened tongue has with noble deeds. But natural affection restrains my zeal, for fear that I may seem to the multitude to incur, in my ardour for speaking about my own affairs, the reproach of a marvel-monger. For on many occasions remembering my father's successes I might have wept my heart out describing and relating how many evils he encountered, and I should not have passed the spot without mourning and lamentation. But in order that there may be no artificial rhetoric (ῥητορεία κομψή) about that part of the history, like senseless adamant and stone I hurry over what befell my father, though I ought to bring it out into an oath like that young man in Homer (for I am no whit inferior to him who said, 'No, by Zeus, and by the woes of my father, O Agelaus'), so as to be and be called a loving daughter (φιλοπάτωρ). But let my filial sentiment (πάθος) be reserved for myself alone, for wonder or wailing,[7] and let the thread of the history be resumed.'

[1] I. 12, p. 27. Cf. XIV. 3, p. 431, where 'a tear springs out' at the thought of her father's ungrateful enemies whom she longs to denounce by name. 'But I restrain my tongue and my panting heart.'
[2] XV. 6, p. 475.   [3] XV. 11, p. 496.
[4] V. 9, pp. 147, 148.   [5] III. 8, p. 91.   [6] IV. 8.
[7] τὸ μὲν πάθος τὸ πατρικὸν ἐμοὶ μόνῃ καταλελείφθω καὶ θαυμάζειν καὶ ὀλοφύρεσθαι. The word πάθος may perhaps have here, as C. S. H. B. translates it, the meaning of 'suffering'. Then the sense would be, 'Let my father's sufferings be left for me to admire and bewail in solitude', and πατρικόν is used subjectively instead of objectively.

In our eyes Anna falls into both the historiographical sins which she deprecates, artificial rhetoric and sentimentality, but to herself without doubt she appeared a model of simple lucidity and self-restraint.[1]

It is of course consistent with this same attitude of mind, this ill-concealed idolization of her father, that she should see in every occurrence the hand of Providence, the eye of God, protecting and watching over the great Emperor. Of this as it affects Anna's personal religious faith we have already spoken. In a question of history-writing it brings us to the great problem of 'fix'd fate, free will, foreknowledge absolute' which may or may not have been discussed by the Fallen Angels 'on a hill retired',[2] but has assuredly affected every narrator ever since. Pagans and Christians alike have hesitated between Fortune and Providence, τύχη and πρόνοια, as the ultimate cause of events. Polybius lays the principal stress on man's own actions. Plotinus has many chapters on Fate and Providence and Chance, while Procopius believes so much in εἱμαρμένη as to doubt the power of prayer to change the predetermined. In the ninth century Nicolas Mysticus ascribes the loss of Sicily to the folly of the Greek admiral and not to God's anger, and Leo begins his *Tactica* by saying that divine protection for the Roman Empire lasted as long as it cultivated the military art and no longer. Attaliates devotes several pages to the statement that God gave victory to the ancient Romans because though pagans they were just and law-abiding and humble before their deity, and will deny it to wicked Christians. He mourns over the inability of the Greek emperors to realize this. Why do they not read history and see that calamities have always come either from God's wrath towards sin or from man's stupidity? Why, when defeated, do they not perceive 'the nemesis of God' and mend their ways?[3] In Anna's own day Theodore Prodromus gives us yet another point of view. Though professing a firm belief in Providence he rails at the injustices of fortune, finally consoling himself with the reflection that even St. Paul could not 'tread the abyss of the mysteries of God'. So Anna herself, though on the whole she believes that God rules all, and that τύχη should be considered a θεία ψῆφος,[4] ascribes misfortunes to the folly of men[5] no less than to 'divine

[1] For her attitude to κομψεία, see III. 6, p. 83, and XIV. 7, p. 448.
[2] Milton, *Paradise Lost*, II. 557, 560.
[3] Attal., pp. 193–8.
[4] XII. 7, p. 363. By the ψῆφος Θεοῦ Botaniates got his crown (Attal. opening address).
[5] XIV. 3, p. 433; XIV. 7, p. 444.

permission'. Like many a Christian before and since she tries
to reconcile opposite theories and combine the 'foreknowledge
absolute' of divine πρόνοια with the 'free will' that alone
makes her hero's actions deserving of praise.

One more topic, closely connected with the Basileus, now
presents itself, namely Anna's pride in the city of her birth.
It is well known that to all Byzantines Constantinople was the
queen of cities, the 'beloved city' from which no wise man was
voluntarily absent.[1] Anna's references to all the palaces and
other glories have as it were a triumphant ring. She tells of
the Purple Chamber and its splendid marbles, and though
princes 'born in the purple' undoubtedly did not get their
names from its colour, we as we read her are content that she
should think so.[2] We enjoy her complacency over statuary in
the streets,[3] over church doors inlaid with silver and gold,[4] over
the 'open-air court paved with marble' near the church of
St. Demetrius.[5] Writing for readers who would need no descriptions she alludes cursorily to Constantine's Hippodrome or
'theatre'[6] with its stone pyramid, to his Forum, to the Bronze
Hands over an archway marking the limits of a criminal's possible reprieve, to the Gates of Blachernae and Charisius and
St. Romanus, and to the different orientation of the Great and
the Mangana Palaces. The topography of medieval Constantinople has been much studied,[7] and cannot be dealt with here.
Here it is enough to assert that though on the whole Anna
prefers to describe people rather than places, yet anything she
says about her beloved Constantinople is none the less clear
and accurate for being tinged with imperial pride. Like her
fiancé Constantine Ducas she might, in the words of Theophylact, congratulate herself because hers was a πατρὶς βασίλισσα
καὶ μεγαλόπολις καὶ καλλίπολις, great beyond compare.[8]

[1] I. 16, p. 38; XI. 9, p. 334. It is ingratitude that makes Gregory Gabras wish
to leave it for his Trebizond home (VIII. 9) and morbidity when the blinded and
defeated rebel, Nicephorus Diogenes, 'shunning residence in the metropolis',
prefers to live on his own estates (IX. 10, p. 265).

[2] VII. 2, p. 190; cf. VI. 8, p. 166. The name Porphyrogenitus undoubtedly
came from the association of 'Tyrian purple' with imperial pomp. As a matter of
fact the colour was nearer scarlet, as can be seen in the illuminations of medieval
manuscripts.

[3] III. 1, p. 72; VII. 2, p. 190.

[4] V. 2, p. 129.   [5] XII. 6, p. 361.

[6] II. 6, p. 54; 10, p. 64; VI. 11, p. 174; X. 9; XII. 6, p. 363; XIV. 6, p. 444;
XV. 10, p. 493; 11, pp. 500, 503. Robert de Clary (f. 122, cols. 1 and 2), describes
the Hippodrome as a flat place with rising tiers of seats all round, 'la ou li Griu
montoient pour eswarder les jus'. Anna gives no such details, though she mentions βαθμούς.

[7] Especially by Ebersolt, Mordtmann, Paspates, and van Millingen.

[8] Theoph., παιδ. βασ. I, 3 (P. G. 126, col. 256). We may compare Thucydides'

37. FILIAL AND OTHER PREJUDICES

WE now approach more directly the subject of Anna's veracity. We have already dealt with the self-pity and desire to play the tragedy queen which makes parts of her autobiography positively unintelligible. As to her filial partiality much has been written and the estimates of various critics will doubtless continue to vary greatly. We have seen that she herself scouts the imputation. Great as her subject was, loving as her heart was, she never let sentiment (so she would have us believe) obscure truth. But for most of us 'the lady doth protest too much, methinks'. Her constant assertions of impartiality[1] seem to any dispassionate reader to point to an uneasy conscience, and when she says, 'Whenever I see my father stumbling I actually transgress the law of nature and cling to truth, holding him indeed dear, but having truth dearer', we begin at once to look, but quite in vain, for the fair-minded criticism of which she boasts. His deceits are a καλὴ ἀπάτη.[2] His escapes in battle, what the unkind might call his running away, are a θαῦμα παράδοξον.[3] On this point Anna may be considered sensitive. In a very lengthy excursus in XV. 3 she defends her father against the charge of cowardice, claiming for him courage (he 'loved danger if ever any one

eulogy of Athens (*Hist.* II. 38). Attal. p. 23, calls Constantinople ἡ εὐδαίμων μεγαλόπολις, Constantine the Rhodian names her 'this city of the world's desire' (*Rev. des ét. gr.*, IX, 1896, p. 38) ; to Prodromus she is ἡ τῆς οἰκουμένης καρδία (*P. G.* 133, col. 1246), to Callicles (Poem XXX. 1) she is ἡ πανευτυχὴς καὶ πανολβία πόλις. For the impression produced by the Constantinople of Anna's day on foreigners we may give two references out of many. First we have Foucher de Chartres, chaplain of Baldwin the Crusader. In *Hist. Hierosol.* I. 9. 1, he says: 'O quanta civitas nobilis et decora! quot monasteria, quot palatia sunt in ea, opere miro fabrefacta! quot etiam in plateis vel vicis opera ad spectandum mirabilia.' [We may compare the visit of Abul Cassim, *Al.* VI. 11, p. 174.] 'taedium est magnum recitare quanta sit ibi bonorum omnium opulentia, auri scilicet, argenti, palliorum multiformium, sanctorumque reliquiarum. omni etiam tempore navigio frequenti cuncta hominum necessaria illuc adferunt negotiatores.' (Cf. what Anna says of the city when her father's troops sacked it, II. 10, p. 64.) Secondly, the *Skalholtsbok* (*Antiquités russes*, II. 416, quoted by Riant, *Expéditions et pèlerinages des Scandinaves*, pp. 68, 69) tells of the splendour of Constantinople and St. Sophia in the the twelfth century as regards relics. On the occasion of the Latin siege of 1204 it is hard to say whether the Greek Nicetas or the French Villehardouin is the more admiring. See *Camb. Med. Hist.* IV, p. 745, and compare also Leib, *op. cit.* pp. 236, 237.

[1] Pref. 2, p. 2; I. 16, p. 40; IV. 8; XV. 3. In XIV. 9, p. 456, she actually declares that she has omitted τὰ πλείω of her father's achievements, and insists that her story shall not be stigmatized as δωροδοκοῦσα, literally 'taking bribes'. In III. 8, pp. 90, 91, she says her object is not to 'write an encomium', but 'to make history'. With XV. 3 cf. Psellus on his mother, *B. G. Med.* V. p. 11.

[2] VI. 10, p. 175.

[3] IV. 7, p. 119. See p. 517 below.

did') no less than wisdom and resourcefulness. In a phrase which strikes us as sad bathos she compares him to a caltrop ('falling he stood'). Yet even this modest compliment she fears may earn for her the reputation of 'bragging', and she asserts once more that truth not partiality makes her praise so 'good' a man. She represents him as almost superhumanly modest, shunning all praise for his exploits,[1] which he only narrated 'to us in the intimate circle'.[2] But his daughter for all her fear of boasting does not hesitate to compare him to Alexander the Great,[3] to the Apostles, and even to Our Lord Himself.[4] His life was a model of sobriety,[5] he toiled for others till he killed himself, he was a Thirteenth Apostle for religious zeal;[6] in fact 'in all things he excelled all', orators in eloquence, military heroes in strategy.[7] Yet all the while the same recurrent note is struck; she claims to be writing not a panegyric but a history, and understating facts rather than exaggerating them.[8]

Out of a tangled mass of high-falutin' sentiment in her famous passage deprecating pathos in history[9] there emerges one interesting and rather novel thought: Anna could wish she was not Alexius' daughter, not because in that case she would have less power of talking about his woes, but because she would have more, as no one would then suspect her of partiality. It is the exact opposite of Psellus' saner view that a person is all the more bound to bestow praise when he knows by 'domestic and intimate experience' that it is deserved, as in the case of his mother.[10]

In conclusion we may say that whether justified or not, whether wearying to the modern reader or not, Anna's admiration of her father's wisdom, ingenuity, foresight, calmness, generosity, eloquence, missionary fervour, piety, courage, intrepidity, strength, daring, and insight keeps up steadily throughout her work. He was certainly a hero if not to his valet at least to his eldest daughter, and in her opinion the greatest writers of antiquity could hardly have done justice to his great deeds.[11]

---

[1] XV. 11, p. 495.   [2] VII. 3, p. 198.   [3] XV. 7, p. 485.
[4] XIV. 3, p. 431; 8, p. 453; XV. 7, pp. 483, 484.   [5] XV. 11, p. 498.
[6] VI. 11, p. 176; XIV. 8, p. 453; XV. 11, especially p. 498.
[7] XV. 8, p. 487; cf. XV. 10, p. 495.
[8] III. 8, p. 91; V. 1, p. 126; XII. 3; XIV. 7; XV. 3. Bryennius says the same in praising his father. *Hyle*, IV. 5, p. 96.
[9] IV. 8, quoted in Ch. 36 above.   [10] B. G. Med. V, p. 3.
[11] VIII. 6, p. 236. She would have approved of the fulsome praise of her father in the already mentioned poems from the Vatican MS. of the *Panoplia* of Euthymius Zigabenus (C. Neumann, *Gr. Geschichtschreiber*, pp. 33–5). Alexius is most pious, a great blessing (εὐτύχημα) for the Greeks, an ingenious general, ἀγχίνους as

This brings us to an even more vital matter by which to test Anna's truthfulness. The last chapter of her book gives a most minute and touching picture of her father's last days and of the anguish caused to her mother and herself by his death. Are we to believe, on the authority of one man[1] writing more than fifty years after the events, that this is all untrue, that Irene and Anna were only concerned with plans to make the dying man support their selfish ambitions, and that all her filial affection was from beginning to end a sham? We may truly blame our authoress for egotism as to her own woes, for exaggerated language, and for the 'bitterness' which she futilely deprecates, but these are flaws in a very different category from deliberate insincerity. If in actual fact she hoped, even after Constantine's death, to succeed Alexius and hated her father undyingly for killing these hopes, why did she write his biography on such eulogistic lines, instead of with the venom that would have relieved her feelings and thrilled her readers?[2]

Let us come down to details. If we are to believe modern critics, Oster and Neumann and Chalandon, Anna wilfully garbles facts as to her mother not only in her last chapter but in her whole book by representing her as a devoted wife.[3] They

a ruler, famous for κατορθώματα and τρόπαια, defender of the faith, &c., and the Trinity are called on to bless him. It is therefore curious to find Anna omitting many incidents of Alexius' life recorded by her husband, especially as his ecstatic eulogies (*Hyle*, I. 6, p. 20, and elsewhere) show precisely the same spirit as her own. We can understand her leaving out the quarrels which attended her father's marriage to Irene, as well as the fact of his previous marriage to one of the Argyrus house (*ibid*. III. 6), or his inglorious if prudent refusal to march against his brother-in-law Nicephorus Melissenus (*ibid*. IV. 31); these things did not specially redound to his credit, and Bryennius' arguments to justify his accession may have been omitted by her as not altogether convincing to her conscience (*ibid*. Pref.). But why should she fail to tell us of Alexius' prowess in Asia Minor on the occasion of his brother Isaac's capture, and their subsequent joint campaign (*ibid*. II. 5–13), his preservation from shipwreck by the Mother of God (*ibid*. II. 27, p. 64), his friendly relations at Constantinople with the captured Urselius and with the grateful Emperor Michael VII (*ibid*. II. 28, p. 64), his gallant defence of the capital (*ibid*. III. 13, p. 78), the important part which he played during the transfer of sovereignty from Michael to Botaniates (*ibid*. III. 19–23), and his success in restoring order and winning popularity in his οἰκεία ἀρχή of the Western Provinces (*ibid*. IV. 30)? Such silence certainly seems to justify her assertion that boasting was *au fond* not her object, and tends to make us feel confident that Anna believes in nearly if not quite all the wonderful qualities of head and heart and arm that she ascribes to her father.

[1] Nicetas Acominatus, who as a devotee of John belauds his hero in a way that throws doubt on his general discrimination and accuracy.

[2] The existence of another view of Alexius due to mere spite is suggested by the Preface of John Cinnamus' *History* (p. 2). He passes over the life of this Emperor with a bare reference, because it has been accurately narrated by those 'who have not composed their history πρὸς ἀπέχθειαν ἐκείνῳ'. Cinnamus never mentions Anna or her husband by name.

[3] See p. 114, notes 4 and 5, above.

assert that Alexius Comnenus all along found a dangerous opponent in his wife Irene Ducas: they take the popular rumour
of his wish to get a divorce so as to marry the Empress Maria,
and his opposition to the coronation of his young girl bride,[1]
as showing a rivalry between himself and her which lasted
throughout the reign.[2] We may say at once that in this first
struggle the principals appear to have been not Alexius and
Irene but Anna Dalassena and John Ducas Caesar, with the
ἀπροφάσιστος μῆνις that existed between them.[3] Also, if we
believe Zonaras and Glycas in their statement that at first
Alexius was not a faithful husband, we ought surely to accept
their subsequent assertion that the passing of years made him
increasingly dependent on his wife.[4]

We read in the *Alexias* that Irene's going into camp with her
husband was an act of self-sacrifice for her and a subject of
derisive gossip to those who wished him ill. Anna herself refers
to τοὺς φιλοσκώμμονας καὶ τὰς φιλολοιδόρους γλώττας,[5] and she
may even have been aware of the currency of such scandal as
Chalandon credits, to the effect that Alexius took her because
he could not trust her influence in Constantinople if left behind.
But scandal is not fact, and there seems no reason why it should
not be true as Anna asserts that the Emperor took his wife away
with him from the comforts of the capital to act as his nurse
and his guardian, either of which functions might easily excite
the contemptuous jeers of Turkish enemies[6] or domestic malcontents.

As to the last scenes of the reign, the desire with which
Nicetas credits Irene of seeing Alexius succeeded not by John
but by Anna and Bryennius is not mentioned by Zonaras, who

---

[1] III. 2, p. 75.
[2] C. Neumann (*Gr. Geschichtschr.* p. 20) says: 'die Kaiserin [Irene] stand gegen
den Kaiser', largely because Alexius wished to humble the Ducas and other great
families who had put him on the throne.
[3] III. 2, p. 72.
[4] This tallies with Anna's account of why Alexius took her with him on campaigns; he needed her to rub his gouty feet, and also to ward off domestic dangers,
'unsleeping guard of the Emperor as she was'. To her daughter, Irene's reluctance
to go with the army is an effect of modesty, which is with some little difficulty overcome by her devotion (XII. 3; XIII. 1; XIII. 4, p. 386; XIV. 4 and 5; XV. 1, 2,
3). The *Anon. Syn. Chron.* says that the virtues of Irene have been recorded in
certain 'writings' (p. 182). Probably this refers to the *Hyle* and the *Alexias*.
Zonaras gives us the interesting information that Irene was alarming; people
approached her husband when he was alone 'without fear', but she 'showed an
imperious and severe nature and vehemently reproved the disorderly' (*Epit.*
XVIII. 29). This agrees with *Al.* III. 3, p. 77 A and B.
[5] XII. 3. So διαλοιδορουμένους τῷ βασιλεῖ καὶ ὑποψιθυρίζοντας in XV. 3, p. 466.
The lampoons of XIII. 1, p. 377, show the same spirit of criticism.
XV. 1. The Turks doubtless thought Alexius was shamming illness.

on the contrary represents the Empress (however fond she might be of her son-in-law) as hoping to reign herself,[1] while the *Anon. Syn. Chron.* merely alludes to it in a passage beginning 'There is a story', &c.[2] It is not too much to say that this whole conception of Irene's relation to her husband and of Anna's relation to them both is supported neither by good evidence nor even by probability.

A harder matter to fathom is Anna's great bitterness as to John, about whom Chalandon[3] can predicate 'admiration presque générale'. She shows this from the first, when in a fashion half absurd and half pathetic she consoles herself with the thought that even in the cradle John was unattractive.[4] 'The baby was swarthy in complexion[5] with a broad brow, lean cheeks, and a nose neither snub nor curving into a hook, but as it were midway between the two. His eyes were dark and showed his secretiveness and sharpness ($\hat{\upsilon}\pi o\kappa a\theta\acute{\eta}\mu\epsilon\nu o\nu$ $\mathring{\eta}\theta o\varsigma$ $\kappa a\grave{\iota}$ $\mathring{o}\xi\acute{\upsilon}$) as far as can be guessed from the body of an infant.' She takes pleasure in reflecting that much of the popular enthusiasm over her brother's birth was probably feigned, though she speaks as if his father's intention to 'bequeath to him the Empire of the Greeks' was perfectly natural.

Putting aside as unproved Nicetas' story that Anna hoped to succeed her father when he died, and accepting the assumption that her brother's rights seemed to her perfectly valid, however much she might regret his and their existence, we may well ask why she is so spiteful about John. She accuses him of having frustrated her father's achievements and ruined by his 'folly' an Empire which according to her he seized with brutal callousness as that father lay dying.[6] As to preceding events, her dark hints about some one very near the Emperor who contributed largely to his ill health, possibly even by attempted poisoning,

---

[1] *Epit*: XVIII. 24. In chs. 26 and 29 he tells us of friction between Irene and John when she was ruling for Alexius and of her love for Anna and Bryennius (making the latter popular and John jealous), but never of any wish of hers for them to succeed. John 'feared for his throne and life' in connexion with his mother, because he thought that, relying on the support of her much loved son-in-law, she meant permanently to keep the reins of empire which her sick husband had delegated to her.

[2] p. 187.   [3] *Jean II Comnène*, p. xxxiii, and ch. i.

[4] VI. 8, p. 168.

[5] William of Tyre, XV. 23, dwells on John's ugliness and dark colouring. Gibbon thinks 'Caloioannes' (his nickname) was ironical.

[6] XIV. 3, p. 433; XV. 11, p. 503. Both Zonaras and Nicetas say that he did not attend Alexius' funeral, a display, in those days, of almost impious disrespect. The story of the signet-ring which he took off his father's hand as a sort of badge of sovereignty is told with different interpretations by Zonaras, Nicetas and *Anon. Syn. Chron.* Anna does not mention it. The importance of such a $\delta a\kappa\tau\acute{\upsilon}\lambda\iota o\nu$ comes out in IV. 5, p. 112.

are in truth so very dark as not to be comprehensible with any certainty.[1] She would like to rail against these κακουργότατοι, but she thinks better of it and leaves us to guess even as to who they are. In view however of her attitude towards the διάδοχος whom she hardly ever mentions and never favourably,[2] we may well believe first that by these 'bosom' enemies of her father she meant her brother John, secondly that Nicetas Acominatus is correct in saying that after his accession she welcomed the efforts of the imperial kinsmen (τῶν ἐκ γένους) to set her and her husband on the throne. Possibly from jealousy, possibly from some more creditable reason, Anna saw only an unworthy Emperor in John, about whose merits his father on the other hand can hardly say enough. To Alexius he seems endowed with every physical and mental quality, strength, beauty, brains, even the 'noble horsemanship' so dear to Byzantines as to ourselves.[3] To Euthymius Zigabenus he is κάλλιστον ἄνθος of the Comnenus house,[4] and Theodore Prodromus is almost nauseatingly fulsome in his praise.[5] These may be interested witnesses on the one side, but we are bound to admit that in this matter Anna for all her staple profession of fair-mindedness is probably equally prejudiced on the other. Embittered by old disappointment over a fiancé and a crown together lost, filled with anger against the filial impiety of a brother whose very birth had overclouded her life, may she not when conspiring against him have seized on some real or fancied grievance in the hopes of driving him from the throne to which she never denied his rights? If this is so, we are surely entitled to hold the definite conviction that the picture drawn for us in the *Alexias* is true, that Anna and her mother truly loved Alexius, and that there is nothing but truth in her sorrowful words, 'the Emperor gave up his sacred soul to God, and my sun set.'[6]

---

[1] XIII. 9, p. 399; XIV. 4, p. 437; XV. 1, p. 462.
[2] As we have seen, she speaks disagreeably of him as a baby (VI. 8, p. 168), and there is acidity in her curt announcement of the birth of his son and heir (XII. 4, p. 356). Even in connexion with her husband who fought for and with him she has no word to say of the many victories which other writers ascribe to John (Pref. 3, p. 3). See, in connexion with the Patzinaks, p. 436, note 6, below.
[3] *Mous. Alex.* II. 44 sqq.
[4] Three poems, published C. Neumann, *Gr. Geschichtschr.* pp. 33–5.
[5] Poems, *passim*.
[6] XV. 11, p. 505. Callicles (Poem XXV), represents John as mourning over his father's death, 7–9, and calling it ἡλίου δύσις (36).

38. OMISSIONS AND INCONSISTENCIES

ON the purely technical side of Anna's composition two points must not be left unnoticed, her omissions and her inconsistencies. First, her lacunae. At several places in the text there are blank spaces in the manuscript, such as when Alexius comes to 'the plains called ——', and to a certain place lying ——.[1] We are told that the devils were enraged with Basil the Bogomile for betraying to the Emperor —— ——;[2] presumably there should follow the name for their secret mysteries; was it deliberately omitted as *infandum*? Or are all these blanks to be explained as cases where she meant as we say to look the thing up, and either forgot or was hindered by the enforced seclusion of which she complains?[3]

Besides this, characters are sometimes introduced without names, e.g. 'the Count who was commandant', 'the man guarding this place', 'those of the priestly register whose names I omit'.[4] This may be ignorance or mere forgetfulness: in one instance she says frankly that time has taken away her recollection of certain names.[5] But over and over again we feel she is making deliberate omissions. It is not only that she revels as we have seen in mysterious self-pity. Even when she is not personally concerned we find her suppressing names that she must have known and hurrying over controversial incidents. What was the court scandal at which she hints, when a eunuch was able to stop an ex-Empress's marriage merely by saying πολλὰ καὶ καίρια?[6] Why did Maria adopt[7] Alexius, and did he really ever think of divorcing Irene to marry her?[8] Who were the 'certain people' to whom Nicephorus Diogenes spoke γνησιώτερον of his plot and whom Alexius vainly tried to win over?[9] When she is telling us how this same conspiracy spread to the highest ranks in the army and the state, including senators and the two nobles Cecaumenus Catacalo and Michael

---

[1] XV. 2, p. 464: 3, p. 469. A complete list of the lacunae (even omitting the last chapter of all, where the text from p. 500 D to the end of p. 507 C is in a very bad state) would be too lengthy to give here. We may signalize as examples those at I. 10, p. 24 A; VI. 7, p. 164 A; IX. 8, p. 262 B; X. 8, p. 292 C; XII. 5, p. 359 A; XIII. 1, p. 379 A: 10, p. 404 B; XIV. 3, p. 433 A: 5, p. 439 A; XV. 3, p. 467 A. In XI. 2, p. 315, an important number is missing after σταδίους.
[2] XV. 8, p. 489.
[3] XIV. 7. If the seclusion was as strict as this, it makes the researches into archives which Oster predicates for her a figment of his imagination.
[4] XI. 11, p. 340; XIV. 5, p. 439; XV. 7, p. 485.
[5] V. 9, p. 148.   [6] III. 2, p. 74.   [7] II. 1, p. 44.
[8] III. 2, p. 72.   [9] IX. 6, p. 257.

Taronites, we come upon a lacuna of about thirty-four letters
which by rights ought to contain the name of another banished
suspect.[1] The incriminating letters found in Diogenes' tent are
vaguely described as 'sent to him by certain people', but the
fact that these people are ἔκκριτοι ἅπαντες is a source of great
embarrassment to Alexius,[2] and it seems likely that Anna could
have revealed their identity if she had chosen. She longs to
catalogue all the ἀγνώμονες whose ingratitude filled her father's
life with trouble, but she restrains her 'tongue and panting
heart'. She declares that the 'folly of those who succeeded to
the throne' stultified her father's achievements so that 'matters
turned to confusion', but we look in vain for any explanation of
the statement.[3] 'The sedition of those at home', not further
specified, is one of the great complications when the Crusaders
are threatening to overthrow the Empire.[4] Anna hints, 'so as
not to tell everything', at a most sinister and powerful 'third
cause' for her father's gout, a cause worse than accidents, worse
even than worry from barbarian Franks; this was the constant
presence near him of some one who 'did not come in contact
with him just once and go away, but was present with him and
clung to him like the worst kind of flavours in jars'. This man
either actually or metaphorically tried to poison the Emperor
and was only foiled by the vigilance of Irene. 'But,' says Anna,
'biting one's tongue one must check one's story and not stray
from the straight road, even though that story is very desirous
to leap up against the utter scoundrels.'[5] Fear of these
unspecified ἐγκόλπιοι ἐχθροί causes Alexius to send for the
Empress during a lull in the Turkish campaign,[6] and they
doubtless are the τινες τῶν ἐναντίων who jeer at him for
cowardice and infuriate not him but his wife.[7] Perhaps some
day the manuscript of a twelfth-century Procopius or Psellus
may be discovered and may throw light on Anna's dark hints.
Till then we can only enumerate them, and in default of a
better accept the explanation offered by most critics, that at
no time during the reigns of her brother and nephew did she
feel safe in speaking out. That her mysteriousness is deliberate
all must be inclined to admit, but whether it is a mere
affectation or does in truth mask hidden treasures of information no human being can say.

[1] IX. 8, p. 262.   [2] IX. 8, p. 261.
[3] XIV. 3, pp. 431, 433.   [4] XIV. 4, p. 434.
[5] XIV. 4, p. 437. A similar hint of treachery and attempted poison occurs in
XII. 2, p. 352, where Irene as regards her husband is called 'a good antidote to
the dangers of the banquet, and against harm in food a salutary medicine'.
[6] XV. 1, p. 462.   [7] XV. 3, p. 466.

Next come the inconsistencies between different parts of her book. Here no occult motive can have been at work, neither love of mystery nor difficulty in getting at facts. She simply is inharmonious with her own self, and the one thing to which this points is a lack of careful revision.[1]

One marked instance is the confused account of Alexius' robbing of the churches.[2] In V. 2 he seems to do the deed twice, once through his brother Isaac for fighting the Normans, once later in view of 'Scythian' enemies. Yet the one restitution narrated (in VI. 3) seems to have taken place soon after December 1, 1083, long before the Patzinak War of 1086, though 'raids of Scythians' are mentioned here also. Whatever these raids may have been,[3] Anna leaves them undescribed.

Again Durazzo is mentioned as early as Book I and constantly afterwards, with the frequent comment that it is also called Epidamnus, but suddenly in XII. 9 she thinks fit to give a detailed account of its surroundings, adding further details in XIII. 3. The same is true of Philippopolis and Mount Haemus.[4] Characters often come in on two occasions and are not described till the second.[5] References are found to past statements that have never been made,[6] and knowledge which the reader does not possess is presupposed,[7] as for instance in the vexed question of Botaniates' heir.[8] Fresh people appear and

---

[1] Inaccuracies, i.e. cases where she disagrees with facts known to us from other sources, do not come under this head, and are dealt with in various connexions as they come up.

[2] See p. 298, below.

[3] Chalandon (*Alexis Ier*, p. 37) speaks of their 'continuelles incursions'.

[4] First described XIV. 8, after being mentioned as early as Books VI. and VII.

[5] So Maria, Irene's mother, in II. 5, p. 54 and 6, p. 55; Patriarch Cosmas in II. 12, p. 68, and III. 3, p. 75; Bohemund, appearing first in I. 14, p. 34, but not called Saniscus till IV. 6, p. 115; Pacurianus, whose Grand Domesticate is promised in II. 4, p. 70, and mentioned in IV. 6, p. 115, but has to be inferred in IV. 4, p. 108; Basil Curticius in I. 9, p. 21, and V. 5, p. 139, possibly also XII. 5, p. 359; Taticius, who plays a big part from IV. 4 onwards, but comes in as an unknown person might in IX. 9, p. 263. If the John Taronites of XIII. 1, p. 376, is the same as the one in X. 2, p. 273, and XII. 7, he is not described till his third appearance (but see Du Cange's note on the third passage).

[6] Anna says Cantacuzenus' scouts 'were barbarians, as my story has already shown' (XIII. 5, p. 391); it is the first mention of the fact. The letter of Alexius to Henry of Germany refers to a previous 'agreement' of which we know nothing (III. 10, pp. 93, 94). A defeat of Cabasilas is alluded to but never described (XIII. 5, p. 390, and 7, p. 395).

[7] Bohemund is made to speak of Norman defeats which Anna has never recorded (XIII. 12).

[8] In II. 2 he chooses as his successor a kinsman, Συναδηνός τις, probably his brother-in-law Theodulus or a nephew. In II. 5 we hear of a young ἔγγονος of his, betrothed to Alexius' niece. In II. 12 he offers to adopt Alexius because he himself has 'neither son nor brother nor any near relation'. In IV. 5 Anna mentions the courage and in IV. 6 the death of a Nicephorus Synadenus as quite a new

play their part without a word of introduction and disappear
again as abruptly, very much in the style of what some one has
called the 'tantalizingly incomplete narratives' of the New
Testament.[1] Contradictory assertions are made in different
parts of the book,[2] two of them curiously enough about the
Diogenes family. Anna first tells us that Leo Diogenes was killed
in the Patzinak campaign and then, confusing him with his
brother Constantine, that he fell at Antioch.[3] At one point she
describes Nicephorus Diogenes as a popular hero,[4] at another
she speaks of 'the hostility of all men' towards him and his
family.[5] Raymond de St. Gilles first appears as 'the Count
Prebentzas', then as 'Isangeles', and there is not a word to show
that they are the same person.[6] Two slightly different accounts
are given of Alexius' ransoming certain crusading counts from
captivity in Cairo.[7] When the Emperor uses Sacred Lots for
the second time, Anna speaks as if it was a new and wonderful
invention.[8] In XI. 6 she promises us a description of Theodore
Gabras' origin and character when she has already given it in
VIII. 9. The story of Gregory Taronites is so inconsequent as
to make one question whether his personality has not been confused with that of Gregory Gabras. At any rate he appears first
as Gregory and then as Taronites, and we hear of his appointment to succeed the general Dabatenus in the Dukedom of
Trebizond, whereas that district was still, when last mentioned,
in the possession of Theodore Gabras, father of the other
Gregory.[9] Aspietes and Tzachas both appear to fall dead and

character, though he must have been related to the Synadenus of Book II,
or identical with him if we assume a slip in the Christian name. See p. 31 above,
note 2.
    [1] e.g. Musaces in IX. 8, Alacaseus in X. 4, and Pegasius in X. 10; Bacchenos in
XII. 7, and the second Contostephanus, who causes the name to be put abruptly
in the plural, in XII. 8, p. 368, though this Stephanus Contostephanus is not mentioned individually till XIII. 7.
    [2] e.g. Bohemund's fleet seems to be twice burnt (XIII. 2, p. 380, and 6, pp. 393,
394). Roger, Robert Guiscard's son, is in two places at once (I. 16, p. 37; III. 12,
p. 97; V. 3, p. 131). Pargiaruch is Sultan before his father has died (VI. 10,
p. 172: 12, p. 179).
    [3] VII. 3, p. 196; X. 2, p. 271; cf. Nic. Bry. I. 6, p. 20, and II. 29, p. 66.
    [4] IX. 6, p. 257, and 8, p. 261.
    [5] IX. 9, p. 264.
    [6] X. 8, p. 290: 11. p. 305. This is accepting Du Cange's identification of the
two, but Prof. Grégoire believes (Byzantion, Tome III, 1926, pp. 511–17) that the
κόμης Πρεβέντζας of X. 8 is not St. Gilles but the Πριγκιπάτος of XIII. 4, Bohemund's
right-hand man sent ahead to prepare his way, as Bohemund after crossing in X. 8
does not come on to Constantinople till X. 11. See p. 465, note 2.
    [7] XI. 7, p. 328; XII. 1, p. 346; the name of Alexius' envoy differs in the two
stories, though the same man may be meant, and we may assume the incident to
be one, not two, as has been said above.
    [8] X. 2, p. 273; XV. 4, p. 471.
    VIII. 9,; XI. 6, p. 326; XII. 7.

some time afterwards reappear on the stage without explanation.[1]

The town of Aulon (modern Avlona) is captured, before Robert Guiscard arrives in Illyria, by Bohemund,[2] who spends some little time there after his defeat at Larissa and before crossing to Italy.[3] So it is to the flag planted 'as towards Aulon' that the Normans who wish to return home repair after the capture of Castoria.[4] Yet as an essential preliminary to his second campaign Robert orders his sons Roger and Guy to take 'all the cavalry' and 'to be zealous to seize ($\kappa a \tau a \sigma \chi \epsilon \hat{\imath} \nu$)' this town. 'And they crossing over [from Italy] took it by assault.'[5] When had the imperial troops recovered it? Anna does not say. In the same way Nicomedia is freed from Turks early in Alexius' reign,[6] and is apparently open for the passage of Taticius and the imperial troops in VI. 10, p. 172. But a very short time afterwards[7] we have the statement, made without explanation or comment, that the Turks ruling at Nicaea 'were holding the city of Nicomedes' and the Emperor wished to drive them out.[8] And to give one more instance of inconsistency (in this case very trifling) we may observe that the causes alleged by Anna for Alexius' gout are various and are never given all together.[9]

In short, the whole composition of the work inclines us to believe first that it was not written, as the French would say, *tout d'un trait*,[10] and that the different parts were not necessarily composed in their chronological order; secondly that the revision was never completely carried out, for what reason, whether

---

[1] IV. 6, p. 117, and XII. 2; IX. 3 and XI. 5. The solution may be in the case of Tzachas that νεκρός (like the 'lifeless' of Jane Austen and Thackeray) means not 'dead', but 'fainting', or as we might say 'for dead', which is possibly the real translation of Acts xx. 9, where Eutychus when νεκρός was revived by St. Paul. As to Aspietes we must suppose that in the earlier passage he does not 'give up his life' like the Zacharias with whom he is coupled, but merely πλήττεται καιρίαν, which we see from XII. 2, p. 350 does not invariably mean receiving a mortal blow, any more than ἔξαιμος points to death.

[2] I. 14, p. 35; III. 12, p. 98. In IV. 2, p. 105; V. 3, p. 131, Anna writes as if Robert himself had taken it, but it is a clear case of 'qui facit per alium facit per se'. He seems to have touched there with his army (I. 14, p. 34; III. 12, p. 98; IV. 4, p. 108).

[3] V. 7, p. 143; VI. 5, p. 158.   [4] VI. 1, p. 153.

[5] VI. 5, p. 159.   [6] III. 11, p. 96.   [7] VI. 10, p. 174.

[8] We must assume that he succeeded, for in VII. 7, p. 205, four years later, we read of Abul Cassim 'arming against Nicomedia', and in X. 5, p. 282, of the Turks 'pressing on it' in their raids.

[9] XIV. 4, and 7, p. 449; XV. 11, p. 496.

[10] It is very striking, as we shall see further in Ch. 73, how Anna will use a word or phrase, which seems to be running in her head, very frequently for the space of a few chapters or of one Book, and then never again. This points to the same conclusion.

indifference or the inertia of old age or death itself, we do not know.

Fortunately, none of the questions involved are serious ones, except for the mystery about Anna's woes and Alexius' 'bosom enemies'; we are merely tantalized by being left in an ignorance that is in fact immaterial. Still, in a work that claims to be above all things a truthful record of the past, we must admit that omissions and inconsistencies, whether wilful or accidental and however small, do mar the perfection of the whole.

39. STATE OF THE EMPIRE IN 1081

WE must now consider Anna as a historian more in detail. We have pointed out that to her Alexius was above all the man who restored the Empire.[1] How did he do this? She would have said in four ways. At home he crushed rebellion; in the church he combated heresy; in the field his armies 'set up many trophies'; in the world at large he taught men to know once more what the Empire really meant. So that Anna's story of Alexius' achievements, together with our study based upon that story, falls naturally under four heads, Domestic, Ecclesiastical, Military, and Foreign Affairs. But before dealing with each topic we must consider what was the actual state of the Empire which in these four ways he had to widen.[2]

At the outset we may remind ourselves that from the nature of the case Anna's information is unique and invaluable. Whatever flaws there may be in her picture, no one else in her time could have drawn it at all, except her own husband, whose similar attempt was cut short by death. As the daughter of an Emperor and wife of a Caesar she was in a position to realize that the Empire needed three things, military successes, good diplomacy, and a strong internal government. We could wish perhaps that she had given us fewer battles and trials of heretics and more events in the daily life of monarch and subjects. But the fact remains that if we want to understand the Byzantine Empire of 1081 to 1118 we have no other picture which for vividness and detail can be mentioned in the same breath with the *Alexias*.

---

[1] I. 6, p. 16; VI. 11, pp. 175, 176; Nic. Bry. makes the same claim for Alexius (Pref., p. 12), who succeeded to the throne ἐν καιροῖς δυσκόλοις. See p. 241 above.

[2] C. Neumann (*Gr. Geschichtschr.* p. 97) points out that, like Anna, Cinnamus claimed the whole Roman Empire for Constantinople; all the Western Emperors from Romulus Augustulus were τύραννοι. In his case it made him utterly indifferent to all geography and ethnography in the outside world.

For the marvellous advantages with which the Eastern Empire started we cannot do better than quote Diehl.[1]

'Placé au point de jonction de l'Asie et de l'Europe, intermédiaire naturel entre le monde asiatique et l'Occident, il se trouvait au point où venaient aboutir et se joindre toutes les grandes voies[2] commerciales alors fréquentées et connues. . . . Dans la mer Noire, par les ports de la Crimée il était à portée des routes fluviales du Dnieper et du Don, qui pénétraient profondément dans la Russie méridionale.'

Not only the capital but Cherson and other ports beside held an important commercial position—'Thessalonique surtout, le centre économique le plus important d'Europe après Constantinople'. From North-East, East, and South-East traders brought their goods to or through the Eastern Empire. It remains to be seen how far its historical development corresponded to these great gifts of Nature.

After the days of Constantine the double Empire of East and West remained for nearly two centuries united in theory though separate in fact, while Visigoths and Huns in turn had their day and ceased to be. Under Zeno I (474–91) the Western Empire was extinguished, and the Roman Senate sent to the Eastern Emperor acknowledging him as ruler of East and West alike. The result was exactly contrary to what might have been expected. Theodoric the Ostrogoth was appointed Zeno's deputy at Ravenna, and except for a brief interval under Justinian who reigned 527–65 and reconquered Africa, Italy, and Spain, the Emperors at Byzantium never had more than nominal power West of the Adriatic.

Great dangers soon threatened the Empire. Within fifty years of Justinian's death not only had the Lombards conquered most of Italy, but the Persians whom he had held at bay had ravaged all Asia Minor, and the Slavs had poured in over the Danube. Heraclius (610–41) cleared Asia Minor, and even conquered Persia itself, while in 626 a large body of Avars and Slavs were beaten back from Constantinople and retired across the Danube. But in 634 he was totally defeated beyond Jordan by a horde of Saracens, who proceeded to conquer Syria and Egypt and finally in 697 took Carthage, the Empire's last stronghold in Africa. The Eastern Empire seemed doomed to extinction, till in 717 a first-rate general, Leo the Isaurian, seized the throne and repelled from Constantinople the 'grand

---

[1] *Byzance*, pp. 87 sq.
[2] e.g. the Via Egnatia.

army of the Saracens', thereby proving himself, as Oman[1] points out, more really the deliverer of Europe than his contemporary Charles Martel, who merely 'turned back a plundering horde sent out from an outlying province of the Caliphate'. Asia Minor was freed from the Saracens, and till the Turks appeared in the tenth century the imperial power remained supreme there. When under Leo's son Constantine V (741–75) the exarchate of Ravenna was captured by the Lombards, this loss seemed small compared to victories over Saracens in the East and Slavs and Bulgarians in the Balkan Peninsula. The final separation between Rome and Constantinople came in 800, when Pope Leo III crowned Charlemagne as Emperor of the West; but here again the Byzantines were too much occupied with the domestic and ecclesiastical activities of their ruler the Empress Irene to pay much heed to this epoch-making event.

As years went on, both the Emperors Leo VI (886–911) and Constantine VII (912–59) had leisure to write about foreign policies and wars instead of desperately conducting them. During their reigns and for a century after, the commercial importance of Constantinople as the principal market or clearing-house between East and West was unique. She was indeed great both in peace and in war, for Nicephorus Phocas and John Tzimisces were successful against the Saracens in Cilicia and Northern Syria as well as in Crete and Cyprus, and also against the Russians in Eastern Bulgaria, and when their ward Basil II finally came to rule alone (976–1025) he gained great triumphs in the Balkans, as his surname of Bulgaroctonos shows. In the regions of Southern Italy, though Sicily remained in the hands of the Saracens, who had captured Syracuse its last important stronghold in 878, he gave to the imperial power a new if delusive appearance of stability, and in Armenia he added certain districts to the Eastern provinces. But this was to be for many years the last display of Byzantine prowess.

Under Zoe and her three husbands and one adopted son Serbia revolted, the Patzinaks made raids across the Danube, the Normans as a formidable new enemy conquered the Theme of Longobardia (Byzantium's last possession West of the Adriatic), and the Seljuq Turks first appeared on the Armenian frontiers. With Zoe and her sister Theodora the Basilian dynasty of 190 years ended, and twenty-four years of anarchy (1057–81) left the Empire shrunken in territory and crippled in resources. The capture of the Emperor Romanus Diogenes

[1] *Byzantine Empire*, p. 187.

by the Seljuqs at Manzikert in 1071 (the very same year that the Normans took Bari, the last imperial town in Italy) was a disaster unparalleled in Byzantine history. His Turkish conquerors spread Westward right to the Aegean and Propontis, and it was left for Alexius I, as Oman points out, to drag the Empire out of the deepest slough of degradation and ruin into which it had ever sunk. Of the whole realm which had once spread, so Anna would have us believe, from the Pillars of Heracles to the Pillars of Dionysus, including the Troglodytes on the South and Thule on the North,[1] there only remained secure to him Thrace, Macedonia, and Thessaly. The Byzantine emperors had for centuries been standing more and more on the defensive, and when Alexius came to the throne he found himself with his back against the wall.

Thanks largely to his vigour and prudence, the Empire during this reign was extended North, South, and West, to the Danube, to Cilicia, and to the Adriatic. To the East and South-East in Asia Minor the 'great scarcity of men to prevent' the Moslem inroads was in part set right by the unwitting aid of the Crusaders, and the new Frankish and Armenian principalities acted as buffers between the Greeks and the Turks. It was not in human power to foretell that the worst misgivings of the Byzantines would be fulfilled, and that within a hundred years other Crusaders would seize the Empire their predecessors had assisted, and would be conveyed by Venetian seamen whose power Alexius' own concessions had so disastrously increased.

Even without being his daughter any biographer of this Emperor must admit his indomitable energy and persistence and the substantial advantages which he gained for his realm both in diplomacy and war. His achievements according to her were only nullified by the 'folly of those who got the sceptre after him', and 'with the Emperor sank all better things'.[2] The 'slavish' nations whom he had restrained by his constant labours from their assault on the Empire of the Greeks, 'by nature mistress of all other races',[3] were able after his death to work their wicked will once more.

But as to the abject state of affairs, due to the ineptitude of his predecessors, when her father came to the throne in 1081, Anna can hardly find strong enough words. The Emperor 'was grieved and distressed because the Empire of the Greeks

[1] VI. 11, p. 176.
[2] XIV. 3, p. 433. Anna uses the neat phrase κενόσπουδος αὐτῷ ἡ σπουδή; as a matter of fact this statement is hard to reconcile with John's military strenuousness as mentioned by herself in Pref. 3, pp. 4, 5. Perhaps she is alluding to the wasteful wars of Manuel, unprofitable even when successful.
[3] XIV. 7, p. 445.

had no adequate army . . . and in the treasuries of the Palace there were no heaps of money stored up. For those who had reigned before him being utterly unsuited by disposition (λίαν ἀτέχνως διατεθέντες) for warlike and military concerns had brought the affairs of the Greeks truly to a bad pass.[1] I at least have heard from actual soldiers and from some older men that none of the cities for ages past had been brought into such a state of abjectness.'[2] Or as she tersely puts it later on: 'Affairs were in desperate straits, with weakness and poverty together oppressing the Empire of the Greeks.'[3] Once again she says of her father: 'He possessed neither troops nor money, for everything had been sacrificed, wasted on things of no profit.'[4] No wonder that his only hope was to attack the problem gradually, facing his enemies successively, and trying in some way to dispose of the less important first.[5] After the Turks had been temporarily subdued and Robert Guiscard had died and the Patzinaks and Comans had been repelled, the Empire might have looked for rest, but for the Crusaders with their troubling of the Empire and their stirring up of the Turks, so that Anna's bitterness against them is great. She could truly say of Alexius that 'not even for a short space did he partake of repose all through the time of his reign, because ever fresh enemies kept springing up continually',[6] but all the others paled before the sinister importance of 'the Celts'. However, with the military and foreign events of his reign we are not now concerned; we will turn to his problems at home.

If Alexius found his path in 1081 bristling with foreign enemies,[7] the internal condition of the Empire was hardly less deplorable: an empty treasury, an army so reduced by the short-sighted economies of his predecessors as to consist mainly of foreign mercenaries, the capital hardened to the sight of blood and revolution, and the country population both harried by hostile raiders and oppressed by the great provincial landowners. The picture is dark indeed.

[1] It is an interesting inconsistency when Anna in another passage, wishing to exalt her father's military merits, says that 'things in former days and the circumstances of the Empire before our times were very easy and considerably lighter ' (XIV. 7, p. 445).
[2] III. 9, p. 91.   [3] V. 1, p. 127.   [4] III. 11, p. 96.
[5] VI. 11, p. 175.   [6] XIV. 4, p. 433.
[7] Oster (A. K., Pt. I, p. 1) has pointed out that in 1081 the Empire was 'ohne Freunde, ohne Bundgenossen'; hence came Alexius efforts to get allies (III. 10). By the year 1108 he was in friendly diplomatic relations with the Serbians, the Pope, the Hungarians, and at least one prince from South Italy, for we read of their having ambassadors (ἀποκρισιάριοι) at his court (XIII. 12, p. 416).

40. ACCOUNT OF PAST EMPERORS

AT this point it may be well to consider the information which Anna gives us about her father's precursors on the throne, corresponding as it does very closely with what we learn from other historians.

For Nicephorus Botaniates, whom her father first served and then deserted, she evinces chiefly contempt; he is a spendthrift, old and vacillating and ruled by his slaves, and his unjust desire to keep the crown from Constantine Ducas has brought its own punishment.[1] The man responsible for the Empire's ruin[2] is to her Romanus Diogenes (1067-71), whose ill-fated figure looms large in her vision. She says (not quite accurately) that her husband began his book with that reign, over which 'various historians' had laboured.[3] Under him Alexius first turned to a military career.[4] (We may note that his kindness to her grandmother Anna Dalassena in this matter is far less dwelt upon by Anna than by her husband in his work.) His defeat at Manzikert was a death-knell to the 'Roman' State, and he seems to Anna so great a personage that even the fortunes of his sons are narrated in much detail.[5] In less important matters we learn that he chose an excellent site for a palace outside Constantinople, and admired the elder Nicephorus Bryennius so much that he adopted him as a brother; also that he issued gold coins with his effigy.[6] His blinding seemed such an outrage to one at least of his devoted followers that he made it an excuse for rebelling.[7] When in his last campaign Alexius is victorious over Saisan, the Turks agree that their territories are to return to the state they were in before the defeat of Romanus

---

[1] Bk. II, *passim*; III. 4; V. 1. The same view is taken by the *Anon. Syn. Chron.* pp. 171, 172. Constantine Manasses (*Syn. Chron.* lines 6717-19) puts the opinion of his day (the reign of Manuel) about Botaniates thus: he loved luxury,

> τὰ δ' ἄλλα πάντα πάρεργα καὶ τὸ μηδὲν ἡγεῖτο
> κἂν τὰ Ῥωμαίων ὅρια στενοῦντο τοῖς βαρβάροις
> κἂν ἐλεπόλεσι πολλαὶ πόλεις κριοκοποῦντο.

Nicephorus Bryennius tells us he committed a crime almost unknown in Byzantine history by debasing the coinage (*Hyle*, IV. 1, p. 87). Attaliates is this Emperor's one champion.

[2] Scylitzes assigns this sinister role to Michael VII (p. 856).

[3] Pref. 3, p. 4; IX. 6, p. 255. Psellus speaks eloquently of his rashness and reckless self-confidence (*Chron.*, Rom. IV, Byz. T., pp. 248 sqq.).

[4] I. 1, p. 3. [5] Books VII and IX.

[6] II. 8, p. 61; III. 10, p. 94 and Du Cange's note; X. 3.

[7] VI. 9, p. 169. It is well known what a guilty conscience Psellus has about this blinding, and how he strives to clear Michael VII from all complicity.

Diogenes.[1] And in her penultimate chapter the same Emperor is brought in as the cause of the terrible desolation still prevailing in Asia Minor.[2]

Among her other references to past emperors we find eight to Constantine the Great; the Forum at Constantinople bears his name, he built the theatre otherwise called Hippodrome or Circus, and appropriated a statue of Apollo as representing himself. His mother St. Helena built a church 'in his name' at Apollonias, and his right to be called the Thirteenth Apostle can be disputed only by Alexius himself.[3] Anastasius Dicorus, Emperor from 491 to 518, had dug a trench below Lake Baane.[4] Basil II neglected learning, and in this statement Anna agrees with Psellus.[5] Under this Emperor her paternal great-grandfather fought against the rebel Sclerus; his joint rule with his brother Constantine is mentioned in connexion with a Bulgarian king, and his prowess in marching into Asia is recorded.[6] One of his early regents, John Tzimisces (969–76), ἐκεῖνος θαυμάσιος, also went across the straits and victoriously transported captive Manichaeans from Armenia to Thrace, to be guards against Scythian inroads.[7] Zoe is only mentioned for the richness of her coffin,[8] but the reign of her third husband, Constantine IX Monomachus, bad as it was for the morals[9] of the court, marks the first beginning of that revival of learning which Anna's father consummated.[10] We may note that though she speaks of the monastery of St. George built by this Constantine she never alludes to his μουσεῖον τῆς νομοθετικῆς[11] and his practical methods of encouraging letters. Still, she does not show the hatred for his anti-military spirit evinced by the soldier Cecaumenus, and merely says that Maniaces rebelled in his reign.[12]

[1] XV. 6, p. 478, referring to Manzikert, 1071.   [2] XV. 10, p. 495.

[3] II. 5, p. 52, and 12, p. 68; VI. 10, p. 174; 13, p. 181; XII. 4, pp. 356, 357; XIV. 6, p. 444: 8, p. 453. We may note that this same title of Thirteenth Apostle was awarded to Constantine V Copronymus by the Iconoclastic Council of 753 (Camb. Med. Hist. IV, p. 14).

[4] X. 5, p. 282.

[5] V. 8, p. 144; Psellus, Chron., Basil II, Byz. T., p. 15.

[6] XI. 1, p. 311; XII. 9, p. 371; XV. 10, p. 495.

[7] XIV. 8; XV. 10, p. 495. Psellus calls him ὁ μέγας ἐν βασιλεῦσιν Ἰωάννης ἐκεῖνος (Chron., Const. IX, Byz. T., p. 128), and says he increased to power the Empire of the Greeks (ibid., Basil II, Byz. T., p. 1).

[8] VI. 3.   [9] III. 8, p. 87. Cf. Psellus' account of his amours.

[10] V. 8, p. 144. Cf. Psellus, Chron., Const. IX, Byz. T., p. 107.

[11] Attal. p. 21.

[12] V. 8, p. 144. Laurent, in his Byzance et les Turcs Seldjoucides, pp. 50 sqq., points out how unfair the Byzantine historians have been to Monomachus. Cecaumenus is one of the worst. Psellus says most people of his time called him Euergetes (Chron., Is. Comn., Byz. T., p. 215).

To her father's uncle the Emperor Isaac Comnenus there are only three allusions, two merely giving his relationship to some other person, one a long extract from Psellus about his war (successful largely owing to his personal valour) against the Μυσοί, to which Anna adds an account of his building a church to St. Thecla in thanksgiving for a wonderful escape.[1] Probably Anna, like her paternal grandmother, felt bitterly towards Isaac for having resigned the throne prematurely and not secured the succession for a member of his own family.[2]

The man who actually did succeed him, Constantine X Ducas, only comes into the *Alexias* twice, and on both occasions merely as a father.[3] But one of his sons, the Emperor Michael VII, plays a large part. He sends Alexius against Urselius and makes him στρατηγὸς αὐτοκράτωρ. It is against him that Nicephorus Bryennius originally rebels. When deposed he becomes first a monk and then an archbishop,[4] but though he and his brothers deserve praise as φιλολογώτατοι, yet the harm done by his foolish betrothal of his son Constantine to Robert Guiscard's daughter outlasts his reign.[5] On the strength of it Robert professes to invade the Empire solely to champion his daughter's rights and reinstate on the throne her future father-in-law, and an impostor is found to impersonate Michael, though Robert's own messenger sees the real ex-Emperor living in a monastery.[6] Michael's wife Maria (married before his death to his successor Botaniates) and his son Constantine have each a considerable share in Anna's story, his wholly creditable, hers of a more doubtful character.[7] We learn that Michael and his Ducas brothers consorted both with Psellus and with the philosopher Italus.[8] Whatever he was to these same

[1] I. 3, p. 8; III. 8; XI. 1, p. 311; cf. Psellus, *Chron.*, Is. Comn., Byz. T., pp. 221 sqq.
[2] She gives no hint however of his haughty contempt to all, even his own relations (Psellus, *ibid.*, Byz. T., p. 224).
[3] III. 2, p. 75; IV. 6, p. 116. Yet all the historians agree in representing his anti-military spirit as ruining the Empire (Laurent, *op. cit.* pp. 56–8). Oman (*Byz. Emp.* p. 250) says he 'disbanded no inconsiderable portion of the army and cut down the pay of the rest' in order to save money.
[4] Nic. Bry. (III. 24, p. 84) says the Patriarch Thomas made him first a monk and then Metropolitan of Ephesus, τὴν καθαρότητα τοῦ ἀνδρὸς γινώσκων.
[5] I. 1, pp. 3, 4; 4, p. 9; 10, *passim*; II. 1, p. 43; V. 8, p. 145. In this last passage, during the struggles of the Greeks to keep the remnants of their Empire in Italy in the teeth of combined 'Latins and Italians' (i.e. Normans and Lombards), he makes an ill-judged choice of a diplomatic envoy and is lenient to his treachery.
[6] I. 12 and 15; IV. 1, 2.
[7] III. 1–4; VI. 8; IX. 5–8.
[8] V. 8, p. 145. Glycas and Zonaras dwell contemptuously on Michael's preference of poor iambics to statecraft (*Bibl. Chron.* IV, p. 330; *Epit.* XVIII. 16). Constantine Manasses (6642–4) makes him out as a most zealous student, working for 'sleepless nights'. Cf. Theophylact (*P. G.* 126, col. 260). See above, p. 179.

full brothers and his uncle John, towards his Diogenes half-brothers he shows the harshness of fear, condemning them and their mother Eudocia[1] to a monastic life. A special kind of gold coin is named after him.[2]

Before we leave these matters of imperial history two points must be considered that concern Anna's immediate family. The first of these is her statement that her father was fourteen when his brother Manuel died.[3] Chalandon as usual believes any-body rather than Anna, and says on the strength of some words of Zonaras that Alexius was seventy when he died in 1118.[4] That puts his birth in 1048, so that when Romanus Diogenes who ascended the throne in 1067 was starting three years later on 'his great campaign against the Persians', which ended in the Manzikert disaster of 1071, Alexius would have been twenty-two. Now not only does Anna state definitely that he was fourteen when his brother Manuel died, and consideration for the bereft mother made Romanus Diogenes keep back this younger boy from going to the front with himself, but she uses the terms νεανίσκος and μειράκιον, which would have been gro-tesque applied to a man in his twenties. Also she dwells more than once on his *youth* at his accession,[5] whereas if we take Zonaras literally he would in 1081 have been thirty-three. But as a matter of fact what Zonaras says is this:[6] Alexius died 'having lived ἔτη ἑβδομήκοντά που τὰ πάντα ἢ ὅτι ἐγγυτάτω, and having reigned out of these 37 years 4 months and a few days'. Does not the vague turn of the phrase about the life, con-trasting forcibly with the accurate calculation as to the reign, show that Zonaras was sure how long Alexius had reigned, but not sure how long he had lived? And after a strenuous reign of continual hardships, he may well have looked 'about seventy' when he was in fact (if we put his birth as Anna does in 1056) fully eight years younger.

The second question, that of the origin of the Comnenus family, concerns Anna's standards whether moral or intellectual only remotely, but it is remarkable that neither she nor her husband, fond as all Byzantines were of giving magnificent pedigrees to their characters, ever tell us anything about the Comneni. Are we to see in this the deliberate silence of a pride which could not bear to admit a humble origin? This is the

---

[1] IX. 6, p. 256. For his generosity to his Ducas kin see Psellus (*Chron.*, Mich. VII Byz. T., p. 263); it is only one of the many virtues which his old teacher belauds on page after page. He never mentions the disastrous Norman betrothal.

[2] XIII. 12, p. 414.   [3] I. 1, p. 3.   [4] *op. cit.* p. 23.

[5] III. 7, p. 85; 9, p. 91; 11, p. 96; V. 1, pp. 126, 127.

[6] *Epit.* XVIII. 29.

view of G. Murnu,[1] and he is inclined to accept (though he cannot verify it) C. Hopf's quotation from Benjamin of Tudela to the effect that Alexius was descended from Vlachs, those nomads of the Balkan peninsula who, in the persons of the present-day Roumanians, still claim to be Romans in race, language, and descent.[2] Psellus puts the home of the Comnenus family at Comne near Adrianople, 'dans une région où l'élément vlaque dans ce temps-là devait être suffisamment représenté', as it was near the mountains. The Vlachs have been proved by N. Jorga and others to have had 'une situation privilégiée sous les Comnènes'. Anna merely mentions a Vlach 'χωρίον near Larissa',[3] Vlach nomads enrolled as recruits in the Greek army,[4] and 'a chosen man of the Vlachs' giving useful information to Alexius in war[5]—with other Vlachs performing the same function for his Coman enemies[6]; therefore nothing as to any 'privileged position' can be learned from her, and to a 'Roman' princess any half-breed nomadic stock would hardly be an ancestry to be proud of. But if Murnu is right in saying that the general Tzintziloukis who served Manuel I was a Vlach (according to his name, which being 'tout à fait vlaque et même dialectal' means 'five wolves'), then the Andronicus Tzintziluces of Anna's eleventh Book is another of the race. To him by Alexius' orders St. Gilles commits Laodicea, but he is besieged there by Tancred and famine forces him to surrender the town.[7] His career is not glorious, but he at least seems to have been a trusted general, one who comes under what Murnu calls 'le régime de faveur des Comnènes'. Whether or no he was in Hopf's phrase a *Stammesgenoss* of Alexius we have not at present sufficient evidence to say.

[1] Paper read before the Congress of Byzantinology at Bukharest (*Acad. Roum. Bulletin*, Tome XI, pp. 212–6).
[2] As a matter of fact they had a considerable admixture of Slavonic blood, the name 'Vlach' being itself Slavonic. In the eleventh and twelfth centuries they were sometimes ruled by Bulgaria, sometimes by Byzantium.
[3] V. 5, p. 138. The *Encycl. Brit.* points out that it is from Anna that we first hear of this Vlach settlement in Thessaly.
[4] VIII. 3, p. 227.   [5] X. 2, p. 274.
[6] X. 3, p. 274. We must not forget that the *Strategicon* of Cecaumenus has a most violent diatribe against the Vlachs as false, treacherous, and cowardly (pp. 74, 75). Since the conquests of Basil II they had been nominally Greek subjects.
[7] XI. 7, pp. 329, 330.

INTERNAL AFFAIRS

41. FINANCE AND LAW

THE various details of Anna's gloomy picture of the Eastern Empire in 1081 must be considered in order, and as we have said, the subject falls naturally into four divisions, of which Internal Affairs constitute the first. What do we learn from Anna about the inner workings of the Empire?

It may be said at the beginning that she displays little interest in the financial conditions of her time, except in so far as they affect the army.[1] In the first of her many panegyrics over her father's achievements she excuses him on several grounds for not trying to fight the Turks and Normans simultaneously. First, even Heracles cannot engage two enemies at once; secondly, Alexius was young; thirdly, he found on his accession a desperate state of affairs. Things, as she loves to say, were ἐν στενῷ κομιδῇ. The Empire after a considerable period of gradual decline was 'by now destroyed, and had come to the last gasp'; the new Emperor had 'no forces, no money, for everything had been already squandered, spent on nothing useful'.[2] Under Nicephorus Botaniates, so she says, the waste had been so colossal that the doors of the empty Treasury could freely be left open.[3]

As to the way Alexius repaired the waste she tells us little. We know that he later on recommended his son John not only to give unstintingly, but to 'receive unstintingly a stream' of money,[4] and if we are to go by Chalandon this unstinted receiving by the sovereign reduced the subjects to bitter poverty. Anna however tells us nothing of that side; 'taxes' and 'confiscations' are mentioned vaguely, and on one occasion Church property is 'borrowed', but of the everyday financial administration in her father's time she gives no picture whatever. Yet

[1] Chalandon blames her for indifference to internal affairs as a whole.
[2] III. 9, p. 91; 11, p. 96.
[3] V. 1, pp. 126, 127. See also VII. 7, p. 204.
[4] Mous. Alex. I. 319. Zonaras (XVIII. 21, 22) and Glycas (IV, pp. 332, 333) talk darkly of 'unlawful' (ἀπαίσιοι or ἀποτρόπαιοι) ways by which Alexius exacted money from his subjects especially the upper classes, but they like Anna give no hint as to what 'lawful' ways would have been. Attaliates speaks of a burdensome corn monopoly (p. 202) as a feature of imperial finance. Leib (op. cit. pp. 86, 87) dwells on onerous taxes exacted even from pilgrims and clergy, and says that under Alexius I, 'L'arbitraire régnait dans les finances.' Zonaras again says (XVIII. 22) that Alexius found the coinage debased and exacted gold for taxes, while he made his payments in bronze, for which he melted down bronze objects. Theophylact speaks of subjects bringing yearly taxes, some silver, some gold, as quite the usual thing (παιδ. βασ. I. 1, P. G. 126, col. 253).

it must have been elaborate and extensive. We know from other sources how costly the Byzantine court-life must have been; the writings of Constantine VII (Porphyrogenitus) impress on us its sumptuousness even in the tenth century,[1] and in Anna's day Constantinople was still the queen of cities.

Again, the incessant wars of the eleventh century were an even greater drain on the imperial treasury. All the time the menace of 'barbarians' on the Eastern frontiers was growing more severe, and the government was torn between the desire to encourage small proprietors in Asia as against the formidable δυνατοί who weakened the central authority, and the necessity for having large bodies of armed men to repel invasion. Agriculture must be fostered, yet the Empire must be guarded. Attempts to repress the great landowners by forbidding them to buy out small proprietors had only driven them to conquest and constant frontier wars, till finally each great noble had a small army of trained slaves.[2] The autocratic Basil II had striven to put this down by heavy taxation of the rich and powerful,[3] but, in spite of all, the *latifundia* had increased and with them the distress of the peasantry.[4] Constantine Monomachus in his turn bled the rich, not for military purposes but for his own pleasures and to secure his own power, also earning the censure of all soldiers by accepting a tax in lieu of military service. None of all this does Anna mention, but it is certain that whatever had been taken in by Constantine IX was no less quickly poured out, and that after the intervening years of waste and anarchy Alexius found nothing in the treasury worth speaking of. No wonder that an imperial tax-gatherer carrying his collection in a βαλάντιον to Constantinople feared to be imprisoned if 'seen with empty hands by those of the imperial treasury'.[5]

Yet though the treasury was empty its officials were as

[1] Especially *De cerimoniis*. So Luitprand, the German envoy to Constantinople, marvelled over its splendour in 949.

[2] See note on slaves above, p. 53.

[3] In a paper on *The attempt of the Arabs to conquer Asia Minor*, read by Sir Wm. Ramsay before the Congress of Byzantinology at Bukharest (*Acad. Roum. Bull.* Tome XI, p. 4), he attributes the survival of the Byzantine power in Asia Minor mainly to the sturdy character of the Anatolian peasantry and 'their resident lords', a great military aristocracy, and says: 'The explanation lies in economics, not in war. Defeat was made possible by waste and extravagance, over-taxation, wrong system of taxation. Every victorious Emperor from Augustus to John Komnenos was an economist, who conserved the immense resources of the Empire and applied them well.' This view hardly agrees with those quoted on p. 266, note 4, above.

[4] Zonaras, XVII. 12, tells us that at one point, driven to desperation by imperial exactions, famine, and a plague of locusts, a whole neighbourhood of small-holders started to emigrate.

[5] II. 6, p. 56.

numerous and important as ever. We know that the Grand Treasurer was called in the ninth century Logothete τοῦ γενικοῦ,[1] but by Anna's time he had got the title of Logothete τῶν σεκρέτων.[2] This word σέκρετα, taken straight from the Latin, has given rise to many commentaries. It seems to have been applied first to the Imperial Council, next to the rooms in the Palace where the various σεκρετικοί (of whom Bury enumerates eleven kinds) sat, and finally to the tribunal before which cases affecting the imperial finances were tried. The σέκρετον housed in a separate treasury-building called γενικόν was, according to Du Cange, known as τοῦ γενικοῦ, and its chief (with financial and judicial duties) as Logothete τοῦ γενικοῦ; but by loose usage he came to be called Logothete or προεστὼς τῶν σεκρέτων as though no other σέκρετα existed.[3] It is in financial matters and judicial matters arising therefrom that Anna Dalassena has full authority by the Golden Bull as Regent in Alexius' absence.[4] In this document even the word δημοσιακός, of 'public' remissions of fines, has like σέκρετον a financial flavour. In Byzantine Greek δημόσιον is a tax and δημοσιώνης a tax-gatherer, like the Latin *publicum* and *publicanus*, and the Tribunal τοῦ γενικοῦ or

---

[1] Bury, *Imperial Administration in the Ninth Century*, ch. C 4 (2).

[2] III. 1, p. 70, and see Du Cange's notes on III. 1, p. 70 A, III. 6, p. 84 B, 85 A, and VI. 3, p. 157 B. In VI. 3, p. 157, Alexius repays to the σέκρετον of [Christ] our Surety what he owed for stripping the Empress Zoe's coffin; here the word must refer to an ecclesiastical treasury. In XV. 7, p. 485 the σέκρετα of the Orphanage, where the accounts were kept, should be translated 'office'. Du Cange points out (note on III. 6, p. 84 B) that in legal parlance σεκρετικὸν ἀξίωμα came to mean 'senatorial rank'. The 'Great σέκρετον' is mentioned as the scene of part at least of the trial of Italus ('Trial of Italus,' *Bull. inst. arch. russe de Constantinople*, Vol. II, p. 41).

[3] In III. 1, p. 70, a nephew to Alexius by marriage is said to have held this post. In III. 6, p. 84, this official is called ὁ κατὰ τὴν ἡμέραν διοικῶν τὰ σέκρετα.

[4] III. 6. In the Golden Bull we may note the use of θέματα in its etymological meaning of 'things deposited' (we might render it 'Fisc'), whereas in XIII. 12 the singular is used throughout in the regular Byzantine sense of 'district'. The wording of the document is difficult. The sentence τῷ δὲ μηνὶ . . . ὃ δόξει ταύτῃ ποιεῖν shows that even in the 'month' which the Logothete τῶν σεκρέτων apparently dedicated to making 'promotions' and awarding 'dignities' in his own department, even then Anna Dalassena had 'full power to do what shall seem good to her'. The next sentence beginning ἀλλὰ καὶ seems at first sight to restrict her power, by enacting that previous arrangements shall stand. It is however possible to translate ἀλλὰ καὶ as 'Nay truly', in which case the sentence confirms instead of limiting her authority, and reads: 'Nay truly if some shall have been appointed to the Treasury or the Fisc [i.e. by the Empress Regent] and shall have gone on in succession and shall have been honoured with large or medium or small dignities, they shall be for the future permanent and not to be moved.' Then follows another ἀλλὰ καὶ ('nay truly' or 'furthermore') introducing a still stronger statement as to her powers. She is responsible to no one; her enactments, mostly to be made in writing and sealed with her own special seal, possess τὸ παντελῶς ἀλογοπράγητον, and to her 'the matters about the taxes and the expenses on behalf of the Empire' are wholly committed (III. 7, p. 85).

τὰ σέκρετα *par excellence* was often called δημοσιακά from the taxation-cases which were there tried. A similar combination of legal and financial powers is indicated in the passage where, after a rebellion in Cyprus has been put down, Alexius sends a man famed for 'justice, incorruptibility, and ταπεινοφροσύνη', to act as κριτὴς καὶ ἐξισωτής.[1] Du Cange in his note suggests that the rebellion had been due to oppressive taxation,[2] so that the duty of this official was to 'equalize' it, by making suitable assessments for all the towns in the island. Certainly after this we find Cyprus a sort of gold-mine from which the Emperor drew as he pleased, with a governor who counts among the sovereign's most important subordinates. Thus he orders the 'Duke' to supply not only ships to transport his envoys on a mission to Baldwin King of Jerusalem, but 'much money of all kinds, of every form and image, and of all kinds of materials for the gifts to the Counts'.[3] The sum raised was so large that the envoys deposited it for safe keeping in the bishop's palace at Tripoli, and a threat of stopping all supplies from Cyprus is held over a recalcitrant vassal's head.[4]

Turning back to Constantinople we observe that in the case of Anna Dalassena her power was limited to finance and the legal matters arising therefrom. This is proved by the simultaneous appointment of her son Isaac to guard Constantinople.[5] We know from Zonaras that her rule was hated[6] as despotic, but we may well believe that her difficulties in balancing her budget were great. The same writer tells us that Alexius himself when in need of money cut down salaries and seized the property of senators and others.[7] Over all the finances, however and whenever brought in, the Emperor had absolute control,[8] and throughout the book Alexius' expenditure of 'sufficient money' (to say nothing of presents in kind, such as *objets d'art*, reliquaries, clothes, and even a candlestick) on

---

[1] IX. 2, p. 250.

[2] It is rather ominous to read in Nic. Acom. *John C.* 3, p. 7, of an undersecretary who grew rich ἐκ τοῦ τάσσειν φόρους.

[3] XIV. 2, p. 424. 'Gold and silver and all sorts of garments' are specified on p. 428 in the same story.

[4] XIV. 2, p. 428. The only other place mentioned as containing 'sufficient gold and money of the imperial treasuries' is Sinope on the Black Sea (VI. 9, p. 169).

[5] IV. 4, p. 109.

[6] *Epit.* XVIII. 24.

[7] *Epit.* XVIII. 21 and 22; Glycas, IV, pp. 332, 333.

[8] In the case of one confiscation from a convicted rebel, the man's 'very fine house' ἐδόθη πρὸς τὴν Αὔγουσταν, who magnanimously restored it to his wife (XII. 6, p. 362). On another occasion the confiscated property is given by Alexius to the army (VI. 2, p. 155). On the Emperor's lavishness see Chs. 16 and 17 above, and Ch. 55 below.

enemies and friends, on salaries and military pay and rewards and bribes, or to seal a treaty, would have strained a Fortunatus' purse.[1] It was presumably to have them 'registered' for taxation that Alexius professed to summon the Manichaeans, who for all their suspicions felt bound to come.[2] He considers himself at liberty to draw for his military schemes, which as he truly said 'wanted much money', on the 'gold and silver' of his family and friends.[3] When this supply is exhausted he dares not try a general levy, 'despairing of the loyalty of the Greeks', so he appropriates Church treasures. In restoring this 'loan' he assigns 'a sufficient sum of gold brought in yearly by the collectors of taxes' to one σέκρετον, and 'a yearly income of sufficient money from the imperial treasuries' to the priests of one of the churches. The restoration is based on the ecclesiastical 'inventories' themselves.[4] When the Venetians are rewarded for naval aid, they get[5] not only 'many gifts' at the time but also a yearly 'χρυσίου ποσότητα ἱκανήν' for all their churches, and to St. Mark's is assigned all rents and taxes from certain workshops, wharves, and 'other pieces of real property' in Constantinople,[6] 'and', Anna adds, 'what was even more, he made their trading free in all the lands under the sway of the Greeks, so that they could traffic uncontrolled and according to their own pleasure, and need not on account of a trading-tax or for any other tax brought in to the public treasury, contribute as much as one obol. They were outside all Greek authority.' Neither Anna nor her father was aware that this fatal concession, markedly strengthening the power of Venice, was a death-blow to the trade of Constantinople, which hereby and increasingly lost her century-long position as the great emporium between East and West.

Other instances of Alexius' frenzied finance occur from time to time and make us feel he is an autocrat indeed. Thus he is not only able to found a new town for the 'commoner sort' of his Manichaean converts at Philippopolis, but he can make donations to them of 'corn-lands and vineyards and houses', confirming these possessions (with power of bequest to descendants or wives) by a Golden Bull.[7] He takes the same steps to make ἀναίρετον the landed property of his Orphanage,[8] where he further-

---

[1] III. 10; XII. 1, p. 347; XIV. 2, p. 428; XV. 6, p. 480, &c.
[2] VI. 1, p. 154.
[3] V. 1, 2; VI. 3, p. 156.
[4] VI. 3,
[5] VI. 5, pp. 161, 162.
[6] See Du Cange's note on VI. 5, p. 161 D.
[7] XIV. 9, p. 456.
[8] XV. 7. It is regrettable that the charter of this institution should not have survived. See p. 113, above.

more spends enormous sums daily on the maintenance of old
and infirm people with their attendants. We have already seen
that in this case we are not told whether he purchased or confiscated the land that seemed specially suitable—only that he
'quickly assigned' it to his beneficiaries. Confiscation was, we
know, a favourite punishment for political offences,[1] but the
Orphanage seems to have been established in a period of calm.
Doubtless the Emperor felt himself entitled to commandeer
land, as he did money from his friends[2] and hospitality for
visitors from compliant monks.[3]

We must repeat that 'gifts' is a word and an idea appearing
in almost every chapter of the *Alexias*.[4] A formidable ex-
Empress, a would-be assassin, a rebel commandant, enemies
and their leaders when they surrender or can be bought off,
ransomed captives, deserving or needy or formidable allies,
converted heretics, meritorious soldiers, new mercenaries, one
and all receive 'sufficient money' or 'plenteous gifts'.[5] Even
men sent to prison may count on the Emperor for bountiful
maintenance.[6] If his financial powers are unlimited so also are
the demands upon him. Thus when a fortress has to be built
in summer heat outside Nicomedia the Emperor acts as his
own contractor, and draws workmen from all sides by 'generous
pay'.[7] If he decides to spend large sums on his fleet, none can
prevent him for all their criticism.[8] The crusading chiefs are
bribed into taking the oath of homage, either by money beforehand or by rewards afterwards,[9] and sometimes in return for

[1] e.g. VI. 2 and 4, p. 157; VIII. 7, p. 236; IX. 8, p. 262; XII. 6. There must
also have been cases of intestacy where properties escheated to the Crown.
[2] V. 2. It is interesting to find Irene making independent use of her own money
in philanthropy in XII. 3, p. 354. Similarly Anna Dalassena is represented as rich
enough to be lavishly hospitable (III. 8, p. 87).
[3] X. 11, p. 302.
[4] In his first poem to John, Alexius speaks of the handing on of the Emperor's
δωρεαί as one of a governor's main duties (*Mous. Alex.* I. 342). Nicephorus Bryennius
is as fully alive as Anna to the necessity for a prince's well-being of great sums to
engage mercenaries or reward successful generals (*Hyle*, I. 7, p. 21, &c).
[5] III. 11, p. 97; IV. 2, pp. 105, 107; V. 1, p. 127; 2, p. 128; 3, p. 131; 7, p. 143;
VI. 5, p. 160; 14, p. 183; VII. 1, p. 189; 6, p. 202; 8, p. 208; IX. 6, p. 256;
7, p. 260; X. 4, p. 281; XI. 1, p. 310; 2, pp. 313, 314, 315, 316; 7, *passim*; 8, p. 332;
11, p. 340; XII. 1, *passim*; 5, p. 357; 7, p. 365; XIII. 8, p. 399; 9, p. 401; XIV. 1,
pp. 419, 422; 3, p. 431; 4, p. 434; 9, p. 456.
Bury (Appendix 12 to Vol. V of Gibbon's *Decline and Fall*) says that the Byzantine Emperors aimed at 'making the Treasury full instead of the Empire rich'; with
these never-ending and ill-regulated expenses falling on each Emperor's shoulders
it is difficult to see how they could have done otherwise.
[6] V. 2, p. 130; VI. 7, p. 165; XIV. 9, p. 457.
[7] X. 5, p. 283.   [8] XII. 4, p. 356.
[9] X. 7, p. 289; 9, p. 298; 11, p. 303, 304. In the last passage quoted Bohemund
is won over by the sight of a room in the palace stored with goods and clothes

service annual subsidies are promised.[1] But over and above all
Alexius and the other generals are in constant want of coin to
pay their troops.[2] At the very outset Alexius when revolting
against Botaniates writes to a hoped-for supporter: 'I need
money and without it it is impossible for anything to turn out
as it should.'[3] On this same occasion his brother-in-law Palaeologus promises to contribute τὴν ἐν κινητοῖς αὐτοῦ θεωρουμένην
περιουσίαν (all fortunately laid up in one convenient spot), and
John Ducas Caesar robs an imperial tax-gatherer in support of
Alexius' cause.[4] Rebellions are costly things, and the Anemas
conspirators were fortunate in finding a rich accomplice from
whose resources they went on 'drawing out of a golden stream'.[5]
Another considerable outlay is entailed by ransoming captured
soldiers, a duty which the Emperor seems to take on himself.[6]
Thus it is probable that war was proportionally hardly less costly
in the twelfth century than now. Yet of all the expenses of Alexius'
reign Anna would have us think that the heaviest and the least
rewarding lay in the large sums demanded for transporting the
Crusaders to the Holy Land. He had given them innumerable
gifts and heaps of gold, he had 'spent sums beyond all number',
and the Empire had profited not at all.[7] Whatever else Anna
felt about finance, she knew at least that such an investment
as this was unsound.

Before we pass on to another topic it may be interesting to
note that though only six out of Alexius' Novels[8] have to do
directly with finance, yet these six are all most important.
Novel 20 deals with fines in matters of contract, and with the
reversion of a property without heirs. Novel 22 is the record
of the Emperor's humble restitution of the Church property
taken by him for military expenses, with an edict forbidding
such spoliation for the future. Novel 30 grants the Island of
Patmos to St. Christodulus for a monastery. Novels 32 and 36

and with gold, silver, and copper coin 'filling the chamber to such an extent that
a man could not walk'. The successors of St. Gilles receive money bribes in XI. 8,
p. 332, and XIV. 2.

[1] XI. 3, p. 315. In XIII. 12, p. 414 (bis), the payment is to be made in gold
coins (λίτραι) of the Emperor Michael VII. Du Cange in his note points out that
λίτραι (Latin librae) were synonymous with τάλαντα.
[2] Alexius gives all the 'properties' of the robbed Manichaeans to 'those who had
toiled with him in the battles that befell' (VI. 2, p. 155). See above p. 269, note 8,
and below, ch. 55.
[3] I. 16, p. 39, and III. 9, p. 92.
[4] II. 6, pp. 55, 56.   [5] XII. 5, p. 359.
[6] VII. 2, p. 190: 3, p. 199: 4, p. 200. In VII. 6, p. 203, he buys back from the
Patzinaks the head of the son of his general Migidenus.
[7] XIV. 2, pp. 422, 423.
[8] Coll. IV in Vol. III of Zachariae v. Lingenthal's Jus Gr.-Rom.

make concessions to the Venetians and Pisans respectively, while Novel 34 contains the invaluable 'Rescripta ad rationales et rationarium antiquum et novum'. We may also note that according to Zachariae von Lingenthal[1] the old custom of tax-collecting by the state had by Alexius' day been changed into that of annual farming. Anna with her marked indifference to all such details tells us not one word of all this,[2] and her father's enactments become all the more indispensable as sources of knowledge.

Turning now to legislative matters, we may note that of Alexius' endeavours to prevent disorder in his Empire by law-making rather than to punish it half-heartedly when rampant we hear little either in the *Alexias* or in the Novels themselves; from the nature of the case his justice (or injustice) was chiefly of a financial kind. Chalandon states that he was compelled to raise money by various unpopular means, not only the spoliation of Church treasure, but also the exaction of heavy taxes even from the clergy, while in order to reward his partisans 'il eut recours aux biens des couvents et les distribua à titre de bénéfices'.[3] Anna never mentions this, and the only lasting confiscations she speaks of are from criminals. Only twice does she allude to any legal enactments at all, once when she says that the secretary John Taronites used freely to criticize τὰ βασιλέως προστάγματα,[4] and again when she says that as soon as external and internal disturbances were quieted Alexius turned 'to law-courts and laws', being 'the best dispenser both of peace and war'.[5] Unfortunately his dispensing of peace interests her less than the other, and she rarely even draws her figures of speech from the law-courts. One of the few instances may be given here. In telling how Alexius justified before a 'great assembly' his action in taking Church property for his cam-

---

[1] *Gesch. des gr.-röm. Rechts*, p. 236. The old system apparently prevailed under Botaniates, *Al.* II. 6, p. 56.

[2] The latest contribution to the study of Byzantine finance is F. Dölger's *Beiträge zur Geschichte der byzantinischen Finanzverwaltung besonders des 10. und 11. Jahrh.* (*Byz. Arch.* 1927) in which he re-edits with introduction and commentary the manuscript (Cod. marc. gr. 173) which W. Ashburner had already published without notes in the *Journal of Hellenic Studies*. He gives four reasons for the special difficulties presented by Byzantine constitutional history: (*a*) Paucity of material; (*b*) Religious preoccupation of most chroniclers; (*c*) Purist dread of technical terms, causing an 'Unart der unscharfen Bezeichnung'; (*d*) Unreliable editions. In connexion with the manuscript, which he cannot date more precisely than between 913 and 1139, he gives a full description of the various offices associated with the imperial finance.

[3] *op. cit.* ch. X, p. 282.   [4] XIII. 1, p. 376.

[5] XIV. 7, p. 449. Zonaras (XVIII. 26) amplifies this by saying that Alexius appointed days when he sat and received judicial petitions, which his ὑπογραμματεῖς read and answered.

paigns (elsewhere euphemistically called 'collecting money with the public consent from all possible sources, according both to the laws and to justice')[1] she says,[2] 'In appearance he sat as a judge on the imperial throne, but in truth he himself was about to be examined. . . . The Emperor sets himself plainly forth as on trial (ὑπόδικος), and sets as judge any who would.' As the proceedings seem to have consisted of a monologue on Alexius' part, while we hear nothing of what the συνέδριον said or thought, it is obvious that this was not a 'trial' in any ordinary sense, and that the word is used merely by analogy.

One legal phrase does occur in Anna's pages too frequently to make reıerences necessary. 'To gain a victory' is almost always τὴν νικῶσαν ἔχειν, the word implied being γνώμην, the *victrix sententia* of a law-court. In one instance the metaphor is completed by the use of a word for voting, εἰ τὴν νικῶσαν ἡμῖν ἐπιψηφιεῖται Θεός.[3]

This rapid survey must suffice. Neither in finance nor in law as such did Anna take any interest; they only appealed to her as providing the material and mental sinews of war for her father's incessant contests.

INTERNAL AFFAIRS

42. SENATE AND OFFICIALS

WE will now turn to more definitely constitutional matters. In a highly important passage Zonaras represents Alexius as oppressing the Senate;[4] Anna does not say this in so many words, but we cannot fail to see that some of the worst conspiracies of the reign arc due wholly or in part to senators, and this argues the Emperor's unpopularity with that body.[5] It is equally noteworthy that Alexius never resorts to severe punishment.

It has often been discussed how much power the senators retained in the eleventh and twelfth centuries in Constanti-

---

[1] V. 2, p. 129.   [2] VI. 3, p. 156.
[3] IV. 5, p. 114. In XV. 11, p. 497 we have τῶν πλειόνων ἡ ψῆφος ἐκράτει.
[4] *Epit.* XVIII. 29. Botaniates would seem to have kept on good terms with the Senate (Attal. pp. 308, 318) and John Comnenus cultivated it in order to counterbalance Irene's power (Glycas, IV, p. 334).
[5] VI. 4, p. 157; IX. 6, p. 257; XII. 5, p. 359. On the occasion of the first conspiracy Zonaras (XVIII. 22) represents Alexius as having seized men (whose innocence the writer implies) simply 'in order that he might rob them of their property'.

nople. Theoretically they still had an important part in choosing the Emperor; practically heredity or military usurpation was the usual determining factor, and the Senate did little more than ratify.[1] Theoretically they had ceased to have legislative power since the days of Leo VI; practically they help to pass decrees, in matters of heresy at least, and join the clergy or the army in an arraignment of their Emperor necessitated by popular discontent.[2] Attaliates speaks of Botaniates reading a Novel before them and getting their approval.[3] The same writer rates their number as ὑπὲρ μυριάδας.[4] Psellus[5] tells us that both Constantine IX Monomachus and Constantine X Ducas democratized the Senate, admitting artisans and barbarians and even slaves. With its aid the civil government hoped to make head against the power of the army, but when a military usurper came to the throne his sympathies were naturally with the troops that had placed him there. So throughout the Alexias we find the Senate more or less in opposition, and we can well credit Zonaras' statement that Alexius 'was zealous to humble' its members.[6] But the matter is complicated by Anna's vague use of the word συγκλητικός to mean any one of rank and importance, (one of the class equally indefinitely termed τῆς μείζονος τύχης), and especially one of the innumerable court functionaries whom the Emperor personally appointed and personally paid.[7] The high-born land-owning families[8] to whom the Comneni themselves seem to have belonged were still important members of the 'senatorial register',[9] and we have more than one indication that Alexius partly hated and partly feared his formidable peers.[10] It may not have been altogether unpleasing to his ear when Gregory Taronites

---

[1] Nicephorus Bryennius (Hyle, I. 22, p. 34) describes the λογάδες τῆς συγκλήτου coming together to discuss affairs in the struggle for the throne between Michael Ducas and Romanus Diogenes.

[2] VI. 3; XV. 8, p. 488: 9, p. 491, and see the 'Trial of Italus' in Bull. inst. arch. russe de Constantinople, Vol. II, p. 42.

[3] p. 314.   [4] p. 275.

[5] Chron., Const. IX. and Const. X. Byz. T. pp. 151 and 238. Under Constantine IX ἡ σύγκλητος διέφθαρτο, while Constantine X ἀφαιρεῖ τὸ μεσότοιχον between τὸ πολιτικὸν γένος καὶ τὸ συγκλητικόν. The Anon. Syn. Chron. describes Botaniates as going still further in this ὕβρις τῆς συγκλήτου, p. 171.

[6] Épit. XVIII. 29.

[7] Attal., p. 122, tells us that Romanus Diogenes 'made the yearly gifts which were attached to the Senatorial dignities' (ἀξιώματα). τύχη in the non-classical sense of 'rank' apears repeatedly in the Alexias.

[8] P. Grenier, Emp. Byz. Vol. II, p. 27.

[9] In III. 6, p. 83, to become part of ὁ συγκλητικὸς κατάλογος is a synonym (in a nobleman's life) for attaining man's estate.

[10] e.g. the Bryennii in II. 6, p. 57 (accounting perhaps for Anna's marriage of policy) and the Ducas family in III. 2.

wrote him 'a long letter attacking the leaders of the Senate', and this may account in a measure for the curious indulgence with which this turbulent noble was treated by the Emperor.[1] On other occasions we find the Senate, true to its old name of βουλή, called together to advise the Emperor on matters of peace or war or to ratify some decision of his.[2] They receive 'gifts and honours' at the birth of an imperial heir,[3] and in short form a rather indefinite luminous circle round the central authority.

Of special officials of many kinds, doubtless all drawn from this senatorial register, we find no lack in Anna's pages. The titles of Caesar or Sebastos, Sebastocrator, Protosebastos, and Panhypersebastos, some of them invented by Alexius, were mostly reserved for members by birth or marriage of the imperial family and did not confer any office[4]; that of νωβελλίσιμος or πρωτονωβελλίσιμος figures as a reward for service and might be given to a foreigner.[5] The posts of Great Drungary of the Fleet and Domestic of the Schools of East or West will be mentioned again when we come to military matters.

[1] XII. 7. The whole story is rather mysterious, and the fact that Alexius' sister had married one of the Taronites family (III. 4, p. 78) does not explain away the many difficulties. Why, if meditating ἀποστασία, should Gregory imprison his predecessor Dabatenus who was departing for Constantinople and had therefore, one might have thought, ceased to be a danger? Did the Emperor know of his rebellious feeling and send him to virtual exile on the Black Sea, like Theodore Gabras in VIII. 9? What was his quarrel not only with the army but with the Senate and the imperial kinsfolk, one of whom, Alexius' nephew, was his own first cousin? And above all, what was his secret power that made this said cousin afraid of being considered his partisan and caused Alexius to treat him as, long before, he had treated Urselius, merely pretending to blind him, so as in some way to satisfy public opinion? and why at the very end was the Emperor able to forgive him openly and shower benefits on him? We turn in vain for light on the subject to the three letters of Archbishop Theophylact to Gregory Taronites and one to Serblias mentioning him (Ser. II, Epp. 4, 26, 37, and Ser. I, Ep. 8, *P. G.* 126, cols. 364, 409, 432, and earlier 321). In all these Taronites appears as a person of great importance, great in peace and war, not only in the neighbourhood of the Black Sea and 'the chief town of the Colchi' (presumably Trebizond), but also in Macedonia, sending instructions to the governor of Berrhoea. His return from Colchis, clearly not the enforced return described by Anna, is a great sorrow to the people there, though a great gain to the Emperor who has in him a watchful guard and counsellor. Alexius will reward his 'good counsel and bravery', and has indeed, with his usual insight into character, always put him 'above all men'. How and when did this man become a rebel who had to be imprisoned ἐπὶ πλείονα καιρόν before being pardoned? See p. 96, note 3, above, and p. 374, below.

[2] II. 5, p. 52; XIV. 2, p. 424. It is ἐκ μέσης συγκλήτου that Alexius is proclaimed σεβαστός under Botaniates (I. 9, p. 22).

[3] VI. 8, p. 167.

[4] I. 9, p. 22; III. 4. In X. 9, and elsewhere καῖσαρ is used regularly of Nic. Bryennius (XIII. 11, p. 405). Callicles (Poem XXXII. 34), makes a dead Norman prince say: τῷ τῶν σεβαστῶν ἄξονι προσέγραφην; he seems to have married into the imperial house. See p. 453, note 6, below.

[5] VII. 8, p. 208; X. 3, p. 274; XIII. 8, p. 399, and 12, p. 416.

In civil affairs the Prefect (ἔπαρχος) of Constantinople[1] seems to have been an important personage, and we have already spoken of another very responsible official, the Logothete τῶν σεκρέτων, as well as of the secretaries and the keeper of the inkstand. Alexius was 'honoured' by Botaniates 'with the dignity τῶν προέδρων', and Du Cange defines this body as consiliarii consilii secretioris.[2] It is the πρωτοπρόεδρος καὶ κατε-πάνω τῶν ἀξιωμάτων, 'chief of official dignitaries,' who ·is sent by Alexius to administer a treaty-oath to Henry of Germany.[3] The office of Great Primicerius, which according to Bury was in the early tenth century merely that of eunuch of the bed-chamber,[4] seems in Anna's days to have involved command over certain Turkish auxiliaries.[5] In the first campaign against Robert Guiscard we also read of a special corps of βεστιαρῖται, 'officers of the wardrobe', who are among the Emperor's 'inti-mates'.[6] Originally their functions were confined to the Palace, and were often purely honorary; thus Maria the Bulgarian, daughter-in-law of John Ducas Caesar and mother of the Empress Irene, held the rank of πρωτοβεστιαρία.[7] The giving of such titles of rank without any duties attached had, so Bury tells us,[8] become gradually more and more a feature of Byzan-tine life. Subordinate officials became co-ordinate and inde-pendent, and titles of offices became mere grades of rank. Thus Alexius writes of sending twenty such honorary ἀξιώματα ac-companied by solid cash to Henry of Germany,[9] while the rank of Protosebastos conferred on the Doge, and of ὑπέρτιμος on the Venetian Patriarch, similarly bring in both cases the appro-priate ῥόγα[10] but no court duties. Enemies actual or potential are thus honoured. Sometimes the comprehensive phrase παν-τοῖαι τιμαί is used, sometimes the exact form of honour is speci-fied. Thus one Turk is made Duke of Anchialus, another becomes Sebastos, as does Bohemund,[11] though his demand for the military prize of the Domesticate of the East is not

---

[1] III. 1, pp. 71, 71; XII. 4, p. 355: 5, p. 360; XIII. 1, p. 376.   [2] II. 1, p. 43.
[3] III. 10, p. 94. This word κατεπάνω was the regular title for a military governor in the Theme of Lombardy.
[4] Imp. Admin. System, ch. D. 1 (5).   [5] IV. 4, p. 109.
[6] Ibid. Many of these official names meet us in the Novel of Alexius concerning images and Bishop Leo (Novel 22, P. G. 127, cols. 972–84), i. e. the Eparch, ὁ ἐπὶ τοῦ κανικλείου, the Primicerius, &c.
[7] II. 5, p. 54; VI. 8, p. 166. Dölger however believes that the βεστιαρῖται were originally military guards and afterwards had civil employment. He thinks the name, which he cannot explain, had only a late and accidental connexion with the imperial βεστιάριον or 'Reichszeughaus' (op. cit. pp. 31 sqq.).
[8] Op. cit.   [9] III. 10, p. 94.   [10] VI. 5, p. 161.
[11] VI. 9, p. 171: 10, p. 174; XIV. 1, p. 419. For 'honours' in general, X. 11, p. 304, and constantly elsewhere.

unnaturally ignored.[1] Finally, the Byzantine equivalent of our Birthday Honours bestowed on 'chiefs of the Senate and army' marks auspicious events in the imperial family.[2]

Governorships of important towns or provinces might be either signs of favour or a polite form of exile,[3] but this takes us away from our present subject. In Constantinople itself other officials mentioned by Anna are the ὕπατος τῶν φιλοσόφων,[4] one body vaguely termed οἱ ἐπὶ τῆς τάξεως, who seem to have done the work of marshals,[5] and another set of τὰ τῶν κοινῶν διοικοῦντες ἐν τῇ πόλει, who corresponded to our police officers.[6] There are also quartermasters for superintending food supplies,[7] attendants on the table or the bedchamber, court cooks and chief butlers,[8] and finally the court doctors.[9] In the narrative of Alexius' last illness we hear of the physician Michael Pantechnes,[10] apparently in regular attendance, and of consultants, among whom Nicolas Callicles was chief. The former was the pupil and both were the correspondents of Archbishop Theophylact of Bulgaria, so they must have been men of some importance. Anna, as we have said, does not seem to have thought them specially efficient, though in a doubtful matter of treatment she 'sided with the opinion of Callicles', perhaps because he had won fame as a poet and has left us verses that show his intimacy with the imperial house.[11]

[1] X. 11, p. 304. [2] VI. 8, p. 167.
[3] e.g. I. 16; VII. 8, p. 209; VIII. 7, 8, and 9; XII. 4, p. 356; 7, p. 364.
[4] Also called προκαθήμενος φιλοσοφίας ἁπάσης (V. 8, p. 145 : 9, p. 147). He was appointed by the Emperor. After Italus was deposed for heresy under the Patriarch Eustratius Garidas, we read in the days of the next Patriarch Nicolas (i.e. between 1084 and 1111) of Theodore Smyrnaeus, an eloquent theologian much admired by Theophylact and Callicles (Sternbach, op. cit. p. 374), occupying this post (P. G. 127, col. 973, Novel 22 of Alexius). Schemmel says that after Theodore the chair remained vacant fifty years (Die Schulen von K'pel im 12. bis 15. Jahrh.). See Du Cange's note on V. 8, p. 145 c.
[5] XIV. 3, p. 432. [6] XIII. 1, p. 378. [7] X. 10, p. 299.
[8] II. 3, p. 47; VIII. 8, p. 238; 9, p. 242; IX. 5, p. 254; X. 11; XI. 9, p. 333; XIII. 1, p. 378; XIV. 5, p. 438; XV. 2, p. 462; 6, p. 476. The chief butler Michael was 'very warlike and one of the Emperor's chief intimates'. Anna gives the alternative name for οἰνοχόος as 'pincernes' (VIII. 9, p. 242).
[9] XV. 11. The only reference to an army doctor is in IV. 4, p. 110.
[10] See Schlumberger, Sigillographie, p. 687, and Diehl in Mélanges Schlumberger, I, p. 116.
[11] See Du Cange's notes on XV. 11, pp. 496 and 497 A, and Sternbach's edition of the Poems of Callicles. There would appear to have been some jealousy between the permanent and the temporary advisers. See p. 219, note 3, above.

INTERNAL AFFAIRS

43. DISAFFECTION

THROUGHOUT his reign Alexius had trouble with the senators and their conspiracies. But in addition to that Anna's whole story points, probably often unconsciously to herself, to an alarming amount of permanent disaffection among his people in general, and she bemoans the ingratitude[1] of his subjects in not realizing all he had done and suffered for them. Military revolts will come in later, but we will consider the civil plots now.

At the very beginning of his career she speaks of the 'manifold and far-reaching confusion' (ὄχλησις) of the Empire,[2] which indeed was διεφθορυῖα ἤδη.[3] Part of this was due to the fact that there was 'no adequate army'[4] and no money to obtain one, but part also to internal confusion. We see Alexius[5] not only patching up a peace with the Turks, but also pardoning the domestic enemy Monomachatus before he can turn his attention to Robert Guiscard. Even then he has to leave his brother Isaac behind to keep Constantinople, 'and if any murmuring words were heard from his enemies as usual, to put them down'; the capital could not be trusted to be true to him in his absence.[6] We hear of murmurings and insolent whisperings and wounding disloyalty;[7] in fact the plotters and τύραννοι were so many that Anna professes to have forgotten their names.[8] The imperial and patriarchal decree of 1026,[9] anathematizing rebels and excommunicating any priest who admitted them to communion, would seem to have been singularly inoperative. Indeed, to Anna the hypocrisy and untrustworthiness of subjects is proverbial.[10] One thing to her credit is the dispassionateness with which she praises the valour while she blames the

[1] XIV. 3, p. 431. [2] III. 6, p. 83. [3] III. 8, p. 88.
[4] III. 9, p. 91. [5] III. 11 and 12.
[6] IV. 4, p. 109. So in V. 2, p. 128, Alexius is said to despair of the 'loyalty of the Greeks', and in V. 2, p. 130 the obstructive Bishop Leo relies on 'ill-disposed men, of whom there then were many, towards the government'.
[7] IV. 4, p. 109; V. 2, pp. 129, 130; VI. 3, p. 155; XII. 4, pp. 356, 357; XIII. 8, pp. 398, 399; XV. 3, p. 466. In XIV. 4, p. 434 Anna speaks of ἡ στάσις τῶν οἴκοι, and in XIV. 7, p. 449, she puts the crushing of 'the seditions of rebels' as only second to the quelling of foreign wars.
[8] V. 9, p. 148. The Anon. Syn. Chron., p. 183, speaks vaguely of many rebellions.
[9] Zach. v. Lingenthal, Jus Gr.-Rom. Vol. III, p. 320.
[10] VI. 8, p. 168. Treachery in an envoy does not seem to surprise her (V. 8, p. 145), nor the need for an emperor to hurry home from the front 'hearing a revolt rumoured' (III. 8, p. 90).

disloyalty of the turbulent men who shook the Empire.[1] Her
spirit was the same as that which made Alexius let so many
potential enemies live on quietly on their own estates.[2] It is
all the more remarkable because of the prevailing Byzantine
atmosphere of suspicion,[3] largely justified in an age of universal
treachery even among friends and kinsmen. Attempts at assassination leave him unmoved.[4] He merely clung to the presence
of the Empress at his side with her 'unsleeping eye'[5] to guard
him. How Anna reconciles this picture of her father's constant
danger and constant watchfulness with her theory of his
wonderful popularity among his subjects[6] we cannot pretend
to explain, unless indeed we assume that it was only the upper
classes and especially the senators who hated him, while the
populace were disposed to love him for the open-handedness
and affability with which all the writers credit him.[7]

Out of all the plots against the Emperor's throne and life
we may believe that of Nicephorus Diogenes, to which Anna
devotes no less than six chapters,[8] to have been the most serious.
It was probably the very gravest danger he encountered in his
whole reign. His daughter tells us that his affairs were 'in
desperate straits', and admits that even he was afraid κατ'
ἄνθρωπον with his subjects 'thus turbulent', with 'the whole of
the political and military order corrupted by the flatteries of
Diogenes',[9] and with his own 'support confined as it were to
some few individuals'. It was indeed a case of 'danger hanging
over his head', when he was liable to be murdered while asleep
or returning from the bath or playing polo, and when his enemy
was in the position of an intimate friend. It would appear that
only the determined armed rally of Alexius' supporters, notably

---

[1] So of Urselius, I. 1, p. 4; Nicephorus Bryennius, I. 5, p. 10; VII. 2, p. 191, and
X. 3, p. 276; Basilacius, I. 7, p. 17, and 9, p. 22; Theodore Gabras, VIII. 9, p. 240.
The chapters in which Cecaumenus (*Strat.* pp. 64–74) deals with would-be usurpers
and rebels are among the most instructive in his book.

[2] So Maria, Constantine Ducas, and Nicephorus Diogenes in Bk. IX. 5–end.
The same liberty had been allowed to John Ducas Caesar by Botaniates (II. 6,
p. 55). Anna is proud of her father's clemency in this respect (IX. 6, p. 256).

[3] See Ch. 12 above.

[4] IX. 5–end, especially 7, pp. 259, 260. See pp. 144 sq. above.

[5] XII. 3, p. 352.

[6] e.g. Pref. 4, p. 8; XIV. 6, p. 444, and 7, p. 448; XV. 11, p. 506.

[7] So Theodore Prodromus (*Epithalamium*, *P. G.* 133, col. 1400) praises him for
πραότης, Zonaras for being reasonable and approachable and better liked when
Irene was not by (XVIII. 29), Ordericus Vitalis for being 'amiable to all' (Pt. III,
lib. 7, ch. 4, *P. L.* 188, col. 519). See p. 48, note 6, above.

[8] IX. 5–10.

[9] The statement that Nicephorus feeling sure of the adherence of the rank and
file laid himself out to win officers and senators is twice given (IX. 6, p. 257, and
8, p. 261).

his kinsmen and connexions and his father's attendants, saved him from a popular rising to dethrone and kill him. By his own showing, in his speech to the malcontents assembled in his tent, he had again and again turned the blind eye to Nicephorus' intrigues and concealed them from the public, leaving him and his accomplices ἐπὶ ταὐτοῦ whenever possible. What he and his biographer ascribe to affection[1] and generosity we may with more plausibility put down to fear. Indeed even Anna inclines to think he consented to the blinding of Diogenes and possibly of Cecaumenus Catacalo. As she truly points out, he could not keep all the guilty men in prison, having 'not sufficient forces to set guards over so many'. For all her word-painting of trembling subjects, standing 'more dumb than fishes' while their magnanimous Emperor first reproved and then forgave them, we get a very deep impression of the impotence of the throne in the face of real danger. Alexius seems to have escaped this time by the skin of his teeth. If Ordericus Vitalis[2] is right in saying that a 'filius Diogenis Augusti' went with Bohemund to Italy in 1105 with other dispossessed heirs of previous emperors so as to stir up hatred against Alexius, it would look as if the twice-shown clemency[3] to Nicephorus had been thrown away. Even if the 'filius' was a fourth Diogenes unknown to us from other sources, gratitude must have been singularly lacking in the whole family.

An aftermath of the story of the Diogenes plot fills two and a half chapters of Book X, when a common soldier impersonates Nicephorus' dead brother Constantine. The attempt fails and the pseudo-Diogenes is captured and blinded.[4] After this disturbance has subsided and Alexius has encountered the far more formidable danger of the crusading hosts we hear of another important conspiracy,[5] hatched by nobles, men very proud of their valour and the splendour of their birth, and comprising in their number several generals and an ex-prefect of Constantinople. This Anemas plot aims at murdering Alexius over a game of chess and seizing the throne. The cat's-paw is the conveniently rich but timid and foolish senator John

---

[1] The Emperor, who saved his life at Dristra (VII. 3, p. 198), would seem to have had an unaccountable liking for this young man in spite of his gross ingratitude. He weeps and groans over his calamities, restores to him his confiscated goods, longs for his society at Constantinople, and pardons even a second plot. Anna can hardly have invented the whole of this (IX. 10).
[2] *Hist. Eccl.* Pt. III, lib. 11, ch. 9, *P. L.* 188, col. 809.
[3] IX. 10, pp. 265, 266.
[4] X. 2, p. 271, to 4, p. 279. See Chalandon on the discrepancy between Nestor and the other Russian chronicles in this matter (*op. cit.* pp. 151 and 267).
[5] XII. 5 and 6.

Solomon, turned into a 'rebel' (Anna would have us think) by the erroneous philosophical teaching of Italus.[1] He fondly believes that his accomplices mean 'to anoint him Emperor', and 'thinking he already held in his hands the empire of the Greeks', promises 'gifts and dignities to his future subjects', a phrase which seems to show that common people also were implicated. The conspiracy must indeed have been widespread, for Anna says: 'The Empire within was full of mutiny' ($\dot{a}\pi o\sigma\tau a\sigma\acute{\iota}a$)[2] in spite of Alexius' lavish bestowal of honours and money to purchase loyalty. There was however the usual leakage and treachery of the plotters against one another. It is unpleasing to read of the great Emperor allowing a resort to threats of torture in order to extract confession, and afterwards to a degrading parade of the criminals, crowned with offal and seated on oxen, through the jeering crowds of the capital. No one finally is killed or even blinded, but we feel that the Emperor has had a second great fright.

The rebellions of Gregory Taronites and Michael of Amastris[3] end surprisingly in complete reconciliation, but as they were wholly military they do not concern us here. In XIII. 1, we get another plot of civilians, and here we may suspect that Anna suppresses more than she reveals. She begins by telling us that when her father heard of Bohemund's landing in 1107 he hesitated to leave Constantinople because 'domestic affairs ($\tau\dot{a}$ $\kappa a\tau$' $o\hat{\iota}\kappa o\nu$) were once more unfavourable to him'. However, he went, and even on his march to the front he encountered the danger of assassination, which would have proved fatal but for the Hand of God and the presence of the Empress. As to this last factor Chalandon assumes that her desire to go back to the capital from Mestus shows her participation in the plot. He considers that this is further proved by her husband compelling her to go on, and by his exclamation when a specially scurrilous lampoon urging her return to Constantinople is found in his tent. 'La première pensée d'Alexis fut d'accuser Irène d'être l'auteur de ce placard.' But surely this is a great twisting of the Emperor's words, which are as follows: "$\tau o\hat{\upsilon}\tau o$ $\dot{\epsilon}\gamma\dot{\omega}$ $\mathring{\eta}$ $\sigma\acute{\upsilon}$", $\pi\rho\dot{o}s$ $\tau\dot{\eta}\nu$ $\beta a\sigma\iota\lambda\acute{\iota}\delta a$ $\dot{a}\pi o\nu\epsilon\acute{\upsilon}\sigma a s$, "$\mathring{\eta}$ $\tau\iota s$ $\tau\hat{\omega}\nu$ $\pi a\rho\acute{o}\nu\tau\omega\nu$ $\check{\epsilon}\rho\rho\iota\psi\epsilon$." Is it not far more natural to infer that Alexius suspected neither himself nor his wife but one of his followers actually present, presumably 'Theodore the brother of Aaron', and did not like to say so more openly?[4] Anna herself ascribes the whole guilt to this Aaron, illegitimate descendant of the extinct Bulgarian dynasty.[5]

---

[1] V. 9.   [2] XII. 5, p. 357.   [3] XII. 7; XIV. 3, p. 431.
[4] Op. cit. p. 274.   [5] XIII. 1, p. 376.

She says he 'incited the rebellious section to murder the Emperor', and brought his brother Theodore into it. The deed was to have been done upon Alexius 'either on meeting him in a narrow place or coming secretly upon him as he slept'; the agent was to be Aaron's savage Scythian slave Demetrius, and the weapon a two-edged sword. When all this, including the authorship of the lampoons, was discovered first by accident and then by confessions extorted from another of Aaron's slaves, the Emperor banished not only the two brothers but also their mother. The story ends abruptly, leaving us with many unanswered questions. The whole conspiracy, Anna tells us, only delayed the Emperor's march five days.

If we stand aghast at the constant evidences of disloyalty among individuals throughout Alexius' reign, it is no less startling to read of whole towns disaffected both in Asia and in Europe.[1] In Alexius' first campaign, when he tries to borrow money from the people of Amasea in Pontus so as to pay the Turks for surrendering Urselius (theoretically the town's enemy as much as the rest of the Empire's), he is shouted down and 'the people of Amasea are moved to rebellion' ($\dot{a}\pi o \sigma \tau a \sigma i a$).[2] Anna ascribes this partly to a few professional agitators, partly to the inherent folly of 'the vulgar crowd', but from her story it is evident that their final acquiescence is induced by self-interest, not loyalty. The calling together by Alexius, as imperial general, of 'all the citizens and especially those of highest rank and well off for money', and the way he tries to cajole them into advancing the sum required, with promises that it shall be faithfully repaid by the Emperor, throw an interesting light on the very slight bond that attached outlying cities to the centre of the Empire. It was touch and go whether the citizens would not set Urselius free, and Anna's picture of the 'great raging crowd' which her father, a small man, subdues by his voice and lifted hand would be worth quoting in full for its vividness, if it were original and not copied almost bodily from her husband's work. In characteristic fashion Alexius, already the arch-diplomat in his daughter's eyes, fills the people with suspicions of their chief men ('who are deceiving you, buying their own safety by your blood') and declares that they are playing a double game with Urselius and the Emperor. He grants them a night to think over the question of giving money, but is so afraid of popular violence that without waiting for

[1] Curiously enough Anna never tells us anything, good or bad, about any towns in Greece.
[2] I. 2, p. 6.

their answer he pretends to blind Urselius, in order to put him so to speak out of the running for a 'tyranny' and bring his supporters to reason. 'And this persuaded the whole populace, whether native or foreign, to contribute to the common fund like bees,'[1] after which Alexius proceeds to bring back to their allegiance the cities and fortresses all round 'that had formerly acted badly'.

Amasea and its neighbourhood, we may reflect, were far from Byzantium and might conceivably sit loosely to the interests of the Empire. But Thessalonica though not very much nearer was certainly far dearer, a most important place in fact, where the army in the *Alexias* assembles again and again. Yet the rebel Basilacius found shelter within its walls, and its doors were closed against Alexius and the Emperor whom he represented. Only a threat that he will assault and sack the town brings the inhabitants to their senses. 'The Thessalonians from fear that the city would be captured and would suffer harm, yielded an entrance to Comnenus.' Basilacius took refuge in the citadel, but 'all those who dwelt in the acropolis and guarded it drove him thence and forcibly handed him over, unwilling as he was, to the Grand Domestic'. We wonder whether Alexius' subsequent activities in Thessalonica 'setting its affairs in order' included punishment for those who had tried to flout his authority.[2]

The next town to play fast and loose with its allegiance is Durazzo, of which we shall speak at greater length later.[3] But here we feel with Anna that the presence of a large foreign population from Venice and Amalfi and other places had lowered the standard of loyalty and made the inhabitants more ready to change sides. After the defeat of Alexius outside their walls they think it prudent to surrender to Robert Guiscard;[4] after his death they do the same to Alexius, who has used his favourite trick of 'sowing dissension' and has followed it up by promises and bribes. On this occasion they murder all the partisans of Robert and 'hand over the fortress to the Emperor, after securing a complete amnesty from him'.[5] Self-interest is their sole consideration, as it is of 'the rulers of the lands and cities held by Robert' in Epirus, when after the Durazzo defeat they speedily 'despair once for all of the Emperor and go wholly over to Bohemund's side'.[6]

---

[1] I. 3, p. 7.   [2] I. 9.   [3] See Ch. 61, below.
[4] V. 1, p. 125.   [5] VI. 6, p. 163.
[6] V. 4, p. 133. Alexius' written exhortations in III. 9, p. 92, before hostilities had begun, to 'the leaders of the sea-towns and even to the islanders themselves'

Everywhere it is the same story. Unless the Emperor is there to terrorize his subjects, not only commandants play him false but cities and provinces also. Trebizond and Antioch and Acrunus are disloyal only in the person of their governors, but in the bitter times of the Coman invasion in aid of the pseudo-Diogenes it is whole towns that are traitors. At Goloe, twice chosen as a safe stronghold by Alexius in the earlier Patzinak War,[1] we read: 'The inhabitants of the town put in chains the man entrusted with the defence of the fortress and handed him over to the Comans, whom they themselves welcomed shouting joyfully.'[2] And the neighbouring towns, 'Diampolis and the rest', follow this example. Yet so venial is this felt to be that as soon as the impostor has fallen and the Comans have retreated Alexius goes once more to Goloe,[3] as a good place for distributing the requisite honours and 'great gifts' to his troops. When in this same Coman campaign the important military station Adrianople (once so hostile to Alexius[4]) and its commandant Bryennius remain staunch, after earnest entreaties from the Emperor to its 'chosen men', we are left in doubt whether it is honour or the expectation of 'many bounties' that influences their action.[5]

One more rebellion on a large scale will conclude the list, that of Crete and Cyprus, which apparently revolted simultaneously. In Crete the inhabitants do not even wait for the arrival of the imperial forces, but turn against their former leader and effect 'dreadful slaughter upon him'.[6] The island is handed over to Nicephorus Diogenes 'for his own dwelling-place'.[7] The reduction of Cyprus takes longer, even though the rebel Rhapsomates is a poor fighter and a wretched rider whom his own soldiers desert for the enemy.[8] Under a new and juster administration it seems to have remained loyal and tranquil.[9]

Before we finally leave the subject of plots against the Emperor, whether by few or by many, it is worth making a special

had failed of effect. The same motive of self-interest doubtless makes the same neighbourhood go over once more to the same Bohemund, after an interval of more than twenty years (XIII. 5, p. 390).

[1] VII. 2, p. 193; 3, p. 198.

[2] X. 3, p. 274.   [3] X. 4, p. 281.

[4] II. 6, p. 57. For troops there see VI. 14, p. 183, &c. It was presumably the head-quarters of the Domestic of the West (Chalandon, *op. cit.* p. 37, note 4).

[5] X. 2, p. 274. In XIV. 8, p. 452, we are informed that the Manichaeans in Philippopolis, who formed the majority of the inhabitants, 'tyrannized over the Christians and seized their goods, paying little or no attention to messengers from the Emperor'.

[6] IX. 2, p. 248.   [7] IX. 6, p. 256.

[8] IX. 2, p. 249.   [9] See Books XI and XIV.

study of one word which Anna constantly uses in this connexion, as indeed do all her contemporaries. In classical Greek
the word τύραννος meant 'an absolute sovereign', referring
rather to 'the irregular way in which the power was *gained* . . .
than [to] the way in which it was *exercised*. . . . However, the
word soon came to imply reproach and was used like our
tyrant.'[1] Sometimes this is the meaning in the *Alexias*, but far
more often Anna gives it the Byzantine sense of 'rebel'.[2] It is
one of her favourite words. Thus the Celt Urselius was τυραννικώτατος τὴν ψυχήν and inclining πρὸς καθαρὰν τυραννίδα; Bryennius had a 'plan of tyranny' just as his father had 'rebelled of
old' (τυραννήσας); Basilacius also was 'most tyrannous', in
aspect as well as soul. Now these three as well as George
Maniaces were all actually rebels against the emperor of the
day, and when Alexius before his revolt mysteriously notifies
John Ducas Caesar (himself stamped by his outward appearance as a former would-be usurper) of his impending τυραννίς
the meaning is the same.[3] But to Robert Guiscard the term of
'rebel' was in no sense applicable. So when Anna calls him or
his son Bohemund a τύραννος,[4] or the king of Germany accuses
the Pope of 'tyranny' for occupying the Papal throne without
his consent,[5] the idea as far as one can distinguish between the
two is rather of seizing sovereignty than of rebelling against it.[6]
The Manichaeans at Philippopolis 'tyrannized over' the Christians, having previously been 'independent rulers' (τυραννιῶντες)
in their Armenian fortresses.[7] The overbearing Scythian slaves,
Borilus and Germanus, are tyrannous[8] in our modern sense
both to the Emperor they flout and the fellow-subjects they
oppress. It would have been a 'plot of tyrannical violence' if
Alexius had taken Church property as a theft 'and not a loan'.[9]
Yet to have an εἶδος ἄξιον τυραννίδος is a fine and desirable

---

[1] Liddell and Scott. In Thucydides both Pericles and Cleon remind the
Athenians that their empire is a 'tyranny', because it has been 'unjustly gained'
(*Hist.* II. 63, and III. 37).

[2] Thus the evil teachings of Italus the philosopher made not a few of his pupils
into τυράννους, and the later history of one of them, John Solomon, shows that
rebellion is meant (V. 9, p. 148; XII. 5).

[3] I. 1, p. 4; 7, p. 17 (*bis*); II. 6, p. 55; 7, p. 57; V. 8, p. 144; X. 2, p. 274 (*bis*).

[4] e.g. I. 10, p. 23 (*bis*); 13, p. 30; 14, p. 34; XII. 9, p. 370; XIII. 2, p. 379; 3,
p. 381; 4, pp. 388, 389; 6, p. 394.

[5] I. 13, p. 31.

[6] Robert is represented as usurping power in Italy, and Bohemund at Antioch.
In the Παιδεία βασιλική of Anna's contemporary Theophylact, the 'tyrant' is a man
who seizes power by violence and bloodshed and then oppresses his people
(II. 6–11, *P. G.* 126, cols. 269–73).

[7] XIV. 8, pp. 451, 452.   [8] I. 16, p. 39; II, *passim*.

[9] VI. 3, p. 155.

thing,[1] though as this is a quotation from Euripides it is perhaps not a fair test of Anna's real sentiments. Usually of course in 'tyranny' rebellion and usurpation of power are conjoined, as in Botaniates' or Abul Cassim's achievement and Nicephorus Diogenes' aspirations.[2] Anna twice draws the distinction between enemies without and τὸ τυραννικὸν πλῆθος within.[3] The Anemas conspirators when convicted are exposed to public derision as τετυραννευκότες,[4] being men who had 'armed their tyrannous hand' to kill the Emperor.[5] Many a time did the Emperor crush 'the seditions of rebels'[6] (τὰς τῶν τυράννων στάσεις). But the full sense of cruel ruthlessness which enters into our word 'tyrant' and is to be found in Thucydides, Aristotle, and Plato[7] is altogether absent from Anna's use of the word and its derivatives.

If open conspiracy and 'tyranny' and popular discontent are common in the *Alexias*, the milder forms of insubordination that take the form of lawless contempt for authority are no less so. In one story indeed, when Theodore Gabras steals his son away from the Byzantine court, our sympathies are wholly with him, and we see not ingratitude but natural feeling when later on the son himself tries to escape, unshaken in his resolve even by the prospect of an imperial bride. Probably there was more than meets the eye, for Anna talks mysteriously of a plot and of an oath on a specially sacred relic and of 'accomplices' who, like the boy himself, are banished. As the story stands it seems emphatically 'much ado about nothing'. But graver breaches of discipline are to be found. Three times we see a civil populace ready to lynch unpopular victims, careless of what the Emperor may say.[8] In very early days we have Alexius' secretary Manganes disobeying his orders in his supposed interest.[9] The freedom of speech and behaviour of Isaac Comnenus[10] towards his sovereign brother would seem excessive even in this demo-

---

[1] Pref. 4, p. 6 as to which see Ch. 5; VI. 7, p. 165. In II. 7, p. 57, there seems to be an allusion to this phrase; cf. Nic. Bry. IV. 15, p. 96. In Nic. Acom. *John C.* 3, p. 7, and 9, p. 21 we find εἶδος τυραννικόν and τὸ εἶδος τυραννικώτατος used in a laudatory sense.

[2] VI. 11, p. 176; IX. 5, p. 255; 6, p. 257 (*bis*); 10, p. 266. So Nic. Bry. (I. 1, p. 16) says Bardas Sclerus had 'been a tyrant' (i.e. rebel) for years, though he never gained the sceptre.

[3] I. 10, p. 23; XII. 5, p. 359.   [4] XII. 6, p. 362.

[5] XII. 6, p. 361.   [6] XIV. 7, p. 449.

[7] 'To a tyrant . . . nothing is inconsistent that is expedient' (Thuc. VI. 85). 'Tyranny is fond of bad men' because it loves flattery (Arist. *Pol.* V. 11, p. 1314). 'The tyrant never tastes of true freedom or true friendship' (Plato, *Rep.* IX. 576).

[8] V. 9, p. 149; IX. 7, p. 260; XV. 10, p. 494.

[9] II. 8, p. 60; 10, p. 63.   [10] VIII. 8.

cratic age, and in the conspiracy of Nicephorus Diogenes we are
startled to see how boldly the young man intrudes on the
Emperor's privacy. In the same story one attendant rebukes
Alexius as 'mad', another applies to the suspect Nicephorus
torture 'that had not been commanded him', and it is the
Emperor's adherents not his emissaries who take the convicted
man and blind him.[1] Even if as Anna suggests this plan was
initiated or approved by her father, the execution of it was their
lawless doing. As to licence of mere words, we may note that
in a friendly critic Anna admires free speech even to her father,[2]
but any man who rails against the imperial kinsmen shows
'complete madness'[3] (ἀπόνοια παντελής). In another quarter,
the speech of Bohemund to Alexius himself as well as to his
envoys is so haughtily discourteous that one wonders they ever
came to terms, even by the mediation of Anna's persuasive
husband.[4] Throughout the history, in cajoling or coercing turbulent subjects no less than in dealing with formidable enemies,
Alexius is like an acrobat walking on eggs.

To sum up, we find internal affairs in the Empire as depicted by Anna a strange mixture of despotism and anarchy,
of theoretical adoration for a semi-divine Autocrator and
flagrant insubordination against him.[5] We see money collected
with difficulty and spent in lavish gifts; we find the Emperor
standing in daily danger from plotting and discontented subjects, yet bound by prudence or sense of dignity to waive all
severe penalties. When we consider that, as Diehl points out,[6]
between 395 and 1453 the Eastern Empire was the scene of
sixty-five revolutions, and that of 107 emperors only 34 died in
their beds, we must indeed admit that uneasy lay the head that
wore the crown of Byzantium. And Anna's pages unceasingly
remind us of the fact.

---

[1] IX. 5-10. So in Bk. II the Scythian court slaves intend to blind Alexius
without any leave from their master Botaniates. In Scylitzes, p. 868 A, we read of
torture applied (without the orders of the Emperor Botaniates) to a peculating
Logothete, so severe that he died under it.

[2] XIII. 1, p. 376.　　　　[3] XII. 7, p. 364.　　　　[4] XIII. 9-11.

[5] See Ch. 7 above and Ch. 57 below. It is an interesting fact that the scribe
of the C manuscript of the *Alexias* makes textual corrections 'quibus cautum est
ne Alexius eiusque frater Isaacius . . . ἀποστάται nominarentur'; Reifferscheid,
Praef. p. vii.

[6] *Camb. Med. Hist.* IV, p. 728.

ECCLESIASTICAL AFFAIRS

44. PATRIARCHS AND CLERGY

ANNA'S attitude to ecclesiastical matters is perhaps the most interesting side of her character, or rather of her mind. We notice at once how keen is her interest in her Church and its theology, far keener on the intellectual side than that of most moderns, to whom doctrinal hair-splittings offer less than no attraction. Next we realize how this writer, who tried so hard to weigh evidence in secular matters, forgot all sense of proportion in inveighing against God-hated heretics, and lost the humane spirit which she theoretically admires. Finally we have to try and discover how far her display of theological learning shows accuracy and real knowledge.

We must begin by a few general remarks on the state of the Greek Church in her day. The religion or superstition of individuals has been already considered; here we must think of the Church and its officers as a political institution. L. Bréhier[1] has pointed out in an interesting way how in the fourth and fifth centuries, while the West was being ravaged by barbarians, the East was the centre of the world. The rich and prosperous Byzantine Empire was the seat of the various Councils, as well as the birthplace of all heresies; it was after Egypt the nursery of monasticism, the source of Christian art, the shrine of the most precious relics, as well as in material spheres the home of manufacture and trade. Suddenly the Persian and Arabian invasions came to change the face of the world. Pilgrimages from the West to Palestine continued even after the infidel captures of Jerusalem (by Persians in 614 and Arabs in 637), but from the days of Charlemagne onwards it was the Franks and not the Byzantines who guarded the Holy Sepulchre. This fact and the long Iconoclastic controversy diminished Byzantine prestige, which had barely recovered in the eyes of Europe when the schism of 1054 finally severed East and West. The days when the Eastern Emperor could summon the whole Church to a Council, act as its chairman and execute its decrees, were for ever gone by. Whether they admitted it or not, Greek Christians were only a part and no longer the whole of the Body of Christ on earth.

Even within the Eastern Empire the Church was not supreme,

[1] *L'Église et l'Orient.*

for except in rare cases the Emperor could always overcome the Patriarch.[1] Their importance varied inversely; if one was strong[2] the other was proportionally weak, but whereas the Emperor apparently could remove an obnoxious Patriarch by his sole authority, it needed the support of a popular revolution for a Patriarch to get rid of an Emperor. The intrigues about the replacing of Cosmas by Eustratius Garidas in the Patriarchate are a clear proof of how much depended on the personality of the rival potentates, the secular and the hieratical. Botaniates is a feeble old man, so he 'obeys the words of the bishop',[3] but Cosmas is himself the tool of the Ducas family,[4] and even his 'height of virtue', or in other words his being 'full of sanctity', is discounted by τὸ ἁπλοῦν καὶ ἄπραγμον of his character, and Anna Dalassena has little trouble in having him persuaded to resign the episcopal throne and enter a monastery.[5] The patriarchs, even if as has been truly remarked almost none resisted the emperor's will with impunity in the long run, could yet make their power unpleasantly felt, as both Photius and Cerularius had in past days shown; it was a mere question of brains and character. The subordinate rôle of the four men who occupied the see in Alexius' reign, Cosmas, Eustratius Garidas, Nicolas Grammaticus, and John Agapetus (or of Chalcedon), is certainly due to their personal inefficiency. Eustratius Garidas was a eunuch and a creature of Anna Dalas-

---

[1] Pope Paschal II (Ep. 437, *P. L.* 163, col. 388), writing to Alexius about reunion, says it is easier for the Emperor to achieve it than for himself, 'quia nostrarum gentium diversitas non facile in unum potest convenire consensum. Vobis autem per omnipotentis Dei gratiam facultas patet, quia clericorum ac laicorum, praepositorum ac subditorum . . . de vestro pendent arbitrio, cum vestrae adsit benignitas voluntatis.' (There is a lacuna in the text after 'subditorum'.)

[2] The Patriarch Cerularius, according to Rambaud, wished to found 'une théocratie grecque', and aspired to wear the purple boots (*Rev. Hist.* III, 1877). His attempt ended in imprisonment and deposition at the hands of the Emperor Isaac Comnenus (1059).

[3] II. 12, p. 68.

[4] III. 2.

[5] III. 4, p. 79. We may note that the *Anon. Syn. Chron.* says that Cosmas retired from old age (p. 182), while Zonaras (XVIII. 21) and Glycas (IV, p. 332) represent him as giving up his post voluntarily, from disapproval of Alexius' methods of raising money. Under the circumstances it is strange to find Anna Dalassena calling Cosmas in to help in quieting Alexius' conscience about the sack of Constantinople (*Al.* III. 5, p. 81).

Scylitzes (p. 860 c) speaks most scornfully of Cosmas when elected after the death of John Xiphilinus: 'The Emperor [Michael VII] chose another, not from those of the Senate, nor from those of the [Great] Church, nor any other of the Byzantines named and famed for word and deed, but a certain monk Cosmas sprung from the holy city, and honoured by the Emperor with the greatest honour on account of the virtue (ἀρετή) belonging to him, for although he was τῆς ἔξωθεν σοφίας ἀγευστος καὶ ἀμύητος, yet he was adorned with various virtues; wherefore overlooking all things [beside] he placed him at the helm of the Church.'

sena's, whose ambitions he had flattered.[1] Three other writers
speak of him as contemptuously as does Anna. She tells us first
of his 'show of virtue' and later on of his gullibility when pitted
against the clever heretic Italus;[2] Zonaras, Glycas, and the
Anon. Syn. Chron. represent him as an uneducated, undistin-
guished man, fitter rather for 'a corner' than for public affairs,
who was deposed against his will.[3] Of his successor Nicolas we
also know little. Krumbacher ascribes to him some verses regulating monastic fasts,[4] but Anna, though calling him ὁ γραμ-
ματικός as well as 'most blessed', only mentions him as assisting
at the trial first of Nilus and then of the Bogomile heretics, and
helping in the drawing of Sacred Lots.[5] The *Anon. Syn. Chron.*
praises his 'poverty and self-denial' and says he founded a
monastery, but Zonaras is not enthusiastic over his learning.[6]
The next Patriarch John does not figure in Anna's pages at
all.[7] Two meagre references to former patriarchs, St. Ignatius
and John Xiphilinus,[8] exhaust all that she has to say about
previous holders of the see. On the other hand, it may be
pointed out that even a patriarch held in low esteem can fix,
with the aid of 'certain chosen members of the Holy Synod
and of the monastic body', the penance for an emperor.[9]
To him matters about the taking of church property, as well
as heretics and their refutation, are naturally brought.[10] He is
the κορυφαῖος of all (thereby enjoying the same title as the 'chief'
apostles, St. Peter and St. Paul[11]); he alone can crown sovereigns, and in the Great Church of St. Sophia he reigns
supreme.[12] The position was a great one; it was only the
occupants of it that were small.[13]

[1] III. 2, p. 75, and 4, p. 79.   [2] V. 9, p. 148.
[3] *Epit.* XVIII. 21; *Bibl. Chron.* IV, p. 332; *Anon. Syn. Chron.* p. 182. The word
γωνία occurs in all three accounts and may be the colloquial word for a cloister.
Cf. *Al.* X. 1, p. 269; XIV. 7, p. 447, and see p. 49, above. Prodromus in a poem
complaining of illness says: ἰδοὺ τελέως ἤργησα καὶ γὰρ ἐγγωνιάζω (C. Neumann,
Gr. Gesch. p. 46). The *Anon Syn. Chron.* says he was deposed 'deservedly'; Glycas says
the cause was unknown. Anna merely mentions his παραίτησις, X. 2, p. 273. In the
'Trial of Italus' Alexius says he himself took up the trial because Eustratius 'rather
dwelt at leisure and preferred peace and quiet to noisy throngs, and turned to God
alone, *Bull. inst. arch. russe de Constantinople,* Vol. II, p. 32).
[4] *G. B. L.* p. 317.
[5] In X. 1, p. 270, at the trial of Nilus we read: 'There were then present all the
body (πλήρωμα) of the Bishops and the Patriarch Nicolas himself.' Cf. XV. 8,
p. 488; 10, p. 492. For the Lots see X. 2, p. 273.
[6] *loc. cit. Epit.* XVIII. 21.
[7] Zonaras says he was versed in λόγοις τοῖς τε θύραθεν καὶ τοῖς καθ᾽ ἡμᾶς (*Epit.*
XVIII. 25).   [8] III. 3, p. 75; X. 10, p. 298.   [9] III. 5, p. 81.
[10] V. 2, p 128; 9, p. 148; X. 1, p. 270; XV. 8 and 10.
[11] X. 2, p. 273; cf. I. 12, p. 29; IX. 9, p. 265.   [12] III. 2; V. 9, p. 148.
[13] Interesting sidelights on the power of the Patriarch are thrown by the 'Trial
of Italus' (*Bull. inst. arch. russe de Constantinople, loc. cit.* p. 64), where we read of a

We will now consider the expression five times used by Anna, 'the Holy Synod'. 'Certain chosen members' of it help to assess the Emperor's penance.[1] His brother Isaac summons to St. Sophia 'the Synod and the whole body (πλήρωμα) of the Church', evidently two distinct units, to hear his intention of taking ecclesiastical treasure for military needs. The 'members of the Holy Synod' are described as ἐπ' ἐκκλησίας συνεδριάζοντες τῷ πατριάρχῃ.[2] When Bishop Leo of Chalcedon makes his second protest against this method of procuring soldiers' pay by robbing churches, he sets himself not only against the Emperor but against the considered opinions of 'the more distinguished members of the Synod'.[3] The trial of Nilus and his Armenian fellow-heretics is instituted by the Emperor, who 'collecting the chiefs of the Church, decided with them that a Synod should be held publicly concerning these men. And there was then present all the body of the bishops and the Patriarch Nicolas himself.'[4] The Synod listens to the accused Nilus, condemns him to a 'perpetual anathema', and reasserts the true orthodox doctrine. Shortly afterwards another obdurate heretic is 'also' handed over by the baffled Emperor to 'the Church' (here it would seem loosely synonymous with 'Synod'[5]), which subjects the man to the same fate as Nilus. Finally, in Anna's last Book the Bogomile heretics are tried before Alexius, 'and there were then present many of the Senate and of the Holy Synod and men chosen from the very Naziraeans (monks) for their learning'.[6] These same judges, described again as 'all of the Holy Synod and chosen men of the Naziraeans and Nicolas himself, the Patriarch of the time', condemn the misguided leader Basil to be burnt.[7]

Du Cange in his note on the first of these passages states that

disciple of Italus who had been set by the Patriarch 'over the monasteries of the West', and by two Novels of Alexius (a) *De jure patriarchae circa monasteria* (*P. G.* 127, cols. 941–5); (b) an unpublished one in a manuscript of Mt. Athos, *De exemptione montis Atho a patriarcha* (Zach. v. Lingenthal, *Jus Gr.-Rom.*, Tome III, Proleg. p. xviii, No. 44).

[1] III. 5, p. 81.   [2] V. 2, p. 128.
[3] V. 2, p. 130.   [4] X. 1, p. 270.
[5] So 'the Church' tries the heretic Italus (V. 9, p. 148). Probably in both these passages only the bishops are meant. Du Cange, in his *Glossarium med. et inf. latinitatis*, defines *Synodus* thus: 'Vox generica est scriptoribus Christianis, quibus fere semper quodvis Concilium episcoporum dicitur'. In the Orthodox Church to-day the word Synod has the same specially episcopal meaning, e.g. in the late Holy Synod of Russia which consisted of Bishops and a Procurator representing the Czar, and in the Greek Constitution drawn up in 1864, which enacts that 'the Orthodox Church of Greece . . . is governed by a Synod of Bishops' (*Encycl. Brit.*, 'Orthodox Eastern Church'). It is therefore safe to conclude that to Anna also a Synod meant 'a council of bishops'.
[6] XV. 9, p. 491.   [7] XV. 10, p. 492.

the name 'Synod' strictly belonged in Anna's day only to the four high ecclesiastical dignitaries who acted as the Patriarch's counsellors, the Great Oeconomicus, the Great Sacellarius, the Great Chartophylax, and the Chartophylax who served as Curator Sacelli. But it is clear from all the places where Anna uses the word that she gives it a wider and more general signification, treating it (as we have said) as equivalent to 'all the body of the bishops'. Other phrases of hers, doubtless including priests if not deacons also, are 'as many as were on the hieratic register' (ὅσον or ἅπαντες τοῦ ἱερατικοῦ καταλόγου, as contrasted with τὸ στρατιωτικόν or ὁ στρατιωτικὸς κατάλογος)[1] and τὸ ἱερὸν τῆς ἐκκλησίας σύνταγμα.[2] From the bishops certain λογάδες (once called γερουσία) seem to have been selected, acting like a Privy Council and liable to be summoned in advance of the main Synod.[3] But on the whole we must own that about the episcopal body, as about the senatorial, Anna gives us disappointingly little information.

Even individuals among the bishops as apart from the patriarchs do not often occupy her stage. We hear twice of Bishop Leo of Chalcedon, once as a contumacious opponent not only of the Emperor's financial methods but also of his and the whole Church's teaching about images, once as a timely apparition helping George Palaeologus in battle. His ignorance, deficiency in dialectics, and obduracy towards his kind sovereign, who finally deposes him, outweigh in Anna's mind his austerity of life and 'the superabundance of his virtue', and she seems to consider exile in Pontus his fitting fate.[4] It is perhaps natural that she should not think very admiringly of bishops when we remember that two at least of the patriarchs she mentions as well as Bishop Leo were men of no learning, and that when the highly educated but otherwise contemptible Michael VII was deposed he first entered the monastic and then the episcopal ranks.[5] The Bishop of Tripoli also plays a sorry part in a matter of trust, though it is perhaps hardly fair to cite him among bishops of the Empire.[6] On the other hand Alexius pays great heed to the accusation made against his nephew John Comnenus by the then 'Archbishop of Bulgaria', whom we know to have been the writer Theophylact of Achrida,[7] and when the

[1] VI. 3, p. 156; X. 2, p. 273. [2] XV. 9, p. 492.
[3] V. 9, p. 148; X. 1, p. 270; XV. 8, p. 488; 9, p. 492.
[4] V. 2; VII. 4, p. 199. She evidently marvels at the devotion to the bishop of her uncle George Palaeologus.
[5] I. 4, 9; 12, p. 28. [6] XIV. 2.
[7] VIII. 7, p. 236. His own four letters to 'the Sebastocrator's son' (P. G. 126, cols. 513, 529-33) throw no light on this, and Anna as usual is far from explicit. The story is mysterious in many ways.

heretic Nilus is tried 'all the body of bishops' as we saw above, is present.[1] The Patriarch of Antioch is the subject of a special provision in the treaty made by Alexius and his son John with Bohemund. The Norman is to have the town, but this is the condition which he accepts: 'I agree and swear by the God honoured in the Church of Antioch that the Patriarch of Antioch shall not be of our race, but whomsoever your Majesties shall appoint, being one of those trained in the great Church of Constantinople';[2] this was indeed an admirable device for the Empire to keep a hold on Antioch. Other provincial bishops mentioned in the *Alexias* are Eustratius of Nicaea, said to be wise both in mundane and in religious matters and specially expert in argument, and the Bishop of Philippopolis.[3] With their aid Alexius makes strenuous efforts to convert the Manichaeans.[4]

Among foreign hierarchs Anna alludes to Herbius, Archbishop of Capua, whom Alexius tries to win over,[5] to the Bishop of Bari whose 'envoy' accompanies the army of Robert Guiscard on his first Illyrian campaign,[6] and to the Bishop of Pisa who commands a fleet and stirs up 'two others of those dwelling on the sea-coast', presumably the Bishops of Genoa and (by a stretch) Florence.[7] In enumerating the witnesses to Alexius' treaty with Bohemund she mentions the Bishops of Amalfi and Taranto (honoured with the favourite episcopal epithet of 'very dear to God'), the former of whom is 'an envoy from the Pope to the Emperor', and signs for the pilgrims who cannot write.[8] It is of course part of Anna's indifference (or ignorance) as to 'barbarians' that she calls Peter the Hermit an ἐπίσκοπος and ἀρχιερεύς[9] and mentions 'bishops' quite vaguely with 'kings and dukes and counts' as commanding the crusading hosts.

In the lower ranks of the clergy we find Anna cursorily alluding both to seculars and to regulars. Not only the Bishop of Taranto but also 'the clergy with him' sign as witnesses to

---

[1] X. 1, p. 270.
[2] XIII. 12, p. 413. For the importance of this see's occupant cf. Nic. Bry. II. 28. Even Isaac Comnenus, himself Duke of the town, stood in awe of him.
[3] XIV. 8, p. 453. This same Eustratius of Nicaea is mentioned by Nicetas Acominatus (*Thes. Orth. Fid.*, *P. G.* 140, col. 136) as tinged with the heresies of his teacher Italus, and deprived of his rank as bishop. It seems hard to credit.
[4] XIV. 8, p. 453. The Preface to the *Panoplia* of Euthymius Zigabenus (*P. G.* 130, col. 21) suggests the danger of theological rivalry between an emperor and his bishops; Alexius refuted heresies but οὐ τὸ τῶν ἀρχιερέων ἔργον σφετεριζόμενος.
[5] III. 10, p. 93.   [6] III. 12, p. 99.   [7] XI. 10, p. 335.
[8] XIII. 12, pp. 415, 416. He is mentioned as an envoy from Paschal II to Alexius in a letter from the former to the latter, pleading for a Council towards reunion (*P. L.* 163, col. 389).
[9] X. 10, p. 299; XI. 6, p. 326.

Bohemund's treaty,[1] and priests (ἱερεῖς) are present with the imperial army, to perform the last rites for the dying.[2] Irene's benefactions to 'those whom from their appearance and their life she knew to be serving God and to be intent on prayer and antiphonal songs'[3] must have extended to the clergy of the various churches like the Chalcopratia.[4] Alexius furnishes 'a large body of clergy and a plentiful supply of lamps to the temple' in his Orphanage.[5] The church of St. Sophia had produced great grammarians and lexicographers.[6] In Anna's few other references to priests their vestments are specially mentioned.[7] Finally on the principle of *corruptio optimi pessima* she feels the public exposure and condemnation of the heretic Blachernites for holding 'tenets foreign to the Church' to have been a peculiarly dreadful necessity, because he was 'in holy orders' (ἱερωμένος), and even the valour and generosity of the 'Latin priest' in his single combat with Marianus Maurocatacalo do not atone in her eyes for his impiety in fighting at all.[8]

ECCLESIASTICAL AFFAIRS

45. MONKS AND CHURCH PRIVILEGES

ON the whole it may be said that Anna shows no sign of being priest-ridden, or even monk-ridden, which was far more common in those days. On the other hand she never displays on her father's behalf that economic and military jealousy of the monastic orders, as of men who would not 'pay, work, or obey', who undersold lay labour and shirked service in the army, of which N. Jorga[9] speaks, and in which he sees the true root of the Iconoclastic movement. By the twelfth century things had calmed down and images had returned to favour, 'mais sans que les couvents, surtout à Constantinople, eussent jamais regagné l'influence que la thaumaturgie des

---

[1] XIII. 12, p. 415.   [2] XV. 7, p. 482.   [3] XII. 3, p. 351.
[4] VI. 3, p. 157. Here 'the performing of hymns' is their special duty.
[5] XV. 7, p. 485.   [6] Ibid.
[7] X. 8, p. 292; XI. 8, p. 331. St. John the Evangelist twice appears thus robed (II. 7, pp. 58, 59; XII. 4, p. 355). A bishop's robe, mitre, and pallium occur in I. 12, p. 28; cf. I. 4, p. 9.
[8] X. 1, p. 270; X. 8.
[9] Paper read before the Congress of Byzantinology (*Acad. Roum. Bull.* Tome XI, pp. 147–50). He draws interesting comparisons between Iconoclasm and the similar attacks on monks and nuns in China in the fifth, sixth, and ninth centuries, in Transylvania under Maria Theresa, and in France at the Revolution of 1789. He might have added, in Spain less than a hundred years ago.

icônes' (rejected by popular sentiment as idolatrous) 'leur avait
assurée'. The great monastery of Laura, founded on Mount
Athos in 969, was for the contemplative life only, and its members were not to mix in state affairs.[1]

Accordingly, in the *Alexias* we find no 'turbulent priest'
powerful enough to cause the Emperor even a fraction of the
vexation experienced by Henry II. The patriarchs were virtually his creatures, the monks were chastened by the memory
of that hundred years' struggle.[2] Yet the part played by the
monastic orders was still very important, not least because 'the
angelic life' was, as we must constantly remind ourselves, the
usual refuge for tired or fallen greatness. The deposed Emperors
Michael VII and Nicephorus Botaniates were both forced into
monasteries;[3] the Emperor Isaac Comnenus had retired to one
voluntarily,[4] and so does Isaac the Sebastocrator just before his
death.[5] The Patriarch Cosmas on leaving his see goes to the
monastery of Callias; into a monastery in Bithynia Alexius'
brother Manuel is carried to die.[6] Anna Dalassena is represented by her granddaughter as yearning for the conventual
life,[7] and by Zonaras and the *Anon. Syn. Chron.* as having already
put on τὸ ἔνδυμα τὸ μοναχικόν.[8] When Alexius' daughter Eudocia
is ill-treated by her husband Iasites her mother's remedy is
expressed in the two words εὐθὺς ἀποκείρει.[9] The same life is
adopted by Eudocia's aunt Theodora, widow of Constantine
Diogenes.[10] The Empress Maria's retirement to the palace by
St. George's monastery of the Mangana (which together with
the Hebdomon had been deeded to her by her second husband
Botaniates) did not indeed imply any taking the veil at first;
this was afterwards forced on her by Alexius,[11] who simultaneously deprived her son Constantine of his imperial insignia. An
earlier palace upheaval had consigned Eudocia Macrembolitissa, Maria's predecessor as Empress, to a convent with her
young Diogenes sons.[12]

[1] Yet Nic. Bry. (*Hyle*, IV. 27, p. 102) speaks of Abbot Symeon of Mt. Athos as the
envoy from Alexius to Basilacius. On the Byzantine monasteries see *G.B.L.* p. 713.
[2] Baynes (*Byz. Emp.*, pp. 91–3) gives an interesting account of how the Icono-
dules headed by Theodore and the monks of Studium tried to assert the Church's
independence of the Emperor in spiritual matters, and how their attempt failed.
[3] I. 4, p. 9, and 12, p. 28; III. 1, pp. 70, 71.
[4] Psellus, *Chron.*, Const. X, Byz. T., p. 237.
[5] Zonaras, XVIII. 24. Even Alexius, according to *Anon. Syn. Chron.* p. 186, dies
τὴν τρίχα κειράμενος, though without abdicating or retiring to a cloister.
[6] III. 4, p. 79; Nic. Bry. I. 12, p. 26.   [7] III. 6, p. 82; 8, p. 88.
[8] *Epit.* XVIII. 21; *Anon. Syn. Chron.* p. 177.   [9] Zonaras, XVIII. 22.
[10] X. 2, p. 272. She 'took up the conventual life, pursuing the ascetic life most
conscientiously and turning to God alone'.
[11] III. 4, p. 80; Zonaras, XVIII. 21.   [12] IX. 6, p. 256; Nic. Bry. I. 20, p. 33.

Sometimes the 'garment of a monk' was regarded merely as a flag of truce, inglorious but reliable. Thus John Ducas Caesar had adopted it to avert the displeasure of his nephew Michael VII, but was justly afraid that soldiers would jeer at him as an 'abbot'.[1] In her own enforced retirement Anna associates only with old soldiers now tonsured, 'who had met with misfortunes and had changed from worldly tumult to the peaceful condition of monks'.[2] Their transformation was doubtless due to prudence rather than to a sense of vocation; revolutions could not harm them now.

Alexius to please his mother keeps a monk in his military tent,[3] and 'certain chosen members of the monastic body' help as we saw above in assigning the penance for the sack of Constantinople. We hear of one monk bringing news (which it is true is not believed) to an imperial general, and of another on whom is fathered a specially virulent lampoon in the Aaron conspiracy.[4] As Cinnamus speaks of monks in camp giving advice to John II[5] and Bryennius shows us Alexius using an abbot as his envoy,[6] we may fairly conclude that many of these individuals accompanied the Greek armies. Their 'gown and cowl' was supposed to be the symbol of virtue, so the Bogomiles dressed as monks, and it was Basil's 'gown' that was first burnt by the executioners. Monkish prayers, as is well known, were thought to have peculiar value.[7]

The treaty between Bohemund and Alexius was attested among others by 'the most pious head of the revered monastery' of St. Andrew's at Brindisi with two of his monks.[8] It is to the scholarly monk Euthymius Zigabenus that Alexius entrusts the compiling of a 'Panoply' against heretics, while the $\kappa\alpha\theta\eta\gamma o\acute{\nu}\mu\epsilon\nu o\iota$ of monasteries help him in training his orphan charges, and Anna speaks of all the learned among the 'Naziraeans' taking part in the controversy with the Bogomiles.[9] There is no hint in the *Alexias* that monastic morals (as well as their standard

---

[1] II. 9, pp. 61, 62, and see the whole story in Zonaras and Nicephorus Bryennius. When this Caesar took part in the Comnenus conspiracy he was living on his own estates, though he had retained the monastic garment (II. 6, p. 55).
[2] XIV. 7, p. 448.   [3] I. 8, p. 19; III. 5, p. 81.
[4] IX. 4, p. 253; XIII. 1, p. 377.
[5] *Hist.* I, 6, p. 8; see also *Alexias*, I. 8, p. 19.
[6] *Hyle*, IV. 27, p. 102. See p. 296, note 1, above.
[7] XV. 8, pp. 486, 487, and 10 p. 494. See p. 69, note 6, above.
[8] XIII. 12, p. 415.
[9] XV. 7, p. 482; 9, p. 490; and 10, p. 492. This word, derived from the Hebrew word *nāzīr*, 'separate', is found in ecclesiastical writings as early as the fourth century. Psellus uses it contemptuously for fighting monks (*Chron.* Theod., Byz. T., pp. 186–7), but in the *Alexias* it is merely a rhetorical term for 'monks' in general. See p. 100, note 1, above.

of learning) were as deplorable as we know them from other sources to have been,[1] causing the reforms of St. Christodulus[2] to be badly needed. Under Alexius also John, Patriarch of Antioch, ventured to attack the imperial custom of granting to great laymen monasteries which were consequently exposed to worldly temptations and relaxations of rule,[3] and at the end of the twelfth century Bishop Eustathius of Thessalonica was still complaining that the monks in his diocese were insubordinate, lazy, luxurious, oppressors of the peasants, and utterly uneducated.[4] Very different is Anna's picture of holy monks depending on the hospitality of Anna Dalassena,[5] and of Iberian nuns accustomed to 'go from door to door' till Alexius gave them 'a great convent, providing also for their food and appropriate garments'.[6] It is true that when Alexius is preparing to restore the church treasures which he had on two occasions, once through his brother Isaac and once personally, 'borrowed' for military needs, the 'curators of the holy monasteries' bring their βρέβια or inventories in which are recorded the 'gifts made of old by many to the holy houses'.[7] This argues riches, and the outcome argues power, among the monks, for Alexius makes handsome restitution and promises never to err in the same way again. In this instance only do we find the Autocrator bowing before the Church,[8] and here the matter was so serious that Alexius

---

[1] See p. 136, above.

[2] In 1088 Alexius, confirming the previous donation of Anna Dalassena, gave him Patmos for the site of a new monastery (Zach. v. Lingenthal, *Jus Gr. Rom.*, Vol. III, pp. 370–5. See Le Barbier, *St. Christodule et la réforme des couvents grecs*, chs. III, IV). This, according to the *Encycl. Brit.*, 'was the origin of the monastery of St. John which now owns the greater part of the southern half of Patmos'. The founder is buried in the church, which contains a chalice and embroidered crown possibly sent by Alexius from St. Sophia.

[3] Chalandon, *op. cit.* ch. x, pp. 282 sqq., deals at some length with this question.

[4] *De emend. vit. mon.* (*P.G.* 135, cols. 729–909). He ascribes much of the evil to rich endowments. The monks revelled in hot baths and fine clothes, and were so fat with over-eating that they had to ride. The Abbot was no better. He excepts the monks of Constantinople from his strictures. Prodromus inveighs against the luxury of ἡγούμενοι (*Poèmes Prodromiques*, pp. 49–71)..

[5] III. 8, p. 88. She was kind to 'priests and monks', καὶ ἄλλως φιλομόναχος οὖσα, so that she listened to the flatteries of Eustratius Garidas (III. 2, p. 75). Loparev, in his Life of St. Cyril Phileotes (reviewed in *B. Z.* VII, p. 480), says she was kind to this saint; Alexius used also to visit him in his cloister 'with his whole family'.

[6] XV. 7, p. 485. The same passage mentions 'the work of deaconesses', but unfortunately without explaining it.

[7] V. 2, p. 129 A and D; VI. 3, p. 156. These curators correspond to the οἰκονόμοι of the twenty-sixth Canon of Chalcedon.

[8] Putting the two 'borrowings' together, we find that he and Isaac make four separate excuses. First, the laws of Justinian (Novel 120, ch. 9) and the canons of the Church allowed their deed, because the money in the Emperor's hands went to conquer 'infidels', an equivalent to ransoming or preserving Christians from bondage, and so to the permitted exception as given by Du Cange (note on

published a Golden Bull 'as a sure protection' to all God's churches, expressing his own repentance and forbidding that such thefts (which according to Anna had been perpetrated by others before him)[1] should be repeated till the end of time. His daughter tells us nothing of this, but the *Anon. Syn. Chron.* gives the curious document in full.[2] The Emperor had done his deed, he says, in all innocence, thinking circumstances demanded it, but God was angry and the cause of His anger was explained to him by 'spiritual and godly men' to be these thefts. So he will make restitution, and he lays on all future emperors 'the bond of God, never to dare to touch sacred things κἂν πᾶσα ἀνάγκη βιάζεται'. For men must use their own possessions and leave God His.

Monasteries, we may observe, were put to various uses. In that of SS. Cosmo and Damian outside the city George Palaeologus keeps his personal property stored, and Irene's mother Maria is found staying; here later on Bohemund was lodged as the Emperor's guest.[3] To the nunnery of the Petriae the Emperor Botaniates consigns the leading women of the Comnenus and Ducas families, pending the result of their kinsmen's revolt.[4] From the 'so-called Pege monastery' as his base Italus

---

V. 2, p. 128 A. See also VI. 3, pp. 156, 157): 'Rerum et cimeliorum ecclesiasticorum alienatio prohibetur, excepta causa redemptionis captivorum.'

Secondly, some at least of the churches despoiled were 'long unused and deserted', so that their property 'ministered to no need'. They came under the 'superfluous possessions' which Justinian (*loc. cit.* ch. 10) allowed in certain cases to be taken. When Anna says that Isaac Comnenus recited to the Synod the 'Canons' on this point, she doubtless means all the relevant civil and canonical ordinances of which Bishop Leo of Chalcedon showed himself deplorably ignorant, consonant as they were with 'economics' and 'justice' (V. 2, and VII. 4, p. 199).

Thirdly, the Emperor did but follow the example of great men of old, Pericles, and David with the shewbread.

Fourthly, he intended to make and did actually make manifold restitution for a very small 'loan'. Anna admits that otherwise it would have been 'a theft or plot of tyrannical violence' (VI. 3, p. 155).

At the same time she wishes us to believe the investigation to have proved that nothing had been taken away except the ornamentations of gold and silver laid on the coffin of the great Empress Zoe, and a few other objects not actually counting for the sacred cult' (VI. 3, p. 156) apparently including other 'silver and gold laid on to the doors of St. Mary in Chalcopratia' (V. 2, p. 127). This can hardly be true, in view of the great opposition aroused and of the handsome yearly sum paid in compensation by Alexius (VI. 3, p. 157). See p. 253, above.

[1] VI. 3, p. 156.

[2] It is also in Zach. v. Lingenthal, *Jus Gr.-Rom.* Vol. III, pp. 355–8.

[3] II. 6, pp. 54, 55; X. 11, p. 302. Palaeologus removes his possessions on the back of the monks' beasts of burden. We have mentioned in another connexion the passage where Nicephorus Bryennius tells us that the two Comneni who were wards of Basil II lived in the Studium monastery, partly for its edifying atmosphere, partly to be near the country for drilling and hunting (*Hyle*, I. 1, p. 17).

[4] II. 5, p. 54. The leave granted them to supply their needs from their own houses must have been a welcome relief to the resources of the convent.

appears to have done his official work as Chief of the Philosophers, after Psellus had become a monk and left his post and
the capital. The Prefect of Constantinople lodges at Thessalonica in a monastery of St. John the Evangelist.[1]

Other monasteries mentioned by Anna are 'the Patriarch's
near Propontis', so called from the Patriarch St. Ignatius who
was once its abbot and was buried there,[2] and the monastic
churches of Christ our Surety at Constantinople and of the Holy
Trinity at Venosa, which contained the tombs of the Empress
Zoe and of Robert Guiscard respectively.[3] But she tells little
or nothing about what went on inside these cloisters, and we
owe our knowledge of their rules and functions in general to
the various *Typika* that have survived from her day. We are
fortunate enough to possess several,[4] notably the *Diataxis* of
Attaliates about the monastery which he founded, the *Typikon* of Pacurianus' monastery near the river Vardar, and in
Constantinople those of Irene's convent of the Cecharitomene
(where the nuns not only fasted and worked but prayed for
the dead of the imperial family[5] as well as sheltering its living
members), and of the Pantocrator and Cosmosoteira. On all
of these we have touched when considering Byzantine philanthropy; here we are regarding them purely as evidences of
monastic activity male and female. We have unfortunately not
got the *Typikon* of the Philanthropos monastery which Alexius
erected to be his burial-place,[6] but we may assume it to have
been one of these same institutions, concerned with the service
of man no less than of God. But of this aspect of monastic life
Anna Comnena gives no inkling; her monks only pray and
sing hymns and perform sacred rites.

We must now say a final word about the privileges of the
Church as a whole. Quite early in Anna's story[7] we read of

---

[1] V. 8, p. 145; XII. 4, p. 355, where the word is τέμενος, here clearly meaning
the monastic buildings attached to the church.

[2] X. 10, p. 298, and see Du Cange's note.

[3] VI. 3, p. 157, and 6, p. 163. The place of Zoe's burial is obscure. See Du
Cange's notes on VI. 3, pp. 156 B and 157 B.

[4] On *Typika*, see *G. B. L.* pp. 316–19; also Oeconomos, *Vie religieuse*, chs. X,
XI; Diehl, *Fig. Byz.*, Series II, pp. 64 sqq.; and *P. G.* 127, cols. 985–1120. See
also Ch. 18 above.

[5] The strictest precedence in honour was observed, and the anniversaries of
some deaths were observed with far greater lavishness (of money spent on the poor)
than others. Among the other minute regulations in Irene's *Typikon* we find that
every nun had to have a monthly bath (cf. pp. 113, 135, 298, note 4, above), and
the eunuch doctor, the only layman admitted within the walls, might prescribe
more if he thought fit (*P. G.* 127, col. 1080).

[6] *Anon. Syn. Chron.*, p. 186; Nic. Acom. *John C.* 2, p. 6. Leib (*cp. cit.* p. 259),
speaks of a monastery hospice for *Latins* promised or actually founded by Alexius
near Nicaea. No records of this remain.   [7] II. 5, p. 52.

Sanctuary, so well known in western Christendom. She speaks
of 'the church of Bishop Nicolas, which they are wont to call
the Refuge up to this day, once built long ago near the Great
Church,[1] for the safety of those convicted upon charges . . . so
that every one convicted upon a charge if he manages to get
into it might thereupon be freed from the penalty of the laws'.
She adds, as though to remind us of the Emperor's claim to be
head of the Church: 'For the emperors and Caesars of old
thought their subjects worthy of much care.' In this church
the most sacred spot is at τὰ εἰσόδια τοῦ ἱεροῦ βήματος (chancel),
and here Anna Dalassena sits on the ground clinging fast to the
'holy doors' and refusing to move.[2] The same idea makes the
womenfolk even of rebels as secure from harm in the ' τέμενος
of the Mother of God' as in a fortress,[3] and causes the dethroned
Botaniates 'fearing the recklessness of the army' to enter St. Sophia and feel safe.[4] The serious trouble and expense which
Alexius, as we have just seen, brought upon himself not only
from the clergy but from senate and army and people by taking
Church property shows the sanctity attached to churches as
such. The Emperor might be the Head of the Church, but he
had no rights over its buildings and no power over its purse.

ECCLESIASTICAL AFFAIRS
46. ORTHODOX DOCTRINE

FROM consideration of the outward mechanism of the
Church we will now pass to matters of dogma, but of
dogma in the abstract as opposed to the practical results on
Anna's character of her religious beliefs, an aspect of her
personality which we have already considered. The purely
intellectual standpoint about doctrine is one which certainly
interested Greeks more than Latins always, and scholars of the
twelfth century more than those of our own times. In Anna's
case such interest was honestly come by, for theological zeal

[1] Du Cange says that from the first St. Sophia had this right of sanctuary.
Note on II. 5, p. 52 c.
[2] II. 5, p. 53. We may compare the classical idea of altars as places of sanctuary,
(Thuc. V. 60 and VIII. 84), and the 'Cities of Refuge' in the Old Testament.
[3] II. 6, p. 55.
[4] II. 12, p. 68. This makes it all the more surprising that one church in the
Palace at Constantinople was apparently treated as a public passage-way, with a
'door freely open to all' into an unroofed court on one side, and other unlocked
doors leading into the imperial bedchamber on the other (XII. 6, p. 361).

was traditional in the Palace at Constantinople and even in its Gynaeceum. As early as the fifth century the orthodox Cyril had been supported by Pulcheria, sister of Theodosius II, while his enemy the heretic Nestorius found a champion in the Empress Eudocia. This rivalry of the royal sisters-in-law may well have set the fashion of theology among the ladies of the court, a fashion kept up by the great Theodora[1] of the sixth century and reaching its height under the lesser Theodora who ended the Iconoclastic movement. The Eastern Empire as we have said was the home of both heresies and councils, so that we must not be surprised to find a Byzantine princess talking glibly of canons and decrees and abstruse dogmas which are mere ghosts of the past to us. With her especially it was a case of 'bon chien chasse de race', for in her own family she had two ardent theologians. Irene could hardly eat her meals for her absorption in the Fathers[2] ('the blessed men', as they are once called) and above all in St. Maximus the Confessor,[3] difficult as he seemed to her daughter to understand. Alexius throughout the history takes upon him the role of Defender of the Faith, 'Thirteenth Apostle',[4] combating heresy in every form, and by precept and example encouraging the study of 'the sacred books'[5] above all other forms of culture.[6] For, as Rambaud has told us, 'la propagande religieuse' was the supreme glory of a Byzantine emperor.[7]

It is the fundamental maxim of Oeconomos'[8] book before quoted that 'l'empire de l'Orient n'était redevable de son unité qu'à l'alliance du christianisme avec l'hellénisme'. This fact

---

[1] She was a zealous champion of the Monophysite heresy, and as such the opponent of her husband Justinian in his enforcement of the decrees of the Council of Chalcedon.

[2] V. 9, pp. 147, 148; XII. 3, p. 351. Possibly the passage about Maria the Protovestiary's acquaintance with Euthymius Zigabenus means that she too was interested in theology (XV. 9, p. 490).

[3] Born at Constantinople about 580, and a distinguished opponent of the Monophysite and Monothelite heresies. Many quotations from him occur in the *Panoplia* of Euthymius Zigabenus (*P. G.* 130), i.e. concerning the Trinity (cols. 95 sq.), Deity (cols. 141 and 204), the Incarnation (col. 229), and the Eutychian heresy (cols. 1021 sqq.). Maximus is one of the nine Greek fathers in the miniature of Cod. vat. gr. 666, of which the other side, with Christ and the Emperor Alexius, is reproduced in Chalandon's book so often quoted.

[4] XIV. 8, p. 453.

[5] These 'sacred books' apparently comprised the Bible and the writings of the Fathers (τῶν ἁγίων) and formed part of general education (X. 1, p. 269).

[6] V. 9, p. 148. So he contended against Bishop Leo, Italus, Nilus, the Manichaeans and the Bogomiles, and trained his son-in-law on the same lines (XIV. 8, p. 453). We also possess a treatise of his against Monophysitism. This zeal is as we might expect his special glory in the eyes of Euthymius Zigabenus.

[7] *L'empire byzantin au Xᵉ siècle.* See Cinnamus, *Hist.* VI, ch. 2.

[8] *La vie religieuse dans l'emp. byz.* p. 11 (opening sentence).

made Byzantium for centuries the natural champion of orthodoxy against heathen philosophy, and against heresies and superstitions within the Church,[1] much though her work was hampered by the 'Caesaropapism' of her Emperor and the low moral and intellectual standard of many among her clergy. When in 1054 East and West separated, the Byzantines felt all the more bound to defend Christianity on their side of the world. Their Erastian views as to Church and State made them tolerant to people totally outside the Orthodox fold (such as the Latin Christians, who had a different faith from themselves, just as they had a different sovereign), but ferocious in their intolerance towards heretics who should have been loyal servants but were not. For like the Athenians of St. Paul's time, very many members of the Eastern Church were δεισιδαιμονέστεροι, and such preoccupation had combined with ignorance to produce a recrudescence of abnormal beliefs. The virulence of Anna's attack on astrology[2] clearly shows that it had a great hold on her contemporaries, in spite of the many attempts of past emperors to uproot it.[3] Just before her own day Michael Psellus, the most important intellectual personage of the eleventh century, had turned from Aristotle to Plato, and with him had revived not only learning in general but also all the recondite doctrines of the Neo-Platonic school.[4] Against these not only Alexius but his grandson Manuel fought the good fight with far more zeal than the clergy under them,[5] and it is abundantly evident that of all Anna's sources of pride over her father this was the deepest and greatest. We will consider in detail the heresies dealt with in her book, after a few preliminary remarks on general points of doctrine.

Anna has on the whole very few references to the universally accepted and non-controversial articles of our faith. She alludes once to the Incarnation in terms that we might use now ('the Only Begotten Who became man for our sakes')[6] and that were probably inspired by the Nicene Creed. She mentions the Transfiguration[7] and Our Lord's miracles (one of

---

[1] For the various Eastern heresies with unfamiliar names we can look at Nic. Acom. *Thes. Orth. Fid.* Bk. IV (*P.G.* 139, Latin version). Among the forty-four attacked by him we find the Carpocrateni, Tessaresdecatistae, Thnetopsychitae, and Parhermeneutae.

[2] VI. 7.

[3] *G. B. L.* p. 627. [4] V. 8.

[5] Nic. Acom. (*Man. Comn.* VII. 5, p. 136) disapproves of theological activities in laymen, even though sovereigns, and seems to admire Andronicus I for refusing to have such subjects discussed in his tent, greatly as he honoured learned men (*Andr. Comn.* II, ch. 5, p. 213). Cinnamus does not take this view.

[6] XV. 7, p. 484. [7] III. 6, p. 84.

them inaccurately, as we saw in considering her Biblical knowledge[1]), and on more than one occasion the incidents of His
Passion.[2] The difficulty caused by the fact that Alexius says to
the Crusaders, apparently on Maundy Thursday, 'Revere the
God slain to-day for us all' may be explained either by seeing
an allusion to 'the presanctified Host consecrated on Maundy
Thursday',[3] or by taking τήμερον more vaguely, as 'at this
season' (which would be quite in keeping with Anna's loose
way of using terms that in classical Greek have a precise meaning), or by supposing that the 'frequent summonings' of Alexius
did not succeed in collecting the Latins together till the next
day, Good Friday itself.[4] The Resurrection comes into the same
passage,[5] and 'the Holy Tomb' figures throughout as the great
magnet for pilgrims to Jerusalem.

In all this there is nothing to arrest our attention. It is only
when she turns to controversial points that Anna becomes im-
passioned. Heretics are always arrogant and obstinate; the
honourable term 'inflexible' (ἀμεταμέλητος, ἀμετάθετος, or ἀμετα-
κλινής) becomes a reproach when applied to them.[6] Bishop
Leo overclouds his 'superabundance of virtue' by ignorance and
obstinacy in false doctrines. A proud barbarian is said to
'breathe forth the spirit of Novatus',[7] the third-century Cartha-
ginian presbyter often confounded with the better-known
Novatian who shared his extreme and harsh views as to the
perpetual exclusion of the lapsed.[8] The blind scholar Didymus
'had arrived at the summit of music and geometry', but spoilt
all his attainments by falling into 'an absurd heresy'.[9] Indeed

---

[1] XV. 7; see p. 196 above.

[2] Maundy Thursday is the day of 'the Mystic Passover' (II. 10, p. 64). The
Lance, Nails, Cross, and Crown of thorns are spoken of in VIII. 9, p. 242; X. 9,
p. 295; XI. 6; XIII. 12, p. 415; XIV. 1, p. 419. In XIV. 3, p. 431 she says it
was Christ, afterwards the Sufferer and the Crucified, who gave manna to the
Israelites and led them across the Red Sea.

[3] See Murray's *Eng. Dict.* s.v. *Presanctify.*

[4] X. 9, p. 295.

[5] Also XIV. 2, p. 428.

[6] X. 1, p. 270; XV. 8, p. 489; 10, p. 492, and cf. σιδήρεος XIV. 9, p. 457. To
the *Anon. Syn. Chron.* the common herd is δεινὸς καὶ δυσμάχητος as to doctrine, a
doubtful merit, p. 179. The heretic Basil is 'a donkey hearing a lyre but not comprehending it' (*ibid.* p. 181). Theophylact applies to all heretics the words in
Matt. vii. 15, about wolves in 'sheep's clothing' (Comm. on *Matt., P. G.* 123,
col. 213), which later writers use specially for the Bogomiles.

[7] VI. 12, p. 179; X. 7, p. 288.

[8] See W. Bright, *Canons of the First Four Councils*, p. 29, note on Nicaea Canon
VIII concerning the 'Novatians or self-styled Cathari'. L. Pullan, *The Church of
the Fathers*, p. 163, says that by preaching that 'the Church cannot forgive mortal
sin' they 'ministered as much to spiritual pride in the unfallen as to despair in the
fallen'. Hence the adoption of the name as the archetype of arrogance.

[9] IX. 10, p. 266. The extant writings of Didymus the Blind, the fourth-century

there is nothing which in Anna's eye heresy cannot spoil; it is a taint, a corruption, an unforgivable sin.[1]

The dead-and-gone Novatus and Didymus, to say nothing of Alexius' living heretical foes, are singled out by name for reprobation. But at least two other heresies, that of Nestorius and that of the Theopaschites, are so to speak glanced at by Anna on more than one occasion. By insisting on the term Theotokos, Theometor,[2] Anna expresses her belief that the B.V.M. was not only the mother of the human nature of Christ but 'the Mother of God'. Possibly she had read in the *Panoplia* of Euthymius Zigabenus[3] the quotation from John Damascene,

writer of Alexandria, i.e. exegetical fragments and treatises *De Trinitate, De Spiritu Sancto*, preserved in Saint Jerome's Latin translation, show practically no signs of the heresies which caused him to be condemned by the Fifth, Sixth, and Seventh General Councils; they contain only a slight trace of belief in the pre-existence of the soul. In the Fifth Council (Constantinople II, 553) he is anathematized in the edict by which the Patriarch Eutychius of Constantinople gave effect to the decrees of the Council. In Canon I of the non-oecumenical Council in Trullo, 692, called by Justinian II to set down the decisions of the Fifth and of the Sixth (Constantinople III, 681) there is a reference to the sentence passed on Origen and Didymus and Evagrius, 'all of whom brought back again the circlings of certain bodies and souls and deranged transmigrations'. In 787, at the Seventh General Council (or Nicaea II), the letter of the Synod to the Emperor and Empress, and also its final decree, anathematize 'the fables of Origen, Didymus, and Evagrius, in accordance with the decision of the Fifth Council held at Constantinople'. Had Anna seen heretical writings of Didymus now lost to us? Or was she simply going by the decisions of the Councils? Probably the latter.

[1] Anna twice applies λύμη to the contagion or taint of heresy (X. 1, p. 270; XV. 8, p. 489). In IX. 6, p. 257; 9, p. 263, she uses it of the evil influence of Nicephorus Diogenes. The Definition of Faith of the Council of Chalcedon, which she may well have studied, has τοῦ ψεύδους λύμη; cf. Nic. Acom. (*John C.*, 12, p. 31) of the λύμη βιοφθόρος of scurrility and luxury. In the 'Trial of Italus' men must avoid contagion even from repentant heretics (*Bull. inst. arch. russe de Constantinople*, Vol. II, p. 57). Zigabenus, in the Preface to the *Panoplia*, speaks of heresies as ἰοβόλα καὶ θεοστυγῆ. Heretics are said (in the *Synodikon for the First Sunday in Lent*, Ouspensky, *Journ. of Univ. of Odessa*, Vol. 59, p. 420) to 'spit forth the venom of loathsome heresy'.

[2] I. 16, p. 38; II. 5, p. 53; IV. 2, p. 105; VI. 9, p. 170; XII. 6, p. 361; XV. 11, p. 501.

[3] *P.G.* 130, col. 1008. This learned monk and his task are thus described by Anna, XV. 9, p. 490: 'I send those who wish to read about the whole heresy of the Bogomiles to the book called the *Doctrinal Panoply*, composed by order of my father. For the Emperor sent for a certain monk called Zygabenus, known to the imperial lady who was my maternal grandmother, and also to all those of the ecclesiastical register. He had arrived at the summit of letters (γραμματική) and was not unmindful of rhetoric, and understood dogma like no one else. On him he enjoined to set forth all the heresies each by itself and after each to write down the refutations of the holy Fathers, including the heresy of these Bogomiles as that impious Basil had expounded it. This book the Emperor named the *Doctrinal Panoply*, and to this day the writings are so called.' This account agrees with what Zigabenus himself, full of admiration and praise for his sovereign's theological zeal, says in his Preface to the work, and also in his three Poems to Alexius, published by C. Neumann in his *Gr. Geschichtschreiber*, pp. 33–5. The quotations from the Fathers are arms collected to 'overthrow the walls of doctrines hated by God and deceiving the people'.

calling Nestorius 'impure, horrible, a Jew in mind,[1] a vessel of dishonour', for denying that Mary was θεοτόκος[2] and for styling Christ 'God-bearer' (θεοφόρος) instead of God incarnate.

The heresy of the Theopaschites is described by the *Encyclopaedia Britannica* as 'a variety of Monophysitism', held by 'those who accepted the formula that in the death of Christ God had suffered and been crucified'. Anna is doubtless alluding to this controversial question when she speaks of τὰ πάθη τοῦ ἀπαθοῦς καὶ σωτῆρος Χριστοῦ.[3] If we turn to Leontius of Byzantium[4] we find a long discussion as to how the Second Person of the Impassible Trinity could be passible, i.e. suffer on our behalf. Arguments and counter-arguments follow at bewildering length, but one thing is made clear: the Divine Nature of each Person of the Trinity is impassible, and though Christ was passible before His Resurrection, He became impassible afterwards, and thereby achieved 'the impassibility of all human nature for all ages'. St. Ignatius puts the matter shortly:[5] Christ, Son of Mary and of God, was first παθητός, καὶ τότε (i.e. after His Resurrection) ἀπαθής. It is surely possible that τότε (after ἀπαθοῦς) may have fallen out of the text of the *Alexias* in the passage just quoted.[6]

[1] Under the circumstances the absence of references to the Jews in the *Alexias* is remarkable. We read of 'Hebrews' in Jerusalem (XI. 6, p. 327), of Zedekiah, the last King of the Jews (VII. 3, p. 195), and of a few men with possibly Jewish names, two Aarons (XIII. 1), Solomon (XII. 5 and 6), and Elias, of whom the three first were conspirators and the last may have been a runaway slave (X. 7, p. 288). Osler (*Life*, Vol. II, p. 403) says: 'In the early Middle Ages the Jewish physicians played a role of the first importance as preservers and transmitters of ancient knowledge. With the fall of Rome the broad stream of Greek science in Western Europe . . . filtered through in three streams—one in South Italy, the other in Byzantium, and a third through Islam. . . . With the Byzantine stream the Jews seem to have had little to do.' Jorga (p. 143) says that Jews took no part in public life at Constantinople.

[2] On the other hand it is instructive to find Italus treated as 'absurd or impious' for *believing in* τὴν Θεοτόκον whereas it is only right to *believe in* Deity (θεότης); he ought to have said that he *believed that* the Theotokos was a virgin and was θεοτόκος κυρίως ('Trial of Italus', *loc. cit.* p. 54).

[3] XIII. 12, p. 415.

[4] *P. G.* 86, 1768 d, chs. vi–xi, and cf. Athenagoras, *Legatio pro Christianis* (*P. G.* 6, col. 908).

[5] *Epistle to the Ephesians* (*P. G.* 5, col. 652).

[6] The dogma involved was one on which the Greek theologians bestowed much thought, as we see from the quotations in the *Panoplia*. It is correct to say that 'God suffered in the flesh', incorrect to say that Deity (θεότης) did so (*P. G.* 130, col. 257). Athanasius said of St. Paul οὐ τὴν θεότητα πεπονθέναι φησὶν . . . ἀλλὰ τὸ πρόσλημμα, i.e. the assumed human flesh (col. 309). The same Father made use of this phrase Θεὸς ὢν ἀπαθὴς σάρκα παθητὴν ἔλαβεν (col. 448). St. John Damascene said, 'The impassible divinity of the Word, joined in hypostatic union with the flesh, when the flesh suffered, remained impassible' (col. 1064). Gregory Nazianzen spoke of Christ as παθητὸς σαρκί, ἀπαθὴς θεότητι (col. 884). Perhaps the best explanation, if such a word can be used, is that quoted by Zigabenus from Athanasius, stating that when we say 'Christ' we refer to the conjunction of the two

Two other theological terms are used by Anna in a technical though not a controversial sense, θεολογία and οἰκονομία. Liddell and Scott thus define the former word: 'the doctrine of the Divine Nature of Christ, opposed to οἰκονομία, His human nature'. Both are the objects of the Bogomiles' derision.[1] Elsewhere Anna often uses οἰκονομία in the non-religious sense of 'arrangement, contrivance', and the like.[2]

ECCLESIASTICAL AFFAIRS

47. THE PAPACY

WE now come to the passages where Anna definitely challenges and condemns some idea as false. The first person of whom she falls foul is the Pope. To begin with, it is noticeable that she never gives him his name, whether it is Gregory VII, 1073–85[3] (whose relations with Robert Guiscard and Henry of Germany are described at considerable length), or his short-lived successor Victor III, 1086–7, or Urban II, 1088–99, whose part in the First Crusade she passes over in complete silence,[4] or Paschal II, 1099–1118, whom Bohemund, according to her, won over by libels on the Greeks but who sends to Alexius an

natures. 'And thus it is possible to say correctly that Christ suffered, since this name signifies two things at once, the impassible Word and the passible flesh' (col. 1104).

In his *Discourse against Armenians* (*Anal. Hierosol.* I, p. 119) Alexius himself deals with this question, saying: 'He suffered in the flesh passible by nature, and not the Deity but the flesh underwent death. For the Deity being impassible in its nature remained impassible, but the flesh suffered being passible. For this reason there are two natures in the one person of Christ, one passible, the other impassible.' With such a father we cannot wonder at Anna's theological meticulousness.

[1] XV. 8, p. 488. The two are coupled together in a quotation from St. John Damascene in Zigabenus, *Panoplia*, col. 188, as follows: οὐδὲ πάντα ἄρρητα οὐδὲ πάντα ῥητά, τά τε τῆς θεολογίας τά τε τῆς οἰκονομίας. The word θεολογία constantly occurs in the *Panoplia* meaning 'Godhead'. In the *Chalcedonian Definition of Faith* (W. Bright, *op. cit.* p. xxxiv) we get τὸ τῆς δι' ἡμᾶς τοῦ κυρίου οἰκονομίας μυστήριον, which Bright translates as 'the sacred truth of the Incarnation' (of the Lord for our sakes). In *Panoplia*, col. 56, we get the phrase that Christ is τὴν τῶν ἀνθρώπων σωτηρίαν οἰκονομῶν. Ottley (*Doctrine of the Incarnation*, p. 565) says this theological use of οἰκονομία was derived from *Eph.* I. 10, where A.V. translates 'Dispensation'.

[2] e.g. V. 2, p. 129; XI. 5, p. 322; XII. 1, p. 347; XIII. 9, p. 401, and 12, p. 408; XIV. 2, p. 427. In the *Prologue* to her will Anna has the curious expression: ὁ τρόπος τῆς οἰκονομίας, meaning in this instance Death (line 11).

[3] I. 13; III. 10, p. 93; and V. 3. Gregory died in the same year as Robert, 1085.

[4] See the reasons she gives for the Crusade in X. 5.

envoy mentioned as a witness to the Norman treaty.[1] In the second place, she is at great pains to represent the Pope as a mere man, with characteristics like other men, capable indeed of most shocking actions. Oster blames her severely for having circulated a wholly untrue report that Gregory VII mutilated the envoys of Henry of Germany,[2] and explains the circumstance on which the report was founded. In this instance prejudice may have made her glad to believe hearsay evidence, but it is hard to see how at her distance she could have verified it, especially as after the events of her fifth Book all connexion with the German Empire seems to have ceased.

But even in the incidents which she describes truthfully her tone about the Papacy is antagonistic and almost contemptuous.[3] The great investiture contest between Gregory and Henry is dismissed in a few words. The Emperor is accused of 'selling benefices for gifts, and bestowing episcopal honours on unworthy men',[4] while the vital fact thus expressed by Chalandon,[5] 'depuis la mort de Léon VIII (965) c'est le consentement de l'empereur [d'occident] qui fait la légitimité du pape', receives from her this cursory notice:[6] 'But the King of Germany accused the Pope of tyranny' [in the sense of 'usurpation of power'] 'because he had seized the apostolic throne without his consent.' If he does not give it up the Emperor will turn him out $\mu\epsilon\theta$' $\ddot{v}\beta\rho\epsilon\omega\varsigma$. We must not forget that since the final breach of 1054 with Rome in the time of Pope Leo IX and the Patriarch Cerularius, the Eastern Christians had had less occasion for exact knowledge about Papal affairs.[7] In this case at any rate Anna represents the Pope as tacitly admitting the Emperor's claim, and glad enough to be reinstated on his throne by Robert Guiscard, though not till after hesitation and

---

[1] XII. 8; XIII. 12, p. 416. In 1091 Alexius was expecting 'mercenaries from Rome' (VIII. 5, p. 230), i. e. from Urban II—and ten years earlier than that he had tried to make an alliance with 'the Pope of Rome' [Gregory VII] 'against Robert' (III. 10, p. 93).

[2] I. 13, p. 31. She calls the Pope a barbarian and $\kappa\alpha\tau\dot{\alpha}\pi\tau\nu\sigma\tau\sigma\varsigma$, and says his deed especially against envoys was 'most monstrous, exceeding barbaric violence', and 'unworthy not only of a bishop, but of any man bearing even the name of Christian'.

[3] She does indeed begin by saying that the Papal throne was 'a noble sovereignty, defended by troops of all sorts ' (I. 13, p. 30), but she at once proceeds to depreciate its possessor.

[4] I. 13, p. 31. We may compare Canon II of the Council of Chalcedon against simony and kindred faults.

[5] Hist. de la domination normande, p. 26. He cites in support Mgr. Duchesne's Les premiers temps de l'état pontifical, p. 346.

[6] I. 13, p. 31.

[7] Letters had however passed between the Byzantine court and the Pope, as a reference to Hagenmeyer's Kreuzzugsbriefe will show. See p. 312 below.

delays and excuses of a mortifying nature.[1] In other ways Gregory is like any other 'barbarian'. He makes mundane alliances and then breaks his oath; he goes to war, 'this man of peace and disciple of the Man of Peace', and is allured by the same bribes as any temporal monarch.[2] About Paschal II she is frankly patronizing. When Bohemund crosses to Italy in 1105 and rouses hatred against Alexius,[3] he first of all manages by a skilful piece of propaganda[4] to 'persuade the archi-hieratical (i.e. Papal) mind that it had been reasonably stirred up against the hostility of the Greeks', and so wins the sympathy of 'many among the more boorish and ignorant' Italians. Then follows the comment: 'For who of the barbarians near and far would not have come of his own accord to war against us, when the archi-hieratical mind was inclined that way, and when a man apparently fair-minded was arming all his horse and men and military forces?' Surely no rabid Protestant could have been more anxious to belittle the Successor of St. Peter.[5]

Her attitude is indeed dictated by Orthodox loyalty, which makes all her remarks about the popes 'tendencious'. It is therefore worth while to consider even at some length what the Greek position then was. We will begin by quoting in full Anna's remarks in Book I, ch. 13.

'This', i.e. the mutilation of the German envoys,

'was the deed of the chief bishop and of one who had become president of the whole inhabited world, as indeed the Latins say and think, for such is their vain pretension. Whereas, when the sceptre passed from Rome hither to our native land and our imperial city, the episcopal rank of sovereignty passed also as a matter of course. And from the beginning the emperors have given the pre-eminence to the bishop's throne of Constantinople, and especially the Council of Chalcedon brought the see of Constantinople up to the highest place, and set the dioceses throughout the world under it.'

As a matter of fact Anna's non-Catholic wish is father to her thought. The question of the relative positions and privileges

[1] I. 13, pp. 33, 34; V. 3, pp. 132, 133.
[2] I. 13; III. 10, p. 93. Thus he gives Robert Guiscard worldly reward for military aid (V. 3, p. 133). Strangely enough Anna does not mention what we know from a letter of his own, that he believed in the pseudo-Michael and did his best to arouse the faithful on that impostor's behalf (Leib, *op. cit.* pp. 16–18).
[3] XII. 1 and 8.
[4] He exhibits some Scythians captured from the Greek army as a proof that Alexius was using heathen savages to fight Christians (XII. 8, p. 367). See p. 88, note 4, above.
[5] Yet she lets us see that a pilgrimage to Rome 'to worship at the shrine of the chief apostles' was common for Byzantine monks (I. 12, p. 29).

of Rome and Constantinople, as established by the Councils of Constantinople I (381) and Chalcedon (451),[1] is so ably dealt with in William Bright's *Canons of the first four General Councils* that we need only quote from his translation and his notes.

First, *Constantinople I, Canon III.* 'However, the Bishop of Constantinople is to have honorary pre-eminence (τὰ πρεσβεῖα τῆς τιμῆς) after the Bishop of Rome, because Constantinople is the New Rome.'

Bright says:

'This is a brief but momentous provision connected with the preceding canon, which had ruled that bishops were not to interfere in the affairs of other dioceses. The word πρεσβεῖα by itself . . . means prerogatives or privileges; but here the qualifying addition τῆς τιμῆς limits its scope to an honorary precedency . . . as distinct from any peculiar authority. . . . Such a precedency, or priority of rank, or primacy of honour, is implicitly recognized as belonging to the see of Rome in regard to all other sees whatever, the Constantinopolitan included, even as in the secular order Old Rome continued to rank above New Rome.'

He continues: 'An absolute priority being reserved to the see of Rome, precedency over all other sees is conferred *de novo* on that of Constantinople.'

We come next to *Chalcedon, Canon XXVIII*:

'We, following in all things the determinations of the holy fathers, do ourselves also adopt the same determination and resolution respecting the privileges (πρεσβείων) of the most holy church of . . . Constantinople, New Rome. For the fathers naturally assigned privileges to the see (θρόνῳ) of the elder Rome, because that city was imperial; and taking the same point of view, the 150 religious bishops[2] awarded the same privileges to the most holy see of New Rome, judging with good reason that the city which was honoured with the sovereignty and senate, and which enjoyed the same privileges with the elder imperial Rome, should also in matters ecclesiastical be dignified like her, holding the second place after her (δευτέραν μετ᾽ ἐκείνην ὑπάρχουσαν).'

The Greeks argued that if the reason assigned by *Chalcedon, Canon XXVIII* for Rome's supremacy (i.e. that it was 'imperial') was once admitted, then, when Empire had obviously ceased to exist at Rome and was in fact flourishing at Constantinople, the claims of Rome to supremacy were as a matter of course transferred to the New Rome her successor. Anna never calls

---

[1] Respectively the Second and Fourth General Councils.
[2] i.e. the Council of Constantinople I, 381. See Bright, *op. cit.* p. 91.

the Emperor of Germany 'Basileus' but only 'Rex', and thus even if it was at Rome that he theoretically reigned, this capital could not in her day be said βασιλεύειν. Against this point of view Bright makes the following statement in commenting on *Constantinople I, Canon III*:[1]

'The reason given, because the city of Constantine is a New Rome, implies that the existing precedency of the Roman see has, like that of the Constantinopolitan, a basis simply political, the imperial majesty of Old Rome itself. . . . Such a representation was unfaithful to the facts. The Church of Rome was what it was, the first of all Churches, for a variety of reasons ecclesiastical as well as political. It owed much to the name of the City, but much also to the names of SS. Peter and Paul.'

As a matter of fact Rome admitted neither the premiss nor the Greek deduction from it. Her delegates claimed, in an early session of the Council of Chalcedon itself, several days before the twenty-eighth Canon was drawn up, that there was an ecclesiastical far more than a political ground for her 'ecclesiastical precedency', and that the Pope occupied the Chair of St. Peter.[2] And even the 'second' place was denied to Constantinople by the Papacy, which always put itself first, Alexandria second, and Antioch third, right down to the Lateran Council of 1215, by which time a *Latin* patriarchate had been established at Constantinople. Still, the twenty-eighth Canon being accepted and still held by the whole Eastern Church,[3] it was possible for a Byzantine princess of the twelfth century without wilful disingenuousness to interpret it in the Greek fashion, and infer from it that with the passing of the political 'sceptre' from the Old Rome to the New, 'the episcopal rank of sovereignty' had also changed its place.[4]

The reason for what may be thought disproportionate length in dealing with this subject must now be given. Without a clear comprehension of Anna's views on the Papacy we cannot fully

---

[1] *Op. cit.*, p. 107.

[2] Bright, *op. cit.* pp. 226 sqq. Pope Leo I had claimed this six years before and Valentinian III had admitted it.

[3] Bright, *op. cit.* p. 233.

[4] S. Salaville in *Échos d'Orient*, XVII (1914), says, according to a review in *B. Z.* XXIII, p. 296, that Theodore of Studium (759–826) 'mit Entschiedenheit für den Primat des Petrus und des Papstes (inkl. Infallibilität) eintrat'. It was a much discussed point, throughout the centuries. Thus Leib (*op. cit.* p. 38, note 1) quotes a twelfth-century Slavonic text translated by M. Jugie, denying that Rome got her supremacy from her position as the capital of the Empire and asserting: 'C'est de la grâce divine que cette primauté a tiré son origine', because Christ said to St. Peter 'Feed my sheep'. Otherwise, argues the old writer, Milan and Ravenna would have had the primacy when the Emperors had their residence there.

appreciate her attitude towards Latin Christians and especially
those of the Crusade. Her position is so to speak a double
one, tolerance for Roman dogmas, wrath at Roman pretensions.
Members of the Latin Church are most emphatically fellow-
Christians,[1] whom not even the Thirteenth Apostle Alexius considers as heretics suitable for his proselytizing attacks; and as
we have already said Anna has no more quarrel with their
separate ecclesiastical allegiance than with their separate political.[2] Even Robert Guiscard and Bohemund, though accused
of 'barbarism' and every kind of perfidy, are never blamed for
schism. Ordinations in the two branches of the Church were
for a long time interchangeable,[3] and a Norman Duke of
Antioch is willing to swear that the 'patriarch' of that see
should always be appointed by the Emperor from the clergy of
St. Sophia: 'Yea, let such an one mount the throne in Antioch
and he shall perform all episcopal acts, in laying on of hands
and the other ecclesiastical functions, according to the privilege
of that throne.'[4] (On the part of Alexius, as we have already
had occasion to point out, this was doubtless a political precaution for strengthening Greek influence, not a religious one.[5])
Leib has devoted his whole book[6] to proving that even after
the rupture of 1054, though the Greek clergy might gird at the
Latin ritual and regulations, there were amicable relations between Rome and Byzantium. Courteous messages and letters
were interchanged,[7] and care displayed for the other's interests;[8]
indeed the first Crusade itself was largely due to Papal sympathy with Greek troubles.[9] Efforts at reunion to be achieved

---

[1] I. 12, p. 29: 13, p. 32; X. 8, p. 291, and 9, p. 295. In III. 10, p. 93, Alexius
addresses the German Emperor as 'most Christian Brother'.

[2] It is only when they in her opinion break deliberate oaths of homage that
they become 'rebels': there is no hint that they are rebels from the Christian Faith.

[3] Celestine III (1191–8) had specially to instruct the Archbishop of Otranto
'que les ordinations doivent être faites par les évêques du même rite'. See Gay,
paper read before Congress of Byzantinology, Bukharest, *Acad. Roum. Bull.*, Tome XI,
p. 135.   [4] XIII. 12, p. 413, date 1108.

[5] After the death of the legate Adhémar in 1098 the Crusaders forcibly set up a
Latin Patriarch at Antioch, and the Greek occupant of the see retired to Constantinople, where he doubtless influenced Alexius in the direction of the stipulation
later exacted by treaty; see p. 294 above and pp. 475–6 below.

[6] E. Caspar, in reviewing it in *B. Z.* XXVI (p. 102), demurs to its statements
as one-sided.

[7] Pope Victor II writes to Anna Dalassena as his dear daughter, prays for her
and her family and exhorts her to remember Rome as her first mother. So Simeon
Patriarch of Jerusalem joins with Adhémar the Legate in addressing to Pope
Urban II a letter in the name of the clergy and laity of both communions.

[8] Alexius refused to countenance the antipope Clement III.

[9] The presence of Byzantine envoys at the Council of Piacenza, held in 1095 by
Urban II, seems to Tout (*The Empire and the Papacy*, pp. 138, 175) a proof of Alexius'
tendency towards 'imploring Latin help against the Turks', but Chalandon

by the calling of a Council were made, however fruitlessly, up to and even after 1204.[1] At Mount Athos 180 monasteries, Greek, Georgian, Armenian, and Latin, existed peaceably side by side. Alexius himself sent presents to the Abbots of Cluny and Monte Cassino, in addition to enriching the churches of Venice and Pisa, both faithful to Rome, while the Norman Count Roger in Magna Graecia founded Basilian houses as well as Cistercian, and the Popes favoured Grottaferrata. The prohibition by the Emperor of the Latin rite of unleavened bread in the Venetian, English, Amalfitan, and French churches of Constantinople was probably only a retaliation for his excommunication by Gregory VII, the champion of Michael VII. When the excommunication was removed (apparently not till the days of Urban II in 1089),[2] so was the prohibition. Not only sovereigns and generals but clergy and common people in the two communions remained on friendly terms,[3] and the bond was always that of common Christianity.[4] Differences of dogma and ritual, the famous 'Filioque' clause, and the Roman unleavened bread are never mentioned by Anna Comnena,[5] and she is prepared to believe that God helped the

(*Alexis Ier*, pp. 155, 156) is probably right in holding (1) that Alexius merely 'pria Urbain II de l'aider à lever des mercenaires', (2) that at this particular Council the Greek envoys had come 'pour reprendre les négotiations touchant la réunion des deux églises'. At the same time it is hard to disregard the statements of Ekkehard of Urach (*Hierosol.* chs. 5 and 6) and Bernold (*Monumenta Germaniae*, Scriptores V, p. 462) that Alexius wrote many letters to the Pope and sent envoys 'ad hunc Synodum' imploring aid 'contra paganos'. Hagenmeyer (*Kreuzzugsbriefe*, p. 41) sees in these letters 'ein nicht unwesentlicher Faktor' towards the First Crusade. See Ch. 68, below.

[1] After the hopes of reunion had been dashed, first by the antipope, then by Urban II's death, and even though the crusade which should have united Latin and Greek Christians had obviously divided them, yet Paschal II resumed negotiations with Alexius. See his letter *Ep.* 437 (*P. L.* 163, cols. 388–9), where he says the first step must be for the Patriarch of Constantinople to accept 'primatum et reverentiam sedis apostolicae'.

[2] Bernold, *loc. cit.* p. 450.

[3] Gay in the paper quoted above says (p. 134) : 'Ce n'est pas entre les chrétiens des deux rites qu'il y a antagonisme et rupture.' *Anon. Gesta Francorum* describes in ch. 39 a joint religious service at Jerusalem for Greeks and Latins, with a procession and 'masses and prayers'.

[4] *Anon. Gesta Francorum*, chs. 4 and 10, shows Bohemund and Tancred in Thrace and Asia Minor refusing to pillage 'Christians'. This is Anna's tone throughout; Greeks and Latins are to her equally 'Christian'. The massacre of Greek Christians by Latin crusaders in a village beyond the river Halys is a unique and puzzling incident (XI. 8, p. 331).

[5] Photius in his *De S. Spiritus Mystagogia* rails for ninety-six chapters against the impiety, madness, arrogance, &c., of what he calls the νέοι πνευματομάχοι, even accusing them of falsifying texts (*P. G.* 102, cols. 280–392)—and Psellus hates the Latin clergy and doctrine (*B. G. Med.* IV, pp. 348 sqq.), but his pupil Theophylact (*P. G.* 126, cols. 221–49) makes light of Latin errors and blames any who criticize them harshly. He even says that he considers those errors 'neither many, nor adequate for dividing churches' (ch. i) and ascribes them 'not to wickedness

Crusaders.[1] She sees no objection to a marriage between
Alexius' nephew and the German king's daughter,[2] and we
know that such alliances were frequent and that the contracts
never contained a word about abjuration on either side.

On the other hand, however harmless Roman Catholics
might be as to ritual and dogma, the very claim of Papal
supremacy marked them out as arrogant and presumptuous[3]
even beyond other 'barbarians', and this is the other side of
what we have called Anna's double position. We shall deal
with the Crusaders later, but we must never forget that her
indignation over the Pope's absurd pretensions predisposed her
to consider his followers as tainted with pride, overbearingness,
and greed of power.[4]

of mind as much as to ignorance' (ch. IV). Euthymius Zigabenus hardly mentions
the Latins in his *Panoplia*. Other Greek writers who dealt with Roman doctrines
without bitterness were George the Hagiorite and John of Kiev, uncle of Theodore
Prodromus, and the same mild spirit was shown on the other side by Anselm and
Grosolano. Orthodox pilgrims went to Rome, as Latins to Constantinople. Even
when the Normans had conquered South Italy and Sicily, 'là où les Grecs étaient
en nombre, le clergé resta grec'. Everywhere 'où il n'est pas question de rivalités
nationales ou politiques . . . le rite latin et le rite grec fusionnent dans l'union la
plus parfaite' (Leib, *op. cit.* p. 99). As long after the schism as 1120 we find the
Abbot of Cluny begging the Patriarch of Constantinople for his prayers, because
though their languages are different they have one Lord, one Faith, one Baptism.
    Early in the same century Guibert de Nogent, though reviling Alexius as a
tyrant stained with awful crimes, and holding the Turkish invasions to be a punishment to the Greeks for their loss of true religion, yet charitably throws the blame
of their heresies on the less heavy air of their country, producing lighter bodies
and subtler minds.
    [1] XI. 6. It may well be, as Leib believes, that the real tension between Greeks
and Latins in the Crusade only began after the death of the tactful legate Adhémar.
The persistent stealing of relics by the Latins must have been another cause; Peter
the Hermit's band pillaged churches in and near Constantinople itself (*An. Gest.
Fr.*, ch. 2).
    [2] III. 10. The contract between Michael VII and Robert Guiscard betrothing
Constantine to Helen still exists (Bezobrazov, *Russian Journ. Min. Instr. Publ.*,1889,
Tome 265).
    [3] Even the mild Theophylact says we must not accept the doctrines of the
Latins κἂν ἀπὸ τοῦ θρόνου τοὺς λόγους ποιῶνται, ὃν ὑψηλὸν ὑψηλοὶ προτιθέασι, κἂν τὴν
τοῦ Πέτρου ὁμολογίαν προβάλλωνται, κἂν τὸν ἐπ᾽ ἐκείνῃ μακαρισμὸν ἐπιφέρωσι, κἂν τὰς
κλεῖς τῆς βασιλείας ἡμῖν ἐπισείωσιν᾽ (*P. G.* 126, col. 241). There is no mistaking the
half-amused resentment over such claims, and 'shaking of the Keys'.
    [4] This attitude of mind in Anna helps to account for her misrepresentation of
the Catholic rules as to fighting clergy, of which we have already spoken.

ECCLESIASTICAL AFFAIRS
FALSE DOCTRINE
48. IMAGES

TURNING now to another controversial question, we find that one name brought forward in the uproar about church-robbery is that of Bishop Leo of Chalcedon, whose real error however was connected with a point in the Iconoclastic controversy. He withstood the alienation of Church treasure largely on the ground that its material was for ever sacred after having borne the likeness of Christ or some saint, and that it was sacrilegious to melt it down for military purposes. As the learned Ouspensky, quoted by Chalandon,[1] says, his theory was that: 'La matière dont sont faites les saintes images reste un objet saint, même lorsque l'image du saint ou du Christ en est effacée.' This was worshipping images λατρευτικῶς, οὐ σχετικῶς,[2] whereas the second Council of Nicaea (otherwise called the seventh General Council) had in 787 decided, while re-establishing the worship of images, that the sanctity of the material was 'accidental' and ceased as soon as the likeness was effaced. Anna's story is that the Emperor 'went on exhorting' Leo to 'change his opinion about images', and she implies that Alexius was supported by the 'more distinguished members of the Synod' when it came to adding after many years the penalty of banishment to that of deposition for the recalcitrant bishop. She states that even in exile he was obdurate, apparently practising some sort of hunger-strike. The account of the matter in the σημείωμα passed at the conference[3] on the subject is very different. According to this report, the Emperor having called together a large number of senators (including members of the imperial family and officials of all sorts, civil and military) together with the Patriarchs of Constantinople and Jerusalem and various bishops and abbots, as well as his brother the Sebastocrator, made a speech saying that 'being just prepared for a campaign' he had thought of leaving the matter 'to God's bishops', but decided it was too serious. Having been ardent from his mother's womb for the faith as handed down by the Fathers, he put all else 'second to the matter in hand'. Then exhorting the assembly to keep an un-

---

[1] Op. cit. p. 111. [2] V. 2, p. 129.
[3] P. G. 127, cols. 972–84, Alexius' Novel 22 taken from a manuscript which once belonged to catechumens of a monastery on Mt. Athos.

biased mind he first calls for prayer and next summons Leo. After Leo has undertaken 'to make his defence with all candour and a pure soul', part of the Canon of the seventh Council is read, as upon 'the Sunday of Orthodoxy' (still a Greek feast, dating from 843). This enacts that honourable worship (προσ-κύνησις) must be paid to images 'but, according to our faith, not the true λατρεία which beseems the divine nature only. . . . For the honour of the image passes to the prototype, and he who worships the image worships in it the person (ὑπόστασιν) of the one depicted.' Questions follow, some put forward by Alexius to elicit the orthodox answers of the council, some apparently asked by members of it desiring information. An anathema is pronounced on those who worship images not σχετικῶς but λατρευτικῶς, and it is decided that 'the likeness of Christ seen in the material (ὕλη) must not be worshipped λατρευτικῶς', and that though 'holy images partake of divine grace', yet the 'likeness' does not share in 'the divine nature' which is ἀπερίγραπτος. At last Alexius sums up: 'Towards Christ Himself the worship is λατρευτική . . . but towards His images it is . . . σχετική, otherwise ὁμωνυμική' (in the words of St. Theodore of Studium), and Leo, overcome by this weight of learning, recants his errors and accepts the dicta of the Emperor and the Council. These two narratives are hard to reconcile. The only possible explanation is that the σημείωμα represents an early stage of the proceedings, i.e. part of the Emperor's 'exhortations' to Leo, while Anna carries the history on farther, and shows us the Bishop relapsing into his old error and meeting with deposition and exile in consequence.

In the opinion of some critics, as we have seen, Iconoclasm was primarily a political movement, inspired by jealousy of the monks.[1] There was also a strong feeling that all the wonder-working images[2] out of which the monks made so much capital

---

[1] See p. 295, above.

[2] N. Jorga in his paper before the Congress of Byzantinology at Bukharest (Acad. Roum. Bull., Tome XI, p. 149), in speaking of the Iconoclasts states: 'Des empereurs dénués de toute passion calculaient bien en s'en prenant aux images sur bois, seuls objets de l'adoration, aux petits tableaux recouverts d'une armure d'argent constellée de pierres précieuses, tout en respectant sur les murs les fresques dont on n'a trouvé une seule grattée.' This directly contradicts Stephanus Diaconus (P. G. 100, cols. 1113 and 1120) who says that under Constantine V Copronymus churches were torn down ὡς ἱερὰς εἰκόνας ἐχούσας, and that the church of the B.V.M. in Blachernae, τὸν πρὶν κεκοσμημένον τοῖς διατοίχοις ὄντα . . . διὰ εἰκονικῆς ἀναζωγραφήσεως with scenes from the Life of Christ, was not only demolished but turned into an orchard and aviary; also Nicephorus the Patriarch (P. G. 100, col. 989) who relates how the same Emperor τοῦ Σωτῆρος καὶ τῶν ἁγίων οὔσας διὰ ψηφίδων χρυσῶν καὶ κηροχύτου ὕλης εἰκονογραφίας ἀπέξυσε. The whole question is a difficult one; indeed, modern critics are not even agreed as to exactly what the icons were, whether statues, figures in low relief, or pictures

led to idolatry and were harmful to the Empire.[1] But on the purely theological side Baynes[2] has pointed out that Icono-

(see above, p. 209, note 2). The words εἰκών, εἰκόνισμα, ἐκτύπωμα, χαράσσειν, γράφειν, στηλογραφεῖν, ξύειν, εἰκονογραφία, and ζωγραφικὴ ἐπιστήμη are used by Byzantine writers with that 'Unart der unscharfen Bezeichnung' of which Dölger complains in another field. When Nicephorus the Patriarch (P. G. 100, cols. 356 sqq.) discusses the meaning of γραφή and ends by saying: ὁ γράφων ἤγουν εἰκονίζων ἄνθρωπον, he leaves us none the wiser. We are not even certain whether the 'holy icon of Christ fixed above the imperial doors' and called 'The Holy Bronze' διὰ τὸν χαρακτῆρα, was a statue in the round or a low relief or a board (such as we find elsewhere called a πίναξ) painted and with metal inlaid; it was taken down and burnt, but this would have been equally possible for all three (Steph. Diac. in P. G. 100, col. 1085). This icon was replaced later, for Zonaras speaks of it as fixed up, with a πέπλος hanging before it (Épit. XVIII. 25). Baynes (Byz. Emp. p. 91) says: 'It may be questioned whether there is satisfactory evidence for any widespread use of statues in the churches of the Eastern Empire even before the Iconoclastic controversy', and Mr. Edwyn Bevan in conversation expressed the same doubt. Diehl, on the other hand (Manuel de l'art byzantin, p. 278), asserts: 'Il est certain ... qu'au début la sculpture tenait une grande place dans les églises', though he admits that theologians always thought painting 'plus sainte' and suspected statuary as pagan: furthermore, Eastern influence tended to make sculpture a mere ornament, a sort of accessory of architecture. Certainly in the instances of religious sculpture which he enumerates there are no statues in the round, only bas-reliefs on stone, ivory, or metal. As far as worship of them (pp. 361 sqq.) is concerned, it could we feel have been quite as well directed to a painted or enamelled picture as to any form of carving. Two other recent writers on the subject are O. M. Dalton (East Christian Art, Oxford, 1925) and L. Bréhier in his already quoted paper before the Bukharest Congress of Byzantinology (see p. 209, note 2, above). Dalton, in his third chapter, gives a learned disquisition on the change in the 'character of glyptic art' in the Mediterranean countries, largely due according to him to Oriental influence with its ignorance of perspective. He says (p. 162): 'The statue was eliminated by the action of aesthetic principles themselves: the process was aided by a popular antipathy to 'graven images' on the part of a large Oriental population, but was not initiated by it, still less by any ecclesiastical prohibition. The definite ban was not imposed by the Orthodox Church until 1453, probably through Mahommedan influence.' Again on p. 167 he states: 'When the cult of "images" was restored, such reliefs' [i.e. 'the crowded figure reliefs of the earlier centuries'] 'did not come back; they were as extinct as the statues; the work which they had done passed finally into the hands of the mosaicist and the painter', and on p. 179 he adds: 'Free sculpture ... practically ceased with the sixth century, though there is allusion to a few official statues much later', notably at Constantinople, down to 'Comnenian times and even later'. Low reliefs in stone, wood, ivory, and metal were as often religious as secular, but in distinctive Christian art all forms of figure sculpture were from very early days in 'a subordinate position' to painting (p. 226), in which we may include mosaics. Bréhier, on the other hand, asserts that statues in Byzantine churches were 'tolérées jusqu'au XVᵉ siècle' though rare, and that a Russian pilgrim of the fourteenth century saw at Constantinople 'un Christ de grandeur naturelle qui est comme une statue et non comme une icône'. His two other quotations from the Itinéraires russes (Soc. de l'Orient latin) hardly prove his point, as the 'angels in stone' and the 'crucifix carved in wood' might just as well be low reliefs as free sculpture.

On the whole, wherever there is no explicit information to the contrary, it seems safer always to take the 'icons' of Byzantine writers, Anna Comnena and others, not as statues or even bas-reliefs, but as pictures painted on panels or enamelled in colours with raised outlines of metal. Probably the miraculous icon at St. Maria in Blachernae belonged to one of these two classes. See pp. 77 sqq., above.

[1] The victories of the Arabs were popularly ascribed by their enemies to their hatred of idolatry.   [2] Byz. Emp., p. 90.

clastic hatred of images not only sought to deprive the faithful
of the religious help of 'sacred pictures . . . the Bible of the
uneducated', but also implied the idea that matter was evil,
which is obviously a form of 'Manichaean dualism'. He puts
the Iconodule argument thus: 'Christ by becoming flesh has
sanctified, has deified, matter; to hold that Christ cannot duly
be represented through the medium of matter is thus really to
deny the Incarnation.' Manichaeism with its cognate heresies
will be treated last of all as most important, but the suggestion
of its connexion with Iconoclasm had to be noted here. It is
indeed curious how interwoven the various 'false teachings'
mentioned in the *Alexias* really are.

Before we close the matter of Images we must say a few words
about it as it concerns the heretic Italus. Though he was, as we
shall see, principally condemned for neo-Platonic ideas, he is
accused by Anna of 'insults to the august images of the Saints',[1]
a charge which seems to have been brought against him in his
trial (of which an account has come down to us), since he denies
having struck an image of Our Lord with a stone or incited others
so to do. But on the other hand he displayed towards images an
undue and excessive reverence, in that like Leo before him he
professed to λατρεύειν the image of Christ, whereas the Catholic
doctrine as we have said is that λατρεία belongs to deity only;
as true believers we κατασπαζόμεθα σχετικῶς τὰς εἰκόνας.[2] The
Synodikon for the first Sunday in Lent, which attacks a number
of heresies prevalent under Manuel I, praises those who worship
images (for the εἰκονομάχος αἵρεσις is μᾶλλον χριστομάχος) but
only those who do so κατὰ σχέσιν.[3] The whole controversy is
summarized by Euthymius Zigabenus,[4] with whose words,
culled by him from various authorities, we may conclude:
'Worship towards Christ Himself is λατρευτικὴ καὶ φυσική . . . that
towards the image of Christ is σχετικὴ καὶ ὁμωνυμική. For I worship the Christ in it, which is σχετικὴ προσκύνησις καὶ ὑποστατική.'

---

[1] V. 9, p. 149.
[2] 'Trial of Italus' (*Bull. inst. arch. russe de Constantinople*, Vol. II, pp. 54, 55). It is
interesting to note that his master Iamblichus taught the innate power of images,
while Porphyry, at any rate in his later works, did not (J. Bidez, *Vie de Porphyre*,
p. 21 and elsewhere).
[3] *Synodikon* for the First Sunday in Lent, pp. 415, 419.
[4] *Panoplia* (*P. G.* 130, col. 1168).

ECCLESIASTICAL AFFAIRS

FALSE DOCTRINE

49. NEO-PLATONISTS

THE story of Italus,[1] like that of Bishop Leo, is an instance
of a man's being accused of one thing when his real offence
lay in another, and furthermore of apparent discrepancy between
the *Alexias* and our other authorities. Italus was primarily not
a heretical theologian but a philosopher,[2] and the charges
brought against him in the 'Report of his Trial' above quoted
do not correspond at all closely to what Anna alleges. As far as
Anna personally is concerned, her disapproval of the heretic is
only a cover for her dislike of the man, 'barbarian' in origin,
speech, and temper. Her description of his violence both with
tongue and hands while browbeating his opponents rather
lacks verisimilitude if we reflect that he was appointed to one
of the most dignified of court offices, that of Chief of the Philosophers, just vacated by the great Psellus. Italus' career in the
Byzantine diplomatic service was cut short 'because he was
detected betraying the interests' of the Empire, but tolerance
for such a lapse is less surprising than the condoning by the
sovereign of sins against the stateliness of philosophy. If he is the
'Lombard' to whom Psellus writes a letter as to the difficulties
of learning,[3] his temperament would seem to have needed in-
citing to activity (such as war) rather than the reverse. But as
Anna represents him he is a violent and unrestrained man, first
an insubordinate pupil to her much-admired Psellus, and then
a lecturer who, though his ostensible subjects were Aristotle and
Plato and the neo-Platonists, yet radiated such a pernicious
influence that he turned his followers into rebels. Perhaps
political unsoundness lay at the root of the errors which the
'apostolic' Alexius felt bound to expose, even with Norman foes
still holding part of his land.[4] The task is first entrusted to

---

[1] V. 9.

[2] Ouspensky discusses the similarity between his teaching and that of Abelard
(*Journal du ministère de l'instruction publique*, September 1891).

[3] In Psellus, *De operatione daemonum, etc.*, p. 164.

[4] This raises a point as to Anna's accuracy. The 'Trial of Italus' (*loc. cit.* p. 30)
gives the date as Indiction V, i.e. between September 1, 1081 and August 31,
1082. But Anna (V. 8, p. 143) says her father deferred the expedition against the
Normans in Castoria in order to deal with the heretic, and Castoria, which was

Isaac the Sebastocrator, but he hands Italus over 'to the Church by command of his brother the Emperor', with the disastrous result that the Patriarch Eustratius Garidas is led astray. For some reason, though Italus had a great following among the nobility and especially its younger members,[1] his teaching aroused such fury among the populace that they wished to kill him and were only restrained by the Emperor. In Anna's account of the matter, these 'destructive' doctrines are 'summarized under eleven headings', and to prevent their spreading their infection further Alexius ordered Italus to denounce these headings from the ambon in St. Sophia, with head uncovered, while the crowd listened and supplied the refrain of cursing.

So far it is only his doctrines that have been anathematized and not himself, but the graver step is found necessary by the Emperor owing to the criminal's impenitence and relapse, in spite of personal exhortations from his sovereign. How long this anathema on the man himself lasted we do not know, but it seems to have been removed[2] privately and not publicly, doubtless from fear of another popular rising against the hated man. The people, clearly, no less than Alexius, thought his dogmas φθοροποιά.[3]

What then did he teach? Anna's charges against him are two: he and his followers believe in metempsychosis and the Platonic doctrine of Ideas (together with 'similar strange doctrines resembling these' but not specified), and they show disrespect to Images. With the latter charge we have dealt already. But intensified study of Platonic and neo-Platonic ideas was part of the revival of learning initiated by the great Psellus,[4] who held Aristotle in very low esteem in comparison,

recaptured by Alexius shortly before December 1, 1083, the date of Anna's own birth, was apparently not handed over by Bohemund for safe-keeping to the Celt Bryennius till the spring or summer of 1083 (see Chalandon, *op. cit.* pp. 88–91). We may well say that it is a small matter, referring to events long before Anna's own day, and that an inaccuracy may therefore be pardoned. But another explanation is suggested later; see p. 323.

[1] V. 9, p. 147 ('the youth swarmed round him'). V. 9, p. 149 ('Not a few nobles were ruined by these destructive doctrines').

[2] This is taking ὑπάγεται in V. 9, p. 149 c, as 'is withdrawn from' (the ecclesiastical anathema) and not 'is subjected to', as in the *C. S. H. B.* translation. The verb may bear either meaning, but in view of the context the former seems more likely; the fate of the doctrines is contrasted (by μέν and δέ) with the fate of the man.

[3] In the 'Trial of Italus' we read that 'the popular rush filled with zeal against the man' was so great that an 'inarticulate roar and shout rose from the concourse of those that ran together'.

[4] Rambaud (*Rev. Hist.* III, p. 264) calls Psellus 'presque un homme de la Renaissance' in this respect.

and he describes the stages[1] of his own intellectual advance as
marked by Aristotle, Plato, Plotinus, Porphyry, Iamblichus,
finally 'stopping at the most wonderful Proclus as in a very
great harbour'. Of these six authors Anna tells us that Italus
studied five, Plotinus (the master of Porphyry and Iamblichus,
and indirectly of Proclus) being rather surprisingly omitted
from her pages altogether. Porphyry comes in again in connexion with the Manichaeans.

Now in the 'Trial of Italus'[2] we find that philosopher accused
of six heresies which correspond exactly neither with Anna's
account nor with the eleven counts specified in the *Synodikon*
already mentioned. The heresies in the first document may be
summarized as follows:

1. Italus deprived the Son of divine ἀξία, apparently by mis-
use of the words ἐπιστροφή and γέγονεν (the passage is very
obscure). He followed the errors of Proclus and Iamblichus.

2. Like the Sabellians he said there was only One Person of
the Trinity.

3. Like the Arians he made the Son inferior to the Father.

4. He said Christ was born a mere man and was afterwards
deified, instead of being God made man; like the Apollinarians
he called him a 'God-bearing man' instead of a 'flesh-bearing
God'.

5. He believed *in*, and not only *truths about*, the B.V.M. (We
have dealt with this in speaking of the Theotokos.)

6. He held that Images were to be worshipped λατρευτικῶς
instead of σχετικῶς. (We have dealt with this under 'Images'.)

These six heresies were abjured by Italus, but for safety's sake
the Council decided that any one associating with him or his
disciples was liable to instant banishment. He afterwards
pleaded guilty to false doctrine under nine κεφάλαια τῆς Ἑλληνι-
κῆς ἀθεότητος γέμοντα, and was ready to abjure it, but denied
that he had struck an image of Christ with a stone. Italus was
deprived of his professorial chair and sent to a monastery 'to
receive the suitable correction', but his disciples came off lightly
and were all acquitted, a circumstance which Chalandon con-
strues as proving that 'le clergé était hostile à ces poursuites
où se trouvaient compromis plusieurs de ses membres'.[3]

---

[1] *Chron.*, Const. IX, Byz. T., p. 108. These six names are also brought in by
him in his *Summary of the Chaldaean doctrines* (*P. G.* 122, col. 1153) as having all
believed, in a greater or less degree, that the Chaldaean oracles were 'divine
voices'.

[2] *Loc. cit.* pp. 30–66. The document is headed τὰ πραχθέντα βασιλικῇ καὶ
συνοδικῇ διαγνώσει ἔν τε τῷ παλατίῳ καὶ τῇ ἁγιωτάτῃ τοῦ Θεοῦ μεγάλῃ ἐκκλησίᾳ
κατὰ τοῦ Ἰταλοῦ Ἰωάννου; cf. p. 318, note 2.

[3] *Op. cit.* p. 313.

Up to this point we have found little that would make a casual reader identify the Italus of *Alexias* V with the Italus of the 'Trial'. Anna never mentions any of his six heresies, though about many of them she felt strongly. The errors of Proclus and Iamblichus and the nine headings 'replete with Hellenic impiety' not further specified may indeed resolve themselves into 'metempsychosis and the Platonic theory of Ideas', and the striking an image with a stone could certainly be called ὑβρίζειν, even if to worship such objects λατρευτικῶς instead of σχετικῶς could not. But is it not possible to conceive of two trials of Italus, of which the Report mentions the first and Anna and the *Svnodikon* the second?[1] For the 'eleven headings' of the *Alexias* may well be the eleven counts of the *Synodikon*, though the first count refers to false teaching about the Incarnation with which Anna reproaches a later heretic Nilus and not the neo-Platonic Italus. The counts are summarized by Chalandon and Oeco-nomos, and the briefest possible abstract must here be given. Anathemas are pronounced upon:

I. New-fangled views on the Incarnation and Christ's two natures and as to how the Logos united Himself with human nature and deified the flesh which He assumed. (This bears a relation to heresy no. 4 in the 'Trial'.)

II. 'The impious doctrines of the Greeks' about souls.

III. The 'folly' of alternative beliefs in metempsychosis or annihilation of souls.

IV. The claim that Ideas are co-eternal with God.

V. Any slight put on the seven General Councils[2] and the Fathers.

VI. Disbelief in miracles.

VII. The following of Greek philosophers instead of merely reading them as a part of education. (An interesting light is hereby thrown on the contemporary attitude of Theology to-wards classical learning.)

VIII. Platonic theories, especially on the existence of Matter coevally with and independently of God, and its taking form from Ideas.[3]

IX. Unorthodox views about the resurrection of the body.

X. Belief in the pre-existence of souls, and in Universalism,

---

[1] As a matter of fact the trial described in the Report was not even the first: we read in its own pages that Italus had already given trouble under Michael VII and been condemned by a Synod.

[2] We may note that metempsychosis was condemned by the Seventh Council, Nicaea II, in 787.

[3] This is stigmatized by Zigabenus in his *Panoplia* (*P. G.* 130, col. 145), quoting from St. Maximus.

i. e. the doctrine that no punishment will be eternal.   XI gives
a *résumé* of the other ten, and is the first to contain the name
of Italus. An anathema is attached.

Of these ten counts, nos. II, III, IV, VII, VIII, and X
have definite reference to Anna's charges of belief in metempsychosis and the theory of Ideas; nos. I and VI are wholly
irrevelant, but nos. V and IX have a slight connexion with false
doctrine about the soul. The matter of Images is dealt with
in the same *Synodikon*, not in the eleven anathemas but in the
preceding blessings.

What then may we conclude from the fact that the *Synodikon*
and the *Alexias* agree fairly well, while the Report of the 'Trial'
is quite distinct? Probably, as in the case of Bishop Leo, that
Anna (who here has the support of the *Synodikon*) carries the
story further than does the other account. The proceedings of
the Synod against both heretics seemed at the time to end in a
triumph for orthodoxy, involving no severe punishment to the
offender, and the Report was drawn up in that spirit. But
both Anna and the compiler of the *Synodikon*, writing under
Manuel I, had reason to know that the triumphs were short-
lived and the punishments only deferred. This hypothesis of
two trials of Italus saves us furthermore from impugning Anna's
chronological accuracy in the matter.[1] The trial described in
the Report was, as its preamble states, in Indiction V; that described by her may well have been a year or more later, while
Alexius was 'planning against Bryennius', the Norman commander of Castoria. In this way we explain the discrepancies
between the six heresies and the 'eleven headings', between the
tame ending of the Report and the dramatic scenes of the
Alexias, and above all between the two dates given. If we argue
that Anna would certainly have mentioned a previous trial of
Italus, we may reply, first, that as she omitted his condemnation by a Synod under Michael VII she may equally well have
omitted his second conflict with the authorities, and secondly,
that we know beyond reasonable doubt of her making such an
omission in the case of Bishop Leo.[2] Why not then in the case
of Italus too?

The after-effects of the teaching of Italus were even more
serious than Anna leads us to infer. The going astray at
this juncture of one man, the Patriarch Eustratius Garidas[3]

[1] See p. 319, note 4, above.   [2] See above, p. 316.
[3] In the 'Report of the Trial' he is merely spoken of as a lover of quiet and the
contemplative life, a man full of ἀρετή, and his orthodoxy is never questioned—
another small proof that this trial was not identical with that described in the
Alexias.

is mentioned both by her and by the *Synodikon*,[1] but from later sources we learn that in Manuel's time a recrudescence of neo-Platonic doctrines affected others of the higher clergy.[2] Nicetas even says that an unorthodox proposition, due to long-ago memories of his master Italus, was uttered by that Bishop Eustratius of Nicaea who helped Alexius against the Paulicians and whom Anna describes as 'a man wise in things divine and secular, more renowned in dialectics than those who frequented the Porch and the Academy'.[3] Whether this story is true or not, the heresy of John Italus was a λύμη indeed.

ECCLESIASTICAL AFFAIRS

FALSE DOCTRINE

50. MONOPHYSITES

IF Anna omits to give us Italus' unsound notions on the Incarnation she makes up for it when she comes to the next heretic Nilus, who with his Armenian followers takes up the whole of chapter 1 of her Tenth Book. We know from the one mention of him in the *Synodikon* that he was a monk: 'On the doctrines impiously taught by the monk Nilus, and on all who share therein, anathema.' Anna puts the same fact thus: 'He was a man clever in making a show of virtue,[4] coming from I know not where, but for some time at any rate he frequented the capital and living in a corner[5] devoted himself to God only forsooth and to himself, continually absorbed in the sacred books.' She then goes on to describe in language very like what she used about Italus the deficiences of Nilus in 'any Hellenic education' and any παιδεία λογική, a circumstance which once more she ascribes to lack of instruction in 'the depth of the divine literature', and which had caused him to 'go astray about the sense of the writings'. Yet he had followers, 'a not ignoble band', and carried his teaching into 'great houses'. He was credited with ἀρετή and an austere life, and also in spite of his defective training with γνῶσις, here probably in the simple

---

[1] V. 9, p. 148; *Synod.*, p. 427 (in the Russian heading).

[2] Oeconomos, *op. cit.* pp. 30 sqq., and Chalandon, *Jean II et Manuel I Comnène*, pp. 640 sqq.

[3] XIV. 8, p. 453; Nic. Acom., *Thes. Orth. Fid., P. G.* 140, col. 136.

[4] The same phrase, ἀρετὴν ὑποκρίνεσθαι, is used of the Patriarch Eustratius Garidas (III. 3, p. 75).

[5] Probably a monastery. See pp. 49 and 291, note 3, above.

sense of 'knowledge', not with the special theological meaning
of esoteric acquirements.[1] Then follows the indictment of his
twofold error as to the Incarnation. He misapprehended the
hypostatic union of Our Lord's divine and human natures, and
he was wrong about how the second of these was deified. With
this matter was connected the doctrine known as ἀντίδοσις or
communicatio idiomatum.

To ordinary laymen nowadays the whole discussion is so
remote and academic that we too must beware lest, like Nilus,
we do 'not even grasp what ἕνωσις is, nor what ὑπόστασις is at
all', and like him fail to 'understand hypostasis or henosis
separately, or again in combination, hypostatic henosis'. There
probably floats through our minds a recollection of Browning's
bitterly satirical lines :[2]

> There 's a great text in Galatians,
> Once you trip on it, entails
> Twenty-nine distinct damnations,
> One sure, if another fails.

Yet if we are to gauge Anna's intellectual standards and
achievements, we must try to get at her point of view, try to
understand what seemed to her of such vital importance. To
begin with, we must examine her usage of the technical terms
about what she calls τὸ μυστήριον, meaning especially the
mystery of the Incarnation. This term occurs in the Definition
of the Faith by the Council of Chalcedon (451), as do also
ὑπόστασις and ἕνωσις which first call for explanation.

(1) ὑπόστασις has a place in the theological teaching on the
Trinity as well as in that on the Incarnation, but Chalandon[3]
is clearly wrong in thinking that Anna is here at all concerned
with the former doctrine; Nilus' errors were, as Oster puts
it, 'Fehler in Christologie'. Murray's Dictionary thus explains
the word Hypostasis: 'Personality, personal existence, person:
(*a*) distinguished from *nature*, as in the one hypostasis of Christ
as distinguished from His two *natures* (human and divine)', &c.[4]
It further defines hypostatic union (ἕνωσις καθ' ὑπόστασιν) as
'union of the human nature of our Lord with the divine, con-
stituting two natures in one person'. Canon Ottley[5] points out
that the term Hypostasis was introduced into theology by

---

[1] We have spoken elsewhere of the contrast which Anna loves to draw between
virtue and learning. See above, p. 137.
[2] *Soliloquy of the Spanish Cloister.*   [3] *Alexis I*ᵉʳ, p. 317.
[4] Zigabenus in his *Panoplia* uses the word throughout as synonymous with
πρόσωπον. This was in accordance with the decision of the Second General
Council of 381 (Constantinople I).
[5] *Doctrine of the Incarnation*, pp. 410 sqq., 576–9, 587–92, 599, etc.

Gnostic writers, and that whereas it was heresy to ascribe to Christ two natures and two hypostases, or one nature and one hypostasis, the Councils laid down the doctrine of two natures, one hypostasis.

(2) ἕνωσις, by which this is reached, is 'union', and must be carefully distinguished from the 'conjunction' (συνάφεια) taught by Nestorius, or the 'commingling' (κρᾶσις) of Eutyches. (Our own Athanasian Creed is directed against these two heresies among others.) The term Hypostatic Union denotes first that the union is real, not simulated;[1] secondly that it results in a single Person.

Other difficult points are as follows:

(3) ἀντίδοσις or *communicatio idiomatum* is defined by Ottley[2] as 'the interpenetration of the two natures of Christ, pervasion of the human by the divine, participation of attributes'. This matter of doctrine is discussed in the works of the St. Maximus[3] whom the Empress Irene specially loved to study;[4] it is therefore natural that her daughter should mention it.

(4) All this was connected with the insistence already mentioned on the dogma that Christ was not merely θεοφόρος (as any inspired man might be said to be) but θεάνθρωπος λόγος, the two natures being vitally united.

(5) τὸ πρόσλημμα,[5] or the human flesh which the Word assumed, was said to be 'deified', having been originally of the substance (οὐσία) of His mother Mary.[6] It was the part of Him that suffered.[7] One of the heresies attacked in the *Synodikon*

---

[1] This sense of basis or reality was the original meaning of the word Hypostasis. It was developed by neo-Platonist and Christian usage into the secondary meaning given above. See the learned disquisition in Zigabenus, *Panoplia* (P. G. 130, col. 121) on the terms ἐνυπόστατος, αὐθυπόστατος, ἑτεροϋπόστατος, and ἀνυπόστατος, and cf. Nic. Acom., *Thes. Orth. Fid.*, Bk. III, especially ch. 4, in P. G. 139.

[2] *Op. cit.* p. 591.

[3] Quoted by Zigabenus, *Panoplia* (P. G. 130, col. 253). So also in the same work (col. 1049) we have a long passage on the subject from St. John Damascene's refutation of the Monophysites.

[4] V. 9, p. 147.

[5] The term occurs in Greg. Naz., *Oratio XL in sanctum baptisma* (PG. 36, col. 424), and *Carminum*, Liber II, Historica, Poem XI, lines 647-51 (P. G. 37, cols. 1073-4). In the second passage he condemns all those

εἰ μὴ σέβοιεν ὡς ἐν ἄνθρωπον Θεὸν
τὸν προσλαβόντα σύν γε τῷ προσλήμματι

δύο φύσεις εἰς Χριστὸν ἐλθούσας ἕνα.

So Callicles (Poem XVI. 53) makes John Comnenus say of Christ, in addressing the Theotokos:

ἐκ σοῦ λαβὼν πρόσλημμα συνδεῖ τὰς φύσεις.

[6] Zigabenus, *Expositio Symboli* (P. G. 131, col. 16).

[7] Athanasius in Zigabenus, *Panoplia*, Tit. IX, col. 309; Greg. Naz., *Oratio XL*; and against Apollinarians in Zigabenus, *Panoplia*, col. 884.

brings in yet another aspect of the doctrine; it was wrong to
say that the assumed flesh differs from the divine nature 'not
in nature only but also in honour' (τῇ ἀξίᾳ), and that it serves
God (λατρεύει Θεῷ) like a great high priest.[1] It was a matter
where the 'twenty-nine distinct damnations' lurked very near.

(6) τὸ θεοῦσθαι, deification, was a term freely used in early
theology referring to what happened as to both Christ's
human nature and our human nature in Him. The first
application is what concerns us here. The Definition of Faith
of the Sixth General Council (Constantinople III, 680–1) says:
'His most holy and immaculate animated flesh was not destroyed because it was deified, but continued in its own state
and nature.' Origen had said[2] that Christ after His Resurrection deified the nature which He had taken, but the more
orthodox view is expressed by Gregory of Nyssa: 'The flesh
which He has assumed and at the same time deified.'[3] The
deification occurred at the Incarnation of the Logos: 'Who,
although He be God and Man, yet He is not two but One
Christ; One not by conversion of the Godhead into flesh but
by taking of the Manhood into God.'[4] He still wears, and will
come again wearing, τὸ πρόσλημμα.[5] He became 'one out of
two opposites, flesh and spirit, of which the one deified and the
other was deified',[6] and ' τὸ πρόσλημμα by the hypostatic union
. . . was deified . . . from the actual union[7] (ἐξ αὐτῆς ἐνώσεως).

This process of union however 'for ever remains a mystery',[8]
and those who speak of it must do so warily. It is a heresy to
say that the assumed flesh is deified φύσει; it is orthodox to say
that union of the two natures is φυσική or κατὰ φύσιν.[9] Deification of τὸ πρόσλημμα was not such as to absorb it; the human
nature remained 'with the grace from above' added.[10] 'God
became flesh, in order that flesh might become God, οὐ τῇ
φύσει ἀλλὰ τῇ καθ' ὑπόστασιν ἐνώσει καὶ τῇ θεώσει.[11] This subtle

---

[1] *Syn.*, p. 427.   [2] *Comm. on St. Matt.* ch. 28 (*P. G.* 17, Pt. II, col. 309).
[3] *Great Catechism*, XXXV (*P. G.* 45, col. 88).
[4] *Athanasian Creed*, simple and clear as compared to the theology of the *Panoplia*.
[5] Greg. Naz. against Apollinarians in Zigabenus, *Panoplia*, col. 885.
[6] *Panopl.*, col. 212.   [7] *Ibid.* cols. 248 and 257.
[8] The first count against Italus in the *Synodikon* is, as we have seen, an attack
on those who try to explain 'the ineffable doctrine of the Incarnation'.
[9] Ottley (*op. cit.* p. 411) says that Cyril used ἔνωσις φυσική as equivalent to
ἔνωσις καθ' ὑπόστασιν.
[10] Ottley (*op. cit.* pp. 591–2) deals with this, and speaks of 'the truth so often
insisted on by Athanasius and others that the Divine Son really appropriates
human nature and makes it His own, and imparts to it by the virtue of His person
a "grace of unction" and a "grace of union" '.
[11] Zigabenus, *Panoplia*, col. 1076: where he further quotes Greg. Naz. as saying
'concerning the deified flesh of the Lord', that it became οὐ . . . θεότης . . . ἀλλὰ
θεός, οὐ φύσει ἀλλὰ θεώσει.

distinction is elaborated in the interesting (and for a theological document singularly lucid) 'Discourse of the great lord and Emperor Alexius Comnenus made by him against Armenians who wrongfully teach that there is one nature in Christ'.[1] The name of Nilus does not occur in this writing, but Anna tells us that a number of Armenians in Constantinople, notably two called Tigranes and Arsaces, were 'incited to impiety' by this man, and 'the Emperor saw that impiety was feeding on the souls of many and that the affairs of Nilus and of the Armenians were closely interwoven',[2] so that he and they were finally tried together. It is therefore relevant to see what Armenian heresy Alexius combats in this 'Discourse'. We find at once that it was a form of Eutychianism or Monophysitism, and the familiar phrase 'Perfect God and Perfect Man' soon enters our mind; God 'deified the assumed flesh ἅμα τῇ ἑνώσει'. Unless we admit that 'the human part of the Lord was not changed in essence (κατ' οὐσίαν)[3] but was deified by the hypostatic union' we must be-

[1] Ed. A. Papadopulos-Kerameus, *Anal. Hierosol. Stach.*, I, p. 116–23.
[2] Anna dislikes Armenians as a race. As heretics we meet them again in XIV. 8, pp. 450 and 452, at Philippopolis, mixed up with the Manichaeans, &c., but their 'salt stream' of doctrine is after this one contemptuous reference not further specified. The animus of her contemporaries against Armenian heresies varied in strength. Alexius favoured Mt. Athos with its 180 monasteries, where Armenian and Georgian monks as well as Latins all lived close to Greeks. On the Roman side, when Bohemund and the other crusading chiefs wrote to Urban II (Hagenmeyer, *Kreuzzugsbriefe*, Ep. 16) begging him to come to Antioch and extirpate the heresies of the Greeks, Armenians, Syrians, and Jacobites, they were probably actuated by political rather than religious animosity (Leib, *op. cit.* pp. 221 sqq.). One Armenian Patriarch at any rate managed to keep on good terms with both Rome and Byzantium; this was Gregory II, son of an Armenian prince, who received a pallium from Pope Gregory VII, and before he took holy orders was made a duke by Alexius. Zigabenus, *Panoplia*, cols. 1173 sqq., attacks Armenians for saying that Christ's body was a phantom and not really human, and as such incorruptible and impassible. They did not reverence the Cross aright, and their faith, rites, and sacraments were all θεοστυγής. Attaliates (p. 97) ascribes Byzantine reverses to divine 'anger against the Armenians who inhabit Iberia and Mesopotamia and as far as Lycandos and Melitene and the neighbourhood, and the men who observe the Jewish heresy of Nestorius, and that of the Acephali' (i.e. those who did not recognize the Patriarch of Constantinople as their head); it is not clear whether he is alluding to one brand of heresy or several. Theophylact has several passages dealing with the conversion of Armenians (*P.G.* 123, col. 1160; *P.G.* 124, col. 284; *P.G.* 126, cols. 345–9, 353–6, 520). It is interesting to find from him that their churches needed reconsecration before the Orthodox could use them. They preached 'the madness' of the one nature of Christ.
Nicetas Acominatus (*P.G.* 140) devotes Bk. XVII of his *Thes. Orth. Fid.* to Armenian errors, but Migne has only edited part of it; the note refers to the 'variae haereses' of which Armenians are accused, but the text is omitted.
On the whole it is probably true, as Laurent (*Byzance et les Seldjoucides*, p. 71, note 5) states, that mutual hatred and an inquisitorial spirit were very common in the Greek and Armenian churches.
[3] In the *Synodikon*, p. 431, a curse is laid on 'those who believe that the deification of the assumed flesh means the transformation of the human nature into

lieve either that the two natures of Christ became one, or that
after the deification of the assumed flesh there were two Gods.[1]
The metaphor of iron, which though heated does not cease to
be iron, is applied to the two natures: 'If then thou admittest
that this' [Christ's flesh] 'was made divine in nature (φύσει
θεωθῆναι), and lost its own (οἰκείαν) nature, then admit that
heated iron has lost its own nature.'[2] And this is a vitally
important point, for if the assumed flesh was 'in essence God',
it was not of like nature with us, and the mystery of the Incarnation[3] is of no avail for us. The right view is to accept
'one Person (ὑπόστασιν) composed out of Godhead and Manhood'; the human and the divine natures were united in Christ
as one indivisible Person, but were not merged.

Into this field of controversy abounding in pitfalls Nilus
boldly stepped. He did not understand the hypostatic union
itself nor the terms that defined it; his views as to the communication of attributes and the deification of the assumed
flesh were unorthodox and he refused to change them even at
the bidding of his pious and persuasive Emperor. So, to deal
with him as before with Italus, 'the leaders of the Church' had
to be called in council by Alexius; once more we have the
Patriarch (now Nicolas Grammaticus) with 'the whole body of
bishops' sitting in judgement. As was inevitable, the Emperor
won, and 'the Synod, in order to free the souls of many from
his corrupt teaching, laid [Nilus] under a perpetual curse and
proclaimed yet more plainly according to the tradition of the
Fathers the doctrine of the hypostatic union'.

This is the last of Nilus in Anna's pages. But 'after him, or
rather with him'[4] another heretic is brought forward 'holding
impious tenets foreign to the Church, although he was in holy
orders'. This is Blachernites, who shared in the 'taint' (λύμη)
of the Enthusiasts, and like Nilus had undermined 'great houses'.
Anna gives us no details as to his errors, but Zigabenus[5] identifies the Enthusiasts with the Massalians, the sect which was so
to speak one of the two parents[6] of the Bogomile heresy, Manichaeism being the other. This will be considered later. We

Godhead, and that the body of the Lord . . . is transformed into the substance
(οὐσία) of Godhead, so as to infer from this either that the Incarnation of the
Lord and His sufferings occurred as a phantom and not a reality, or that the Godhead of the Only Begotten suffered'.

[1] 'Two natures and two persons' constituted the Nestorian heresy.
[2] Pp. 117–18. The same metaphor and the same *reductio ad absurdum* occur in
Zigabenus, *Panoplia*, col. 1076, and in Theophylact, Ser. I, Ep. 20 (*P. G.* 126,
cols. 353–6).
[3] The word used is οἰκονομία; see above, p. 307.
[4] X. 1, p. 270.	[5] *Panoplia*, col. 1273.	[6] XV. 8, p. 486.

need only say now that Blachernites, the solitary Enthusiast or
Massalian depicted by Anna, was as impervious as Nilus and
Basil the Bogomile to the instructions of Alexius. He was consequently 'handed over to the Church, and they too, after
examining him further, recognized that he was unshakable, so
they subjected him and his doctrines to a perpetual curse'.

The Armenians, as we have seen, reappear as helping to per-
vert Philippopolis, and with them the Jacobites, whose doctrine
is described as a river 'from the most foul fountains of Jacob'.[1]
Such is Anna's only allusion to the famous sixth-century monk
Jacobus Baradaeus who fought so manfully for the Monophysite
teaching against Emperor, Council, and clergy, that the Church
of his foundation still exists in the East and still bears his name.
Leib[2] seems to regard the Jacobite movement as due to the
desire of 'le parti national syrien' to make itself independent
at Antioch of the 'parti melkite', subordinated to Constantinople by the Council of Chalcedon; if this is so, Anna as a loyal
daughter not only of the Church but of the Palace had a double
reason for hating these 'foul fountains'.

ECCLESIASTICAL AFFAIRS
FALSE DOCTRINE
51. MOSLEMS

AFTER studying Anna's meticulous learning in the case of
heresies with which she was familiar it is interesting to
turn to her strangely wild statements about the Mohammedan
religion.[3] In the first place she represents the Turks, whom she

---

[1] XIV. 8, p. 452. See above, p. 328, note 2, on the Jacobites at Antioch. The
name 'Jacobite' given to the sect by its enemies is first found in a synodal decree of
Nicaea in 787. We append an extract from the discourse entitled περὶ αἱρέσεως
τῶν Ἰακωβιτῶν of Philip the Solitary (P. G. 127, col. 885). He says that the monk
Jacobus 'accepted the doctrine of Eutyches', who taught (a) that after the
Incarnation Christ's two natures were mixed (κραθῆναι) into one', and (b) that God
was passible (hence the name Theopaschitae). We cannot sum up the whole
subject better than in his dictum (ch. x): 'He who denies the hypostatic union
in Christ on account of the difference of natures is a Nestorian; he who denies
the difference of natures in the hypostatic union is a Eutychian; he who proclaims
the hypostatic union and the difference of natures in the unity of the Holy Trinity
proclaims the imperial and blameless faith.'

[2] Op. cit. p. 183, note 3.

[3] Yet we learn from Villehardouin and others that there had always been a
mosque at Constantinople for visitors and prisoners, so ignorance was inexcusable.
Cf. in the contemporary Chanson de Roland (1115–20) the current idea of the
Mohammedans as worshippers of a Trinity: 1. Mahumet, 2. Apolin, 3. Tervagan,
see Ch. de R. (MS. Oxford) stanza CLXXXVII, ll. 2570–91.

calls indifferently Turks, Arabs, Saracens, Ishmaelites, and
Hagarenes, as very ready to be bribed into a change of religion,[1]
and the conversion of 'those who perform mysteries (ὀργιάζουσιν)
by the rites of Mahomet' is a task zealously undertaken by the
'most hieratic, most didactic and apostolic' Emperor.[2] These
same Moslems are ἀθεώτατοι and intercourse with them defiles
true believers,[3] for Anna's ideas of their tenets are lurid indeed.
Her words on the subject are worth quoting in full.[4] 'The
Ishmaelite barbarians [are] slaves to drink and wine and Dionysus. For this race yields to Dionysus and Eros, and is most
passionate in every sort of sensuality, and their passions are not
circumcized together with their flesh. They are nothing else
but slaves and triple slaves of the ills of Aphrodite. Wherefore
also they worship and honour Astarte and Astaroth, and set
great store by the image of the Star,[5] and the golden Chobar
that is found among them.' In these strange gleanings from
Phoenician mythology Anna does not seem to realize that
Astarte and Astaroth are one and the same deity whom later
writers[6] identified with one still more famous, the goddess
described by Zigabenus[7] as 'Aphrodite whom in their own
tongue [the Saracens] call Chabar' (written 'Chobar' by our
authoress), meaning 'The Great'. But in any case the whole
passage is an absurd travesty of Mohammedanism, which in
its essence as held by Mahomet himself was 'emphatically a form
of Judaistic Christianity', and the worst that could be said of it
was that it was 'influenced by the traditions of the Parsees and
of the heathen Arabs'.[8] As to its ethics, Anna ignores the
Prophet's rule of total abstinence and often speaks as if drunkenness were peculiarly the vice of Moslems, who were fitly
symbolized by vines.[9] Their reputation in her mind for bravery
and skill on the one hand and deceitfulness, arrogance, and

---

[1] So the Σιαούς or envoy sent by the Sultan to Alexius (VI. 9, p. 170) is baptized
and the 'archsatrap' Elchanes, apparently with his 'blood-relations' (VI. 13,
p. 181). Perversion to Mahommedanism, on the other hand, is a 'mad enterprise'
(VI. 9, p. 169). Foucher de Chartres (I. 16, 5) narrates the baptism of part of
the Turkish garrison of Antioch.

[2] VI. 13, p. 181. See also Const. Porphy., de Cerim. II. 49 (C.S.H.B. Vol. I, p. 694).

[3] III. 11, p. 95; V. 2, p. 128.   [4] X. 5, p. 284.

[5] From Zigabenus, Panoplia, col. 1333, we infer that Anna means Lucifer, called
there τὸ ἑωσφόρον ἄστρον.

[6] See The Syrian Goddess (trans. from Lucian by H. A. Strong), note 7, p. 44.

[7] Zigabenus, Panoplia, loc. cit.

[8] L. Pullan, Church of the Fathers, p. 12. We may note here that Anna never once
attacks the Jewish tenets which were such a bugbear to many medieval theologians.

[9] VI. 12, p. 179; IX. 3, p. 251; X. 5, p. 284; XV. 1, p. 461. So Cedrenus,
pp. 727 C, 744 A, B, describes both Maniaces and Catacalo as having easy victories
over the 'Saracens' because the latter had been drinking all night and were ὑπὸ
μέθης σφαλλόμενοι or οἰνωμένοι.

cruelty on the other belongs rather to 'Foreign Affairs'. Here we are dealing only with their theology, and we may note that Anna's misstatements meet us again in the *Panoplia* of Ziga-benus. He says, in the passage just quoted: 'The Saracens up to the times of the Emperor Heraclius served idols, worshipping the Dawn-bringing star (Lucifer) and Aphrodite, whom in their own tongue they call Chabar, and this word means the Great.[1] But then a false prophet Mahomet rose among them, great and notorious for his blasphemies.' Hereupon follows an account of Mahommedan teaching and ritual, as contrasted with Christianity. But as Anna does not go into such details we need only say here that Zigabenus displays little accurate knowledge as to those he is attacking.[2] When Manuel Com-nenus shortly before his death displeased the clergy of his day by wishing to remove the anathema[3] from the 'complete' (ὀλόσφυρος) God of the Mohammedans, he was showing not only tolerance but more intelligence about the subject than the professional theologians,[4] who as Chalandon says were 'd'une ignorance rare quant à la religion des Musulmans',[5] an ignor-ance which Anna fully shared.

The river Chabar in Ezek. i. 3 is Χοβάρ in the LXX, and clearly comes from the Hebrew כבר 'to be great'.

[2] Zigabenus has an argument (of course finally triumphant) with a Saracen in the *Disputatio de Fide* printed in *P. G.* 131, col. 20.

[3] According to the formula of abjuration which every convert from Islam had to pronounce, and which was engraved on a marble tablet in St. Sophia. A Vatican manuscript contains this formula (together with others for Jews, &c.) under the name of Nicetas Acominatus (*P. G.* 140, cols. 124–36).

[4] Nic. Acom. *Manuel C.*, VII. 6 and 7, and Nic. Acom. *Thes. Orth. Fid.*, Bk. XX (*P. G.* 140). In the formula of abjuration (see last note) we find the following passages relevant to our text:

(a) ἀναθεματίζω Μωάμεδ and his family, and the Koran and its teaching about Paradise, the Old Testament, and Christianity.

(b) ἀναθεματίζω τοὺς τῷ πρωϊνῷ προσκυνοῦντας ἄστρῳ ἤγουν τῷ ἑωσφόρῳ καὶ τῇ Ἀφροδίτῃ· ἣν κατὰ τὴν Ἀράβων γλῶσσαν Χαβὰρ ὀνομάζουσι, τουτέστι μεγάλην.

(c) καὶ ἐπὶ πᾶσι τούτοις ἀναθεματίζω τὸν Θεὸν τοῦ Μωάμεδ, περὶ οὗ λέγει, ὅτι αὐτός ἐστι Θεὸς εἷς ὀλόσφυρος [ὃς] οὐκ ἐγέννησεν οὐδὲ ἐγεννήθη.

(We are reminded of the inscriptions about the God Who was not begotten neither begat which are still to be seen round the Palace at Seville, put up by Moorish workmen unknown to their so-called Christian master Pedro the Cruel.) After this the convert expressed his faith in Christianity and asked for baptism.

In Bk. XX of the *Thes. Orth. Fid.* Nicetas accuses Saracens of sensuality and all-night carousing. He also replies to their accusation that Christians were idolaters for worshipping the Cross and images by saying that Moslems kiss the Sacred Stone, 'and this which they say is a stone is the head of Aphrodite whom they worshipped and called Chabar'. Those who look carefully can see ἐκ γλυφίδος ἀποσκίασμα of the goddess (*P. G.* 140, col. 109).

[5] Chalandon, *Jean II, etc.* p. 661 note. He adds: 'Soit qu'ils ignorassent l'arabe, soit qu'ils ne connussent pas la doctrine musulmane, [les Grecs] se contentaient le plus souvent de diffamer leurs adversaires auxquels ils reprochaient toutes sortes d'absurdités et d'inepties.'

ECCLESIASTICAL AFFAIRS

FALSE DOCTRINE

52. MANICHAEANS AND MASSALIANS

WE now come to the great polemical triumphs of the book, those gained by the Emperor over the Manichaeans (including Paulicians) and their offshoots the Bogomiles, triumphs which allow Anna to display her theological learning to the full.

When the Manichaeans first meet us in our pages, their race is not mentioned at all and their αἵρεσις only in passing. They are merely brave but undisciplined soldiers who after a defeat 'return home in disorder', and refuse to be lured even by the offer of 'gifts and honours' into returning to the standards.[1] After the collapse of the last Norman army at Castoria,[2] Alexius does not wish to go back to Constantinople before subduing τούτους τοὺς ἀποστάτας[3] (whom in this passage she calls alternately Manichaeans and Paulicians, though later on she distinguishes between the two[4]) who were 'a stain on the glorious trophy of the Western wars'. But being anxious, because of their fierce recklessness and headstrong valour, first of all to avoid a rupture with them μὴ χεῖρόν τι μελετήσαιεν, and secondly to punish only their leaders and get the remainder for his army,[5] he resorted to stratagem. On a pretence of registration the chiefs are brought before him ten at a time and arrested, their goods are distributed to Alexius' army, and their wives imprisoned. The rest of the body, some of whom are baptized by their own desire, are pardoned and sent home to Philippopolis under the supervision of a court official; only the ringleaders, 'those responsible for this great madness' (ἀπόνοια),[6] are sent to island prisons.

As a direct result of this act of violence a baptized Manichaean named Traulus, living at court and married to a θεράπαινίς of the Empress, deserts Constantinople and his wife and escapes North to the Danube, where he marries a Patzinak

---

[1] IV. 4, p. 109; V. 3, p. 131. Curiously enough, Zonaras describes Alexius as driving 'illegally serving' Manichaeans out of the army, 'for an ancient law once for all forbids the Manichaeans to serve' (XVIII. 23).
[2] VI. 2.
[3] Either 'deserters' or 'heretics', probably the former from what follows.
[4] XIV. 8, p. 450, but see XV. 8, p. 486.
[5] He actually does this in XIV. 9, p. 456.
[6] Here again the 'madness' may be either desertion or heresy.

princess and ultimately brings that nation of raiders upon the
Empire.[1] For the time being 'the Emperor, treating the affairs
of the Manichaeans cursorily (ὁδοῦ πάρεργον ποιησάμενος), had
them once more in treaty with him (ὑποσπόνδους)',[2] in spite of
the fact that Traulus spurns 'a Golden Bull of pardon'; but
when the inroad of the renegade and his followers with the
Patzinaks finally came, it was a grave matter, 'for the
Manichaeans are by nature a very warlike race, and ever
longing like dogs to feed on the blood of men'.[3] Still even
in this Patzinak war certain Manichaeans fight 'very ardently'
on the Emperor's side,[4] and on a later occasion 'Romanus of
the Manichaeans' is one of Alexius' closest attendants in camp.[5]
It is not however till Book XIV that Anna explains the past
history of this interesting body of men. John Tzimisces[6] who
reigned 969–76 transported conquered Manichaeans as captive
slaves from Pontus and Armenia into Thrace, to guard the
Empire against Northern incursions. They did indeed come up
to their reputation as 'formidable forces' and were 'very staunch
guards' in keeping back 'the Scythians',[7] till Alexius could bring
the latter 'to total destruction', but were otherwise as 'free and
unruly' at Philippopolis as in the days of their virtual independence (τυραννιῶντες) in their native land. Now for the first time
we are taught to regard them as dangerous heretics. Speaking
of the decline of Philippopolis, Anna ascribes it first to conquest
by Northern enemies and then says:

'And in addition to other things it suffered from the presence of many
impious men. For Armenians possessed this city, as well as the so-
called Bogomiles about whom themselves and their heresy we will
speak in due season later on, and also those most accursed Paulicians,
being a branch of the Manichaean sect.[8] As their name implies, they
sprang from Paul and John, who having laid hold on the impiety
of Manes handed it down unadulterated to those who were of their

---

[1] VI. 4.
[2] VI. 5, p. 158. The same words ὁδοῦ πάρεργον ποιεῖσθαι recur in XIV. 8,
p. 453, also about the Manichaeans, but there Alexius treats the 'secondary matter'
of their conversion, as 'greater' than his 'work' at the moment, which was war
with the Comans.
[3] VI. 14, p. 182. The same phrase is applied to the Comans in X. 2, p. 272,
and is probably purely conventional.
[4] VII. 3, p. 193.   [5] XIII. 1, p. 377.
[6] XIV. 8, p. 451. Theophanes (quoted in Du Cange's note on IV. 4, p. 109 c),
writing early in the ninth century, says Constantine Copronymus (740–75) did
this, so there seem to have been two transportations.
[7] Anna says that Tzimisces turned these men who were ἀντιμάχους as heretics
into συμμάχους in war, and set them as ἀξιομάχους forces against the enemy. The
play on words is not easy to translate (XIV. 8, p. 452).
[8] From this point onwards she identifies the two sects entirely, and only uses
the word 'Paulicians' once more, in XV. 8, p. 486.

party. Therefore I should have liked to run over the teaching of
the Manichaeans and to unfold it briefly, and furthermore to be
zealous in the upsetting of these most godless doctrines. But partly
because I know that the heresy of the Manichaeans is laughed at by
all, partly because I am pressing on to the history, I leave on one
side the arguments against them.'

She adds that Porphyry has reduced the 'foolish teaching of the
.Manichaeans to utter absurdity' (a rather startling statement
which we shall analyse later). After devoting a few lines to
Porphyry and Plato she returns to the Manichaeans. 'As for
these pupils of Manes, and of Paul and John the sons of Callinice, because they were uncivilized and brutal in mind, and
reckless to the point of bloodshed', they had been, as we have
seen, brought into Thrace by Tzimisces as useful guards, but
their disposition was unaltered. 'For the whole of Philippopolis
except for a few men was made up of Manichaeans, and they
tyrannized over the Christians there and plundered their goods,
paying little or no heed to the messengers sent by the Emperor.
Therefore they increased and all the regions round Philippopolis
were heretic.' The presence of Armenians and Jacobites caused
a 'confluence of all ills, for as to doctrines the rest disagreed
with the Manichaeans, but in rebellion[1] they agreed'. Whereupon Alexius, oblivious of the threatening Comans, performed
a 'truly most apostolic action', and earned the title of Thirteenth
Apostle by using his tongue, sharpened through long study of
holy writ, against these heretics. 'He tried to lead the Manichaeans away from their salt stream of religion and fill them
with sweet doctrine. Therefore from morning till afternoon or
evening, sometimes till the second or third watch of the night,
he would summon them and teach them the orthodox faith,
refuting the distorted nature of their heresy.' In this good work
he was assisted by Bishop Eustratius of Nicaea, by the Bishop
of Philippopolis, and by Nicephorus Bryennius Caesar, his own
pupil in theology. A very large number were converted and
after confessing their errors to a priest were baptized, even
though at first many were obdurate, 'bringing forward quotations and testimonies from the sacred writings and thinking
thereby to establish their hateful doctrine'. Alexius showed his
evangelical zeal by foregoing sleep and food and 'persisting in
the summer season in a tent out-of-doors'. Finally his 'dialectical warfare'[2] (λογικὴ ἅμιλλα) enables him to set up a trophy
'against the heretics, by his most pious arguments'. Their three

---

[1] ἀποστασίαις, which may equally well mean 'unorthodoxy'. See p. 333, note 3.
[2] XIV. 9, p. 454.

leaders, Culeon,[1] Cusinus, and Pholus, remain 'adamantine against yielding to argument', showing themselves 'ingenious in tearing the Divine Word to pieces and in busily interpreting it in an extravagant sense'. As they resist all the Emperor's 'premisses' and objections and pay no heed when he 'destroys their counter-arguments like the web of a spider', he sends them to Constantinople virtually as prisoners. Culeon finally consents to become 'a tame sheep of our fold', but the other two, 'being the most blasphemous of all Manichaeans' and showing symptoms of 'clear melancholy',[2] were thrown into prison, where they finally died.

After the departure of these three from Philippopolis Alexius went on with his great task and 'each day brought over to God sometimes 100, sometimes more', till 'myriads and thousands of innumerable men' were converted, and 'whole cities and lands, subjugated by all sorts of heresies', were brought back by him 'in various ways to our orthodox faith. For the principal men he thought worthy of great gifts, and he enrolled them among the leaders (λογάσι) of the soldiers.' To the 'commoner sort' and the agricultural labourers he gives the even more material reward of a new town, called Alexiopolis after himself, with 'corn-lands and vineyards and houses'. There he settles them and their families, and 'with a golden bull he confirmed his donations to them' and their heirs after them.

These passages have been given at length, so that we may realize what a formidable body the Manichaeans seemed to Anna and her father, dour opponents whether in arms or in arguments. As to their doctrines she is merely abusive instead of giving any details. Professor Burkitt[3] has pointed out that we know the Manichaeans principally from the misrepresentations of their enemies,[4] but Anna apparently thinks it a waste of time to represent them at all. Such slight criticism as she makes of their Dualism with reference to Porphyry and the Platonists will come into another chapter; it will be wiser now to turn to the other sects which sprang from them, the Paulicians, Massalians (or Enthusiasts), and Bogomiles.

As we have said above, Anna is far from clear as to the difference between Manichaeans and Paulicians, so we turn to Zigabenus in quest of further information. He argues at great

---

[1] He had been a captain over the 2,800 Manichaeans at Durazzo, and had led these insubordinate soldiers home after the disaster (IV. 4, p. 109; V. 3, p. 131).

[2] i. e. 'madness', equivalent to the ἠλιθιότης earlier in the chapter.

[3] *Religion of the Manichees*, pp. 11 sqq.

[4] Among many other theologians the Patriarch Photius (*P. G.* 102, cols. 16–264) wrote four books against the Manichaeans.

length[1] against the Paulicians and gives us their tenets, or rather his version of them. Like Anna, he believes the name[2] to have been compounded from those of Paul and John the two sons of Callinice, who were born in Samosata, a city infected with the Manichaean heresy. Led by these two the sect (according to Zigabenus) twisted the words of Scripture, believed in two principles and thought Matter wholly evil, did not accept the Incarnation as real or duly honour the B.V.M., would not worship the Cross, disbelieved in the two great sacraments, had no proper priesthood, rejected Jehovah and the Old Testament, and in morals were dissolute and drunken. We may note that almost all these aberrations are similarly credited not only to the original Manes, but also to the kindred heresies of Massalians and Bogomiles, to say nothing of the Mohammedans. It was easier to stigmatize a religion as κατάπτυστος or θεοστυγής than to probe its depths.[3]

When we come to the arch-enemy Basil the Bogomile and his fellow scoundrels, we are informed that if one parent of their doctrine was Manichaeism, the other was the heresy of the Massalians or Enthusiasts.[4] Anna only refers to the Massalians once, in this connexion,[5] and once to the 'taint' and the 'impiety' of the Enthusiasts, which led into κακοδοξία and doctrines 'impious and foreign to the church' the priest Blachernites, a man associated with the Monophysite heretics, and punished like them by a 'perpetual anathema'.[6]

We get the identification of the two sects in Zigabenus.[7] The name of Massalians, he says, 'changed into the Greek tongue means Euchitae, suppliants', because of their insistence on prayer; 'they are also called Enthusiasts, as experiencing the

---

[1] *Panoplia*, cols. 1189–1273. Oeconomos (*op. cit.* p. 39) points out that they were really Adoptionists, holding Christ to be not God's Son, but an angel adopted by Him.

[2] The *Cath. Dict.* says that the origin of the name is obscure; it occurs first in 719, in the Acts of the Armenian Synod of Duin. The *Encycl. Brit.* says that the Bogomiles 'are also known as Pavlikeni'.

[3] F. C. Conybeare published in 1896, with an English translation, the Armenian text of the Paulician *Key of Truth*. He speaks of them as 'the extreme left wing of the Iconoclasts', the great 'party of revolt against the revived paganism of the eighth century'. This agrees with what has been said above.

[4] The *Encycl. Brit.* says: 'The word [Bogomile] is a direct translation into Slavonic of Massaliani, the Syrian name of the sect corresponding to the Greek Euchites. The Bogomiles are identified with the Massaliani in Slavonic documents of the thirteenth century.' The article goes on to say with truth: 'It is a complicated task to determine the true character and the tenets of any ancient sect; . . . the heretical literature has to a great extent either perished or been completely changed.'

[5] XV. 8, p. 486. [6] X. 1, p. 270, and see Ch. 50 above.

[7] *Panoplia*, col. 1273.

workings of a certain demon and believing them to come from the Holy Spirit'. The same writer, in the title of his *Confutatio*,[1] speaks of 'the blasphemous and varied heresy of the Massalians and of the Phundaitae also called Bogomiles and Euchitae and Enthusiasts and Encratetae and Marcionists'. Later on in Anathema I he speaks of the wide spread of 'the Massalians or Bogomiles', and in Anathema II of 'the heresy of the Massalians or Luco-petrians and Phundaitae and Bogomiles'. Nicetas adds three more aliases, Euphemitae, Martyriani, Sataniani.[2]

Out of this bewildering wealth of names one fact emerges, that their Orthodox opponents in the twelfth century did not know how to distinguish between the many allied sects. The most authoritative information about the Massalians comes from a manuscript, published by Fr. Diekamp, of a seventh-century writer.[3] Of the various accusations brought against them under eighteen heads the most striking are as follows: they say that Satan and demons inhabit men, they disregard the two Sacraments and believe only in the efficacy of prayer (i. e. of the *Paternoster*), they utter strange talk of visions, man's perfectibility, &c., they shun ordinary life in all its forms (e. g. labour, marriage, public worship), and they are so anti-social as to harbour runaway slaves. All these charges are repeated by Zigabenus in the two works just cited and by Nicetas in his *Thesaurus Orthodoxae Fidei*. Further enormities are their Sabellian belief in one Hypostasis of the Trinity and of a second Trinity in the seventh Heaven; their sham clerical elections and guileful adoption of 'the habit of monks, desiring thereby to escape notice and deceive the multitude',[4] their acceptance of additional scriptures, their scorn for the Cross and images, and also for churches as 'the abode of demons', and above all their rejection of the true doctrines of the Incarnation and Transubstantiation. On moral grounds they are reprobated for idleness,

---

[1] *P. G.* 131, col. 40.

The *Encycl. Brit.* ('Enthusiasm') says: 'A Syrian sect of the fourth century was known as the Enthusiasts; they believed that by perpetual prayer, ascetic practices and contemplation, man could become inspired by the Holy Spirit, in spite of the ruling evil spirit which the Fall had given to him. From their belief in the efficacy of prayer ($\epsilon \dot{v} \chi \dot{\eta}$) they were also known as Euchites.'

Psellus, in his *De operatione daemonum* (chs. II–V), speaks scornfully of the Euchitae, saying that whereas Manes accepted two principles ($\dot{a} \rho \chi a \dot{\iota}$), the $\delta \eta \mu \iota o \nu \rho \gamma \acute{o} s$ of Good and the $a \dot{v} \tau o \nu \rho \gamma \acute{o} s$ of Evil, this sect had three, the Father and two Sons; he also violently attacks their abominable rites.

[2] *Thes. Orth. Fid.*, Bk. IV, Ch. 36 (*P. G.* 139, cols. 1329 sqq.).

[3] The monk Georgius, *B. Z.* IX, pp. 20–23.

[4] *P. G.* 130, col. 1288, and *P. G.* 131, col. 41, $\tau \hat{\omega} \kappa \omega \delta \acute{\iota} \omega \tau \grave{o} \nu \lambda \acute{v} \kappa o \nu \kappa \rho \acute{v} \pi \tau o \upsilon \sigma \iota$, and col. 45, $\tau \grave{o} \psi \epsilon \upsilon \delta o \mu o \nu a \chi \iota \kappa \grave{o} \nu \sigma \chi \hat{\eta} \mu a \mu \epsilon \tau a \mu \phi \iota \acute{a} \zeta o \upsilon \sigma \iota$; cf. Anna's words about the Bogomiles, XV. 8–10.

hard-heartedness, immorality, perjury, &c., especially those who claim to be 'perfect'.

Modern critics have dwelt on the anti-social tendencies of this sect. Pullan[1] speaks of their lives spent in begging and no work, and also of their mystic dances which made them the 'nearest ancient Christian parallel to the dancing dervishes of modern Turkey'. Oeconomos[2] says the Massalians came from the Gnostics through Manichaeism, and by their disapproval of marriage and the Sacraments cut themselves off from the civil and religious life of the community. The last outcome of these various heresies was the sect of the Bogomiles, who may be said to have been Paulicians in dogma and Massalians in morals, and this is the sect which inspires Anna with the greatest abhorrence, indeed with an almost unaccountable savagery. She may be said to 'see red' whenever she mentions them.

ECCLESIASTICAL AFFAIRS
FALSE DOCTRINE
53. BOGOMILES

WE will first take Anna's account of the Bogomiles. They do not appear in her pages till her fourteenth Book, and then only in passing; their heresies were added to those of the Armenians and Jacobites as the sore affliction of Philippopolis.[3] But in Book XV we have the better part of three chapters devoted to them.[4]

The last theological contest of her father's reign (a contest we may note in which he needs and obtains more ecclesiastical assistance than ever before[5]) is waged with these Bogomiles, who combined two 'very evil and contemptible doctrines', namely, the δυσσέβεια of the Manichaeans or Paulicians, and the βδελυρία of the Massalians. Their heresy was 'new, never before known to the church'. Or rather 'it seems it existed even in the times before my father but was unperceived, for the race of the Bogomiles is most artful in counterfeiting virtue'. They guilefully assumed the monastic habit and appearance, and were attacked by Alexius like 'a serpent lurking in its hole', on an occasion when peace abroad allowed him to apply him-

---

[1] *Church of the Fathers*, p. 318.
[2] *Vie religieuse, &c.*, pp. 39, 47.
[3] XIV. 8, p. 450.
[4] XV. 8–10.
[5] XV. 8, p. 488; 9, p. 492; 10, p. 492.

self 'to more spiritual things'. The leader Basil[1] had taken for
followers twelve 'apostles', and 'certain female disciples, women
of bad character and altogether vile', and the heresy spread
'like fire'. Diblatius, one of the band, is induced by imprisonment and torture to betray his comrades, and 'the archsatrap
of Satanael' (i. e. Basil) is summoned to Court. But fear or some
other sinister motive (Anna we may remark calls it 'holy dissimulation') makes Alexius wary in dealing with him. Instead
of arguing with the heretic publicly as he had with other lost
sheep, the Emperor and his brother Isaac pretend to become
his friends and disciples, and lead him on to a full exposition
of his doctrines, which a shorthand writer takes down behind
a curtain. 'So that accursed [θεοπληγής] man joined together
all things speakable and unspeakable, and omitted no abominable [θεομισής, later θεοστυγής] doctrine, but even despised our
dogma of Christ's Divinity and made out all the Incarnation
as illusory.[2] Furthermore, he called the holy temples, alas, the
temples of demons, and he treated and considered as of no
account what we say is the consecrated body and blood of Him
who is both the first High-priest and the first Sacrifice.' The
Emperor proceeds to hold a Conference of the Senate, the Army,
and the Church under the Patriarch Nicolas, and the charges
against Basil are read. The heretic however, 'inflexible, true-
bred Bogomile', refuses to abjure even under threats of torture,
prison, and death. 'He clung to the demon with closed teeth
and embraced his Satanael.' The Emperor pleads again and
again with him, but the story ends in his being condemned by
the leaders of the Church, and burnt alive in the Hippodrome.
Anna's complacency over the execution is in modern eyes the
greatest blot upon her book, and she does not improve matters
by adducing puerile proofs of Basil's guilt, as we have seen
when discussing Superstition.[3] Before his death he was carefully segregated 'so that he should not have freedom to talk to
any man and communicate to him his own defilement', a taint
so 'foul' that "αἰδώς" prevents our princess from sullying her
womanly and royal tongue with his doctrines, and makes her
refer the curious to the *Panoplia* of Zigabenus. The matter of
Basil's followers, the twelve disciples and others who included
many from 'the greatest houses',[4] was even more serious and
was dealt with before their master's death. At one moment

[1] Glycas says he was an ἰατρός (IV, p. 334).
[2] For this technical use of θεολογία and οἰκονομία see above, p. 307.
[3] See Ch. 11, above.
[4] The same is said of Italus and Nilus and Blachernites. Heresy was clearly an
aristocratic foible.

Alexius contemplated the burning of them all, but for fear some
Christians might be mixed up with the heretics he allowed them
to choose between a pyre with a cross and a pyre without, and
in this strangely simple way he satisfied himself as to the sheep
and the goats. The former who marched to the Cross were
dismissed 'with many words of encouragement', the latter,
'most godless', were imprisoned till they either recanted under
daily exhortations or died in their errors. Captivity was also
the fate of the Bogomiles present at their leader's death, saved
by Alexius from popular lynching. The account of Basil's own
execution is painful reading.[1] His misplaced belief in angels to
rescue him and his momentary hesitation in face of the fire,
unaccompanied however by any yielding, for he was 'as though
of adamant', inspire in us neither the superstitious fear felt by
the executioners nor the scornful horror evinced by Anna, but
rather an admiring pity. Of his share in the matter rather than
Alexius' may we use Anna's concluding words: καινοπραγία τις
καὶ τόλμη παράδοξος. To her it is 'the last work and labour of
those great labours and successes of the Emperor';[2] to us it is
an exhibition of *odium theologicum* at its worst.

Examined more closely, Anna's charges against the Bogomile
doctrines resolve themselves into three: heretical views as to
Christ's two Natures and the Incarnation, scorn of churches as
the abode of demons, and disbelief in Transubstantiation. With
all three we are familiar from our study of what she calls the
'impiety' and the 'wickedness' of the Paulicians and Massalians.
Still it is not easy to see any connexion between these three
tenets and the immorality, hypocrisy, and madness at which
Anna darkly hints,[3] any more than to understand why the
heresy should have been so popular on the one hand and such
a source of unreasoning fear to the Court on the other. In no
other instance does Anna display such childish superstition or
such vindictive prejudice, and we can almost see her shudder
with disgust and terror as she writes.[4]

---

[1] See p 520 below.   [2] XV. 10, p. 495.

[3] Basil is κάκιστος and the 'archsatrap of Satanael' (XV. 8, p. 487); μοναχὸς
καὶ πολλαχὸς τὴν κακίαν (*ibid.*). He is also vain (XV. 8, p. 488) 'foul' (*ibid.*),
'demoniac' (*ibid.* p. 489), 'impious' (9, p. 490), 'mischievous' (10, p. 492), 'mad'
(10, pp. 493-4), 'abominable' (10, p. 493).

[4] Her explanation of an untimely earthquake and of stones falling from heaven
on Basil's cell is as follows: 'these were reminders, it seems, of the demons round
Satanael, who were enraged and thought it dreadful that he had betrayed the'
[lacuna in text] 'to the Emperor and had brought on keen persecution against the
error' (XV. 8, pp. 489, 490). May we not assume that Anna wishes to indicate
the prevalence among the Bogomiles of unholy and awful rites (such as those with
which Jews and Christians credited one another all through the Middle Ages),
and that the missing word is a name for these? When Basil stands perplexed before

Other writers of Anna's day or a little later show the same unexplained hatred. It is true that the five Anathemas apparently directed against the Bogomiles in the *Synodikon*[1] are not abusive; but Zigabenus[2] cannot sufficiently revile the 'ridiculous mysteries' of the sect (all of them 'wizards, and corrupters and destroyers'), or their 'pernicious and pestilent' leader, 'full of corruption, and the instrument of all evil'. They are accused of every conceivable heresy, Paulician, Sabellian, Adoptionist, Manichaean, Massalian, and what not. They are dualists, they reject the Old Testament, twist the New Testament into absurd meanings, deny the Incarnation, despise images, the Cross, and the Sacraments, consider churches as habitations of demons,[3] and pray only the Lord's Prayer over and over again. Finally, like the Massalians, the Bogomiles 'dress as monks and assume their habit like a bait, hiding the wolf with the garment, so that, being readily received because of their habit and getting an opportunity for discourse, they may unsuspected in their friendly speeches drop poison into the ears of their listeners'. In his concluding paragraph Zigabenus once more praises the 'most wise and magnanimous Emperor' for having unmasked this dreadful heresy, burnt its chief teacher, 'having the assent

the pyre, it is because 'the devil that had seized his soul poured profound darkness on him' (XV. 10, p. 493). So mighty is the man for evil that the 'executioners feared lest perhaps the demons round Basil might do some strange wonder by the permission of God', in saving him from the fire. They therefore hurry his end (*ibid.* 494) and the very flames testify his guilt by leaping forward and consuming him utterly.

The constant recurrence of the name of Satanael may be elucidated from Zigabenus' *Panoplia*. He says the Bogomiles believed that God had two sons, of whom Satanael or Satan was older and more powerful than the Word, and after his expulsion from heaven made our world as it is, and formed Man 'out of earth mixed with water' (*P. G.* 130, cols. 1293 sqq.).

[1] pp. 425-6. The five errors are (1) Making Christ an 'adopted angel', and the Holy Spirit inferior to the Father. (2) Saying that the Devil made the visible world and Man. (3) Denying Transubstantiation. (4) Refusing to worship the Cross. (5) Scorning images as idols.

[2] *Panoplia*, Tit. XXVII. In the heading to Tit. XXVII he explains that 'Bogomile' means in Bulgarian 'one who desires the mercy of God'. From other sources we know that a Pope Bogomile lived in Bulgaria about the middle of the tenth century, and his heresy was attacked by his contemporary Cosmas, whose polemic *Against the Heretics*, written in old Slavonic, has been edited by M. G. Popruzenko (St. Petersburg, 1907). The sect survived the conquest of Bulgaria by Basil II in 1018, and members of it were to be found there and in Serbia and Bosnia down to the fourteenth century. Zigabenus also attacks the 'heresy of the godless Phundagiatae, who call themselves Christopolites, but in the West are called Bogomiles' in a separate treatise in *P. G.* 131, col. 48.

[3] Thus in *Panoplia*, col. 1313 the Bogomiles are represented as saying that Satan lived first in the temple at Jerusalem, and then went to St. Sophia. We may compare the 'Satan's seat' of *Rev.* ii. 13, a term which the writer applied to the great Pergamos Altar, but which many an ardent Protestant would think not too strong for St. Peter's at Rome.

of all men in office whether clergy or laymen', and spared no pains to hunt down any disciples that might be left. As a matter of fact even after his drastic measures we hear from Nicetas Acominatus of two bishops convicted in 1143 as guilty of 'the most foul heresy of the Bogomiles', while in 1147 the Patriarch of Constantinople is deposed largely for having befriended a preaching Bogomile monk.[1]

One more testimony to the sentiments inspired by this particular heresy shall be cited from the *Anon. Syn. Chron.*[2] The writer tells us that the Devil stirred up Basil 'forerunner of Anti-Christ', who in the stereotyped phrase was τῷ κωδίῳ κρύπτων τὸν λύκον; indeed like the cuttle-fish he emitted blackness 'that he might escape the notice of the hunter', and Alexius' horror over the heresy is vividly depicted. Basil is obstinate, vain, and the deceiver of many, and his death at the stake is a fit 'prelude to the everlasting fire', a suitable end to a 'rotten tree not bearing good fruit'.

What lies behind all this? It is hard to say, but a tentative suggestion may be made. In view of the peculiarly intimate footing of monks in the houses and with the womankind of the pious of those days, was it not a plausible suspicion that under the protection of the monastic habit these heretics wormed their way into families for evil purposes? 'They which creep into houses, and lead captive silly women laden with sins' have always filled the right-minded with special fury and aversion; they have seemed to them 'seducing spirits', holding the 'doctrines of devils',[3] 'false teachers who privily bring in damnable heresies',[4] 'deceivers who subvert whole houses'.[5] Among Basil's followers were women of the worst character,[6] and charges of immorality practised under the plea of 'perfection', as well as those of utter scorn for the married state, were as we have seen freely brought against the various allied sects. Anna will not 'sully her tongue' with describing the Bogomile tenets. Is it not then conceivable that the virulence of her father and herself against these Bogomiles was due to the exalted moral standard which the Byzantine Court was taught to admire in Anna Dalassena, which Alexius (as may be seen from his enact-

---

[1] Chalandon, *Jean II, etc.* pp. 635 sqq.
[2] pp. 178–81.
[3] 1 *Tim.* iv. 1; 2 *Tim.* iii. 6. Zigabenus indeed quotes both these texts in the beginning of his diatribe against the 'many-named sect of the Massalians or Bogomiles' (*P. G.* 131, cols. 40, 41), and in Anathema VI attacks their condemnation of marriage. But he does not make any specific charge of immorality.
[4] 2 *Pet.* ii. 1.
[5] *Tit.* i. 11; cf. XV. 9, p. 490, 'The evil had sunk καὶ εἰς οἰκίας μεγίστας.'
[6] XV. 8, p. 487.

ments and letters) strove to reintroduce into monastic life, and which Irene championed and enforced in the *Typikon* of her Convent? If Italus was condemned rather as a neo-Platonist than as a heretic, the Bogomiles may have been held 'accursed' and 'God-hated' on moral rather than theological grounds, for 'foul' lives rather than for 'impious' doctrine. It is no answer to say that from them partly sprang the Cathari (Albigenses)[1] to whose example of austere and simple living the Christian Church owed so much. Their principles may have been so lofty as to impose 'a strain on human nature which few men could have been expected to bear',[2] and their practice under temptation may have collapsed, or they may merely have been misjudged. But wherever men with peculiar privileges and in a peculiar garb 'creep into houses', there is sure to arise, with or without justification, the suspicion, animosity, and jealous dread which permeate Anna's pages.[3]

ECCLESIASTICAL AFFAIRS

FALSE DOCTRINE

54. DUALISM

FINALLY, before we leave the subject of Anna's theological knowledge, we must consider her general attitude towards the Dualism which lay at the root of so many heresies.[4] When she is telling of her father's polemics against the Manichaeans at Philippopolis, she says she would like to describe the heresy, but she is 'pressing on to the history', and is 'aware that the

---

[1] M. E. Hirst, *The Quakers in Peace and War*, pp. 23 sqq.

[2] E. Holmes, *The Albigensian or Catharist Heresy*, p. 27.

[3] It may be interesting to quote from a recent French criticism of the Bogomiles. R. P. Guérin Songeon, in his popular *Histoire de la Bulgarie* (1913), says on p. 215 of the Bogomiles in Bulgaria: 'Tout patriote devait être bogomile. Philippopoli, où Tzimiscès avait transporté une nouvelle escouade d'Arméniens dualistes, fut le foyer de ce nationalisme hérétique. . . . Traqué en Bulgarie, le bogomilisme passa en Serbie et en Bosnie. En sapant l'amour de la patrie, en prêchant la lutte des classes, en supprimant toute morale, cette doctrine anarchique acheva de décomposer les peuples de la presqu'île et fut le meilleur auxiliaire de la conquête ottomane. Au moment de l'arrivée des Turcs, les neuf dixièmes des bogomiles embrassèrent l'islamisme et saluèrent comme des libérateurs les ennemis de la civilisation chrétienne.' *B. Z.* XXVI, p. 200, contains a notice of a new book by J. Iwanow, *Bogomilenbücher und Legenden* (Sofia, 1925). The reviewer says the writer has been led 'zu dem sicheren Schluss dass die abendländischen Katharer und Patarener ihre Lehre von den Bogomilen übernommen haben'.

[4] If we are to believe Holmes (*op. cit.* p. 100), Christianity itself is 'dualistic to the core'.

heresy of the Manichaeans is laughed at by all'.[1] She continues:
'Furthermore I know that not only those of our faith[2] but
actually the Porphyry who raged against us in many chapters
himself reduced to utter absurdity the foolish teaching of the
Manichaeans by very scientifically investigating concerning the
two Principles [ἀρχῶν], although his Rule of One [μοναρχία]
compels him to bring his readers to the Platonic Unit [ἑνάς], or,
in other words the One [τὸ ἕν]. Now we indeed honour the
Rule of One, but not that which One Person circumscribes.[3]
Nor have we admitted the One of Plato; this is ineffable among
the Hellenes and secret among the Chaldeans; for they hang
from it many other principles both of and above the world.'

The passage, short as it is, bristles with difficulties and technical terms, and needs careful study.

At the first blush it reads as if Anna were alluding to some
definite writing of the philosopher Porphyry against the Manichaeans, and no such has come down to us. In his *Life of Plotinus*
he describes his master's battles against the Gnostics, who as
is well known[4] claimed to reach perfection through γνῶσις or
knowledge of the invisible world, and taught that the visible
world of matter was evil. These Gnostics were so numerous
about the middle of the third century that they could easily
form part of Plotinus' audience at Rome.[5] But though they
ostensibly came to learn, they began attacking their master's
idol Plato and were felt to require drastic treatment. Porphyry
says:[6]

'There came against [Plotinus] many of the Christians, and heretics
raised up out of old philosophy . . . who . . . bringing forward

---

[1] XIV. 8, p. 451. According to Sir T. Arnold (*Camb. Med. Hist.* IV, p. 287), it
was not 'laughed at' by the Moslems but severely persecuted.

[2] αὐλή, literally 'court', is probably here equivalent to 'faith', as also in XIII. 12,
p. 406; see p. 497 below.

[3] Reading οὐχ ἦν ἕν πρόσωπον περιγράφει (instead of the οὐχὶ . . . of the edition
princeps of 1651 or the οὐχ ἦ . . . conjectured by Reifferscheid). This makes it a
correct quotation from Greg. Nazianzen and from Zigabenus after him (*P. G.* 36,
col. 76; *P. G.* 130, cols. 25 and 61), as well as being in accordance with the technical use of περιγράφειν. We may note that the better Florentine manuscript (F)
of the *Alexias* ceases before this point in Book XIV, so that we have to rely on the
inferior Coislinianus (C), where, as may be seen in the Paris Bibl. Nat., the text
has been emended, ι being written with blacker ink in a space that might originally
have held two letters. Reifferscheid, (*Praefatio*, p. vii) makes C out as equivalent
to the Tolosanus which Possinus handled in 1651 and which Oster describes as
'spurlos verschwunden'.

[4] Eug. De Faye, *Gnostiques et Gnosticisme*, tome 27 de la Bibl. de l'École des
hautes études (Sc. rel). Cf. Bouillet, *Ennéades de Plotin*, and *Vita Plot.*, ch. 24.

[5] Earlier in the same century Hippolytus or Origen included them in the *Contra
haereses* (*P. G.* 17, col. 3159, 3343). In the second century St. Irenaeus had waged
war on them, and two centuries later they were still a danger, as we see from
Epiphanius (*P. G.* 41, cols. 329–64).   [6] *Vita Plot.*, ch. 16.

revelations (ἀποκαλύψεις) of Zoroaster' [and others] . . . 'deceived many being themselves deceived, saying that Plato had not reached to the depth of intelligible substance (τῆς νοητῆς οὐσίας). Wherefore Plotinus, making many refutations in his lectures (συνουσίαις) and writing a book which we entitled πρὸς τοὺς γνωστικούς, left us to judge the rest. . . . And I, Porphyry, made frequent refutations in reply to the work of Zoroaster (πρὸς τὸ Ζωροάστρου).'

He showed the book to be a recent forgery 'composed by those who devised the heresy, to make men think (εἰς δόξαν) that the doctrines which they chose to proclaim came from the ancient Zoroaster'. Plotinus' book against the Gnostics is identified by Fabricius[1] and later writers with *Enneas II*, Book IX, which though it does not contain the word 'Gnostic' is headed 'Against those who say that the Demiurge of the world is evil, and that the world is evil'. Two modern writers among others have written vivid descriptions of this struggle between neo-Platonism and Gnosticism. Carl Schmidt[2] says of the book of Plotinus just mentioned: 'Platonischer Monismus und gnostischer Dualismus stehen sich hier in ihrer ganzen Schroffheit gegenüber', for the Gnostics taught of a good God side by side with a bad Demiurge and of a pure κόσμος νοητός unequally yoked with a material κόσμος αἰσθητός. J. Bidez[3] says, 'La poussée des gnostiques était violente à Rome même, vers le milieu du 3ᵐᵉ siècle', and continues: 'Brandissant apocalypses et révélation, c'est à Platon qu'ils s'en prenaient. A son royaume des Idées pures, ils opposaient un panthéon resplendissant d'émanations lumineuses.'[4] Amelius, fellow-pupil with Porphyry of Plotinus, 'fit du gnostique Zostrianus une refutation systématique en 40 livres'. This importance attached by Christians and non-Christians to the destruction of Gnosticism[5] explains the subsequent violence of the attacks on Manichaeism[6], which in the words of Oeconomos[7] 's'est assimilé les principaux éléments du gnosticisme expirant', or, to quote Schmidt once more, 'ja nur eine neue Auflage des Gnosticismus

[1] *Bibl. graeca*, V. 687.
[2] *Plotin's Stellung zum Gnosticismus* (Texte und Untersuchungen zur Geschichte der altchrist. Litt. XX, Neue Folge, V, 1900, ed. Gebhardt and Harnack).
[3] *Vie de Porphyre*, pp. 44, 45.
[4] Epiphanius says that Bardesanes, following Valentinus, 'πολλὰς . . . ἀρχὰς καὶ προβολὰς [emanations] διηγήσατο' (P. G. 41, cols. 992, 993). Irenaeus says Valentinus began with a Dyad and taught of emanations therefrom (P. G. 7, cols. 560 sqq.).
[5] The names of a great many Gnostics of various shades have come down to us (e.g. Bardesanes, Basilides, Valentinus, &c.) in various polemics directed against them; this in itself proves how much they were feared.
[6] Zigabenus couples Manes and Valentinus together (*Panoplia*, cols. 305–9).
[7] *Op. cit.* p. 39.

war', and owed to that origin its 'gewaltigen Siegeszug durch den Occident im 4ten Jahrhundert'.[1]

Whatever else Manes did or taught he certainly preached Dualism; and his two principles, Good and Evil, are assailed by his opponents from Epiphanius[2] right down to Zigabenus[3] and Nicetas.[4] Two recent writers have made statements worth quoting. Professor Burkitt[5] says: 'Eznik of Kolb, the Armenian writer of the fifth century, writing against Zoroastrianism, treats Manichaeism as a variety of Persian religion', or in other words 'as another religion found in Persian lands which is Dualistic in character, which nevertheless the Persians persecuted'. Dr. Pullan[6] says of Manichaeism that it 'started from the old Persian belief that the world is a battle-ground between Light and Darkness, which are opposed as good and evil'. From this, as we have seen above, the Manichaean heretics in the Christian Church came to deny the Incarnation and prohibit Image-worship, because both are dependent on Matter, which is evil.[7] To this point however Anna does not allude. 'The impiety of Manes' and 'the most godless doctrines' of his followers (a heresy

---

[1] *Op. cit.* p. 24.

[2] *P. G.* 42, *Haer.* 66, especially cols. 30 and 41. He puts the matter very clearly.

[3] *Panoplia*, cols. 305 sqq., especially col. 315. In col. 1305, as in col. 317, the Μανιχαϊκὴ παραφροσύνη is accused of denying the Incarnation.

[4] *Thes. Orth. Fid.*, Bk. IV, ch. 33, *P. G.* 139, cols. 1316–24. Characteristically he gives alternative names for the heretics; Manichaeans are called Cubrici (because Manes was originally Cubricus) and 'Ακουανῖται from a teacher Acouas. He summarizes the usual teaching of the founder, i.e. the two Principles (God=Good =Light, and Matter=Evil=Darkness) and the doctrines derived therefrom; that the God of the Old Testament is not the God of the New; that Christ was only a phantom and only seemed to suffer, and that there is no resurrection of the body. To this he adds not only belief in metempsychosis, and in ἔμψυχα plants, trees, &c., but also the worship of the Sun, Moon, and Stars (a charge apparently peculiar to this critic; when Pullan, *op. cit.* p. 178, makes the same statement he quotes no authority). He says that Manes, who called himself the Paraclete, undertook to cure a Persian prince, and failing was flayed alive by the king. The chapter ends with a statement that by law Manichaeans cannot inherit either under a will or from an intestate, but their goods go to τὸ δημόσιον ταμεῖον. Yet 'their heresy still flourishes'. A treatise against the Manichaeans written in the time of Justinian by Bishop Zacharias of Mitylene, and published by Cardinal Pitra in *Analecta Sacra*, vol. V, p. 69 (1888) says: 'Evil is not a substance (οὐσία) but a transgression of divine law. If then evils are not by nature and God is the maker of natures, there is one sole ἀρχή.' So Gregory of Nyssa protests that Evil is οὐχ ἀρχή, ἀλλὰ τοῦ ἀγαθοῦ στέρησις (*Panoplia*, p. 313). Bishop Methodius similarly says that evil is 'ignorance or indifference concerning [God]' (*P. G.* 18, col. 345). It is of course the existence of evil which all along has given colour to Dualism, and the efforts of the old theologians to explain it away are interesting.

[5] *Religion of the Manichees*, p. 72. He goes on to point out that Dualism is not confined to Zoroastrianism, nor is Manichaeism a mere variant of that religion. But this hardly concerns us.

[6] *Church of the Fathers*, p. 178.

[7] See Baynes, *Byz. Emp.*, p. 90. Zigabenus, *Panoplia*, cols. 317, 429, bears on this, and cf. col. 1308.

'laughed at by all' and stigmatized as 'foolish teaching'), all this resolves itself in her pages simply into the charge of Dualism.[1] So when we are tempted to wonder whether Anna, in saying that 'Porphyry . . . reduced to utter absurdity the foolish teaching of the Manichaeans', could possibly be making a confusion between the great Neo-Platonist and Bishop Porphyry of Gaza, we are met with three objections. First, though Bishop Porphyry *preached* against the Manichaeans[2] he does not seem to have *written* anything. Secondly, the Pagan philosopher was too well known and too much admired in the Middle Ages for such a confusion to be at all probable.[3] Thirdly, even though Porphyry does not appear to have written directly against the Manichaeans (whose name does not appear in his works), he certainly controverted their main tenet and was a bitter enemy of their forerunners the Gnostics. The end of Anna's sentence, that he showed the folly of Manichaeism 'by very scientific investigations concerning the two principles', need not mean that he 'attacked the Manichaeans, but only the dualism which was associated with their name'.[4]

[1] XIV. 8, pp. 450, 451.

[2] See his Biography by Mark the Deacon, translated by G. F. Hill (1913).

[3] Admiring allusions to Porphyry as a philosopher and writer explaining Aristotle and inspiring men's minds occur in two epigrams ascribed to Leo the Philosopher (*circa* 900 A.D.) published respectively in J. F. Boissonade's *Anecdota graeca*, II, p. 473, and *Anth. Pal.*, IX, No. 214. Psellus quotes his opinion with respect in his *Summary of the Chaldaean doctrines* (*P. G.* 122, col. 1153), and studied his writings along with those of Plotinus, Iamblichus, and Proclus (*Chron.*, Const. IX, Byz. T., p. 108). The same writer also alludes three times to Porphyry, once as 'the wise', in discussing Homer (C. N. Sathas, *Sur les commentaires byzantins*, Ann. Ass. études grecques, 1875, pp. 207, 216–7); and Bidez (*op. cit.* p. 135) tells us that the pupils of Psellus used Porphyry as a help towards understanding popular writers. The same critic says: 'C'est grâce à Porphyre qu'Aristote va exercer désormais en logique une souveraine autorité' (p. 62). The 'logic of Porphyry' was an integral part of Dialectics in the West (*Camb. Med. Hist.* V, p. 765), and cannot have been unknown in the East. St. Augustine, who had himself been a Manichaean, has much to say about Porphyry's *De regressu animae* in his *De civit. dei* (X, XII, XIII, XXII), and Bouillet thinks Porphyry helped to form St. Augustine as a philosopher. But this is not relevant to our subject, as Anna's theological instructors had probably never read a line of the Bishop of Hippo. What is more to the point is that Porphyry's fifteen books against the Christians (to which Anna alludes as his 'raging against us in many chapters') were thought powerful enough to be burnt in 448 by order of the two Emperors of the day, and were controverted, according to St. Jerome, who speaks of his blasphemy and 'impudence', by Methodius, Eusebius, and Apollinaris; Methodius indeed consecrated 'decem milia versuum' to the task, *P. L.* 22, cols. 666, 923 and three extracts from a prose work of his κατὰ Πορφυρίου are given in *P. G.* 18, col. 345. Socrates calls the Arian heretics Porphyrians as a term of great reproach. Finally, we may mention a fresco in the Viale Manzoni which V. Daniel (*Revue belge de philol. et d'hist.* III, 1923) explains for the first time as representing not Job and his wife, nor Odysseus and Penelope, but something out of Porphyry's *De antro nympharum*.

[4] I owe this explanation to the kindness of Prof. D. S. Margoliouth, from whose unpublished letter I am permitted to quote.

This brings us to the various technical terms used by Anna in this connexion, 'principles', μοναρχία, and 'the Platonic ἑνάς or τὸ ἕν'. The two principles of Good and Evil need not be further dwelt on. Porphyry wrote two books περὶ ἀρχῶν, of which we only possess one sentence, preserved by Proclus[1], to the effect that Mind is αἰώνιον, but τὸ ἕν is before παντὸς αἰῶνος. He is also quoted by Cyril as saying in his *Lives of the Philosophers*[2] that Plato makes God or the One or the Good the cause of all things, and in the Letter to his wife Marcella[3] he acknowledges one supreme deity. The works of his master Plotinus are full of 'the One or the Good';[4] so are those of Proclus[5] and Damascius.[6] Psellus in his short summary of the teaching of the Chaldaeans begins with the words μίαν ἀρχὴν τῶν πάντων δοξάζουσι, καὶ ἓν αὐτὴν καὶ ἀγαθὸν ἀπογυμνοῦσι, and ends with the statement that Aristotle and Plato 'accepted the greater part' of the Chaldaean doctrines, while the School of Plotinus, Iamblichus, Porphyry, and Proclus 'accepted them without criticism as divine voices'.

It need hardly be said that all these later philosophers derived their notions of the Good and the One from their model Plato.[7] In the *Parmenides*, *Sophistes*, and *Philebus* we find the One and the Many appearing again and again, and the terms μονάς, ἑνάς, and ἕν are too closely associated in our minds with Plato to need discussion here. But the word μοναρχία used by Anna calls for a word of comment. Pullan[8] says: 'The word Monarchia had been used by St. Irenaeus[9] to signify the sovereign unity of the Godhead, and it was meant to repudiate the Gnostic theory of numerous divine emanations.'[10] Porphyry himself seems to have fastened on it for attacking Christianity,

---

[1] *In Platonis theologiam*, ed. Portus, 1618. The same thought comes in Porphyry's ἀφορμαὶ πρὸς τὰ νοητά, ch. xliii, §§ 1, 5 (ed. Mommert, pp. 41–3). Mind is πολλά, the One must be before τῶν πολλῶν.

[2] Only Bk. I exists whole. The rest is fragments.

[3] Ch. 18, *Opuscula*, ed. A. Nanck, p. 286.

[4] *Enn.* II. 9; III. 3 and 8; V. 4; VI. 8 and 9.

[5] *In Parmen.*, translated in *Chaldaean Oracles of Zoroaster*, p. 30, published by Theosoph. Soc.

[6] περὶ ἀρχῶν, translated by A. Chaignet *passim*, e. g. §§ 1, 49, 125.

[7] Syrianus, in his *Comment. ad Metaph. Aristot.* XIII. 7, says, 'Unum et Bonum idem sunt apud Platonem'.

[8] *Op. cit.* p. 133.

[9] St. Jerome tells us that Irenaeus wrote a book 'De monarchia, sive quod Deus non sit auctor malorum' *P. L.* 23, col. 649.

[10] Pullan also refers to the passage where Tertullian (*P. L.* 2, cols. 157–9) says the word was used as a sort of catchword by 'imprudentes et idiotae', who did not really understand it, and emphatically denies that a Monarchia excluded the having the Son as 'particeps'. But here again we must not ascribe Anna's ideas to any Latin influence.

and we find him saying that 'God could not rightly be called
μονάρχης unless he ruled over [other] gods, μονάρχης γάρ ἐστιν
οὐχ ὁ μόνος ὢν ἀλλ' ὁ μόνος ἄρχων'.[1] This polytheistic view is combated at great length by Zigabenus. In his Preface to the
Panoplia, he says that of the three theories about God, ἀναρχία,
πολυαρχία, and μοναρχία, the first two are Greek absurdities and
the third only is tenable, and this thesis is expanded whenever
occasion serves. But a modern reader will heartily agree with
his quotation from Dionysius the Areopagite,[2] that ἡ θεαρχία,
though sometimes spoken of as a μονάς or a ἑνάς, sometimes
as a τριάς, is really understood by none.

Anna at any rate has no doubts or trepidations as to her
powers of grasping and uttering theological subtleties, and she
proceeds at once from the dogma of μοναρχία to those implied
in the words πρόσωπον and περιγράφειν. The first she uses like
Zigabenus as synonymous with ὑπόστασις or Person, a term
applied sometimes to the Three Persons of the Trinity, sometimes to the One Person in Two Natures of our Lord. As to
περιγράφειν and its opposites they refer to the teaching expressed
in the Athanasian Creed, that God is 'incomprehensible', i.e.
cannot be circumscribed. So Zigabenus quotes from John
Damascene the dictum that if there were many gods τὸ ἀπερί-
γραπτον would be impossible for each, and δεῖ τὸν Θεὸν ἀπερί-
γραπτον εἶναι καὶ πάντα πληροῦντα καὶ ἐν ἑαυτῷ περιγράφοντα.[3]

Finally Anna turns to occult matters and with much
assurance tells us that 'the One of Plato' is ἄρρητον among
the Hellenes and ἀπόρρητον among the Chaldaeans.[4] Does she
really mean anything by this? It seems doubtful. In the
first place we must remember that 'Chaldaean' has always, for
some strange reason, been very loosely used. Kroll suggests
that 'jeder Occultismus chaldäisch genannt werden konnte',[5]
Burkitt[6] says, 'Chaldaeism had come to mean little more than
astrology',[7] and even to-day a correspondent of Professor Margoliouth's told him that 'one of her friends could speak Chaldaic
fluently'. Porphyry's works have many allusions to Chaldaeans.

[1] Macarius Magnes, IV. 20, ed. C. Blondel, Paris 1876, p. 199.
[2] *Panoplia*, (*P. G.* 130, col. 45).
[3] *Panoplia*, col. 44.
[4] XIV. 8, p. 451.
[5] Pauly-Wissowa, *Real Encyclopädie*, Vol. III, col. 2045.
[6] *Op. cit.* p. 73.
[7] According to Rambaud (*Rev. Hist.* III, p. 266), Psellus, who afterwards himself
wrote on Chaldaean Oracles, accused John Xiphilinus and Cerularius 'de verser
dans les superstitions chaldéennes'. Iamblichus (*de comm. math. sci.*, ed. N. Festa
p. 66) says that οἱ μαθηματικοί were called 'Chaldaeans' by the Assyrians. On
Babylonian wisdom, see Nock in *Essays on the Trinity* (1928), p. 66.

He says that they engaged in speculations about the heavens and like the Jews worshipped the Supreme Deity; that Pythagoras who consorted with them in Babylon learnt from them 'what are the principles of all things', and that importance should be attached to certain initiations of Chaldaean theurgi.[1] Aeneas of Gaza[2] tells how Porphyry 'wrote a whole book in which he puts forth the Oracles of the Chaldaeans', and we know that he also wrote about Julian the Chaldaean philosopher, who according to Bidez[3] was the originator under Marcus Aurelius of 'un système de gnose païenne', a mixture of various beliefs of West and East including fire worship and belief in angels and demons. The *Chaldaica Logia*, edited by Kroll,[4] have been described as a 'mixture of Pythagorean Platonic and Jewish teaching', but show no sure signs of neo-Platonic influence. On the other hand the Doctrines of the Chaldaeans as summarized by Psellus seem to the uninitiated pure gibberish, with their Paternal Depth, and Teletarchs and Fountains, and Gods ζωναῖοι and ἄζωνοι. The connexion between Manichaeism and Chaldaean learning is not made clear even by modern critics,[5] and we may be sure that Anna did not recognize it, or she would not have spoken so admiringly of Psellus for 'having mastered the learning of the Hellenes and Chaldaeans'. Probably even in her day Mesopotamia was a blessed word, and we shall gain little by probing her vague generalities farther.

Two couples of words deserve a brief notice before we close this investigation. Anna says the doctrine of the One is ἄρρητον to Hellenes and ἀπόρρητον to Chaldaeans. The antithesis seems to be between 'ineffable' and 'secret' (or 'esoteric'). The former word in its mystical sense can be traced back to Plato[6] and is found in Damascius (where his translator, Chaignet, paraphrases it as 'que la parole humaine est impuissante à

---

[1] *Life of Pythag.*, chs. 6 and 12, and *De regressu animae.* See Bidez (*op. cit.*). St. Augustine (*De civ. Dei*, X. 27) says Porphyry got some of his opinions 'a Chaldaeis magistris'.
[2] Fabricius, *Bibl. gr.* I, p. 309; V, p. 744.
[3] *Op. cit.* p. 88.
[4] *De oraculis Chaldaicis*, Bresl. philol., Abh. VII. 1.
[5] G. Krüger (*B. Z.* XXII, p. 477) says that the 123rd Homily of Severus of Antioch, published by Kugener and Cumont, shows 'the close connexion of Manichaeism with the Chaldaizing Mazdaism of the Babylon of that time', and Pullan (*op. cit.* p. 178) says Manichaeism was compounded of Persian Dualism 'overlaid with Babylonian theories connected with the worship of the stars'. But no proofs are adduced by either writer. In the sixth century with equal vagueness Damascius (περὶ ἀρχῶν, § 125) said, 'Les Babyloniens semblent avoir négligé le principe Un de tout et en avoir établi deux', trans. A. Chaignet, *Problèmes et Solutions*, Vol. II, p. 128. [6] *Sophistes*, 238.

rendre'[1]), Porphyry,[2] and Proclus.[3] But its most technical
meaning so to speak and the one to which Anna probably
alludes, belongs to Valentinian Gnosticism, which started everything from an unnamed (ἀνονόμαστον) Dyad, ἧς τὸ μέν τι καλεῖ-
σθαι "Ἄρρητον, τὸ δὲ Σιγήν.[4] What idea this conveyed to our
authoress it is impossible to conjecture. From the way that she
hurries over these sublime matters, we may perhaps infer that
the 'ineffable' and the 'esoteric' were in truth equally obscure
to her, and that she would have been among those towards
whom Pythagoras made ἀπορρήτους his λόγους as fit only for the
brotherhood to hear.[5]

Her other pair of words, ἐγκοσμίους τε καὶ ὑπερκοσμίους (ἀρχάς)
is also an echo of Gnosticism. The two are used in the second
century by Basilides[6] and three hundred years later by Proclus,[7]
on each occasion with reference to the origin of all things. How
any one could 'hang' them from the One of Plato is a mystery
which Anna does not explain.[8]

We may now say good-bye to her polemical pretensions, and
turn with relief to something less wholly remote from us and our
sphere of interests than these theological hair-splittings. But
one thing must clearly be burnt into all her readers' brains,
namely that the danger of falling into heresies unawares was
to the Byzantines of the twelfth century a very real nightmare.
Everywhere 'the troops of Midian prowl, and prowl around'

[1] περὶ ἀρχῶν, §§ 2, 3, 49, and see Chaignet, vol. I, p. 10, note 4.
[2] e. g. Life of Pythag., ed. A. Nauck, p. 49.
[3] In I Euclidis librum (ed. G. Friedlein), pp. 90, 141.
[4] Irenaeus, v. Haer., Bk. I (P. G. 7, col. 560). Another form of Gnostic cosmogony was an Ogdoad, ἄρρητον being one of the first four things from which the
next four emanated (ibid., col. 568).
[5] Iamblichus, de comm. math. scientia, ch. 24 (ed. N. Festa), p. 75. So Proclus
(In I Euclidis librum, p. 90) speaks of ἀπορρητότεροι λόγοι. Psellus, in his Summary
of Chaldaean doctrines (P. G. 122, col. 1152), says that 'in each soul there is an unknown ἰδιότης ῥητοῦ καὶ ἀπορρήτου (secret) συνθήματος'. It is a little suspicious that
Anna finds excuses for not going into detail about either the Manichaean or the
Bogomile heresy. One had been exposed already and the other would sully her
tongue. Is not this the same spirit that makes pupils in examinations, as was once
said in a report, 'cloak ignorance with verbiage'?
[6] Basilides divided τὰ ὄντα into κόσμος and ὑπερκόσμια (Contra haereses P. G. 17,
col. 3310).
[7] In Crat. 169, ed. G. Pasquali, p. 93. Here we meet with πατρικὴ αἰτία and
πηγή, which he elsewhere couples with ἀρχή (In Tim. 242 D), ed. E. Diehl, III,
p. 14.
[8] She may possibly be referring to the passage of Irenaeus about the προαρχή,
and the ἑνότης and μονότης which τὸ ἐν οὖσαι προήκαντο . . . ἀρχὴν πάντων . . . ἦν
Ἀρχὴν ὁ λόγος μονάδα καλεῖ . . . ἤ τε μονότης καὶ ἑνότης, μονάς τε καὶ τὸ ἕν, προήκαντο
τὰς λοιπὰς προβολὰς τῶν Αἰώνων (P. G. 7, col. 565). This is hard to reconcile with
col. 560 on the Dyad, but the whole matter is beyond our scope except in so far as
it illustrates how audaciously in her handling of terms and doctrines Anna exercised
herself in great matters which were too high for her.

as they write. And even if a man had lived his whole life in perfect orthodoxy, was there not always the peril that some evil enemy, like Browning's monk, might

> trip him, just a-dying,
> Sure of heaven as sure can be,
> Spin him round and send him flying
> Off to hell, a Manichee?

MILITARY AFFAIRS

55. INTRODUCTION, NUMBERS AND PAY

WHEN we come to consider Anna's attitude towards military affairs, it is difficult to know how much to say and how much to omit, as her interest in Alexius' campaigns is only one, though the principal, aspect of her devotion to him and to the Empire which they served to 'widen'. It is not unfair to say that his successes in the field are not remarkable. Robert defeated him at Durazzo, and Bohemund after being twice victorious was obliged to withdraw not so much because Alexius relieved Larissa as because he corrupted the Norman army. Years later the same enemy was brought to terms not by arms but by famine. In the Patzinak war the terrible Greek disaster at Dristra was only after a considerable time compensated by the success at Lebunium. In the Turkish fighting Alexius took no part till nearly the end of his life, and even then his triumph lay rather in a profitable treaty than in any brilliant victory. It is therefore peculiarly instructive to see how Anna as a historian regards her father's military career. In addition to countless passages about his 'strategy', 'trophies', and the like, she three times gives us a summarized picture of his varied combats and successes.

First, in looking back to the Crusade she starts with an outline of Alexius' position at that time. The Westerners were ambitious and terribly numerous, and the Emperor knew that 'all the Greek forces would not suffice against a fraction of them, even if they were collected into one body; how much less then when most of them were scattered, some guarding the gorges[1] towards Serbia and Dalmatia, others those towards the Danube, so as to watch for the attacks of the Comans and Dacians, while

---

[1] This need to watch his frontiers must never be forgotten in estimating Alexius' attitude to the Crusaders (Chalandon, *Alexis Ier*, p. 163).

many were entrusted with the defence of Durazzo, so that it might not again' (i.e. as in the first campaign of Robert Guiscard) 'be captured by the Celts'. Anna then tells us how he 'restrained with promises and gifts' the less formidable of his enemies (evidently those coming from the North), and devoted himself wholly to resisting the Western Crusaders without, and the unnamed traitors within. On every occasion indeed he 'made a stand against what was very urgent, like one notable among doctors using the rule of his art'.[1]

Secondly, the public announcement by Eustathius Camytzes of her father's Turkish victories elicits from her this comment:[2]

'In truth as far as fortune went, he had had to do with bad luck (δυσχερέσι πράγμασι ὡμιλήκει), adverse both to him and to the interests of the Greeks, and had been utterly swamped by a flood of misfortunes, but his valour (ἀρετή) and alertness and activity stood firm and was stubborn against every misfortune. For on none of the former emperors even up to our day did there descend such a complexity of troubles and such mischief from all sorts of men at home and abroad as we have found in the case of this Emperor. For either it was necessary, with God's permission, that the affairs of the Greeks should be in evil case . . . or else the Greek power had come to this condition from the folly of previous rulers; at any rate a throng of troubles and a disturbance swelling like the sea had come together in the times of my father's reign. For at the same time and all together the Scythian from the North and the Celt from the West and Ishmael from the East had been stirred up, apart from the dangers on the sea, and leaving out the barbarians who ruled the waves and the innumerable pirate ships, which either the rage of the Saracens built, or the greed of the Vetones and their ill will towards the Greek empire constructed.[3] And all cast envious eyes on her; for the empire of the Greeks, being by nature mistress of the other nations, has what is slavish as her constitutional enemy (ἐχθρωδῶς διακείμενον) and whenever this can seize an occasion, it attacks her now from this side and now from that by land and sea. And things in former days and the circumstances of the Empire before our times were very easy and considerably lighter, but in my father's time, as soon as he had mounted on the imperial chariot, immediately from all parts dangers rushed in together. Then the Celt was roused and showed the point of his spear and the Ishmaelite bent his bow, and all the Nomadic race and the whole Scythian tribe pressed on with myriad wagons.'

[1] XIV. 4, pp. 434, 435.   [2] XIV. 7, pp. 444, 445.
[3] Anna here makes her only important allusion to the pirate vessels which infested the Mediterranean from the first days of the Arab invasion, and for many centuries afterwards. The 'barbarous Vetones' were, so Du Cange tells us in his note on XII. 9, p. 370 c, the Slav pirates of Narenta on the Illyrian coast, who on being driven from Italy by the Lombards had settled on the Eastern shores of the Adriatic and waged incessant war with the Venetians.

Anna as usual fears the charge of partiality in praising her father, and meets it by reiterating her statement as to 'the Emperor's perils on behalf of the welfare of the Greeks, and . . . the struggles and misfortunes . . . which he endured on behalf of the Christians'. As usual also she appeals to first-hand testimony in confirmation.

Thirdly, at the end of the Emperor's last campaign, in which he made with the Turks a treaty that restored the imperial boundaries to the condition they were in 'before Romanus Diogenes wrapped round him the reins of empire and was defeated in that great defeat',[1] Anna once more asserts her father's claims to having saved the state.

'Since the barbarians came over the boundaries of the Empire, from the very accession of Diogenes[2] who marched against them and was unlucky as men say from the word Go, not till the reign of my father was the barbarian hand[3] destroyed, but swords and spears were whetted against Christians, and there were battles and wars and slaughters. For cities disappeared, lands were ravaged, and all the realm of the Greeks was defiled by blood of Christians. Some fell pitifully by arrows and spears, some were driven away from their homes and led captive to the cities of Persia. And fear seized all, as they hurried to hide in caves and groves and mountains from the evils falling on them. Among these some lamented over their sufferings in being led away to Persia, while others still going about (if indeed any remained in the Greek borders) deeply groaning bewailed one a son, one a daughter. One wept over a brother, one a nephew dying untimely, and like women they would drop down hot tears. And at that time (τότε) there was no condition without tears and groans. And except for a few, I mean Tzimisces and the Emperor Basil, from the early days (ἔκτοτε) till my father no emperor had dared under any circumstances to touch Asia with the tips of his feet.'[4]

On this somewhat highfalutin passage of Anna's we have an interesting commentary in her father's first poem to John.[5] He too enumerates the external and internal enemies with whom

---

[1] XV. 6, p. 478.   [2] 1067 A. D.

[3] χείρ, which may also be translated 'band' or 'violence'.

[4] XV. 10, p. 495. It is clear that ἔκτοτε refers vaguely to a remote past time, probably as early as the seventh century, when the barbarians began their inroads; it cannot refer like the τότε in the previous sentence to the ten years of chaos between Manzikert (1071) and Alexius' accession (1081), for the two Emperors mentioned both reigned before that period, John Tzimisces 969–76, and Basil II 963–1025. Cf. ἐν τοῖς τότε χρόνοις in III. 3, p. 77, where it is best translated 'in our times' or 'in these latter days'. As we see elsewhere Anna is apt to give a wide meaning to many words that in Classic Greek have a precise signification. It is curious that in this passage she never says that her father set things right again, though she doubtless implies it.

[5] Mous. Alex. I, 282 sqq.

he had contended, Scythians, Italians and Persians, the rising in Crete and Cyprus, and the hostile attacks on Mitylene, Rhodes, and Chios.[1] He too makes us feel the horrors of the Crusading invasion with its μυρίος στρατός.[2] Whether truthful or not his picture and his daughter's agree together; to himself and to her he appeared emphatically a conquering hero.

Before we consider Alexius' military career in detail some preliminary points in connexion with the Byzantine army must be disposed of. The first are numbers and pay.

If Anna's figures are to be believed, armies in her day were often of considerable size, but the more we study them the more random and untrustworthy do these figures seem. Thus Robert Guiscard puts his 30,000 men on to 150 ships, and during the siege of Durazzo loses from famine and disease some 10,000 footmen and 500 mounted officers; the Pope and the German king lose in battle 'more than 30,000' from their two armies.[3] Clearly such numbers are fantastically large. The rebel Bryennius has a right wing of 5,000 which we can well believe, but Godfrey de Bouillon has 10,000 horse and 70,000 foot, and the Crusading contingent that followed later has 50,000 cavalry and 100,000 infantry, figures which certainly seem incredible.[4] The Sultan sends Alexius 7,000 Turkish mercenaries,[5] while the Manichaeans present at Durazzo only amount to 2,800, among whom there are 300 casualties.[6] The combined Venetian and Greek fleets lose 13,000 drowned and many more captured at Corfu,[7] and of Turkish soldiers 50,000 march out on one expedition and 80,000 heavy-armed on another.[8] The emir Tzachas has a fleet at sea and an army of only 8,000 on land,[9] yet is a most formidable foe. In the Patzinak and Coman campaigns the numbers are suspiciously high. The chief Tzelgu is said to put a 'mixed army of about 80,000' into the field; 30,000 auxiliaries are offered to Alexius if he will but make peace; at the Taurocomus ridge 'about 7,000' Comans fall and 3,000 are captured.[10] It is even more obviously

---

[1] Cf. Anna's account in IX. 2; VII. 8; and XI. 5, p. 321.
[2] *Mous. Alex.* I, 330 sqq. Cf. *Al.* X. 5.
[3] I. 13, p. 33; 16, p. 37; IV. 3, p. 108.
[4] I. 5, p. 11; X. 9, p. 293; XI. 8, pp. 331.
[5] V. 5, p. 137.   [6] IV. 4, p. 109; V. 3, p. 131.
[7] VI. 5, p. 161.
[8] VI. 10, p. 171; XI. 3, p. 318. We may note that in XIV. 1, p. 421, the army of Asan is 24,000, but shortly afterwards the figures given are 50,000 in XIV. 4, p. 433, and 40,000 in XIV. 5, p. 439.
[9] VII. 8, p. 206.
[10] VII. 1, p. 188; 2, p. 192; X. 4, p. 280. Five thousand deserters, αὐτόμολοι, come over to Alexius in VIII. 5, p. 231.

guess-work when Anna puts down enemies merely seen approaching as 36,000 or 40,000, or informs us that 6,000 Patzinaks were told off for plunder.[1] It is not surprising that such statistics given after so many years should inspire little confidence, but they seem so utterly absurd (bearing no relation to facts or probabilities as far as we can gauge them) that we wonder why Anna took the trouble to repeat or perhaps invent them at all. We can only suppose her influenced by an inherent belief that the larger the enemy's army, the more glorious the victory, so that it became a point of honour to exaggerate the numbers of Scythians or Turks.

One thing is certain. Throughout the book, from financial necessity armies whether large or small are frequently disbanded, especially at the approach of winter, and the collecting of them is a serious and costly matter.[2]

This brings us to what, as we have hinted before, was the great crux of the whole military situation—Alexius' perpetual difficulty in raising money to pay his troops.[3] He had none in the treasury to begin with, and we wonder from what source he raised 'considerable sums' to send to the Venetian doge as early as 1081.[4] His drafts on the property first of his family and then of the Church (a general levy being a thing he dared not attempt) met only with temporary success.[5] Conquerors alone can effectively exact $\phi\acute{o}\rho ovs$;[6] and without a hope of lawless plunder none of the ill-paid armies[7] of the day could have been kept together. Communications between an army and the home treasury took so long that profitable bargains might be nullified by lack of funds.[8] Demands for arrears or for higher pay might become so serious as to produce mutiny.[9] There was no army of unpaid conscripts, and except in the case of certain

---

[1] VII. 3, p. 196; VIII. 1, p. 221; 4, p. 228.

[2] II. 3, p. 49; V. 1, p. 127; VI. 14, pp. 183, 185; VII. 11, p. 217; XII. 4, p. 356, etc.

[3] Leo (Tactica, XIX. 17) says that if crews are not well supplied they will mutiny or else plunder their friends. Cf. Archidamus the Spartan, 'War is not an affair of arms, but of money' (Thuc. I. 83; VI. 34), and the similar sentiments of Cecaumenos, $\lambda\acute{o}\gamma.$ $vov\theta.$, p. 94.

[4] III. 9, p. 91; IV. 2, p. 107; V. 1, p. 126. Further large sums to Venice are mentioned in VI. 5, p. 161, after a great naval victory.

[5] V. 1 & 2; VI. 3.

[6] IV. 3, p. 107. Robert Guiscard starts for his Illyrian campaign $\tau\grave{\eta}v$ $\chi\acute{\omega}\rho av$ (of South Italy) $\dot{a}\rho\gamma\upsilon\rho o\lambda o\gamma\acute{\eta}\sigma as$ $\dot{a}\pi a\sigma av$ $\kappa a\grave{\iota}$ $\phi o\rho o\lambda o\gamma\acute{\eta}\sigma as$ (I. 16, p. 38).

[7] In theory they were paid annually (VI. 14, p. 183). But Bohemund's men had four years owing (V. 7, p. 143).   [8] I. 2, pp. 5, 6.

[9] V. 7, p. 143; cf. V. 2, p. 128. In the old Greek armies pay was deliberately kept back to render desertion (whereby it would be forfeited) less likely (Thuc. VIII. 45).

provincial landowners in Asia no sort of feudal tenure. It was
a case for all, Greek and mercenaries alike, of 'being a slave
for pay' (ἐπὶ μισθῷ δουλεῦσαι).[1] It is startling to a modern ear
to hear of soldiers receiving money 'that they may fight coura-
geously',[2] but as military service was then almost entirely a
matter of sale and barter and personal inclination, it was perhaps better that the commercial aspect should have been thus
clearly stated. The first step taken by the Crusaders is to sell
their lands to pay for troops,[3] and Bohemund, much hampered
by poverty and consequent want of men, is peculiarly sus-
ceptible to the attraction of a stupendous bribe.[4] War then,
as now, was the most expensive luxury in which an empire
could indulge.

MILITARY AFFAIRS

56. OFFICERS AND MEN

THE army has enormous importance in Alexius' history. As
we have seen, it was the army that gave him the crown;
its wishes counted far more than those of the civil population,
and in the sack of Constantinople he can restrain the 'native'
quite as little as he can the 'barbarian' forces.[5] When Alexius
has to justify himself in a purely ecclesiastical matter, or
even to try a heretic, τὸ στρατιωτικόν is summoned no less
than the Senate and the Church.[6] At Anna's birth honours
and gifts are bestowed on 'the leaders of the army'.[7] These
same leaders are frequently consulted, sometimes in positively
humble terms, by the generals commanding them, even when
the general is their Emperor.[8] In an age when military usurpa-

---

[1] V. 7, p. 143. The term θητεῦσαι is used of the Normans who join Alexius'
forces, pay being here not mentioned (VI. 1, p. 153). See p. 107, note 8, above.
Butumites is advised by the Emperor to 'hire' (μισθοῦσθαι) the Crusading stragglers
as a garrison for Nicaea (XI. 3, p. 317).
[2] XI. 11, p. 340. Leo (Tactica, XIX. 71) advises bestowing 'gifts and honours'
on brave soldiers, but not till after the battle, when cowards are to be punished.
[3] X. 5, p. 285.
[4] X. 11, pp. 301, 303. On a later occasion he suggests that money only would
get back Laodicea (XI. 11, p. 340).
[5] II. 7, p. 57; 10, p. 65.
[6] VI. 3, p. 155; XV. 8, p. 488.   [7] VI. 8, p. 167.
[8] IV. 5, p. 112; VII. 1, p. 189; VIII. 1, p. 221; 3, p. 227; X. 2, pp. 273, 274;
4, pp. 277, 281; 9, p. 295; XIV. 2, p. 424. Romanus Diogenes similarly consults
'the best of the generals' in Nic. Bry. I. 13, p. 26. Leo (Tactica, XIX. 36) says an
admiral should consult his ἄρχοντες before battle.

tions were of common occurrence (as much so indeed as in the history of the kings of Israel), it is obvious that officers and especially popular ones required firm yet careful handling, none the less if they were of the imperial family. Alexius did his best to be in very truth Commander-in-Chief with sole authority, but the way in which he 'summons' one general after another, and gives them definite instructions on every point, serves to show that independent action on their part was to him a never-ending subject of uneasy fear.[1]

Military officers are first mentioned by Anna just after Alexius' accession. We read: 'in the treasuries of the Palace there were no heaps of money stored up, with which he might engage allied troops from other countries.' So he calls to Constantinople the various commandants from Asia Minor (Dabatenus of Heraclea and Burtzes of Choma being specially mentioned), enjoining on them to leave just enough men behind to guard the towns, and to bring all the rest and 'as many fresh recruits as they could', to help in the Illyrian campaign.[2]

Here we must point out again at the risk of repetition, first that the highest commands were very apt to be given to members of the imperial family, secondly that pardoned rebels often occupied responsible military posts, and thirdly that while no officer was allowed to act on his own initiative but only under the Emperor's orders, the Emperor was no less bound by custom to consult his (so to speak) General Staff. The various titles of Great Domestic of the East or of the West,[3] Great Drungary of the fleet,[4] decurion,[5] tagmatarch,[6] dux of the fleet,[7] σπαθάριος,[8] thalassocrator,[9] phalangarch or protostrator,[10] toparch or topoteretes[11] need more careful investigation than

---

[1] Chalandon (*op. cit.* p. 280) considers that the strong hand which Alexius, a soldier-emperor following after two civilians, tried to keep on the army by acting as his own Commander-in-Chief and giving the best posts to his relations or henchmen, was the cause of the constant revolts among the officers mentioned by his daughter.

[2] III. 9, p. 91. Cf. III. 11, p. 96; V. 1, pp. 126, 127; VII. 7, p. 204.

[3] I. 4, p. 9; II. 4, p. 50; IV. 4, p. 108, and 6, p. 115; VI. 4, p. 157; VII. 1, p. 189; 2, p. 191; cf. Nic. Bry. I. 3, p. 18. Chalandon believes that the official headquarters of this officer were at Adrianople. In the ninth century there had been seven military commands called Domesticates (Bury, *Imp. admin. system*, ch. C. II).

[4] III. 4, p. 78; VI. 11, p. 174; X. 4, p. 279; XIII. 1, p. 376.

[5] III. 11, p. 95.   [6] XI. 5, p. 322.

[7] VII. 8, p. 206; 9, p. 209; IX. 1, p. 246; X. 7, p. 288; 8, p. 290; XI. 10, p. 335.   [8] II. 11, p. 64.

[9] IX. 1, p. 247; 3, p. 250; XI. 5, p. 322. As we have said, military and naval commands are throughout interchangeable (e.g. Cantacuzenus in X. 2, XI. 9 and 11, XIII. 5 and 6).

[10] V. 7; VII. 3, p. 196.

[11] III. 9, p. 92.

space permits. At any rate Anna uses them consistently and with apparent accuracy, though she likes to vary her terms by synonyms.[1] She is of course fully alive, and makes her readers so, to the monstrous impertinence of Bohemund in asking to become Domestic of the East,[2] yet we find Taticius the son of a Saracen captive, a man therefore 'not of free condition', holding the post of Great Primicerius, and commanding a special body of mercenaries, the Bardariote Turks.[3] We also have a Scythian ('very wise and practising virtue and truth') as Grand Hetaeriarch over the foreign Palace Guards, and Du Cange believes that one title, that of ἐξουσιοκράτωρ, was distinctive of the officer commanding the Alan auxiliary troops.[4] Indeed of Alexius' officers surprisingly many are foreign by birth. The 'Celts' Urselius, Umbertopulus, Peter Aluph, and Roger,[5] the Armenians Ariebes, Philaretus, and Aspietes,[6] the Turk Camyres, the Sarmatian Uzas with his son, and the Scythian or Sarmatian Caratzes[7] play important parts in the imperial army. The Turkish generals Elchanes and Scaliarius fight and die for the Empire,[8] and the 'most warlike' Monastras, 'dear to Ares' and praised as having 'much experience in military matters', is a half-breed.[9]

If the officers are partly of foreign extraction, the troops are

[1] στρατοπεδάρχης and στρατηγὸς αὐτοκράτωρ seem to be loosely equivalent (I. 1, p. 4; 2, p. 5; II. 1, p. 43; IX. 2, p. 250; XI. 1, p. 311; XII. 2, p. 350). In XIII. 2, p. 379, it is hard to distinguish between λοχαγοί, ἀρχηγοί and συνταγματάρχαι. The commandant of a fortress is indifferently δοῦξ, ἡγεμών, στρατηγός, τοπάρχης, τοποτηρητής, or κουράτωρ (III. 9, p. 92; VII. 8, p. 205; XI. 5, pp. 323, 324).

[2] X. 11, p. 304.

[3] IV. 4, p. 109 (and see Du Cange's note). He was 'of the same age as' and had been 'brought up with' Alexius (Nic. Bry. IV. 20, p. 99); XI. 3, p. 317.

[4] VIII. 7, p. 237; cf. I. 5, p. 11; XIII. 6, p. 393. The name ἑταιρεία was given to the soldiers (largely foreign) in personal attendance on the Emperor, and bound to protect him against plots (Bury, op. cit. p. 106). They are mentioned as fighting at Manzikert under the traitor Andronicus Ducas (Nic. Bry. I. 16, p. 29). The excubitors, originally also Palace Guards and one of the four τάγματα guarding the capital (Bury, op. cit.), are described by Anna as going out on active service with their commander (IV. 4, p. 109).

[5] I. 1, p. 3; II. 4, p. 50; IV. 4, p. 109: 6, p. 117; V. 5, p. 136; 7, p. 143; VI. 14, p. 183; VIII. 7, p. 236; X. 2, p. 273; XI. 6, p. 324; XIII. 4, p. 387: 9, pp. 400, 402: 12, p. 416.

[6] V. 5, p. 136; VI. 9, p. 168; VIII. 7, p. 236. There is a long article by J. Laurent in the Mélanges Schlumberger (vol. I, pp. 159–68) as to the identification of Anna's Aspietes (IV. 6, p. 117, and XII. 2) with the Oschin of Matthew of Edessa and the Ursinus of Albert of Aix. Laurent believes there were two Armenian princes called Aspietes.

[7] V. 5, p. 137; 7, p. 142; VII. 3, p. 195; 9, p. 213; 10, p. 214; VIII. 5, p. 232; 7, p. 237; X. 4, pp. 279, 281; XV. 6, p. 476.

[8] VI. 13, p. 181; X. 2, p. 274 (where it is tempting to insert καὶ before τοῦ Ἐλχάν, so as to bring in the two men); XIII. 5, p. 390.

[9] VII. 9, p. 213; 10, p. 314; VIII. 5, p. 232; X. 2, p. 274; 4, p. 281; XI. 2, p. 314; 9, p. 334; 11, pp. 339, 340; XII. 2, p. 348; XIV. 3, p. 429; 5, p. 441.

predominantly so. Oman[1] says: 'After Manzikert we find foreign mercenaries always forming both a larger and a more important part of the Imperial host than in the flourishing days of the Macedonian dynasty. Franks, Lombards, Russians, Patzinaks, Turks were enlisted in permanent corps, or hired from their princes as temporary auxiliaries. It is no longer the old Byzantine army which we find serving under Alexius Comnenus and his successors, but a mass of barbarian adventurers, such as the army of Justinian had been 500 years before.' Later on he gives a reason for this:[2] 'The Comneni were centralizers, and preferred to manage affairs from head-quarters rather than to trust their forces to the strategi of the themes. They preferred to raise bodies of troops for general service rather than to localize the corps. A dangerous proportion of the army was for the future composed of foreign mercenaries.'[3] Furthermore the Comneni 'found native troops hard to raise, now that the old Asiatic recruiting ground was gone', and had also learned 'a great respect for Western valour', so that 'they enlisted as many Western mercenaries as they could get together'. Finally 'to supplement the Western spear [they] called in the Eastern bow', so that 'thousands of horse-archers hired from the nomad tribes' (Turks, Patzinaks, and Comans) 'rode in their hosts', till 'the native corps began to take quite a secondary place'. The old hatred of mercenaries displayed by Polybius throughout his work, and in a more modified form by Thucydides,[4] had entirely disappeared, and as we have already seen one of Anna's grievances against her father's spendthrift predecessors is that they had left him no money for engaging assistance of this kind,[5] what she once calls 'horsemen and footmen coming out of all lands'.[6]

Yet mercenaries can never be wholly trusted. The Franks in Alexius' army go over to Bryennius in the middle of the battle, and the Nemitzi (Germans) in Constantinople betray the city to their master's enemy.[7] Dalmatian allies watch the course of

[1] *Art of War*, I, p. 223. The system of substituting money payments for personal service or the provision of local militia had been started by Nicephorus II Phocas (963–9), and carried to its extreme under Constantine IX Monomachus (1042–55). See Laurent, *Byzance et les Turcs Seldjoucides*, p. 50, note 4.
[2] *Op. cit.* I. p. 227.
[3] See F. Dölger's review in *B. Z.* XXVI, pp. 102–13 of a new book by P. Mutavciev (Sofia, 1923) dealing with στρατιῶται as opposed to 'Söldner' and discussing 'Soldatengüter', πρόνοια or οἰκονομία, and the like.
[4] *Hist.* VII. 48.
[5] At the same time she realizes that heterogeneous δυνάμεις ἐκ διαφόρων ξενικῶν τε καὶ ἐγχωρίων are less reliable (II. 9, p. 61) and less easy to control (II. 10, p. 64; III. 2, p. 73. See following paragraph.
[6] VIII. 3, p. 227.   [7] I. 6, p. 14; II. 9 and 10.

events at Durazzo and go home without fighting.[1] Even the
'warlike' Manichaeans, descendants of Armenian captives
settled in Thrace, leave the colours after a defeat and cannot
be bribed to return; later on they join the Patzinaks against
the Empire.[2] On the whole the 'godless' Turks are the most
staunch of the hirelings.[3] On one occasion we hear of 500
invaluable horsemen from Flanders, and we find Bulgarians,
Vlachs, Alans, and 'Sarmatians skilled in archery' who justify
the trust reposed in them; Alexius again is eager for 'mercenary
troops from Rome'.[4] Scythians are fatally given to plunder and
to deserting,[5] good fighters though they are. The Venetian
sailors as a body remain loyal to the Greek side, but Pietro
Contarini goes over to Robert.[6] The distrust which all three
armies, Patzinaks, Greeks, and Comans, feel of each other
is entirely justified by the intrigue and deceit and treachery
that marks the whole Patzinak campaign; at one point 5,000
mountaineers come over to Alexius, and at no point does any
one believe any one else's word.[7] The Comans play the same
sinister part in the rebellion of the pseudo-Diogenes.[8] Always
the hired allies of to-day, often obtained after immense trouble
and delay, might be the enemies of to-morrow.[9]

Let us see what else besides casual mercenaries an emperor
had to rely on. When Alexius as the general of Botaniates went
against Bryennius, the West, with its 'Macedonian and Thracian regiments', its 'cavalry of the theme of Thessaly', and
'the veteran remnants of the old army of Italy, which had
long served under Maniaces',[10] had gone over to the rebel;
so to the loyalist side was left only 'quite a scanty army', i.e.
'Immortals who had very recently (χθès καὶ πρώην) taken up
sword and spear, and a few soldiers from Choma, and a
Celtic force amounting to but few'. The Emperor's officials
summon allies (a euphemistic word for 'mercenaries' throughout the book) from the Turks, but Alexius does not await their
arrival.[11]

---

[1] IV. 6.   [2] V. 3, p. 131; VI. 2 and 4.
[3] I. 4, p. 10; 6, passim; II. 6, p. 56; IV. 2, p. 105; V. 5, p. 137; 7, p. 142;
VIII. 3, p. 226; X. 4, p. 280; XI. 2, p. 316.
[4] V. 7, p. 142; VII. 6 and 7; VIII. 3, p. 227; 5, p. 230; XIII. 6.
[5] I. 5; VII. 2, p. 192; VIII. 5, p. 231; XV. 4, p. 470; 6, p. 476.
[6] VI. 5, pp. 160, 161.
[7] Books VII and VIII.   [8] X. 4, p. 281.
[9] V. 1, p. 125; 2, p. 128; 3, p. 132: 7, p. 143; VI. 1, pp. 153, 154; 9, p. 170;
VIII. 3, p. 226; XI. 2, p. 316; XII. 4, p. 356. Cf. Thuc. VII. 13; VIII. 28.
[10] Oman, op. cit. I. p. 224, where 'John' Maniaces should be 'George'; cf. Oman,
Byz. Emp., p. 246.
[11] I. 4. Bryennius however says Alexius set out σχὼν μεθ' ἑαυτοῦ τοὺς ξυμμάχους
Τούρκους (Hyle, IV. 4, p. 90).

This corps of Immortals is later described by Anna as 'the most distinctive (ἰδιαίτατον) among the Greek forces',[1] and its creation is fully narrated by her husband.[2] He says, 'I ought to explain who these Immortals are. The Emperor Michael [VII], or to say truth the eunuch Nicephorus the logothete, seeing that the army of the East had all become subject to the Turks and was now at an end, took pains to form a new (νεόλεκτον) army as best he could, and collecting some of the soldiers from Asia who had been scattered and were serving for pay, he put cuirasses on them and gave them large oblong shields,[3] and helmets to wear and spears.' They receive careful training from a specially chosen commander, who 'as soon as they could ride with safety and bear arms competently', tests them by strenuous sham-fights at a gallop, giving to the best the rank of officers and also the name of Immortals, which was subsequently attached to the whole corps.[4] The story is thus recounted by Oman:[5] 'So wholly had the army of the East been cut off' (through the ravaging of the Asiatic themes, 'the great recruiting ground of the Imperial army', by the Turks since Manzikert)[6] 'that in 1078 Michael Ducas, by collecting all the scattered and disbanded survivors of the old corps from the Asiatic side of the Bosphorus, and supplementing them with recruits, only obtained a division of ten thousand horse, the so-called Immortals, with whom the future Emperor Alexius Comnenus made his first great campaign.' The Immortals therefore were born subjects of the Empire; so were the few soldiers from Choma, which has been clearly proved to have been a district not far from the Phrygian Laodicea ad Lycum.[7]

---

[1] II. 9, p. 62. Du Cange, in his note on I. 4, p. 10 A, seems to take ἰδιαίτατον as 'most permanent'.   [2] Loc. cit.

[3] θυρεός=scutum, as opposed to ἀσπίς, the round shield.

[4] Neither he nor Anna mentions the fact that the name came from the famous Persian horsemen known as 'Immortals' (Oman, Art of War, I, p. 28). Du Cange, in his note on I. 4, p. 10 A refers to Procopius, De bello Persico, I. He himself explains the name 'quod pacis aeque ac belli tempore militarent'.

[5] Op. cit. I, p. 223.

[6] Oman (op. cit. I, p. 222) points out that 'Thirty years after Manzikert when the armies of the Crusaders marched from Nicaea to Tarsus, right across the ancient heart of the Empire, they nearly perished of starvation in a land of briers and ruins'.

[7] Note on III. 9, p. 92 B, and see XI. 5, p. 324. Du Cange ridicules the interpretation of χῶμα=earth, mound, making 'soldiers from Choma'=native-born, indigenous. But his suggestion that Choma was the ancient Lycia seems hardly less fantastic. Ramsay (Hist. Geogr. of Asia Minor, p. 136) and the map of Asia Minor (ed. J. G. C. Anderson in Murray's Handy Classical Maps) identify the modern village of Homa or Khoma ('which retains the Byzantine or Turco-Byzantine name') with Siblia, a little North of the river Maeander and about twenty miles North-West from Apamea. It must not be confused with Chonae: Nic. Acom. mentions both as distinct places (Man. C. VI. 1, p. 115).

Alexius therefore had two contingents of Greek soldiers, the Immortals and the Chomatenes, and one of 'Celtic' (i.e. Norman) mercenaries, doubtless the remainder of the army with which the defeated Urselius had once encountered him.[1] (Soldiers, as we have said before, were seldom loath to change sides.[2]) In the battle of Calaure[3] against Bryennius, Alexius himself retains the 'so-called Immortals and some of the Celts', while Catacalo[4] commands 'the Chomatenes and Turks'. The said Chomatenes are routed by a body of 'Scythians', Alexius with the Immortals is driven off the field, the 'Franks' surrender to Bryennius,[5] and the day is only saved by the arrival of fresh Turkish aid for Alexius, who thereupon returns to the fight. The Immortals seem on this occasion to have shown the bad effects of their hasty training, though one of them performs an act of great if futile daring by seeking Bryennius in single combat.[6] When we next meet them they are guarding Constantinople for the Emperor Botaniates, to whom as fellow-countrymen or fellow-Greeks ($a\vec{v}\tau\acute{o}\chi\theta ones$) their faith and loyalty are irrevocably pledged.[7] Alexius is advised not to attempt the task of seducing either them or the 'Varangians from Thule' . . . because 'those axe-bearing barbarians' (further depicted as 'dangling their swords from their shoulders') having received 'in succession the one from the other as a paternal tradition, and as it were a trust and inheritance, fidelity to the emperors and the guardianship of their persons, preserve their fidelity to him unshaken, and will not endure so much as a mere word about betrayal'. We will return to the Varangian guard presently. Here they with the Immortals exemplify the only motives that were thought sufficient to keep troops loyal

---

[1] I. 1–3.   [2] I. 5, p. 12.

[3] So VI. 1; IX. 2, p. 250, &c.

[4] Not otherwise described. There was in the same battle a Tarchionites Catacalo serving under Bryennius (I. 5, p. 11). Oman describes these Chomatenes as 'garrison troops' and the Turkish mercenaries as 'all horse-archers'.

[5] 'Dismounting and giving him their right hands, as is their ancestral way of swearing fealty' ($\tau\grave{a}s\ \pi\acute{\iota}\sigma\tau\epsilon\iota s\ \delta\iota\delta\acute{o}\nu a\iota$) (I. 6, p. 14).

[6] I. 5, p. 11.

[7] II. 9, p. 62; cf. II. 10, p. 64. It is hardly necessary to make the reminder that to be autochthonous was the proudest boast of the Athenians (Thuc. I. 28; II. 36). Similarly Anna throughout uses 'Ρωμαῖοι with a ring of pride. We may note that both she and her husband pass by in silence the far less favourable opinion held of the Immortals by others. Thus Attaliates (306) says that when the Emperor Botaniates wished to set the East in order, and the Greek troops from Constantinople did not wish to go beyond Nicaea, 'he summoned also other soldiers whom they called Immortals, being not easy to count in number and well trained in the bow, and supposed to possess the other arts of war through experience, by reason of continual practice; and as they were enslaved by disorder and disloyalty the Emperor was zealous to make them stronger and stauncher by friendly words and exhortation and even more by the kindness of gifts'.

—affection as of fellow-countrymen,[1] and a sense of ancestral pride. The Immortals play no further part in the history, but when Botaniates is at the very end of his tether, his slave Borilus wishes to make a stand against the incoming Comneni with 'those who dangle their swords over their shoulders' (i.e. the Varangians) 'and as many as sprang from Choma'.[2] It is this last band from which Alexius fears a counter-revolution.[3] Again, in the enumeration of the troops ready at hand in 1081 for use against Robert Guiscard we have the familiar combination of names. We are told that Alexius 'was grieved and distressed because the empire of the Greeks had no adequate army; for there were not more than 300 soldiers, and these were from Choma, all feeble and inexperienced in war, and a small number of foreign barbarians, the kind accustomed to dangle their sword from their right shoulder'. After this the men of Choma only come in once more, as supplying decarchs for the army.[4] So we can now devote our attention to the Varangian Guard.

Riant[5] tells us that as a result of the many attacks on Constantinople between 860 and 971 by 'les princes scandinaves de Russie', the emperors started a Varangian Guard to imitate the Scandinavian *hird*. It is certain that Byzantine chroniclers first speak of Βάραγγοι under Romanus III (Argyrus), 1020–34,[6] and Riant believes the Guard to have been at the beginning 'uniquement composée de Scandinaves'.[7] But after 1066 Eng-

---

[1] As a matter of fact, some Immortals revolted in Cyprus with Rhapsomates (IX. 2, p. 250) against Alexius when Emperor, but if their leader was equally Greek and αὐτόχθων they may have felt justified.

[2] II. 12, p. 67.   [3] III. 1, p. 71.   [4] III. 9, p. 91; 11, p. 95

[5] *Expéditions et pélerinages des Scandinaves*, p. 97.

[6] Cedrenus (p. 735 c) speaks of τῶν εἰς παραχειμασίαν διεσπαρμένων Βαράγγων on the accession of Michael IV who succeeded Romanus III. In p. 787 A they appear coupled with the Franks, and in p. 792 D the writer has this sentence: οἱ φυλάσσοντες ἐν τῷ παλατίῳ στρατιῶται Ῥωμαῖοί τε καὶ Βάραγγοι (γένος δὲ Κελτικὸν οἱ Βάραγγοι μισθοφοροῦντες Ῥωμαίοις).

[7] Bury (note on Gibbon's *Decline and Fall*, Vol. VI, p. 155) endorses this, saying that the Chronicle of Nest speaks of the Baltic as the Sea of the Variagi, and that in the λόγ. νουθ. of Cecaumenus (p. 97) Harold Haardrade is called 'son of the king of Varangia', i.e. Norway. He adds: 'The formation of the Varangian Guard at Constantinople and the inclusion in it of other Teutons (Danes, English, &c.) led to an extension of the meaning of Varangian from its original limitation to Norwegians or Scandinavians.' Gibbon (*op. cit.* vol. VI, p. 412) says of the Greeks in Constantinople at the time of the Latin Siege 'the firmest hope was in the strength and spirit of the Varangian Guard'. Villehardouin calls them 'Englois et Danois avec leurs haches'. They may have been the special 'ethnic' or 'barbarian' guards of Attaliates (p. 294) who while living in the Palace get drunk and revolt against Botaniates. They are forgiven, but some are sent to garrison distant forts. Anna speaks vaguely in XII. 6, p. 361, of 'those to whom is entrusted the guarding of the Palace' (who on this occasion lead away convicted conspirators). In XIV. 3, p. 432, she distinguishes the 'axe-bearing barbarians' from 'the soldiers collected of every language', though the two corps combine to

lish exiles went to offer the crown of their native land to the King of Denmark, and when it was refused they proceeded onwards to Constantinople. They built and garrisoned for Alexius Cibotus on the Asiatic side, and were subsequently merged by the Emperor in 'l'ancienne garde',[1] which had also been swelled by Norman nobles from England and France who had quarrelled with their kings, as well as adventurers from Apulia and Sicily. The services of Harold Haardrade to the Empire, mentioned only by Cecaumenus,[2] are not said to have affected the Varangian Guard in any way, but it is interesting to find from the *Knytlinga Saga* how large a part the Guard played during the visits to the capital of Eric the Good and Sigurd I. Eric in 1102 was on his way to the Holy Land, so Alexius feared he might lead his countrymen away to go with him, and therefore only allowed them to visit the Norwegian king in small bands till he himself was reassured by Eric's behaviour.[3] But in 1110 Sigurd was returning from Palestine, so he was not a formidable magnet; indeed he ended by leaving some of his men behind to 'grossir la garde vœringue',[4] and taking relics home instead. On the other hand Saxo says that some of the Varangian guard entered Bohemund's service before the second siege of Durazzo; these are probably Anna's 'men in the Greek service from the island of Thule' who had gone over to the Norman prince and came with him to Aulon. They may have returned to the Emperor the

form a guard of honour round the Emperor. So also in the scene in IX. 9, p. 263, where the Varangians are *par excellence* 'those appointed of old guardians of the imperial person'. Other terms for guards in the *Alexias* are ἐξκούβιτοι (IV. 4, p. 109), βεστιαρῖται (*ibid.*; see p. 277, note 7, above), and ἑταιρία (I. 5, p. 11; VIII. 7, p. 237), but Anna does not differentiate their functions. A special bodyguard of six, two of them sons of the former Emperor Romanus Diogenes, are chosen by Alexius at the front in VII. 3, p. 195.

[1] Some English names have been found in epitaphs of members of the Varangian Guard. In a note of Gibbon's (*op. cit.* Vol. VI, p. 89) he quotes from Codinus, p. 90, Βάραγγοι κατὰ τὴν πατρίαν γλῶσσαν . . . ἤγουν Ἰγλινιστὶ πολυχρονίζουσι ('wish a long life'). Ord. Vit. (Pt. III, lib. 7, ch. 4, *P. L.* 188, col. 519) says Alexius received refugee 'Angli' who came by sea after Harold's death 'and commended to them publicly the principal palace and the royal treasures; nay he made them guardians of his own life and of his possessions'. Cinnamus (I. 3, p. 4) says that the 'axe-bearers' are ἔθνος Βρεταννικόν.

[2] λόγ. νουθ. p. 97. He was at Constantinople 1043–4 after helping Geo. Maniaces (still loyal) in Sicily in 1038 (Bury's note on Gibbon, *op. cit.* Vol. VI, p. 184).

[3] The Saga represents Eric as haranguing the Varangians in order to impress on them their privileges in guarding the Emperor, and their duties of loyalty, sobriety, and courage (Riant, *op. cit.* pp. 159 sqq.). He was rewarded by money and relics, and a lodging in the Blachernae Palace.

[4] As well as sixty warships, still displayed at Constantinople forty years later. Anna mentions none of the three visitors Harold, Eric, or Sigurd. Possibly Eric is one of the 'kings' said by her to have gone on the First Crusade (X. 10, p. 299).

spring after the Treaty, when the rest of the Norman army was disbanded.[1] Turning to another estimate of the Varangians,[2] we find that Zonaras does not give them a very glowing testimonial for faithfulness. He represents them as revolting against Botaniates after the blinding of Bryennius, 'planning to kill him', but being put down and glad enough to beg and receive pardon.[3] They also seem easily gulled by John Comnenus into a premature belief in his father's death, though here they do make an effort to guard the Palace as is their duty.[4] Anna's specific references to this Guard, except for her one eulogy on their loyalty,[5] deal almost entirely with their peculiar arms. They are axe-bearers (πελεκυφόροι), and they have two-edged swords 'upon their shoulders'.[6] Now as these axes were not the missile Frankish kind, but heavy and two-handed such as the Danes introduced into England,[7] it is clear that if they wielded these they could not at the same time 'brandish' a sword, giving the ordinary meaning to the word κραδαίνειν always used of these men, but must have 'dangled' it from their shoulder on a bandolier.[8] Their appearance should excite awe,[9] and their bravery in battle is undoubted even if marred by 'inexperience and heat'.[10] Their honourable career ended with the Latin invasion of Constantinople in 1204.

As to the arms of other troops we find a monotonous recurrence of the same terms, helmets (once in dire military straits replaced by silk caps), shields (which may be fourfold), swords,

---

[1] XII. 9, p. 370; XIV. 1, p. 419.
[2] See note above referring to Attal., p. 294.
[3] Epit. XVIII. 19, a great contrast to Al. II. 9, p. 62.
[4] Epit. XVIII, 29.
[5] II. 9, p. 62. This eulogy is belied by XII. 9, p. 370, if Bohemund's 'men from Thule' were the Varangians.
[6] II. 12, p. 67; III. 9, p. 91; IV. 6, pp. 115, 116; IX. 9, p. 263; XII. 6, p. 361; XIV. 4, p. 432. The term 'captain of the Varangians' occurs in IV. 6, p. 115; cf. VII. 3, p. 195. Oman says that at Durazzo the Varangians 'rode to the battle spot like the thegns of the West', but then dismounted and marched forward shoulder to shoulder (op. cit. I. 166). On this occasion they carried shields (IV. 6, p. 115). Nic. Bry. mentions the curious equipment of 'the guards about the court from the barbarous land near the Ocean' (Hyle, I. 20, p. 32), and dwells on their time-honoured privilege of guarding the palace (ibid. II. 14, p. 52, and III. 5, p. 71). Albert of Aix (IV, ch. 40, P. L. 166, col. 503) speaks of 'Danai' [Danes] 'bipennium armatura dimicare peritissimi' in Alexius' army when he goes to Philomelium. The same writer says the Alemanni with Peter the Hermit (whom Anna calls Νορμάνοι: X. 6) had double axes (I. ch. 18, loc. cit. col. 401).
[7] Oman, op. cit. I. 115.
[8] I am indebted to Prof. Oman for this explanation. It would appear that they knocked down an enemy with the axe and dispatched him with the sword. κραδαίνειν of a spear may be translated 'wield', always with a sense of motion (XIII. 2, p. 379; XV. 3, p. 468).
[9] XIV. 3, p. 432.
[10] IV. 6, pp. 115, 116.

daggers, cuirasses (sometimes a scale corslet), greaves, lances, bows and arrows.[1] The swords were sharp and powerful enough to cut off an enemy's hand or even head,[2] spears set in rest by horsemen could pierce through chest and spine, and arrows could cause terrible wounds.[3]

Defensive armour is what is mainly implied in the word πανοπλία (though in classical Greek it included sword and lance), and a fully armed man is κατάφρακτος.[4] We constantly hear of generals arming themselves and their followers 'excellently'.[5] The sight of shining equipment may paralyse a barbarous Scythian host, and the envoys of the vainglorious Hugh of France, hoping to impress the Greeks, are 'clothed in golden armour, greaves and all'.[6] Yet its weight may be a severe handicap, especially to a Norman soldier when dismounted; his huge shield and peaked boots are fatal hindrances to rapid movement.[7] For this reason it was expedient to shoot at the Norman horses rather than at their riders. Alexius in the campaign of 1108 against Bohemund gives this as a definite order to his generals,

'knowing that as far as their cuirasses and iron coats went they were hard to wound or rather altogether invulnerable . . . For the Celtic armour (ὅπλον) is an iron coat, ring wound round ring, and the material of good iron, so as to turn off even a considerable dart . . . And as an addition to their defence there is a shield, not round but oblong, beginning very broad and ending in a sharp point. It is slightly hollowed, in outward appearance smooth and shining and sparkling, with a bronze knob. Therefore any dart, whether Scythian or Persian or launched by arms of giants, would be beaten off, and would bound back to the sender.'

On this account it is futile to shoot at the men, but if their

---

[1] I. 11, pp. 25, 26; II. 10, p. 64; IV. 6, p. 117; VII. 3, p. 197; VIII. 5, p. 232; X. 7, p. 288; 8, pp. 291, 292; 9, pp. 295, 297. The θυρεός (long shield) of X. 9, p. 297, occurs again in XII. 3, p. 353 in a figurative sense of Irene's virtues, coupled with ἀσπίς (buckler).

[2] I. 6, pp. 14, 15; 8, p. 20; IV. 6, p. 117; VII. 9, p. 211; XII. 2, p. 350. In IX. 9, p. 263, we read of 'heavy iron broadswords'.

[3] IV. 4, p. 110; XII. 2, p. 350.

[4] XIII. 5, p. 390; 6, p. 394; XIV. 6, p. 442; XV. 6, p. 478.

[5] καλῶς or καρτερῶς, I. 4, p. 10; V. 5, p. 138; VII. 2, p. 189; VIII. 5, p. 232; IX. 1, p. 247; XI. 7, p. 329; 8, p. 331. Alexius is σιδηροφορήσας in VII. 11, p. 217. Yet to receive the Crusaders he scorns armour and wears only imperial robes (X. 9, p. 295). The 'colour' of a Greek general's ἀμφίων may refer either to gilt (or coloured) armour or to the wearer's cloak, surtout, &c. (X. 8, p. 293). On one occasion Alexius has to substitute silk 'cloaks and caps' for armour 'since he had not sufficient iron for every one' (VIII. 5, p. 232).

[6] VI. 14, p. 184; X. 7, p. 288; cf. XIII. 2, p. 379; XV. 6, p. 478. So Nic. Bry. (II. 27, p. 63) describes the Turks fleeing before the ἀστραπή of Greek weapons. See also Al. I. 8. p. 20.   [7] V. 6, pp. 140, 141; XI. 6, p. 325.

horses are wounded they may throw their riders, and 'a Celtic man on horseback is irresistible and could even break through a Babylonian wall, but when he gets off his horse he becomes the sport of all that will'.[1]

One other piece of Frankish equipment is the tzangra or crossbow which Anna describes in a very clear and intelligible way. She calls it 'a barbaric bow and wholly unknown to Hellenes', and considers its effect 'truly δαιμόνιον'. But we should never guess from her text what is abundantly evident from Du Cange's note, that in her day it was thought to be a despicable mode of fighting, 'viro strenuo indignum', and fit to be classed with the use of poisoned weapons.[2]

MILITARY AFFAIRS

57. ALEXIUS AS COMMANDER-IN-CHIEF

WE have now dealt with the officers and men of the Byzantine army, and come at last naturally to its head.

On the personal characteristics of Alexius Comnenus as a general, his courage, prudence, cleverness, and devotion to his men, we have already touched. A few words will suffice as to the other features of his military career. He began this as subordinate to his brother Isaac, whom Anna once describes as 'entrusted with all the forces of the Eastern and Western commands',[3] but whom Chalandon believes to have been Domestic of the Schools for the East only. Then by two successive emperors, Michael Ducas and Nicephorus Botaniates, Alexius is made στρατηγὸς αὐτοκράτωρ (also called stratopedarch) [4] and Domestic of the Schools (also described as 'Great Domestic of the Western and Eastern armies', though as a matter of fact Nicephorus Melissenus seems to have been all-powerful in the

---

[1] XIII. 8, pp. 397, 398. The *Encycl. Brit.* (art. 'Heraldry') uses Anna's words 'smooth and shining' (λεῖος καὶ στίλβων) in support of the statement that armorial bearings on shields were unknown in the eleventh century. This seems a somewhat arbitrary deduction from these two adjectives. We must not forget that hundreds of years before this the Carians had given the Hellenes crests on helmets and devices on shields. (Herod. I. 171.)

[2] X. 8, p. 291. Du Cange quotes Joinville as praising certain 'beaux faiz d'armes' on the ground that 'nul ne tiroit d'arc, d'arbaleste, ne d'artillerie'. Prof. Grégoire has pointed out (*Byzantion*, Tome III, 1926, pp. 311–17) that tzangra is undoubtedly a Byzantine corruption of *cancer*, which (because of the shape) was the name for a crossbow in Low Latin.

[3] I. 1, p. 4. Also Duke of Antioch (II. 1, p. 43).

[4] I. 1, p. 4; II. 1, p. 43.

East).[1] After overcoming three enemies, Urselius, Bryennius, and Basilacius, he is made Sebastos and 'honoured with the dignity of proedros'. Relying on the support of his soldiers he enters Constantinople by craft and deposes Botaniates. No military skill is needed for this, and when shortly afterwards we hear that he 'chased [the Turks] out of the borders around Bithynia and all Thynia, and out of those of Nicomedia',[2] the credit belongs to his troops, those troops of whom Anna speaks so contemptuously, rather than to the Emperor who gave orders from his capital. However from this moment onward, first with Robert Guiscard, then with Bohemund, and repeatedly with the Turks, there is almost incessant fighting, in which he often took a personal part during the forty-seven years of his reign. And always in every campaign he was his own Commander-in-Chief, appointing and removing generals and commandants,[3] arming and training recruits whose military exercises he even shared when advanced in years.[4] Again and again in war Alexius goes on horseback along the ranks encouraging the troops,[5] and on two occasions at least his personal bravery caused him to be actually wounded.[6] Anna impresses on us that even when he might seem to be 'a spectator' in a campaign, he was in truth at the side of the fighters with his whole heart and soul, and shared with them in the same sweat and toil'.[7] Besides having to conduct affairs both military and diplomatic from a distance, and to supply stimulation and good counsel about every action, every siege, every plan of operations,[8] we find him personally studying the ground, designing siege-

[1] I. 4, p. 9; II. 1, p. 43, and 8, p. 59; VI. 4, p. 157; VII. 2, p. 191. His grandfather Manuel had held supreme command in the East, XI. 1, p. 311.

[2] III. 11, p. 96.

[3] XIII. 7, and throughout the history.

[4] e.g. V. 3, p. 130; VII. 10, p. 214; XII. 1, p. 348; 4, p. 355; XIII. 2, p. 379; XV. 3, p. 468, &c. He keeps his forces supplied with arrows and furnishes siege engines (XI. 2, p. 312; XIII. 8, p. 397).

[5] Even in his last campaign (XV. 3, p. 468).

[6] IV. 6, p. 117; VII. 9, p. 212. We may compare Thuc. V. 9, where the Spartan general Brasidas boasts 'I will show you that I can not only advise others but fight myself'. It is interesting to note that Anna says her father received his head wound at Durazzo (IV. 6, p. 117); Alexius himself (Mous. Alex. II. 80, 81) speaks of his κράνος τρωθέν at Phthia, south of Larissa, to which his daughter does not represent him as ever going. Other important generals killed or wounded or captured through their own daring are the Emperor's brother Isaac Comnenus (III. 3, p. 78), the Grand Domestic Pacurianus (VI. 14, p. 183), George Palaeologus (IV. 4, p. 110), Eustathius Camytzes (XIV. 5 and 6), and Alyates (XIII. 5, p. 391).

[7] XIII. 8, p. 398; cf. IX. 4, p. 251. For his attention to detail as a commander cf. VIII. 1 and 3; XI. 2, p. 312; 10, p. 335, and above all his New Parataxis.

[8] III. 9, p. 92; IV. 1, p. 103; XI. 2, p. 312; XIII. 4, p. 386; 5, pp. 389, 391; 7, pp. 395, 396.; 8, pp. 397, 398; XIV. 2, 3, and 5; XV. 3, p. 369.

engines, drawing maps, superintending fortifications even in intense heat and acting as his own paymaster, in short keeping up the closest personal contact with his officers and his men.[1] As in the very beginning the way he had braved all dangers with his soldiers was a strong argument for their choosing him as Emperor,[2] so to the very end he fought whether in body or in spirit with his men. Once when the season of year and his own ill-health kept him from actual warfare, he remained in hastily improvised winter quarters 'in order to encourage them all'; when he cannot ride into battle, he drives in the midst of his troops and cheers them by smiles.[3]

Great stress is laid by Anna on the outward signs of royalty on a campaign. The tent of the commander formed a sort of sacred centre to the army, and all the more so if he was the Emperor.[4] To keep the general's tent[5] standing is the supreme effort of an army resisting an overwhelming attack,[6] and when Alexius' tent was upset in the Patzinak campaign 'it seemed a bad omen to those who were not loyally disposed towards the Emperor'.[7] Zonaras[8] tells us that Romanus Argyrus as Emperor had a tent 'full of all sorts of wealth and imperial magnificence', and Alexius seems to have taken on a campaign not only a tent which proved large enough to hold all the malcontents who had conspired with Diogenes as well as the Emperor's loyal adherents, but also a gilded throne, on which in Anna's phrase φοβερὸς προὐκάθητο.[9] The tent as we have seen was accessible to all, but one sign of sovereignty, the βασιλικὴ σημαία par excellence, is most jealously guarded; the standard with its concomitant of silver-studded staves is the symbolic

---

[1] VIII. 3, p. 227; IX. 1, p. 245; X. 5, pp. 282, 283; XI. 2, p. 312; XIII. 2, p. 379.

[2] II. 7, p. 58.

[3] XIV. 3, pp. 429, 430: 5, p. 438; and XV. 1–7.

[4] In I. 7 and 8 Alexius leaves his tent brilliantly lighted and steals out of it himself, knowing that his enemy Basilacius would attack it first of all.

[5] III. 8, p. 90. In later passages we find 'the imperial tent and all the stores' coupled together (IV. 7, p. 118; VII. 3, p. 195, and 11, p. 215), and in XV. 1, p. 461, it is pitched last, in the middle of all the other tents. In XI. 7, p. 329, the pitching of the general's tent is the phrase used to denote the encamping of an army.

[6] IX. 4, p. 253. The capture of the imperial tent at Manzikert by the Turks is specially mentioned by Nic. Bry. (I. 17, p. 31).

[7] VII. 3, p. 194. τοῖς μὴ εὔνως ... διακειμένοις κακὸς οἰωνὸς ἔδοξεν.

[8] Epit. XVII. 12.

[9] IX. 9. The statement that, once inside the tent, the malcontents 'had their place assigned to them in rows', suggests a very large tent indeed. This is borne out by XI. 3, p. 317, where, when Alexius receives the Crusaders' homage at Pelecanus, he does so in a tent 'in size such as no one at that time had ever yet seen'. In XIII. 1, p. 376, the imperial tent is called ἐρυθροβαφής.

mark of the imperial presence.[1] Flags, especially a great number of them waving, strike terror into the foeman's heart.[2]
To 'snatch the flag' from a standard-bearer's hands, 'whirl
it round a few times, and then bend it to earth', is a noble
deed of daring, likely to prove the turning-point of a battle.[3]
So sacrosanct indeed is a commander's standard that its place
may even be taken in action by the holiest of relics, such as
the veil of the Virgin,[4] one of the sacred Nails of the Passion,[5]
or a 'golden standard of St. Peter'.[6] The divinity that hedged
a king was never more emphatically asserted than in this
particular matter, and we like to think of the Byzantine
Emperor marching forth amid his loyal soldiery, with trumpets
sounding, flags flying, and a host of devoted horse and foot
guarding him on every side.[7]

There is however another side to all this, a wholly different
aspect of Byzantine military affairs which we must never forget.
This in a word is the amazing untrustworthiness of the army.
Alexius owed to his troops his elevation to the throne,[8] yet
throughout his history we find him exposed not only to
civilian plots and disloyalty but also to insolence, treachery,
and mutiny from his soldiers. After the defeat of Durazzo 'all
the distinguished and picked soldiers of the Greeks' go over to
Bohemund.[9] The 'Celt' Umbertopulus had been one of Alexius'

---

[1] V. 6, p. 140; VI. 11, p. 175; VIII. 2, p. 224. In VI. 1, p. 153, the approach to the
standard symbolizes the adoption of imperial allegiance by defeated enemy troops.
XI. 2, p. 314, the putting 'staves and flags' round the walls, and the proclamation
of Alexius with 'trumpets and horns', alike serve to mark the capture of Nicaea
by Manuel Butumites. In VIII. 5, p. 233, the presence of 'the man holding the
imperial standard' by the side of the Coman contingent helps to keep their loyalty
steady.

[2] VI. 14, p. 184; VIII. 1, p. 223: 2, p. 224; XI. 2, p. 313. The impaled heads
of slain Turks are paraded 'as if flags' by the Crusaders outside Nicaea, with a
view to inspiring terror from afar (XI. 1, p. 311).

[3] V. 7, p. 142.

[4] Alexius carries this himself in battle, though his weapons hamper him, and
a strong wind nearly tears it from his grasp. Rather than that it should be captured by the Patzinaks, he rolls it up and hides it in a bush (VII. 3, pp. 196, 198).

[5] XI. 6, p. 327.

[6] This is carried to the First Crusade by Count Hugh, brother of the French
king (X. 7, p. 288). Du Cange (note, ad loc.) points out that it was a usual gift
from Popes to Christian champions.

[7] See XIV. 5, p. 438. The commander's horse shared in his splendour. That
of Bryennius at Calaure had 'purple trappings and gilded head-gear', with 'the
men holding the swords which customarily accompany kings running beside'.
Its capture by Alexius, together with the swords, enables him to persuade his
army that Bryennius is dead. 'He sent out that gold-adorned horse and the
swords wielded on both sides of the sovereign's person, and commanded a very
loud-voiced man to run through the army in every direction and shout out
that Bryennius had fallen' (I. 5, p. 13). So of the imperial horses at Larissa in
V. 6, p. 140.

[8] II. 7, p. 57.   [9] V. 4, p. 133.

chief helpers in his usurpation;[1] yet he rebels, drawing after him 'a not ignoble crowd', among whom is another distinguished general, the Armenian Ariebes.[2] The Emperor waives 'the penalties of the laws', imposing only banishment and confiscation of goods, and Anna passes hurriedly from the subject.[3] Nicephorus Diogenes[4] corrupts 'the whole of the political and military order', especially the more prominent members,[5] among whom we find the famous old general Cecaumenus Catacalo,[6] and Alexius' adherents stand ready to oppose armed force to armed force. Nicephorus himself and his brother Leo (who died in his loyalty) had held honourable military positions in the Illyrian and Patzinak campaigns,[7] and Nicephorus had been made Governor of Crete.[8]

The man who impersonates another Diogenes and does great harm to the Empire with Coman aid is a common soldier,[9] who comes 'from the East, poor and wearing a goatskin', and he reckons on treacherous assistance from the governor of Adrianople as an ex-rebel, though in this instance the ex-rebel (Nicephorus Bryennius) remains true to Alexius, and the pretender's scheme is crushed.[10]

Even during the Crusade, when common anxieties should

---

[1] II. 4, p. 50. He fought for the Emperor at Durazzo (IV. 4, p. 109) and against the Patzinaks (VI. 14, p. 183).

[2] VIII. 7, p. 236. Ariebes held the citadel of Achrida against Bohemund (V. 5, p. 136).

[3] Zonaras (XVIII. 23) mentions the additional punishment of a 'mocking triumph'. Yet the Celt is given another military command (X. 2, p. 273).

[4] IX. 5–10.

[5] Anna tells us that he 'did not take so much trouble about the rank and file of the army, for they had all already turned to him, but he turned wholly towards the chiefs, and showing great concern over the officers and the select men enrolled in the Senate, he won them over' (IX. 6, p. 257, repeated in IX. 8, p. 261).

[6] N. Banescu, in a paper on Katakalon Kekaumenos read before the Congress of Byzantinology at Bukharest (*Acad. Roum. Bull.*, Tome XI, pp. 29, 36), states his belief that the Cecaumenus Catacalo implicated in Diogenes' plot was not the πάππος of the author of the *Strategicon*, as he would have had to live over 100 years in that case, but the military hero of Sicilian, Armenian, and Balkan wars between 1038 and 1057. At the time of the conspiracy (1094) he was doubtless an old man, led to rebellion by sympathy with the nobles and officers who resented Alexius' autocracy. Banescu considers that Alexius dealt gently with him, allowing him to be blinded (see Anna's version of the matter IX. 9, p. 265) instead of putting him to death.

[7] IV. 5, p. 112; VII. 2, p. 190: 3, pp. 195 (*bis*), 196, 198.

[8] IX. 6, p. 256.

[9] X. 2. He is described as οὐ τῶν ἐπιφανῶν ἀλλὰ τῆς κάτω τύχης, also as ἐκ τοῦ χάρακος or χαρακηνός. Du Cange takes these last epithets to mean *gregarius miles* from χάραξ a camp, and Reifferscheid supports this view by spelling the words χάρακος and χαρακηνός without capital initials. It is however probable that Χάραξ, capital of a district of Susiana, and its cognate adjective, are what Anna had in mind.

[10] X. 3 and 4.

have made all Greeks cling together, Alexius fears that Michael
the Butler, a discontented 'intimate' of his own trained by himself from childhood, may if left in a centre of military activity
make τὸ ὁπλιτικόν mutiny.[1] During the Crusade also we find
the Emperor, perhaps short of officers, allowing an important
command to be given to Eustathius Camytzes,[2] last heard of
as exiled and imprisoned for participation in the rather mysterious conspiracy of Gregory Gabras.[3] From this moment, we
may add, Camytzes is one of the most prominent of the Greek
generals, even allowed when wounded to sit down in the presence of the Empress Irene.[4] His fellow-conspirator, George
son of Decanus, is also pardoned and given a responsible post.[5]

At a later period the Anemas conspiracy involves several of
the Emperor's most important officers;[6] indeed Anna herself
intercedes for the Anemas brothers so that her father 'may not
be deprived of such soldiers'. Not long after this another soldier
revolts, this time at his post in distant parts. This Gregory
Taronites Duke of Trebizond rebels, writes abusive letters
against other generals and the Senate, is captured, goes to
prison, and is suddenly and unaccountably pardoned.[7] So also
some years later is the commandant of Acrunus, whose story is
very similar.[8] Soldiers 'set over the defence of the capital',
when taken at a great emergency to the front, cannot be trusted
to follow their Emperor into a pitched battle with the Patzinaks.[9] The guarding of captives is evidently an unpopular task
which a general may well be reluctant to impose on his own
men,[10] and prisoners of all sorts escape with surprising ease.[11]

It is of course a sense of this prevalent disloyalty, coupled
with the fact that universal service was unknown, that even
a good general might be τῆς στρατιωτικῆς παιδείας πάμπαν ἀμύητος, and that young nobles like every one else needed training
from experienced teachers in shooting and wielding a spear and

---

[1] VIII. 9, p. 242; XI. 9, p. 334.   [2] XI. 5, p. 324.
[3] VIII. 9.   [4] XIV. 6, p. 443.
[5] VIII. 9, and XIV. 3, p. 431.
[6] XII. 5, 6, especially 6, p. 363. Castamonites and George Basilacius may have
been smarting under disgrace after defeat or under family wrongs (I. 7–9 ; VII. 3,
p. 195 ; 8, p. 206). But Curticius was one of Alexius' most trusted generals (I. 9,
p. 21 ; V. 5, p. 139; VI. 12, p. 178; VII. 1, p. 189; 3, p. 195 ; 11, p. 218;
VIII. 1, p. 189 ; 6, p. 235). Michael Anemas had had a command in the Coman
War (X. 2, p. 274).
[7] XII. 7. See above p. 96, note 3 ; p. 276, note 1.
[8] XIV. 3, p. 431.   [9] VIII. 1, pp. 221, 223.
[10] VIII. 6, p. 234 ; IX. 8, p. 262.
[11] VII. 2, p. 193; X. 2, p. 272; 4, p. 278; XII. 7, p. 264. In II. 5, p. 54, guards
are bribed to bring news. In XII. 7, p. 365, a prisoner tries at least to corrupt his
gaolers.

in horsemanship,[1] which makes Alexius raise during the Patzinak war the corps of Archontopules. Of them Anna writes:[2] 'This battalion of Archontopules was first invented by Alexius. For when the Empire of the Greeks had no army because of the negligence of previous emperors, he collected from all quarters the sons of fallen soldiers,[3] and trained them to arms and called them Archontopules, as being the sons of Captains (archons), so that being reminded by their name of the noble birth and courage of their parents, they too might be mindful of ardent valour.' She then compares them to the Sacred Company of the Thebans, whom in error she calls Spartans. The heavy losses among these brave but inexperienced youths are a desperate grief to Alexius.[4]

Even where soldiers are not actually disloyal, their lack of discipline as we understand it is very striking. The commandant of Larissa adopts to Alexius a hectoring tone which seems even to Anna παρρησιαστικώτερον,[5] and when in the Patzinak campaign Nicephorus Bryennius is 'witty' in a speech to his Emperor, we should call it merely impertinent.[6] Generals may find it necessary to lie to their troops in order to keep them from plundering.[7] The traitor Neantzes cuts off in his sovereign's presence the head of an enemy informing against him, and Alexius has to bear this insolence.[8] After Lebunium Synesius comes δυσχεραίνων to his sovereign, chiding him severely for not having had the prisoners killed; the prisoners are finally put to death, and the Emperor suspecting the agency of Synesius has him arrested, but is soon persuaded by the imperial kinsmen to let him go.[9] Constantine Gabras, one of a very turbulent family, declines the task of 'trenching off the passages' of Bohemund's army, and Anna's only comment is that he was hoping for higher work, which indeed he subsequently gets.[10] Though Imperator as well as βασιλεύς, the Emperor could not safely count on loyalty or even on respect from his men.[11]

---

[1] I. 14, p. 34; V. 3, p. 130; VIII. 9, p. 241; IX. 2, p. 249: 6, p. 257; XI. 9, p. 333; XII. 1, p. 348; and 2, p. 348; 4, pp. 355, 356; XIII. 2, p. 379; XIV. 1, pp. 419, 420; XV. 3, p. 468. For the rawness of recruits see I. 4, p. 10; 14, p. 34; III. 9, p. 91; V. 1, p. 126. Leo (*Tactica*, VII. 9) said a soldier must be able to jump on to a horse and shoot in any direction from horseback at full gallop. This is still the modern Persian ideal.

[2] VII. 7, p. 204.

[3] For this idea of hereditary devotion cf. IV. 4, p. 109; V. 5, p. 136; VII. 3, pp. 195, 196; IX. 9, p. 262; XIII. 1, p. 378.

[4] VII. 7, p. 204.   [5] V. 5, p. 138.   [6] VII. 2, p. 191.
[7] VII. 8, p. 206.   [8] VII. 9, p. 211.   [9] VIII. 6.
[10] XIII. 7, p. 395; XIV. 3 and 5; XV. 4, p. 473.
[11] For earlier times cf. Ch. IX of M. Rostovtzeff's *Social and Econ. Hist. of the Roman Empire* (1926). For insubordination in civilians see Chs. 7 and 43 above.

MILITARY AFFAIRS

58. HORSES.—GREEK FIRE

ONE thing must never be forgotten in reading the *Alexias*, namely that, as Bury says, 'the strength of the army lay in the heavy cavalry'.[1] The use of horses in sport or as a proof of good breeding has been already dealt with; Anna's metaphors[2] and stock phrases alone would show us the importance of the animal every day of a man's life. But in war he was essential, and her mentions of horse-archers, mounted spearmen, and cavalry-charges would fill a good-sized book.

Oman has pointed out how from Justinian onwards the Byzantine army became more and more preponderantly a cavalry force,[3] yet in Anna's day it still contained a considerable number of foot-soldiers, as did the armies of its foes. Robert Guiscard's forces according to Anna consisted of 'armed horsemen and infantry and light-armed troops'.[4] She elsewhere calls them 'forces of cavalry and infantry passing number'.[5] In Alexius' march on Constantinople he relies on τὸ ὁπλιτικόν, which is here ἡ κρείττων στρατιά as distinguished from 'the chosen men of the cavalry'.[6] On another occasion it is as it were a promotion for light-armed and heavy-armed infantry to ride as lancers against the enemy.[7] In two engagements dismounted horse-archers advance sending out 'a thick shower of

[1] Note to Gibbon, *op. cit.*, Vol. VI, p. 99. Robert Guiscard on rising to power triples his cavalry and doubles his infantry (I. 11, p. 24).

[2] A rebel is a man who 'gets rid of the bridle' (VI. 9, p. 169) (cf. Nic. Bry. III. 1, p. 68). So too ἀνασειράζειν (XI. 8, p. 331), ἐπιστομιζόμενος (X. 2, p. 271), ἀχαλιναγώγητος (X. 6, p. 287; XIV. 7, p. 449). If a man goes in any direction he 'bends his rein' (VIII. 5, p. 232, and elsewhere, as also in Nic. Bry., e.g. I. 14, p. 28), if he goes back he 'saddles his horse for return' (V. 7, p. 143; VI. 14, p. 185), &c. See p. 133 above, and p. 511, note 6, below. Gallant warriors gallop 'with loosened rein' (I. 6, p. 14, and *passim*), or 'letting out their whole rein' (VII. 10, p. 215). The beginning of action is 'when the horses are stirred to prick up their ears' (I. 5, p. 11 A); history is a horse which must be controlled (I. 16, p. 40); the State is a chariot where the ruler holds the reins (III. 7, p. 85; VII. 2, p. 191; 8, p. 208; XII. 3, p. 351; XIV. 7, p. 445); cf. p. 133 above.

[3] *Op. cit.* I. pp. 174, 187, 193, 196.

[4] I. 16, p. 37; III. 12, p. 99.

[5] IV. 1, p. 102. F. Dölger, in his review of Mutavciev's book mentioned above (*B.Z.* XXVI. p. 107) says of the Byzantine army: 'Die auf Soldatengütern angesiedelten Stratioten waren *Reiter*', whereas 'die Akriten' on the borders were 'ohne Pferd'.

[6] II. 10, p. 63. In IV. 4, p. 109: 5, p. 112, τὸ ὁπλιτικόν is apparently used for Alexius' whole army, though it included horse-archers (IV. 6, p. 115).

[7] III. 11, pp. 95, 96.

arrows', while their συνασπισμός adds to their formidable might; on the second occasion their spare arrows are carried on mules.[1] It is noteworthy that the shooting of Nicephorus Bryennius Caesar, comparing favourably in Anna's eyes with that of Teucer, the two Ajaxes, Heracles and Apollo, is performed on foot from the walls of Constantinople.[2] But the Turks on the other hand always shoot from horseback, making dashes 'like hurricanes', and are liable to break anything but the most serried ranks; even in flight they can pierce with their arrows [3] 'either the horse or the horseman' pursuing them. In sober fact, a horse was as valuable as a man if not more so.[4] The fatigue or fall of his wounded horse puts a soldier, especially a heavy-armed Frank, out of action, so that orders are frequently given to aim at the enemy's horses, not at the men.[5] Repeatedly throughout the *Alexias* we hear of resting horses,[6] turning or leading them out to graze or drink,[7] sparing them and feeding them up for future use.[8] At the second siege of Durazzo Bohemund's lack of food for his horses, which had to be brought from Italy in special boats, is no less serious than the shortage for his men;[9] Alexius' forward march is similarly hampered in devastated Asia Minor.[10] Cavalry-charges (ἱππασίαι) are the almost invariable opening of a battle,[11] and horsemen in small bodies are admirable for annoying the enemy,[12] though in a gorge infantry can easily repulse them, and certain kinds of ground render

---

[1] VII. 10, p. 214; XI. 2, p. 313.   In IV. 6, p. 115, the Varangian Guard dismount, as they always did before battle, and march on συνησπικότες, only opening out occasionally to let the horse-archers pass through them for a charge.
[2] X. 9.   [3] XV. 3.
[4] XIII. 9, p. 399; XIV. 6, p. 442. The horse of Bryennius (I. 5) afterwards saves Alexius' life at Durazzo by his wonderful agility (IV. 7). Like Richard's Barbary, 'so proud that Bolingbroke was on his back', (*Rich. II*, Act v, sc. 5), Sguritzes seems to have had no objection to a change of owner.   A Turk leaps 'like some leopard' on to an enemy's horse in I. 6, p. 15.
[5] I. 6, p. 15; 9, p. 21; VII. 3, p. 198|; 4, pp. 199, 200; 8, p. 207; X. 9, p. 296; XIII. 8, p. 398; XIV. 5, p. 440; 6, p. 442; XV. 4, p. 472. Cf. Nic. Bry. II. 12, p. 49. In Nic. Bry. II. 6, p. 44, Alexius is constrained to ride a mule. In *Al*. VII. 3, p. 197, the Emperor is very careful not to wound his own horse in hacking at 'three Scythian foot-soldiers' who seize his bridle and his leg. In V. 4, he tries to block the Norman horses with wagons and lame them with caltrops. In VI. 14, p. 183, Pacurianus is killed by his horse dashing him against a tree in a charge. In VII. 11, p. 217, Alexius wins the day by rolling wheels against the Patzinak horses. A wounded horse caused the capture of Romanus Diogenes at Manzikert (Nic. Bry. I. 17, p. 30).
[6] I. 6, p. 16; 11, p. 26; IV. 7, p. 119; VII. 11, p. 217; XI. 2, p. 315.
[7] VII. 3, p. 195; X. 4, p. 278; XI. 7, p. 329.
[8] I. 7, p. 18; XV. 2, pp. 465, 466.
[9] XIII. 2, pp. 380, 381; 8, p. 399.
[10] XI. 8, p. 331; XV. 4, p. 471.
[11] *passim*, e.g. VI. 10, p. 172.
[12] IV. 6, p. 115.

them useless.[1] The old reputation of Thessalian horsemen[2] was equalled by Turks and Normans.[3] Single combats by horse-men bearing lances furnish some of Anna's most exciting epi-sodes,[4] and choice war-horses notably Arabs are mentioned more than once.[5] Alexius makes horseback charges in person, and even when 'gripped by ague' rides along the lines to inspire confidence in his men.[6] Besides horses, an army had mules and oxen to carry the baggage or do other hauling, and wagons are also mentioned in this connexion.[7] In the Patzinak campaigns[8] we not only hear a great deal of the ἄμαξαι or ἁρμάμαξαι that played a vital part in the Scythian tactics,[9] but we also have allusions to the wagons of Greek countrymen, with their wheels and axles.[10] Alexius when his gout prevents his riding goes to the front in a 'covered chariot, grasping the basket-work frame (λύγος) in his right hand';[11] Irene accom-panies the army in a mule-borne litter.[12]

Before we leave external equipment entirely, one method of warfare in which Byzantines delighted must not be passed over. Very frequently Anna tells us of ships and stores and towns and gates and siege-instruments being burnt (the ships twice in bravado, to show there is no turning back),[13] and though on some occasions the method was clearly only hurling fire-arrows or setting fire to brushwood soaked with oil or pitch,[14] yet she has some references to the famous Greek fire, strictly

---

[1] V. 7, p. 142; VI. 10, p. 173; X. 3, p. 275. Ground is cleared for cavalry sorties outside a city in XI. 11, p. 340. We may recall the sufferings of the Athenian horses at Decelea (Thuc. VII. 27).

[2] I. 5, p. 11.

[3] So the Celts under Taticius advance 'like fire' with lance in rest and rout the Turks (VI. 10, p. 172). Alexius begs for 500 Frankish horse (VII. 6, p. 202; 7, p. 205). ἀνὴρ Κελτὸς ἐποχούμενος is ἀνύποιστος τὴν ὁρμήν (V. 4, p. 135; 6, p. 140, and XIII. 8, p. 398). Cf. X. 3, p. 277. The Normans in the campaign of 1108 seem to have been all mounted. They attack at full gallop and their charges stop the Scythian archers of the Greek army from shooting (XIII. 6, p. 392). See p. 133 above, especially note 10. For the Turks see XV. 3, p. 469 and elsewhere.

[4] e.g. I. 6, p. 14; XII. 2, p. 350; XV. 3, p. 469, and elsewhere.

[5] VII. 7, p. 205 : 9, p. 212; XIV. 2, p. 429; XV. 6, p. 478.

[6] VII. 9, pp. 212, 213. So Cantacuzenus and King Baldwin each gallop out and try to prevent their men flying (XIII. 5, p. 391; XIV. 2, p. 427).

[7] VII. 10, p. 214; VIII. 4, p. 229; 5, p. 233; 6, p. 235; XI. 11, p. 340; XIII. 3, p. 383; XV. 4, p. 472; 6, p. 477. In XIV. 6, p. 442, the baggage animals seem to have been horses.

[8] Books VI–VIII.

[9] They not only cut the bodies of fallen enemies by the scythes fastened beneath, but serve as 'towers' for the ranks.

[10] VII. 9, p. 212; 11, pp. 215–17, 218; VIII. 4, p. 229. So we read of ploughs drawn by oxen (XIV. 9, p. 456).

[11] XIV. 5, p. 438.   [12] XII. 3, p. 353.

[13] IV. 6, p. 114; XIII. 2, p. 380; cf. XIII. 5, pp. 391–4.

[14] IV. 4, p. 110; 6, p. 116; X. 9, p. 294; XIII. 3, pp. 382, 385, 386; 5, p. 391.

speaking a liquid, which Oman[1] enjoins on us to distinguish
carefully from the 'inflammable substance attached to ordinary
missiles'.[2] In connexion with the second of Bohemund's
abortive devices, when the besiegers are smoked out 'like a
swarm of bees', Anna speaks of fire which could be blown
from tubes against an enemy. Oman tells us that 'the composition was a great State secret',[3] and indeed the *Alexias*
gives no details that might convey useful information. It
merely says that when Bohemund mined, the Durazzo garrison
countermined, and when the enemy came in sight through
a hole they 'burnt their faces with fire. Now this fire had
been prepared by them by the following contrivances. From
the pine and certain other such evergreen trees inflammable
resin is collected. This is rubbed with sulphur and put into
tubes of reed, and is blown by the men using it with violent
and continuous breath. Then in this manner it meets the fire
on the tip and catches light and falls like a fiery whirlwind on
the faces opposite it.'[4] Later on in the siege liquid fire, πῦρ
ἔνυγρον, is mentioned[5] as applied to the heaped-up, oil-soaked
brushwood. Oman sees in these passages an allusion to two
kinds of Greek fire, one 'a powder composed of resin mixed
with sulphur' blown into the besiegers' faces, and the other
'a much more complicated and formidable substance' in liquid
form. We may remark that the danger to the user of blowing
inflammable powder down a tube lighted at the end would
seem to have been scarcely less than to his enemy.[6] When
Taticius and Lantulph attack the Pisan fleet they have ships
fitted at the prows with tubes (concealed in animals' heads) for
discharging fire in battle, but whether as a powder or a liquid
we are not informed.[7] As however it was powerful enough to
set not only 'rudders' on fire but even 'three huge ships', it

[1] *Op. cit.*, II. 46–8.
[2] Leo (*Tactica*, XIX. 58) speaks of iron caltrops or nails with lighted tow attached.
[3] Const. Porphyr., *de Admin. imp.*, ch. 48 (Vol. III, p. 216), deals with Greek
fire; so does Leo in his *Tactica*, XIX. In ch. 13 (*loc. cit.* p. 84) Constantine says
that the recipe for the Greek fire should be refused to a barbarian, along with
other outrageous requests such as an imperial robe or crown, or a bride from the
imperial family.
[4] XIII. 3, p. 383; p. 404 below.   [5] XIII. 3, p. 385.
[6] Bury, in his edition of Gibbon, *op. cit.* Vol. VI, p. 11 note, says: 'It is certain that
one kind of Greek or marine fire was gunpowder' The recipe is preserved in the
ninth-century *Liber ignium ad comburendos hostes* (ed. F. Hofer, *Hist. de la Chimie*,
I, 1842).'
[7] XI. 10. The phrase used is ἀφίεσθαι πῦρ, also βάλλειν. The animals' heads
'belched forth' the fire, which if discharged 'amiss' was liable to 'go out' without
accomplishing anything. In Thuc. VII. 53 a burning ship is propelled against
an enemy fleet: this was the old method, less deadly than the new, because less
accurate.

was doubtless the deadly liquid of which Oman speaks. Anna
as usual wishes to give her father credit for inventiveness, though
possibly her words ('they were not accustomed to such apparatus') only mean that this contrivance, whereby fire 'having
by nature an upward course' could be sent in any direction,
was new to the Pisans in particular.[1] At any rate, if she did
believe the device to be an original one of her father's she was
mistaken, for already in the tenth century Leo the Wise (or if
we go by Krumbacher Leo the Isaurian in the eighth) had[2]
prescribed the fitting of fire-tubes on to all war vessels, as well
as the provision of hand-squirts for fire and fire-filled jars for
projectiles, to say nothing of other jars full of snakes and scor-
pions. Schlumberger says that when Nicephorus Phocas went
out against the Saracen pirates in 960 he had 2,000 such 'fire-
bearing vessels'.[3] Another way of using this most formidable of
all weapons was, as the reference to Leo shows, to hurl break-
able jars of liquid fire against the enemy, either from some sort
of engine, or by hand like a modern grenade. Anna writes of
the inhabitants of Tyre when besieged by the Crusaders:[4] 'In
one night they filled many earthenware jars with liquid pitch
and threw them against the engines ($\mu\eta\chi\alpha\nu\acute{\eta}\mu\alpha\tau\alpha$) standing near
the city. And when these were of course shattered, this liquid
was poured out on the wood,[5] on to which they threw lighted
torches and then again other jars containing much naphtha[6],
which caught fire and straightway turned into a flame reaching
to heaven and reduced their engines ($\mu\eta\chi\alpha\nu\acute{\alpha}s$) to ashes. Then
at the time when day began to shine, the fire also shone forth
with it, rising like a tower into the air from the wooden pent-
houses' ($\chi\epsilon\lambda\tilde{\omega}\nu\alpha\iota$, literally 'tortoises').[7]
    Finally one instance may be mentioned, where ordinary fire is
effectively used by Alexius. In one of his Turkish campaigns

---

[1] XI. 10, p. 336. Or possibly in the animals' heads there was something new
(XI. 10, p. 335). Both hand-squirts and mechanical apparatus might be used to
discharge liquid fire.

[2] *Tactica*, XIX. 6, 51, 54, 56-60.

[3] *Récits de Byzance et des Croisades*, 2ᵉ Série, p. 39. Schlumberger believes that this
deadly liquid fire, partly made of explosive oil, was largely responsible for arresting
the Saracen expansion in Eastern Europe, such panic terror did it inspire. Atta-
liates says Constantine Monomachus had ships furnished $\tau\tilde{\omega}$ $M\eta\delta\acute{\iota}\kappa\omega$ $\pi\upsilon\rho\acute{\iota}$ (p. 21).

[4] XIV. 2, p. 426.

[5] This was obviously brushwood piled up by Baldwin in his desire to take the
third zone of the 'outworks' mentioned earlier in the chapter; his preparations
were through his carelessness turned against himself.

[6] This explains the 'naphtha and pitch' got ready by the besieged Geo. Palaeologus at Durazzo (IV. 4, p. 110).

[7] Oman quotes the *Itin. Regis Ricardi* as saying that Greek fire could only be put
out by sand or vinegar (*op. cit.* II. 48).

the enemy defeated in open fight take refuge in a dense and marshy reed-bed, where the Greeks cannot follow. The Emperor sets a ring of soldiers all round, lights a fire at one side, and seizes on all those who try to escape by the other.[1] These unheroic tactics are complacently recounted by his daughter.

MILITARY AFFAIRS

59. THE NAVY

AS to the Byzantine navy, a few words must suffice. C. Neumann pointed out in 1898[2] that the history of the Byzantine navy had never been adequately written. P. Grenier, in his *Empire byzantin* of 1904, has one short passage on it. Since then Bury, in his edition of Gibbon (1909-14), has given us a brief appendix on the subject,[3] Baynes has devoted a few pages to it in his *Byzantine Empire*,[4] and Diehl brings it into Ch. XXIII of the *Cambridge Mediaeval History*, Vol. IV.[5] Oman, in his new 1924 edition of *The Art of War*, passes the matter almost wholly by.

As an opening we may quote Baynes's dictum that the Byzantine Empire like Republican Rome 'only took to the sea under compulsion',[6] and in the course of centuries its fleet was

---

[1] XIV. 5, p. 441.   [2] *Hist. Zeitschr.* Vol. 45, pp. 1–23.
[3] Vol. VI, App. 5.   [4] pp. 143–9, 217–20.
[5] It should be noted that this writer assigns a higher value to the Greek fleet than do most Byzantinists. He says that it 'saved Constantinople in the great siege of 717', and that from the close of the ninth century till the beginning of the twelfth 'Byzantium was the great sea-power of the Mediterranean'. Its end, according to him, only came when Constantinople neglected naval construction and hired foreign vessels, finally in the thirteenth century considering the maintenance of a fleet 'as a useless expense' (pp. 741–2).

[6] *Op. cit.* p. 143. It is interesting to read the opening words of Leo's *Tactica* XIX, περὶ ναυμαχίας. The Emperor in his Preface to the whole book says the art of war is vital and has decayed. In XIX. 1, addressing an imaginary admiral, he says: 'Now we will give directions about naval warfare, having found nothing laid down about it as rules (κεκανονισμένον) in ancient works on Tactics.' He says he will 'shortly' (actually in seventy-five paragraphs) explain what he has read σποράδην and known 'by brief experience', and learnt from the deeds or sufferings τῶν πλωΐμων στρατηγῶν. His maxims are full of sound sense, and dwell more than once on the necessity of adapting one's own mode of warfare to that of the enemy, whose various methods are described, or to circumstances (16, 43, 68, 69, 73). An admiral should know his men personally and exhort them to courage (18, 19, 21, 31). The necessity of careful preparation, training, order, and vigilance is emphasized (20, 25, 26, 29, 74), and signals and formations are studied (39–42, 44–6, 70). No navy wins without two requisites, good soldiers and God's favour (34, 50, 72, 75). Characteristically the Byzantine Emperor advises the avoidance of a general attack when possible (32, 33), and advocates the practice of feigning flight and taking the enemy at a disadvantage (47–9, 61).

inferior to that of the Vandals, of the Arabs,[1] and of the Italians. Even Cecaumenus, though pronouncing that 'the Fleet is the glory of the Empire' (τῆς 'Ρωμανίας), speaks of venal, sluggish admirals and ill-equipped ships, and recommends that naval commands should be given to superannuated military men.[2] Neumann, Baynes, and Bury elucidate the situation somewhat by pointing out that there were two fleets, the imperial and the provincial or thematic, and that the final decay of both in the eleventh century was due respectively to the anti-military policy of the Emperors between Basil II and Alexius I (who all had the example of Romanus Lecapenus to show them that great admirals might be formidable subjects, no less than great generals), and to the Seljuq conquests which annihilated the three maritime themes, the Aegean, the Samian, and the Cibyrrhaeot.[3] Certainly there was one moment in the tenth century when Constantine VII Porphyrogenitus could claim θαλασσοκρατεῖν as far as the Pillars of Hercules,[4] and Nicephorus Phocas could boast to the envoy of the German king 'navigantium fortitudo mihi soli inest'.[5] But besides the regular navies of hostile nations, the Byzantines were constantly suffering from the heterogeneous pirates and sea-rovers infesting the Mediterranean, recruited even from 'Scandinavian freebooters' who 'penetrated through the straits of Gibraltar'.[6] If Moslem piracy had diminished since the Norman conquest of Sicily, it had not ceased; indeed it had in a sense been aggravated by the same practice among the Norman conquerors, of whom Crispin and Guynemer and many others came to the Mediterranean by sea, as well as among the Italian seamen.[7] Even all through the first Crusade Riant tells us[8] there were a number of Northern

---

Odds should never be faced (66, 67). New devices are to be concealed, for fear the enemy might copy them (63). The section ends with saying that a successful admiral will be rewarded not only by the Emperor, but by God whose 'inheritance' he is defending (75).

[1] Grenier believes the death-blow to Byzantine supremacy in the Mediterranean was the pillaging of Thessalonica by the Arabs in 904 (op. cit. Vol. I, p. 163).

[2] λόγ. νουθ., pp. 101-3. Just before this he describes the army as 'the glory of the Emperor and the power of the Palace'. Baynes (op. cit. p. 149) says: 'The soldier always took precedence of the sailor, and in this . . . New Rome but preserved the traditions of the older Western capital.' The strategi of maritime themes were paid less than the others (Diehl, op. cit. p. 744).

[3] Baynes, p. 146, says of this Cibyrrhaeot theme: 'Here was the Empire's outpost against the Saracens.' The district of Cibyra in Pamphylia was probably a shipbuilding centre. Cf. Ramsay, Historical Geography of Asia Minor, p. 420.

[4] De them., Vol. III, p. 58.   [5] Liutprand, Legatio, ch. 11 (P. L. 136, col. 915).

[6] Baynes, op. cit. p. 145. 'Some of these robbers', he points out on p. 219, 'thus gained money to go on pilgrimages in honour of Our Lady.'

[7] J. Laurent, Byzance et les Turcs Seldjoucides, p. 106, note 2.

[8] Expéditions des Scandinaves, p. 138.

vessels 'demi-corsaires, demi-marchands', committing 'pira-
teries' along the Syrian and Anatolian coasts,[1] and Anna
herself mentions the Greek naval police on the watch against
pirates in the Adriatic.[2] Neumann is of opinion as regards the
two fleets, imperial and provincial, that the latter did most of
the work, being always ready for action, while the former
(though larger, at any rate in the tenth century) only came out
for a great war. At the end of the eleventh century, he says:
'Ueberall spürt man das Fehlen jener kleinasiatischen Provin-
zialflotte.'

Alexius (to his credit be it spoken) all through his reign
steadily increased the imperial fleet, collecting some ships and
building others. As to the size and character of the fleet,
'anchored according to custom' outside Constantinople during
his own rebellion and won over for him by Palaeologus as an
essential factor towards his success,[3] we have no information.
There were clearly enough sailors to make a loud 'acclamation'
for the new Emperor, and to guard the Capital from any 'who
might attempt to cross from the East'. Yet certainly at first
Alexius had to rely on 'the navy of the whole State' of Venice,
enlisting by immense bribes its aid against Robert Guiscard.
In the first sea-fight off Cape Pali the Venetians sustain the
combat with the Normans unaided; 'Maurice[4] with the Greek
fleet' is not mentioned till the naval action of the next spring.[5]
When Robert's second invasion is expected, Alexius has still not
enough ships of his own and hires some from Venice.[6] But by the
time of the first Crusade he has vessels sufficient for the sending of
two separate bodies of the Crusaders straight by sea to the Holy
Land,[7] and a 'Greek fleet' is waiting off Antioch when Taticius
decides to bring his troops home,[8] while Alexius does not hesitate to pit his navy even against the redoubted Pisans and

[1] Alexius sends John Ducas against 'the satraps of the Turks and the barbarians
infesting the sea-coast' (XI. 5, p. 322).
[2] In X. 7, p. 288. Nicolas Maurocatacalo, Dux of the Fleet, is anchored off
Durazzo τὰ πελάγη περισκοπῶν ὡς μὴ λάθοιεν αὐτὸν λῃστρικαὶ νῆες παραπλεύσασαι.
For Anna's mention of the 'barbarous Vetones' see above, p. 354 and note 3. Cf.
Nic. Bry. III. 3, p. 70; his own father had fought Italian pirates. Baynes believes
that the danger from corsairs was one of the reasons why the Byzantines did not
care to invest capital in oversea commerce, which gradually passed into the hands
of the Italian Republics (op. cit. p. 218).
[3] Palaeologus exhorts them ἑτεραλκέα τὴν νίκην ποιησαμένους αὐτῷ (sc. to Alexius)
προσελθεῖν. II. 11, p. 65.
[4] Spoken of by Nic. Bry. (II. 26, p. 63) as 'having the greatest possible experience in naval matters'.
[5] IV. 3, p. 107. Chalandon even puts this action off for nearly two years, till the
spring of 1083 (op. cit. p. 91, note 3).
[6] VI. 5.   [7] X. 10, p. 299; XI. 8, p. 332.
[8] XI. 4, p. 319.

Genoese.¹ He not only commandeers ships 'from all the lands
under the sovereignty of the Greeks', but he has 'a good number' (ἱκανά) built under his own direction at Constantinople.²
When an invasion by Bohemund is possible though not imminent, he collects such a large fleet 'from the Cyclades Islands
and the sea-coast cities of Asia and from Europe itself' that
many of his subjects murmur, doubtless at the expense which
they would thereby have to bear.³ In policing the seas or
helping in sieges or cutting off an enemy's supplies the Greek
navy in the *Alexias* plays an honourable if minor part.

As to the kinds of ships mentioned by Anna they are surprisingly many: triremes, pirate-vessels, war (or 'long') ships,
dromonds, i.e. light or 'running' craft, 'sermones' (whatever they
may have been), freight-ships, horse-transports, skiffs (sometimes small enough for inland waters),⁴ pinnaces,⁵ and
'merchantmen of heavy tonnage' (μυριοφόροι ὁλκάδες), as well as
ναῦς and πλοῖα in general. For going up the Hebrus Alexius
uses an ἀμφίρυκον πλοῖον⁶ which Du Cange says was equivalent
to ἀμφίρρυτον, a boat so small as to be washed on all sides by
the waves, up to the very gunwale. Important people seem
often to have used small boats; Tzachas gets away in an
ἀκάτιον, Robert Guiscard and Count Hugh each escape from
shipwreck on a σκάφος, and it is an imperial μονήρης, a special
one 'set apart for the empresses', that conveys Irene to and
from her husband's camp.⁷ In such an inconspicuous boat
Bohemund returns to Italy after the humiliating treaty, and
Alexius visits the shipbuilding yards, or slips into his capital at
the end of the final Turkish campaign so as to avoid a public
entry and reception.⁸ Robert Guiscard after his naval defeat at
Butrinto goes to Cephallenia in a μονήρης γαλέα.⁹ One class of
boat which seems to have been reserved for the second in command in a fleet is 'called by sailors' an ἐξκούσσατον, from the

¹ XI. 10 and 11.
² XI. 10, p. 335. Some of these are fitted with fire-projecting tubes.
³ XII, 4, p. 356.
⁴ III. 11, p. 95; XI. 2, p. 313.
⁵ VI. 13, p. 181, and VII. 8, p. 205. The word is ἀγράρια from *peregre*, a small
fast-sailing boat with a sharp prow used by the Emperors for going across the
Bosporus, i.e. 'abroad'. See Du Cange on VI. 13, p. 181.
⁶ VIII. 3, p. 227; 4, p. 228. Camytzes crosses from Damalin to Constantinople
in a boat of this kind (XIV. 6, p. 443).
⁷ III. 12, p. 98; IX. 1, p. 248; X. 7, p. 289; XV. 1, p. 462: 2, p. 463. So a
Peloponnesian count 'wings his own μονῆρες with oars' to dash against the Pisans
(XI. 10, p. 336). It is however in a bireme that Bohemund comes from Antioch
to Corfu in a coffin (XI. 12, p. 341).
⁸ XI. 10, p. 335; XIV. 1, p. 419; XV. 7, p. 482.
⁹ VI. 6, p. 162.

Latin *excusatum*.[1] Du Cange in a long note explains this as an *oneraria navis*, immune ('excused') from certain fiscal burdens;[2] it is not an altogether convincing derivation, but the point is hardly worth further discussion.

Scouting, according to Bury,[3] was done by μονήρεις or galleys (γαλαῖαι, a less usual form than γαλέαι). So the second Drungary of the fleet is left on the watch 'with his excussate μονήρης'.[4] After Bohemund's death the Dardanelles are guarded by sailors 'making sallies in swift light boats' (διὰ δρομάδων κούφων νηῶν), while the hostile Italian fleet sends out 'swift scout ships' (κατάσκοποι δρομάδες) to get news of Alexius' whereabouts.[5] Rafts, ferries, and a pontoon-bridge all figure in Anna's pages,[6] but call for no special attention.

Compared to modern vessels all the Byzantine vessels were small and unseaworthy, and incapable of withstanding storms; the weather was often a deadlier foe than a hostile fleet. The unseasonable snowstorm and wind which wrecks Robert Guiscard's first fleet, as it tries to cross the Adriatic 'in battle array', gives rise to one of the finest passages in the book, a passage which will bear comparison with Masefield's famous *Dauber*. What concerns us here is however not Anna's style, but the actual way in which the ships are battered to pieces. 'The winds were destroying' [literally 'eating up'] 'the sails, and the yards were shattered and fell on the deck,[7] and the boats were sinking, crews and all. So some of the ships with their sailors were engulfed in the waters, some were carried against the headlands and dashed to pieces. Then the hides wrapped round the turrets came loose through the rain, and the nails came out of their proper places, and thereupon the skins growing heavier quickly upset those wooden turrets and falling down sank the ships.'[8] Even in calm weather the vessels of the eleventh century were liable to capsize if not properly

---

[1] The 'second count' in the expedition of Nicolas Mavrocatacalo has such a boat, also called a κάτεργον (X. 8, p. 290); the 'second Drungary of the fleet' under the Contostephani brothers has one with one bank of rowers, another instance of a μονῆρες for a man of high position (XII. 8, p. 369).

[2] X. 8, p. 290.

[3] *Loc. cit.* The only passage where the word 'galley' occurs in the *Alexias* it has no suggestion of scouting (VI. 6, p. 162). Leo (XIX. 74) recommends having small dromonds for the watch (cf. 29) and μονήρια and γαλέας ready for emergencies.

[4] XII. 9, p. 369.   [5] XIV. 3, pp. 429, 430.

[6] VIII. 4, p. 229; XIII. 6, p. 394; XIV. 7, p. 447; 9, p. 454.

[7] We may compare the storm that broke up the Pisan fleet: 'The waves dashed, the yards creaked, and the sails were torn through' (XI. 10, p. 336).

[8] III. 12, p. 98. Other devastating storms occur in X. 7, p. 288; XI. 10, pp. 336, 337; 11, p. 338. Irene cannot get back to Europe 'because the sea [of Marmora] was not navigable' (XV. 2, pp. 463, 464). A favourite expression is that vessels are ἡμίθραυστα.

ballasted : 13,000 (!) Venetians are thus drowned, 'by rushing all together to one side'.[1]

From the ships we pass to those on board them. Neumann[2] points out that the crews (he might have added, 'like the land forces') came from three sources, native Greeks, 'im Reich angesiedelte Barbaren', and foreign mercenaries.[3] Baynes states that 'in the *Tactica* of Leo VI' (giving it the later date and not the earlier suggested by Krumbacher) 'the crews are soldiers and sailors too',[4] but that the two arms were differentiated 'in the expedition of 902'. As a matter of fact we plainly see from the *Alexias* that the distinction between soldiers and sailors, as between generals and admirals, was never absolute. Only in one place is there a definite contrast drawn between 'those of the fleet' (who 'being unversed in fighting on land' are panic-stricken and useless in a siege) and 'the land soldiers' (ἠπειρῶται στρατιῶται).[5]

On the whole we may say that the Byzantine navy was always complementary to the army. Anna herself, by her shorter descriptions, stilted phrases, and evidently diminished interest,[6] makes us feel that battles at sea, partly no doubt because her father never took part in them, are of secondary importance to those on land. Only the action with the flagship of ὁ κόμης Πρεβέντζας and the use of fire-ships against the Pisans rouse her to any real enthusiasm, and she shows from first to last little knowledge of naval ways.[7]

[1] VI. 5, p. 161. In VII. 8, p. 210, a commander seems to have waited for sailing till he 'found the sea low-waved'. This is prescribed by Leo, *op. cit.*, 2, 27.

[2] *Op. cit.* p. 6.

[3] Diehl, *op. cit.* p. 742, says that the Mardaites from Mt. Lebanon and some Varangians served in the fleet: also that the native sailors were rewarded with hereditary fiefs.

[4] *Op. cit.* p. 148. The *Tactica* (XIX. 13) makes the upper bank of rowers the fighters, armed like land soldiers (65). The lower bank has spears (62). This was the classical custom. Spartan 'hoplites who will themselves handle the oars' are spoken of by Thucydides (VI. 91). It seems to him anomalous for naval actions to have 'almost the appearance of a battle by land' (*ibid.* I. 49; VII. 62, 63) through having decks crowded with special soldiers.

[5] XII. 8, pp. 367, 368. As always, the most important person on a boat was the steersman (οἰακοστρόφος, II. 7, p. 57; πηδαλιοῦχος, X. 8, p. 290; κυβερνήτης, X. 2, p. 271). Words used for sailors are πλωτῆρες (III. 12, p. 98) and τό ναυτικόν or οἱ ναυτικοί (III. 12, p. 97; XI. 5, p. 323) who may be used to garrison a town. In some passages 'the rowers' seem to be contrasted with the other men on board (IX. 1, p. 248; X. 7, p. 288; 8, pp. 290, 293; XI. 5, p. 323). We hear of rowing 'noiselessly' (III. 11, p. 95) or the reverse (XII. 9, p. 369); also ceaselessly (VII. 8, p. 207); also of holding water (III. 12, p. 98).

[6] Const. Porph. *de Admin. imp.*, has only one chapter dealing with the fleet (51 in Vol. III), and Leo's *Tactica* has only one Constitution.

[7] X. 8; XI. 10. One point involving her accuracy may be noticed here. She gives the Venetians in Robert's two Illyrian campaigns credit for five naval victories and one defeat (IV. 2, 3, p. 107; VI. 5). Of these five victories Chalandon

MILITARY AFFAIRS
60. BATTLES AND AMBUSCADES

OUR study of the Byzantine navy has taken us a little aside from our main subject, which is Military Affairs seen by Anna as the medium of her father's glory. We have spoken of his untiring persistence, like a caltrop indeed, in sharing every side of his army's labours. Before we go into details of life on a campaign, it may be well to recapitulate very briefly the principles which he held up before him, as they are to be gleaned from his daughter's encomiums.

It has been said so often as scarcely to brook repetition that the Byzantine mind admired cleverness above all things; not for nothing was their chief church dedicated to Wisdom. So that though Anna is proud of her father's courage she is even prouder of his tricks and diplomacy in war, his feigned flights, his playing off a weaker foe against a stronger one, his stratagems to conceal his inferior numbers, and the rest.[1] Above all does she gloat over his skill in performing two characteristically Byzantine transactions,[2] ὑποποιεῖσθαι, 'to win over' (usually by

believes the second to have been a small incident grossly magnified (*op. cit.* p. 91, note 3), and the fifth (after the defeat) to have been a pure invention, because we know that the Venetians deposed their Doge in punishment for the destruction of their fleet (p. 93, note 3). It is however possible that they got ready another. Their 'dromonds and triremes and small ships' were probably not all in action together, and Anna leaves the length of the interval between defeat and victory quite vague. In the absence of better evidence we will believe Anna. The other suggestion (p. 71, note 3), that Alexius' negotiations with the Venetians (IV. 2, p. 105) began earlier than his daughter seems to say, is more plausible.

[1] See above, Ch.21 and pp. 153, 245. In VI. 11, p. 175, the humouring of the weaker of two enemies is erected into a principle. In I. 3, p. 7, he has the 'Palamedes-like device' of pretending to blind Urselius, and the same comparison is applied by his daughter to his dealings with Botaniates (II. 2, p. 47). In I. 5, p. 13, he falsely proclaims his enemy's death; in I. 7 and 8, he deceives Basilacius, and in V. 5 and 6, Bohemund, by concealing his own position; in I. 4, p. 10, and X. 4, p. 281, he hides the inferior numbers of his army; in V. 5, p. 139, he orders a feigned flight, and Anna says he often did so (XV. 3, p. 467). (For other generals who conceal their numbers see XI. 2, p. 313; XIII. 9, p. 401; XIV. 1, p. 421; XV. 1, p. 461: Cf. Thuc. V. 8.) In VII. 2, he plays a mean trick on the Patzinak envoys. In VIII. 1, p. 223, he deceives the enemy by dressing up his men in prisoners' clothes; in XI. 2, p. 314, he outwits the Crusaders by a μηχανή or δρᾶμα. In X. 4 he approves the acted lie of Alacaseus. He exhorts Palaeologus to use 'every device' (III. 9, p. 92).

[2] II. 3, p. 48; V. 7, p. 143; VI. 4, p. 158; 6, p. 163; 12, p. 178; VII. 6, p. 202; VIII. 4, p. 228; 5, p. 230; X. 11, 306; XIII. 4, p. 387. In XI. 3, p. 315, his two captured generals adopt the same methods with the Turks. See also IX. 2, p. 249; 6, pp. 257, 258; 8, p. 261; XI. 4, p. 319 (*bis*); 8, p. 332; XII. 5, p. 360; XIII.

fair means or foul), and ἀπαιωρεῖν, 'to keep amused' some opponent while acting behind his back. Again and again we hear of the Emperor endeavouring to 'win' some one away from his proper allegiance by promises or by money down, or by circulating untruths or arousing discontent, and though he is not invariably successful it never seems to discourage him from fresh efforts of the same kind. He does not draw the line even at bogus letters to sow dissension.[1] As to keeping his foes amused, it is a performance on which Anna loves to dilate.[2] In short, like Cinnamus she holds that to win a victory δι' ἀπάτης or ῥᾳδιουργῶν is as good as any other way;[3] all that matters is the winning; and as a fact her father's military successes were

12, p. 411; XIV. 2, p. 424. In Books VII and VIII Alexius holds out revenge, booty, and pay, as inducements to bring over the Comans to fight their former friends the Patzinaks. Anna cannot help admiring as γενναῖος the Norman count who refuses to desert Bohemund and enter her father's service (VI. 1, p. 154), and the Venetians are equally loyal to Alexius (VI. 5, p. 161); but large sums of money buy the homage of the Crusaders. In VI. 5, p. 159, Alexius' attempts upon Robert Guiscard's son Guy met with ultimate failure, as the later history shows (XIII. 4, 5, 9, and 10), but temporary success, if we are to believe the *Chanson d'Antioche* (see Chalandon, p. 92) and a possible interpretation of Callicles' Poem XXXII. (See Ch. 67, below.) In XI. 11, p. 339, the 'soldiers of Tancred stood firm and Cantacuzenus ὑποποιούμενος τοὺς Κελτοὺς οὐκ ἔπειθε. The πανουργία of Alexius in XIII. 4, is also unsuccessful. But see XIV. 3, p. 432, where he wins the Turks. The policy of the Athenians of splitting up hostile combinations is alluded to by the Syracusans in Thuc. VI. 77, and Alcibiades practises it (*ibid.* VIII. 45).

[1] XIII. 4. In this connexion we may quote Oman (*Art of War*, I. 202): 'There is ample evidence, not only from the records of chroniclers but from the chapters of Leo's *Tactica*, that the East-Romans felt no proper sense of shame for some of their over-ingenious stratagems in war.' He instances negotiations only intended to lull the enemy 'into a belief in the certainty of peace' and thus to make an attack easier, and also the sending of 'bribes into the hostile camp'. Leo recommends two ancient tricks 'that were already 1,000 years old in his own day. The first is that of addressing treasonable letters to officers in the enemy's camp and contriving that they shall fall into the hands of the commander-in-chief in order that he may be made suspicious of his lieutenants'. It is interesting to find Alexius putting into practice this doubtfully moral maxim of a bygone Emperor, his predecessor on the same throne.

[2] VI. 10, pp. 174, 175. The people of Tyre act like this to Baldwin (XIV. 2, p. 426), and so do the Comans to Alexius (X. 4, p. 281). The word ἀπαιωρεῖν (equivalent to μετέωρον ταῖς ἐλπίσι ποιεῖν, XIV. 2, p. 426) may indeed be taken as expressing in one word much of the diplomatic ideal of Anna's day. (We must note that in X. 2, p. 272; XIII. 3, p. 381; and XV. 11, p. 501, the word has either a slightly or a wholly different meaning.) Pulchases the Turk does it to Alexius (VI. 12, p. 179); Alexius does it to the Patzinaks (VIII. 5, p. 230); the mother of Tancred does it to the imperial admiral (XII. 8, pp. 366, 367). So when Bohemund asks for the Domesticate of the East the Emperor 'fawns on him with fine hopes' (X. 11, p. 304). Again, it is hardly necessary to say that to return the same answer to each of two rival suitors is a trick of venerable age; Robert Guiscard practises it towards the Pope and the German king (I. 13, p. 33), just as centuries before the men of Camarina had so dealt with the Syracusans and Athenians (Thuc. VI. 88). In VIII. 7, Alexius sends letters of different meaning to his nephew John Comnenus and to the latter's subordinates at Durazzo.

[3] V. 5, p. 138; 6, p. 141; XIII. 4, p. 387; XV. 3, p. 467. In I. 4, p. 10, she says of him κλωπετεύειν τὴν νίκην ἐβούλετο. Cf. Thuc. V. 9 on κλέμματα in war.

more often won by stratagems of various sorts than by open
attacks. With a heterogeneous and doubtfully loyal army such
as we have described, this was probably inevitable. If he was
ever and indeed usually successful we, like his daughter, may
reasonably ascribe it to his own qualities of 'strategic skill'[1]
and his conviction that anything, 'craft' or even 'roguery', was
better than defeat.[2] Even his zeal as a converter of heretics
did not make him neglect either learning or strategy,[3] though
temporarily he 'took up the apostolic contest instead of the
strategic'.[4] This paragon indeed 'in all things excelled all, in
didactic discourse he outstripped those who busied themselves
about speech,[5] in battles and strategies he surpassed men
admired in arms'.[6] For in her eyes 'the first of virtues is the
wisdom of generals in gaining a victory without danger'; a good
leader is resourceful, ever devising something πανοῦργον καὶ
στρατηγικόν , something brilliant (ὀξύ τι), and condescending to
any stratagem against superior numbers.[7] His advice to the
Crusaders runs characteristically on the same lines. They must
rely on solid ranks and ambushes, and if victorious must not
pursue the enemy far or in disordered fashion; neglect of these
maxims spells ruin.[8] A general's first duty according to the
experts of the day was to keep his men safe.[9]

As to the nature of his military operations, they were threefold; Anna herself divides them into 'sieges, ambuscades, and
fights in regular battles'.[10] But before we deal with these in detail
something must be said about the preliminaries to all military

Attal. (p. 108) says that to the general must be attributed the good or bad
success of an army. See I. 1, p. 4; 2, pp. 4, 5; 4, p. 10; 5, p. 11; 7, p. 18; X. 11,
p. 306; XIII. 4, p. 386 (bis); 5, p. 391; XIV. 8, p. 453. So Polybius (I. 84, 6) extols
στρατηγικὴ δύναμις over 'unreasoning military routine'. The phrase is constantly
used in the Alexias not only of Alexius but of other generals, especially Bohemund.
We may contrast IX. 2, p. 249; XII. 2, pp. 348, 349. She also says, 'The race of
Celts has never made use of strategic order and science at all' (XI. 6, p. 325). On
Alexius as a general see above, chs. 55 and 57.

  [2] XIII. 4; XV. 3.
  [3] Though she does not say so, we may assume that he was familiar with Leo's
Tactica. Its twenty-one divisions deal with all the matters in which Anna displays
such interest: arms, training, camps, sieges, marches, battles, and above all with
the different παρατάξεις of Saracens, Turks, Bulgarians, Scythians, Gauls, Lombards, and Slavs, all enemies of the Empire.
  [4] XIV. 8, p. 453.
  [5] Taking λόγοις and λόγον as referring specially to oratory, rather than to
learning in general.
  [6] XV. 8, p. 487.   [7] XV. 3, p. 467.
  [8] X. 10, p. 301; 11, p. 305; XI. 3, pp. 317, 318; 8, p. 332. Bohemund pursues
the fleeing Greeks ἀκρατῶς, so his unguarded camp is sacked, and the rest of his
cavalry defeated (V. 6, p. 140; cf. Thuc. VIII. 105).
  [9] VI. 10, p. 172; 13, p. 180. Cf. ἀγωνίζου . . . φυλάττειν τὸν λαόν σου (Cec. Strat.
p. 10).
  [10] V. 1, p. 126.

undertakings of whatever nature, namely, study of the ground, scouting, the pitching of a camp, and the choosing of times and seasons.

The first point, topography, is evidently one which interests Anna, and she is fond of describing 'the lie of the land' (τοῦ τόπου τὴν θέσιν) and the attention paid to it by the various generals.[1] To pursue this topic in detail would take us too far. We will only give two instances. A situation 'near a fortress . . . having the river on one side and being marshy on the other' is the spot chosen by Alexius for one of his camps in the Patzinak War, a choice not made till he has himself examined the river-bed and banks on both sides and explained the topography to his officers.[2] Again, when Alexius is anxious to defend his borders against the Dalmatians, he studies the ground in person, 'going everywhere on foot, and gazing about him with his own eyes, lest some unguarded spot should escape him' in this locality of gorges 'hilly, riven, thickly wooded, and wellnigh impassable'.[3]

Connected with this careful study of the ground we must note the dependence on scouts, who with deserters from the other side were a general's only source of information.[4] Cecaumenus is insistent on their value: 'in war let there be with thee scouts many and faithful and active.'[5] Some valuable news must have been got by those who executed the ἀκροβολισμοί of which we hear so constantly, but the reliance was mainly on scouts specially sent out to reconnoitre, men to 'run ahead', as they are once called.[6] They go out 'in all directions' to ascertain the movements of the Patzinaks;[7] one scout by receiving a signal and passing it on enables the Emperor's forces to attack Castoria from the lake side and the land side simultaneously.[8] Scouts watch for fleets[9] as well as armies,[10] and a pretence of advancing to κατασκοπῆσαι the enemy's lines affords an excellent

---

[1] I. 5, p. 11; 7, p. 18; IV. 5, p. 111; V. 5, p. 138; 7, p. 141; VI. 1; X. 3, p. 275 (bis); 5, p. 282. For an unfavourable situation see VI. 10, p. 173.

[2] VIII. 3, p. 227. Similar localities are chosen by Cantacuzene in XIII. 5, p. 392; 6, p. 394.

[3] IX. 1, p. 245.

[4] We may compare the scouts who appear throughout all Polybius' History (e.g. in the sea battle of I. 53) and the 'currours' of Froissart, constantly sent out to ascertain the position and numbers of the enemy.

[5] Strat. pp. 9 (bis), 26. So at Cynossema the Athenians were nearly overwhelmed by the Spartans because their 'scouts had failed them' (Thuc. VIII. 103).

[6] VIII. 2, p. 223. [7] VI. 14, p. 184.

[8] VI. 1, p. 153. Here the topography is most important.

[9] VII. 8, p. 208; XII. 8, p. 368.

[10] VIII. 4, p. 229; XIV. 3, p. 429; XV. 6, p. 479. In IV. 1, p. 103, they are set on the walls of Durazzo to watch for Robert Guiscard. In XIII. 5, p. 391; 6, p. 394 (bis), Cantacuzenus' scouts are apparently 'barbarians'.

opportunity to a traitor for going across and revealing his master's plans.[1] In one instance we hear of one body of scouts being followed by another to keep them up to the mark, the two duties of such men being vigilance and careful observation,[2] so that even the great Alexius is said to watch for his Turkish enemy 'like a scout'.[3]

From scouting we pass to the pitching of camps, to which Anna often refers. This usually demanded 'trenches and a palisade',[4] and this feature of an encampment is mentioned so often as to make enumeration unnecessary and effectively to contradict Oster's statement,[5] that 'die Befestigung des Lagerplatzes .. nur bei sehr vereinzelten Gelegenheiten ausdrücklich und, wie es fast scheinen möchte, als ungewöhnlich hervorgehoben wird'.

The last preliminary matter to be considered is the time and season which appeared most appropriate for fighting in the eyes of Anna's contemporaries. All through the *Alexias* we find the assumption that winter is a close time for fighting,[6] while summer heat is hardly less objectionable for any military operations.[7] The disregard of seasons by the Patzinaks was one of the most disconcerting features of their raids.[8] On one occasion we are told that, the summer being over and the autumn equinox just passed, 'this season seemed favourable for taking the field',[9] a point of view with which those familiar with Asia Minor, where the weather is at its best in late September and early October, would undoubtedly sympathize. But we cannot help reflecting that, with winter and summer both barred, campaigns must have been extremely short.[10]

On the other hand the length of each fighting day must have been very great, for we constantly hear of councils,

---

[1] VII. 9, p. 211.   [2] XIV. 1, p. 421.   [3] XV. 3, p. 466.

[4] In I. 4, p. 10, their absence is specially mentioned. In XV. 1, p. 461, the Greek 'tents' do not seem to have been fortified, but the army is at the time taking the offensive. For the usual practice see I. 7, p. 18; II. 6, p. 57; IV. 3, p. 108; V. 5, p. 138; VII. 8, p. 207; VIII. 3, p. 227; 4 pp. 229, 230, and many other instances of a τάφρος or a χάραξ.

[5] *A. K.*, Pt. III, p. 28.

[6] e.g. V. 1, p. 125; IX. 1, p. 246, and often elsewhere. This was, as is well known, the principle on which the old Greeks conducted their campaigns, notably in the Peloponnesian War; they never fought in winter. In I. 16, p. 37, Robert Guiscard in winter chooses the shortest possible sea journey for crossing to Illyria.

[7] IX. 1, p. 246; X. 5, &c.

[8] VII. 2, p. 190. As has been pointed out by Dieter (*B. Z.* III. pp. 386–90) this passage is copied from Psellus (*Chron.*, Basil II, Byz. T., p. 12), and may possibly be wholly inaccurate as applied to the Patzinaks.

[9] XV. 3, p. 468.

[10] It should be pointed out that the winter was used for training (Leo, *Tactica*, VII. 2).

marches, and the like taking place in the night. Generals
ponder all night over their plans,[1] or even go out then for
reconnoitring,[2] while the self-indulgent drown care in drink,
and women pray and sing 'holy hymns' in churches.[3] As in
other lands, the carrying of secret messages,[4] private diplomacy,[5] sudden surprises of an enemy,[6] all this takes place while
the world is asleep. It is at night that Alexius fears the men
of Amasea will set the captured Urselius free,[7] at night that he
himself escapes out of and into Constantinople.[8] In the darkness hostile attacks or pryings are feared and hostile forces slip
away,[9] while other men remain hidden in ambush or on the
watch,[10] or a commander makes his preparations and issues his
instructions for the morrow.[11] By night deeds of violence are
attempted or executed,[12] so that those in high places especially
need the 'unsleeping eye' of devotion near them.[13]

In all this there is nothing exceptional, and if the use of
night for drawing up documents, organizing military hymn-
singings and processions, trying siege appliances, marching,
holding councils, or arguing with heretics seems more frequent
in the *Alexias* than is customary with us, we must remember the
difference of climate and the desirability of avoiding the day's
heat. On the other hand the turning of night into day by the
anxious watchers round Alexius' dying bed is one of the many
touches of nature in Anna's final chapter that make the whole
world of wives and daughters kin.

We will now take up in reverse order Anna's threefold division of military operations, and deal successively with battles,

[1] I. 2, p. 6; II. 9, p. 61; III. 2, p. 73; VII. 10, p. 214; 11, p. 215. In XV. 6,
p. 477, the Sultan after a repulse 'grieved through the whole night'.
[2] IV. 1, p. 103. But the phrase διὰ πάσης νυκτὸς καὶ ἡμέρας may be merely a
conventional one, as in VI. 1, p. 152, it occurs with the word μαχόμενος, and in
V. 9, p. 147, is applied to the way Alexius and Irene 'toiled over the study of' the
holy books. In XV. 11, p. 499, it is probably used literally of Irene's devoted
nursing.
[3] II. 5; III. 8, p. 88; V. 8, p. 144. In XIII. 1, p. 378, we hear of night prayers
said by a man.
[4] II. 4, p. 50; 6, p. 55; VI. 10, p. 171; X. 2, p. 274; 4, p. 278.
[5] II. 4, p. 50; IX. 8, p. 261; X. 2, p. 272.
[6] III. 11, p. 95; IV. 6, p. 114; VII. 10, p. 214; IX. 5, p. 254.
[7] I. 2, p. 7.
[8] II. 4, p. 51 : 5, p. 52; XV. 7, p. 482. So Diogenes wishes to leave the imperial
camp at night (IX. 7, p. 258). By night Alopus escapes from Mitylene and Tzachas
from Chios (VII. 8, pp. 205, 210), and a Greek general tries to get into Adrianople
unperceived by the Comans (X. 3, p. 276).
[9] X. 4, p. 281; XI. 4, p. 321; 6, p. 326; XIII. 9, p. 401; XV. 4, p. 470.
[10] V. 5, pp. 139, 140; VII. 3, p. 195.
[11] VII. 10, p. 214; VIII. 1, p. 221; XIII. 6, p. 394; XV. 6, p. 477.
[12] VIII. 6, p. 234; IX. 5, p. 254; XI. 2, p. 315; XIII. 1, pp. 377, 378.
[13] XII. 3, p. 352; XIV. 4, p. 437.

ambuscades, and sieges.[1] When we come to details of fighting we at once note the conscientious way in which Anna describes the right wing and the left wing and the centre, both of friends and foes, how they were composed and how they behaved.[2] Yet for the average reader the result is merely wearisome.[3] Whether it is Homer or some Attic historian that she is imitating, as Miss Gardner and Stemplinger would respectively have us think, it cannot be said that her battle scenes are the most successful parts of her work. Their mere number would make it impossible to speak of them all, even supposing it added at all to our knowledge of her. If we are to single out a few more interesting than the rest, we may choose the night battle with Basilacius,[4] the defeat at Durazzo with Alexius' wonderful escapes,[5] and the victory of Lebunium where the army is kept alive by peasants acting as water-carriers.[6]

We must, however, spend a little time on the question of the 'new $\pi\alpha\rho\acute{\alpha}\tau\alpha\xi\iota\varsigma$' or battle array of Alexius which seemed to his daughter so superhumanly wonderful. First we must note that the noun $\pi\alpha\rho\acute{\alpha}\tau\alpha\xi\iota\varsigma$ and the verb with its various derivatives are great favourites[7] with Anna and with her husband, but with a not perfectly uniform meaning.[8] Usually it is 'line of battle', and as such occurs too often to make references necessary. Sometimes 'formation' comes nearer to it,[9] sometimes we must translate 'tactics'.[10] Once $\dot{\alpha}\gamma\omega\nu\acute{\iota}\alpha\iota\ \dot{\epsilon}\kappa\ \pi\alpha\rho\alpha\tau\acute{\alpha}\xi\epsilon\omega\varsigma$, 'regular battles', are contrasted with 'sieges and ambushes'; on two occasions the 'line' is distinguished from horse-archers and other

---

[1] V. 1, p. 126.
[2] We may compare the battle of Manzikert in Nic. Bry. I. 16, p. 29.
[3] See Alexius' campaigns against Urselius, Bryennius, and Basilacius in Book I, the siege of Constantinople in II. 10, the war against Robert Guiscard and Bohemund in Books IV and V, the Patzinak and Coman campaigns of Books VI, VIII, and X, the final contest with Bohemund in Book XIII, and the struggles with the Turks constantly recurring throughout the history, from the beginning of Alexius' reign to the very end.
[4] I. 7 and 8.   [5] IV. 4–8.   [6] VIII. 5.
[7] In the first book they occur six times, in 5, pp. 10, 11; 7, p. 17; 8, p. 20; 9, p. 21; 13, p. 33. The noun can usually be translated 'line', and the verb means 'to post'. In IV. 4, p. 109; V. 5, p. 139, $\tau\grave{o}\ \sigma\chi\hat{\eta}\mu\alpha\ \tau\hat{\eta}\varsigma\ \pi\alpha\rho\alpha\tau\acute{\alpha}\xi\epsilon\omega\varsigma$ comes to mean 'each man's place in the line'. Sometimes it is plural, 'lines' (IV. 6, p. 115; IX. 10, p. 265). In her characteristic way of repeating a word at short intervals, Anna uses some form of $\pi\alpha\rho\acute{\alpha}\tau\alpha\xi\iota\varsigma$ three times in X. 3, p. 275, three times in XI. 3, p. 317, and three times in XIII. 6.
[8] Similarly Phalanx in Byzantine Greek is no longer a technical term for a definite military force; it merely means 'troops' in larger or smaller bands.
[9] VI. 10, p. 171; X. 9, p. 296; XV. 3, p. 470. In XV. 3, p. 469, the plains of Dorylaeum are said to be large enough $\pi\rho\grave{o}\varsigma\ \pi\alpha\rho\alpha\tau\acute{\alpha}\xi\epsilon\iota\varsigma$. In XII. 2, p. 348, $\pi\alpha\rho\alpha\tau\acute{\alpha}\xi\epsilon\iota\varsigma$ are contrasted with $\mu\acute{\alpha}\chi\alpha\iota$.
[10] VI. 14, p. 182, Pacurianus is $\pi\alpha\rho\acute{\alpha}\tau\alpha\xi\iota\nu\ \delta\iota\alpha\mu\eta\chi\alpha\nu\acute{\eta}\sigma\alpha\sigma\theta\alpha\iota\ \pi\sigma\iota\kappa\iota\lambda\acute{\omega}\tau\alpha\tau\sigma\varsigma$. So is the blinded Nicephorus Bryennius (VII. 2, p. 191).

mounted fighters.[1] The commander generally takes his position
in the centre τῆς παρατάξεως.[2] When Alexius rouses up the
citizens of Rusium 'and even the peasants with their private
wagons' to support his fighting troops, the enemy is dismayed
to see τὴν διττὴν παράταξιν.[3] In the battle of Lebunium the Greek
'line' becomes crescent-shaped,[4] as the wings rush forward. In
two later passages the verb ἀντιπαρατάσσεσθαι is used of resisting
calamity or danger.[5] Finally we get the word παράταξις in a
sense combining the ideas of all three words given above, line,
formation, and tactics, as where Cecaumenus says, παρὰ πάσας
τὰς παρατάξεις ἡ Ῥωμαϊκή ἐστι κρείττων,[6] or where Alexius devises
one so novel and wonderful as to impress all beholders. What
then was his καινὴ παράταξις? It is worth a little trouble to
discover, especially when Oster summarily dismisses it as a
revival of the forgotten method of marching 'in hohlen Vier-
ecken',[7] surely a most inadequate explanation.

As we have seen, inventiveness was a quality which Anna
loved to claim for her father, but which we cannot always
admit. Thus his σύνταγμα which was φοβερὸν θέαμα seems
merely to have been a return to the solid serried ranks where
each man knew his place;[8] his καινὴ στρατηγία in the last war
with Bohemund is clearly only the adoption of defensive warfare instead of offensive,[9] while the πολέμου σχῆμα so carefully
enjoined on his troops is just a clearing of the road by horse-
archers, previous to the slower advance of the main body.[10]
But in the final Turkish campaign Anna harps on the
novelty of her father's tactics[11] which, when he finds a plain
large enough, he puts into practice, after having with painful
thought worked them out on parchment.[12] The solidity of
the formation causes Alexius himself to consider it a divine
inspiration, and the experienced archsatrap Monolycus, struck
with equal admiration, guesses its originator. It advances
like 'some living fortified city (πεπυργωμένη)', and prisoners,
women, and children are in the middle. The Greeks can
resist attacks while keeping the παράταξις unbroken, and
this is its peculiar virtue. With vehemence Anna protests

---

[1] V. 1, p. 126; VII. 8, p. 207; 10, p. 214; 11, p. 216; XV. 4, p. 469; 5, p. 474.
[2] IV. 6, pp. 114, 115; VI. 14, p. 184; VII. 3, p. 195; XIV. 5, p. 441.
[3] VII. 10, p. 213.   [4] VIII. 5, p. 232.   [5] XII. 3, p. 353; XV. 8, p. 489.
[6] Strat., p. 10.   [7] A. K., Pt. III, p. 28.   [8] XIII. 2, p. 379.
[9] XIII. 4, p. 386.   [10] XIII. 8, p. 397.
[11] XV. 3, pp. 468–70; 5, p. 474; 6, p. 477; 7, p. 481.
[12] Anna says (XV. 4, p. 469) he had studied the *Tactics* of Aelian, a Greek writer
who dedicated to Hadrian this work from which Psellus compiled extracts; G.B.L.
p. 636. Attaliates describes Romanus Diogenes sitting in his tent διαγράφων τὸν
πόλεμον (p. 113).

against the idea that this invention resembled anything known before. The παράταξις passed on solidly and steadily, it could be halted at a word, in its serried ranks and closeness (συνασπισμῷ καὶ ἀλληλουχίᾳ) it was like the 'unshaken mountains', in its movements it resembled 'a great living creature'. It was emphatically 'new and marvellous to all, and such as no one has ever yet seen, or in writing history has handed down to posterity'.[1] If, as Oster thinks, hollow squares such as the ancients knew well had fallen wholly into oblivion by Anna's day,[2] this language might not be unnatural or excessive, though it is not easy to suspect our learned princess of such historical ignorance. But even so, it does not help us to translate one very difficult passage.[3] Anna has described the Turkish παράταξις as unique, because the right wing, left wing, and centre were all disjoined, and could attack an enemy on all sides with arrows, 'such first-rate archers are they'. Then comes this sentence: 'Turning then his attention to this, that much experienced Emperor himself made the formations (τὰς παρατάξεις), and placed his phalanxes, οὕτως ὡς τοὺς μὲν ἀπὸ τῶν δεξιῶν τοξεύειν ὅθεν αἱ ἀσπίδες προβέβληντο, τοὺς δὲ ἡμετέρους ἐκ τῶν ἀριστερῶν βάλλειν ὅθεν τὰ ἀσκέπαστα ἦν τοῦ σώματος.' Taking τοὺς μέν as 'the Turks', contrasted with τοὺς δὲ ἡμετέρους,[4] we propose the following translation: 'So that the enemy should shoot with his right hand towards the spot where the shields were held in front, and that our men should shoot with their left hands towards where the uncovered part of the enemy's body was.' That is to say, Alexius made the Greeks adopt a wholly new method of shooting, holding their bows in their *right* hands, and pulling the strings with their *left*, so that thereby the shields on their left arms were brought round to cover their bodies.[5] It may be noted, first that the instinct of soldiers is always to shoot straight before them, perpendicularly to their own line of battle, and secondly that Thucydides dwells on the tendency of armies to thrust to the right 'because every soldier individually fears for his exposed side, which he tries to cover with the shield of his comrade on the right (τοῦ ἐν

[1] XV. 7, pp. 481, 482.
[2] We must note that her phrase 'he again drew up that new παράταξις and placing all the prisoners with the women and children in the middle he departed', hardly reads as if the hollow square, with non-combatants in the middle, was the *essence* of the scheme (XV. 4, pp. 473–4: 6, p. 477).
[3] XV. 3, p. 470.
[4] The *P. G.* translation takes τοὺς μέν as meaning 'some of the Greeks' and τοὺς δὲ ἡμετέρους of the rest who held their shields out. This seems indefensible.
[5] The lines would look 'fortified' (XV. 4, p. 474) because the shields covered the bodies more than in ordinary armies.

δεξιᾷ παρατεταγμένου)'.[1] If our rendering is correct the arrangement had indeed all the novelty which Anna predicated of it, and even if 'angels' had nothing to do with it, the reader, like Monolycus, is 'struck with wonder at that new disposition of the battle-array' whereby panic and breaking of the ranks seems to have become a thing of the past.

Another suggestion has however been made by a distinguished Greek scholar, namely that Alexius' novelty consisted in confronting the Turks with a slanting line, which whenever it was attacked wheeled round, so as always to present a series of shield-covered left shoulders, while discharging arrows against the uncovered right breasts of the enemy. This position of the Greek line (not parallel to the Turkish but sloping away at an angle, with the soldiers forced to shoot not perpendicularly to their own front[2]) would make their shots fall slantwise on their foes, and their rapid yet steady wheeling round, to correspond with any movement in the lines opposed to them, may well have caused the impression about which Anna grows rhapsodical, that 'moving they remained motionless and standing they advanced'.[3] Clearly solidity and unbrokenness was the strong point of this particular order of battle, and a sloping, constantly turning line seems a likely way to achieve it. In short, either explanation makes fair sense and neither is entirely satisfactory, though the second presupposes less breach with ordinary ways of fighting than the first.

So much for 'contests in battle-array'. The next division of warfare, the placing of troops in ambush, so as to leap out suddenly on the enemy, is something that Anna would be sure to admire. Indeed it was such an important part of Byzantine military science as to compensate, in one instance at least, for incompetence in personal fighting.[4] Feigned flights were of course closely connected with it. As early as his second campaign we find Alexius practising this against Bryennius; he 'pretended to fly, drawing the enemy by little and little into the ambushes'.[5] At Larissa 'he toiled all day, calling on God for aid, [pondering] how he should lay his ambush',[6] and the successful plan is later described in minute detail.[7] Robert Guiscard treacherously puts men in ambush to seize an unsus-

[1] *Hist.* V. 71.
[2] See above on the soldier's natural instinct.   [3] XV. 7, p. 481.
[4] XIV. 1, p. 420. 'To place an ambush to the best advantage' is given in V. 3, p. 130, as one of the parts of military training.
[5] I. 6, p. 15.   [6] V. 5, p. 138.
[7] V. 5, pp. 139, 140. In V. 6, p. 140, he issues from his night-long ambuscade and attacks Bohemund's undefended camp.

pecting friend;[1] by lying in wait the Patzinaks deal destruction to Alexius' Archontopules, and the Turks to the Crusaders.[2] The setting of ambushes (an art in which they were sorely deficient) as well as watchfulness against Turkish tricks is strongly enjoined on these same Crusaders by Alexius,[3] who himself had in past times 'worked for the destruction' of the Patzinaks δι' ἀκροβολισμῶν καὶ λόχων, that is to say, by never coming to close quarters, but going ahead to all the towns the enemy wished to take and waylaying him on the road.[4] 'Streams and marshy places' help in this matter,[5] and even the worst defeat may be transformed into success by 'men lying in wait' to attack the conquerors and 'turn back the flight' of their own men.[6] It is one of the glories of Alexius' new παράταξις in his last Turkish campaign that Monolycus' ambuscades of light-armed men wholly fail to surprise or break the solid Greek lines.[7] The two verbs used by Anna are 'to set λόχους' and ἐφεδρεύειν, both amounting to the same thing. Ships lie in wait for hostile fleets[8] with more or less vigilance and efficiency, and the same methods are practised on land by the troops whom Alexius sends ostensibly to meet, and really to mount guard over, the Crusaders.[9]

Before we leave this subject we may refer to the vigorous warning given by Alexius in his first poem to his son John against the dangers of an ambush,[10] and may also point out that in Byzantine as well as Classical Greek λόχος has two meanings, 'ambush' and 'body of troops', the latter not invariably uniform in number.[11] Even in the Alexias it is sometimes doubtful whether a commander 'sets' an ambush, or 'draws up' his troops in line, but in the Hyle of Bryennius we find two plain instances of the two different meanings. Once he talks of some one 'falling into an ambush' (λόχοις περιπεσών),[12] once of a commander 'drawing up his army by companies' (παρατάττων τὸν στρατὸν . . . κατὰ λόχους).[13] To establish one's own main body

[1] I. 11, p. 25.
[2] VII. 7, p. 204; X. 6, pp. 286, 287. The Turks fear the like for themselves (XI. 2, p. 315).
[3] X. 11, p. 305; 10, p. 301; XI. 6, p. 325.   [4] VII. 6, p. 203.
[5] I. 11, p. 25; XI. 2, p. 315.   [6] VII. 11, p. 217.
[7] XV. 5, p. 474. Before this, in XIV. 5, p. 440, a Turkish ambush proves disastrous to the imperial troops under Camytzes.
[8] X. 7 and XIII. 7.
[9] X. 5, p. 285; 7, pp. 288, 289; 9, p. 294. Forays were to be prevented 'by moderate shootings at a distance' on the part of the Greeks.
[10] Mous. Alex. I. 262.
[11] See on Phalanx and Parataxis, p. 393, notes 7, 8 above.
[12] Hyle, I. 11, p. 25. This is the usual meaning throughout the book.
[13] Ibid. I. 17, p. 30.

firmly as against surprises and to hamper the enemy by men placed in ambuscade were the two sides of a careful general's preparation for action.

MILITARY AFFAIRS

61. SIEGES: DURAZZO

COMING to Anna's third division of military activities, it hardly needs remarking that fortresses and sieges play a very great part in Byzantine warfare.[1] Durazzo twice over, Castoria, Nicaea, Antioch, Laodicea, Tyre, all provide Anna with material of this nature, and it is clear that to her this is the most interesting side of military operations.

The two sieges of Durazzo (in classical language Dyrrachium or Epidamnus) occupy twenty-two chapters wholly or in part,[2] to say nothing of many passing allusions. A glance at the map will show why from mere situation the place was important,[3] but Anna is at pains to tell us with what peculiar strength nature and art had endowed it, though curiously enough she never speaks of the Via Egnatia, of which one branch starting from it made its position unique. She first mentions this town as having the rebel Bryennius for its Duke,[4] then as 'the metropolis of Illyrium' from which as his starting-point the next rebel, Basilacius, advanced to Thessalonica.[5] The note of its great significance in civil war is thus at once struck. But even greater is its role when foreign invaders attack the Empire. Its capture is the prime object of Robert Guiscard in the first Norman invasion, and of Bohemund in the third. Robert plans to besiege it by sea and land, and undeterred by a shipwreck establishes his troops, augmented by those who had previously crossed under Bohemund, 'inside the ruined walls of the city called of old Epidamnus'.[6] This seems to Anna a good occasion for a display of learning. Rather surprisingly she never alludes to the sinister importance of Epidamnus in connexion with the

[1] Leo, in his *Tactica* (XV. 2), speaks most respectfully of siegecraft. He says: 'A siege requires the bravery of a general, and a mind sharp and strategic and sensible, and preparations of engines, and security (ἀσφάλεια) in sitting down against a town or fortress or stronghold, and that this security shall be produced with much attention' (προσοχή).

[2] III. 12; IV. 1–8; V. 1; VI. 6; XII. 9; XIII. 2–11.

[3] L. Heuzey, *Mission archéologique de Macédoine*, p. 363, says it was in the Normans' eyes 'la clef de l'empire grec'.

[4] I. 4, p. 9. 'Using as his base the city of Durazzo he overran all the West.'

[5] I. 7, p. 17.   [6] III. 12.

Peloponnesian War,[1] but begins its history with speaking of its destruction in the wars between Pyrrhus and the Romans.[2]

The siege of Durazzo is then minutely described, and Alexius instructs his brother-in-law the governor George Palaeologus, who has succeeded the traitor Monomachatus, to crown the walls with unnailed boards, so as to give no footing for enemies mounting on scaling ladders.[3] Other instruments of siegecraft are mentioned, not for the first or the last time in Anna's history: wooden turrets and 'stone-throwing instruments', and siege-engines (ἑλεπόλεις) in general.[4] When in addition they see the formidable army of the besiegers encamped round 'the whole circuit of the walls', panic almost seizes the garrison, who realize that this is no mere raid, but a serious attempt of the Normans upon the Empire. We here get one of the many instances where parleying takes place between besieged and besiegers; the wall is so low that men can speak 'from above' and be heard below, and a man paraded round the exterior can be seen clearly enough to be detected as an impostor[5] by those within. The siege goes on, and the naval victories of the Venetians help Palaeologus little. Famine and disease beset the Normans,[6] but in spite of this the Emperor, when finally

[1] Thuc. *Hist.* I. 24 sqq.

[2] On this Heuzey (*op. cit.* p. 372) comments: 'Rien . . . ne vient confirmer la tradition byzantine sur l'abandon de la place à la suite des expéditions de Pyrrhus.' Indeed references to it in Polybius, Plautus, Diodorus Siculus, and Catullus give reason for supposing that its career of maritime importance was never interrupted. Of 'Amphion and Zethus' we have spoken on p. 200.

[3] III. 9, p. 92. This seems to have been made permanent, for these 'unnailed' boards reappear in the second siege of Durazzo (XIII. 10, p. 403), once more aimed at foiling men who should mount διὰ κλιμάκων. On this second occasion the boards chiefly harass the Greeks, as they prevent the besieged from 'bending over the wall' to talk to their friends. It is possible that Anna makes a mistake in bringing in the device twice, and that it really only served once. In that case this affords another instance of defective revision.

[4] II. 8; p. 61; IV. 1–4; VI. 13, p. 180; VII. 3, p. 194; XIV. 1, p. 421, and often elsewhere.

[5] IV. 1, p. 104. So at Adrianople (X. 4, p. 279) and Tyragium (XV. 6, p. 480). In II. 9, p. 62, Gilpractus the leader of Botaniates' German troops ἄνωθεν προκύψας promises John Ducas Caesar to betray Constantinople to the Comneni. Cf. XI. 4, p. 318. In XI. 6, p. 324, men are let down over the battlements of Antioch by cords.

[6] In IV. 3, pp. 107, 108, we learn that Robert's ships were 'anchored in the Freshwater River' (εἰς τὸν Γλυκὺν ποταμόν) near which his troops were encamped. Heuzey points out (*op. cit.* pp. 365 sqq.) that this clearly refers to the exit of the waters of the lagoon (see p. 400 below) under the bridge into the Bay of Durazzo. He says: 'Le mot γλυκύς s'appliquait particulièrement aux eaux de mer plus ou moins adoucies par l'écoulement des ruisseaux et des rivières, comme le montre Strabon (324) à propos du γλυκὺς λιμήν situé sur la même côte de l'Adriatique.' Strabo's Sweet Harbour was the outlet of the river Acheron (modern Gurla), and as it is almost 200 miles South of Durazzo cannot be, as is said in Pauly-Wissowa's *Real-Encyclopädie*, the place where Robert harboured his ships. The name is (as one might expect) a common one. We may compare the 'Sweet Waters of Europe' and the 'Sweet Waters of Asia', both near Constantinople.

able to take the field in person, is met before he reaches Thessalonica with the news that his deputy has been hard pressed by the besiegers.[1]

Further details afterwards come to Alexius, how Robert had collected 'much material in the plain' (probably brushwood for burning the town) and had encamped his main body about a bowshot from the walls of Durazzo, posting other soldiers 'in the mountains and glades and heights'. After a brief encampment by the river Charzanes (now Erzan) Alexius hurries forward to the church of St. Nicolas 'four stadia away from Durazzo'. Here he studies 'the lie of the land' and the following description follows. 'There was a neck of land stretching out from Dalmatia to the sea, ending in a promontory like a peninsula (χερσόνησος) on which the aforesaid church had been built. Now the slope of this neck, sinking gradually into the plain in the direction of Durazzo, has on the left the sea and on the right a lofty overhanging mountain.' Here Alexius 'brought together all his forces (τὸ ὁπλιτικὸν ἅπαν) and pitched his camp', sending for Palaeologus, who arrives 'with ships of war'.

At this point it may be well to consider the geographical situation. At first sight it is tempting to take Anna's 'neck' as the land on whose South point Durazzo stands, land running parallel to the coast (from which it is separated by a lagoon), and to believe that Alexius' camp was near the neck's Northern extremity. Both on the North and on the South the lagoon is cut off from the sea by a low-lying bar, but whereas the Southern one has been pierced to give an exit for the lagoon waters and contains a bridge, the Northern bar has been left solid, and at its Western extremity ends in the hilly point of Cape Pali (Anna's Pallia or Pales).[2] This point in its turn is connected with the 'neck' by a strip of sand. On Cape Pali we should then place the church of St. Nicolas. Roughly speaking we get a parallelogram sloping from South-East to North-West, the four sides being the coast, the 'neck', and the two bars; Cape Pali is at the North-West angle, Durazzo at the South-West. As a matter of fact the 'neck', which is a mere strip when it leaves the headland of Cape Pali, expands Southwards from a point about four miles North of the town, until when it nears the Bay of Durazzo it is sufficiently broad for a range of hills on the West along the sea, and on the East (near the lagoon) for flat fields capable of holding Robert's army of 30,000 men.

But tempting as this identification is, this particular 'neck' does not fit in with Anna's description nor with the rest of the

[1] IV. 4, p. 110.   [2] IV. 2, p. 105; X. 7, p. 289.

story. If we suppose ourselves to be looking North from its
Southern extremity, the sea is indeed on the left, but there is no
'lofty overhanging mountain' on the right; all the 'mountains'
on this neck are on the West side and overhang the sea. If we
turn round and look South from the neck's Northern end, the
mountains on the right are there, but not the sea on the left,
and even if we strain 'sea' into meaning 'lagoon' and suppose
that after Robert crossed the bridge to go to mass in St. Theodore's church he had to cross back again to fight,[1] we must
admit the impossibility of Alexius' whole army after its defeat
getting away by the two narrow strips which prevent Cape Pali
from being an island. Furthermore, the name of 'San Nicolo'
is assigned in sixteenth-century maps to a church *on the mainland* East of Durazzo beyond the bridge, and William of Apulia
further localizes it by saying it was near Petra,[2] the important
'κλείσουρα'[3] close to the bay, where Pompey set up his camp.[4]
We are therefore reluctantly constrained to follow Heuzey in
making Anna's 'neck' and her 'promontory like a peninsula'
into something much tamer, namely 'le chaînon montagneux'
on the mainland 'ayant à gauche la mer et à droite des crêtes
plus élevées'.[5] Viewed across the lagoon this chain does 'sink
gradually into the plain, in the direction of Durazzo', and on
these foothills Alexius must have pitched his camp. Palaeologus
could obviously not reach him by land, as Robert's army lay
between Durazzo and the mainland, but though Heuzey describes the Norman as 'maître de la mer', he could not patrol the
whole of the open roadstead which is Durazzo's only harbour.[6]
So by sea Palaeologus reaches Alexius and a council of war is
held. The older men advise trusting to famine to overcome the
enemy; 'and by shooting at a distance to hem in' (στενοχωρῆσαι)
Robert; the younger men clamour for battle, and Rehoboam-
like Alexius yields to them. But he endeavours to secure success
by dividing his attacking forces into two (ἐξ ἑκατέρου μέρους
ἐπεισπεσεῖν) and sending some through the lagoon (τῶν ἁλυκῶν)

---

[1] IV. 5, p. 114.
[2] Gul. Apul. *Rer. Norman.* IV. 460 sqq.
[3] XIII. 5, p. 391.
[4] Caes. *de Bello Civ.* III. 42.
[5] Heuzey, *op. cit.* p. 368. He truly comments on Anna's 'exagération à en faire
une presqu'île ou un promontoire'. It makes us feel that her topographical knowledge in this campaign is disappointingly hazy, when we consider that Durazzo
was the scene of her hero-uncle's finest exploits and that these must certainly have
been among the 'narratives' which she got from his own lips (XIV. 7, p. 447).
[6] Gul. Apul., *op. cit.* V. 305, says, 'Castrorum dederat tutum vicinia portum',
but unless we apply 'portus' to the almost landlocked lagoon (see again below)
this may be taken as mere exaggeration on the part of Robert's admiring chronicler.
Both Anna and William would seem to have drawn on the Bishop of Bari's envoy
to Robert (III. 12, p. 99).

to take the Normans in the rear. These land on the West side of the lagoon and attack Robert's camp on the East of the town, where the suburb of Exo-Bazari now stands. Simultaneously a sortie is made by the garrison. On the mainland East of the bridge matters at first go well for the Greeks. The right wing of the Normans is repulsed and driven into the sea by the Varangian Guard, and is with difficulty rallied by Robert's warlike wife Gaita. But this is the last success Alexius was destined to win that day. The Varangian Guard, marching on foot in his van, advance 'through inexperience and hotheadedness' too far from the main body: they are suddenly attacked by Robert's horsemen, and those that are not killed in the charge are burnt in the church of St. Michael, which Heuzey locates in the village of Shimmihl, the Albanian form of the saint's name. From this moment all goes ill for the Greeks. Many fall in fight, the Turkish mercenaries fly, and the Dalmatian allies march off. Finally, Alexius with the remnants of his defeated army gets back to the river Charzanes[1] and thence across the mountains to Achrida. 'Such', says Oman,[2] 'was the fate of the last important attempt made by infantry to face the feudal array of the eleventh century. . . . The supremacy of the feudal horseman was finally established.'

The next move in the game is that 'those inside Durazzo, because most of them were settlers from Melpha and Venice ',[3] open the gates and let the Normans in. It may have been in punishment for its treachery that Alexius later granted financial privileges in Durazzo to those other Venetians who had helped him so valiantly at sea.[4] At any rate, immediately after Robert's death we find the town brought back to the Empire by Alexius' assiduous diplomacy and held for several years by Irene's brother John Ducas, as commandant.[5] He is followed by

---

[1] The marshes and swamps near this river (XIII. 5, p. 392) may have hindered the Norman pursuit.

[2] Op. cit. I, p. 167.

[3] In VI. 6, p. 163, men from Amalfi are mentioned, but it is probable that Anna means not two towns, but one, and that one Amalfi. Heuzey says of Anna's period 'Nous trouvons la ville de Durazzo . . . servant comme autrefois de point de rencontre entre l'Orient et l'Occident. Sa population, comme celle de l'antique Dyrrhachium, est mêlée d'étrangers et surtout d'Italiens' (op. cit., p. 363). See p. 446, note 2, below.

[4] VI. 5, p. 161.

[5] VI. 6, p. 163; VII. 9, p. 209. Heuzey remarks of these dukes (loc. cit.) that 'leur puissance qui s'étend sur toute l'Illyrie tend à en faire des rebelles et des compétiteurs dangereux', so that we four times find Alexius putting some of his family in this important position. As to John Ducas, we must take Anna's 'eleven years' as a mistake for 'seven', i.e. 1085–92, unless we consider that the word ἐνδιατρίψας in VII. 9, p. 209, partly refers to residence under Norman domination and not solely to his years of command.

Alexius' doubtfully loyal and militarily unsuccessful nephew
John, son of Isaac the Sebastocrator. Finally the 'Dukedom'
passes to this John's younger brother Alexius,[1] who defends the
town against Bohemund,[2] while the Normans ravage the
country round, and the admiral Contostephanus reprehensibly
lets reinforcements for their army slip by him at sea.[3]

It is at this juncture that Anna thinks fit to portray the
situation and strength of Durazzo (περί τε τῆς θέσεως καὶ τῆς
ἀσφαλείας),[4] this 'ancient Hellenic city' with which we have been
familiar since her first Book. Her description of the Adriatic
is accurate (from the point of view of a vessel coming from the
South) in so far as the coast does bend slightly East as well as
North in the immediate neighbourhood of Durazzo. But the
whole trend of the Dalmatian shore is from South-East to North-
West, and this we certainly should not infer from her words.
More accurately she brings in the course of the river Drymon[5]
(now the Black Drin) in a hundred outlets from Lake Lychnitis
or Achrida, through many windings into the Adriatic at Elissus,
which, as a modern map with altitudes clearly shows, 'looks
down as one might say across the plains to Durazzo', the coast-
lands between the two being flat and full of streams. It stood
on a ridge, as a μετέωρον πολίχνιον καὶ πάντη δυσάλωτον, and was
therefore at first able to 'give great assistance to Durazzo by
land and sea'.[6] Durazzo indeed needed assistance, for Bohemund 'with skill exceeding that of Demetrius Poliorcetes
brought all mechanical devices' (literally 'travail-pains', ὠδῖνες)
'to bear on this town'. Like his father Robert, he destroys his
ships to show there is to be no thought of return.[7] His camp
is pitched 'opposite the gate opening towards the East, above
which there is a bronze horseman'[8] (very much on the same

---

[1] XII. 4, p. 356.   [2] XII. 9; XIII. 2-11.
[3] XII. 8, p. 366: 9, p. 370; XIII. 2, p. 381.   [4] XII. 9.
[5] XII. 9, p. 371. As is the case with many near-Eastern rivers (e.g. the Hermus
and Maeander in Anatolia) the river Drin has apparently been known to change
its course. The map of Turkey in the 11th edition of the *Encycl. Brit.* makes
it flow out considerably to the North of Alessio (Elissus); in the *Times Atlas* published after the war it passes right by it. The statement that Lake Achrida (ancient
Lychnitis) had been drained by the Bulgarian King Samuel into 'a hundred
ditches, which we call bridges (γεφύρας)', has caused Du Cange to emend the text
to στρουγάς (cf. V. 4, p. 135), a local word for 'ponds', from which the modern
town of Struga, at the place where the Drin leaves the lake, gets its name. But
surely if Liddell and Scott admit that γέφυρα in Homer may mean not only
'bridge' but 'dam', and after Homer 'tunnel', it is not much stretch to make it
mean 'ditch' or 'canal', just as the word 'dyke' may be used either for an embank-
ment or for the water kept in thereby. See Murray's Dictionary.
[6] As it is not mentioned after this passage we may fairly assume that Bohemund
was not long in either capturing it or blocking its activities.
[7] XIII. 2, p. 380; cf. IV. 5, p. 114.   [8] XIII. 2, p. 380.

ground that his father had occupied sixteen years before), and
he gradually draws closer his cordon round the town. The little
careful touches which Anna here bestows on her picture of the
campaign, giving gates and statues and public buildings[1] in
the city, remind us that it had once been the sphere of influence
of her uncle and informant George Palaeologus.[2] But even apart
from personal reasons for interest, Anna must have felt as we
do that it was a notable siege.

For a whole winter and summer Bohemund, after making a
careful study of the ground, 'was constructing military engines,
preparing penthouses' (literally 'tortoises') 'to bear towers and
battering-rams, and some for digging and others for filling up'
(sc. trenches).[3] Then with famine and disease oppressing him
he put them into use, and Anna gives a vivid account of three
separate operations, though in one place she finds his contrivance 'hard to explain'. First, on the Eastern side of the town
by a device 'indescribably wonderful' he applies battering-rams
swung from a leather-covered penthouse that had been rolled
close up under the walls and fixed in the ground. But the
garrison throw open their gates in scorn at 'this theatrical siege-
making' and burn the penthouse by fire which they hurl from
above (Anna, we may remark, cannot resist so good an occasion
for a Homeric quotation and a piece of archaeological information).[4] Next Bohemund makes a mine, carefully secured from
attack or collapse by a penthouse above and props below. Once
more the historian feels bound to describe τὰ τῆς θέσεως τοῦ
τόπου[5] which made mining possible, how on the North side the
town wall, near the 'ducal seat' or Praetorium, 'was on a
mound, I mean not a rocky mound but an earthy'. But Duke
Alexius countermines and drives back the besiegers, on their
final breaking through, by fire blown in their faces as though
against 'a swarm of bees'. Thirdly Anna tells of Bohemund's
great and wonderful wooden turret[6] that had taken a year to
build, prefacing the story with two interesting facts as to the

---

[1] e.g. 'The ducal seat which is called Praetorium' (XIII. 3, p. 382). This knowledge of the internal topography of the town makes all the more strange her
ignorance as to that of the neighbourhood outside. See p. 401, note 5, above.
  [2] XIV. 7, p. 447.   [3] XIII. 2, p. 380.
  [4] XIII. 3. The covering of the penthouse is 'ἐπταβόειον as is said in Homer',
and the battering-ram was invented at Gades.
  [5] XIII. 3, p. 382. Heuzey (op. cit. p. 365) says that the Romans 'dans leurs
camps retranchés, qui sont devenus souvent le modèle de leurs places fortes,
plaçaient ordinairement le praetorium et la porte prétorienne sur le front même
du camp, sur la face la plus accessible'. It is interesting that the Roman name
Praetorium should have survived to Anna's days.
  [6] XIII. 3, pp. 383 sqq.

construction (σχῆμα) of the Durazzo fortifications. In the first place 'its wall is not so high as the towers' (literally 'yields a little to the towers', ὑποχαλᾶται τοῖς πύργοις), 'but the towers rise in a circle on the outside of it to a height of over eleven feet, having an ascent by a spiral stair and strengthened with battlements'; secondly the wall is so broad that 'horsemen even more than four in number could ride along it safely shoulder to shoulder'. As to Bohemund's turret, it seems to have been an elaborate structure in several stories, intended 'to overtop the height of the city's towers by five or six cubits', and Anna is amazed at the 'optical' (we should be inclined to say 'trigono-metrical') skill displayed by 'these barbarians' in their calcula-tions. It is rolled up on wheels which are afterwards removed, and is full of men who in addition to shooting 'constant arrows' are to lower gangways on to the walls. But Duke Alexius' men make a scaffolding over against it, even taller than itself, inside the wall and discharge liquid fire therefrom. Not content with this they heap up in the space between the town and the besiegers' erection 'all sorts of inflammable stuff', saturated with oil, and to this they set fire, so that far from being able to bridge the chasm with gangways, the Normans are mostly burnt inside their own turret walls. Anna concludes her tale with the words: 'So much then for the gigantic turret and the siege by the barbarians.'[1]

During the rest of Book XIII we realize that the siege of Durazzo goes on, and we are never told in so many words that it is raised, though this follows as a natural consequence from the treaty between Alexius and Bohemund.[2] It cannot how-ever have been a very close beleaguering, for the Emperor gets letters from the commandant Duke Alexius,[3] even before Bohe-mund's overtures for peace are forwarded by nephew to uncle.[4] Finally the Norman allows one of the imperial envoys to enter and see the commandant, who apparently had never wanted for supplies,[5] and with this ends Anna's story of Dyrrhachium.

---

[1] XIII. 4, p. 386.   [2] XIII. 12.

[3] XIII. 7, p. 396. He like Lantulph complains to the Emperor of the admiral Isaac Contostephanus for negligence in allowing soldiers and supplies to reach Bohemund by sea.

[4] XIII. 8, p. 399.

[5] An apparent inaccuracy occurs in XIII. 7, p. 396, where we are told that though the South winds were favourable and the North winds unfavourable to ships coming from Lombardy to Illyria, yet 'the South wind blowing violently did not allow [the ships] to come to shore at Durazzo'. As the roadstead at Durazzo (which has no real harbour) faces South, this seems strange till we remember that, as Heuzey (op. cit., p. 360) says, such a roadstead could only protect from the North and East winds, and that 'dès que le temps menace de tourner au Sud-Ouest ou

It has been minutely dealt with here, as affording an excellent instance of several of her characteristics. Interest in siegecraft, the desire to display historical knowledge, a keen eye for topography, and a certainty that her father's advice was always sound, such are the things we especially notice in the long-drawn-out narrative.

MILITARY AFFAIRS

62. CHRONOLOGY OF THE DURAZZO CAMPAIGN

THE sieges of Durazzo lead us naturally to a question of chronology, for the events of Robert Guiscard's first campaign in Illyria are in many ways hard to arrange in order.

The date of his departure from Italy for Durazzo is not uniformly given. There is no particular difficulty in supposing that he 'planned'[1] to start in winter (deciding to sail from Brindisi to Durazzo, because 'he preferred the quickest journey, . . . for it was the winter season and the sun . . . was drawing near to Capricorn'[2]), but did not as a matter of fact start till later. Now the actual crossing, the news of which had reached Alexius in Constantinople by August 1081,[3] is first placed by Anna 'in the season of summer, when the sun had already passed Cancer and was hastening to Leo when, men say, is the rising of the dog-star'[4] (i.e. about twenty-three days or more after the sum-

au Sud, l'ancrage n'est plus tenable dans cette baie ouverte'. Ships that cannot be hauled on shore must get away. It is in connexion with the grave question of winds that Alexius makes a map of the Adriatic for his admiral, Isaac Contostephanus. A strong South wind was dreaded in one's teeth at sea, or as driving one too vehemently on shore. To this day the roadstead of Durazzo has no moles or breakwaters, and Heuzey tells us that soundings reveal no traces of any ancient construction of that sort. Ships going South from Durazzo to Avlona would probably row close to the shore.

    [1] ἔμελλε, ἐβουλεύσατο (I. 16, p. 37).
    [2] i.e. to the winter solstice of December 21.
    [3] In II. 10, p. 64, we hear that Alexius took Constantinople 'in the month of April 6589 of the 4th indiction', i.e. 1081, and in III. 6, p. 83, 'in August of the same indiction' he got the news both of the crossing and of Robert's 'defeat' by the Venetians (IV. 2, p. 105 ; 4, p. 108), news which caused him to 'leave Constantinople at once in the month of August of the 4th indiction'.
    [4] III. 12, p. 98. See p. 212, note 5, above. Murray's Dictionary, s.v. Dog-days, says that in the latitude of Greenwich the cosmical rising of Procyon ('the Fore-runner Dog') in Canis Minor takes place about July 27, and in the latitude of the Mediterranean countries somewhat later; while that of Sirius ('the Dog' itself) in Canis Major occurs (in the two latitudes respectively) about August 11 and somewhat earlier, the heliacal risings being in both instances a few days after the cosmical. The Encycl. Brit., s.v. Canis Major, quotes a writer of 1675 as saying that 'the greater

mer solstice of June 21, which would make it July 14 at the earliest), so that his shipwrecked forces were saved from starvation by the fact that 'the corn-meadows and fields and orchards were laden with produce';[1] but it is also said by her to have been so much earlier that his forces were already encamped outside Durazzo 'on June 17 of the 4th indiction',[2] after he had had a seven-days' rest from the effects of the shipwreck.[3] We can only reconcile the two statements by believing that Anna used 'the rising of the dog-star' vaguely for 'the height of summer', and applied it to the second week in June.

This point is however a small one compared to the next discrepancy. As soon as Alexius hears of Robert's invasion he summons Turkish and Venetian allies,[4] orders the Grand Domestic Pacurianus to follow him, and starts from Constantinople 'in the month of August of the 4th indiction'.[5] He then marshals his heterogeneous army (palace-guards, Macedonians, Thessalonians, Turks from Achrida, Manichaeans, Vestiaries, Franks and Varangians), chooses his officers, goes to Thessalonica, parleys with Robert, summons Palaeologus from the besieged city, and fights a disastrous battle on a certain October 18. Now Anna tells us it was 'the 18th of October of the 5th indiction', which, as the indiction began with the Byzantine year on September 1, would be our October 18, 1081. But to this date there are several objections. In the first place, could a new Emperor, who had mounted a not very stable throne in April, not only establish his position at home but

---

part of the Antients' assigned the heliacal rising of the dog-star to 'the time of the sun's first entering into Leo', which Pliny, Varro and Columella variously put at twenty-three, twenty-nine, and thirty days after the summer solstice of June 21, i.e. July 14, 20, and 21. (Murray's Dictionary, s.v. *Cancer* and *Leo*, says the sun enters Cancer on June 21, and Leo about July 21.) This would seem to fit Procyon better than Sirius, but we must remember that owing to the precession of the equinoxes 'all the phenomena now take place later in the year than in ancient times' (*op. cit.* s.v. *Dog-days*). Furthermore, Anna is far more likely to have used 'the dog-star' to mean Sirius than Procyon, as the classical writers ascribed to the former potent and even baleful properties, connected with the 'dry, hot, and dusty season' of the (very variously calculated) Dog-days (*Encycl. Brit.*, *loc. cit.*), and cf. Callicles' poem XXXIII, possibly spurious, where the 'Dog-Star which burns the whole earth up', is said to 'run alongside of the sun' in August). In any case she can hardly be referring to any date earlier than July, in which month Lup. Protosp. (Muratori, *SS. Rer. Ital.* V, p. 451) also says Robert landed. The *Anon. Bar. Chron.*, however (Muratori, *op. cit.* V. p. 153), says he left Corfu ten days before the end of May, and Malaterra (*Hist. Sic.* III, ch. 24) gives May as the date of his arrival at Otranto, but does not specify when he left it.

[1] III. 12, p. 99.   [2] IV. 1, p. 102: 2, p. 105.
[3] III. 12, p. 99.
[4] IV. 2, p. 105. Chalandon (*op. cit.* p. 71, note 3) thinks the negotiations with Venice must have taken place earlier. See p. 386, note 7, above.
[5] IV. 4, p. 108. This is, as we said above, August 1081.

collect a considerable army and march it across the Balkan peninsula before October 18 of the same year? In the second place (unless we believe with Chalandon that Anna got her dates at this point entirely mixed), we can hardly put aside the passage where, after describing Robert's first naval defeat by the Venetians (of which Alexius had heard before leaving Constantinople),[1] she tells us that Robert, prevented 'during the winter' from launching his ships, and cut off by the combined Greek and Venetian fleets from receiving reinforcements or supplies from Lombardy, was attacked at sea, 'when spring was already at hand[2] and the raging of the sea had ceased', by the imperial navies and again defeated. 'Then Robert realized that he must draw up his whole fleet on dry land', an operation which is later described as having them 'anchored in the River Glykys'; this was undoubtedly the exit for the lagoon waters—referred to above—into the Durazzo bay, near the flat land where his troops were encamped East of the town.[3] Two months of naval preparations at Hiericho (the ancient Oricum some seventy miles farther South) are rather vaguely mentioned, and the Normans are said to have lost 10,000 men from famine and disease in the course of three months. At any rate, Anna must be writing about the summer, as she says that the 'Freshwater River' dried up so much that Robert had great trouble in refloating his ships and getting them down to the Bay.[4] Thus if we accept the facts of this chapter at all, we are

---

[1] IV. 2, p. 105, and IV. 4, p. 108. Chalandon gives July 1081 for the date of this battle (op. cit. p. 74, note 5).

[2] Du Cange's note on these words in IV. 3, p. 107 B is 'Anno Scilicet MCLXXXII', obviously a misprint for MLXXXII. This second naval battle between the Venetians and the Normans at Durazzo is said by Chalandon (p. 91, note 3) to be mentioned by no other historian, and he therefore assumes that Anna not only confused the dates but exaggerated a skirmish between a few boats into a real battle. This seems to depend on the assumption that the Venetian fleet returned to Venice directly after the battle of July 1081. This is not stated by Anna, who merely says that they repaired to their own vessels, and after resting several days sent envoys to Alexius with news of their victory. The ships are first described as ὑποκεχωρηκότες just before the fall of Durazzo (V. 1, p. 125). The envoys were sent back to Venice with money for the doge and 'those ruling under him', but there seems no reason to suppose that the whole fleet returned home too. In the absence of positive evidence to the contrary, we may take as true Anna's narrative in IV. 3, p. 107, namely that throughout the winter of 1081–2 the Venetian fleet aided by a Greek fleet, now first mentioned, with its commander Maurice, blockaded Robert's army in Durazzo, and in the spring of 1082 seriously defeated his forces at sea.   [3] IV. 3, pp. 107, 108; p. 399, note 4, above.

[4] IV. 3. The country between Durazzo and Hiericho was probably all in Robert's power, thanks to Bohemund's successes (I. 14, p. 35) so that intercourse between the two towns was possible both by sea and land. Anna evidently admires Robert's ingenuity in making a channel; Heuzey however (op. cit. p. 366) says 'ce travail ne dut être qu'un jeu pour les Normands habitués aux estuaires de l'Océan'.

bound to believe that over a year, from the summer of 1081 to the October of 1082, elapsed between Robert's arrival at Durazzo and his activities on land, and that the Emperor's defeat and the fall of the town as narrated in the subsequent chapters both occurred in the autumn of the second year. If so, we shall have to emend Anna's date for the battle[1] from '5th indiction' (1081) to '6th indiction' (1082). The chief Western authority for the date of the battle is the *Anonymi Barensis Chronicon*, where we read in truly remarkable Latin as follows :[2]

Mill. LXXXII. Ind. V. Venit Alexius Imp. et commisit bellum cum Robb. Dux fer. III. in die S. Luce Apostoli et Evangeliste; et terga vertit ipse Imp. vicitque ipse Dux.

As the chronicler begins his year on September 1, he gives to the last four months of every year a date greater by one than in our reckoning, e. g. his October 1082 would be our October 1081,[3] and his year 1082 would end on our August 31, 1082. This would seem to show that Anna and he both agree in placing the battle on October 18, 1081. But he distinctly says that it was fought 'feria III', which means 'Tuesday', whereas

---

[1] IV. 6, p. 114. Curiously enough Du Cange in his note on IV. 6, p. 116 B, says of the Durazzo battle 'Errat Anna, cum ait initum Indict. 4, nam hoc anno mense Octobri currebat Indictio 5'. In the editio princeps of 1651 from which Du Cange got his text, Anna says Ind. 5 in this passage, so Du Cange must have made a confusion between this sentence and the one in IV. 4, p. 108, where Alexius starts from Constantinople in the August of Ind. 4.

[2] Muratori, *op. cit.* Vol. V, p. 154; and cf. Lup. Protosp. (*ibid.* p. 45). Malaterra, in his *Hist. Sic.* (*ibid.* pp. 582–5), gives May 1081 for Robert's arrival at Otranto (III. 24), mentions the battle of Durazzo as occurring in October without any year (III. 27), and tells of the surrender of the town to Robert without month or year (III. 28). Wm. of Apulia, in his *Hist. Normann.*, mentions the Durazzo battle without month or year. Petrus Diaconus (*Chronicon Casinense*, Bk. III, ch. 49, Muratori, *op. cit.* Vol. IV, p. 465) says that 'in this year' (1081) Robert crossed from Italy. Then follows the statement that Alexius with 170,000 men was defeated by him. No year is given, and the numbers of the army are so fantastic as to vitiate the authority of the passage. Ordericus Vitalis (Pt. III, lib. 7, ch. 4, *P.L.* 188, col. 520) says of Robert and Durazzo that 'in fine mensis Junii urbem obsedit', without giving the year. After collecting a large army and sending messengers everywhere to get more men 'Mense Octobri Alexius Dyracio appropiavit' and his defeat follows, but here again no year is specified. In any case so much of Ordericus' information about the Emperor is incorrect (e.g. that he reigned thirty years instead of thirty-seven) or doubtful (e.g. that it was Raimundus Flandrensis who opened the gates of Constantinople to the Comneni when Anna says Gilpractus a German, II. 10; and that Alexius for twenty years was as kind to the daughters [plural] of Robert 'ac si ipse genuisset eas') that it would be unwise to pin our faith to any chronology of his, but in this instance he gives none. Zonaras, XVIII. 22, implies that the Durazzo battle was fought soon after Alexius' accession, but he is so hazy about Robert's movements that our confidence is shaken as to his whole story of the campaign.

[3] The note in Muratori, *loc. cit.*, speaks of 'haec consueta nostro auctori annorum anticipatio, qui . . . exorditur ab septembre'.

in 1081 October 18 fell on a Monday, and not on a Tuesday
till 1082.[1] His two indications of time are therefore incom-
patible; either he meant 'feria II', or the whole incident should
be transferred to his next year, Mill. LXXXIII, Ind. VI, and
belong in our reckoning to October 1082. Since this latter supposition fits in with what we have said above, first as to the
inadequate time allowed for Alexius' military preparations between August and October of the same year, secondly as to the
difficulty of explaining away Anna's circumstantial account of
Robert's activities (or rather afflictions) in the winter and
summer after the first naval battle,[2] we shall adopt it, with the
necessary correction of Anna's ἐπινεμήσεως πέμπτης into ἕκτης
in IV. 6, p. 114 D.

After this it is easy to assume that Anna, having brought
Robert's adventures down to the summer of 1082 in the third
chapter of Book IV, turns back in the fourth chapter without
warning to her father's doings from the summer of 1081, when
he had just heard of the first naval battle.[3] If we accept August
1081 as the date for his leaving Constantinople, we must according to our recently explained theory give him a year for con-
solidating his army, probably at Thessalonica.[4] In any case
the battle was fought in the autumn (of whatever year), and
Anna represents Robert as meaning to put off the resumption
of the Durazzo siege 'till the following spring', when traitors
within, hearing of his intentions as well as of his victory followed by the withdrawal of the Greek and Venetian fleets,
saved him the trouble by surrendering the town. Robert enters,
cares for his wounded, and 'because winter was already present
at that juncture' resolves to spend it in collecting troops, and
then 'when spring should appear' to attack the Emperor with
vigour.[5] Surely this points to the surrender of the town in

---

[1] See calendar in *L'Art de vérifier les dates*, Vol. I.

[2] By the autumn of 1082 Robert would have had time to recover from the naval
disaster of July 1081 with its serious 'effet moral' on his tribute-paying Illyrian
neighbours (even Chalandon, *op. cit.* p. 91, note 3, refers this first sea-fight to 1081,
however mythical he may consider the second one), and to be in the formidable
state of vigour described in IV. 4, p. 110, when 'putting in motion all his engines
suitable to siege warfare Robert approached the walls' of Durazzo with 'noble
soldiers' and was able to inflict a crushing defeat on the Greek army (IV. 6–8).

[3] Like many writers she often finishes off a subject, and then turns back to
another which is anterior in time. So in Book V about Bohemund's campaign,
in Book VI about Turkish affairs, and in Book XI, chs. 9 and 10 about events in
the first Crusade. See Chalandon, *op. cit.*, p. xvi.   [4] IV. 4, p. 110.

[5] V. 1, p. 125. The phrases are: (1) εἰς τὸ ἐπιὸν ἔαρ τὴν πολιορκίαν ταμιεύεται,
(2) ἐπεὶ χειμὼν ἤδη παρῆν, (3) ἦρος ἐπιφανέντος, in a future sense. Similarly Alexius
makes preparations to redeem his failure ἦρος φανέντος, also in a future sense (V. 1,
p. 126). We find him at Achrida and Diabolis, probably at Thessalonica, and
finally in Constantinople (V. 1, p. 126; 3, p. 131).

the autumn, and by our supposition it should be assigned to our October or November 1082. Chalandon[1] prefers to trust *Anon. Bar. Chron.* which gives the capture as occurring 'octabo die stante Feb.' of his year Mill. LXXXII.[2] As we have already detected one inaccuracy in this chronicler, and as another Latin authority[3] gives the date as January 1082, we will venture to disbelieve both, and put the event in the autumn of that same year.

The difficulties of chronology are however not over. While preparations on both sides were proceeding, the king of Germany, instigated by Alexius, threatened Lombardy, to which Robert returned in haste[4] leaving Bohemund to carry on the war. Robert's actions in Italy are recounted till he is joined at Salerno by Bohemund, who describes the events of the Illyrian campaign after his departure. This means that the story goes back to the immediate consequences of the fall of Durazzo. The sequence of events is not very clear, but the following suggestions may be made:

(1) That ch. 4 of Book V, which begins with Bohemund's arrival in Italy, carries us back (in consequence of what he told his father) to the events of April to June 1083, during the first three months of the Norman siege of Larissa. These events included Alexius' departure from Constantinople in May,[5] and his two defeats by Bohemund.

(2) That ch. 5 returns from the Emperor, ingloriously sheltering in Constantinople, to Bohemund and his deeds of the preceding winter between November 1082 and April 1083, while Alexius was still collecting troops.[6] The various towns which Bohemund took are enumerated. We hear of three months spent on the river Vardar, and then 'he goes to Larissa

---

[1] *Op. cit.* p. 83, note 4.   Muratori, *loc. cit.*

[3] Lup. Protosp. (Muratori, *op. cit.* V. p. 45).

[4] V. 3. Wm. of Apulia says Robert returned to Italy a year after he left it, and Lup. Protosp. under the year 1082 places his departure soon after the capture of Durazzo (Chalandon, *op. cit.* p. 84, note 7). Why should not the date be the late autumn of 1082, instead of April or May as Chalandon supposes? We may note that modern critics differ greatly on the subject. Chalandon says the spring of 1082; the *Encycl. Brit.*, s.v. *Robert Guiscard*, says Robert was recalled from Illyria 'to the aid of Gregory VII, besieged in St. Angelo by Henry IV (June 1083)'; Tout (*Empire and Papacy*, p. 135) gives May 1084 as the date when Robert 'advanced to the walls of Rome' to help Gregory VII in consequence of 'Henry's invasion of Apulia'.

[5] Chalandon (*op. cit.* p. 86, especially note 1) says May 1082; Du Cange, in his note on V. 4, p. 133 D, says May 1083, which we accept.

[6] The way the story is told makes this break in the chronology natural. In V. 4, p. 133, the chief object is to confront Bohemund with Alexius; after the latter has returned to his capital, his daughter, in V. 5, p. 136, has leisure to go back to the Norman's achievements from the beginning of his sole authority.

intending to winter there'.[1] This may be explained as meaning
that he hoped to capture it and make it his winter quarters
for the next winter, 1083–4, but found it obstinately defended
by the Greek commandant Leo Cephalas. At any rate he
seems to have arrived there on April 23, 'on the very feast
day of the great martyr George', and left troops there which
carried on a six months' siege, while he himself went North-
West again, to encounter Alexius in the two battles described
in the previous chapter. After these defeats, Alexius acted
as he had done before meeting Bohemund at all, and stayed
to collect a large army at Constantinople.[2] Finally he succeeded in raising the siege of Larissa,[3] in October 1083 if we
accept Anna's statement of a six months' siege which began
in April, and this date agrees with her incidental remark
that Bohemund was eating grapes when the fortunes of war
finally turned against him.[4] This leaves two months (October–
December 1083) for Alexius first to go to Thessalonica and stir
up mutiny among the troops of Bohemund (who is therefore
obliged to return to Italy for money),[5] next to retake Castoria
from the Norman Count Bryennius,[6] and finally to reach Constantinople just in time for the birth of his daughter Anna on
December 1 'of the 7th indiction', that is to say, December 1,
1083.[7] We may note that this supremely important event is
narrated by Anna in ch. 8 of Book VI, after one of her curious
parentheses in which from VI. 5, p. 159, to VI. 7, p. 166, she
gives the story of Robert Guiscard's second Illyrian campaign
and death, from the autumn of 1084 to July 1085.

The whole question is a difficult one, which Riant[8] hardly
solves by contemptuously denouncing the 'cent preuves du sans-
gêne d'Anne Comnène à l'endroit de la chronologie'. If she is
not impeccable, neither are the other chroniclers of her day,
and we claim that it is possible, with the above emendation of
one word in her text, to make out a consistent narrative. A

---

[1] V. 5, p. 137.
[2] V. 5, p. 137. πλεῖον μισθοφορικόν, including 5,000 picked Turks 'with highly experienced leaders'.
[3] V. 6 and 7.   [4] V. 6, p. 141.   [5] V. 7, p. 143.   [6] VI. 1.
[7] VI. 8, p. 166. As we have said above (ch. 49) the trial of Italus in Indiction 5, of which we have the full report, is probably anterior to that described by Anna in V. 9. This second trial took place apparently during Alexius' stay in Constantinople in the summer of 1083, when he was collecting troops. Anna says he 'was planning against Bryennius', who was holding Castoria (V. 8, p. 143), and though we are only told of this general's command there after his valour at Larissa in October 1083 (V. 6, and 7, p. 143) it is quite conceivable that he was the commandant in the preceding spring after its capture, which occurred before Bohemund reached Larissa on 23 April 1083.
[8] *Inventaire des lettres historiques des croisades*, Arch. de l'Or. lat. I, p. 88, note 40.

chronological table is appended below,[1] and the subject need not detain us further. It only remains to say that by a strange coincidence the chronology of Alexius' second campaign against Bohemund also presents a difficulty. Anna tells us that her father went to collect troops at Thessalonica to fight against Bohemund, 'in the month of September of the 14th indiction, being the twentieth year since he girded round him the reins of Empire'.[2] The indiction points correctly to the period between

---

[1] The suggested order of events is this:

I. 16. Dec. 1080.	Robert *plans* to cross.
II. 10. Apr. 1081.	Alexius takes Constantinople.
IV. 1 and 2. June, 1081.	Crossing of Robert.
IV. 2. July, 1081.	Venetian naval victory.
III. 6, and IV. 4. Aug. 1081.	Alexius leaves Constantinople to collect army at Thessalonica.
IV. 3. { Spring, 1082.	Second Venetian naval victory.
{ Summer, 1082.	Robert loses 10,000 men from disease.
IV. 6. Oct. 18, 1082.	Battle of Durazzo.
V. 1. Oct.–Nov. 1082.	Durazzo betrayed to Robert.
V. 5. Nov. 1082–Apr. 1083.	{ Bohemund at Achrida, three months on Vardar, Castoria, Tricala, Larissa. Alexius preparing army at Constantinople.
V. 5. Apr. 23, 1083.	Bohemund leaves army to blockade Larissa.
V. 4. { Apr.–May, 1083.	Bohemund besieges Joannina.
{ May, 1083.	Alexius leaves Constantinople.
{ Summer, 1083.	Alexius is twice defeated near Joannina, goes to Constantinople.
V. 5. { Summer, 1083.	Hears of siege of Larissa (six months).
{ Summer, 1083.	Bohemund goes back to Larissa.
V. 5–7 { Oct. 1083.	Alexius raises siege of Larissa.
{ Oct.–Dec. 1083.	Returns to Thessalonica. Tampers with troops of Bohemund.
VI. 2. Oct.–Dec. 1083.	Takes Castoria.
V. 4, and VI. 5. Oct.–Dec. 1083.	Bohemund goes to Italy.
VI. 8. Dec. 1, 1083.	Alexius returns to Constantinople.

In VI. 5, p. 159—VI. 7, p. 166, Anna gives the story of Robert's second Illyrian campaign, 1084–5, and death. From this parenthesis she goes back nearly two years—from July 1085 to December 1083. V. 5 is specially difficult in chronology.

(1) p. 136 C—p. 137 B. *Events of November*, 1082—*April 23*, 1083. (ἐπεὶ δὲ τοῦ 'Ρομπ.—παραχειμάσαι βουλόμενος.)

(2) p. 137 C–D. *Ditto*, involving a repetition as to Larissa. (καταλαβὼν δὲ τὴν μεγαλόπ.—ἐπολιόρκει αὐτήν.)

The mention in p. 137 C of Castoria, as if between Tricala and Larissa, is strange, for Castoria was really the head-quarters from which Bohemund started for Pelagonia, Tricala, and Larissa (p. 137 B). We probably ought in p. 137 C to read (instead of 'Castoria') 'Phaloria', a town West of Tricala or Tricca.

The first time Bohemund's arrival at Larissa is mentioned, it is said he 'wished to winter there', the second time the date, April 23, is given.

(3) p. 137 D. *Siege of Larissa: April–October*, 1083. (ὁ δὲ ταυτηνὶ—μηοὶν ἕξ.)

(4) p. 137 A—end, p. 140. *Events of June–October*, 1083. (δηλοῖ δὲ—τῆς νυκτὸς ἐκεῖτο.)

The siege of Joannina by Bohemund, Alexius' hasty exit from Constantinople, May, 1083, two defeats near Joannina, and return to Constantinople are presupposed. The news of the siege of Larissa reaches him in Constantinople (June, 1083?), but he cannot start at once. After he does, the story goes straight on.

[2] XII. 3, p. 351.

September 1, 1105 and August 31, 1106, but the calculation from Alexius' accession would lead us to 1101. If 'and fourth' has not dropped out of the text after 'twentieth', we must conclude either that Anna made a slip of the pen, or that in characteristic fashion she used 'twentieth' loosely as a good round number.

MILITARY AFFAIRS

63. SIEGES AND FORTRESSES

BEFORE we entirely leave the subject of sieges, we may observe that the walls of medieval strongholds were clearly able to offer prolonged resistance to all the implements and engines known to contemporary siegecraft.[1] Famine was usually a more powerful foe than any ἐλέπολις, and many sieges of long duration figure in Anna's pages in addition to the two of Durazzo. That of Nicaea, a strongly fortified town with thick walls, undertaken by the Crusaders and the Greek troops jointly,[2] gives Alexius an opportunity for two characteristic acts. First he invents new siege-engines, 'most of them not according to the laws of mechanics, but according to other principles that seemed to him good, which indeed caused wonder to all the counts'.[3] Next he holds secret negotiations with the Turks behind the backs of his allies, and by stealth introduces men into the city from boats.[4] Once in, these men under Butumites win the inhabitants by promises from the Emperor and hold the town. A little later the siege of Antioch, fortified by towers and 'battlements and parapets', is a sort of turning-point in the

---

[1] Thus Larissa held out six months (V. 5, p. 137) and Acrunus three (XIV. 3, p. 431), Mitylene three (IX. 1, p. 246), and Adrianople forty-eight days (X. 3, p. 276; here, however, the besiegers probably had no engines).

[2] X. 11, p. 306; XI. 1. St. Gilles makes a brave but futile attempt against the Kneeling Tower with a two-storeyed turret (μόσυν) constructed with skins and withes, the kind 'which those who have more experience in mechanics call a Tortoise'. Logs are thrust into holes made in the walls and set on fire, and the tower kneels even more but does not collapse. Other attacks with arms and penthouses, and the levelling of the ditch outside the walls, are equally without result.

[3] XI. 2, p. 312. To these μηχανημάτων ἐπίνοιαι, not inferior to those of Archimedes and Palamedes, the Emperor's faithful servant Euthymius Zigabenus alludes in the preface to his Panoplia (P. G. 130, col. 20).

[4] XI. 2, p. 313. Riant (Expéditions, etc. p. 144) considers the way these boats were carried on wagons to be launched on the lake was such an essentially Viking idea as almost to prove that there were Scandinavians among the imperial troops. The scheme was originally due to Alexius' observation that 'the Sultan was bringing in sufficient forces and all his necessaries with ease over the adjoining lake'. This is a neat piece of reconnoitring.

story, because from the thick of it Taticius went home, affording the Crusaders a permanent grudge against Alexius, and depriving Anna of a source of reliable information.[1] Here intrigue and famine and superstition all play their part,[2] and this is also interesting as one of the instances where a citadel holds out after the rest of the town is captured.[3] Other sieges, of Tyre,[4] Laodicea,[5] Chios and Smyrna,[6] Mopsuestia and Tarsus,[7] and Otranto,[8] present points of interest upon which we cannot enter now. Suffice it to say that Tancred like his uncle Bohemund is great at siegecraft,[9] but that the most ingenious deed in this whole field is characteristically that of the besieged Alexius, who at Chorlu drops cartwheels from the battlements to roll with deadly effectiveness against the horses of the Patzinak besiegers.[10]

This brings us in conclusion to what we may call the reverse side of the subject, the strongholds fortified and held against besiegers. Generals, admirals, and governors of districts may be called on at any moment to help in building or rebuilding or strengthening some fortress,[11] and as much 'valour and boldness', not to say ingenuity, is shown in defence as in attack.[12] Any one who neglects to establish himself in a stronghold if possible is a fool, and the man who fails to defend it is 'ignoble'.[13] The

---

[1] XI. 4, p. 319.

[2] We may note that at first the Franks and Greeks seem to rely on starving the town into submission; they dig a trench, set their baggage in it, and besiege the city three months. No engines or assaults are mentioned, only ladders by which they finally enter after the surrender (XI. 4).

[3] Cf. V. 4, p. 133, of Joannina; V. 5, p. 136, of Achrida; VI. 13, p. 180, of Apollonias; VII. 3, p. 194, of Dristra; XI. 11, p. 339, of Laodicea. Cf. Cinnamus, I. 8, p. 10. At Durazzo the two commands are distinct *Al.* IV. 8, p. 122.

[4] XIV. 2.

[5] XI. 7 and 11. This town has its citadel revictualled by Bohemund, while Greek troops are actually in possession of the rest. 'Effective blockade' seems in Anna's day to have been rarely achieved.

[6] VII. 8; XI. 5, p. 322.   [7] XII. 2.   [8] XII. 8.

[9] XII. 2, p. 349; 9, p. 370.   [10] VII. 11.

[11] So Bohemund in V. 4, p. 133; 5, p. 137, and the Duke of Cyprus in XI. 7, p. 330; 10, p. 338. On the second occasion he digs trenches all round Seleucia and leaves not only a garrison, but a fleet on guard in the harbour. In the gorges bordering on Dalmatia Alexius erects on foundations of tree-trunks πολίχνια of bricks or stones wherever the ground permits, and measures the distances himself (IX. 1, p. 245). Eumathius Philocales rebuilds and repopulates Adramyttium destroyed by Tzachas (XIV. 1, p. 420). Alexius after his parley with Bolcanus leaves men 'to rebuild the torn-down cities' (IX. 4, p. 252), and intends to carry on the work himself (IX. 5, p. 253). In the height of summer he superintends the building of the 'Iron Fort' to protect a newly dug trench near Lake Baane in Asia Minor (X. 5). He applies himself to ἀσφαλίσασθαι some fortresses against Bohemund and κατοχυρῶσαι others, but the difference is purely rhetorical (XII. 3, p. 354).

[12] So of Duke Alexius at Durazzo in XIII. 3.

[13] XIV. 5, pp. 439, 440.

words used are πολίχνιον,[1] φρούριον,[2] ὀχύρωμα[3] κάστρον, καστέλλιον, and πολισμάτιον,[4] and we find the fortresses which they denote scattered all over the Empire,[5] some no doubt of the 600 which Justinian is said to have repaired. Cecaumenus has thirteen consecutive chapters about the holding of such posts, as well as scattered allusions,[6] and from the very beginning of the *Alexias* to the end we are never allowed to forget that the Empire had more and more learnt to rely on walls, not men. Alexius wins in his struggle against Urselius not by pitched battles but by capturing fortresses, and Robert Guiscard's campaign opens in the same way.[7] All enemy strongholds must be destroyed.[8] Sometimes fortresses serve as prisons,[9] often as places of refuge for defenceless peasantry or for generals awaiting reinforcements,[10] always as bulwarks against an invading foe.[11] Nature and art, water and walls, serve to protect Anchialus on the Black Sea,[12] Nicomedia in Bithynia,[13] Castoria on its ridge running into a lake,[14] Nicaea by the side of Lake Ascania.[15] Tyre has three concentric outworks as well as 'unshakable walls', and Philippopolis has its three hills 'each girt round with a great and lofty wall' as well as with trenches.[16] Yet to remain in one's fortress without making sorties was a clear confession of weakness, and as such would justify attack.[17]

It is not surprising that places so valuable should demand, as we see on countless occasions, scrupulous care in the choice of commandants, and that the keeping of the keys is a solemn

---

[1] e.g. XIV. 5, p. 440, and *passim*. Elissus is a μετέωρον πολίχνιον καὶ πάντη δυσάλωτον (XII. 9, p. 371).

[2] e.g. I. 2, p. 4.   [3] e.g. XI. 7, p. 329.   [4] XIII. 12.

[5] e.g. V. 5, p. 137. The word κωμόπολις means a 'village' whether fortified or not, and occurs too commonly to need references.

[6] *Strat.* pp. 26–35.   [7] I. 2, p. 4; 16, p. 38: cf. VII. 8, p. 209.

[8] V. 5, p. 137, &c.

[9] So a nameless φρούριον in I. 11, p. 26; Amasea in I. 2, 3; Tebenna in XII. 7, p. 364; Philippopolis in VIII. 9, p. 242.

[10] Coloneia in XII. 7, p. 365, and fortresses in general in the Patzinak invasion VII. 1, p. 188.

[11] e.g. the various places in Asia Minor held by toparchs against the Turks (III. 9, p. 92). Alexius makes desperate efforts to keep the φρούρια south of Adrianople from falling into the hands of the Patzinaks (VII. 6, p. 203).

[12] X. 3, p. 275.   [13] X. 5.   [14] VI. 1, p. 152.

[15] XI. 1 and 2. It has a famous 'kneeling' Tower, and the Fort of St. George is in the immediate neighbourhood (VI. 11, p. 176; XI. 2, pp. 313, 314).

[16] XIV. 2, p. 426; 8, p. 450.

[17] In XI. 7, p. 329; XIV. 1, p. 421, failure by the holder of a fortress to make a sortie is held to prove that he has run away or is a negligible quantity. So Cecaumenus (*Strat.* p. 17). Bryennius allows sorties from Adrianople against the Comans (X. 3, p. 277). Palaeologus (IV. 4, p. 110) makes a sortie and is wounded, Alyates does the same and is killed (XIII. 5). In XIV. 3, p. 431, we find the governor of Philadelphia marching out from his post to active warfare.

responsibility.[1] Antioch was the domain of Alexius' brother
Isaac, and we must remind ourselves that Durazzo had successively four members of the imperial family for Duke.[2] The
toparchs still holding Asiatic towns and provinces against the
Turks in the dark days of 1081 are among the first to be summoned by the new Emperor to his support.[3] Everywhere we
perceive the power for good or evil of these commandants, able
as they often were to make themselves independent of the
central authority.[4] It might be for the time an easy way for
an emperor to get rid of a turbulent subject,[5] and the man in
question might regard such a command as exile,[6] or even as
too tame a task,[7] but we are never without the feeling that in
the hands of these commandants and behind their stone walls
the destinies of the Empire were placed. Freeman once pointed
out that the primitive ideal of a suitable residence is a stronghold perched on a high hill, while in more peaceful and commercial times men put their towns by rivers or on the sea. If
this is true, then certainly Anna had not advanced beyond the
primitive stage. A strong tower into which the righteous
runneth and is safe would have been her first requisite.

This ends our survey of Anna as a military historian. Though
her account of foreign affairs is necessarily bound up with her
account of the army, yet it has seemed wiser to separate the
two, and to consider her descriptions of battles and ambuscades and sieges independently of the people against whom the
operations were conducted. And the conclusion of the whole
matter seems to be that these descriptions, though not the finest
specimens of her art, are often lucid, instructive, and even
interesting. Many a modern war correspondent might be glad
indeed to achieve the like.

[1] So of Butumites at Nicaea (XI. 2, p. 314) and Alexius himself at Choerobacchae (VIII. 1, p. 221). We may compare Anna Dalassena and her sons' door-
keys in II. 5, p. 51.

[2] Alexius' brothers-in-law Palaeologus and John Ducas, and his two nephews
John and Alexius Comnenus, sons of his brother Isaac the Sebastocrator. See
Ch. 61, above.

[3] III. 9, p. 92. They are ordered to leave 'sufficient soldiers' behind as garrisons
and to come to Constantinople with every other possible veteran or recruit.
One of them is mentioned later as having owned πολίχνια in the heart of Asia
Minor (XV. 4, p. 471) and another becomes Duke of Trebizond (XII. 7, p. 364).
Governors are described indifferently by various names (III. 9; VII. 8, p. 205;
XI. 5; see p. 360, note 1, above). In the case of one such governor we are
specially told that he was ἀρειμάνιος (XI. 5, p. 323).

[4] VI. 9; VIII. 9; XII. 7; XIV. 3, p. 431; 8, p. 451. See the implication in
X. 2 and 3 about Adrianople and Nicephorus Bryennius.

[5] VIII. 9.   [6] I. 16, p. 38.   [7] XIII. 7, p. 395.

FOREIGN AFFAIRS

64. THE EAST

WHEN we approach the last of Anna's historical interests, foreign affairs, we are once more compelled by lack of space to omit more than we include. Foreigners were to her, broadly speaking, either enemies or mercenaries, and as such they come before her in a purely military or diplomatic light. But they cannot be passed over altogether, and we will try if possible to understand her attitude to each race as men even more than as fighters, with a side-glance on her father's behaviour to each. The foreign nations which Anna once describes as attacking the Emperor from the East, North, and West[1] fall naturally into these three geographical groups.[2] We will begin with the first.

The Eastern foes are called by her Arabs, Turks, Hagarenes, Saracens, Ishmaelites, or Persians, as the fancy of the moment dictates, and once she speaks of 'Turcomans dwelling in Asia',[3] but as a matter of fact the Mohammedans who appear in her pages are probably all Seljuq Turks. This tribe, which first made its appearance in Turkestan at the end of the tenth century, gradually came Westward till 'in 1055 Tughril Beg entered Bagdad and was proclaimed Sultan'.[4] Another element was thereby added to the kaleidoscope of the Eastern world, where the Empire had contended successively first with Persians and Armenians and then with the various Arab or Saracen hosts, Ummayads, Abbasids, and Fatimites. When Tughril Beg died in 1063 'he left to his successor Alp Arslan an empire which eight years later stretched from the Hindu Kush to the shores of the Mediterranean'.[5] Ani, capital of

---

[1] XIV. 7, p. 445.
[2] The South plays very little part in Anna's history. Egypt is mentioned rhetorically in V. 6, p. 141; VI. 11, p. 176; 13, p. 182; geographically in I. 4, p. 10; VII. 5, p. 201; XV. 7, p. 485; and as the home of astrology and such-like arts in VI. 7. Ethiopia figures once in a proverb (IX. 6, p. 257). Cairo, under the usual medieval name of Babylon, is mentioned in XI. 7 and XII. 1. Rhetorical references to the Babylon of antiquity occur in XIII. 8, p. 398; XIV. 2, p. 423; and XV. 10, p. 494.
[3] XIV. 6, p. 442.   [4] Camb. Med. Hist. IV, p. 304.
[5] Ibid. p. 277. In this article H. Loewe ascribes largely to the Seljuqs 'the failure of the Crusaders to make any lasting impression on the East', and on the other hand 'an unconscious influence of East upon West' through intercourse in the Holy Wars (ibid. p. 299). In his opinion their appearance saved Islam from impending destruction (p. 302).

Armenia, which had for centuries been the buffer-state protecting the Empire against Eastern invasions, fell in 1064, during the fatal reign of Constantine X (Ducas). The Seljuqs poured into the Eastern provinces, and the gallant attempt of Romanus IV Diogenes (stepfather of the new Emperor Michael VII Ducas who had succeeded to the crown at fourteen) to stem the tide ended in his defeat and death at Manzikert in 1071. We need not here quote in full Anna's statements about the Turkish encroachments, but we shall do well to remind ourselves that when Alexius ascended the throne in 1081 the Turks had advanced up to the Bosporus; his first military action was to recover Bithynia and the town of Nicomedia, and confine the enemy by arms and by a treaty to the further side of the river Draco;[1] Nicaea, Iconium and Smyrna, to mention merely three of the most important towns in Asia Minor, still lay in the Sultan's power. Only on the Black Sea were the Greeks still masters, holding in particular the key stronghold of Trebizond, while in the South Antioch was at least nominally theirs.[2]

[1] This is a small and very winding river rising in the hills North of the Ascanian Lake near Nicaea, and flowing out into the Bay of Astacus, in the sea of Marmora, near the ancient Helenopolis (Ersek).

[2] Alexius' brother Isaac at one time (1074–9) bore the title of Duke of Antioch (II. 1, p. 43). See above, p. 29, note 2. Schlumberger, *Sigillographie de l'Emp. Byz.*, p. 307–8, gives a list of sixteen Byzantine Dukes of Antioch from 976 to 1085. When this town first comes plainly before us in the *Alexias* it is in the hands of Philaretus, an Armenian who had been loyal to Romanus Diogenes if not to his successors on the throne (VI. 9). Laurent (*Byzance et les Turcs Seldjoucides*, p. 10) points out that our knowledge as to the exact extent of the power of the Turks in Asia Minor after Manzikert is extremely vague. Take for instance their province of Bithynia; the authorities, Greek, Arabic and Armenian, differ as to its capital, size, and political status. 'Il paraît sage', says Laurent, 'de renoncer à dresser d'après les sources un inventaire géographique détaillé des possessions turques et byzantines dans l'Asie occidentale en 1081.' It is clear that Michael VII after his deposition in 1078 was able to become Bishop of Ephesus, still 'a glorious and famous church' (Attaliates, p. 303), and Anna herself speaks of Greek Governors of Pontus, Paphlagonia, and Cappadocia (to say nothing of Choma) in 1081 (III. 9, p. 92). Indeed there was still enough of 'Asia' unoccupied by Turks for Nicephorus Melissenus to desire it as his share of Empire if the Comneni 'should sway the affairs of the West' (II. 8, p. 59). The historians incidentally mention Greek generals in various Asiatic places, one even as far East as Mesopotamia (Nic. Bry. III. 15, p. 79). As Laurent says, up to 1081 the Arabs made raids rather than conquests: 'il faut . . . ne pas prendre l'itinéraire de leurs destructions pour celui de leurs conquêtes.' It is however certain that the Byzantines, by their fatal habit of recalling troops from the Eastern frontier to combat domestic foes (*ibid.* pp. 22, 23), and by their crushing of Armenia with its potential help against the invaders, themselves let in the Turkish deluge which ultimately submerged the country. In 1050 Byzantine Asia had 'une importance capitale dans l'Empire. Trente ans plus tard elle n'était plus qu'un désert' (*ibid.* p. 105), as we see from the sufferings of the Crusaders. The Emperors had set themselves to humble the provincial nobles, had diminished the army, had failed to pay their troops, and had alienated the Armenians. Furthermore, with pirates on the one side and Turks on the other, the Byzantines in Asia Minor were indeed between the upper and the nether millstone. The rapid success of the Turks in arms between 1071 and 1081 'était dû aux

Relations were complicated by the fact that on the principle of 'Out of two evils choose the least', Alexius frequently as we have seen got Turkish help against other enemies. When sent to conquer Urselius, he only succeeds by winning over the Turk Tutach (whose Sultan he declares is 'friendly' to his own Emperor) and bribing him to surrender the Norman rebel into his hands.[1] On later occasions, too numerous to quote in full, Turkish mercenaries play an important part in the Greek armies.[2] But Turks in the mass are held up to us as formidable enemies, very warlike, highly skilled, and utterly relentless,[3] though with the commendable impartiality which she professes in her Preface Anna is quite ready 'to praise enemies', even 'most godless' Turks.[4] Indeed what might be called her anti-barbarian complex is never so little marked as in the case of these Easterners. They have been bad and destructive neighbours to the Empire, and like 'all barbarians' they 'ravage everything' and are 'ready for slaughters and wars',[5] but they are brave and skilful, and can boast of ἀνδραγαθήματα like Christians.[6] All nations as compared to the Greek Empire, 'by nature their queen' (δεσπότις), are 'slavish' and therefore 'hostile',[7] and like many other barbarians Turks have a 'deceit-

fautes de Byzance et à la trahison ou à l'indifférence de ses sujets', and even after this they owed their advance 'à l'inaction, à l'impéritie et à la division des chrétiens'. Alexius Comnenus, the one Emperor who might have overcome them, was fatally hampered by his Norman enemies (ibid. p. 111).

Of the four groups into which the Seljuqs split, in Kirman, Syria, Iraq and Kurdistan, and Rum or Asia Minor (see Camb. Med. Hist. IV, pp. 314, 315), only the second and fourth figure in the Alexias. The Seljuqs of Syria confronted the Crusaders, the Seljuqs of Rum fought Alexius also. At one moment however Bohemund and one Seljuq chief were allied together against Alexius and another Seljuq, an incident which Anna does not mention, but which as Loewe says is 'one of the instances which show that political considerations were more important than religious differences, not only among the Crusaders but also among the Muslims' (ibid. p. 315).   [1] I. 2.

[2] I. 4, p. 10; II. 6; IV. 2, p. 105; 4, p. 109; 6, p. 117; V. 5, p. 137; 6, p. 141; 7, p. 142; VIII. 3, p. 226; X. 4, p. 380; XI. 2, p. 316; XIII. 6. So also Bohemund has two 'Saracen counts' among his officers (V. 5 and XIII. 5).

[3] Leo (Tactica, XVIII. 61) says the Turks only differ from the Bulgarians as fighters by their greater cruelty. Laurent (op. cit. p. 106, note 3) quotes a long string of writers, Eastern, Greek, and Western, to prove their savage brutality. We should hardly infer it from the Alexias, though Anna believes that Turkish cruelty to Peter the Hermit was one cause of the First Crusade (X. 5, p. 283).

[4] III. 11, p. 95. The word seems rather a statement of fact, like our 'infidel', than a criticism (cf. V. 2, p. 128). So in XI. 7, p. 328, when the Turks 'pressed on to the siege of Jaffa, for such is ever the nature of barbarians' the blame is at least tinged with admiration. We have already spoken of the one exception as to her fairness, in rating them as drunken and immoral.

[5] IX. 3, p. 251; X. 5, pp. 282, 283; XI. 5, p. 321; XIV. 1, p. 421; XV. 10, p. 495. But cf. XIV. 5, p. 439, of a Turkish general avoiding needless bloodshed.

[6] V. 5, p. 137; XI. 8, pp. 331, 332; XV. 5, p. 474; 6, p. 478.

[7] XIV. 7, p. 445. Anna could certainly never have been blamed by Plutarch as φιλοβάρβαρος, as was Herodotus. See T. R. Glover's From Pericles to Philip, p. 3.

ful nature from of old ', and are given to treachery,[1] besides being apt to 'consider themselves as all but overtopping the clouds';[2] but we may set against this their often-shown chivalry to prisoners taken in war. The imperial general Rodomerus had evidently not suffered in his captivity with the Turks, but had learnt their language;[3] they admire another brave foe and show chivalry in begging him to save his life by surrender,[4] and on at least one occasion the Sultan of Cairo releases prisoners without ransom.[5] If Moslems are ready to go over to the enemy or to exact 'tribute' from those they conquer, so are Christians.[6] It is true that in war-time Turks make weird cries like wolves or dogs, they shout and yell and beat drums and wear strange clothes,[7] but they are also 'most ingenious' ($\mu\eta\chi\alpha\nu\iota\kappa\dot{\omega}\tau\alpha\tau\omicron\iota$),[8] 'splendid archers' ($\tau\omicron\xi\iota\kappa\dot{\omega}\tau\alpha\tau\omicron\iota$),[9] and 'experienced in war' ($\dot{\epsilon}\mu\pi\epsilon\iota\rho\omicron\pi\dot{\omega}\lambda\epsilon\mu\omicron\iota$).[10] They do indeed ruthlessly kill the earliest Crusaders and make a wall of their bones, but it seems to have been in reprisals for wanton brutality to infants and old people.[11] On a later occasion it is the cold-blooded cruelty (even to children) of the imperial general Eumathius Philocales that stirs up the whole country against the Greeks.[12] On the whole the impression left on our mind is expressed in a favourite dictum of the Great War: 'The Turk fights like a gentleman.'[13]

When we go into the matter a little more minutely we find that the first Turkish campaign, narrated in III. 11, is characteristic in two ways: Alexius does not go to the front in person, and he concludes matters with diplomacy; these two phenomena strike us again and again.

---

[1] VII. 8, p. 209.   [2] XV. 6, p. 479.

[3] XI. 3, p. 315. So Nic. Bry. (I. 19, p. 32) represents the behaviour of the 'leader of the Persians' to the captured Romanus Diogenes as a model of clemency and courtesy.

[4] XIV. 5, p. 440.

[5] XI. 7, p. 328; XII. 1, pp. 346, 347. These are probably two variants of the same story. The second account gives more details, i. e. that there were 300 prisoners, that they had suffered great hardship in their prison, which was $\delta\epsilon\iota\nu\dot{\eta}$ $\tau\hat{\omega}\nu$ $\pi\dot{\alpha}\lambda\alpha\iota$ $\gamma\epsilon\gamma\epsilon\nu\eta\mu\dot{\epsilon}\nu\omega\nu$, and that Alexius 'greatly admired the barbarian's' [i.e. the Sultan's] 'spirit'.

[6] VI. 9, p. 170, and cf. VI. 1; XI. 11, p. 339, and cf. IV. 3, p. 107.

[7] XIV. 5, p. 439; 6, pp. 443, 444; XV. 5, p. 475; 6, p. 476. Probably the 'foreign and barbarian dress' of Bohemund, when he came in a coffin from Antioch and startled the people of Corfu, was Turkish (XI. 12, p. 342).

[8] XV. 1, p. 461.   [9] XV. 3, p. 470.

[10] XI. 8, p. 331.   [11] X. 6, pp. 286, 287.

[12] XIV. 1, p. 420. Chalandon points out (op. cit. pp. 12, 98, 136), that the Armenian Samuel of Ani considered Malek Shah, the Sultan Tapares of Anna's Book VI, the ideal sovereign, and that Matthew of Edessa praised his goodness and thought his death a loss to the whole world.

[13] We may note that Anna does not think it beneath the 'grandeur' of her history to bring in Turkish names, as she does in the case of 'barbarian' Franks.

In Book VI Anna carries on her story about the Turks from 1085 right down to 1092,[1] and then in Chapter 14 returns to 1086 and the beginning of the Patzinak War. During Alexius' struggle with Robert Guiscard, the Moslems had gradually got back again to the Bosporus, and Alexius' old enemy Solyman of Nicaea[2] had gone South and seized Antioch, succeeding the last Byzantine duke, an Armenian named Philaretus, in 1085 and leaving Abul Cassim to hold Nicaea. The death of Solyman in battle against Tutuses, brother of the great Sultan Malek Shah, is followed by the virtual independence of 'all the Satraps that were holding towns and fortresses',[3] and the raids of Abul Cassim round Nicaea cause Alexius to send forces against him.[4] Meanwhile negotiations have been going on between the Emperor and Malek Shah, the nominal sovereign of all these petty princes. Once more Alexius uses diplomacy rather than force, and while ostensibly considering the Sultan's offer of substantial aid in return for an alliance by marriage, he hoodwinks the Turkish envoy completely. By a flattering reception he induces him to be baptized and makes him in return Duke of Anchialus. Later on another Turk, Abul Cassim, is lured by Alexius to Constantinople. 'Plentiful gifts' are promised and given him, and he is kept amused with 'baths and horse-races and hunting', with sight-seeing, and 'an equestrian contest for his benefit in the theatre' (i.e. circus), while Alexius' men are rapidly building a fort[5] to overawe Nicomedia. Abul Cassim finally returns to Nicaea and is besieged for three months by Prosuch, acting for Malek Shah. Once more Alexius is true to type; he resolves to help Abul Cassim, on the ground that 'when two enemies of the rule of the Greeks are fighting one another it is wise to come to terms with the weaker', so as finally to crush both. So he sends troops to try and raise the siege of Nicaea,[6] and at some later period fails to close with a renewed offer from Malek Shah,[7] that in return for a Byzantine princess as a bride for his son[8] the Turks would support the Empire against all enemies.

[1] VI. 9-13. [2] See III. 11. [3] VI. 10, p. 171.
[4] Anna believes that he was 'yearning to annex the sceptre of the Greek Empire' (VI. 10, p. 172).
[5] Chalandon (p. 101, note 1) says this was Cibotus, which the Varangians built for him.
[6] VI. 11, p. 176. Chalandon (p. 101) dates this as 1086. The final withdrawal of the besieging Turks does not take place till VI. 12, p. 177.
[7] Chalandon (p. 135) believes the date to have been 1092, the year of Malek Shah's death. In that case we must assume, as he does, that Anna tells us nothing about either Abul Cassim or Malek Shah during a space of six years (1086-92). Tzachas (see p. 423, below) comes on the scene in 1088.
[8] Anna here shows unusual aversion to Turks. Such a marriage would have been 'wretched', bestowing a crown 'sadder than all poverty' (VI. 12, p. 178).

Before the Greek envoy can carry Alexius' evasive answer to
the Sultan, the latter is killed,[1] and anarchy reigns in Asia
Minor, each emir[2] making himself independent.

Into all the ramifications of the campaign as told in Books
VI, VII, VIII, and IX there is no time or space to go. Cyzicus
lost to the Empire since 1081 is regained, and the Satrap
Elchanes comes over to the Greeks and is converted to Christianity by Alexius, the ἱερατικώτατος and διδασκαλικώτατος of
emperors.[3] But solid successes are non-existent, and in 1088
during the Patzinak War (1086–91), when Asiatic affairs are
already so serious as to demand the immediate dispatch of
the best imperial cavalry, the 500 horsemen newly come from
Flanders, to the Eastern front rather than to the Western,[4]
Tzachas the Emir of Smyrna begins troubling the Empire by
land and especially by sea.[5]

After Alexius early in 1091 has gained a slight success over
the Patzinaks at Choerobacchae,[6] we are told that Tzachas has
not only raised a new fleet but has been intriguing with 'the
Scythians' (who were to seize the Chersonesus while he
hemmed in the imperial forces from the other side of the Dardanelles), and trying to seduce Alexius' Turkish mercenaries.
With Abul Cassim threatening Nicomedia[7] Alexius would have

---

[1] VI. 12. Anna says he was murdered when drunk by Chasii (assassins) paid
by his brother Tutuses. This seems to be a confusion with the fact that about a
month before Malek Shah's death the great Vizier Nizam-al-Mulk was thus
assassinated (Camb. Med. Hist. IV, p. 308). Matthew of Edessa says Malek
Shah was poisoned by his wife (Chalandon, op. cit. p. 135, note 3). Anna's
Turkish history in this Book is not of the soundest; she mentions 'Pargiaruch
the newly made Sultan' in 10, p. 172, whereas he does not really succeed his
father till some time later (12, p. 179). One dramatic incident (VI. 12,
pp. 177, 178) bears the stamp of truth. Abul Cassim loads fifteen mules with
gold and goes to Malek Shah, hoping to buy his consent to the retention of
Nicaea by himself. But Puzanus has forestalled him, and the Sultan declines to
reopen the case, saying, 'Now that I have once committed the authority to
the Emir Puzanus, I do not wish it to be taken away from him. Let [Abul
Cassim] go to him and give his money to him and say all that he wishes. And
what seems good to [Puzanus] shall be my pleasure too'. What seems good to
Puzanus is to strangle Abul Cassim with a bowstring, but Anna sees the Sultan's
hand in the deed. The whole story, of the rivalry, the bribes, the plausible yet
cruel monarch, the savage penalty for ambition, is true to all we know of the East
down to far later times.

[2] Anna seems to use 'satrap', 'emir', and 'sultan' interchangeably for the same
office. Cf. VI. 12, p. 180, with VII. 7, p. 205. We find the title 'exousiast' in
XI. 7, p. 328, and the verb in III. 11 p. 95. 'Saisan' also is probably not a name
but a rank (see p. 426, note 5, below). Anna only differentiates the 'Great Sultan'
of Bagdad.

[3] VI. 13.   [4] VII. 7, p. 205.
[5] VII. 8.   [6] VIII. 3, p. 226.

[7] VII. 7, p. 205. Chalandon, op. cit. p. xvi, shows that in VI. 12 Anna antici-
pates the events of 1092 including Abul Cassim's death, and returns in VI. 14
to events in Europe in 1086; in VII. 7 Abul Cassim is still alive.

three enemies on his hands at once. The great danger to the Empire was however checked by Alexius' brilliant victory at Lebunium over the Patzinaks, and for the better part of two Books Anna makes only one casual reference to the Turks.[1] But Book IX opens with the ominous news, brought to Alexius when enjoying a brief respite at Constantinople from troubles in Dalmatia and troubles in his own court circle, that Tzachas is venturing to call himself βασιλεύς, and once more aiming at a conquest of the Empire by sea.[2] John Ducas is now (1092) sent from Durazzo to Asia Minor, and after three months takes Mitylene. Thereupon peace is made and hostages exchanged, but this consideration deters neither side from injuring the other. Anna is duly shocked at the way in which Tzachas violates his oath to spare the people of Mitylene on his departure, but she has no criticism to make when Constantine Dalassenus attacks him after the peace.[3] On the whole Greek perfidy succeeds the best, and Tzachas has to remain inactive in Smyrna while John Ducas fortifies Mitylene and recovers several of the islands before he is summoned back by the Emperor to suppress revolts in Crete and Cyprus. Tzachas seizes the opportunity of his absence to make fresh naval preparations, and Alexius once more resorts to diplomacy, stirring up against him his son-in-law Kilidj Arslan, with the suggestion that Tzachas was too 'much experienced' to have any real designs on the Empire, but was in fact coveting the Sultanate of Nicaea. Tzachas in ignorance of this intrigue goes to see Kilidj Arslan, who makes him drunk at a banquet, stabs him, leaves him for dead, and concludes a treaty with the Emperor.[4]

This is in 1092, and for four years we hear practically no more of the Turks. Then in 1096 comes the Crusade, and from that time till after the death of Bohemund[5] in 1109 or 1111[6] they appear as the enemies primarily of the Franks and only secondarily of the Greeks. The Emperor however represents himself, possibly in reference to his early fighting as a youth, as one who had had 'knowledge for a long time back of the method of warfare of the Turks',[7] and as such he gives good and often neglected advice to the Crusaders.[8] At Nicaea he

---

[1] VIII. 9, p. 240.
[2] He is said to have treated Smyrna as his 'royal residence' and his 'private lot' (IX. 1, p. 245; XI. 5, p. 321).
[3] IX. 1, and see p. 151, above.
[4] IX. 3, pp. 250, 251; cf. IX. 1, p. 245.   [5] X. 5 to XIV. 1.
[6] Chalandon, p. 249, note 6.   [7] X. 10, p. 301.
[8] X. 11, p. 305; XI. 3, pp. 317, 318; XI. 8. Turkish ambushes are specially to be dreaded (X. 6, p. 287; 10, p. 301).

sends Butumites to negotiate directly with the Turks, and when they have been induced to surrender by lavish promises he enrols some of their 'satraps' in his army,[1] being apparently more willing to deal honestly with them than with his supposed allies the Crusaders. In the same spirit Anna displays little enthusiasm over the joint victory of Crusaders and Greeks at Dorylaeum[2] and the other successes (on one occasion over the redoubted Kilidj Arslan), which allowed the combined army to reach and besiege Antioch. When Bohemund tells Taticius that the counts attribute to the Emperor's treachery the rumoured arrival of fresh Turks from Chorassan, it may have been an uneasy conscience quite as much as hunger and fear that made the Greek general beat a hasty retreat from the camp;[3] it is the sort of craftiness that might well have occurred to Alexius. After this Anna's information about the Crusade is less reliable, but she certainly represents the Turks as equal on the whole to the Christians in bravery and determination.[4]

In the meanwhile after his capture of Nicaea in 1097 Alexius has fresh trouble, both from Tzachas at Smyrna and also from Tangripermes at Ephesus, and thus has a good excuse for delaying his own march to join the Crusaders. Finally the Turks are driven back by John Ducas from the West coast, and this encourages Alexius to advance in person from Pelecanus, where he had remained during and after the siege of Nicaea, to Philomelium beyond Polybotus. But the same report of the fresh Turkish host from Chorassan which had been used by Bohemund to terrorize Taticius convinces Alexius of the hopelessness of saving Antioch. He therefore starts back to the capital with a large body of 'captured barbarians and Christian refugees',[5] leaving small segments of his troops to check the Turkish advance.

In Books XII and XIII there is no mention of Turks[6] till we get to the treaty between Alexius and Bohemund, with the latter's solemn promise to defend his liege lord against all comers as long as he is himself 'free from any barbaric and Turkish war', and furthermore to turn all lands he may capture 'whether

---

[1] XI. 1, 2.   [2] XI. 3, p. 317.   [3] XI. 4, p.319.

[4] XI. 4, p. 320, of the 'few brave men' who hold the Citadel of Antioch. It is not until the Sacred Nail is found that the Crusaders can rout the Turks (XI. 6, p. 327) and proceed to Jerusalem.

[5] XI. 6. These refugees come 'saving their bodies and as much money as they could carry'. There are women among them.

[6] Except for XII. 7, p. 365, where Gregory Taronites intrigues with Tanisman, and the ransoming of the Frankish counts at Babylon (i.e. Cairo) in XII. 1 (cf. XI. 7), a story redounding to the credit of the Sultan's generosity as much as to that of Alexius.

Turkish or Armenian, Pagans or Christians', into vassal states of the Empire.[1] Finally Bohemund dies and Alexius immediately applies himself to repairing the barbarians' ravages 'on the coast of Smyrna and as far as Attalia'.[2] Forces under Eumathius Philocales rebuild Adramyttium which Tzachas had totally destroyed, but their achievements are neutralized by great cruelty which enrages the inhabitants and brings down upon them the formidable army of the Archsatrap Asan of Cappadocia. In the fighting which takes place from Philadelphia as a base, the Greeks are uniformly successful. Many Turks are killed or captured or drowned in the Maeander, and Eumathius 'plentifully rewards' his men. This seems to have given the Emperor a fresh desire to join the Crusade, but it dies out in plans and negotiations, and soon he is fully occupied in dealing vicariously with the Turkish peril on the Ionian coast. In 1111 Constantine Gabras,[3] the new governor of Philadelphia,[4] confronts the advancing Emir Saisan (a chief not otherwise specified),[5] defeats him, and makes him sue for peace. Then once more Anna records a diplomatic triumph for her father. The Turk, who is depicted as fully alive to the Emperor's greatness, sends envoys to the Chersonesus, where Alexius was wintering so as to keep guard over his Empire by sea and land. They are overawed by the enthroned Imperial Majesty with his guard of honour, and Alexius takes advantage of this frame of mind. In his daughter's words:[6] 'Having ascertained what the Sultan wished, inasmuch as he realized that not all the things demanded by them would profit the empire of the Greeks, he wrapped much persuasiveness round his words, and made very clever explanations to them, till by much speaking he persuades them to acquiesce in his desires'. The treaty is concluded, but Anna though reiterating her praise of her father's devoted patriotism gives us no hint of the terms.

In any case he was not to enjoy peace for long. An army of 50,000 Turks is announced 'from all the lands of the East and Chorassan itself'.[7] So in 1113 Alexius, now nearly sixty and crippled with gout, took the field in person against the Turks for the first time since his accession.[8] The initial brunt of the

[1] XIII. 12, pp. 407, 409.
[2] XIV. 1, p. 419.   [3] XIV. 3.
[4] Eumathius Philocales, the former Governor, becomes Duke of Cyprus (XIV. 2, p. 424).
[5] Unless we identify him with the 'Sultan Saisan' of Chorassan (XIV. 3, p. 431). But Du Cange takes Saisan as a title merely; see his note on XV. 1, p. 460 A, and see p. 423, note 2, above.
[6] XIV. 3, p. 432.   [7] XIV. 4, p. 433.
[8] XIV. 5. In XI. 6, at Philomelium, he seems not to have been in action at all.

fighting is borne by Eustathius Camytzes, but after one success
he is defeated and captured. Then Alexius tries his fortune
and wins a victory at Acrocus near Cotiaeum. The enemy's
subsequent attacks are repelled, and Camytzes escapes to
Alexius, who sends him to Irene at Constantinople with the
good news of triumph, soon afterwards returning thither himself.

Coman raiders and Manichaean heretics next engross his
attention,[1] and when he is desirous to go against the Turks he
is bedridden with 'the wonted suffering in his feet'.[2] We must
observe that throughout Book XV one of the two Turkish
leaders, a second Saisan, otherwise Kilidj Arslan II, son of the
Kilidj Arslan of the previous wars, is notorious for youthful
insolence and conceited folly. He allows his courtiers to mock
at his invalid opponent and his nurse-wife in what we can only
call theatrical skits,[3] he fails to realize that no trick devised by
'the highly ingenious' could possibly deceive Alexius,[4] he is
contemptuous of the new *parataxis*,[5] and after his capitulation
he neglects to his own undoing the Emperor's advice and the
subsequent warning of a dream.[6] The marching and counter-
marching in chapters 1 and 2 makes dull reading, however
much it meant 'brilliant victory' for the Greeks. In chapter 2
however we get a dramatic account of three successive messengers coming in haste to announce that the Turks are getting
nearer. We almost feel the panic which Irene was too brave
to show, as the Emperor dispatched her homewards fleeing
before the dreaded foe. But nothing decisive happens (to the
malign amusement of the disloyal), and the Empress rejoins
her husband at Nicomedia.[7]

We next follow the newly trained Greek army on its march
towards Iconium. The men are instructed to make only short
dashes for foraging purposes, and nothing special occurs till
Alexius reaches Dorylaeum and puts into practice the new parataxis which we have already discussed at length. Here we will
only quote Anna's words about Turkish methods of fighting.
She describes their battle array[8] as different from others, in that
'the right wing and the left wing and the centre are separated
from one another . . . and whenever any one makes an onslaught
on the right or left wing, the centre leaps upon him and the
part of the whole battle array (παράταξις) behind the centre,
and like hurricanes they throw the troops opposed to them into
confusion. As for their weapons of war, they do not use spears

---

[1] XIV. 8, 9.   [2] XV. 1, p. 460.   [3] XV. 1, p. 461.
[4] *Ibid.*   [5] XV. 5, p. 475.   [6] XV. 6.
[7] XV. 3.   [8] *Ibid.*

at all, as do the men called Celts, but encircling the enemy on all sides they shoot at him with bows. And so their fighting is at a distance, for when [a Turk] pursues, he captures [his enemy] by his bow, and when pursued he conquers by his arrows. For he shoots his arrow and the arrow flies and strikes either the horse or the horseman, and because it is launched by a mighty hand it passes through the whole body; such splendid archers are they'.[1] Against these redoubtable foes Alexius uses his new parataxis with great effect and to the admiration of the wiser among the enemy. The Sacred Lots however order a retreat from Philomelium, and he starts for the capital, with prisoners, women and children in the middle of his hollow square. The line remains unshaken under all the Turkish attempts to break or terrify it, and finally the enemy sues for peace. Courtesies are exchanged: the Sultan kisses the Emperor's foot, and the Emperor throws his own cloak round the Sultan's shoulders. By the treaty now made the Turks are to return to the boundaries that obtained before Manzikert, and the Sultan departs content with 'very much money',[2] only to be blinded and strangled in Iconium by his bastard brother. Thus the star of the last Turk mentioned by Anna sets in darkness, and Alexius returns triumphant to Constantinople, one of the few Emperors who had ever 'dared to touch Asia at all even with the tips of his feet'.[3] His mantle as an Asiatic conqueror descended on to his son John, whose frequent campaigns against the 'barbarians' round Antioch and elsewhere, in the company of his brother-in-law Bryennius Caesar, cause Anna to recite in her Preface a string of Asiatic place-names.

We have dwelt on these Eastern foes at some length, for to Anna they are hardly, if at all, inferior in importance to Robert and Bohemund. Even though in her heart she may prefer a good Turk to an inferior Christian, still the Turk was the hereditary enemy of Church and State,[4] and to victories over

---

[1] We may compare the description of Turkish fighting in Leo's *Tactica* (XVIII. 55, 58). 'In battle they do not make their array (παρατάσσουσιν) in three parts like the Greeks, but in different bands, in clumps (δρουγγιστί) fitting the parts one to the other at a little distance from each other. . . They rejoice rather in fights from afar, and ambushes and encirclings against the enemy, and feigned retreats and turnings and scattered lines.'

Anna gives us one vivid picture of Turks laying waste the land, then surrounding their enemies who could not get out for food or water, and finally defeating them in hand-to-hand fight (XI. 8, pp. 331, 332).

[2] XV. 6, p. 478.   [3] XV. 10, p. 495.

[4] We may note that of real knowledge about the history or culture of Eastern nations she has little. Aleppo, Edessa, Damascus, Bagdad, Mesopotamia, and Chorassan are all mentioned casually. 'Horses of noble breed from Damascus and Edessa and Arabia' seem to be her only associations with the places named

him whether military or diplomatic many of her best passages are appropriately devoted.

Before we finally leave the East we must say a word about the Armenians, formerly enemies, then in theory subjects of the Empire, and as cordially disliked by Anna as by many of the Greeks nowadays.[1] Laurent, while clearly showing with what unwise harshness this country had been treated by various emperors, admits that 'Les Arméniens installés dans l'Empire pour le défendre, l'avaient souvent trahi',[2] and he gives a long list of instances. He adds: 'Le fait est que les Arméniens ne tenaient pas en place dans l'Empire; pour échapper au formalisme administratif ou au prosélytisme religieux des Grecs, ils se donnaient à une vie libre, errante et vagabonde; . . . la guerre civile, à son défaut le brigandage, voilà quelle était leur occupation favorite.' As we have seen, Anna has a horror of their Monophysite heresy,[3] and she also dislikes them as human beings. Philaretus is guilty of the double crime of rebellion and apostasy to Mohammedanism;[4] Ariebes plots against Alexius, and it is a Turco-Armenian half-breed who tries to stab the Emperor in the Palace riding-school;[5] 'a certain Armenian' betrays Antioch to Bohemund; later 'the Armenians' side with Tancred against the Empire, and he has Armenian recruits,[6] while last but not least Aspietes, sprung of the royal Arsacid house, from whom great things might be expected because of his noble birth and his personal bravery, proves himself when 'far from his master's hand' a broken reed as a governor, drunken, lazy and incompetent.[7]

(XIV. 2, p. 429). The 'luxury' of Assyrians invented chess, and their women had round faces (III. 3, p. 77; XII. 6, p. 360). The Chaldaeans are famed for occult learning (V. 8, p. 144; XIV. 8, p. 451), and the walls of ancient Babylon were a type of strength (XIII. 8, p. 398; XIV. 2, p. 423). In one passage she says that her father extended the Empire to the Euphrates and Tigris, a considerable exaggeration (VI. 12, p. 176), unless we consider the Frankish and Armenian principalities as parts of his dominions, nominally at least.

[1] Krumbacher (Sitzungsber. zu München, 1893, p. 246) gives a medieval Greek proverb ''Αρμένιον φίλον, χείρον' ἐχθρὸν μὴ θέλε', and talks of the 'üble Meinung' of Byzantines to Armenians, of whom they were jealous in trade and in all high official, military and legal positions. He also quotes Cassia, who in the first half of the ninth century wrote a collection of Gnomes and Epigrams; one begins as follows:

Τῶν 'Αρμενίων τὸ δεινότατον γένος
ὑπουλόν ἐστι καὶ φαυλῶδες εἰς ἄγαν.

[2] Op. cit. pp. 50 sqq.
[3] X. 1 and XIV. 8. It was from Armenia that Tzimisces had brought the Manichaeans to Philippopolis.
[4] VI. 9, p. 168.   [5] VIII. 7, p. 236; IX. 7, p. 259.
[6] XI. 4, and 9, p. 334; XII. 2, p. 348.
[7] IV. 6, p. 117, and XII. 2. We should add by way of exception that Pacurianus though Armenian is a good Grand Domestic (II. 4, p. 50). Like Aspietes he is of noble birth.

To Armenians as forming a state Anna's only reference is in the treaty between Alexius and Bohemund where she includes them among 'those who have never served the Greek Empire' (τῇ 'Ρωμανίᾳ),[1] and it is not quite clear what she means. We must of course rule out the tenth-century Armeniac Theme in Asia Minor (stretching along the Black Sea and including Sinope), to which she four times alludes;[2] that was nowhere near the territories under discussion. If in the treaty she refers to Greater Armenia, it had had, among its centuries of chequered history under national or foreign rulers, Roman, Persian, and Arab, at least two periods (633–93 and 1021–64) when the Byzantines held the power.[3] At the end of the second of these, it was finally subjugated by the Seljuq Turks. If Anna's phrase is not purely rhetorical, she is probably speaking of what Macler terms Armeno-Cilicia, a 'new Armenian State' founded and ruled from 1080 to 1340 by the so-called Rupenian princes, kinsmen of the Bagratid dynasty just extinct in Greater Armenia. The 'Crusading leaders stood in every kind of relationship to the new Armenian kingdom. They befriended and fought it by turns'.[4] Though its constituent members might once have been as Armenians subject to Byzantine rulers, yet as new petty princes, who had taken to the Taurus Mountains for shelter against the Turks, they might consider themselves as in fact entitled to claim entire independence.

One word must be said in conclusion about the Iberians. Anna represents Iberian nuns as frequently visiting Constantinople, and their chronic state of poverty is finally ended by Alexius who bestows on them 'much care'. This includes 'a great convent and food and suitable clothes'.[5] The Iberia meant is of course not Spain, but the Caucasian Georgia of modern times, which had been independent under its own rulers throughout its history (in spite of attacks by Basil II and other Byzantine emperors), till the Turkish hordes overwhelmed it. From the first it had had close ties with the Greek Empire, and the early Georgian Church had sought spiritual guidance from Byzantium. Under pressure from Turkish inroads it was appropriate that refugee nuns should make their

---

[1] XIII. 12, p. 409.   [2] I. 2, p. 6; XI. 8, pp. 331, 332, and 12, p. 342.
[3] Camb. Med. Hist. IV, pp. 154, 155, 164–6 (F. Macler).
[4] Ibid. p. 167. In XIII. 12, p. 412, the territory of two of these 'Rupenian Armenians' is specially excluded from Bohemund's share because they have become Alexius' 'men'.
[5] XV. 7, p. 485. The Anon. Syn. Chron. also mentions (p. 178) these Nuns in the Orphanage, as being 'of other tongue but of the same customs and faith'.

way to the religious metropolis of the Eastern world. And on quite a different occasion the fact that his mother was an Iberian made it more natural for the Sultan's envoy to Constantinople to accept as a donation from the Emperor 'divine baptism', 'many gifts', and a dukedom.[1]

FOREIGN AFFAIRS
65. THE NORTH

ANNA'S interest in Eastern races is virtually confined to Turks and Armenians, and her attitude is respectful enmity to the first and antipathy to the second. In the North she mentions many more different peoples, of whom some are in friendly relations with the Empire. Thus Alans[2] have confidential places at court[3] and serve in the imperial armies.[4] The ex-Empress Maria and her kinswoman married to Alexius' brother Isaac belong to this race, as does the second wife of Theodore Gabras.[5] The 'Dacians', as Anna terms the Hungarians, provide the bride of her brother John.[6] Their ancient but disregarded treaties with the Romans are mentioned,[7] and they form part of the invading Patzinak army,[8] so that the marriage was doubtless one of political 'convenience'. Through their territory (Οὐγγρία) Alexius will allow the Norman soldiers to go home if they will from Castoria.[9] In the only two other places where the name occurs, Anna tells us that the Crusaders with Peter the Hermit came to Constantinople 'through the Dacians' (later expressed as 'through the parts of Hungary'),

---

[1] VI. 9.

[2] 'Iranian nomads first met with North of the Caspian, and later [c. first century A.D.] spreading into the steppes of Russia' (*Encycl. Brit.*, s.v. *Alani*). We may note that Anna never once mentions the growing power of Russia itself.

[3] I. 16, p. 38; II. 4, p. 50.

[4] XIII. 6, p. 393. They are μαχιμώτατοι and have a special commander called ἐξουσιοκράτωρ. See Du Cange's note on XIII. 6, p. 393 A. In XV. 2, p. 464, one seems to be a scout.

[5] VIII. 9, p. 240. Cf. II. 1, p. 44.

[6] XIII. 12, p. 416. Tzetzes says this Empress was ἐξ Ἀλαμανῶν (G. Hart, *op. cit.* p. 221). Anna correctly calls the Hungarian ruler a Krales. The *Anon. Syn. Chron.* p. 181, says Alexius asked the Krales or 'King of Paeonia' for a wife for John.

[7] III. 8, p. 89.

[8] VII. 1, p. 188. Their ἔφοδοι are coupled with those of the Comans in XIV. 4, p. 434. In III. 8, p. 89, in a passage copied from Psellus (*Chron.*, Is. Comn., Byz. T., p. 222), Anna speaks of the 'Getae' as living beyond the Danube; these were called 'Dacians' by the Romans. The Province of Dacia set up by Trajan was bounded on the West by the river Theiss, and did not comprise the modern Western Hungary, which formed part of Pannonia.

[9] V. 7, p. 143.

and she enumerates these same Dacians among 'the very rich tribes' who live on the slopes of Mount Haemus.[1]

The Bulgarians similarly receive from Anna slight but not unfavourable attention, and there is no sign in the *Alexias* of that horror of the race which comes out in the epistles of their metropolitan, Archbishop Theophylact.[2] Maria, the daughter-in-law of John Ducas Caesar and mother of the Empress Irene, was a Bulgarian princess,[3] and Bulgarian men and officers serve in the Greek army.[4] The first and the last kings of Bulgaria, Mocrus and Samuel Mocrus, are brought in so as to date certain facts in Balkan history.[5]

The half-Latin half-Slavonic Vlachs and their possible kinship with Alexius have been dealt with already.[6] The Serbians and Serbia only appear in the *Alexias* twice, first as vague equivalents of and then as neighbours to Dalmatians and Dalmatia,[7] who under the leadership of Bodinus and Bolcanus give the Empire a great deal of trouble.[8] A learned Russian, Petroff, wishes to identify these two chiefs; the learned Frenchman Chalandon proves at great length that this is wrong,[9] and the evidence seems to support him. At any rate in the *Alexias* it is

[1] X. 5, pp. 284, 286; XIV. 8, p. 452. Peter the Hermit did indeed come through Hungary, but not across the Adriatic first as Anna supposes. See Du Cange's note on X. 5, p. 285 D. Chalandon (p. 169) suggests that Peter's sufferings (prior to his arrival at Constantinople) 'from the Turks' (X. 6, p. 286) really means 'from the Hungarians', because the Byzantines often called the Hungarians Turks. On his previous pilgrimage, many months before, be had 'suffered dreadful things from the Turks and Saracens who were laying all Asia waste' (X. 5, p. 283).

[2] *P. G.* 126, cols. 308, 508, &c. In the *Alexias* (VIII. 7, p. 236) this prelate complains to Alexius of treachery in the latter's nephew John Comnenus, who as Governor of Dyrrachium was as we might say the principal layman of the see of Achrida, though of course not a Bulgarian.

[3] 11. 6, p. 55. Another Bulgarian had married the Emperor Isaac Comnenus. Her brother Aaron was governor of Ani, where an inscription records his building a wall and remitting a tax (Laurent, *op. cit.* p. 31).

[4] VIII. 3, p. 227; 4, p. 229. If as Du Cange says the traitorous Aaron brothers were sprung from Bulgarian kings, it shows that noble Bulgarians were among the courtiers closest to the imperial person, XIII. 1.

[5] VII. 3, p. 194; XII. 9, p. 371. We have already noted (p. 240, note 1) that Anna follows a recognized convention in calling the Bulgarian monarch alone of all the world outside Byzantium by the majestic name of Basileus. One result of Basil's conquest of Bulgaria was to make Constantinople and not the Eastern provinces the most important part, because the centre, of the Empire. But the conquest also served to bring the Patzinaks into immediate and perilous contact with the Greeks. On neither of these aspects of the history does Anna touch.

[6] See p. 265, above.

[7] IX. 4, p. 252; XIV. 4, p. 434. A correspondingly vague use of the word Dalmatia is to be seen in IV. 5, p. 111, where Durazzo is placed in it.

[8] As a matter of fact the year 1071, so disastrous to the Empire at Manzikert, had also seen a formidable insurrection in Serbia, while the taking of Bari in Italy by the Normans had encouraged the Dalmatians 'to secure practical independence' on their side of the Adriatic (*Camb. Med. Hist.* IV, p. 325).

[9] Chalandon, *op. cit.* pp. 142–5.

Bodinus, an 'exarch of the Dalmatians',[1] who with a colleague called Michael welcomes Monomachatus the treacherous Greek governor of Durazzo,[2] and who basely deserts the Greek army in its great defeat outside that town.[3] So far the Dalmatians are assumed to be allies of the Empire,[4] but in 1092 when John Ducas goes to Asia Minor he has already spent many years at Durazzo in combating the encroachments of the Dalmatians, taking their fortresses, and sending numerous prisoners to the Emperor.[5] Bolcanus and Bodinus are now both mentioned, the former as having 'authority' in Dalmatia, the latter as being 'very warlike and full of roguery' ($\dot{\rho}\alpha\delta\iota o\upsilon\rho\gamma\iota\alpha\varsigma$), always trying to increase his territory at the expense of the Empire, but captured in the end by John. After this we only hear of Bodinus once again, but of Bolcanus many times, a threatened attack of the Dalmatians in 1091 being described first as led by the former[6] and then as owing its alarming character to the latter.[7] The extremely rugged 'passes between Dalmatia and our country' have to be fortified under the Emperor's own eye,[8] and the holding of them takes up valuable soldiers.[9] Unfortunately John Comnenus, the successor of John Ducas at Durazzo, is not equal to his task. He is twice beaten[10] by Bolcanus, 'dread in speech, dread in action', and his younger brother Alexius succeeds him as governor. Even the Emperor is no match for the crafty diplomacy of the 'most knavish' Dalmatian ($\pi o\nu\eta\rho\dot{o}\tau\alpha\tau o\varsigma$), who on his advance against the Empire two years after the end of the Patzinak War (i.e. 1093) tries to throw the blame of the disturbance on 'the satraps of the Greeks' for invading his lands,[11] and shows a desire to make peace which is merely hypocritical. For a whole year his promised hostages are not forthcoming. After the first defeat of John Comnenus (who is surprised at night by the supposedly friendly Bolcanus) Alexius again takes the field in 1094, eager to check and to punish the ravaging and burning and other destructions that have reached his ears.[12] On his way to the West he is stopped by the Diogenes conspiracy, but at last he confronts Bolcanus, who is awed by 'the Greek battle array and

---

[1] I. 16, p. 40. Chalandon calls him 'prince de Serbie', *op. cit.* p. 140.
[2] III. 12, p. 97.   [3] IV. 6, p. 118.
[4] IV. 5, p. 112; VI. 7, p. 166.   [5] VII. 9, p. 209.
[6] VIII. 7, p. 236. This is his last appearance; we are not told how soon he had been released after his capture by John Ducas. Ordericus Vitalis, quoted by Chalandon (*op. cit.* p. 142), says he was still in power when the first Crusade began in 1096.
[7] VIII. 7, p. 237 (*bis*).   [8] VIII. 7, p. 236; IX. 1, p. 245.
[9] XIV. 4, p. 434.   [10] IX. 4, p. 453; XII. 4, p. 356.
[11] IX. 4, p. 252.   [12] IX. 5, p. 253.

the serried ranks and the pomp of generalship'[1] into begging once
more for peace. This is granted, and Anna wishes us to believe
that her father's motive was a love for his fellow-Christians,
and a dread of ἐμφύλιος μάχη. Hostages are actually given by
Bolcanus,[2] and Alexius, 'having peacefully settled matters
naturally made to be accomplished by war and steel, returned
to the capital'. Is it cynical to see in all this a confession that
the Dalmatians were too powerful to be conquered in war?
Only on one other occasion do we hear of them, when Alexius'
preparations to withstand Bohemund on his arrival (preparations
which include the sending of his nephew Alexius to Durazzo)
are interrupted by the bad news of John Comnenus' second
disaster.[3] After this Bolcanus and Dalmatia alike fade out of the
history, leaving on us an impression of a people who no less than
the Turks were 'from of old bad neighbours' to the Empire.[4]

Even worse are the Patzinaks and the Comans who, sometimes jointly, sometimes separately, sometimes indeed in opposition to each other, pour over the Danube in no less than five
of Anna's Books.[5] Anna calls them impartially 'Scythians', and
draws no distinction between their characteristics.[6]

About the Patzinaks much has been written, and it seems
clearly established that they were a Turkish tribe from North
of the Caspian, who at the end of the eleventh century had long

---

[1] IX. 10, p. 265.

[2] Anna correctly uses the word ζούπανοι of his chief nobles from whom the
hostages are selected (IX. 10, p. 265).

[3] The passage is as follows: 'Hearing of the defeat of John son of the Sebastocrator, who had been sent before this against the Dalmatians, [Alexius] dispatched
sufficient forces to his assistance. Therefore Bolcanus being most knavish straightway makes overtures of peace to the Emperor and sends the requested hostages'
(XII. 4, p. 356). The situation is very similar to that in IX. 10, but on the whole
it seems better to take the words as referring to a later incident, one which (if the
chronology of the chapter is correct) did not occur till 1106.

[4] We have already (p. 354, note 3, above) dealt with the pirates of the Dalmatian
coast (XIV. 7, p. 445), and need not return to them here. As to Albanians, the
name only occurs twice. The man who succeeds Palaeologus as civil governor
(not military) of Durazzo is an Albanian (IV. 8, p. 122), and Albanians are coupled
with 'those from Dalmatia' as potential allies for the Emperor against Robert
(VI. 7, p. 166).

[5] The Patzinak War lasts from VI. 14 to VIII. 6; Coman raids in support
of the pseudo-Diogenes occupy three chapters of Book X, and they appear again
XIV. 8 and 9.

[6] Other Scythians are the Sarmatians (or Mysi, III. 8, p. 89), but Anna only
mentions them incidentally. They gave trouble under the Emperor Isaac Comnenus (ibid.), they were skilled archers (V. 7, p. 142), they drove the Patzinaks
Southward (VI. 14, p. 182), yet joined the army of the Patzinak Tzelgu against
the Empire (VII. 1, p. 188). Two of Alexius' captains were of the race (VII. 3,
p. 195; X. 4, p. 281). Kadlec (Camb. Med. Hist. IV. 183) takes the names Scythians
and Sarmatians as following one another in time but identical in meaning.
Anna twice has Οὐζᾶς meaning 'Hun' (V. 7, p. 142; VII. 5, p. 201), but one man
who bears this nickname is also called a Sarmatian (VII. 3, p. 195).

been established between the Don and the Danube, acting as middlemen between the Russians and the Byzantines. The advice given by Constantine VII to his son, to keep on friendly terms with the Patzinaks,[1] proves that in his day they were already a power to be reckoned with, but they did not come into immediate contact with the Empire till Bulgaria was crushed and the Greek troops got back to the Danube. As time went on the Patzinaks took every opportunity of crossing the river and gradually extending their domain Southward. Many, so we learn from all the chroniclers, were enrolled in the imperial army, but that did not prevent the tribe as a whole from harrying Greek territory.

A small spark in Alexius' reign lighted up the conflagration. One of the Manichaeans with whose kin Alexius had dealt harshly escapes from Byzantium and goes Northwards. There he joins himself to 'the Scythians living near the Danube', marries (in spite of having left a wife behind him) the daughter of one of their chiefs, and invites them to attack the Empire.[2] As to the campaign which now follows Anna is our sole authority, so that we have no means of testing her accuracy. Chalandon[3] has worked out her chronology so carefully that we will not attempt to do it again; we will merely accept his pronouncement that the eclipse mentioned in VII. 2 is that of August 1, 1087. This dates the invasion of Tzelgu, 'a prominent chief of the Scythian army', and Solomon of Hungary, with their host of over 80,000 men, as occurring in the spring of the same year.[4] With the varying success of the fighting we need not here deal. Alexius thinks the Patzinaks important enough for him to fight in person, to use trickery of a peculiarly unpleasing because sanctimonious kind in negotiation,[5] to consult his officers anxiously as to plans, and to win allies by any means whatever. Even so he suffers a terrible defeat at Dristra. In this battle the Scythians advance with their scythe-armed chariots[6] and work havoc among the Greek army, who when enemy reinforcements are reported turn and fly. Alexius performs marvels of valour, but finally beats a retreat to Beroe, where the Patzinaks allow him to ransom his prisoners,[7] while

---

[1] de Adm. imp., chs. 1–8. They also figure in ch. 37 (Vol. III, pp. 67–74, 164–7).
[2] VI. 4, p. 158. In VI. 14, p. 182, Anna explains that their original move Southwards had been caused by their being 'continually despoiled by the Sarmatians'.   [3] p. 105, note 1.   [4] VII. 1, p. 188.   [5] VII. 2.
[6] They could not fight without these, and they also used them both to carry their families, and as 'towers' to strengthen their line (VII. 3, p. 196; 6, p. 203; 9, p. 211; VIII. 5, p. 232; XIV. 7, p. 445).
[7] They talk of killing prisoners (VII. 4, p. 200), but the Greeks actually do so (VIII. 6).

the adventures of George Palaeologus in his escape give a sparkle of interest after the gloomy battle scenes.

A new 'Scythian' tribe now comes on the stage. These are the Comans or Polovtzes, a Turkish tribe first found in the Ural Mountains, who from friends of their Patzinak kinsmen speedily turn to foes over a question of booty. A series of confusing transactions follow. The Comans go 'home' and then return again, and the Patzinaks make peace with Alexius and break it. Furthermore the Emperor has to contend not only with this enemy alarmingly near Byzantium but with treachery in his own army[1] and a bad attack of ague.[2] A slight success arouses wild enthusiasm at Constantinople, but the 'barbarous' hordes[3] are still near, and it is discovered that the Turk Tzachas has been intriguing with them. A severe winter adds to the trials of the Greeks, and the next spring (1091) matters are so serious that Alexius, after collecting recruits howsoever and wheresoever he can, summons the 500 horsemen of Flanders back from Asia Minor to his aid. At this critical moment there appears a body of Comans, and unstable as they have hitherto proved as allies,[4] they are yet eagerly welcomed by Alexius, who however keeps a river between them and his own troops.[5] The Patzinaks in alarm make overtures both to the Emperor and to the Comans, but their hour has come. The humble turning of the Greeks to God is rewarded; they gain a complete victory, and the Patzinaks are so nearly annihilated that after one more defeat under John II history hears of them no more.[6] From a modern point of view the success is marred by the murder of the prisoners, though at the time this has the good effect of terrifying Alexius' formidable allies the Comans, who

---

[1] The Scythian deserter Neantzes betrays Alexius' plans to his countrymen (VII. 9, p. 211), and later on shows lawless insolence 'worthy of a barbarian soul'.
[2] VII. 10, p. 213.
[3] Their appearance inspired alarm and disgust (VIII. 1 and 2; XII. 8). Scythians glare 'barbarously' (XII. 8, p. 367). We do not however hear of any act of theirs as barbarous as Alexius' impaling the heads of slain enemies on spears (VIII. 2, p. 223).
[4] Anna talks contemptuously of their 'easily led' and 'easily gulled' character (VIII. 4, p. 228). They are also 'deceitful' and 'reckless' ($\delta\xi\acute{v}$) (VIII. 5), and 'like true barbarians they are full of light-mindedness and fickleness in the course of nature' (X. 3, p. 276).
[5] VIII. 4.
[6] VIII. 5. If Zonaras (XVIII. 23) is right in saying that Alexius, after selling many as slaves, put a number of the sturdiest Patzinak prisoners with their wives and children into the theme of Moglena, and that they were there to his day, some portion of the nation must have become assimilated to the Empire. Bury (*Encycl. Brit.*, 'Later Roman Empire') says they were 'exterminated by John Comnenus in 1123'. Anna characteristically gives the credit for their disappearance to her father, and never mentions them in her Preface in enumerating the wars waged by her brother and husband.

fearing a like fate retreat hastily across the Northern ranges. Alexius is generous or prudent enough to send all their promised booty after them.[1] This is in 1091, and we do not meet the Comans again till two Books later,[2] when in 1094 they make the claims to sovereignty of a pretender (purporting to be a son of Romanus Diogenes) into an excuse for invading the Empire.[3] It is interesting to note that this man comes across them at Cherson, where they have gone 'wandering as usual' for the 'sake of trade'. The Sacred Lots decree that Alexius shall march in person against the enemy, who, we may remark (though described as savages 'longing to batten on the blood of men, to be glutted with human flesh, and to bring back much booty'),[4] are welcomed by many of the Northern towns. But the campaign resolves itself into individual acts of rather foolhardy bravery, and a most elaborate ruse concocted to entrap the pretender. With all this the Comans have little to do, and when the pseudo-Diogenes has been finally captured and blinded, they retreat rather tamely homewards.[5] Once more only do they appear in Anna's pages. They cross the Danube in 1114, as recorded in the last chapters of Book XIV,[6] but the very rumour of the Emperor's advance makes them turn and flee; jumping on rafts they re-cross the river and apparently another stream also before the Greek troops can catch them up. Anna's comment is so characteristic that it must be given in full:

The Emperor was grieved that the barbarians had not been overtaken by his armies, but he nevertheless considered this a piece of victory that he had driven back the barbarians by the mere sound of his name, and also that he had brought over many from the Manichaean heresy to our faith, thus setting up a double trophy, against the barbarians by his arms, and against the heretics by his most pious words.

Certainly nowhere do we find any contempt for any of these Northern foes as fighters either expressed or suggested.[7] Even the final defeat of the Patzinaks was chiefly, Anna thought, due to moral causes.[8] Indeed in the passage where their battle formation is described her words show nothing but admiration. 'They know by natural intelligence how to fight and stand

[1] VIII. 6. [2] A raid by them is rumoured in VIII. 7, p. 236. [3] X. 2.
[4] Ibid. p. 272. This stock phrase is as we have seen also used of the Manichaeans (VI. 14, p. 182). [5] X. 4.
[6] The report of their intention causes Alexius to go to Philippopolis in XIV. 8, p. 449.
[7] Their only foibles in the field are yelling in battle and turning prematurely to plunder.
[8] VIII. 5; cf. VII. 3.

in a phalanx', their lines are well knit and fortified by their covered chariots 'as with towers',[1] and even their women are valiant in the fray. Whatever faults the Greeks committed as combatants, that of despising their enemy was not one.

FOREIGN AFFAIRS

66. THE WEST IN GENERAL

AFTER the East and the North there remains to be considered the last and greatest source of danger to the Empire during Alexius' reign and for long afterwards, namely the West. We will take its various constituents in order.

With the extreme North-West Anna has little to do. Riant[2] has proved conclusively that Norwegians or Danes were to be found in all the armies and navies that fought round the Mediterranean, both before and during the first Crusade. But except for her references to the 'axe-bearing barbarians' of the Varangian Guard[3] Anna never mentions Scandinavia, unless indeed the 'kings' who arrive at Constantinople after Godfrey de Bouillon included Eric the Good or Sigurd I of Norway.[4]

By her term Thule she probably means vaguely all the countries bordering on the North Sea,[5] but when she adds the word 'island' she is doubtless thinking of Britain.[6] She tells us that Bohemund (in 1107) landed at Aulon 'bringing an immense army of Franks and Celts, and all the men in the Greek service from the island of Thule, men who at that time had come over to him through force of circumstances'.[7] Ordericus Vitalis[8] says that King Henry I would not let Bohemund come to England, 'metuens ne sibi electos milites de ditione sua subtraheret', but the prince may well have had recruits both from Normandy and Britain (especially those Anglo-Saxons who still

---

[1] VII. 3, p. 196 ; 6, p. 203.   [2] *Expéditions etc.*, ch. III.
[3] See pp. 588 sqq.
[4] Eric went to the Crusade in 1102 and stopped in Constantinople on his way; Sigurd came there on his way home from Jerusalem which he reached in 1106 (Riant, *op. cit.* pp. 159–61, 195 sqq.).
[5] She says the Varangians came from Thule (II. 10, p. 62 ; 11, p. 66). In VI. 11, p. 176, she uses 'famous Thule' rhetorically to mark the Northern limits of the Empire in its palmy days.
[6] II. 11, p. 66; XII. 9, p. 370.
[7] ὅσοι ἀπὸ τῆς Θούλης νήσου στρατεύονται Ῥωμαίοις τότε δὴ αὐτῷ προσχωρήσαντες διὰ τὴν τοῦ καιροῦ δυναστείαν (XII. 9, p. 370). δυναστεία in late Greek often = δύναμις. This sentence, as we saw in Ch. 56, hardly agrees with Anna's praise of Varangian loyalty.
[8] Quoted by Du Cange in his note on XII. 9, p. 370 A.

resented the conquest of fifty years back), malcontents who
had entered the Varangian Guard at Constantinople but now
took the opportunity of joining Bohemund. We need not dwell
on the 'Celtiberians' in the Norman prince's army, for Anna
never speaks of Spain elsewhere, and seems to have no knowledge of the Moorish culture there or even of the Christian
struggle of the Reconquista actually taking place in her day.[1]
But she does say that Bohemund had many soldiers 'of the
Germanic race',[2] and we must examine very briefly what she
knew about Germans.

As we have pointed out before, her information on the subject
is hazy, and she gives a garbled story of the Pope's maltreatment
of German envoys.[3] But she is quite aware of the standing
subjects of contention between the 'king' (whom she never
deigns to call Emperor) and the Papal see: first the Investiture
Contest,[4] then the German claim to appoint and dominate the
Pope.[5] Furthermore she gives a most spirited picture of the
subsequent battle between king and Pope (placed, as Du Cange
says, by 'all the German chroniclers' in 1080) when both armies
'played the man' and the whole plain 'was like a sea from the
blood of the slaughter'. The combatants waded in it and many
of the 30,000 who fell were smothered in this ghastly 'river of
gore'.[6] The fate of the day was decided by the death of
'Lantulph' (Rudolph), one of the two Saxon princes whom the
Pope had won to his side by crowning them 'kings of the whole
West'. The German monarch considered further fighting for
the time unnecessary, and when he afterwards wished to besiege
Rome he first tried to enlist the support of Robert Guiscard,
who however sent the envoys away without committing
himself.[7]

We next hear of King Henry just before the outbreak of
hostilities between Robert and Alexius. The latter sends him
a fulsome letter full of 'honeyed words, and all sorts of promises'
to ask his aid,[8] a letter which Anna lets us perceive was not

---

[1] She says that the battering-ram originated at Gades (XIII. 3, p. 382).
[2] XII. 9, p. 370. In XI. 12, p. 342, he announces his intention of enlisting
Germans together with Lombards and Latins and Franks, all 'men mindful of
Ares'.
[3] I. 13. See Oster, *A. K.* Pt. II, pp. 52 sqq., and p. 308, above.
[4] I. 13, p. 31. [The Pope] 'accused King Henry of not giving benefices gratis,
but selling them for gifts, and entrusting the episcopate to unworthy men'.
[5] *Ibid.*   [6] I. 13, p. 33.
[7] I. 13, pp. 33, 34.
[8] III. 10. Anna as it were apologizes for this by saying that her father was
'not remiss as to the people close to [Robert] behind his back' (p. 93), and that he
knew that 'above all others the king of Germany was able to do anything he wished
against Robert' (*ibid.*).

the first. As a specimen of diplomatic bombast this letter to the 'most Christian brother' of the Emperor is of considerable interest; but the humility of its tone is the really surprising part. Alexius praises Henry's piety, admits to feeling 'insecurity and unrest' from fear of Robert, and pleads for assistance almost on bended knees. He is sending money and purple stuffs now by a responsible envoy, and will send more money and many 'dignities' (ἀξιώματα) with their appropriate 'salary' (ῥόγα), presumably for the German nobles, if only the king will swear to an alliance with the Emperor. A German marriage with Alexius' heir presumptive, son of his brother Isaac, is almost timidly suggested, and the letter concludes with an enumeration of the various relics and other objects sent as 'pledges of friendship' (δεξιωμάτων ἕνεκεν), and with fervent invocations of blessings on the king, 'lover of God's true name'. This letter apparently proved abortive, for after his Durazzo defeat the Emperor writes again to Henry.[1] The text is not given, but we see that the proposed marriage has not been carried out, and that the German must be urged to attack Robert's Lombard possessions 'according to the existing compact'. This time Henry complies, and Robert hurries back to Italy to meet the new danger, joining his forces with those of the Pope. Before battle can be joined, the king learns how very serious and indeed crushing the defeat of his ally Alexius had really been, and 'departed to his native land, considering this (the best form of) victory, not to expose himself to dangers for no profit' Robert contents himself with plundering the German camp and sending a few of his men to pursue the retreating king, apparently in vain. And in this very unheroic fashion Henry passes out of Anna's pages; as regards Robert and the Pope the German sword[2] has proved to Alexius only a broken reed.

From Teutons we proceed to the Latin races of the West, those races between whom Anna hardly deigns to discriminate, and who are all in her eyes the 'barbarians'[3] *par excellence*. She

---

[1] V. 3.

[2] The Nemitzi who garrison Constantinople in II. 9 and 10 are Germans according to Du Cange, though Ordericus Vitalis (Pt. III, Lib. 7, ch. 4, *P. L.* 188, col. 519) says their leader was Raimundus Flandrensis. They change sides with cynical indifference.

[3] Bury (*Hellenistic Age*, pp. 25 sqq.) says that this contemptuous attitude towards 'barbarians' arose in Greece as a dogma after the Persian Wars; up to that time βάρβαρος had merely meant 'non-Greek', in no depreciatory sense. The Stoics and Christianity, especially as set forth by St. Paul, combated racial intolerance with more or less success. But it remained very prevalent in the Byzantine Empire and men justified their exclusivist tendencies from the Old Testament. We have mentioned the fact that Archbishop Eustathius of Thessalonica thought it necessary to state that God made Barbarians as well as Greeks, and hears their prayers no less

calls them indifferently Latins, Franks, or Celts,[1] thereby denoting any one from the other side of the Adriatic, and predicates for them all a number of most unpleasant vices. They are so 'greedy for gain' (ἐρασιχρήματοι) that they will 'sell for an obol even what they hold most dear',[2] including their wives and children.[3] They are 'unstable and easily led', and their thirst for money makes them 'lightly upset their contracts for any cause that occurs'.[4] Or again: 'Such is the race of Celts, changeable and in a swift turning-point of time carried in opposite directions, and you may see the same man sometimes boasting that he will upset the whole earth, sometimes cringing and brought down to the very dust, especially when he falls in with stronger minds.'[5] Franks will change sides in the middle of a battle, and no man can rely on them as allies.[6] Insolence (ὕβρις), a peculiarly barbarian trait that marked the Latins and especially the Crusaders as a whole,[7] is strikingly displayed by the Celt Urselius,[8] by Italus, chief of the philosophers,[9] and above all by Pope Gregory VII.[10] Tancred makes extravagant boasts 'after the manner of his race',[11] who are 'naturally loqua-

(*P. G.* 135, col. 708). Zonaras (pref., 1) says some writers spoil their histories by dialect or 'barbarous' words. Nicetas Acominatus, after describing the capture of Constantinople by the Latins in 1204, lays down his pen, for 'History, most glorious creation of the Hellenes', must not be called on to chronicle 'the deeds of barbarians' (*Alex. Duc. Murz.* 6, p. 373). Attaliates (p. 107) describes Franks generally as 'rejoicing in blood and murder'.

[1] It is chiefly about the Crusaders that she is so contemptuously indeterminate. She uses 'Sicilian' quite accurately (V. 8, p. 143) for the people of the 'island lying near Italy', and 'Italians' and 'Lombards' all belong to the Peninsula. In one place (XI. 12, p. 342) she strings together as separate peoples Lombards and Latins and Germans and Franks, but as it is a rhetorical passage we need not assume that she distinguished between all four; certainly in other places she does not.

[2] VI. 6, p. 163; 7, p. 165; X. 5, p. 283; 6, p. 286 (*bis*); XI. 3, p. 316; XIV. 2, pp. 424, 428.

[3] XI. 2, p. 312. As we have seen, the giving and taking of bribes was by no means confined to the Latin races. Greeks from the days of Thucydides had been constantly addicted thereto.

[4] X. 5, p. 283; XIV. 2, p. 423. So the Pope and Robert break their oaths like true 'barbarians' (I. 13, p. 32). [5] XIII. 10, p. 402.

[6] I. 6, p. 14; XI. 6, p. 325. Untrustworthiness is one of Anna's favourite accusations against 'Latins', e.g. XIV. 2, p. 428.

[7] X. 10, p. 300; XIV. 2, p. 423. Hugh even calls himself βασιλεὺς τῶν βασιλέων (X. 7).

[8] We may compare the ὕβρις καὶ πλεονεξία which Polybius attributes to foreign troops (*Hist.* I. 81. 10, 11). In *Al.* 1, p. 3, the word is not used but the sense is there.

[9] V. 8 and 9. He is accused of 'barbaric folly', making him despise all teachers and even the great Michael Psellus. He bullied and struck his dialectical opponents and could not be a good teacher because of his temper. In his arguing ὕβρις ξυνεπόδιζεν ὕβριν, 'violence followed on violence'. We are twice told of his 'uneducated and barbaric character'. [10] I. 13, p. 31 (three times).

[11] X. 9, p. 294; XIV. 2, p. 423, and 4 *passim*. Cf. Robert's boasts V. 1, p. 126.

cious and verbose'. With this goes the haughty conceit that
never owns to a fault, and the overweening ambition that is
never satisfied[1] and stops at nothing,[2] though Anna admits that
Latins are brave and daring,[3] especially on horseback.[4]

On three occasions Anna gives her candid opinion on the
matter. 'The race of the Celts, as far as one may judge, is
always very hot and quick, but when it has embarked on an
enterprise, it is unrestrainable.'[5] And again: 'All the barbarian
race' (here referring to the Norman Bohemund in particular)
'is impossible to hold back from the enterprise on which it has
started, and nothing, however burdensome, will it not bear,
when once it has launched itself on voluntary hardships.'[6]
Finally, when the Crusaders think of leaving Antioch to its
fate, we read:

'Not only in other respects is the race of Celts headstrong and
imprudent, but as to strategic order and science it has never used
them at all. Rather when war and battle are at hand their courage
shouts aloud and they know no restraint (and this is true not only
of the common soldiers but of the leaders too), rushing irresistible
into the midst of the enemy's phalanxes, if their opponents yield
entirely. But if as often happens the enemy set their forces with
military skill and cleverly follow after them, all their boldness is
turned into its opposite; for to tell the whole truth the Celts at
their first onslaught are invincible, but after this they are very
easy to overcome, both because of the weight of their arms, and
from the passionateness and heedlessness of their disposition.'[7]

Many of these accusations are reiterated in Anna's descriptions of individual men. But enough has been said to show
that, however much her father might appreciate 'Celts' as mercenaries and dread them as opponents, to his daughter they
were always the lesser breeds without the law. Whenever she
brings in some of their national peculiarities, whether it is their
act of homage 'holding out their right hands, as is their ancestral
manner of pledging their troth',[8] or the way they grow their
hair,[9] or their custom of ordeal by single combat,[10] or 'the art

---

[1] X. 6, p. 287; 10, p. 300; XI. 7, p. 328; 12, p. 341; XIV. 4, p. 434.
[2] XIV. 7, p. 445.   [3] IV. 6, p. 116; VI. 1, p. 154; 14, p. 184.
[4] V. 6, p. 140; X. 3, p. 277; XI. 6, p. 325; XIII. 8, p. 398. So Callicles
(Poem XXXII. 1, 5) speaks of κόμπος ἐξ ἱππασμάτων in connexion with a dead
Norman prince, a 'trophy-winning horseman'.
[5] X. 5, p. 286: cf. XI. 2, p. 314, ἀφορμή='enterprise', is a favourite unclassical
expression of Anna's, and ἀκάθεκτος='unrestrainable' is applied by her to the ὁρμή
of various foes (IV. 4, p. 108; VIII. 3, p. 226; XI. 9, p. 333).
[6] XI. 12, p. 341.   [7] XI. 6, p. 325.   [8] I. 6, p. 14.
[9] VI. 7, p. 165. Robert grew a beard for a vow, 'being ever anxious to keep the
customs of his own race'. Contrast Bohemund, XIII. 10, p. 404.
[10] V. 5, p. 137.

of war as it is among the Italians',[1] or the practice of challenging all comers, so vividly described by the 'pure Frank, one of the nobility', who has just insulted the Emperor to his face,[2] or their habit of calling their enemies opprobrious names,[3] we cannot fail to detect the ring of contempt. Manuel Comnenus as we know aspired to be a knight like those of Western chivalry, but in the days of Alexius such a wish would have seemed utter madness, 'barbaric folly' indeed.

When we consider the various 'Latin' races separately, we find that of Italians Anna has little to say whether in blame or praise. The remains of George Maniaces' 'Italian' army serve first the rebel Bryennius and then Alexius.[4] The 'Italians' who are called in 'to alliance' by the Sicilians when 'revolting against the rule of the Greeks'[5] were doubtless some of the Southern Italians who had made themselves independent.[6] But the whole story as told by Anna differs curiously from that in Cedrenus[7] and Zonaras.[8] They represent Maniaces as sent from Constantinople to assist one of two warring Saracen brothers who are ruling Sicily in 1031. Before he reaches the island the brothers have made peace and called in help from Africa against the Greeks. But Maniaces defeats 50,000 'Carthaginians', takes thirteen Sicilian cities, and 'gradually advancing reduced the whole island'. Another African army comes and is defeated, but its leader is allowed to escape, and Maniaces' anger against the careless Greek admiral causes the latter to intrigue for and obtain the disgrace of his commander-in-chief. On the ground of intended 'rebellion' ($\dot{\alpha}\pi o\sigma\tau\alpha\sigma\dot{\iota}\alpha$) Maniaces is summoned back to the capital and imprisoned. This is apparently in the opinion of the two historians Maniaces' only visit to Sicily, for when he is restored to favour by the Empress Zoe, and sent back to his post in 1042 to try and

---

[1] V. 8, p. 143.   [2] X. 10, and XI. 3, p. 317. Cf. Scott's *Count Robert of Paris*.
[3] XII. 8, p. 367.

[4] I. 5, p. 11; VII. 9, p. 210. As a matter of fact it is not accurate to call these soldiers 'Italians' or 'Latins' at all. Cedrenus (p. 756 D) plainly shows that these 'troops in Italy' were Greeks, and as such anxious to go with Maniaces across the Adriatic, 'thirsting to see their own homes'. In any case, as the career of Maniaces ended with his death in 1043, and the two campaigns alluded to in the text were in 1078 and 1090 respectively, it is clear that the name of the general must have clung to the contingent long after the men who actually fought under him were dead.   [5] V. 8, p. 143.

[6] Cedrenus (p. 756 C) speaks of 'Italy around Capua and Beneventum and Naples', as if the separateness and independence of these three towns was an accepted fact even in 1042. In XIII. 4, p. 387, Anna alludes to Μαϊστρομίλιοι at Naples as if these were a family, but Du Cange (note *ad loc.*) explains them as the imperial Magistri Militum, who had shaken off the yoke of the Empire.

[7] pp. 740–4, 755 B–757 C.
[8] *Epit.* XVII. 15 and 22.

regain for the Empire its old territories, it is in Italy only that we hear of him from them, and it is in Italy that, incensed by news from home, he has himself proclaimed Emperor, supported by 'many of the army as a warlike man'. Now in all this there is no hint of any enemies in Sicily for the Greeks except Arabs, whether local or imported from Carthage. When Maniaces fought, he 'pitched his camp against the Hagarenes'; when he was disgraced, 'the island not long after passed to the Hagarenes, only Messina . . . remaining to the Greeks'. It is true that Cedrenus represents Maniaces as building citadels in all the captured Sicilian towns and putting in 'sufficient guards so that the natives (οἱ ἐγχώριοι) should not be able to get back the cities by craft'; also that after his recall 'the natives having summoned forces from the Carthaginians attacked the cities and destroyed the citadels, overpowering the guards, and recovered all the cities except Messina'. But as Sicily had been in Saracen hands long before the taking of the last fortress in 965,[1] we should not naturally take 'natives' for true Greeks. Anna[2] puts the matter thus: 'The Sicilians, when they revolted from the rule of the Greeks and turned to wars and battles against them, summoned the Italians to an alliance . . . but when, while Monomachus was wielding the sceptre of the Empire of the Greeks, the famous[3] George Maniaces seizes Sicily as a usurper' (τυραννήσας τὴν Σικελίαν κάτεσχε), some of the Italians who had originally come to help the Sicilians escaped home. The first sentence distinctly ascribes the war of 1038–40, not to an attempt by the Greeks to regain Sicily from the Saracens, but to a revolt of the Sicilians against a 'Greek rule' that for seventy years had entirely ceased to exist. The second sentence represents Maniaces at the time of his usurpation as having 'seized' Sicily as well as Italy. As to the second point Anna is probably right; any attempt to confute her from the other two writers resolves itself into an argument from silence.[4] But as to the

---

[1] Tout (*Empire and Papacy*, p. 103) describes Sicily as 'entirely Saracen since the capture of Syracuse' (877 or 878).

[2] V. 8, p. 143.

[3] Except for calling him ἐκεῖνος Anna pays no tribute to the brilliant career of Maniaces first in the East and then in Sicily (Cedrenus, pp. 727, 741–4).

[4] The same silence as to any visit of Maniaces to Sicily in 1043 is to be seen in Lup. Protosp. (Muratori, *op. cit.* Vol. V, p. 43), and also in *Anon. Barensis Chron.* (*ibid.* p. 151), who says 'Maniaki se fecit Imp. in Italia' (1042 Ind. 10) and speaks of him at 'Odronto' in the following year. So Psellus (*Chron.*, Const. IX, Byz. T., p. 124) confines Maniaces' action to τὸ πρὸς ἡμᾶς τμῆμα of Italy only. But again such silence is not conclusive, and still less need we trust the highly coloured picture of 'Maniacus' (as a monster of cruelty to young and old and even to monks) in Gul. Apul., *de Normannis*, Bk. I, concluding lines. Here Tarentum is the scene of Maniaces' assuming the purple.

first point (though the matter presents great difficulties), she receives support from an unexpected quarter. Gaufredus Malaterra,[1] in describing how Maniaces (in 1038) conquered Sicily, says that there were in Messina 'strenuissimi suae' (i.e. Greek) 'gentis milites' who made a sortie and attacked him. They were defeated by his allies, the chronicler's admired Normans, and Maniaces marched through the island 'omnia subjugando'. At Syracuse his attack was resisted by 'Arcadius quidam qui urbi principabatur' (obviously another Greek), and he finally fought a battle against 60,000 'Siculi'. If we put these statements alongside of Anna's, it would seem that the men of Greek blood in Sicily, oppressed by Saracens as one might have supposed them to be, were far from well disposed to the Empire. If Maniaces came ostensibly to free them from the Saracen yoke, they would appear to have turned against their liberators and to have summoned Italian aid rather than obey Byzantium as of old.

Later on we have τὰ τῶν Ἰταλῶν,[2] meaning first 'the people of the Italians', then in the next sentence 'the ways of the Italians'.[3] Italians are also correctly said to occupy the coast of the Adriatic opposite to Illyria.[4] Only one other time are they introduced in a body, when Bohemund uses the Scythians captured from the imperial army as exhibits to stir up 'the Italians round the Pope'.[5] As to individual Italians we hear little. We have fully dealt with Italus in another connexion, and also with the Pope and his subordinate clergy, secular and regular.

Turning to the various Italian towns, we find Brindisi figuring as an important port,[6] together with Bari[7] and Otranto.[8]

---

[1] *Historia Sicula*, I. 7, 8 (Muratori, *op. cit.* Vol. V, p. 551).

[2] She never calls Italy affectedly 'the land of the Ausones' as does *Anon. Syn. Chron.* p. 178. 'Lord of the Ausones' is a title given by Callicles to the Emperor. (Poems XII, XXIV, and XXXII.)

[3] V. 8, p. 145. In the first sentence we read that under Michael Ducas VII, 'the peoples of the Latins' [here meaning 'Normans'] 'and of the Italians were struggling against the Greeks, and the occupation of all Lombardy' [described in V. 8, p. 144, as ἔτι ὑπὸ Ῥωμαίους τελοῦσα] 'and Italy was contemplated'. This occupation actually occurred when Bari, the last Greek town in Italy, was taken by the Normans in 1071, the very year of Michael's accession. In the second sentence Italus is sent to Durazzo on a diplomatic errand 'as understanding the ways' [or possibly 'the language'] 'of the Italians'. But he 'was detected betraying our interests', an act of perfidy which is soon forgiven with the strange and uncertain clemency of those times.

[4] XII. 9, p. 370. [5] XII. 8, p. 367.

[6] I. 15, p. 35, ἐπίνειον τῆς ὅλης Ἰαπυγίας εὐλιμενώτατον. Robert sails from there I. 16, p. 37; III. 12, p. 97.

[7] Hugh and Bohemund sail from here X. 7, p. 288; XII. 9, p. 369.

[8] I. 14, p. 34; 16, p. 37, &c. Robert's second crossing is made from there (VI. 5, p. 159). It is vainly besieged by Contostephanus (XII. 8).

Salerno comes in as Robert's capital,[1] and Melpha is the district round it.[2] Pisa and Genoa like Venice had fleets and might be useful allies or dangerous enemies. Rome is frequently mentioned, almost always in connexion with the Pope; pilgrims land at Cotrone (Croton) from the Eastern Empire to go thither, while Beneventum is a half-way house between Rome and Salerno, between the Pope and Robert.[3] Robert is buried[4] in a monastery at Venosa.

So far we have not found much of interest in Anna's statements about Italy as distinct from Sicily. Probably her only first-hand knowledge came from the envoy of the Bishop of Bari,[5] and he flourished nearly forty years before she actually wrote her history. In any case, except as the starting-point of Robert and Bohemund Italy did not much concern her. It is however necessary to say a few words on her use of the terms Lombardy, Apulia,[6] and Venetia, as thereby hangs a tale of Byzantine pride and its fall. The word Lombardy needs explanation, and we must start by reminding ourselves that the kingdom of Lombardy and the theme of Lombardy were in two quite distinct parts of Italy. Du Cange[7] has pointed out that in a charter of Charlemagne Lombardy is said to be another name for the whole of Italy, but that in Constantine Porphyrogenitus, *De Themat.* it means the theme of Longobardia as it existed in the middle of the tenth century, made up of Calabria and Apulia. Certainly its modern use as equivalent to the Po valley would have been unintelligible to Anna, though historically that is not without foundation, as Pavia was the capital of the old Lombard kingdom which reached from the Alps to Terracina. This kingdom existed from 568 till 774, when Desiderius was deposed by his son-in-law Charlemagne. During these two centuries the Byzantine Empire kept at least a partial

---

[1] I. 12, 13, 14, 15; V. 3, pp. 132, 133; VI. 5, p. 158.

[2] I. 12, p. 30. Du Cange says that Anna uses the wrong word here and means Amalfi, which is certainly much nearer Salerno than Melfi is. This view is supported by the fact that in V. 1, p. 125, we read of settlers ἀπὸ Μέλφης καὶ Βενετίας in Durazzo, and in VI. 6, p. 163, the foreigners are called Ἀμαλφηνοὶ καὶ Βενέτικοι, looking as if Anna confused the two towns. See p. 402, note 3, above.

[3] I. 12, p. 29: 13, p. 32. For 'mercenaries from Rome' see VIII. 5, p. 230. Once we read of marbles 'brought by previous Emperors from Rome' to Constantinople (VII. 2, p. 190).

[4] VI. 6, p. 163.

[5] III. 12, p. 99.

[6] Of any distinction between Northern and Southern Italians such as the *Anon. Gesta Francorum* (ch. 2) makes by using the terms 'Lombardi et Longobardi' there is no trace in Anna: she only has the one word Λογγιβαρδία throughout, and the adjective Λογγίβαρδος, only used twice, in XI. 12, p. 342; XV. 7, p. 485.

[7] Note on I. 11, p. 24 C. The statement of Fuchs (*op. cit.* p. 34), based on Tzetzes, *Chil.* VI. 683, that 'Longobardenland' = 'Norditalien' is, as appears from the last note, untrue of the *Alexias* at least.

hold on what was later called the Lombard Theme, and when Frankish or Italian kings, or after 961 German emperors, were ruling the North as delimited above, the South was comparatively unaffected by all the changes of dynasty.[1] The great danger to Calabria and Apulia in the early ninth century was from the Saracens who overran those parts with seemingly irresistible force. But by 890 we find the Greeks once more in possession of the all-important town of Bari, and ruling the theme of Lombardy by a Catapan.[2] The Saracen peril was over, but the colonies (if we may use the word) of men truly Lombard by race, left over in Apulia from the days when these Northern invaders had poured Southwards along the Apennines, were not only troublesome neighbours to the Byzantines, but indirectly the cause of their ruin. In 1017 during a border war these Lombards called Norman adventurers to their aid, and this was the beginning of the end for the theme, Lombard in name but Greek in citizenship. The Normans settled in Southern Italy. Robert Guiscard was invested in 1059 by Pope Nicolas II with the dukedom of Calabria and Apulia (or, as Anna puts it, 'having ascended to the ducal eminence he was named Duke of all Lombardy') to be held as a fief of the Holy See,[3] and in 1071 Bari, the last Byzantine possession on the Western side of the Adriatic, was lost to the Empire. If Robert did, as Anna alleges, offer to Alexius before the Battle of Durazzo that on certain conditions he would 'reckon Lombardy itself as belonging to the Emperor',[4] the conditions were 'wholly impossible

[1] L. Gay, in his *L'Italie méridionale et l'Empire Byzantin*, gives a more detailed account. He says that in 774 Italy was divided into three states. 'Italie franque, Italie pontificale, Italie lombarde', with the Byzantine territories only 'morceaux épars' among the Lombards and in the next century cut off from connexion with Constantinople by the Saracen command of the sea, pp. 3, 4. He then spends seventeen chapters in telling how Basil I (867–86), first as the ally then as the enemy of the Frankish Emperor Louis II, began to restore the sway of Byzantium in South Italy, and his successors went on with the work in the teeth of Saracen, Lombard, German, and Papal opposition. 'Dans les dernières années de Basile II, entre 1020 et 1025 la puissance byzantine est à son apogée.' Its rapid and final decline was due to the Normans, pp. 431 sqq. Chalandon (*Hist. de la domination normande*) points out that when the eleventh century opened Calabria was still Greek in language, law, and Church ritual, and that under Basil II the Lombardized Apulia was won back for the Empire. Even after the Normans came Byzantine influence did not disappear. Robert Guiscard allowed the Greek administrative organization (official names, &c.) to survive in Calabria and Apulia, and the former province long kept its Greek language and the Greek rite performed by Greek clergy.

[2] From κατεπάνω, used by Anna with τῶν ἀξιωμάτων in III. 10, p. 94.

[3] I. 12, p. 27. In June 1080 Gregory VII was driven by necessity to confirm this donation, and according to Anna added regal dignity to Robert's titles (I. 13, p. 32), 'though before this he [the Pope] had not been friendly towards him'. In 1081 Herman, a step-nephew of Robert's, is 'prefect' (ἀρχηγός) of Lombardy, and not only separate from but hostile to Robert (Du Cange on III. 10, p. 93 A), but this implies no connexion with Byzantium.   [4] IV. 6, p. 113.

and injurious to the rule of the Greeks', and in any case Robert's
decisive victory made the whole bargain fall to the ground.
Longobardia had for ever ceased to be a Greek province,[1] and
when Anna uses the term she refers neither to the old Lombard
kingdom nor to the theme of later days, but somewhat vaguely
to the territory of the hated Norman, with Salerno (captured by
him in the past) as the seat of his 'ducal rank'.[2] Yet con-
servatism is so strong in her that when Robert parades the
pseudo-Michael through the towns of Southern Iraly, Anna talks
of his stirring them up 'to revolt'[3] (πρὸς ἀποστασίαν) just as
though their tie with Byzantium had not been already finally
severed. This however is purely rhetorical imperialism; when
she comes to details she accepts facts as they are. Calabria she
never mentions, and Apulia is used by itself or with Lombardy
to describe Robert's realm. He ruthlessly impresses recruits of
all ages and exacts hostages 'from Lombardy and Apulia', he
appoints his son Roger 'archon of all Apulia' in his absence;
by his audacity he had become master of 'all the towns and
lands of Lombardy, besides Apulia itself'; to Apulia his dead
body is carried back.[4] Nowhere does Anna advance the smallest
claim to this province as even theoretically part of the Empire.

Still more remarkable is the way she talks of Venice. Venice
had been virtually independent for nearly three centuries, and
Anna does not attempt to deny it. If the agreement of 810
between Charlemagne and Nicephorus I had left the Venetians
technically vassals to the Eastern Empire,[5] this theory as years
went on had less and less relation to fact. Certainly in 1081
their ostensible lord Alexius had to buy Venetian support at
sea by 'offers and gifts', reward with 'a thousand benefits' the
messengers who brought news of victory, and send 'sufficient
sums to the Duke of Venice and those ruling under him'.[6] The

[1] When in V. 8, p. 144, Anna says that in the days of Maniaces (1042–3) Lombardy 'was still reckoned under the Greeks', she clearly implies that it afterwards
ceased to be so.
[2] V. 3, p. 132. The previous Lombard prince of Salerno, Mascabeles (the
Gaimarus of Latin chroniclers), had evidently paid no allegiance to the Empire
(I. 11, p. 24).   [3] I. 15, p. 37.
[4] I. 14, p. 34 ; 16, pp. 37, 38 ; IV. 1, pp. 103, 104 ; VI. 6, p. 162. In III. 12, p. 99,
she correctly says that Pyrrhus fought the Romans there, and in XII. 9, p. 370,
she mentions 'the land of the Apulians' as being on the opposite coast of the
Adriatic from Dalmatia.
[5] It seems probable that they were actually and not only formally dependent
till 840, when they made their first contract on their own account with other
Italian cities under the auspices of Lothar. They had learnt through the weakness
of the Eastern Empire that they must fight Slavonic and Saracen pirates alone, and
when the Emperors grew stronger in the tenth century it was too late to reimpose
their authority.
[6] IV. 2, pp. 105–7. The 'Duke' at this moment was Domenico Selvo, who had

Venetians make their terms with the Emperor 'through envoys' as between equals, and Alexius responds with a golden bull. On their second appearance as indispensable allies at sea, this curious state of relations is even more marked. Alexius promises Venice 'a manifold reward', her sailors feel themselves bound by 'covenants' with him, acting not as obedient subjects but as trusty allies,[1] and in the end his munificence to them is lavish. Gifts and honours are showered on them; the Doge has the rank and income of Protosebastos, the Patriarch those of 'Most Honourable'. Various Venetian churches get yearly grants of gold, and to St. Mark are assigned rich revenues from real property in Constantinople. This was royal bounty indeed for service rendered. But however great the naval skill of the Venetians may have been,[2] the reward seems excessive, and disaster subsequently fell upon the Empire from its gift to another state of the absolute right of free and untaxed trading. This was the fortunate lot of Venice 'in all the lands under the authority of the Greeks'. As Anna expresses it, her citizens were 'outside all Greek authority',[3] and the Empire lived to rue the day. For over a century the Jeshurun of the Adriatic waxed fat, and finally kicked against its benefactress in the treachery of 1204.

FOREIGN AFFAIRS

67. THE WEST. THE NORMANS AND GUISCARD

AT last we come to the Normans, who first in the harassing Illyrian campaign and then in the Crusade loom so large in Anna's eyes that she seems to see a Norman[4] in every

married a sister of Michael VII. He was probably specially interested in exposing the pseudo-Michael. Anna characteristically seizes the occasion of this first mention of Venice to bring in a bit of archaeological learning—that to Venetian invention was due the 'blue' colour in the horse races at Constantinople (IV. 2, p. 105 B, and see Du Cange's note).

[1] VI. 5, pp. 160, 161.

[2] Anna praises this skill in them (IV. 2, and VI. 5), as dispassionately as (later on) in the 'barbarian' Pisan fleet (XI. 10, p. 336).

[3] VI. 5, p. 162.

[4] She uses 'Normandy' (and 'Norman') with some accuracy as the birthplace of Robert (I. 10, p. 23; 11, p. 24), and famed for horsemanship (X. 3, p. 277). But the 'Νορμάνοι' who behaved so ill under Peter the Hermit (X. 6) were probably Germans ('Alamanni', Anon. Gesta Francorum, ch. 2), and the Νορμάνων φοσσάτον led by two chiefs from Flanders, which Anna says arrived in Constantinople after the death of Godfrey at Jerusalem, is pronounced by Du Cange (note on XI. 8, p. 330 D) to have really consisted of Lombards, with some German and French

Westerner. Peter the Hermit and Godfrey de Bouillon, Hugh of Vermandois and Raoul and Baldwin, they are all to Anna 'barbarians' of the same evil breed.[1] If Raymond of St. Gilles stands out from the rest, it is not as a Provençal, for she would not have known the difference, but as the one man of them who made himself acceptable to her father.

The keynote is struck in the very first chapter. Urselius the Celt, known to us through other writers as Roussel de Bailleul, having 'swelled out into great fortune', becomes a 'grievous rebel, most tyrannous in soul', and ravages 'almost all the lands of the East'. He shows himself 'pre-eminent' even over men of great military experience, he swoops down 'like a hurricane' or 'in the manner of a thunderbolt', and is 'irresistible in his attacks'. All these qualities, which of course only enhance those of his victorious opponent, reappear again and again in Anna's pages when she talks of some notorious 'Frank'.

Urselius is soon conquered, but Alexius' next Norman foe, Robert Guiscard, dominates the scene from the middle of Book I to the middle of Book VI.[2] So important is he that his personality is twice fully described,[3] to say nothing of judgements on him incidentally introduced.[4] He first appears as 'an irresistible evil and incurable disease' brought on the Empire by fate, or 'to speak more piously' by the permission of Providence. He is 'that braggart Robert famed for his tyrannical soul, whom Normandy produced but whom evil (φαυλότης) of every form nurtured and fostered'. Yet Anna is fair-minded enough to put down his invasion of the Empire not only to his own coveting of its sceptre but largely also to the folly of Michael VII in affiancing his son to Robert's daughter, in that 'foreign and barbarous marriage contract'[5] which gave the Norman an excuse for interfering in Byzantine affairs. 'Now

counts added. If the leaders were counts of Flanders at all, they must have been brothers of the Robert Count of Flanders who having been to Jerusalem before the First Crusade (VII. 6, p. 201) had promised and duly sent 500 horsemen to the Emperor's aid (VII. 7, p. 205; VIII. 3, p. 227). For the question of Alexius' letter to Count Robert see p. 457, note 1, below.

[1] Wm. Miller, in his article on Anna Comnena (*Quarterly Rev.*, January 1920), points out that Anna's birth occurred 'at an interesting moment in the history not only of the Greek Empire but of Christendom . . . the time when [or rather two years after the time when] the Medieval West and the Medieval East first met; when the Normans . . . first crossed the Adriatic and Ionian seas to attack the Greek Empire'.

[2] Only Book II, dealing with Alexius' accession, has no mention of Robert.

[3] I. 10, p. 24; VI. 7, p. 165.

[4] IV. 8, p. 121; V. 1, p. 126.

[5] I. 10, p. 23. As other foreign betrothals were not at all uncommon, this passage shows that Anna resented the idea of this particular one partly because of its fatal consequences, but partly from personal jealousy. See p. 12, above.

this Robert was Norman by race, obscure in rank,[1] tyrannical in mind, very crafty (πανουργότατος)[2] in soul, noble in fight, most formidable in attacking the wealth and abundance of great men, unfailing in achievement, turning the objects of his aim into inevitable facts. And in body he was so tall as to surpass the tallest, ruddy in complexion with tawny hair, broad shoulders, and eyes which almost emitted sparks.'[3] Above all he was 'well proportioned from the top of his head to his feet', and his shout like that of a Homeric hero 'would put many myriads to flight'.[4] Anna winds up this description, full as it is of admiration virtually wrung from her, by saying: 'He was of course a slave to no man, subject to none of all the world; for such are great natures, men say, even if they are of humble rank.'

Then follows a description reminding us of David in the Cave of Adullam or Robin Hood in Sherwood Forest. 'Coming from Normandy with a few horsemen (there were five horsemen and thirty footmen in all) he departed from his native land and spent his time in the ridges and caves and hills of Lombardy, ruling a robber-band and attacking wayfarers, sometimes taking their horses, sometimes also other articles, and weapons.' But worse is to follow. 'In his case the prelude to livelihood was bloodshedding and many murders,' and we have the grim story first of Robert's treachery and savage cruelty to his rich father-in-law Mascabeles, otherwise Gaimarus of Salerno, whose teeth and eyes he knocks out,[5] then of his growing ambitions for Empire and his belief, real or pretended, (for like Odysseus he is 'a man of many wiles') in the cause of the pseudo-Michael. His wife Gaita, subsequently the Amazon of the Durazzo battle, here surprisingly appears as restraining him from war 'against Christians',[6] but he gets round her objections and those of his counts, and proceeds on his lawless path, aided by well-chosen alliances of his own and by the fortuitous quarrel between the German king and the Pope which made the latter glad to enlist Norman support.[7] In his contract with Gregory Anna repre-

---

[1] I. 10, p. 23; IV. 1, p. 104. This same point is insisted on about Bohemund (X. 11, pp. 301, 303).

[2] Zonaras calls him ἀνὴρ πανοῦργος καὶ πολεμικώτατος (XVIII. 22).

[3] I. 10, p. 24. There is a lacuna here, where we should expect to find the colour of the eyes.

[4] Robert boasts that by this ἐμβόημα he could 'all but shake the earth, and confound whole phalanxes' (V. 1, p. 126).

[5] I. 11. The wealth of details in these early stories seems disproportionately great. However, it all serves to show that from the beginning Robert was τὰ πάντα δεινός, πολυτροπώτατος, κακουργότατος and ῥᾳδιουργότατος (I. 11, pp. 25, 26; 12, p. 29). The treachery to Mascabeles seems to be alluded to in Cec. Strat. pp. 34–5.

[6] I. 12, p. 29; 15, p. 35; IV. 6, p. 116.   [7] I. 12 and 13.

sents Robert as utterly false and perjured:[1] when he comes back later from his triumphant Illyrian campaign and keeps his word in helping the Pope, it is simply because his own Lombardy is threatened.[2] Even in collecting troops, hostages and 'tribute' his barbarity is unparalleled, worse than Herod's,[3] though Anna grudgingly admits the 'daring and force and bravery and untameable spirit', common to him and that 'on-rushing thunderbolt' Bohemund. Indeed the son and father together are 'pungent smoke preceding a fire', only to be compared to the insect-pests of the Prophet Joel.

Nothing stops Robert, not even the news from Constantinople that Alexius has succeeded Botaniates on the throne and that the deposed Michael is alive and well, so that all cause for a war based on the late Emperor's supposed injuries to the house of Ducas and the Norman bride is at an end. Robert merely threatens the news-bearer with death and supports the pseudo-Michael with greater ardour than ever, though Anna would have us know that in this too he was treacherous and double-faced.[4] At last he sails with a large host from Brindisi to Corfu and, except for sinister intrigues with Monomachatus the Governor of Durazzo,[5] we hear nothing further of him till the middle of Book III, when Alexius has been already a few months on the throne.[6] Learning of the danger at hand, the Emperor makes his mother Regent, collects troops and invites allies from all parts to encounter the foe, and does his best by diplomacy to get rid of the treacherous Monomachatus and hinder the inhabitants of the Illyrian coasts from joining Robert and swelling his army.[7] The greatness of the peril shines out in Alexius' imploring letter to the German king,[8] and in his coming to terms with the Turks as the lesser enemy, so as not to 'fight against two'.[9] Then follows the fine description of Robert's crossing and the great storm which met him after leaving Corfu, 'as though God were wrath against Robert's unrestrained overweening insolence'.[10] However, while the fleet

[1] I. 13, pp. 32, 33. He does, however, order his son Roger to give aid to the Papal See if required (I. 14, p. 34).
[2] V. 3.   [3] I. 14.   [4] I. 15; III. 9, p. 91.
[5] I. 16.   [6] III. 6, p. 83; 9, p. 91.
[7] III. 9, 10. He fears 'the generals and counts hurrying to join' (Robert).
[8] III. 10. Robert is 'that murderer, that guilty one, enemy of God and of Christians', who is causing the Empire 'insecurity and unrest in no small degree'. He is ἀδικώτατος and God will punish him. Curiously enough, though she brings into the letter one of Robert's nephews Bagelard, and represents Alexius as trying to win over Bagelard's half-brother 'Herman, prefect of Lombardy,' she loses the golden opportunity of telling us how cruelly Robert had dispossessed both these princes of their rightful lands (Du Cange's notes on III. 10, pp. 93 A and 94 A).
[9] III. 11.   [10] III. 12; IV. 2, p. 105.

is wrecked Robert himself gets safe to land 'undismayed and confident, methinks, that his life would last long enough for him to compass fighting against whom he would'. With a certain inconsistency Anna ascribes the preservation of some of his followers partly to the time of year when the crops were ripe and saved them from starvation, but chiefly to 'the almighty power of God' whose great enemy Robert was.[1] At any rate he lands, collects a large army and besieges Durazzo, and like Milton's Satan he is in truth the hero of Book IV, far more than is the new governor George Palaeologus, Anna's admired uncle, or even the Emperor himself. Robert covets the Empire;[2] 'from extreme poverty and obscure rank, he had through energy of nature and pride of spirit' become lord of Lombardy and Apulia, and then come 'into the desire of more, as is apt to happen to insatiable souls'.[3]

In the battle of Durazzo he shows himself 'very high souled, a great lover of danger', though in Anna's eyes his 'bitterness', his 'wrath', his 'passion' and his 'anger' overcloud even his gallant readiness to kill or be killed in every fight.[4] Yet when one of his soldiers indignantly disclaims a charge of cowardice, Robert listens to reason and forgoes his wrath,[5] so that we understand the devotion with which he was evidently served.[6]

The surrender of Durazzo by its foreign inhabitants speedily follows, and Anna allows us once more to see the human side of Robert in his care for his wounded. It is perhaps this which elicits from her a comparison between Robert and her father.[7] 'They were both of them adepts at foreseeing and comprehending everything, and were ignorant of none of the arts of war, but were accustomed to all sieges, all ambuscades and fights in battle array. In enterprises of force they were active and noble, and were hated by all the captains under heaven, a match for each other in wisdom and manliness'. After this Robert withdraws his formidable activities to defend his own

---

[1] III. 12, p. 99.   [2] IV. 1, p. 103. It is no mere raid he is making.
[3] IV. 1, pp. 104, 105.   [4] IV. 8, p. 121.   [5] IV. 8, p. 122.
[6] So of his followers in I. 11 and IV. 6, and his 'weeping son' in VI. 6, p. 162. We note however that one of his soldiers betrays his plans to the Emperor and his son Guy intrigues with Alexius (I. 15, p. 36; VI. 5, p. 159). Callicles' Poem XXXII tells us of a knight born in France, who after fighting in Illyria against the Emperor Alexius had been won over by him and made Sebastos. The heading is 'To the tomb of Roger the Sebastos', but one is tempted to substitute 'Guy', first because of the latter's intrigues mentioned by Anna, revolving round an 'unusual honour' and a 'marriage contract' (cf. line 35 of the Poem, where the dead man says: καὶ κῆδος ἔσχον ἐκ μεταρσίου γένους), secondly because the Chanson d'Antioche as Chalandon points out (Alexis Ier pp. 92, 182) represents Guy as living at the Court of Alexius in 1097 'en qualité de neveu et de sénéchal'. It is true that he was back in Bohemund's camp in 1107-8 (Al. XIII. 4-10).   [7] V. 1, p. 126.

possessions in Italy[1] and finally goes to Salerno 'to rest himself from his many toils',[2] while Bohemund fights with the imperial army. But this is only a brief interlude. Though appalled 'as if struck by a thunderbolt'[3] by the news of his son's reverses, yet 'even so Robert planned nothing ignoble, or unworthy of his own valour and daring. Rather indeed was he kindled all the more to fight, and thoughts and cares greater than before filled his mind. For the man was a staunch defender of his own counsels and plans, and was in no wise willing to give up in matters where he had once come to a resolution, and, to tell the whole truth, undaunted[4] and thinking that everything was easy for him to seize at the first assault.' So he collected a large army, and on encountering the Venetian fleet 'started the fight as he was sure to do'.[5] When defeated in the first encounter he was so 'warlike and ardent for battles' as to court another. Once more he loses, but soon afterwards self-confidence in the Venetians allows him to surprise them and to seize their un- ballasted and top-heavy ships. The captive crews are treated by the Norman with ghastly cruelty and mutilation, except such as are held for ransom. Anna takes evident pleasure in narrating these horrors.

'But Robert could not keep quiet,' though his activities were shortly to be ended by death. Fever seizes him in Cephallenia, and in fulfilment of prophecy he dies near a place called 'Jeru- salem',[6] from which according to Dante he mounted to Para- dise, as did also Godfrey de Bouillon. Anna has no views as to this but, pleased to show her medical knowledge, 'cannot say precisely' whether he died of fever or pleurisy; the cause assigned by various Latin chroniclers, namely poison admini- stered by his wife Gaita at Alexius' suggestion,[7] is not so much as hinted at here. The body is taken in the teeth of a great storm to Italy and buried in the monastery of the Holy Trinity at Venosa. Robert had lived seventy years and been Duke for twenty-five.[8]

The relief which Alexius felt at Robert's death must have

[1] On taking leave of his army in Illyria he is made by Anna to utter this shrewd maxim: 'It is not right to seize the goods of others and through negligence lose our own' (V. 3, p. 131).

[2] V. 3, p. 133.   [3] VI. 5, p. 158.

[4] This word ἀκατάπληκτος and variants upon it may almost be said to give Anna's ideal of the perfect hero, the Greatheart of Bunyan. See p. 142 above.

[5] VI. 5, p. 160. The untranslatable ὁποῖος ἐκεῖνος.

[6] VI. 6, p. 162. Ather, the actual scene of his death, is also an Old Testament place-name (Joshua xv. 42; A.V. Ether, but Cod. Alex. gives variant Ἀθέρ.).

[7] See Du Cange's note on VI. 6, p. 162 D.

[8] Or twenty-six, if we date the dukedom from the Synod of Melfi 'in the summer of 1059' (Tout, op. cit. p. 115).

been so immense that we are hardly prepared for the dispassionate tone of Anna's second detailed description of her father's worst foe.[1] 'Now Robert, as rumour went and some said, was an exceptional chief, clever,[2] fine in countenance, polished in speech, quick in words, with a powerful voice, easy of access. In stature he was tall, he always wore his hair cut close to his head, and he had a thick beard, so anxious was he always to observe the customs of his own race.[3] He preserved the beauty of his face and of his whole body to the end, and was proud of these things, because through them he thought his appearance worthy of a throne.[4] He treated with honour all those who were most loyally disposed to him. But he was very parsimonious, very fond of gold, very keen at a bargain, very fond of possessions, and on top of this very fond of glory.'[5] These foibles brought him 'much reproach from all', whereas the Emperor in his turn was blamed for rashness in having fought him in the field, instead of trusting to the local inhabitants to wear him down, 'shot at from all sides'. Anna emphatically controverts this idea as underrating the adversary, and says: 'For Robert's valour and proficiency in war and steadfastness of will are known to all; the man was of those who are conquered not easily, but rather with great difficulty, as under reverses he only appeared the more courageous',[6] with which words of generous admiration the description abruptly ends. When Anna next mentions Robert it is to make the astounding statement that 'Alexius when he turned his reins towards Illyria by great labours utterly vanquished Robert and his son Bohemund, and delivered the Western provinces from very great misfortune'.[7] So strangely in course of time do defeats and questionable tricks of diplomacy become transformed by pious memory into victories, and the operations of nature into achievements of some honoured man. Intrigue and famine checked Bohemund's career on two different occasions, and death stopped Robert's, but to Anna these princes were both victims of her father's bow and spear.[8]

---

[1] VI. 7, pp. 165, 166.

[2] The epithet describing Anna's favourite mental quality—ἀγχίνους.

[3] i.e. to keep a vow till he had conquered the Eastern Empire. See Du Cange on VI. 7, p. 165 D, and above p. 59, note 2.

[4] Quoted from Eurip., Aeolus, Frag. 15. Cf. Pref. 4, p. 6, where it is used in connexion with Nicephorus Bryennius Caesar.

[5] The five superlatives give an effect that translation wholly fails to reproduce: φειδωλότατος, φιλοχρυσότατος, ἐμπορικώτατος, φιλοκτεανώτατος, φιλοδοξότατος.

[6] This defence of her father is probably a hit at George Palaeologus, who had advised against fighting (IV. 5, p. 112). [7] VI. 9, p. 168.

[8] It is interesting to observe the growth of this legend about Bohemund in Anna's history. In V. 7 she represents Alexius as raising his siege of Larissa, but

FOREIGN AFFAIRS
68. THE WEST. THE CRUSADERS

THIS might seem the right place to consider the subsequent career of Bohemund, but he is so much the archetype to Anna of all the Crusaders that it is perhaps better to treat him last as the most important of that band. In his first conflict with Alexius he has indeed no distinguishing feature, he is merely his father's true son,[1] and we gather little personal knowledge of him in the Larissa campaign.[2] But from 1097 when he comes among the Crusading bands to Constantinople, till his treaty of 1108 with Alexius and his death not long afterwards, he is seldom absent from Anna's stage. To her the First Crusade is grouped round three men, her father, Raymond of Provence, and Bohemund. All else is subsidiary, and as our subject in hand is Anna's view of things rather than objective facts, we are spared any attempt at writing a history of the Crusade, which has already, as Miss Lees[3] truly says, been treated 'from many different points of view, racial, religious, political, economic, military, romantic'. But a few words of general introduction may serve to show why the Holy War meant one thing to the Crusaders and something totally different to the Byzantines.

Bréhier[4] has stated that pilgrimages from Western lands to the Holy Places had gone on increasing from century to century. Nothing had stopped them, no matter in what infidel hands Palestine might be. When the fanatical Shiite Hakim destroyed the Holy Sepulchre in 1009 and persecuted the Christians, it only arrested the pilgrims for a few years. Men thought it wiser

---

compelled to tamper with the enemy's troops before he can get rid of him out of the country. Yet in VI 9, p. 168, she speaks as if he had conquered him completely, and in X. 5, p. 285; 9, p. 294, Bohemund's chief motive for joining the Crusade is said to be his 'ancient grudge against the Emperor', a wish to 'pay him back for that glorious victory which he won against him' at Larissa. Alexius at the time of Bohemund's arrival in Constantinople does not think it prudent to remind him of anything worse than 'reckless deeds', and 'that hostility' (X. 11, p. 302), but in XIII. 12, p. 406, the Norman is made to admit defeat at Alexius' hands in a vague expression which may refer equally well (and equally untruly) to the indecisive campaign of 1083 or to Bohemund's being obliged by famine to abandon the siege of Durazzo in 1108. It is instructive to read the other side in the *Gesta*, ch. 6, Alexius 'valde timebat' Bohemund 'quia olim eum sepe cum suo exercitu ejecerat de campo'. It is as the son and representative of Robert that Bohemund here concerns us; his independent career is dealt with in Ch. 69 below.

[1] I. 14. See last note.   [2] V. 4–7.
[3] Ed. of *Anon. Gesta Francorum*, 1924, p. xxii.   [4] *l'Église et l'Orient*, ch. II, III.

to make their pious journeys in bands and not alone, but make them they did, and though after the schism of 1054 the Eastern Church tried hard to hamper such proceedings, the steady stream continued, till the Seljuq Turks swept Westward and took Jerusalem in 1070. The disaster of Manzikert in 1071 gave the final blow to these pilgrimages, and the Crusades were principally an attempt to have them renewed. In 1073 Michael VII seems to have suggested to Gregory VII an Occidental expedition to help Constantinople and Jerusalem against the Turks. But it was not till Urban II became Pope in 1088 that this idea actually took shape, and in all probability by that time Alexius I neither solicited nor even desired Western intervention.[1] His grievances against the Turks were primarily political; if his own subjects desired to worship relics he had plenty in Constantinople, and it was his interest to make sure

[1] See above, p. 312, note 9.

In spite of Bury's note (on p. 261 of Vol. VI of Gibbon, *op. cit.*) calling it 'doubtless genuine', we are following Chalandon (*Alexis Ier*, pp. 325 sqq.) and Riant in rejecting the supposed letter of appeal from Alexius (whose name is never mentioned) to Robert I, Count of Flanders, as largely if not wholly spurious. Hagenmeyer in 1901 (*Kreuzzugsbriefe*, p. 25) said that 'der Inhalt des Briefes all echt anzusehen ist', but allowed of the possibility of its having been deliberately worked up in Flanders into an *excitatorium*. H. Pirenne, writing six years later in the *Revue de l'instruction publique de Belgique* (Vol. 50, 1907), believed that the letter 'dérive d'un original authentique' written by Alexius in 1090 after the Greek reverses at Mitylene and Chios, to remind Robert of aid promised in a personal interview in 1089. This date (1089) for Robert's return from Jerusalem is arrived at by Pirenne from the presence or absence of his name in the Flemish charters; from 1087 to early 1090 it is replaced by that of his son Robert II. This agrees with the dates in the *Alexias* as established by E. de Muralt (*Essai de Chronographie byzantine*), and Pirenne thinks Anna errs only in placing the interview of her father and Robert at Beroe (VII. 6, p. 201) where he probably only made a short stay after the battle of Dristra in 1087, and not in Constantinople as does Guibert de Nogent. Guibert in his *Gesta Dei per Francos* only professes to give excerpts in his own words, and the date of our other source for the letter, the *Historia Hierosolymitana* of Robert of Reims, is very uncertain. It is therefore impossible to be sure what the original Greek letter really said, or when it was translated and remodelled by some Latin; Pirenne says 1095-6, after the Council of Clermont but before the Crusade; Chalandon says 1098-9, when the Crusade was in full swing. Chalandon elsewhere states that to modern Greek historians the Crusade appears a calamity, taking up in combats with the Crusaders the Greek troops that should have been fighting the Turks (*op. cit.* p. 159). It must however be said that the *Anon. Syn. Chron.* (pp. 183-5), after giving a vivid picture of Alexius' dangers from East and West through the inefficiency of past Emperors, says that he tried to make the Italians his friends, sending messengers to 'the bishop presiding over the older Rome' and to various Christian princes telling them that τὸ ἔθνος οὐκ ἀνεκτόν was holding the Holy Sepulchre. This made many leave their lands for the cause, and they came to Constantinople in thousands. Then Alexius, 'by divine aid and the help of these [sc. Crusaders] and his own efforts', succeeded in driving 'the Persians out of the Greek lands'. The picture of the relations between the Emperor and the Crusaders seems to have become rose-coloured in the course of years; this Chronicle was not written till after 1261, and by contrast with 1204 the First Crusade might well appear all harmony to the writer.

of Nicaea and Antioch rather than to concern himself about the fate of Jerusalem.

To the Byzantines the Crusaders, huge bodies of men, women and children, preceded by portents, speaking uncouth tongues, liable to plunder for their daily needs, were the most terrible kind of barbarians, alarmingly numerous,[1] and engaged on a work which interested the Empire hardly at all, except in so far as it helped to 'widen the dominion of the Greeks' and restore their lost possessions. Alexius hoped to use them as mercenaries like Urselius and the rest, and was ready to pay them well, but he never liked them. Anna puts this matter quite clearly. Whatever his private feelings might have been, her father 'had sent many Greek armies with the Crusaders against the Turks, for two reasons: first that they might not become a prey to the Turkish sword because he cared for them as Christians,[2] secondly so that organized by us they might destroy some of the Ishmaelite towns and give others according to contract to the Emperor of the Greeks, and thereby widen the dominion of the Greeks'. When first Bohemund and then Tancred 'clung tight to the city of Antiochus' and other towns, the Emperor felt he had spent money and toil in vain.[3] The

---

[1] Theophylact (Ser. I, Ep. 11 : *P. G.* 126, col. 324) describes himself as hardly in possession of his senses after the διάβασις or ἐπίβασις of the Crusaders; Time had however as usual taught him to bear the Frankish 'insults'. See the similar passage in *Mous. Alex.* I. 330 sqq. Even a Latin chronicler thinks it natural of Alexius not to have let the Crusaders enter Constantinople *en masse* (Foucher de Chartres, I. 8, 9). Again, Stephen of Blois does not resent the Emperor's fear of the 'infinita populorum turba' at Nicaea and his effort to keep them in confinement (Hagenmeyer, *Kreuzzugsbriefe*, Ep. IV). In I. 13, 4 Foucher gives a curious list of the component nationalities of the Crusading army. Though they could not understand each other, yet they 'were as brothers in the love of God'. The names are 'Franci, Flandri, Frisi, Galli, Allobroges, Lotharingi, Alemanni, Baioarii, Normanni, Angli, Scoti, Aquitani, Itali, Daci, Apuli, Iberi, Britones, Graeci, Armeni'. The modern visitor to the Assembly of the League of Nations, looking at the delegates of fifty-four countries and hearing all round in the galleries a babel of tongues, can sympathize with the bewilderment which these heterogeneous and unexpected guests must have caused at Byzantium, a sensation not diminished by their turbulence and discourtesy.

[2] Anna was bound to say this of the Thirteenth Apostle.

[3] XIV. 2, pp. 422, 423. As to the whole course of the Crusade up to the siege of Antioch, Chalandon (*Hist. de la Ière Croisade*, p. 124, *etc.*) asserts with truth that Anna's account is at least as trustworthy as that of the Latin chroniclers. Oster blames Alexius for not having grasped the full significance of the Crusade and put himself at the head of East and West in this sacred adventure (*op. cit.* Pt. II, p. 47). This is surely being wise after the event. The Emperor's fear and suspicion of the 'barbarians' as they advanced on the capital, his secret relief when the bands of Peter the Hermit spurned his advice and went prematurely to Asia Minor (even if we disbelieve the *Gesta's* grim 'gavisus est valde' (ch. 2), when he heard of their destruction by the Turks), and his outraged feelings against the arrogant Hugh, the plundering and bellicose Godfrey, and the insufferable Bohemund, to say nothing of the 'numberless host' led by 'kings and dukes and counts and

Byzantines could not foresee the calamity of 1204, and the consequent desirability of as it were putting a ring through the nose of this bull that might gore them; and without this foreknowledge were they not bound to do as Alexius did, keep on as friendly terms as possible with these savage hordes when present, and heave a deep sigh of relief when they saw the last of them? 'Egypt was glad at their departing, for they were afraid of them.' This is precisely the spirit of Anna's Books X and XI.[1] And in justice to the Greeks we must remember that others felt the same about the Crusaders. Plenty of tales of insubordination, bitter passions, and savage cruelty may be extracted from the Latin chroniclers themselves, and many a recent writer endorses the opinion of old de Peyssonnel,[2] that wherever the Normans went, whether as conquerors or Crusaders, they differed little in violence from the Goths and the Huns.

On the whole it is remarkable that Anna should have been so little prejudiced rather than so much, and that she tells the story of the Crusade with such comparative dispassionateness. Bohemund it is true rouses anger in her; but Godfrey and Hugh, Raoul, Tancred and Baldwin all meet with justice, even if cold justice, at her hands.[3] More important in considering

---

even bishops'—all this was not only pardonable but inevitable, and the outcome must have seemed to Alexius to justify his worst apprehensions; 'no advantage had accrued to the Empire of the Greeks from these great toils and pains and expenses' (XIV. 2, p. 422 D).

[1] By a curious contrast, while Anna devotes over one and a half Books to the Crusade, Zonaras dismisses it in fifteen lines.

[2] *Observations sur les peuples Barbares*, p. 173. We may compare the bitter remarks on the savagery of the 'Latins' in the 'so-called Holy War' in a life of St. Anastasius, edited by Sathas in *Archives de l'Orient Latin*, II, p. 426. Gibbon gives the same picture. Bréhier, in the introduction to his edition of the *Histoire Anonyme de la première Croisade* (Paris, 1924), says of the writer: 'Comme ses contemporains il trouve justes et raconte froidement les massacres les plus horribles, la décapitation des prisonniers turcs, la violation des sépultures musulmanes, l'égorgement de la population sans défense dans les villes prises d'assaut'. We may however question whether the two tales of pointless savagery that Anna gives about the Crusaders, first the barbarities inflicted by the 'Normans' with Peter the Hermit on Turkish children and old men (X. 5, p. 286), and then the gratuitous massacre of a friendly Christian population, priests and all, by the army under the leadership of St. Gilles (XI. 8, p. 331), are not too highly coloured to deserve implicit belief (see p. 92, note 8, above). But the aspersions on the morals of the Westerners, though put by her into the mouth of Peter the Hermit, probably represent her real feelings on the subject (XI. 6, p. 326). Foucher (I. 11, 8, and I. 15, 13) says the same of his fellow soldiers.

[3] Thus she ascribes the friction between Godfrey's followers and the people of Constantinople to a natural if groundless suspicion on the part of the newcomers that their chief had been seized (X. 9, p. 294). They therefore made destructive attacks on various buildings; yet we feel that in Anna's mind this mild violence only showed up by contrast the sacrilegious sack of the capital by her father's own troops fifteen years before (III. 5).

her truthfulness is the fact that she ascribes to Peter the Hermit
and not to Pope Urban II the initial movement which led to
the Crusade.[1] This is interesting, because later critics give Peter
less and less of a place in the genesis of the expedition, and the
Pope more and more. But even this is a minor point. The big
matter at issue between Anna and the Latin chroniclers is
whether Alexius did or did not keep his word with the Crusaders. To the Latins he appeared just as perfidious, crafty,
and oath-breaking as they did to him, and there is much to be
said for both sides. At any rate (unless we accept the theory
that Alexius first called them in, which is never a plea advanced
by the Crusaders themselves), he was the only party who could
reasonably complain of experiencing ingratitude.[2] One of
Anna's great charges against the Westerners is that, after her
father had lavished time and money and trouble upon them,
they showed themselves 'very stiff-necked and bitter', and entirely callous as to his sufferings 'on behalf of Christians'.[3] She
even makes a violent onslaught on them on the strange ground
that their verbosity, with the endless standing to listen entailed
on him thereby, had been one main cause of her father's
gout. They were ambitious, insolent, reckless, greedy, and unrestrained; but worse than all, they were wordy 'above every
race of men', and in their 'immense loquacity' they outraged
court etiquette, showed no consideration for the time or inclina-
tions of others, and kept the Emperor standing for hours when
he was wishing to go to bed. And because of their well-known
'hot temper' he thought it wiser to bear it.[4]

When she first brings the Crusaders on the scene, and there
is no question of her father or his gout, she gives a very calm
and just account of the different motives[5] inspiring them, rang-
ing from true piety to blatant ambition. Some came so as to
be as we might say in the fashion, selling their lands to get
equipment and followers, 'for each of the Celts was anxious to
excel the rest'. Bohemund and others 'of the baser sort' thirsted
for power, even for the imperial power, while Bohemund him-

---

[1] X. 5. Contrast Foucher, I. 5, 11. For her inaccuracies after Taticius left
Antioch see p. 231, note 8, above.

[2] This seems to be the meaning of ἀπανθρωπία as displayed by the Crusaders,
together with ὕβρις (XIV. 2, p. 423).

[3] XIV. 2, p. 422, and 7, p. 445. Yet Chalandon, *Alexis I*er, p. 157, points out that
the Crusaders did as a matter of fact accuse the Emperor of ingratitude as well as
perfidy: they possibly felt that in fighting the Turks they were pulling his chestnuts
out of the fire, whether he had invited them or not.

[4] XIV. 4. For the whole passage see p. 519, below. So also in X. 9, p. 294,
we read of τὸ φύσει λάλον τε καὶ μακρηγορώτατον τῶν Λατίνων.

[5] X. 5, p. 285; X. 9, p. 294.

self had the additional motive of attempting to avenge his
Larissa failure. But 'the simpler souls' including Peter the Hermit, did truly wish to 'worship at the Lord's tomb and inquire
into the truths about the sacred places'. Nothing could be
better put.

In general Anna is cynical as to the religious fervour of most
of this great unmanageable host, but what is much more on
her mind is to retort on them the charges of bad faith which
they brought against Alexius. Is it perhaps a subconscious
feeling of guilt that makes her call the Crusaders at Nicaea
every conceivable bad name, 'changeable', 'unstable' (bis),
'untrustworthy', 'unrestrained', variable as the currents of
Euripus?[1] Are these and the euphemistic phrases of 'trick'
or 'comedy' all uttered to justify the way her father treated his
allies (actuated as she admits by fear of their 'immense number'), going behind their backs to make terms with the Turkish
enemies, and instil into them suspicion of Western cruelty?
Curiously enough the Latin chroniclers[2] do not blame Alexius
in this matter of Nicaea, so it was perhaps successfully kept
secret from them, as Anna implies. Indeed all through the siege
and capture of this town they represent him as giving the promised supplies, generously distributing goods and money, and
finally appointing Greek troops to march on with the host.[3]
Raymond d'Aguilers is the devoted adherent of the Count
of Provence just as the author of the Gesta is of Bohemund;
but both they and the more impartial Foucher develop their
principal bitterness against the Emperor at a later stage, in
connexion with Antioch.[4] Foucher ascribes the deaths of the
Crusaders, on the march through Asia Minor and during the
long siege, to starvation (caused by Turkish devastation of
the country) and bad weather and enemy attacks, all sent
propter peccata nostra,[5] and he does not begin to call Alexius the

---

[1] X. 11; XI. 2.　　　　　　[2] e. g. Gesta, ch. 8; Foucher, I. 10, 8–10.

[3] The first letters of Stephen of Blois and Anselm of Ribemont speak of perfectly cordial relations up to this date between Greeks and 'Latins' (Hagenmeyer,
Kreuzzugsbriefe, Epp. IV, VIII). So also does the letter from the counts to the Pope,
incorporated by Foucher in I. 24, 1–14, the passage abusing Alexius being an
evident interpolation (Chalandon, op. cit. p. 205). So also do Alexius' own letters to
the Abbot of Monte Cassino in Aug. 1097 and June, 1098. He says that his 'imperium'
has helped the Crusaders 'non ut amicus vel cognitus sed ut pater', claiming truly
that no one else 'post Deum' could have done so (Riant, Epistula Spuria Alex. Comn.
ad Robertum, pp. 43–5. Zonaras (XVIII. 23) makes the curious statement that the
Crusaders sold Nicaea to Alexius for much money. Presumably this refers to the
largesses of which all the Latin writers speak.

[4] The letter from the counts saying that Bohemund meant to keep Antioch was
perhaps the last straw which caused Alexius to intrigue with Egypt and make
special overtures to St. Gilles (Chalandon, p. 206).

[5] I; XI. 8, and XV. 13.

perturbator et tyrannus of all 'pilgrims' till the moment when the conflict between him and Bohemund, initiated in connexion with Antioch, had led to the Norman invasion of Illyria in 1107.[1] Even the *Gesta* with its strong anti-Greek bias admits that Alexius gave the Crusaders at Constantinople and else-where an adequate 'mercatum' and good advice, to which they only responded by lawlessness and pillage;[2] it is the desertion by the Greeks at Antioch that this chronicler cannot forgive,[3] and indeed Anna's conscience does not seem to be altogether easy as to this, and even less as to her father's failure to join the Crusaders in the Holy Land. Her excuses are most plaus-ible, but why does she make them at all?[4] May we not see the same desire to exculpate Alexius and represent him not as the offending party but as a type of injured magnanimity when the innocent counts whom he rescues from captivity in Cairo are set down as 'enemies and hostile, breakers of their oaths and promises to him'?[5] It is, we are forced to believe, an instance of the famous maxim: 'No case: abuse the plaintiff's attorney.'

This brings us to what was really the crux of the situation, the oath of homage taken by the Crusading chiefs to the Emperor. Did they swear it? and if so, what did they swear? It is a remarkable fact that the oath, though alluded to in all accounts of the Crusade, is actually given in few. Anna's ver-sion is as follows:[6] '[Godfrey] going to the sovereign swore the oath which he was asked for, namely that whatever cities and lands or fortresses he should capture, which formerly were reckoned under the empire of the Greeks, he would hand over to the general sent by the Emperor for this very purpose'. Riant[7] gives the formula from Robert of Reims, remarking truly that it is 'far from seeming so authentic': 'Iuro quia nun-quam per me aut per meos vitam aut honorem amittet' (*sc.* Alexius), 'aut quidquid hodie iuste aut iniuste possidet.' Ekke-hard of Urach[8] says the Crusaders swore to the Emperor 'ut urbes quasque suo imperio defractas pristinae ditioni si vince-rent redderent, ipsique vicissim tam armis quam stipendiis regiis infra metam eandem se foveri non dubitarent'. Foucher gives no particulars, but treats the oath as perfectly natural.[9]

---

[1] *Ibid.* II; XXXVIII. 3.   [2] Chs. 2, 3, 5.   [3] Ch. 16.

[4] The 'promise to come behind with forces', cast by Bohemund in the Emperor's teeth (XI. 9, p. 333) is never explicitly admitted by Anna, but never denied. The Latin chroniclers assert it freely. For Anna's sensitiveness on the subject see p. 143, note 7, above.   [5] XII. 1, p. 347.

[6] X. 9, p. 298. This corresponds closely with Albert of Aix and William of Malmesbury. See Du Cange's note, *ad. loc.*

[7] *Expéditions des Scandinaves*, p. 198, note 1.   [8] Ch. 14.

[9] *Op. cit.* I. 9, 2.

'Erat enim omnibus hoc necesse, ut sic cum imperatore amici-
tiam consolidarent, sine cuius consilio et auxilio nostrum iter
nequivimus expedire, neque illi qui nos erant subsecuturi eodem
tramite.' Like Anna he represents the Emperor as lavishly
rewarding all who took the oath.[1] But the fiery writer of the
Gesta views the matter very differently. The oath is to him only
to be excused as a terribly painful necessity to which the counts
submit because 'volentes nolentesque humiliaverunt se ad
nequissimi imperatoris voluntatem', and were 'coacti necessitate'.[2] As to what they actually swore the writer says nothing,
but he concludes in these words: 'Imperator quoque omnibus
nostris fidem et securitatem dedit; iuravit etiam quia veniret
nobiscum pariter cum suo exercitu per terram et per mare, et
nobis mercatum terra marique fideliter daret ac omnia nostra
perdita diligenter restauraret, insuper et neminem nostrorum
peregrinorum conturbari vel contristari in via Sancti Sepulcri
vellet aut permitteret.' To this side of the oath Anna makes
Bohemund allude in condensed form, when writing to Alexius:[3]
'After promising to come behind us with a large force thou hast
not been willing to confirm thy promise by deeds.' The suffering of the Crusaders from famine at Antioch is laid at the
Emperor's door, and the final reproach is that 'even Taticius,
that faithful slave of thy power, who had been given to us as
a help, left us in this danger and went away'. Such then were
the undertakings assumed on both sides; it remains to be seen
how they were fulfilled.

To begin with we will give Anna's statement as to which of
the Crusaders took the oath. The allegiance of Peter the Hermit
was obviously not worth getting. The first arrival of note was
Hugh, brother of the King of France. He according to both
Anna and Foucher was led to Constantinople by the imperial
troops sent to meet him, and kept there a virtual captive[4] till
in Anna's words he 'became [the Emperor's] man, swearing the
oath customary to Latins'. Next Godfrey de Bouillon comes
and refuses vehemently to put himself 'into the position of a
slave'.[5] Fighting ensues and Count Hugh pleads with Godfrey

---

[1] Anna represents both the Greeks and the Crusaders as applying the term
δουλεία to the homage sworn (X. 10, p. 300; XI. 11, p. 340). So Tancred's mother
professes δουλεία to the Emperor (XII. 8, p. 366). The lavish rewards for the oath
were one of the ways in which Alexius was drained by the Crusaders of 'innumerable
gifts and heaps of gold', and of 'sums beyond all number' (XIV. 2, p. 423).

[2] *Op. cit.* Ch. 6.

[3] XI. 9, p. 333, and see Du Cange's note *ad loc.*

[4] X. 7, p. 289, changing the punctuation of *C. S. H. B.* and of Reifferscheid's text
into ἄνετον μέν, οὐκ ἐλεύθερον δὲ παντελῶς. Foucher, I. 6, 3, 'non omnino liber'.

[5] X. 9.

to follow his example. Once more he rejects the idea with scorn, but being once more worsted in arms he submits to his fate and swears. Other chiefs, part of Anna's numberless host of 'kings and dukes and counts and even bishops', pour in upon the Empire and are reluctantly persuaded to take the oath by Alexius,[1] who gets Godfrey to witness it. Baldwin was apparently among the number, as well as the 'Frankish noble' who insolently sat down on the Emperor's chair. We hear of no rewards administered at the moment, but only sage counsel as to how to wage war with Turks. Finally Bohemund enters the capital,[2] and between the lines of his interviews with the Emperor we read their mutual animosity and suspicion. But when the oath is offered, Bohemund, from an interested desire to gain Alexius' goodwill, and 'furthermore being by nature a perjurer', takes it without visible reluctance and receives a large share in the riches which are now lavished, together with more good advice, on all the subservient counts. 'And thus by both money and words he (sc. Alexius) softened their rude natures.' Yet all cannot have sworn, for after the capture of Nicaea the Emperor solicits and obtains the homage of other 'counts'.[3] Tancred, on the ground of owing allegiance only to his uncle Bohemund, remains obdurate the longest, but finally swears also.[4]

Before we deal with the rather perplexing case of Raymond of Provence we may observe that on this general oath the history of the Crusade turned. Nicaea was restored to the Emperor (even if not strictly by the action of the Crusaders[5]), but Antioch was not, and Laodicea not permanently, and to Alexius this seemed a sufficiently grave breach of contract to release him from his own promises. Even Bohemund admits that Antioch was Alexius' due, but tries to prove that the Emperor had turned traitor first.[6] Later on Alexius, then Cantacuzenus, then Duke Alexius and other imperial representatives, revile Bohemund as an 'oath-breaker',[7] one who has 'proved false to his vows and despised the covenant of peace'. The Emperor piously points out through his envoys that the 'breaking of those oaths has not turned out well for Bohemund', and Bohemund 'has his own conscience suitably convicting him'.[8] Small wonder that when this great enemy was finally humbled, special care should be taken to make him pay homage once more, with every outward

---

[1] His diplomacy and persistence are dwelt on by his daughter: he demolished all their excuses and 'pursued them by every sort of method' (X. 10, p. 300).
[2] X. 11.   [3] XI. 3.   [4] XI. 3, p. 317.
[5] X. 11, p. 306; XI. 2.   [6] XI. 4, p. 319.
[7] XI. 9, p. 332; 11, p. 340; XIII. 8, p. 399; 9, p. 400.
[8] XIII. 9, p. 400; 11, p. 405.

form of reverence and humility.[1] Certainly, if as has been said
the whole civilization of Western Europe was founded on the
oath, the statement is no less true of Anna Comnena's conception
of the First Crusade. And nowhere does the importance attached
to it come out more clearly than in the story of the one Crusader
for whom Anna has a good word, Raymond de St. Gilles, Count
of Provence, whom she calls Isangeles.

His mode of entering her pages is strange, though (even if we
take it as it is usually taken) not uncharacteristic of her. In
Book X, ch. 8, she describes the coming across the Adriatic
in a 'pirate ship of large tonnage' of the Count Prebentzas,
usually translated 'of Provence'.[2] He falls in with the imperial
fleet, and after a fight the Crusaders 'yield, though reluctantly',
and the count surrenders 'himself, ship and all, with those under
him'. They all come to land and we hear no more of the
Count Prebentzas as such. Three chapters later, after Godfrey
and Bohemund and many others have arrived at Constantinople, we get this abrupt sentence: 'But [the Emperor] loved
St. Gilles exceedingly and kept him for a while with himself.'[3]
This love is based on the count's great superiority to his fellows
in intellect, sincerity, chastity and truth;[4] 'he excelled all the
Latins in all things, as much as the sun the stars.' To him
Alexius imparted his fears of Bohemund, and St. Gilles after
promising zealous heed went to join the other Crusaders in
Asia Minor, συνταξάμενος τῷ αὐτοκράτορι.[5] This phrase has been
used a few lines back of all the Crusaders and would seem to
mean 'having paid homage', as it clearly does in the scene
at Pelecanus. 'The Emperor . . . wishing that all the counts
who had not yet sworn should also take oaths to him, enjoined
on Butumites . . . to counsel all the counts . . . not to start on
the road to Antioch πρὸ τοῦ συντάξασθαι τῷ βασιλεῖ.' And again

[1] XIII. 9.
[2] This incident follows directly on the statement that Bohemund crossed to
Cabalio (X. 8, p. 289). Prof. Grégoire (see above, p. 254, note 6) has suggested that
the name Πρέβεντζας may be a mistake for Πριγκιπάτος, who as one of Bohemund's
most trusted officers is the recipient of a bogus incriminating letter from Alexius
(XIII. 4, p. 388) and is identified by Du Cange with the Πριντζίτας who signs the
treaty between Alexius and Bohemund (XIII. 12, p. 416), having apparently
seceded to the Greek side, as Marinus of Naples and Roger the Frank (XIII. 4,
p. 387; 12, p. 416) had done. One argument in favour of this theory is that
Principatus would naturally come over as the follower, and herald at Constantinople,
of his chief Bohemund shortly before mentioned. Another is that the discrepancy
between the first and the second pictures of St. Gilles would vanish, if the Comes
Prebentzas and Isangeles were not one and the same person.
[3] X. 11, p. 305. This Count, usually known to us as Raymond of Provence,
was called St. Gilles after an abbey of that name, and Anna transliterates this as
Isangeles. See Du Cange's notes on X. 8, p. 289 D; X. 11, p. 305 A.
[4] See XI. 6, p. 327.   [5] X. 11, p. 305.

Tancred 'himself also takes oaths, and indeed, συνταξαμένων ἀπάντων τῷ βασιλεῖ, the latter gives them Taticius to go with them.[1] Though the common late Greek meaning of 'taking leave' is possible, or even the classical one of 'coming to an agreement',[2] the context seems to show that homage is denoted. If so, Anna's version of St. Gilles' proceedings disagrees with that of Raymond d'Aguilers,[3] who says that the Count of Provence totally refused to swear fealty. The writer of the *Gesta* supports this, but says that his refusal to be approached 'de hominio' did not prevent his swearing to respect the Emperor's life and honour and to make others do the same.[4]

We cannot reconcile these two versions; we must simply choose between them, as also between Anna's account of his sea-crossing (if indeed he is the Πρεβέντζας of X. 8) and the Latin chronicler's statement that he came by land through Dalmatia. If Anna as a devoted daughter had a bias in favour of making every one in her pages pay Alexius homage, the count's faithful chaplain had an equally powerful motive for representing him as the one strong independent prince. Certainly throughout the story St. Gilles remains on good, indeed intimate, terms with the Emperor,[5] and when he dies Alexius' envoy goes to his heir 'to prepare him to swear to the Emperor to keep true fealty (πίστιν) towards him, such as his deceased uncle St. Gilles preserved to the end'.[6] Putting all the arguments together we may surely, without considering Raymond d'Aguilers as a 'faussaire dangereux' or even a wilful 'menteur',[7] believe him to have been led astray by vicarious vainglory, and may accept the fact that Alexius' one trusted Crusader, Anna's favourite Isangeles, did not stand out in obstinate isolation, but took and kept the oath of homage even more zealously than the rest.

---

[1] XI. 3, pp. 316, 317.

[2] II. 5, p. 52; V. 3, p. 132; VII. 3, p. 194; VIII. 9, pp. 240, 241; XI. 1, p. 309; 5, p. 322; XIV. 5, p. 438. So in Nic. Bry. I. 12, p. 26. But in X. 10, p. 301; XII. 1, p. 347; XV. 6, p. 479, Anna may mean either homage or farewell. In the *Anon. Syn. Chron.*, p. 187, the word denotes farewell.

[3] *Historia Francorum qui ceperunt Ierusalem*, ch. 11. Foucher (I. 9, 2) says 'Raimundus id facere tunc' [i.e. when other counts swore] 'recusavit', which seems to imply that he yielded later.

[4] *Op. cit.* ch. 6. It has been suggested that the *Gesta* here merely copies from Raymond's Chronicle. In *Gesta*, ch. 30, we find St. Gilles with the other counts inviting the Emperor to come to Antioch 'ad recipiendam civitatem et [ut] conventiones quas erga illos habebat expleret'. They assuredly did this to keep their oath, and St. Gilles' motives are not distinguished from those of the rest.

[5] XI. 7. 8.

[6] XI. 8, p. 332. The same argument is used with St. Gilles' bastard son Bertrand and his son after him (XIV. 2, pp. 425–8).

[7] See the criticisms mentioned by Chalandon, *op. cit.*, Introd. p. xxxiii.

One other point occurs in connexion with St. Gilles. In the *Alexias* the use of the word ἧλος points to an interesting conflict between Byzantine and Frankish credulity. In classical Greek it means a 'nail', and is so used by Anna in speaking of Robert Guiscard's ships,[1] and in reference to the Crucifixion, where cross and nails and lance are mentioned together.[2] But in the story where Gregory Gabras steals a relic, to make his oath more solemn, and hides it 'in his bosom', this sacred ἧλος is described as that 'with which the wicked men pierced my Saviour's side'.[3] At the first blush one would take this to mean the Sacred Lance, which the Byzantines believed to have been safely housed in Constantinople long before the First Crusade began, but as we shall see presently Anna probably refers to one of the Sacred Nails. However, all this does not explain the discrepancy between the *Alexias* and the Latin chronicles as to the relic found at Antioch by the Crusaders; the former speaks of ' ὁ ἅγιος ἧλος ', committed as 'holy and divine' to the care of St. Gilles[4]; the latter have no doubt that this was no mere nail but the unique lance of the Roman centurion. Which are we to believe?   Leib[5] here translates the phrase[6] by 'un clou sacré' and adds this note: 'Il est curieux de voir la transformation opérée par les sources grecques; elles remplacent la lance par le clou (certains interprètent, le fer de la lance). C'est que la sainte lance était censée se trouver déjà à Constantinople parmi les nombreuses reliques: en 614 à St. Sophie, au Xe Siécle et au début du XIe dans l'église de la Vierge du Phare.' He also refers to J. Ebersolt who in his *Sanctuaires de Byzance*[7] gives a full account of the bringing of the Lance from Jerusalem to Constantinople in 614, of its two successive habitations (St. Sophia and the church of the Pharos), and finally of its being catalogued in the latter place in the year 1200 by the keeper Nicolas Mesaritis.   Ebersolt carefully distinguishes the λόγχη from the ἧλος, also mentioned by Mesaritis, 'le saint clou qui avec trois autres avait percé le corps du Christ et avait trempé dans son sang', and adds a note that, though Mesaritis only mentions one nail, 'il en existait plusieurs autres à Constantinople; des clous sont signalés à plusieurs reprises au palais'. It may well have been one of these that Gabras stole and hid in his bosom, unless Anna used 'my Saviour's *side*' loosely for any

---

[1] III. 12, p. 98.   [2] XIII. 12, p. 415.
[3] VIII. 9, p. 242. The word ἐγκόλπιος seems here to have a general meaning, not its special sense of 'pectoral' cross, i.e. a cruciform reliquary, as in III. 10, p. 94. Cf. II. 5, p. 53.
[4] XI. 6, pp. 326, 327.   [5] *Rome, Kiev et Byzance*, p. 242.
[6] XI. 6, p. 326.   [7] pp. 10, 24, 26-7.

part of His body. If she really means 'side', the nail must have been one of Ebersolt's 'plusieurs', which may be interpreted not (as Ebersolt implies) to mean 'le saint clou avec trois autres' only, but to include at least five, i.e. the generally accepted four in the feet and hands and another driven in to fasten down the 'side'.[1] In any case she clearly intends us to believe that the relic found at Antioch was not, as Latin chroniclers arrogantly claimed, the unique Sacred Lance[2] which for nearly five centuries had been in safe keeping at Constantinople, and on which Bohemund swears in his treaty with Alexius;[3] she would of course not mind admitting the possibility of the Crusaders having discovered another nail.

In conclusion then we will assume that, though the two phrases used by Anna in the Gabras story and in Bohemund's oath are confusingly alike,[4] yet the first relic, of a size to be ἐγκόλπιος,[5] was a 'nail' and the second the Sacred Lance. If this is so, Anna uses ἧλος in its classical sense throughout.

[1] Zonaras (XIII. 3) says that Constantine the Great, when appropriating to himself a statue of Apollo, fastened on to the head τινὰς τῶν ἥλων οἳ τὸ σῶμα τοῦ κυρίου προσεπαττάλευσαν τῷ σωτηρίῳ σταυρῷ. If these as seems probable represented the rays of the sun-god (Anna calls the statue ’Ανθήλιος, XII. 4, p. 357), there must have been a considerable number of nails. Prof. Dawkins has pointed out in conversation that one medieval legend speaks of a bag of nails taken out to Calvary, all of which acquired sanctity though only four (or if the feet were crossed only three) were actually used. He also says that in a modern Greek song there is an allusion to a fifth nail called τὸ φαρμακερόν or 'deadly', because it pierced the Saviour's side, the whole conception being evolved from folk-lore and showing not an enlargement of but a divergence from the Gospel story.

[2] It is interesting to note that Foucher (I. 18, 1, 2) represents Bishop Adhémar as sceptical about the genuineness of the relic, while the *Gesta* declares the Bishop was so entirely convinced that he himself carried 'the Lance of the Saviour' into battle (ch. 29).

[3] XIV. 1, p. 419. He swears on it τῷ νῷ, as contrasted with the Gospels which were actually 'brought out', and the way it is joined with the Crown of Thorns, the supreme Byzantine treasure, would seem to show that Anna thought of these sacred relics as both in the same place, XIII. 12, p. 415.

[4] (a) τὸν ἅγιον ἧλον, δι’ οὗ τὴν τοῦ ἐμοῦ σωτῆρος πλευρὰν οἱ ἄνομοι ἔνυξαν (VIII. 9, p. 242).

(b) τῆς λόγχης, δι’ ἧς τὴν τοῦ σωτῆρος ἡμῶν πλευρὰν οἱ ἄνομοι ἐξεκέντησαν (XIV. 1, p. 419).

[5] We must not forget that relics were more often than not only *portions* of some sacred object, notably of the True Cross. See Du Cange's notes on II. 5, p. 53 c; III. 10, p. 94 d; XV. 11, p. 496 c. But in the case of the thing 'found' at Antioch it is obvious that the Crusaders spoke of the entire article, not of a reliquary containing a piece of it.

FOREIGN AFFAIRS
69. THE WEST. BOHEMUND

WE come at last to what is for Anna the *fons et origo malorum* in the Crusade and its aftermath, namely the overweening arrogance, greed, treachery, perjury and all the rest of Bohemund 'surnamed Saniscus',[1] the terrible Robert's even more terrible son, whose conflict with Alexius lasts twenty-seven years.[2] It is, as we have said before, not till he is a Crusader that he incurs Anna's venomous attacks. Then no colours are too dark for painting him, even though by this true aristocrat his low birth and poverty are contemptuously taken as some excuse.[3] Desire to improve his fortunes, crazy ambition either to seize the imperial sceptre or by becoming Grand Domestic to use the Greek troops for winning a principality in the East, an 'ancient grudge' against the Emperor—such are his motives of action.[4] But the Emperor is a match for him, 'understanding of old his deceitful[5] and treacherous nature', as well as 'the unfriendliness and malice of the man'.[6] So when he takes the oath of allegiance Anna seems prepared to believe that he did not intend to keep it. Like other Latins he is unstable, greedy, venal, while he displays the further vices of craft, suspicion, and callous disregard of his followers' lives.[7] Yet Anna is fair-minded enough to balance his good and evil qualities as follows:[8] 'By nature the man was a knave and quick at handling situations, in knavery and valour surpassing all the Latins who then passed through, as much as he was inferior to them in forces and money; indeed he excelled them all in superabundant activity in mischief.'[9]

True to his nature, though he was fully aware of the duty of surrendering Antioch, he yet 'coveted it for himself' and resorted to a double trick to secure it; he got Taticius and the Greek troops away by the fear of famine coupled with the

---

[1] IV. 6, p. 115.   [2] 1081–1108.   [3] X. 11, pp. 301, 303.
[4] X. 5, p. 285; 6, pp. 287, 288; 9, p. 294; 11, p. 304; XI. 12, p. 341; XII. 1, p. 345.
[5] His 'accustomed lying' is mentioned as an accepted fact in XI. 9, p. 333.
[6] X. 11, pp. 301, 302.   [7] X. 11.
[8] X. 11, p. 304. πονηρὸς καὶ ὀξὺς πρὸς τὰ συμπίπτοντα, . . . πάντων ἐκράτει κακεντρεχείας περιουσίᾳ.
[9] He certainly showed this in sending supplies and penetrating himself into Laodicea, which Greek troops were actually besieging (XI. 11, p. 340). Anna also tells of his reckless bravery, coupled with arrogance, in V. 6 and 7, and XI. 3, pp. 317, 318.

scare of a pretended plot against them,[1] and he induced the
Crusaders to promise the possession of the town to whichever
count first brought to terms the Turkish officer opposite his
place in camp, knowing all the time that 'a certain Armenian'
opposite himself had agreed with him to open the gates.[2]
Once installed as governor he refuses to surrender the city to
Alexius and even sends his nephew Tancred to seize Laodicea,
thus coming into open conflict with the Empire whose vassal he
was, and insolently justifying his treachery by the Emperor's
alleged desertion.[3]

In short, Bohemund is emphatically πονηρότατος, 'most
knavish',[4] and possesses a 'knavish soul',[5] to say nothing of the
minor faults of discourtesy[6] and blatant venality.[7] He was
indeed 'always the same Bohemund and never changed one
whit for the better',[8] and it seems superfluous energy for the
Emperor to go on reproaching him whenever he gets the opportunity.

Over the matter of Bohemund's Turkish captivity (1100–3),
which Anna never mentions, we need not linger.[9] Turning to
a lighter side of his career we find that the last chapter of
Book XI ends with a detailed description of a τέχνη on his

---

[1] We feel that even Anna does not think her father's man played le beau rôle here.
[2] XI. 4.
[3] XI. 6, p. 327; 7, p. 330; 9, pp. 332, 333; 10, p. 337. His argument is cogent:
'How is it just that what we gained with our own sweat and toil we should thus
lightly surrender?' (p. 333). So speaks Tancred in XII. 2, p. 348.
[4] A distinction which he shares with the Dalmatian Bolcanus (XII. 4, p. 356).
[5] XI. 10, p. 337.   [6] Ibid.
[7] He implies to Cantacuzenus that he is ready to sell his ill-gotten gains to the
Emperor, adding 'Be sure that without money thou canst not get even a castle'.
(XI. 11, p. 340; cf. X. 11).   [8] XI. 9, p. 333; 10, p. 337.
[9] A point of chronology is here involved. XI. 9 gives us the negotiations of
1103 between Alexius and Bohemund and the subsequent march into Cilicia
of Manuel Butumites. But XI. 10 carries us back to the expedition of the Pisan
fleet, which the Pisan chroniclers date for us as occurring in 1099. Anna says the
Greek fleet went after it in April (XI. 10, p. 335), and if we retain in the opening
sentence of the chapter the πρός which C. S. H. B. and the Teubner text alike
cut out, (ἐξερχόμενοι οἱ Φράγγοι πρὸς τὰ Ἱεροσόλυμα) we get the proper sequence;
the Crusaders, on their way from Antioch which they captured June, 1098 to
Jerusalem which they reached 6 June, 1099, made overtures to the Bishop of Pisa
and got aid from his fleet. But the story ends before the chapter does, with the
words: 'Such were the doings of the Pisan fleet', and Anna in characteristic
fashion returns to Bohemund and the year 1103, so that the episode of the
Genoese fleet in XI. 11 is in truth 'after the course of a year', i.e. in 1104. For
her sudden transitions see Ch. 62, above. Chalandon, ignoring this habit of hers,
discovers erroneous chronology in the passage (op. cit. p. 215, note 1). In XI. 11
we find Cantacuzenus (in the year 1104) besieging Laodicea, which had been
beleaguered by Bohemund in 1099 but abandoned by him when the Pisans left
him (XI. 10, p. 337 A–C), and which at the end of 1102 during his captivity had
been captured for him by his nephew Tancred (XI. 7, p. 330; 9, p. 332; and
cf. Chalandon. pp. 216, 218, 221–.).

part, which Anna calls 'very ignoble but very clever'. Having
neither army nor fleet to continue the struggle with the Greeks,
he gives out that he is dead, and at the end of 1104 escapes in
a coffin on a bireme from the harbour of Antioch. In order to
add verisimilitude by a smell of decay, he keeps a dead cock
on his chest, and makes his attendants go through periodic
lamentations, while he himself lies like a corpse, breathing only
through holes in the lid, and being fed by stealth. Anna cannot
get over her amazement at such audacious ingenuity, and her
style gets more and more lyrical and antithetical. Finally, at
Corfu he gets out of his hiding-place, beards the governor, and
'with a haughty glance and manner, and speaking in a haughty
and wholly barbaric voice', sends messages of insolent defiance
to the Emperor, threatening that he will stir up all Italy to war
against him, and will even take Byzantium. The concluding
words of XI. 12 are: 'To such a pitch of boasting forsooth was
the barbarian wrought up.'

In the next Book we find Bohemund trying in every possible
way to forward his dreams of empire. He marries one daughter
of the King of France, and gets another sent to Antioch as the
bride of his nephew Tancred. He collects troops by fair means
or foul, 'travelling round all the lands and towns' with violent
abuse of Alexius as a Pagan who is leagued with Pagans against
Christianity. The rumour which had formerly been spread
abroad at Antioch, probably by Bohemund himself, that Alexius
had called in Curpagan and his Turks to relieve the town while
the Crusaders were besieging it, was doubtless circulated again.
As an object-lesson to show his own piety and magnanimity,
Alexius decides at this juncture to send home laden with gifts
the counts whom he had delivered from their prison in Cairo.
These go round Southern Italy calling Bohemund an inveterate
liar,[1] and pointing to their own treatment by Alexius as a proof.

Not long afterwards however Bohemund is able to give a
somewhat similar object-lesson telling directly against Alexius.
While he himself is expected with great terror in Illyria, one
of his nephews (a brother of Tancred) defeats the Greek forces
at Otranto and captures six of their Scythian mercenaries.
These are sent to the Pope as a proof that Alexius used barbarians in war against Christians, and their fierce aspect acts
as admirable propaganda. As Anna puts it half admiringly,
'craftily (πανούργως) methinks did he handle the question of the
war against the Christians', for when once he had convinced
the Pope, 'a man apparently reasonable', of Alexius' iniquities

---

[1] XII. 1.

in this direction it was easy to win over 'boorish and ignorant men'. The army which he collected was so large and heterogeneous, Franks, Celts, English, Germans, Spaniards, that the very report of it threw the Greek admiral into a panic. Even the famous sea-captain Lantulph 'turned aside' and allowed the Norman fleet, convoyed like a moving city by a ring of huge merchantmen, to cross unmolested and to disembark its forces. After plundering far and wide Bohemund settles down like a greater Demetrius Poliorcetes to besiege Durazzo scientifically.[1] His ingenuity and determination receive full credit from Anna throughout her story of the siege; only at the beginning does she condemn his 'tyrannical mind' and his ambition that ignored even monitions from on high.[2]

In the episode of Alexius' attempt to sow dissension between Bohemund and his counts by bogus letters, we feel that the Norman comes out better than the Greek. Alexius, so says his daughter, thought Bohemund too 'full of knavery and energy' (πονηρία καὶ δραστηριότης) to make open fighting advisable, so he resorts to this trick, hoping that rage would make his enemy 'revert to his barbaric customs' of savage vengeance against the incriminated chiefs. But instead of this Bohemund reflects for six days, and then either from sharp-sighted perception of the truth or from a realization of what is expedient decides on ignoring the matter and leaving the counts unmolested.[3]

Once more as regards the two great antagonists it is a case of 'Greek meeting Greek', or in Anna's proverb 'Cretizing to a Cretan'.[4] It is probably respect for his wits quite as much as for his courage that makes her call Bohemund[5] 'most warlike', and 'most like a tyrant', one who when disaster befell him 'was in no wise cast down, but rather seemed more confident' (θαρραλεώτερος). When he is finally driven by hunger and disease to sue for peace, his negotiations with the imperial envoys are so described as to bring out what Anna probably considers his two main characteristics, arrogance and the caution which springs from a crafty nature. He insists on hostages and oaths and safe-conducts with wearisome iteration; he is careful not to let the envoys spy out the nakedness of the land; he insolently refuses to hear any reproaches over the past, and he claims, with a haughtiness that 'takes ill' and is affronted at any opposition, an honourable reception by the Emperor as though almost

---

[1] XII. 8 and 9.   [2] XIII. 2 and 3.
[3] XIII. 4.   [4] X. 11, p. 304.
[5] XIII. 6, pp. 393, 394, τυραννικώτατος. For the various shades of meaning, partly of blame, partly of praise, attached to this word, see pp. 286–7 above.

on equal terms.[1] The envoys contest the minor points but yield
on all the larger, and both sides swear on the Gospels.[2]

In the following chapter [3] Bohemund's sudden submissiveness
to the envoys, even in the matter of a place whither to transfer
his camp, calls forth from Anna a diatribe on the Celtic race,
unstable and unaccountable, now boasting, now servile. But
when he finally reaches the Emperor, the historian evidently
thinks the time has come for a detailed picture of her villain-
hero. We give it in full:

'Now this man, to put it shortly, was such that no one has been seen
like him, neither barbarian nor Hellene, for when seen he was a
marvel to the eyes, and when named he was a terror. And to
describe the barbarian's appearance in detail, he was so great in
the height of his body as to exceed the tallest man by nearly a cubit,
small of abdomen, but broad in his flanks and shoulders, expansive
of chest and powerful in his arms. As to the whole condition of his
body he was neither denuded of nor burdened with flesh, but perfectly proportioned and so to speak formed according to the canon
of Polyclitus.[4] He was strong in his hands, steady in the tread of
his feet, solid in his neck and back, and he appeared to any one
keenly interested in him somewhat round-backed, not because the
spinal vertebrae of the back had suffered any injury, but he was
formed so it seemed somewhat like this from birth. His skin in all
the rest of his body was very white, but his face was ruddy with the
white. And his hair was yellowish, but did not hang down to the
middle of his back like that of other barbarians, for the man had
no passion for long hair, but was cropped to his ears. As to his
beard I cannot say whether it was red or some other colour, for the
razor went over it till the chin was smoother than any chalk; yet it
appeared to be red too. His eyes were blue, and displayed at the
same time spirit and dignity, and his nose and nostrils breathed
the air freely.'

Then follows an obscure sentence (with one lacuna and one
possible misreading) to the effect that his broad nostrils corresponded to his broad chest. She continues:

'For nature had given him passages through his nose for the breath
that surged up from his heart. Now in this man something sweet
appeared, but was impaired by alarming qualities on all sides. For
as a whole throughout all his body the man was harsh and brutal
both in size and looks, as it seems to me, and his laugh would have
been a snorting in others. In soul and body he was such that both

---

[1] This is in spite of the fact that he describes himself as going to the Emperor
χάριν οἰκονομίας καὶ θεραπείας τῆς πρὸς αὐτόν (XIII. 9, p. 401).
[2] XIII. 9.   [3] XIII. 10.
[4] We may note that Alexius and Irene, in their daughter's eyes, even excelled
this Canon (III. 3, p. 76).

anger and love raised their heads in him, and both looked towards
war. His intellect was resourceful and crafty[1] and could elude all
attack. For his speech was precise and he gave answers affording
no handle anywhere, and being such as he was and so great he was
inferior only to the Emperor, both in position and eloquence and
in the other gifts that come from nature.'

The treaty between the Greeks and Normans fills all the last
chapter of Book XIII, and in its purely conventional language
tells us nothing further as to what Anna thought of Bohemund.
And when she mentions his death six months later she makes
no comment whatever.[2] But indeed, having once depicted him
in full, as 'inferior only to the Emperor', what more could she
find worth saying about him?

We however who are not Alexius' daughter may well spend
a few moments on the treaty accepted by Bohemund with such
reluctance[3] and enunciated by Anna with such pride. For one
thing it closes an episode about which H. Hagenmeyer wrote
in 1913:[4] 'Eine eingehende kritische Behandlung des Feldzuges
Boemunds gegen Alexios . . . steht noch aus; es wäre ein dank-
bares Thema für eine Monographie, in der auch das . . . längere
Gedicht des gleichzeitigen Tortarius seine Würdigung und Ver-
wendung finden müsste,' referring to the unpublished poem of
Radulphus Tortarius,[5] *De obsidione Dyrrachii.*

As portrayed by Anna the campaign is somewhat lacking in
interest, all but the chapter devoted to Bohemund's ingenious
though unsuccessful siegecraft.[6] But the treaty evidently seemed
to her of the highest importance, and occupies what appears to
us a disproportionately large share of her pages.[7] We must
however admit that it is extremely lucid for all its repetitions,
grandiloquence, and diplomatic tall talk. Bohemund begins by
laying down the usual maxim of International Law, that war
vitiates all contracts. Therefore former agreements between
him and the Emperor do not hold, nor must he be reproached
for the past. He is now wiser, and will make 'this second agreement', becoming if permitted the vassal[8] of Alexius and his son
John. This he swears by God and His saints before witnesses,
and he will receive a copy of the contract in a Golden Bull
signed by the Emperor. His homage (πίστις) involves defending

---

[1] πανοῦργον once more.   [2] XIV. 1, p. 419.

[3] He is finally induced to sign by the persuasive Nicephorus Bryennius Caesar
(XIII. 11). Zonaras (XVIII. 25) says it all took place 'near Colonea Europea'.

[4] In his edition of Foucher de Chartres, p. 518, note 1.

[5] A manuscript in the Vatican, Reg. Christ. 1357, ff. 124–32.

[6] XIII. 3.   [7] XIII. 12, pp. 406–16.

[8] Five words are used for this: λίζιος, ἄνθρωπος, οἰκέτης, ὑποχείριος, and δοῦλος.
One of the verbs employed is θεραπεύειν.

the Empire with his troops against Christians and Pagans, unless impeded by illness or private war, in which case he will send some general in his stead. The promise, which is to be held 'pure and uncorrupted' all his life, is given in return for various specified lands and cities. Not only the joint Emperors' lives but their honour and their 'imperial limbs' and their possessions must be defended, and Bohemund will never seize or hold any part of the Byzantine territory except what is specifically given him. In lands once under the sway of Constantinople, any conquests made by Bohemund shall either be surrendered to an imperial delegate or administered for the Emperor at his pleasure. No treaty harmful to the Empire shall be made by Bohemund with 'any other Christian'; and he will not 'become the man of another', on the same ground brought forward by Tancred when refusing to swear to Alexius,[1] i.e. that one 'lordship' is enough for one man to serve. No deserters from Alexius' sway shall be received, and barbarian enemies who make their submission to Bohemund shall at once swear fealty through him as proxy. Even lands that 'have never served the Greek empire' are to be considered as part of it ('whether Turks or Armenians . . . Pagans or Christians'), and their inhabitants as the 'men' of the joint emperors, not to be supported in any insubordination; Tancred is to surrender, on pain of war with his uncle, the cities which he holds. The commandants of the towns assigned to Bohemund are to become 'sureties for these agreements', by swearing similar fealty and taking most solemn oaths to abjure Bohemund's service, if 'downright madness and frenzy' should make him forsworn. They too must defend the sovereign when necessary, taking 'dreadful oaths'[2] of loyalty like their superior. These oaths shall be administered at once to the Normans who are with Bohemund, and if Alexius will send representatives out to Syria the forces there shall swear too.[3] So in the same way can an oath be taken in Lombardy from all who wish later to cross the Adriatic. Bohemund will be on warlike or peaceful terms with his Eastern neighbours as his suzerain pleases; he will regard Turkish deserters as belonging to the Emperor, and will only retain captives when taken in war by his own 'pain and fatigues'.

Then follows the really vital part. Bohemund is to keep the dukedom of Antioch for life[4] if he remains loyal, but the Patri-

---

[1] XI. 3, p. 316.
[2] φρικαλέοι ὅρκοι (XIII. 12, pp. 410, 411).
[3] The idea of proxy comes more than once into this treaty.
[4] Certain towns are excepted, and certain others elsewhere are given in exchange.

arch there must always be a Greek priest from St. Sophia, and Laodicea is specially retained for the Empire. If the writer of the *Gesta*[1] is right in saying that as early as 1097 Alexius promised Bohemund, 'si libenter ei iuraret, XV dies eundi terre in extensione ab Antiochia retro daret et VIII in latitudine', all we can say is that the execution was long delayed, *de iure* if not *de facto*. At any rate Anna herself admits[2] that in the greatest issue of all Bohemund came off victor. He was to keep Antioch, and the fact that he could not bequeath it like Edessa[3] was a minor consideration, as was also the Emperor's retention of the hotly contested Laodicea.

The pact concludes with every kind of solemn asseveration of good faith, and every form of oath then held most sacred, sworn on the holiest objects of reverence visible and invisible,[4] before a host of witnesses whose names and offices are given with the utmost minuteness. Nothing has been omitted that could impress and awe the reader. 'God and men and the most high angels' attest the solemnity of the transaction;[5] bishops and monks, knights and foreign ambassadors, a notary and a eunuch of *nobilissimus* rank, all sign as witnesses, while the unlettered 'leaders of the pilgrims'[6] make their mark. Never surely was any covenant more solemnly signed, sealed and delivered. As to its subsequent fate (for it was never kept) no blame can be attached to Bohemund, who went home after receiving the usual 'sufficient money' and died[7] in a short time. And we can readily understand how Tancred, refusing to be bound by his uncle's treaty, 'clung to Antioch and considered it altogether as belonging to him'.[8] But on the other hand we feel it natural that the oath-breaking of 'these barbarian Franks', on whom according to Anna he had lavished care and

---

[1] Ch. 6.

[2] Chalandon curiously sees in the whole treaty 'le triomphe définitif d'Alexis sur Bohémond' (p. 249) because of the limitations put on the boundaries of the dukedom of Antioch. This is not our reading of the text. Probably each party tried to consider itself the winner.

[3] With Edessa Bohemund was to receive an annual subsidy (twice emphasized) of 200 gold 'talents' with the effigy of Michael VII (Ducas). See Du Cange's note on XIII. 12, p. 414 c. Bohemund undertakes to send an envoy for this to Constantinople yearly.

[4] The sufferings of Christ, the Cross, the Gospels, the Crown of Thorns, the Nails and the Lance. [5] XIII. 12, p. 411.

[6] It is interesting to find the περεγρῖνοι petitioning Alexius about lands, as though admittedly his vassals (XIII. 12, p. 414). In Foucher's account of the treaty (II. 39, 2) Alexius swears to protect the pilgrims by land and sea, 'ne quis eorum diriperetur vel male tractaretur'.

[7] XIV. 1, p. 419. Anna says in six months, but Chalandon on the authority of the Latin chroniclers gives an interval of three years, and believes the date of his death to be 1111 (*op. cit.* p. 249, note 6). [8] XIV. 2, p. 422.

money, should have 'rent in sunder the soul of the Emperor'.[1]
First he tried reproaching Tancred with 'injustice and violation
of oaths', as well as with 'ingratitude towards the Greeks', but
the 'mad barbarian cursed of God' refused in insulting and
boastful terms even to listen.[2] So by the advice of the Senate
and army Alexius resolves to try to gain allies against Tancred
among the other Crusaders. Bertrand the son of St. Gilles
swears fealty, but Baldwin king of Jerusalem (then in process
of besieging Tyre) meets the falsehood of the Greek envoys
with double dealing of his own.[3] Neither he nor Tancred comes
into the story again, and when Tancred died in 1112 all idea
of the treaty's ever being executed was finally abandoned.

Such then is Anna's version of the relations between her
father and the Crusaders, of whom Bohemund was to her the
chief. On three points it differs materially from that of the
Latin chroniclers, two comparatively trivial (whether St. Gilles
took the oath and whether the relic found at Antioch was a
Lance or a Nail), but one vitally important, affecting our whole
conception of her father. Which broke faith first, Alexius or
the Crusaders? Was Alexius or Bohemund the greater knave?
Even from his daughter's own story we are inclined to give at
least the chronological precedence in duplicity to the Emperor,
and to believe that from the very first he was trying to circum-
vent his detested allies, till he finally deserted them in their dire

[1] XIV. 2, pp. 423, 428.
[2] Alexius tries to set St. Gilles' son against Tancred by this accusation (XIV. 2,
p. 425). Insolence is Tancred's chief characteristic. He is the last to take the oath
of homage and brawls in the Emperor's presence (XI. 3, pp. 316, 317). He is the
first openly to 'break the oath' by wresting Laodicea from an imperial general
(XI. 7, p. 330), and he acts all along as Bohemund's âme damnée. But with her
strange fair-mindedness Anna depicts him as a devoted and obedient nephew
while Bohemund is alive (XI. 3, p. 316; 7, p. 330; in XII. 1, p. 346, he
even lets his uncle choose a wife for him, and in XIII. 11, p. 405; 12, p. 410,
it is assumed he will do Bohemund's bidding); a brave and energetic soldier
(XI. 5, p. 320; XII. 2, p. 348), στρατιώτης φερεπονώτατος, and a never defeated
master of siegecraft (XII. 2, p. 349), as well as ῥωμαλεώτατος τῶν κατ' αὐτόν,
famed for strategic experience, a true 'thunderbolt-bearer' (ibid.). His mother as
guardian of Otranto is brave and resourceful, and outwits the Greek admiral
who attacks the town (XII. 8). One curious touch is that Anna professes
ignorance as to whether she or her husband was related to Bohemund by blood
(ibid. p. 366). Similarly it is strange to find her calling Roger the πρωτότοκος
son of Robert (V. 3, p. 131), when in reality Bohemund was the eldest, the only
son of the first wife Alberada, as we learn from Malaterra, I. 30 (Muratori, op. cit.
V. p. 557).
[3] XIV. 2. Baldwin does not come well out of this story. He is taken in by the
Tyrians and fails from indolence and over-confidence to capture Tyre, and though
he saw through a falsehood of Butumites' and 'reproved him bitterly as a liar',
he yet fatuously hoped to get money from the imperial envoys and use it against
Alexius to help Tancred. Butumites insisted on service before payment and Baldwin sent him away. He is indeed changed for the worse from the reasonable and
brave count of X. 10, p. 300; XI. 7.

need at Antioch. But in fairness we must remember that the Crusaders (and especially the gigantic, cunning, unscrupulous, and overbearing Bohemund) seemed to him quite as much savages as Red Indians did to the early American settlers. If he used fraud and not force to get the better of them, it may have been necessity rather than preference that dictated his actions, because, in Anna's familiar phrase, 'not having sufficient forces against such numbers ἐν ἀμηχανίᾳ καθίστατο',[1] a frame of mind not heroic but very human.

[1] VII. 6, p. 203, and often elsewhere.

VI. ANNA AS A WRITER

70. *KOINH* AND GRAMMAR

WE have now come, after our attempted exploration in the various paths of Anna's morals and mind, to a viewpoint distinct in character from any we have yet approached. Here the question is not What did Anna feel and think? but How did she express it? In short we come to her Style. When we reflect that on the style of her predecessor Psellus a learned Frenchman has recently written a volume of 614 pages,[1] it might seem as if such a subject had better be left to form a separate book. But if the style is the man (or the woman), we are in duty bound to say at least a few words about Anna Comnena's.

It would take an exhaustive study to compare it with that of her contemporaries, in order to estimate her superiority or the reverse. Most of the Byzantine Greeks of about her time are hard reading, and she certainly is one of the hardest. Taking them at random, we observe that her husband Bryennius, at least for the first half of his work, is far easier than Anna; so also is Attaliates. Zonaras is sometimes obscure, sometimes very clear; the *Anon. Syn. Chron.* is on the whole easy, and Psellus very difficult, while at the other end of the rather wide period we have Nicetas Acominatus, often almost incomprehensible. Theophylact and Theodore Prodromus[2] writing on current topics present difficulties of a special kind. One handicap of course they all had in common: they were trying to perpetuate a classical language which was no longer the spoken tongue of their time. And their faults are just what we might expect: artificiality, phrases elaborately recondite, verbs heaped with prefixes because the plain root-meaning had become obscured, quotations and allusions to pad out the 'shrunk shank' of their style.

This question of the Byzantine literary κοινή has called forth a flood of literature. Suffice it to say with Renauld that the term, as used by Psellus, meant 'la *langue de la tradition écrite*, langue de savants, qui reposait essentiellement sur l'imitation du vocabulaire et des formes de l'ancien grec . . . langue conventionnelle qui . . . subsiste encore aujourd'hui sous le nom de *langue puriste*

---

[1] E. Renauld, *Étude de la langue et du style de Michel Psellos*, Paris, 1920, with a *Lexique choisi de Psellos* as a separate volume.

[2] A. Maiuri, in his article *Una nuova poesia di Teodoro Prodromo in greco volgare* (*B. Z.* XXIII pp. 397–407), suggests that Prodromus used sometimes to write his poems 'in lingua volgare' and translate them into 'lingua letteraria'.

ou *langue savante*.'[1] This critic then enumerates the features which distinguish the κοινή from Attic Greek, new words, new meanings, corrupted grammar, looser syntax, all of which he sums up as 'l'admission de tournures de la basse grécité'.[2] Krumbacher[3] gives an even shorter definition of the κοινή: 'Sie steht auf einer Mittelstufe zwischen der attischen Reinsprache und dem schwankenden Idiom des Volkes.' And we can see for ourselves that different authors occupy different positions on this 'middle step', Anna Comnena being, in her own opinion and that of her age, a perfectly pure 'Atticizer'.[4] Few critics however would agree with her; in her most elaborate passages, those over which she obviously laboured most and of which she was certainly most proud, she reminds us of the comparison drawn by Rohde between the erudite Byzantines, with their fine phrases and displays of learning, and the 'Vogel Strauss, der trotz seiner prächtigen Federn nicht fliegen könne'.[5] Grenier,[6] after dwelling on the marked division in eleventh-century Constantinople between the language of the learned (founded on the classics to which two centuries before men's minds had been turned back by Photius) and the language of the people, sums up the characteristics of Byzantine literature[7] as follows:

---

[1] *Op. cit.*, Introd., p. iii. He contrasts it with 'ce que les philologues appellent κοινή sans autre qualificatif, la *langue de la tradition orale*'.

[2] Prodromus even if on occasion he composed in the popular Greek of his day, yet throughout his writings professes as a classical scholar to despise it.

[3] *G. B. L.*, p. 789.

[4] Pref. 1, p. 1, τὸ Ἑλληνίζειν ἐς ἄκρον ἐσπουδακυῖα. Zonaras says of her τὴν γλῶτταν εἶχεν ἀκριβῶς ἀττικίζουσαν (XXVIII. 26). To Theodore Prodromus she is the Tenth Muse (*Epithalamium*: P. G. 133, col. 1401). Her attitude to the common speech of her day is interesting. She calls it sometimes ἡ συνήθεια (IV. 4, p. 109; VI. 3, p. 156; 13, p. 180; XI. 11, p. 339), sometimes ἰδιῶτις γλώττη or λέξις (VII. 5, p. 201; X. 2, p. 272; XII. 6, p. 362), and quotes verbatim a verse composed in it (II. 4, p. 51). (Cf. also VII. 3, p. 198; and XII. 6, p. 362 of similar songs.) So Cecaumenus (*Strat.* p. 49) speaks of monks as ἰδιῶται τῷ λόγῳ, recalling 2 Cor. xi. 6. But Anna also uses κοινὴ διάλεκτος in this sense, and not in that taken by Renauld from Psellus (III. 4, p. 80; VIII. 3, p. 227). Once she talks of ἡ νῦν γλῶττα ἐκβαρβαρώσασα as having changed the name Lychnitis into Achrida (XII. 9, p. 371); once she speaks of the 'Persian dialect' (VI. 12, p. 178); and twice she calls the Scythian language a διάλεκτος which Greeks could not understand (VII. 9, p. 211 (*bis*); VIII. 5, p. 232), where there is no sense as in our word 'dialect' of a patois but rather of a distinct language. But on one occasion she introduces a 'word commonly used by the soldiers' (VII. 1, p. 188), namely κοπός, probably for σκοπός in the sense of 'aim' or 'object', and legitimately to be translated 'little game'. W. Miller, in his article on Anna (*Quart. Rev.*, January 1920), translates it 'fatigue-parties'.

When Anna transmogrifies foreign names in a way that to Gibbon shows her 'proud ignorance so dear and familiar to a polished people', we need to remind ourselves of Bury's comment on this: 'A reader, ignorant of the pronunciation of modern Greek, might easily do injustice to Anna'.

[5] *Der griechische Roman*, p. 333.   [6] *Empire byzantin*, Vol. 1, p. 329.

[7] He makes the interesting observation that up to the Crusades Byzantine

On the one hand learning, adherence to tradition, and love of form; on the other want of life or observation or the sense of truth and beauty. In Anna's case the indictment is grossly exaggerated, but it has enough verisimilitude to make a good foundation for any critical study of her style. An elaborate investigation of Renauld's kind would be quite impossible here. We will content ourselves with pointing out in her writings certain peculiarities of construction and phraseology in which she diverges from classical Greek, usually in company with her contemporaries, and then a few of her more personal and individual qualities.

At the outset we will dismiss her love for quotations and allusions, and especially for Biblical and Homeric phrases, with which we have dealt in considering her education. All the writers of her period quoted the Bible and Homer and displayed their knowledge of history and mythology, some more and some less copiously;[1] it was the sign of having been properly brought up, just as in old days Members of Parliament plumed themselves on citations from Virgil and Horace. We may also omit the tendency to point a moral which we see in all Byzantine writers,[2] for this is connected with their view of Divine Providence, and of that we have already spoken. This feature, involving the careful enumeration of causes for events, is, we must repeat, to be found in Thucydides, the model for all later historians, as is also the putting into men's mouths of 'sentiments proper to the occasion'.[3] It is with humbler matters that we propose to deal here—grammar and vocabulary.[4]

First, grammar. As in the *Strategicon* of Cecaumenus so in the *Alexias* moods are chaotic,[5] indicative, subjunctive, and optative being used in the same sentence with no difference of meaning.[6] Plural verbs after a neuter plural noun are common.[7] Tenses are loosely used too often to make references necessary. Genitives absolute refer to the subject or object of

---

literature was familiar to no one outside the Eastern Empire except the Arabs; Greek was as much an unknown language to the Western part of Europe, as Latin to the Eastern, *ibid.* p. 334.

[1] Thus Bryennius and Zonaras quote little, Psellus fairly often, Theophylact very frequently.

[2] Nicephorus Bryennius and Attaliates in particular do this very markedly.

[3] Thuc. I. 22.

[4] It should be said at the outset that the references in the notes are meant to be illustrative, not exhaustive, from this point onwards.

[5] We may remark that as to genders and cases Anna is more careful than Cecaumenus.

[6] e.g. XIII. 12, pp. 410D, 411A. So aorist optative and future indicative in X. 8, p. 293 A.

[7] e.g. III. 6, p. 84 B, C, and often elsewhere.

a sentence;[1] demonstrative pronouns take the place of reflexive, and the reflexives themselves are promiscuous.[2] The verb χρᾶσθαι is followed by an accusative or a genitive.[3] We have εἰς for ἐν and ἐν for εἰς,[4] and διά with the genitive meaning 'made of' or 'at'.[5] In one sentence the same pronoun, αὐτῷ, refers to two different people.[6] We get ὡς ἵνα introducing the object of a verb of promising, without any causal, final, or consecutive force.[7] We have a redundant ἄν with the optative in the protasis of a conditional relative clause.[8] We find the form ἐφεύροσαν in the third person plural of the second aorist,[9] and the feminine of πᾶς used in agreement with a masculine noun as in modern Greek,[10] while 'the editorial we' makes Anna speak of herself as τὴν γλῶτταν ἐκδακόντας where we should expect the feminine singular.[11] But over and above all these comparative trifles we have changes of subject in the middle of a sentence, broken constructions, and omissions of principal verbs, all making the *Alexias* very difficult to construe.[12] In this respect Anna is certainly as bad a sinner as any of her contemporaries, and to these defects is doubtless due the aversion hitherto shown to putting her into English.[13]

---

[1] IX. 9, p. 262, where διαφημισάντων in a parenthesis refers to the subject of the long main sentence as expressed by the relative clause ὁπόσοι . . . παρῆσαν. Also XII. 5, p. 358 B; 7, p. 365 B, and often elsewhere.

[2] τούτῳ for ἑαυτῷ, VIII. 1, p. 223; τούτου for ἑαυτοῦ, XII. 2, p. 348; ἐκείνης for ἑαυτῆς, XII. 2, p. 351; τούτοις for ἑαυτοῖς, XIII. 6, p. 392; σφῶν for ἡμῶν αὐτῶν, XI. 4. p. 319; ἑαυτόν for 'myself', XIV. 2, p. 425.

[3] XI. 12, p. 340; XV. 11, p. 499.

[4] XI. 10, p. 335, and often elsewhere; XV. 11, p. 499.

[5] Both in XI. 11, p. 339 B.   [6] XI. 9, p. 333 D.

[7] XIII. 12, p. 409 C.

[8] XI. 12, p. 342 B, and see Goodwin's *Greek Grammar*, edition of 1894, §§ 1437–9.

[9] XV. 2, p. 464 D. Psaltis' *Greek Grammar* gives a similar form ἦλθοσαν as appearing in Greek chroniclers generally.

[10] XII. 8, p. 367 D.   [11] XIV. 4, p. 438. So also in X. 2, p. 271.

[12] Thus in VI. 11, p. 175 C, 'the weaker enemy' is the subject of γένηται, but we have to supply 'Alexius' before the next four subjunctives. In XI. 6, p. 324 B, the sentence starts with ὁ βασιλεύς as subject, but when we get to the principal verb φθάνει we find it has acquired a fresh subject, Γελίελμος, and the Emperor becomes the object as τοῦτον. A few lines later (p. 325 A) the sentence λογισμὸν . . . φυγῆς has no principal verb, and the nominative participle λαμβάνων refers in sense to the Emperor, last mentioned in the genitive. In III. 7, p. 86 B we have to put in as subject 'Anna Dalassena' before θαῦμα ἦν in a kind of apposition to her own 'past life'; in III. 8, p. 88 B, the sentence beginning τὸ δὲ ἦθος has no principal verb.

[13] See p. 3, note 2, above.

71. VOCABULARY—FOREIGN WORDS

NOW as to vocabulary. Here our subject falls under three heads, foreign words, unclassical words, and words unclassically used.

Professor R. M. Dawkins in an unpublished paper from which he has kindly authorized quotation[1] says: 'When Byzantium got a Roman Emperor[2] and a court in which Latin was the language, and when the whole machinery of Roman government, together with Roman Law and Roman military art, was settled in the East, . . . a long series of words passed at this period from Latin into Greek.' It appears that up to the reign of Justinian Greek writers tried to keep out Latin words, but in the eighth and ninth centuries a large number of technical and official Latin words are found, when and because Latin had disappeared as the official language;[3] Latin words had still to be used in many subjects hitherto dealt with in Latin, because no Greek substitute had ever been found. In the legal writings of Justinian we can trace the change in the public mind as to the two languages; in his great works Latin is used, but the larger part of his Novels are in 'this common Greek tongue'.[4] In the fifth century inscriptions on the walls of Constantinople begin to be in Greek, till finally Latin only survived on coins or in court acclamations. But many Latin words had been by this time incorporated into the Greek language. Of one set of such terms Professor Dawkins says: 'The army of the Empire was peculiarly a Roman institution with naturally a full set of Latin terms, very many of which were taken over, together with the army organization, by the Byzantine Empire.' Oman[5] speaks of 'the extraordinary mixture of Roman, Greek, and Teutonic words' in the military terminology in the days of Maurice (586–602), but in the *Tactica* of Leo (probably, as has been said, the Isaurian, 717–41, but possibly the Wise, 886–911) Latin technical phrases are invariably translated into Greek, to ensure universal comprehension.

This is not all. With the commercial contact of East and West, existing even before the Crusades, a fresh set of words derived from the Latin crept into the Byzantine vocabulary. We must therefore carefully distinguish in the *Alexias* between the Latin

---

[1] *Latin Words in the Modern Greek Vocabulary.*   [2] i. e. Constantine.
[3] Freeman (*Some points in the later history of the Greek language: J. H. S.* III) compares this to 'the flood of French words which entered English when English overcame French as the language of this land'.
[4] *Novel* 7, ch. 1.   [5] *Art of War*, I, p. 177.

terms which the Byzantines had inherited from the period between Constantine and Justinian, and the Low Latin terms
which expressed medieval ideas. There are also a few that
come from sources other than Latin. We must therefore divide
Anna's foreign words into three groups, non-Latin, Old Latin,
Medieval.

(a) Of non-Latin terms we find fairly few. Anna correctly
calls the officials in Serbia and Dalmatia 'qui proximam a rege
potestatem habebant' by the name of ζούπανοι,[1] and the Hungarian king by that of κράλης.[2] Turkish rulers are 'emirs' or
'sultans' or 'exousiasts' or 'satraps'. The last word, used as
early as Xenophon's day, is once less correctly applied by Anna
to Greeks.[3] Μουσούλμανος is from the Arabic,[4] ἀββᾶς and σάβ-
βατον from the Hebrew,[5] ζατρίκιον (chess) from Persia, said to
be its place of origin.[6] The word κουλά, citadel,[7] is nearly certainly derived from the Arabic cale (which gives us the modern
village of Kula near Philadelphia in Asia Minor) and not, as
Du Cange supposes, from the Latin collis.[8] Σαγούδαοι in Asia
Minor (XV. 2, p. 264) is by its name (derived from the Turkish
for 'willow') 'a striking proof of the extent of the Seljuk power
along the Dorylaion route'.[9]

(b) Old Latin terms are very numerous. First we get many
titles or names of office, such as Καῖσαρ and Αὔγουστα, applied
throughout by Anna to her husband and her mother, the
'Domestic' of the East or West, and the 'Grand Primicerius'.
We also have νωβελλίσιμος,[10] δούξ used in many passages for
various forms of leadership by land and sea, and giving rise[11]
to the derivatives δουκικός and δουκάτον; ῥήξ for kings, e.g. of
Germany or Jerusalem; πρίγκιπες for princes,[12] κόμητες for
Frankish counts repeatedly and twice for Greek officers;[13] σπαθάριος, 'guardsman';[14] καβαλλάριος, 'horseman',[15] Μαΐστρομίλιοι,

---

[1] IX. 10, p. 265 C, and Du Cange's note.
[2] XIII. 12, p. 416.
[3] IX. 4, p. 252. Σιαούς in VI. 9, p. 170, probably = Mod. Turk. tchaoush,
'sergeant'. [4] XIV. 3, p. 432; 6, p. 442.
[5] II. 4, p. 51; 9, p. 62; VI. 8, p. 166; VIII. 2, p. 223. [6] XII. 6, p. 360.
[7] XI. 5, p. 320; 11, p. 339. So in Cec., Strat. p. 64. In VII. 1 we have τὸ τοῦ Κούλη
πολίχνιον as the name of a fortress near the borders of Thrace and Macedonia.
Ramsay (Historical Geography of Asia Minor, pp. 211–12) says the word 'is still used
in Turkish in the sense of a single house standing apart among the fields away from
a town, and therefore like a castle'.
[8] Note on XI. 5, p. 320 B. [9] Ramsay, op. cit. p. 209 note.
[10] X. 3, p. 274; XIII. 8, p. 399; 12, p. 416. In VII. 8, p. 208, we get the unpleasing hybrid Protonobellisimos. [11] XIII. 12.
[12] III. 10, p. 93. [13] X. 3, p. 276: 8, p. 290.
[14] II. 11, p. 64. Allied names are ἐξκουβίτης and βεστιαρίτης, both denoting men
in a corps of guards (IV. 4, p. 109). We may compare νοτάριος in XIII. 12, p. 416.
[15] XIII. 12, p. 411. Anna knows this is a Norman term.

magistri militum, for the governors of Naples.[1] Then there are names connected with the imperial administration: παλάτιον, the hybrid χρυσόβουλλον and σέκρετον very frequently, ὀφφίκιον, 'office', and ῥόγα, 'salary',[2] κομμέρκιον, 'a trading tax',[3] and λίτρα, 'a talent of gold', defined by Liddell and Scott as the Sicelo-Greek version of *libra*.[4] In other fields we have φόρος for *forum*, πραιτώριον for 'ducal seat',[5] πόρτα for 'gate',[6] σίγνα for 'marks',[7] μανουάλιον for 'candle-stick',[8] σκάλαι for 'wharves',[9] κέλλα for a monastic 'cell',[10] φάμουσον for a 'lampoon',[11] κέντρον for 'centre',[12] βρέβιον for an ecclesiastical inventory.[13] The word κλείσουρα used by Anna for a 'gorge' or 'pass'[14] is explained by Oman as 'a corruption of the Roman *clausura*; it consisted of an important mountain pass with a fortress and garrison'. Other military terms are φόσσατον,[15] κουράτωρ for 'commandant,'[16] κόρτινα, a wall between towers,[17] κάστρον or καστέλλιον very frequently; in the naval sphere we get ἐξκουσσάτον,[18] a name due, according to Du Cange,[19] to the fact that Venetian freight-boats were *excusati*, that is, enjoyed certain exemptions. Month-names are Latin; we get April, June, August, October, November, December.[20] Finally we can close the list with the word τύρβη for 'tumult',[21] which seems to be peculiar to Anna, a translation coined by her for the occasion.

(c) Medieval terms are the most scanty of the three groups; in fact there are only four certain ones, κονόσταυλος ('constable'),[22] λίζιος ('vassal'),[23] σεργέντιοι ('foot soldiers', from *servientes*),[24] and περεγρῖνος ('pilgrim', not 'stranger').[25] We ought

---

[1] XIII. 4, p. 387. Cf. μάγιστρος τὴν ἀξίαν (II. 4, p. 50).
[2] III. 6, pp. 84, 85: 10, p. 94; VI. 5, p. 161. This word, 'that which is asked for', had in the sixth century meant 'largesse to the people'. There is of course no classical Latin equivalent; it is merely derived from *rogare*.
[3] VI. 5, p. 162.   [4] XIII. 12, p. 414.
[5] XIII. 3, p. 382; XIV. 6, p. 444. Strabo has φόρον.   [6] VI. 11, p. 176.
[7] XIII. 12, p. 416.   [8] XV. 6, p. 480.   [9] VI. 5, p. 161.
[10] XV. 8, p. 489.   [11] XIII. 1, p. 377. Dion Cassius has φαμῶσον.
[12] VI. 3, p. 156.   [13] *Ibid.*
[14] V. 7, p. 141; VIII. 7, p. 237; X. 2, p. 272; XIII, 5, p. 391. Oman, *op. cit.* I, p. 185.
[15] In VIII. 5, p. 231 (*bis*), it means a 'camp', but it is equivalent to 'armed band' in XI. 2, p. 312; 8, p. 330 (*bis*); 11, p. 340. In X. 4, p. 281, it might bear either sense.   [16] VII. 8, p. 205.
[17] XI. 1, p. 309.   [18] X. 8, p. 290; XII. 8, p. 369.
[19] Note on X. 8, p. 290 C. He refers to Justinian's *Novel* 59, ch. 2, where ἐξκουσσάτον is a tax paid for any immunity.
[20] II. 10, p. 64; IV. 2, p. 105; 4, p. 108; 6, p. 114; VI. 8, p. 166; XIII. 1, p. 376. We may contrast the pedantry of John Cinnamus (*Hist.* I. 10, p. 15), 'the month which the Hellenes call Xanthic, and the Romaioi April'.
[21] XIV. 7, p. 448.   [22] V. 6, p. 140; XIII. 4, p. 389.
[23] XIII. 12.   [24] XIII. 9, p. 401.   [25] XIII. 12, pp. 414, 416.

perhaps to include γαλέα for galley,[1] as this does not appear in Greek till the tenth century and the original in classical Latin only means a 'helmet', never any kind of vessel. Anna also gives us παγανός, not in the classical sense of 'rustic', nor in that of 'citizen' as opposed to soldier, which we find as early as the sixth century, but meaning 'Pagan' as opposed to Christian; this, she informs us, was a 'Latin' (i.e. Norman) usage.[2] Finally it may be accepted as a fact that her name τζάγγρα is an attempt to transliterate 'cancer', applied in Low Latin to a cross-bow.[3]

72. VOCABULARY—UNCLASSICAL WORDS OR USAGES

On the whole we must admit that Anna uses very few foreign words. This is not so as to non-classical Greek words, of which she has many. Beginning at random, we note that κρησφύγετον is not Attic, and she may have got it either from Herodotus or from Lucian.[4] Several unusual expressions seem to come to her from Polybius: διόπτρα, an instrument used in signalling or measuring; πειθανάγκη, compulsion disguised as persuasion;[5] συρφετώδης ὄχλος, the vulgar herd;[6] ὁρμητήριον as a base of operations;[6] and ῥοπὰς λαμβάνειν, to turn;[7] while her use of ῥᾳδιουργία as 'roguery' (not 'laziness' or 'lewdness' as in Xenophon, or specifically 'fraud' as in Plutarch), and her favourite word πανοῦργος, 'crafty', employed (as Liddell and Scott express it) 'in a less positively bad sense' than in the Attic poets, may be ascribed to the same source.[8] From Plu-

---

[1] VI. 6, p. 162.
[2] XII. 1, pp. 346, 347: 8, p. 367; XIII. 12, pp. 406, 409. When Bohemund called his Scythian captives Pagans, he was 'mocking both at their name and their appearance'; clearly the classical idea of boorishness still clung to the word. It is interesting to see from Du Cange's note on XII. 8, p. 367 c that Constantine VII Porphyrogenitus (911–59) was so ignorant of its derivation as to say: παγανοὶ κατὰ τὴν τῶν Σκλάβων γλῶσσαν ἀβάπτιστοι ἑρμηνεύεται.
[3] X. 8, p. 291; see p. 369, note 2.
[4] I. 15, p. 36; VII. 3, p. 195; IX. 1, p. 248; XI. 12, p. 341; XIV. 2, p. 427; XV. 4, p. 473.
[5] (a) XIII. 3, p. 384; Polyb. X. 46. 1. (b) XV. 8, p. 487; Polyb. XXI. 42. 7. The word πειθανάγκη occurs in Alexius' poem to his son John (Mous. Alex. I. 93).
[6] (a) X. 9, p. 294; Polyb. IV. 75. 5. (b) I. 4, p. 9; IX. 1, p. 246; XI. 11, p. 339; Polyb. I. 17. 5.   [7] XI. 12, p. 342; Polyb. I. 20. 7.
[8] (a) I. 12, p. 29; VII. 9, p. 209; XII. 1, p. 345; XIII. 4, p. 387; Polyb. XII. 10. 5. Alexius uses ῥᾳδιουργία in line 393 of his first poem and ῥᾳδιουργεῖν in lines 365, 366, but here there is, as perhaps in Anna's phrase in XIII. 4, p. 387, a distinct suggestion of deceit. (b) We get the adjective in X. 2, p. 271; 9, p. 294; XI. 12, p. 341; XII. 8, p. 367; XIII. 10, p. 404; XV. 3, p. 467, with the noun in I. 12, p. 29; XIII. 4, p. 387, and the in verb XIII. 3, p. 382; XIV. 2, p. 426; Polyb. V. 75. 2 &c.

tarch's vocabulary she borrows frequently; she would appear to have carefully studied him. Among the words used by her and first found in his writings, as the dictionary will show, are ἀμεριμνία, 'freedom from anxiety', with derivative verb and adverbs;[1] ἀπαγόρευσις for 'exhaustion' with the corresponding participle 'growing weary of';[2] ἀρειμάνιος, 'war-mad';[3] παρανάλωμα, 'prey', whether of the sword or of disease or of famine.[4] Her proverb πρὸς Κρῆτα κρητίζων occurs twice in Plutarch.[5] From him she gets her unclassical use of the classical word δημοσιεύειν, as 'to make public', not (as in Xenophon) to 'confiscate'. She brings it in three times and the kindred adjective δημόσιος once, when speaking of her mother's reluctance to 'make public' her person or her charms. She also has his phrase οἰκουρεῖν 'to stay at home', as well as the adjective οἰκουρικός first found in Lucian.[6] Other Plutarchian words are ἐμφορεῖν, 'to fill';[7] προκαταρκτικός, 'antecedent' of a cause of disease;[8] κατακληροῦσθαι, 'to take as one's share';[9] ῥέκτης, a 'worker';[10] σκαιωρία, 'mischievous scheme';[11] ἀνδραγάθημα, 'exploit';[12] χαρτίον, 'a little paper';[13] μεγαλουργός, 'energetic';[14] and ψυχρήλατος, which Plutarch applies to red hot iron 'quenched in cold water', and Anna to iron made into a statue, very much as Euthymius Zigabenus describes Alexius as sharpening his tongue against heresy 'like hot iron hardened in cold water', καθάπερ σίδηρος θερμὸς ὕδατι ψυχρῷ στομωθείς.[15]

One other class of words shows a less fortunate result of Anna's close study of this favourite author, i. e. various long

---

[1] VI. 10, p. 171; VIII. 6, p. 234; 8, p. 239; IX. 1, p. 247; XIV. 1, p. 419; XV. 1, p. 460. In IX. 5, p. 254; XIV. 1. p, 421; XV. 6, p. 480, we have ἀπεριμερίμνως.

[2] XV. 11, pp. 504, 505.   [3] XI. 5, p. 323, and elsewhere.

[4] III. 12, p. 99; IV. 2, p. 106; 3, p. 108; V. 1, p. 125; 3, p. 132D; X. 6, pp. 286, 287B; XI. 4, p. 319, &c. In II. 3, p. 48, it is followed by a dative instead of a genitive. Elsewhere it is often replaced by ἔργον in the same sense: V. 3, p. 132A; VI. 3, p. 156; VIII. 5, p. 233; X. 6, p. 287A; XIV. 6, p. 443; XV. 1, p. 462, and cf. Attal. pp. 21, 106; Nic. Bry. I. 17, p. 31.

[5] X. 11, p. 304; Plut. Aemil. 23; Lysand. 20.

[6] (a) XII. 3, p. 351. For 'confiscate' she has δημεύειν in XII. 6, p. 362, and the cognate substantive in VI. 4, p. 157. In X. 1, p. 270, the passive δεδημοσίευτο may be translated 'was brought forward in public'; the C. S. H. B. translator takes it as 'damnatus est', in allusion to an ecclesiastical anathema; (b) XII. 3, p. 351; XIV. 7, p. 446.

[7] XI. 12, p. 342 (bis); XIV. 8, p. 453.

[8] XIV. 4, p. 437; XV. 11, p. 498. She contrasts it with the Aristotelian συνεκτικός, 'essential', in the superlative.

[9] XIII. 2, p. 380.   [10] I. 2, p. 6: 12, p. 28; X. 8, p. 292.

[11] XII. 6, p. 360. It is to be noted that the word only occurs in Plutarch in a doubtful passage of Lysand. 25 where Sintenis reads σκευωρία. Anna also has σκαιώρημα in the same sense (IX. 3, p. 250).

[12] I. 1, p. 3; XI. 8, p. 332; XIII. 7, p. 395, &c.

[13] XV. 4, p. 471.   [14] X. 5, pp. 282, 283.

[15] XIV. 4, p. 436; Pref. to Panopl. Dogm. (P. G. 130 col. 21).

and clumsy compounds, such as προσαπαιτεῖν ('to demand besides'),[1] ἐπιδράσσεσθαι ('to lay hold of') instead of the simple form,[2] ἐπινυστάζειν ('to nod over'),[3] ἀφιλοχρηματία (the 'not being greedy for money'),[4] παρακολούθημα ('consequence') with its cognate verb,[5] and finally περιαυτολογία ('talking about oneself'), out of which she gets the even more unpleasing verb περιαυτολογεῖν.[6]

Other uncouth late Greek compounds for which we need not blame Plutarch are found in such numbers in the *Alexias* that we can only give specimens; e.g. παλαιοχώριον, 'ruins of a fort'; πολυκύμαντος, 'swelling with many waves'; συνεξυφαίνεται, of weaving a story together; ἐπωρύεται, of the sea howling round one; ἐπανανήξομαι, 'I will swim back';[7] διευτρεπίζειν, 'to prepare thoroughly';[8] ἀποκρισιάριος, 'ambassador', as in modern Greek;[9] περιυλακτῶν θυμός, a curious way of expressing indignation or courage 'that howls around';[10] παραπορεῖν, 'to go astray';[11] ἐναυθεντεῖν, 'to be independent';[12] ἰχνηλατεῖν, 'to track with stealth',[13] and the contemptuous συγκίνησις, 'crowding together', applied to the Crusading hosts.[14]

As reflecting her ideals, we note the unclassical ἀνύστακτος, 'watchful',[15] and ἀπαιωρεῖν, 'to keep in mental suspense'.[16] In military matters she has the late Greek τὸ προμετώπιον for the 'vanguard',[17] ἀκρόστεγος for the 'pointed' roof of a penthouse,[18] ἀποστράτευτος for a 'retired soldier',[19] ποδοκοπεῖν of 'hacking down' a fortress from below,[20] and finally ἐναγκαλίζεσθαι, 'to set (a spear) in rest', occurring in almost every battle-scene.

In social matters she uses the word μεγιστᾶνες for 'chiefs' or more usually 'nobles', and most characteristically she gives us the active of the classical verb δημοκρατοῦσθαι (meaning 'to live in a democracy') in the scornful phrase of sinister implication,

---

[1] X. 10, p. 300.   [2] XIV. 2, p. 426; 7, p. 445; XV. 6, p. 479.
[3] XII. 3, p. 353 (*bis*); XIII. 6, p. 393: 7, p. 395.   [4] IX. 2, p. 250.
[5] X. 3, p. 276; 5, pp. 283, 285; 11, pp. 304, 306.
[6] Pref. 1, p. 1; VII. 3, p. 198; XII. 3, p. 351; XV. 3, p. 468; cf. Nic. Bry. IV. 15, p. 96, and Psellus' *Fun. Or.* on his mother *B. G. Med.* V, p. 11.
[7] All five in Book XIV, ch. 6 and 7.   [8] XIII. 3, p. 385.
[9] XIII. 12, p. 416.   [10] VII. 9, p. 212; VIII. 8, p. 239; XI. 6, p. 325.
[11] XI. 6, p. 327.   [12] V. 3, p. 132; XII. 2, p. 349.
[13] VII. 1, p. 188; XIV. 6, p. 442.
[14] X. 5, pp. 283, 285; 6, p. 288. So the verb of the Byzantine mob in V. 9, p. 149. The noun is applied in the same sense to the Crusaders in *Mous. Alex.* I. 330.
[15] XII. 4, p. 356, and often elsewhere. As an adverb it comes twice in one sentence in XIV. 3, p. 429.
[16] VI. 12, pp. 178, 179; XII. 8, pp. 366, 367, &c.
[17] XI. 7, p. 328. As an adjective it means 'in front' or 'facing' according as it is applied to one's own side (VIII. 5, p. 232; XIII. 6, p. 392), or to the enemy (X. 3, p. 275).   [18] XIII. 3, pp. 383, 385.
[19] XV. 7, p. 484.   [20] IV. 4, p. 111; XI. 1, p. 311.

οἷον δημοκρατοῦντες, 'as though ripe for a revolution'.[1] Among useful late words we may note her δισύλλαβος for 'short' of a letter,[2] ὁμόχθων, 'compatriot' on the analogy of αὐτόχθων,[3] συμποσοῦν, 'to reckon',[4] and the intensive adverb παρευθύ, 'absolutely at once'.[5] Again, μηδ' ἀντωπῆσαι ἰσχύοντες is not classical, but it is expressive.[6] As to σχεδογραφία, such writing on tablets (σχέδη) of passages to be parsed and analysed was, Anna tells us, a comparatively new educational method; it is therefore inevitable that the name should be new.[7] Two more late phrases may be mentioned. The βοσκηματώδης βίος[8] applied by Anna to a life of purely animal existence is interesting because it appears in her father's first poem, referring to the life of children.[9] And the words δι' ἐγχορήγου (once followed by ὕλης), used of building operations in two passages which have sorely exercised Du Cange, become quite simple when we realize that χορήγι in modern Greek means 'cement'.[10] The harbour near the Bucoleon at Constantinople and the fortress constructed by Cantacuzenus in his siege of Laodicea were made of concrete; the mystery is explained.

Finally in a Christian writer we naturally get terms which would have conveyed nothing to a Pagan Greek. ἀποκάρσις, clerical tonsure,[11] βάπτισμα or φώτισμα for 'baptism',[12] are new words for new ideas.

But Anna does not content herself with new words; she tries to put new wine into old bottles by using classical words in a non-classical meaning, and of this the instances are legion.

As a generalization we may say that she uses words in a less accurate way than do the Attic Greeks whom she professes to imitate. It is a well-recognized fact that in a Silver Age the sense of words breaks down and becomes wider and vaguer; furthermore, in the case of the Byzantines purist tendencies led to a dislike of technical terms or of the use of any one word with a consistent and invariable meaning.[13] This is

---

[1] VI. 12, p. 180. Byzantine writers use the active form in reference to the starting of riots by the δῆμοι or circus-factions.
[2] VIII. 8, p. 238.   [3] III. 1, p. 71; XIII. 6, p. 392.
[4] I. 16, p. 37; IV. 3, p. 108; VII. 7, p. 204; XI. 1, p. 310; 5, p. 323; XIV. 4, p. 433; 9, p. 455. It is usually in the passive.   [5] XI. 8, p. 331.
[6] V. 4, p. 135; XI. 2, p. 316; 3, p. 318. In IX. 10, p. 265, we get μηδ' ἀντωπῆσαι δυνάμενος.   [7] XV. 7.   [8] XII. 3, p. 350.
[9] Mous. Alex. I. 175. The adjective is found in Marcus Aurelius (τῶν εἰς ἑαυτόν, IV. 28, ed. Stich, p. 39) as a sort of midway epithet between 'brutal' and 'childish'.
[10] III. 1, p. 72; XI. 11, p. 339; δι' ἐγχορήγου ὕλης = 'of material mixed with cement'. Byzantius, Dict. français-grec (1856), s.v. Ciment, spells it χορίγι.
[11] V. 8, p. 145.   [12] XIV. 8, p. 454, and elsewhere.
[13] F. Dölger, Beiträge zur Gesch. der byz. Finanzenverwaltung, p. 11.

very marked in Anna's terms of relationship. In her pages ἀπόγονος is 'son' (not 'descendant of some lower generation'), θεῖος is 'cousin' (not 'uncle'), and πρόγονος is 'father' (not 'ancestor');[1] ἔγγονος is a younger relation[2] not near enough to be counted among a man's γνήσιοι, who are merely his 'near kin' or his 'intimates',[3] with no sense of 'lawfully begotten' as in the classics. A γαμβρός may be a 'father-in-law'[4] or any 'connexion by marriage'.[5] An ἐξάδελφος can be not 'nephew' or 'cousin', but 'brother',[6] and ἐξαδέλφη similarly denotes an indeterminate relationship.[7] In somewhat the same way μεῖραξ, which originally meant 'a young girl', is the term applied to Alexius on his accession and to the valiant Marianus Maurocatacalo, both full-grown men.[8] A similar want of precision in words of every-day life is to be seen in νέωτα, no longer 'next year', but applied by Anna to any later date, especially 'next day'; in δείλη for any time of day, not as originally 'late afternoon'; and in ἔκτοτε vaguely for 'in past time' or 'from the early days';[9] in θάτερος used not as 'the other of two', but 'each' or in plural 'both',[10] and in κατὰ κράτος, which ought to mean 'by storm' or 'with all one's might', but recurs constantly in the *Alexias* as 'utterly' with the verbs of conquering, ἡττᾶν, τρέπειν or νικᾶν.[11]

---

[1] VI. 9, p. 169; VII. 2, p. 191; XV. 4, p. 471.

[2] II. 5, p. 51, and cf. II. 12, p. 67.

[3] XII. 7, p. 365. In VI. 4, p. 157; XIII. 5, p. 390, the idea of 'kindred' is weakened to that of 'household'. In Nic. Bry., Preface, p. 9, we have γνησιότης for 'close connexion' and the adverb γνησιώτατα in the same sense; he uses the phrase γνησίως διακεῖσθαι πρός, 'to be on intimate terms with', in II. 29, p. 66. So Anna has γνησιώτερον in the sense of 'more intimate' in IX. 6, p. 257; cf. X. 4, p. 278. But in XIII. 9, p. 401, Bohemund demands to be met by the γνησιώτατοι of the Emperor's relations and in the end has to put up with τινες τῶν πορρωτέρω συγγενῶν, which makes the meaning of γνησιώτατοι as 'nearest' perfectly clear. Cf. *Anon. Syn. Chron.*, p. 187, where John is proclaimed Emperor at the hands of 'the subjects and the near kinsmen' (or 'household', τῶν γνησίων). See p. 28, note 5, above.

[4] IX. 3, p. 250.

[5] III. 2, p. 71; XII. 7, p. 364.

[6] XV. 8, p. 488, unless we believe the word to be a slip for αὐτάδελφος.

[7] In II. 1, p. 44; 3, p. 48, it is not clear whether Isaac had married the niece or the first cousin of the Empress Maria.

[8] III. 7, p. 85; 9, p. 91; X. 3, p. 277. In I. 1, p. 3, μειράκιον means a boy of fourteen.

[9] (a) IX. 5, p. 254, and elsewhere very frequently. In X. 9, p. 295 τήμερον probably='at this season' and not 'today'. (b) XII. 6, p. 360; XIV. 5, p. 440. (c) XIV. 7, p. 446; XV. 10, p. 495. Cf. the equally vague phrase ἐν τοῖς τότε χρόνοις='in these latter days' (III. 3, p. 77, and see above, p. 60, note 1, and p. 355, note 4).

[10] θατέρων τῶν ποδῶν. XIV. 6, p. 443; καθ' ἑτέραν πλευράν. XV. 5, p. 475.

[11] e.g. V. 4, p. 134; VI. 5, pp. 160, 161: 9, p. 168: 10, p. 172; VII. 5, p. 200: 9, p. 212: 11, p. 217; VIII. 1, p. 222; XI. 3, p. 318: 5, pp. 323, 324: 7, p. 328, and XIII. 6, p. 393. So in Nic. Bry. I. 14, p. 28; III. 3, p. 70: 14, p. 78, and Cinnamus, *passim*.

Curious changes of meaning are evident in all the words about oaths and treaties; τελεῖν, πληροῦν and the like mean not to 'fulfil' but merely to 'make' a contract,[1] and 'to sue for peace' is softened into such phrases as ἐρωτᾶν (or some similar word) τὰ περὶ εἰρήνης.[2] μικροψυχεῖν means 'to show folly' and not faintness of heart or body;[3] ἀθυμία is 'madness' not 'despondency';[4] συμπάθεια is not 'sympathy' but 'pardon',[5] and ἀπάθεια not 'want of passion' (whether as a vice or a virtue) but 'immunity'.[6] εὔνοια throughout means 'loyalty', 'obedience' rather than 'goodwill' in general, and the same is true of its cognate adjective and adverb.[7] φιλοτιμεῖσθαι is not to love honour, but to bestow it, and the nouns derived from it mean a 'reward' or a 'gift';[8] πόρισμα once has its classical signification of 'corollary',[9] but on two other occasions it appears as an 'object of gain';[10] τύχη as 'rank' occurs frequently;[11] once it is equivalent to the Latin Fortuna, a tutelary deity.[12] The Attic phrase, τὰ πρῶτα φέρειν, 'to win the first prize', has come to mean a holding of high position.[13] An ἔποικος is no longer a 'settler from outside' but merely an 'inhabitant'.[14] The Thucydidean ἐκεχειρία, 'armistice', is extended to denote any absence from interference, and may be translated 'respite', 'facility', 'a free hand', and so on.[15] The word πανήγυρις never means

---

[1] IX. 3, p. 251; X. 8, p. 292; 10, p. 300 (bis); XIII. 11, p. 406; XIV. 3, p. 432; XV. 6, p. 478.

[2] VII. 2, pp. 192, 193; IX. 4, p. 252; XIV. 3, p. 432; XV. 6, p. 477, &c.

[3] VI. 7, p. 166; XI. 3, p. 317. The noun in X. 2, p. 274, may possibly keep the classical meaning of 'poor-spiritedness', though 'folly' gives the better sense. In XIV. 4, p. 437, the idea of 'faint-heartedness' is clear.

[4] XII. 7, p. 365.   [5] IX. 9, p. 264 (four times), and elsewhere; Attal. p. 124.

[6] VI. 4, p. 158; IX. 2, p. 249; 7, p. 259; X. 8, p. 292; 11, p. 306; XI. 2, p. 313.

[7] I. 8, pp. 19, 20; II. 4, p. 49; V. 2, p. 128; VI. 8, pp. 166, 168; VII. 3, p. 194; VIII. 1, pp. 221, 223; X. 9, p. 295; 11, p. 306; XII. 4, p. 355; XIII. 4 (four times); 10, p. 403; XIV. 1, p. 419; XV. 3, p. 468 (three times). Anna is proud to count herself among ὅσοι περὶ τὸν αὐτοκράτορα εὖνοι (XII. 3, p. 353; cf. VIII. 9, p. 242; IX. 7, p. 260). The original sense of 'kindliness' is retained in Preface 2, p. 3, and in XIII. 6, p. 393, in the adverb.

[8] I. 12, p. 27; II. 12, p. 67; VI. 8, p. 167; VII. 6, p. 202; X. 3, p. 277; XI. 2, p. 314; 8, p. 332; 10, p. 338; XIV. 1, p. 422; XV. 6, p. 478. Cf. Nic. Bry. IV. 1, p. 87. Three times φιλοτιμία occurs in the proberb of making a 'virtue' of necessity (VI. 10, p. 173; XIII. 8, p. 399; 9, p. 402). The use of the word in late inscriptions to denote lavish expenditure is well known, but there is no instance in the Alexias.   [9] XIII. 6, p. 394.   [10] X. 5, p. 285; XII. 8, p. 367.

[11] VIII. 1, p. 221; X. 2, p. 271; XI. 9, p. 334; XII. 8, p. 368; XIII. 6, p. 393.

[12] XIII. 12, p. 409. In XIV. 1, p. 420, she speaks of a man's εὐτυχία or 'luck'.

[13] II. 6, p. 55; IX. 8, p. 261; X. 2, p. 273; XII. 2, p. 350: 5, p. 359; XIII. 4, p. 388; XIV. 9, p. 456. In XV. 8, p. 488, τὰ πρῶτα ἐσχηματίζετο seems to mean 'he gave himself airs of the greatest importance'.

[14] VIII. 7, p. 237; IX. 3, p. 251; X. 3, p. 274; 4, p. 280; XIII. 5, p. 390; XV. 6, p. 480 (bis).

[15] V. 5, p. 139; VI. 10, p. 174; 12, p. 179: 14, p. 182; VII. 2, p. 190; 3, p. 194; XI. 1, p. 312. On her Thucydidean vocabulary see Reifferscheid, Praef. p. xxvii.

'festival' and has almost lost the derived sense of 'market', (though a shade of such a meaning hovers round it) and has become 'supplies'.¹ Among other more or less military terms diverted from their original use, we have ἀμφίον (a rare classical word for 'clothing'), used in the plural for 'armour'.² The term χλαμύς, 'soldier's mantle', comes in Byzantine Greek to denote first armour and then an armed man;³ so σκευή which to classical writers meant 'dress' or 'tackle' acquires a military flavour in the *Alexias*, being constantly used in the plural for 'baggage'.⁴ The verb κραδαίνειν keeps its warlike sense, but with a difference; it is not 'brandish' (as in poetical Attic) but 'dangle', as we have seen in speaking of the Varangians and their swords.⁵

This is but one of the verbs which Anna uses in an unclassical manner. In classical Greek συναράσσειν and συγκροτεῖν are used of objects which can actually be knocked or welded together; in the *Alexias* over and over again it is a metaphorical 'clashing' and the accusative which follows is μάχην or πόλεμον. The expressive χεῖρα διδόναι, 'to surrender', from *manum dare* which originally meant to hold out one's hands to be fettered, is unclassical;⁶ ναυλοχεῖν has lost all sense of naval ambush, and with its cognate noun refers to sea-fights of whatever kind.⁷ καταλαμβάνειν is as a rule no longer to 'catch up with', but simply to 'arrive at';⁸ φθάνειν is 'to come' in a general way, often with an accusative of the object that is reached and only very rarely with any signification of anticipating another's action. καρτερεῖν means not to 'endure' as in classical Greek, but 'to

¹ VII. 6, p. 203; X. 5, p. 285; 9, p. 298, but cf. XIII. 7, p. 396. In the Latin chroniclers *commeatus* and *mercatum* show just the same development of meaning. See p. 131, note 10.
² VI. 14, p. 184. Cf. XV. 6, p. 478, where the corresponding word is ὅπλα. In X. 8, p. 293, χρῶμα τῶν ἀμφίων may refer either to the colour of clothes, or the gilding or painting of armour. In VIII. 1, p. 223 seq., X. 11, p. 303; XII. 1, p. 346; XIV. 1, p. 420; XV. 9, p. 492; 10, p. 494; 11, p. 505, the meaning is 'garments' in general. In VIII. 5, p. 232; XV. 6, p. 478, ἀμφίον is a 'military cloak', which might be of silk.
³ XIII. 9, p. 401 C. So in medieval French 'une cotte' means the man inside the coat of mail. See Du Cange's note.
⁴ XI. 4, pp. 318, 320; 5, p. 324; 8, p. 331; XIV. 6, p. 442. In XI. 10, p. 336, the singular has the old sense of 'apparatus'.
⁵ See p. 367, above. When Anna speaks of δόρατα κραδαινόμενα (XIII. 2, p. 379) we get the old sense of brandishing, as motion is distinctly implied. So also XV. 3, p. 468, and elsewhere.
⁶ XIV. 5, p. 440 (*bis*). We may compare διὰ μακρῶν χειρῶν in XII. 7, p. 365, 'by slow efforts', from the Latin *longa manu*.
⁷ VII. 8, p. 207; XI. 10, p. 336; XII. 8, p. 368.
⁸ This use is too common in the *Alexias* to need references. In XIII. 3, p. 384, the noun κατάληψις is applied to intellectual apprehension, as in the Stoic philosophers. In XII. 7, p. 365; 8, p. 366, we get προκαταλαμβάνειν='anticipate'.

await' as in modern;[1] τυποῦν in Attic is 'to stamp or mould', but Anna uses it in the passive as 'to have decreed to one'.[2] In three places she employs μετέρχεσθαι not in the classical prose sense of 'to seek' or 'pursue as an enemy' or 'approach in prayer', but rather in the Pindaric meaning of 'to woo', much as Americans say 'to get after' some one from whom one wants something.[3] Of the various renderings of συντάσσεσθαι we have spoken in considering the Crusaders' oath of homage.[4]

Twice we get an unusual use of τιθέναι; τίθημι φυλάττειν, 'I promise to keep',[5] and the phrase about Bohemund, ζῶν ἔτι ὡς περὶ κατοιχομένου αὐτοῦ τὴν οἰκουμένην διέθετο', which may be translated, 'while still living he set the world thinking of him as dead'.[6] ἐξελαύνειν and συνελαύνειν have acquired new meanings. The former is not to 'drive out', but to 'round up' as helpers,[7] the latter is not to 'drive together' but to 'coerce' or 'reduce'.[8] Anna's σῴζειν is nearer to the modern Greek 'to be enough' than to the Attic 'to save'. On various occasions she writes of δυνάμεις μηδὲ τὸ πολλοστὸν σῴζουσαι, 'forces not amounting to a fraction' of the enemy's.[9] The curious phrase, σῴζουσαι ἐλπίδες, means not 'hopes of safety', but 'sufficient', or 'satisfactory' (coming almost to the same as 'last') hopes.[10] Three more verbs may be cited: βάπτειν in the late figurative sense of dipping into a person's mind[11]; ἐξορχεῖσθαι, sometimes meaning to 'betray' as in Lucian, sometimes to 'say by way of prelude' or 'begin to tell'; and διαφέρειν, 'to belong'.[12]

Adjectives with new meanings are not so common, but we get γοργός no longer as 'grim' but as a term of praise, 'quick' or 'prompt';[13] ῥητοί not as 'specified' but as 'few';[14] ὑποβρύχιος not as

---

[1] X. 4, p. 280; 6, p. 286; 7, p. 289, &c. It is followed either by an accusative of the direct object, or by an infinitive of purpose.

[2] XI. 2, pp. 314, 315; XIII. 12, p. 414.

[3] III. 2, p. 74; XIII. 4, p. 389; 9, p. 400.   [4] See pp. 465–6 above.

[5] XIII. 12, p. 407.   [6] XI. 12, p. 341.

[7] VII. 11, p. 218; VIII. 4, p. 229; 5, p. 233.

[8] VI. 10, p. 171; X. 2, p. 272; 9, p. 297; 10, p. 300 (bis); XI. 1, p. 311; 2, p. 313; 6, p. 324; 7, p. 330; XII. 7, p. 364; 8, p. 367; XIII. 5, p. 390; 11, p. 405. In XIII. 2, p. 379, it merely denotes in the passive the assembling of troops. In VII. 8, p. 207, the old classical meaning reappears.

[9] IV. 2, p. 105; VI. 13, p. 180; 14, p. 183; VII. 1, p. 189; VIII. 4, p. 228.

[10] VII. 3, p. 197; VIII. 5, p. 234; XI. 6, p. 325; XIV. 5, p. 440; XV. 6, p. 476. In XIII. 12, p. 408, ἐπανασῴζειν= to make good.

[11] IV. 5, p. 114; X. 11, p. 302.

[12] (a) Pref. 1, p. 1; I. 11, p. 25; XIII. 1, p. 378, and the Prologue to her Will, line 32. In I. 16, p. 38; II. 2, p. 45; 7, p. 59; VII. 9, p. 211; XV. 8, p. 489, it = 'betray'. (b) XIII. 12, p. 409; XIV. 2, p. 422.

[13] VII. 2, p. 192, and the ad verb in VII. 3, pp. 197, 198; 9, p. 212; X. 8, p. 291; XI. 9, p. 334; 10, p. 336 (bis); 11, p. 338; XIII. 10, p. 403. So in Modern Greek a γοργοκάμηλος is a dromedary. Cf. Nic. Bry. III. 25, p. 84. See p. 139, above.

[14] IX. 8, p. 261; X. 6, p. 287.

the Homeric and Platonic 'under water' but as 'concealed';[1] εὐπρόσοδος (in speaking of property) not as 'accessible' but as 'productive'.[2]

Finally we come to a few nouns that present some special interest. We have spoken of ῥοπὰς λαμβάνειν, 'to turn', as taken from Polybius; elsewhere Anna has ῥοπὴ καιροῦ, 'the turn of the scale' at a crisis.[3] ἀφορμή in classical Greek means a 'starting point' or 'pretext' or sometimes 'resources', and in Plutarch has the Stoic sense of 'disinclination' as opposed to ὁρμή. But in the *Alexias* the idea conveyed is nearer to the modern Greek meaning of 'cause', and may be translated 'enterprise'.[4] One very favourite word of Anna's is περιωπή, denoting not a 'look-out place' but a 'summit', and especially a 'throne', imperial,[5] ducal, or ecclesiastical.[6] Her use in one place of γέφυραι as 'ditches' and not 'bridges' or 'dams' is so peculiar that Du Cange wishes to alter it to στρουγαί, 'ponds', but it seems possible to keep the present reading on the analogy of 'dyke', which is not only a ditch but also the bank bounding a ditch.[7]

Lastly, there is Anna's new use of old words, denoting new things. ἄνθρωπος comes first to mind, meaning 'vassal' like the mediaeval Latin 'homo' which gives us our 'homage'.[8] Then follow the ecclesiastical terms, μονή invariably for a special dwelling, i.e. a 'cloister', τέμενος for a 'church' not merely a 'sacred enclosure', and ἐκκλησία in a religious sense; πρόνοια for Divine Providence, seldom the more general 'forethought';[9]

---

[1] II. 1, p. 45; 4, p. 49; III. 6, p. 82; IX. 6, p. 257; X. 11, p. 306; XI. 4, p. 319 XIII. 4, p. 388.

[2] XV. 7, p. 483. Sophocles's Dictionary gives a ninth-century writing as the first instance of this usage. 3 II. 7, p. 59; XI. 5, p. 323; XIII. 10, p. 402.

[4] ἐπὰν ἀφορμῆς δράξοιτο 'when it takes up an enterprise' (X. 5, p. 286). So in XI. 12, p. 341, ἐφ' ὅπερ ἂν ἐφορμήσειε 'on whatever enterprise it has started'. In Nic. Bry. I. 22, p. 34, the noun has the old sense of 'opening', and in III. 14, p. 78, of the same author, 'pretext'.

[5] III. 2, p. 74; 8, p. 87; 9, p. 92; V. 9, p. 148; VI. 8, p. 168; VII. 2, p. 190; IX. 1, p. 245; 6, p. 255. In II. 7, p. 57, we have the mixed metaphor 'helmsman of the imperial throne'.

[6] I. 12, p. 27; 13, p. 31. So in general, III. 5, p. 80. In XIII. 9, p. 401, as 'imperial seat' it has the synonyms κλίνη and σκίμπους and in the next chapter θρόνος. Nic. Bry. I. 3, p. 18 speaks of the imperial περιωπή, and the term πατριαρχικὴ περιωπή comes in the Trial of Italus (*Bull. inst. arch. russe de Constantinople*, Vol. II, p. 33). We must not forget to mention that in XII. 6, p. 363, Anna gives the word its old sense of an actual 'watch-tower'.

[7] XII. 9, p. 371 c, and see Du Cange's note; also above, p. 403, note 5.

[8] X. 7, p. 289; XIII. 12, *passim*. So 'hominium' in *Gesta*, chs. 6 and 21.

[9] Quotations to prove the point about πρόνοια are superfluous; in this Anna resembles Cecaumenus and his *Strategicon*. In XV. 7, p. 484, we have the word three times in another non-classical sense, 'provision', and the middle verb is thus used a few lines later. In XI, 5, p. 321; XII. 3, p. 353; 4, p. 356; XIV. 1, p. 419, we may translate 'care'. See also p. 243 above.

χειροτονία not for a 'showing of hands' but for ecclesiastical ordination as in modern Greek, μάνδρα for a figurative 'flock', αὐλή not for 'court' but for 'religious body' or 'faith',[1] ἐπιτιμία and πένθος referring to Church penance, and οἰκονομία for 'dispensation', alluding specially to the Incarnation,[2] as in the Definition of Faith of the Council of Chalcedon.[3]

Such then are some of Anna's unusual words, for most of which we may consult Liddell and Scott in vain. But when we consider what a small proportion they bear to her whole vocabulary, and remember the elaborate glossary required by the average modern Englishman in reading Chaucer, not 600 years removed from him, the real wonder is not that we are sometimes baffled by her phraseology, but that we understand it at all. Our great Greek dictionary was primarily made to deal with writers who lived from three to five centuries before Christ; it is indeed a striking proof of how little literary Greek has changed that with that dictionary's aid we can understand all but a comparatively few words of a twelfth-century author.

Anna Comnena may have *spoken* in a form more akin to modern Greek, but as to her *writing*, a Jesuit composing Latin to-day might ardently wish that he could use his 'dead' language as well as she used hers.

73. TRICKS OF STYLE

FROM grammar and vocabulary we will turn to weightier matters of style, and try to get a general impression of Anna's individuality as a writer. Nobody nowadays would join in Gibbon's vitriolic condemnation of her,[4] virtually amounting to the famous judgement passed by one nineteenth-

---

[1] Pref. 4, p. 6; XIII. 12, pp. 406, 413; XIV. 8, p. 451; 9, p. 457. In XIII. 12, p. 416, αὐλή has the old sense of 'court'.

[2] III. 5; XV. 8, p. 488. In V. 2, p. 129, we must translate it 'economics'. In XII. 1, p. 347, it means 'financial assistance'; but in XI. 5, p. 322; XIII. 9, p. 401; 12, p. 408, and elsewhere, it has the classical sense of 'management' or 'arrangement', merging in XIV. 2, p. 427, into that of 'contrivance', here a euphemism for a lie. The verb is used throughout the *Alexias* in the original meaning. See p. 307 above.

[3] Bright's *Canons of the First Four General Councils*, p. xxxiv. In the *Prologue* to her Will Anna uses οἰκονομία=Fate (line 11).

[4] Thus he speaks of her 'elaborate affectation of rhetoric and science', her 'perpetual strain of panegyric and apology', her 'artificial and pedantic style', her 'vice of long-windedness', and says that 'in chronology she is loose and inaccurate'. Indeed he hardly ever quotes from her without some phrase of abuse.

century English statesman on another—'pompous, egotistical, tiresome, and inaccurate.' The readers of the *Alexias* from cover to cover are probably never likely to be very numerous, for the book is hard and it is long. But those who do the deed will endorse Chalandon's tribute to 'la verve et la chaleur qui animent presque chaque page . . . et donnent au récit un intérêt continu', and will agree with Diehl's dictum, 'c'est un livre absolument remarquable'.[2] Even the cautious Krumbacher[3] calls it 'das erste grössere Denkmal der litterarischen Renaissance', which began with Psellus and lasted all through the Comnenus dynasty into that of the Palaeologi.[4] Criticism to her admirers seems rather like finding spots in the sun. Still, that there are spots cannot be denied. We are not now concerned with her truthfulness or historical accuracy, merely with the way she tells her story, and it must be confessed that she has various tricks of style (such as long digressions, heaping up of synonyms, rhetorical questions, and terribly involved sentences) which do detract from the pleasure of reading her.[5] She also wearies us by her love of grandiloquent names for simple things, 'armour-bearers of Ares' or 'a soldier wholly full of Ares' for 'warrior';[6] 'paying the common debt' for 'death' and being 'counted with the living' for an escape from mortal danger;[7] 'a thrice-repeated lunar revolution' for 'three months',[8] &c. A storm is 'war threatening from the clouds', and a calm sea 'offers its back' to travellers;[9] spring has to

---

[1] *Op. cit.* p. xxi.   [2] *Figures byzantines*, II, p. 52.
[3] *G. B. L.* p. 276.

[4] Oster, who is inclined to patronize Anna Comnena, might, we feel, learn something from her as to style. Nothing in all her pages is more cumbrous than his summary of her qualities in *A.K.* Pt. III, p. 56: 'Wir haben in der Alexias ein quellenmässiges, mit Verständniss und Liebe aufgefasstes, mit feiner ächt weiblicher Beobachtungsgabe oft bis ins kleinste Detail ausgemaltes Spiegelbild eines immerhin noch sehr lebensfähigen Staatsorganismus und seines Trägers . . . Somit ist die Alexias trotz ihrer Mängel ohne Frage eine der hervorragendsten, ja nach Zonaras geradezu die hervorragendste Leistung des Byzantinismus im Gebiete der Geschichte und sichert der Verfasserin auf immer eine ehrenvolle Stellung in der Litteratur.'

[5] Oster, *op. cit.*, Pt. III, pp. 63–5 and 72, mentions a number of these tautologies, digressions, and questions. The cumbrous sentences probably did not strike him, but they are many. The opening sentence of IX. 9 in Reifferscheid's edition is 16½ lines; that of XIV. 2 is of 21. The second sentence of XII. 7 literally translated reads like German: 'And a tower there was, one of the near-the-in-Blachernae-Palace-situated walls of the city.' In the matter of rhetorical questions she does but copy her husband.

[6] I. 8, p. 21; V. 4, p. 135; XI. 9, p. 333; XII. 2, p. 349; XV. 4, p. 473; cf. XI. 12, p. 342. Similarly armour 'glitters in rivalry with the starry beam', (VI. 14, p. 184).

[7] I. 8, p. 21; VIII. 9, p. 240; XIV. 1, p. 419.

[8] IX. 1, p. 246; XI. 4, p. 318; 6, p. 327. The word σεληνιακός is Plutarchian.

[9] IV. 3, p. 107; VIII. 3, p. 226.

come 'smiling', and men 'sharpen their teeth and their knives'
(or 'not their swords only but their hearts') ;[1] large trees are
οὐρανομήκη ;[2] ships are 'winged' by their commanders with their
sails or their oars, or by means of the latter are 'made as it
were into polypods'.[3] A Scythian runner has 'winged feet',
and so has a rumour.[4] A man raised to high position is 'set
up on magnificent pedestals' ;[5] the Empress Irene is 'a resting-
place (καταγώγιον) of holiness',[6] as her daughter Maria is of
'every virtue', and Anna herself of 'mighty ills'.[7] When men
are besieged they have to feed on 'flesh forbidden by the law',[8]
and when they are drowned in a river they are always 'swept
away by the eddies'. Above all, the varied operations of war
or sea-travel inevitably call forth some Homeric phrase.[9]
Warriors are 'dear to Ares' like Menelaus, they are 'mindful
of fierce valour' as in the *Iliad*, and when they go on a journey
they 'loose their stern-cables'[10] and 'sail the watery ways' in
the best Homeric fashion.

Now all this is wholly intentional on Anna's part. She speaks
of the 'grandeur' (ὕφος) of her history as requiring a careful choice
of words; indeed she three times apologizes for introducing
'barbarian' names and justifies herself by Homer's example.[11]
And it is natural that we should find her specially bombastic
and specially given to rhetorical flourishes when she is concerned in self-conscious fashion with the weighty matter of her
own woes; her wail over the death[12] of her brother Andronicus
and the end of Book XV are good instances of this. Other places
where we find her faults of style in an exaggerated degree are
the various occasions when she eulogizes her father,[13] and the
long chapter in which she gives his treaty with Bohemund.[14]
We know that she was proud of having, by her study of the
classics in poetry and prose, 'polished off roughnesses of speech'[15]
in herself, and we may well believe that though she professes
to hate 'artificiality'[16] of diction, she deliberately laid aside when

---

[1] VI. 14, p. 184; IX. 1, p. 246; XI. 10, p. 336.
[2] IX. 1, p. 245; XV. 6, p. 476. Herodotus uses this epithet for trees in II. 138.
[3] X. 8, p. 290; XI. 10, p. 336; XIII. 7, p. 396.
[4] XII. 9, p. 372; XV. 4, p. 471.　　　　　[5] XII. 2, p. 350.
[6] XII. 3, p. 351.　　　　　　　　　　　　[7] XV. 11, pp. 504, 506.
[8] XI. 9, p. 333; cf. V. 5, p. 138.
[9] VII. 8, p. 209: cf. *Iliad*, VII. 282, 293; VII. 11, p. 215: cf. *Iliad*, II. 1, 2.
[10] This special phrase occurs so often both in Anna and in Homer that I have
not attempted to count it in the writings of either.
[11] VI. 14, p. 182; X. 8, p. 289; XIII. 6, p. 393.　Even astrological terms would
'cloud' her story (VI. 7, p. 165).　　　　　　　[12] XV. 5.
[13] e.g. IV. 8; XIV. 7; XV. 3, and many other passages.
[14] XIII. 12, possibly written however by some imperial 'under-secretary'.
[15] XV. 7, p. 486. See p. 178 above.
[16] III. 6, p. 83; IV. 8, p. 121; XIV. 7, p. 448. See p. 243 above.

she 'arrived at rhetoric' the literary qualities which we now admire most, purity of style, clearness, and simplicity, and learnt to bury ideas under verbiage.

Among the minor characteristics of her writing which irritate the modern reader, first and foremost comes her love for long words, especially superlatives, and for compound verbs and nouns. Barber[1] says that in the first century A. D. the Greeks turned back to Attic writers and despised the Hellenistic largely because of the latter's preference for compound verbs over simple; one may wonder what they would have said to Anna. Some of her compounds have already been noted as unclassical; others might be made into a long list. Alexius is described with three adjectives compounded with 'danger'.[2] To Robert Guiscard are assigned five superlatives in one place, two in another, and single ones in three more,[3] as though to some 'lindísima, distinguidísima y exquisitísima' lady in a Madrid society paper; to a Scythian slave three and to her uncle Isaac the Sebastocrator two.[4] In XII. 5 three compound verbs with κατά occur within three lines.[5] Anna is φιλομήτωρ καὶ φιλοπάτωρ, and her father is φιλομήτωρ,[6] as indeed he claims for himself in writing to his φιλοπάτωρ son John.[7] He is moreover ἱερατικώτατος and διδασκαλικώτατος in dealing with infidels, and φερεπονώτατος as is also Tancred;[8] in his adaptability to changing circumstances he is described as συμμετασχηματιζόμενος τοῖς πράγμασι.[9] A general chooses for attacking a town men who are τειχεσιπλήτας (the Homeric epithet for Ares), and φιλοκινδύνους;[10] another general speaks to the Emperor ἐπιφωνηματικῶς.[11] Taticius is περιφανεστάτη κεφαλή of the expedition sent against the Pisan fleet, Irene is περιφανέστατος φυλακτήρ to her husband;[12] Anna defends herself πρὸς τοὺς φιλοσκώμμονας καὶ τὰς φιλολοιδόρους γλώττας.[13] The 'Latin race is φιλοχρηματώτατον and ἀχαλιναγώγητον, 'not to be restrained'.[14] 'More in detail' is

---

[1] Hellenistic Age, pp. 34–5.

[2] μεγαλοκίνδυνος, πυκνοκίνδυνος, φιλοκίνδυνος, VI. 11, p. 176; XIII. 4, p. 386.

[3] The group of five has been given above, p. 455, note 5 (I. 11, p. 25; 12, p. 29; 14, p. 34; IV. 3, p. 108; VI. 7). So Nicephorus Bryennius has three superlatives for his own father in Hyle, IV. 1, p. 87.

[4] (a) XIII. 1, p. 378. (b) φιλολογώτατος καὶ μεγαλεπηβολώτατος V. 9, p. 148.

[5] XII. 5, p. 357 D.   [6] III. 7, p. 86; VI. 8, p. 167; XV. 11, p. 496.

[7] Mous. Alex., I, heading.

[8] VI. 13, p. 181; XII. 2, p. 349; XIV. 4, p. 434, and cf. 436.

[9] XIV. 4, p. 435. The slightly simpler form, μετασχηματίζεσθαι, found in Plato and Aristotle, is used by Anna in XIV. 7, p. 448.

[10] VI. 13, p. 181; cf. XI. 1, p. 311.   [11] VII. 2, p. 191.

[12] XI. 10, p. 325; XII. 3, p. 352.

[13] XII. 3, p. 353; cf. Pref. 2, p. 2; VI. 3, p. 157; and XV. 3, p. 466, διαλοιδορούμενοι τῷ βασιλεῖ καὶ ὑποψιθυρίζοντες. This last word is also used in VI. 3, p. 155, of disloyal criticism.   [14] X. 6, p. 287.

λεπτομερέστερον,[1] and 'to deliberate intently', usually coming slowly to a conclusion, is γνωσιμαχεῖν.[2] The list might be prolonged *ad infinitum*, for there is hardly a page without a dozen such words, but three more shall suffice. The tax assessor sent to set the finances of Cyprus in order is said to have had a reputation for three essential if cumbrously named virtues, δικαιοπραγία, ἀφιλοχρηματία, and ταπεινοφροσύνη.[3]

Besides these words, which are jarring in themselves to the modern ear, we find a number of harmless phrases which she brings in again and again to a wearisome extent.[4] It is also very noticeable that these expressions occur so to speak in clumps; she will use a word or phrase two or three times in one Book, often very close together, and then not again for scores of pages. This is true of ἐν στενῷ κομιδῇ,[5] καθάπερ τινὰ κλῆρον,[6] the expression already alluded to of 'loosing the stern cables' (λύσας τὰ πρυμνήσια),[7] and many others. We are all apt to have, as we say, words running in our heads at certain periods, and this very marked feature of Anna's style helps to prove what we have already suggested, that she composed her history in sections, probably at considerable intervals of time. In some Books, especially the later ones,[8] the repetitions are very marked. Book XII in its fifth and sixth chapters gives us τύραννος ('rebel') twice, and τυραννικός once, three different compounds of ἐγείρειν, three instances of κορυφαῖος (one being

---

[1] VII. 2, p. 191; X. 2, p. 271.

[2] II. 4, p. 49; V. 1, p. 125: 3, p. 131; IX. 7, p. 258; XI. 1, p. 310; XIII. 4, p. 389.

[3] IX. 2, p. 250. Translation is not easy, as we have not got such portmanteau words in English. We may say 'Just dealing, incorruptibility, and courtesy', the last word conveying the idea of the New Testament *virtue* of 'humility', not of the classical *vice* of 'low-mindedness'.

[4] Her husband sins in this way. He has the phrase βουλὴν βουλεύεται συνετήν or the like in II. 14, p. 51; 16, p. 54; 17, p. 55; 21, p. 58; 24, p. 61, to take only one of his Books. Anna copies him in I. 11, p. 25; II. 5, p. 51; VI. 1, p. 152; X. 5, p. 284; XI. 4, p. 319; 7, p. 329; XV. 4, p. 471. In VI. 12, p. 178 she has the similar phrase λογισμὸν λογισάμενος; in XIII. 1, p. 378 we find παρήγγειλαν παραγγελίαν, and in X. 5, p. 282 ἐπίνοιαν ἐπινοεῖται.

[5] Thus ἐν στενῷ κομιδῇ (or variants) occurs once in I. 2, p. 6; 4, p. 10; II. 11, p. 64; III. 9, p. 91; V. 2, p. 127; then twice in VI. 11, p. 175, once in VI. 13, p. 180, and without κομιδῇ in VI. 12, p. 178. After that she gives the phrase a rest till IX. 8, p. 261, and we get it again in XI. 1, p. 310; 6, p. 324, and (without κομιδῇ) 7, p. 330; then again in XIII. 6, p. 393; 8, p. 399.

[6] II. 2, p. 45; 9, p. 62, and twice in VI. 12. Variants occur in VI. 4, p. 158; VIII. 9, p. 240; XI. 5, p. 321; XII. 7, p. 364, with the same meaning. Cf. *Mous. Alex.* I. 44; II. 36; Nic. Acom. *John C.* 3, p. 8.

[7] Four times in VII. 8; twice in X. 8, p. 290; three times in XI. 10, &c.

[8] We must not forget σφάλλω, twice used within a few pages in Book IX to show how Nicephorus Diogenes was 'overthrown' by God's power (IX. 7, p. 258; 8, p. 262), κλονέω seven times in Book I, κοραδοκέω three times in I. 15, p. 35, and ἀκρατῶς three times in chs. 5 & 6 of Book V. For other repetitions in the first eleven Books, see Appendix I at the end of this chapter.

in the superlative), four of κοῦφος in less than a page, and
φόνιον πνέων twice.[1] In chapters 3 and 7 we get three cases of
advising τὰ λώονα.[2] In Book XIII we have μιαιφόνος three
times in the first chapter, δρᾶμα (in a sinister meaning) or some
derivative three times in chapter 1 and three times in chapter 4,
φλυαρία or φλύαρος three times in chapter 1, the phrase ταραχὴ
ἀμήχανος, 'indescribable confusion', twice in one sentence in
chapter 3, and πτῶσις ('collapse') in chapters 8 and 9.
καταφρονητικῶς διατίθεσθαι occurs once in chapter 1, and again
(in the comparative) in chapter 9.[3] The last chapter containing
the Treaty has two instances of repeated words; ἀπροφασίστως
occurs twice, and ὁλόκληρος twice. Book XIV is also full of
repetitions, εὐτυχία twice in chapter 1, πλατῦναι (of 'broadening'
the dominions of the Greek Empire) twice in chapter 2;
warriors are three times called σταθηρός between pp. 440 D and
442 D; ἀποδιδόναι κόσμον (to 'restore order') comes twice in
chapter 1; ἐπιβρίθειν, a Homeric word for 'falling heavily',
three times in chapter 7; ἀπερρυηκώς, a classical but rare
expression for 'dead', twice in chapter 7; τεκμαίρεσθαι ('to
judge') in chapters 7 and 8; ἁλμυρός ('salt', as applied to false
doctrine) twice in chapter 8. In Book XV περιγίνεται is used
twice within a few lines in chapter 3 in two different ways,
both classical.[4] Then we have λάφυρα ('booty') twice in
chapter 4; ἀντέχεσθαι μάχης or πολέμου in the same fourth
chapter three times within a few lines; ἀποσκώπτειν twice
in chapter 5; γυρόθεν περίζώσας of the Turkish tactics three
times in chapter 6; πρόνοια or its verb four times in chapter 7
in the unclassical sense of 'provision for temporal wants'.[5] In
this Book too the word σφαδάζω, which occurs four times in
Book I, four times in Books II–XII, and four times in Book XIII,
now reappears in three passages.[6]

Other stock phrases of Anna's are the being 'whirled away
in the eddies of the stream' of which we have already spoken,[7]

[1] This last phrase occurs again in XIII. 1, p. 377, very shortly afterwards. It is
also found much earlier (VI. 12, p. 178.)
[2] The verb, as again in XV. 6, p. 478, is συμβουλεύειν. We meet the phrase with
ὑποτίθεσθαι in XI. 8, p. 332; XIII. 5, p. 391; XV. 6, p. 480.
[3] καταφρονητικῶς is found with ἔχειν in I. 6, p. 14, διακεῖσθαι in X. 11, p. 302,
and with διατίθεσθαι in VI. 5, p. 160; XI. 5, p. 323, and XV. 6, p. 479, as well as
in the two passages of Book XIII just referred to.
[4] XV. 3, p. 467: (a) 'excels' followed by the genitive, (b) 'comes as an advantage to' followed by the dative.
[5] We have already mentioned ἀπαγόρευσις and its kindred participle in XV. 11,
pp. 504, 505, and καταγώγιον used metaphorically in XV. 11, pp. 504 and 506.
[6] XV. 4, p. 473; 5, p. 475; 10, p. 494. See Appendix II at the end of the
chapter.
[7] VI. 13, p. 181; IX. 5, p. 253; XI. 6, p. 327; XIII. 6, p. 394; XIV. 1, p. 422.
See p. 499 above.

'setting up trophies', a Thucydidean phrase which she works to death,[1] and 'not having sufficient forces against such numbers', usually joined with the statement that the person in question was ἐν ἀμηχανίᾳ.[2] She likes the Stoic word οἰκουμένη with its feeling of grandeur and vastness;[3] she is pleased with her phrase about Bohemund, 'always the same',[4] and even more so with those about her father, ὁποῖος ἐκεῖνος δεινός or ὁποῖος ὁ ἐμὸς βασιλεὺς περὶ τὰ τοιαῦτα, or the like.[5] She may be said to overwork beyond all limits λαμπρός as an adjective,[6] the various compounds of σύρειν and σπᾶσθαι as verbs, and καιρός as a noun. For καιρός the C. S. H. B. Index to the Alexias (which is seldom complete) gives twenty-three references. Her fondness for the word is shown early, for it occurs three times in her Preface. Among the bewildering wealth of phrases into which it enters we will select only two, πρὸ καιροῦ which once means 'for a long time past', and once is the usual 'prematurely',[7] and καιροῦ καλοῦντος, 'if the crisis should call'.[8] Once or twice the best translation of the word is 'the decisive moment',[9] and one very ominous phrase in an age when poisoning was rife is 'the critical times of the banquet'.[10] The elliptical expression τὴν νικῶσαν ἔχειν, 'to gain the day', is

---

[1] II. 1, p. 43; III. 8, p. 90; V. 1, pp. 125, 126; VI. 2, p. 154; VIII. 2, p. 224; XI. 4, p. 319; 5, p. 322; XIV. 7, p. 448; 9, p. 454; XV. 3, p. 467, and elsewhere. Cf. Nic. Bry., Pref. 7, 10, and 12; I. 24, p. 37; Anon. Syn. Chron., p. 183*.

[2] I. 3, p. 7; VII. 6, p. 203; 7, p. 205; 11, p. 215; VIII. 4, p. 229; 5, p. 234; IX. 3, p. 251; 8, p. 262; X. 3, p. 275; XI. 6, p. 325; 7, p. 329; XIV. 1, p. 421; 4, p. 434 (cf. Attal. p. 25), the expression not being uniform, but the meaning always the same.

[3] e.g. Pref. 4, p. 8; XV. 11, p. 506, and elsewhere. She uses it twice in XI. 12.

[4] αὖθις ἐκεῖνος or αὖθις Βαϊμοῦντος XI. 9, p. 333; 10, p. 337; XIII. 11, p. 405. Cf. XII. 7, p. 365, of Gregory Taronites.

[5] VI. 10, p. 173; VII. 6, p. 203; VIII. 1, p. 221; X. 11, p. 302; XI. 11, p. 339; XII. 7, p. 365. It is also applied to Bohemund, V. 6, p. 141; XI. 3, p. 316; 10, p. 337; Robert, VI. 5, p. 160 (bis); John Italus V. 8, p. 145; Irene, XII. 6, p. 362; and Bryennius Caesar, XIII. 11, p. 405.

[6] Its primary meaning is 'brilliant' as of a victory (XIV. 5, p. 441; 6, p. 444; XV. 1, p. 462, and elsewhere), but it is also applied to a voice (X. 1, p. 270 (bis); XIV. 6, p. 444); thanksgivings (XV. 7, p. 482); a reception (X. 7, p. 288); a hero (I. 9, p. 22); and even to repentance (V. 8, p. 146), melancholy (XIV. 9, p. 457), and persecution (XV. 8, p. 489). For σύρειν and σπᾶσθαι, see Appendix II at the end of this chapter.

[7] XI. 1, p. 311; XV. 10, p. 495.

[8] I. 13, p. 32; IV. 4, p. 109; X. 5, p. 283; XV. 2, p. 466. So in Anon. Syn. Chron., p. 179; Nic. Bry., Pref., p. 8. We have already spoken of the phrase ἐν (μιᾷ or ὀξείᾳ) καιροῦ ῥοπῇ, 'in a swift turning-point of time' (II. 7, p. 59; XI. 5, p. 323; XIII. 10, p. 402).

[9] XII. 6, p. 360 (bis); XIII. 4, p. 387; 7, p. 396; XIV. 5, p. 438; 7, p. 445; XV. 3, p. 468. Cf. Attal. p. 321. In XII. 9, p. 370, we get the expression διὰ τὴν τοῦ καιροῦ δυναστείαν = through force of circumstances.

[10] XIII. 3, p. 352. We may note that Anna never refers to Eph. v. 16, τὸν καιρὸν ἐξαγοραζόμενος, but her husband does (Hyle, II. 21, p. 59).

properly a legal term with γνώμην understood, but Anna uses it promiscuously.[1] 'To set baggage in place' is τὰς σκευὰς (to which as we have said she gives an unclassical meaning) ἐναποτίθεσθαι or κατατίθεσθαι, and this phrase she brings in four times in one Book.[2]

A few more of her favourite expressions will suffice. Her characters do things θᾶττον ἢ λόγος in instances too numerous to quote,[3] or act ἐν ἀσκέπτῳ χρόνῳ ('in an instant'),[4] while 'recently' is the right translation of the picturesque phrase χθὲς καὶ πρώην.[5] When things have gone wrong we are told that a man ἠνιᾶτο καὶ ἤσχαλλε; suspects when not proceeded against are left ἐπὶ ταὐτοῦ, 'as they were',[6] and, to conclude, we three times get the expressive word ἀποπηδᾶν of 'rejecting' good counsel,[7] twice in connexion with obdurate heretics.

From this mass of material two general conclusions may be drawn, first that whereas repetitions are usually left in through negligence, Anna's revision was not at all a careful one, possibly because death or old age cut her work short, secondly that she loved long words and would usually have preferred 'caudal appendage' to 'tail'. Connected with this liking for what seems to us bombast is her constant use of antithesis and similar tours de phrase. Urselius 'was blinded and yet not blinded'.[8] Anna Dalassena's appearance was 'revered by angels, feared by devils';[9] she had the reality of Empire and her son only the 'outward form'; he was 'an instrument of Empire, not Emperor'.[10] Isaac Comnenus when enforcing the unpopular

[1] VIII. 4, p. 230; 7, p. 237; XI. 3, p. 317; 5, p. 320; 7, p. 328, and often elsewhere.

[2] XI. 4, pp. 318, 320; 5, p. 324; 8, p. 331. In XI. 10, p. 336, the word σκευή reappears twice, once singular and one plural, in the old sense of 'apparatus', but in XIV. 6, p. 442, αἱ σκευαί are 'baggage' once more.

[3] e.g. VII. 9, p. 212; VIII. 3, p. 227; 4, p. 229; 9, p. 241; X. 10, p. 299, &c. So Nic. Bry IV. 9, p. 93.

[4] IV. 6, p. 117; IX. 1, p. 246; 9, p. 262; XIV. 1, p. 421.

[5] I. 4, p. 10; IX. 2, p. 249.

[6] (a) III. 9, p. 91; VI. 12, p. 177; VIII. 3, p. 226; IX. 1, p. 246; XV. 3, p. 466; cf. Nic. Bry. III. 4, p. 71. (b) IX. 8, p. 262; 9, p. 264; XIII. 4, p. 389.

[7] V. 9, p. 149; XIII. 12, p. 412; XV. 8, p. 488. We may note that she is not quite so fond as her husband of calling danger προύπτος or ὑπόγυος, but she often does so, especially in Books II (3, p. 47; 4, p. 49; 5, p. 53) and IH (9, p. 92; 11, p. 95). We also find the phrase in V. 4, p. 136; VII. 2, p. 192; IX. 9, p. 264; 10. p. 265, and ὑπόγυος θάνατος in X. 3, p. 277. In VI. 9, p. 169, we have a variant, ὑπὲρ κεφαλῆς τὸν κίνδυνον ἐφιστάμενον ὁρῶν.

[8] I. 3, p. 7. Cf. Callicles Poem XXII. 42, σιγῶν λαλῶ σοι καὶ βλέπω σε μὴ βλέπων.

[9] III. 8, p. 88. In the Golden Bull appointing this lady Regent there is a passage ordering that all her enactments 'written or unwritten, reasonable or unreasonable' are to be carried out, but this double antithesis may be ascribed to the official secretary, not to Anna who copied the document.

[10] III. 7, p. 86.

measure of taking Church treasure for military expenses says:
'I am compelled to compel those whom I do not wish to
compel.'[1] Alexius in the same matter looks like the judge, but
is really the prisoner in the dock.[2] When he played a trick on
his soldiers he 'scared' them 'without (real) fear';[3] Anna
describes herself as περιγράψαντες μᾶλλον ἢ γράψαντες her father's
notable deeds.[4] Efficiency is expressed in this or a similar
elaborate formula: 'He did not say and not do, nor did he
promise and not bring his promise into effect.'[5] We read of
a fortress as 'a city in front of a city and a wall before a
wall'.[6] In another military scene we have a priest of the
Latin race, that race which is 'no less sacerdotal than warlike',
behaving as a 'worker' (or later a 'general') rather than
'priest', and turning 'fighting into a priestly office'.[7] Bohemund's
escape from Antioch[8] in a coffin seems to Anna a fit occasion
for a string of antitheses. He was outwardly a corpse, inwardly
a living man; he was dead as far as lying at full length was
concerned, alive inasmuch as he breathed. Though 'not yet
dead and only dead in appearance, he did not hesitate to live
with dead bodies' (i.e. one dead cock laid on his chest). From
Corfu he taunted the Emperor with the words: 'By thee and
thy men I was accounted dead, but by myself and my men
alive . . . I have died when living, and I lived after having
died.' The wearisome iteration only ends with the chapter.

It is everywhere the same. Some undertakings are a matter
of πάρεργον, others of ἔργον.[9] At Tyre ἀμέλεια is displayed by
Baldwin, ἐπιμέλεια by the besieged inhabitants.[10] Three times
over, possibly four, we have the phrase κενόσπουδος ἡ σπουδὴ
γίγνεται, 'the labour is in vain'.[11] A small city is contrasted with
its 'huge' founder;[12] when a rebel is pardoned by the Emperor
the change is from bondage to freedom, from death to the
receipt of gifts.[13] Homer's phrase about bringing the blameless
under blame suggests another similar one; men 'lay the irre-
proachable under reproach'.[14] In the same passage the Empress
goes into camp 'half unwilling and half willing'.[15] ἀντίμαχοι may

---

[1] V. 2, p. 128. [2] VI. 3, pp. 155, 156.
[3] ἀφόβως ἐμορμολύττετο. VIII. 2, p. 224.
[4] X. 2, p. 271. Once more we have the editorial 'we'. See p. 484, above.
[5] X. 4, p. 278; Cf. I. 7, p. 18; XIII. 4, p. 389, and elsewhere.
[6] X. 5, p. 282.   [7] X. 8.   [8] XI. 12.
[9] i.e. of secondary or primary importance (XIII. 3, p. 383; XIV. 8, p. 453).
We get πάρεργον alone in V. 8, p. 144; VI. 5, p. 158; XV. 7, p. 486.
[10] XIV. 2, p. 426.
[11] XI. 9, p. 334; XIV. 3, p. 433; XV. 2, p. 465, and possibly XV. 11, p. 500,
where the text is imperfect.   [12] XIV. 8, p. 450.
[13] XIV. 3, p. 431.   [14] XII. 3, p. 353.   [15] Ibid.

become σύμμαχοι, and be ἀξιόμαχοι δυνάμεις.[1] θράσος ἀντὶ θάρσους means 'rash daring instead of valour';[2] the Turks 'dreaming of conquest had instead been conquered';[3] when Saisan is blinded with the end of a candlestick Anna cannot resist saying that 'the receptacle of light became an instrument of darkness and blinding'.[4] Basil the Bogomile is a 'solitary but manifold in evil' (μοναχὸς καὶ πολλαχὸς τὴν κακίαν)[5] while the ἀπειροπόλεμοι have small chance against the ἐμπειροπόλεμοι.[6]

Finally, as we might expect, Alexius himself reaps the full harvest of this literary device of his daughter's. Of his wonderful new battle-array one might say that 'moving it remained immovable, and standing it proceeded'; it was like 'the unshaken mountains' in solidity and like 'a great living creature' in its motions. And as for the Emperor himself, 'fleeing he conquered and pursuing he was victorious; falling he stood, and while casting down he was himself erect'.[7]

Among other flowers of speech in the *Alexias* we get a few puns, not of a very high order. There is the impostor Ῥαίκτωρ ὁ ῥέκτης ('doer of evil deeds')[8] and Manganes οἷον μαγγανευόμενος ('as it were playing tricks'), while a castle 'keep' may be said to 'keep' its owner prisoner.[9] Bohemund hoped to drive Alexius truly into a 'wolf's mouth' at Lycostomium,[10] Nilus is a Nile of evil,[11] and the foolish plotter John Solomon was 'inspired by the Anemas brothers' whose name suggested ἄνεμος, 'wind'.[12] Finally Anna twice plays on her mother's name with its meaning of 'peace'.[13]

If after this we ask ourselves whether Anna had any sense of humour, the answer is probably in the negative. Her descriptions may make the modern reader smile, as for instance Irene reading the Fathers at the court meals,[14] the people expecting from a prophecy that the Emperor was to die, but feeling it to be adequately fulfilled when 'the wild lion living in the palace had a fever for four days and then breathed his last',[15] or the unfortunate rebel who was no horseman, so that 'if he chanced to have mounted and then wished to ride forth he suffered from

---

[1] XIV. 8, p. 452.   [2] XV. 3, p. 466.
[3] XV. 2, p. 464.   [4] XV. 6, p. 480.
[5] XV. 8, p. 487. So Nicephorus Bryennius contrasts νουνέχεια and συνέχεια in one sentence (Pref., p. 12), and 'war-lover and mother-lover' in another (I. 12, p. 26). He admires antithesis quite as dearly as his wife.
[6] I. 4, p. 10. So in Nic. Bry. I. 10, p. 24.
[7] XV. 3, p. 467. Cf. V. 4, p. 136: 'Such was [Alexius] defeated and conquering, flying and again pursuing.'
[8] I. 12, p. 28.   [9] I. 11, p. 26; II. 8, p. 60; 10, p. 63.
[10] V. 6, p. 141.   [11] X. 1, p. 269.
[12] XII. 5, p. 359.   [13] XII. 3, p. 354; XV. 11, p. 506.
[14] V. 9, p. 147.   [15] VI. 7, p. 165.

confusion and shaking'.[1] But it is doubtful whether she saw any fun in these things herself. When she does applaud some joke, like the pretended blinding of Urselius, who 'groaned like a lion roaring',[2] or the 'jest both clever and mild, mixed with fear'[3] when Alexius scared his own reinforcements by Greek soldiers dressed up in Scythian clothes, or the contrast between a tiny Scythian gaoler and huge Norman captive at which 'great laughter arose from all',[4] we find it hard to share her amusement. And when she records with apparent gravity her pre-natal obedience to her mother, who reinforced her order, 'Wait for thy father's arrival', by making the sign of the cross over the yet unborn baby, and with equal gravity adds the comment 'which even in the womb foreshadowed very plainly my future loyalty towards my parents',[5] or when she tells us as a proof of the Bogomile Basil's awful wickedness that 'the fire as though enraged against him devoured that impious man so thoroughly that there was not even a smell', we may believe her to be perfectly serious. With every desire to see in her a sense of humour we cannot persuade ourselves that she writes these absurdities otherwise than in sober earnest.

APPENDIX I.—REPETITIONS OF WORDS IN
BOOKS I–XI (*inclusive*)

ἀναπαύω (and compounds). I. 3, p. 8: 6, p. 16: 7, p. 18. Also
    V. 1, p. 125, 126; XIV. 6, p. 444: 9, p. 455; XV. 4, p. 472.
ἀναρριπίζω. V. 4, p. 135: 5, p. 136. Also X. 9, p. 297.
ἀντιποιέομαι. V. 3, p. 131 (*bis*), 132.
ἁπλόω. I. 3, p. 7: 4, p. 10.
ἀποθαρρέω. VII. 9, pp. 210, 213 (*bis*): 11, p. 215.
ἀποστρέφομαι. IX. 10, p. 265 (*bis*).
διαλαμβάνω περί. VI. 9, p. 170: 12, p. 177. Also XI. 7, p. 328;
    XIV. 2, p. 424: 5, p. 438. Without περί VIII. 7, p. 237 (*bis*).
διοικονομέομαι. I. 6, p. 15: 7, p. 18.
ἐν ἀναβολαῖς εἰμί. VII. 7, p. 204: 8, p. 205. Also VIII. 5, p. 231.
ἐξόχως φιλέω. IX. 5, p. 255: 6, p. 256: 7, p. 258.
ἐπαγωγός. III. 1, p. 71: 2, p. 74. Also II. 1, p. 44.
ἐρεθίζω. VI. 5, pp. 158, 159.
ἔφοδος. VI. 5, pp. 159, 160 (*bis*).
κατασυστάδην. VII. 9, p. 210: 11, p. 215.
κατορθόω. XI. 4, pp. 319 (*bis*), 320 (*bis*).
κρότος. I. 3, p. 7: 4, p. 9.
λογοποιέω. III. 1, p. 72: 2, p. 74: 9, p. 90.

---

[1] IX. 2, p. 249.   [2] I. 3, p. 7.
[3] VIII. 2, p. 224. Cf. George Palaeologus' feeble practical joke in Nic. Bry.
IV. 39, p. 107.   [4] XIII. 6, p. 395.   [5] VI, 8, p. 166.

μερικός. VIII. 5, p. 234: 6, p. 236.

περινοστέω. VII. 8, p. 210: 9, p. 210. Also X. 2, p. 271; XI. 12, p. 342; XII. 3, p. 354.

προμηθεύομαι. VIII. 5, p. 233: 7, p. 236. Also IX. 6, p. 256; X. 7, p. 288: 10, p. 299: 11, p. 304; XI. 7, p. 328: 10, p. 337; XII. 1, p. 345.

προσδόκιμος. VII. 6, p. 202: 9, p. 209: 10, p. 214. Also VIII. 1, p. 221; XIV. 5, p. 439.

σχέσις. II. 8, p. 59: 11, p. 66.

τὸ φρονοῦν αὐτῷ τῆς ψυχῆς συναγαγών. VI. 5, p. 159: 6, p. 162. Also IX. 5, p. 254, and cf. X. 8, p. 292.

ὑποβρύχιος. II. 1, p. 45: 4, p. 49. Also III. 6, p. 82; IX. 6, p. 257; X. 11, p. 306; XI. 4, p. 319; XIII. 4, p. 388.

ὑπόληψις. X. 11, pp. 304, 305 (bis).

ὑποτυφόμενος σπινθήρ. III. 9, p. 91: 11, p. 96.

φιλαρχίας ἔρως. III. 7, p. 85: 9, p. 91.

χρονοτριβέω. I. 2, p. 5: 11, p. 24.

ὡς ἐξ ἑνὸς συνθήματος. VIII. 5, p. 232: 6, p. 234. Also XI, 2, p. 313.

APPENDIX II.—FAVOURITE VERBS

ἀναδέομαι. I. 5, p. 12: 6, p. 14: 12, p. 27; II. 12, p. 67; III. 8, p. 87; VI. 5, p. 160: 10, p. 172: 14, p. 182; VII. 2, p. 191: 9, p. 209; X. 10, p. 301; XII. 7, p. 365.

σπάομαι (and compounds). I. 1, p. 3: 2, p. 5 (bis): 5, p. 12: 8, p. 20: 9, p. 21: 12, p. 28; II. 1, p. 44: 6, p. 55; III. 8, p. 90; V. 9, p. 148; VI. 7, p. 166: 8, p. 168; VII. 3, p. 197; VIII. 5, p. 233: 9, p. 240 (bis); IX. 6, p. 258; X. 4, p. 280: 5, p. 282: 11, p. 301; XIII. 6, p. 392: 12, p. 411; XIV. 7, p. 449; XV. 4, p. 469. Also in many other places of 'drawing' a weapon.

σύρω (in various forms). Pref. 1, p. 2: I. 5, p. 13: 6, p. 15: 9, p. 21: 13, p. 33: 15, p. 37; II. 6, p. 55; III. 3, pp. 76, 77: 8, p. 90; IV. 6, p. 115; V. 1, p. 127; VI. 3, p. 155: 13, p. 181; VII. 2, p. 190: 3, pp. 195, 196, 197: 5, p. 201: 6, p. 203: 10, p. 215: 11, p. 216; VIII. 7, p. 236; IX. 4, p. 253: 9, p. 264; X. 1, p. 269; XIII. 1, p. 377: 6, pp. 393, 394: 8, p. 397; XIV. 7, p. 448; XV. 3, p. 466: 7, p. 483: 8, p. 487.

σφαδάζω. V. 4, p. 134: 5, p. 137: 7, p. 142: 8, p. 145; VII. 1, p. 189; X. 3, p. 276: 8, p. 293; XI. 5, p. 321; XIII. 4, p. 386: 6, p. 394: 7, p. 395: 8, p. 398; XIV. 3, p. 431; XV. 4, p. 473: 5, p. 475: 10, p. 494.

ὑποποιέομαι. VI. 4, p. 158 (ter); VII. 5, p. 200; VIII. 4, p. 228: 5, p. 230; IX. 2, p. 249: 6, pp. 257, 258: 8, p. 261; X. 11, p. 306; XI. 4, p. 319 (bis): 6, p. 258: 8, p. 332: 9, p. 332: 11, p. 339; XII. 5, p. 360; XIII. 4, p. 387: 12, p. 411; XIV. 2, p. 424.

74. METAPHORS AND PROVERBS

ONE way in which a writer may show humour is in the choice of comparisons, but here again Anna if tried in the balance will be found wanting. Her metaphors and similes are of every sort and description[1] except the humorous. Indeed they are mostly so commonplace that they need not occupy us long. They fall into fairly stereotyped groups. We find converted heretics compared to 'tame sheep',[2] fierce enemies to hunting dogs,[3] crowds to bees or wasps,[4] slow-marching soldiers or feeble opponents to ants,[5] a prisoner to a lion in a menagerie,[6] warriors to lions or leopards or wolves or boars or other wild animals,[7] thin arguments to a spider's web,[8] a grasping man to an octopus,[9] and men digging mines to moles.[10] The whole animal kingdom is ransacked for comparisons. Insect-pests are fit pictures of the all-destroying Robert and Bohemund, and frightened men stand 'dumber than fishes'.[11] Alexius escapes from his enemies 'like a soaring falcon',[12] Psellus rose above captious controversy 'like an eagle',[13] news runs through a country 'like a bird',[14] and Constantine Ducas has eyes like a hawk.[15] Figures of hunting and shooting and fishing are common.[16] In other parts of the world of nature we get beauty compared to roses, fair skins to milk, and height to cypresses.[17] Fire with its accompanying smoke is used to repre-

---

[1] In this she does not resemble her husband, who has few figures of speech.
[2] XIV. 9, p. 457.
[3] VI. 14, p. 182. Obdurate men return to their vomit like dogs (VII. 6, p. 204).
[4] I. 3, p. 7; 6, p. 15; VI. 5, p. 159; XII. 2, p. 349; XIII. 3, p. 383. Cf. Nic. Bry. III. 6, p. 73; Attal. p. 25.
[5] XIV. 2, p. 424; XV. 7, p. 481.
[6] I. 3, p. 8; cf. a retreating soldier 'roaring like a lion' (XIII. 6, p. 393).
[7] I. 6, p. 15; 7, p. 18; 13, p. 32; V. 7, p. 142; VI. 12, p. 179; VII. 4, p. 200; IX. 6, pp. 256, 257; X. 10, p. 299; XI. 1, p. 310; 3, p. 318; XIII. 3, p. 381; XIV. 9, p. 455; XV. 4, p. 473; 5, p. 475; 6, p. 476. So Alexius says to John in Poem I, line 166:

$$\text{ἔσῃ πεποιθὼς οἷα γενναῖος λέων,}$$

and the figure recurs a hundred lines later.
[8] XIV. 9, p. 455.
[9] X. 11, p. 304. So in Nic. Acom. *John C.* 2, p. 6. In *Anon. Syn. Chron.*, p. 179, the reference is to the emission of sepia to darken matters.
[10] XIII. 3, p. 382.   [11] I. 14, p. 35; IX. 9, p. 264.
[12] II. 4, p. 51.   [13] V. 8, p. 145.
[14] X. 4, p. 280.   [15] III. 1, p. 71.
[16] II. 1, pp. 43, 44, 45; 2, pp. 46, 47; V. 4, p. 136; 8, p. 146; VI. 7, p. 166; VII. 8, p. 210; 9, p. 211; XI. 6, p. 326; 10, p. 335; XIV. 2, p. 426; 9, p. 455; XV. 1, p. 461; 2, p. 464; 4, p. 470; 8, p. 487.
[17] III. 1, p. 71; 2, p. 74; 3, p. 77.

sent danger and trouble of all sorts (as well as swift, vigorous action), and thunder and lightning figure in the same way.[1] Great numbers are like the stars or the sands or spring leaves and flowers, or a man's 'own hairs';[2] snowflakes may typify crowds or a shower of arrows or incessant cares,[3] successful warriors attack like fire or a hurricane or a thunderbolt.[4] Robert Guiscard at Durazzo is 'like some winged horseman,[5] Alexius is like an unshaken tower,[6] even a pillar of fire.[7] Troops in firm array are 'as it were walls of adamant' or like 'the unshaken mountains'.[8] Comparisons to mythological personages, Giants, Ares, Heracles, Orpheus, occur too often to need considering; they form part of the equipment of every Byzantine writer. In her last chapter Anna likens herself to the Pythia with her tripod.[9] To the Games we get more references than can be quoted, especially where a 'start' is in question.[10]

Illness is a 'beast' and twines round the victim 'like some twisted serpent',[11] and on the other hand misfortunes befalling the State are like diseases and injury to the body.[12] Smouldering sparks fanned into a flame portray the revival of political and literary activity,[13] and the vanquished retreat 'like sand slipping away under one's feet'.[14] Foolish criticism or feeble fighting is as 'the pastimes of children',[15] and unstable people are like the variable currents in Euripus.[16] Figures from sea-faring occur more frequently than any other, often indicated by just one

---

[1] Pref. 1, p. 7; I. 14, p. 35; II. 3, p. 47; III. 9, p. 91; VII. 2, p. 192; IX. 10, p. 266; X. 11, p. 304; XI. 10, p. 336; XII. 2 (*bis*) ; 5, p. 357; XIV. 4, p. 436; XV. 8, p. 487. So of men 'as though thunder-struck' in VI. 5, p. 158; IX. 5, p. 254.

[2] VII. 3, p. 198; X. 10, p. 299; cf. *Mous. Alex.* II. 75.

[3] IV. 2, p. 105; XI. 11, p. 340; XIII. 8, p. 397; XIV. 5, p. 438.

[4] I. 1, p. 4; 14, p. 35; III. 3, p. 77; 8, p. 89; VI. 10, p. 172; VII. 3, p. 198; XI. 10, p. 336; XII. 2, p. 350; XIV. 5, p. 441; XV. 1, p. 462; 3, p. 469. Alexius' glance is like a whirlwind (III. 3, p. 76).

[5] IV. 6, p. 116.   [6] V. 4, p. 134; X. 4, p. 280.

[7] XV. 5, p. 474. He is also like a caltrop, standing upright however thrown (XV. 3, p. 468).

[8] XV. 6, p. 477; 7, p. 481. A determined man, or one who sternly represses emotion, is like adamant (IV. 8, p. 121; XV. 10, p. 493) or iron (XIV. 9, p. 457).

[9] XV. 11, p. 504.

[10] I. 6, p. 15; III. 12, p. 98; V. 8, p. 144; VI. 8, p. 168; IX. 9, p. 263; X. 5, p. 283; XI. 1, p. 311; XV. 10, p. 495; 11, p. 501. So ἐναποδύεσθαι and similar words convey the idea of stripping for a contest (VII. 9, p. 210; IX. 1, p. 248; XI. 11, p. 339; XV. 3, p. 467; 8, p. 469. So ἐπαλείφειν = encourage (VII. 10, p. 214; XII. 8, p. 366).

[11] XIV. 7, p. 449.

[12] I. 10, p. 22; III. 9, p. 91; XII. 5, p. 358. So insatiable ambition is like a gangrene (IV. 1, p. 105), and impiety like an infectious disease (X. 1, p. 270).

[13] III. 9, p. 91; 11, p. 96; V. 9, p. 148.   [14] I. 1, p. 3.

[15] IX. 2, p. 249; XV. 3, p. 466.   [16] II. 3, p. 48; XI. 2, p. 312.

word.[1] Disasters are hurricanes, and enemies arise in a 'cloud'.[2] Alexius and Irene were the sun and moon of the world.[3] Heretical evils like a flood engulf men in their eddies.[4] Anna's attempt to do justice to her father's great deeds is like 'touching the Adriatic with the tip of her finger'.[5] Again, her narrative journeys like a horse along a high road and digressions must be checked.[6] The flowing stream of time sweeps the past into oblivion, and History has to be the opposing bulwark;[7] we are forcibly reminded of Watts's hymn:

> Time, like an ever-rolling stream,
> Bears all its sons away.

The ship of Count Hugh is 'as it were spat up' by the angry sea;[8] it is despicable to 'behave like a drunkard';[9] men in military metaphor take the 'signal'—literally 'key-note' (ἐνδόσιμον) —and obey.[10] Such are some of Anna's picturesque touches, given each in a single word.

Among the more interesting figures of speech we may count the phrase 'like a paternal inheritance', which is very variously applied to things good and bad, material and spiritual.[11] Again, Raymond of Provence excels the other Crusaders 'as the sun

---

[1] So 'helmsman' of an Emperor or a Patriarch (II. 7, p. 57; III. 4, p. 79; 6, p. 82; IV. 5, p. 114; V. 1, p. 127). We may compare Nic. Bry. I. 4, p. 18, and the Pref. to the Panopl. of Zigabenus (P. G. 130, col. 20). Also κλυδώνιον or κλύδων of public disturbance, with the figure of the ship of state (III. 6, p. 83; 9, p. 92; VI. 3, p. 155; X. 2, p. 271; XV. 11, p. 501; cf. Nic. Bry. I. 19, p. 32), and 'sea' of an unlimited extent, like 'la mar de' in Spanish. So I. 1, p. 3; III. 8, p. 87; V. 9, p. 148; XIV. 4, p. 434; 7, p. 446; XV. 11, pp. 503, 506. Zigabenus (Panopl., loc. cit. col. 1332) speaks of a 'sea of impiety' and works out the figure at some length. Alexius in Mous. Alex. I. 16–19 speaks of sailing well over the sea of life, 'fleeing from the wave and the unstable surge'. Cf. Psellus Chron. Const. IX, Byz. T., p. 107.
Other marine metaphors in single words are: ἐνθαλαττεύεσθαι (I. 13, p. 33), ἀποπνίγοντες (V. 5, p. 138), κυμαίνεσθαι (III. 11, p. 95, and often elsewhere), ζάλη (XIV. 3, p. 431), κατακλύζειν (XII. 5, p. 357), γαληνιαῖος (XIV. 7, p. 448), and ἀντιπνεῖν (I. 16, p. 40). In XIV. 9, p. 455, there is an elaborate simile with κύματα. So Pref. 4, p. 7. ζάλη occurs in this sense in Callicles' Poems, XI. 3; XXII. 65; XXIII. 8; and XXVI. 24.
[2] e.g. V. 2, p. 129; XV. 8, p. 486; 11, p. 506.
[3] XV. 11, p. 506. So in Zigabenus' Second Poem on Alexius, C. Neumann, Gr. Geschichtschreiber, p. 34.
[4] X. 1, pp. 269, 270.   [5] VIII. 6, p. 236; X. 2, p. 271; cf. Attal. 318.
[6] Pref. 3, p. 3; I. 16, p. 40; XIV. 4, p. 438; XV. 11, p. 495. Metaphors from riding are too frequent to warrant enumeration here. See p. 376, note 2, above.
[7] Pref. 1, pp. 1, 2; I. 13, p. 31.   [8] X. 7, p. 289.
[9] XI. 3, p. 317. παροινεῖν perhaps from Plut. Alcib. 38.
[10] II. 4, p. 49; X. 2, p. 273; 4, p. 278; cf. Nic. Acom. John C. 3, p. 8.
[11] II. 2, p. 45 (bis); 9, p. 62; VI. 12, pp. 179 and 180; X. 3, p. 277; 11, p. 305; XI. 8, p. 332. Theophylact reminds his pupil Constantine Ducas that he (C. D.) had inherited affection towards him (T.) ὡς πατρῷον κλῆρον (Ser. II, Ep. 63, P. G. 126, col. 481). So of a luxurious life in Psellus (Chron., Const. IX., Byz. T., p. 112) and of illness in an unpublished poem of Theodore Prodromus. The simile is a very favourite one with Callicles.

the stars';[1] the haughtiness of Gregory VII to King Henry is 'as though he were a demigod discoursing with a mule',[2] both statements giving noteworthy indications of Anna's personal feelings. The changes of fortune and of the popular mind are as unaccountable as the way a die or potsherd falls; a battle stands 'upon the balance' and so do two rivals; and bad men 'roll the wheel of envy' against the innocent.[3] Heretics must be lured into the open 'as a snake lurking in its hole by the secret spells of enchanters'.[4] The Emperor's domestic foes clung to him as bad flavours cling to jars.[5] Small ills heaped on great remind Anna of the honey-cakes served up as dessert to sated epicures.[6] Varied ills are a 'mixed drink', κυκεών, the word applied to Circe's potion in *Odyssey* X.[7] Constantine Ducas (and here we have another personal touch) hated the idea of marrying the Norman Helena 'as infants do those who frighten them'.[8] Enemies may by God's help be 'scattered into foam, like waves when they dash against a rock'.[9] Anna herself has suffered from 'streams of misfortunes . . . like rivers flowing down from high mountains'.[10] Many of these comparisons are apposite enough. But on the whole we must repeat that the figures of speech in the *Alexias* are disappointingly common-place and conventional, affording no insight into the writer's mind. Except for two or three they might have been used by any writer at any period.

Finally we come to Anna's use of proverbs. The *C. S. H. B.* edition gives a partial list of the *Proverbia et Similia* in the *Alexias*,[11] but with many of them we have already dealt as figures of speech[12] or as allusions and quotations.[13] Some again are merely picturesque expressions which we use ourselves

---

[1] X. 11, p. 305. So Nic. Bry. of his own father (*Hyle* IV. 5, p. 91).

[2] I. 13, p. 32.

[3] I. 3, p. 7; 5, p. 10; 16, p. 38; VI. 5, p. 158; VII. 3, p. 196; IX. 9, p. 264.

[4] XV. 8, p. 486.   [5] XIV. 4, p. 437.   [6] X. 2, p. 272.

[7] XII. 5, p. 357; XIV. 4, p. 435; XV. 1, p. 460. Cf. Attal. p. 309. We get 'mixing a cup of death' in Pref. 3, p. 5; X. 11, p. 302; XI. 3, p. 315, and 'smearing the cup with honey', perhaps as an antidote to actual poison, in XIV. 4, p. 437. Cf. the phrase 'he smeared the cup with sweets' of the guileful Emperor in XV. 8, p. 488.

[8] I. 12, p. 30.   [9] III. 9, p. 92.

[10] XV. 11, p. 507.   [11] Vol. II, p. 823.

[12] e.g. especially ἐκ πρώτης ἀφετηρίας or βαλβίδος with ὅ φασι sometimes added: we may translate colloquially, 'from the word Go' (IV. 1, p. 103; 4, p. 108; XI. 1, p. 311; XIII. 5, p. 390; XV. 11, p. 495).

[13] e.g. the fox's skin (IX. 5, p. 254; 6, p. 257); the spindle of Fate (IV. 8, p. 121); a Cadmeian victory (XIV. 6, p. 443; 9, p. 455; XV. 3, p. 467); the Euripus currents (II. 3, p. 48; XI. 2, p. 312), the Nile floods (X. 1, p. 269, in a sort of pun, and XV. 11, p. 499); the arrogance of the heretic Novatus (VI. 12, p. 179; X. 7, p. 288); and the speed of a Lydian chariot (VI. 14, p. 185); ff. 200, 202 above.

without dignifying them with the name of proverbs or even 'similia'.[1] Of more important proverbs we find however quite a number. The same thought which makes Anna describe her father proudly and Bohemund angrily as 'always the same', finds vent elsewhere in 'the crab never learnt to walk straight' of deceitful enemies[2], and 'the Ethiopian did not grow white',[3] the last being of course a Biblical allusion.[4] Wasted arguments are 'singing to a deaf man',[5] meanness is 'splitting cummin' (the tiny seed of spice eaten with food).[6] The equivalent of our 'when Greek meets Greek' is found in πρὸς Κρῆτα κρητίζων.[7] Straining every nerve is πάντα κάλων κινεῖν, first found in Lucian,[8] and casting off disguise is τὴν σκηνὴν ῥίπτειν or διαρρηγνύναι,[9] i. e. to throw down or tear in pieces the back wall of a stage. The Latin proverb *ex pede Herculem* is the best rendering of 'recognizing the garment from its hem and the lion from his claws'.[10] The dog returning to its vomit is of course a scriptural quotation, but it is interesting to find Anna's theological guide Zigabenus applying it to the Bogomile heretic Basil, whereas she uses it of the Scythians.[11] The expression for despising death is a curious one; men fight ὡς τηνικαῦτα γεννηθέντες καὶ τεθνηξό-

---

[1] e.g. 'sharing common salt' (II. 7, p. 58); 'the tips of' fingers, feet, or ears to denote the barest possible use (VIII. 6, p. 236; XIV. 2, p. 423; XV. 10, p. 495); 'smoke before fire' (Pref. 4, p. 7; I. 14, p. 35; XII. 2, p. 348); 'under the tooth' where we say 'under one's breath' (II. 4, p. 50); 'to his beard' where we say 'to his face' (IV. 2, p. 106); 'swifter than birds' (XI. 12, p. 341; XIV. 2, p. 427); 'drop by drop' of troops collecting (XV. 1, p. 460); 'beating the air' (VI. 10, p. 173); 'assuming various colours' of a character (I. 16, p. 39). 'To have heads equal' is only a stronger form of our 'to be equal' in fight (I. 13, p. 33); for a person in the last stage of exhaustion to have 'her soul hanging in her nostrils' is hardly more forced than the 'life hovering on the lips' familiar in the death-bed scenes of novels (XV. 11, p. 501).

[2] VI. 4, p. 158; IX. 1, p. 247. Also to be the same χθὲς καὶ πρότριτα 'yesterday and three days ago' (II. 2, p. 45; VI. 4, p. 158). We may compare *Heb.* xiii. 8.

[3] IX. 6, p. 257. So in *Anon. Sym. Chron.*, p. 180.   [4] *Jer.* xiii. 23.

[5] XI. 7, p. 330; XIV. 2, p. 427. So in Nic. Bry. I. 13, p. 27, and IV. 35, p. 105. In Theophylact *P.G.* 126, col. 324, and *Anon. Sym. Chron.*, p. 181, we get 'a donkey hearing a lyre'.

[6] II. 4, p. 51. This has nothing to do with the tithing mint, anise, and cummin of *Matt.* xxiii. 23, where the idea is of ceremonial scrupulosity. The 'cummin-splitter' figures in Aristophanes, *Wasps*, 1357.

[7] X. 11, p. 304. St. Paul gives the Cretans the character of 'liars' as a well-known fact (*Tit.* i. 12). We might also translate 'the biter bit'.

[8] II. 7, p. 57; III. 9, p. 91; X. 11, p. 304; XI. 7, p. 330; XIV. 2, p. 428. So in Nic. Bry., Pref., p. 8; II. 14, p. 51, and 17, p. 55, and Attal. p. 28. Glycas has the proverb twice, I. p. 39; IV. p. 292. In *Barlaam und Joasaph* (ed. Boissonade, *Anecd. Gr.* IV, pp. 9 and 232) we twice get πάντα λίθον κινήσας, τὸ τοῦ λόγου, equivalent to our 'leaving no stone unturned'.

[9] XII. 8, p. 366; XV. 6, p. 480.

[10] XIV. 3, p. 432; XV. 10, p. 494. In *Don Quijote*, Pt. I, ch. iv, we find this form of the proverb: 'Por el hilo se sacará el ovillo.'

[11] VII. 6, p. 204; *Prov.* xxvi. 11; *Panopl.*, *P.G.* 130, col. 1332.

μενοι;[1] to decide one way or the other is to eat 'flesh either of wolf or of lamb'.[2] 'Flying from the smoke he fell into the fire' and 'flying from a wolf they met with a lion' are two ways of putting our 'out of the frying-pan into the fire',[3] and when Alexius says, 'We have given two and taken one', we feel it to be a good phrase for a bad bargain.[4] 'Making a virtue of necessity' appears as making necessity a φιλοτιμία;[5] 'Not even the gods fight against necessity' is quoted as a proverb.[6] Affairs standing 'on a razor's edge' is an expression found first in Homer, then in Herodotus,[7] and often in the poets. 'Of two evils choose the less' is our version of Anna's 'thinking the less bad course, as men say, the better',[8] as 'the next best way' is of her δεύτερος πλοῦς.[9]

On the whole it is remarkable how many of these proverbs and proverbial phrases have survived from the twelfth century right down to our own day. Only three are quite foreign to us, and we will now give them. (1) The 'popular saying: Let an evil thing return to its own author'[10] has no modern equivalent; the Psalmist's prophecy that mischief will return upon the mischievous man's 'own head' is about the nearest.[11] (2) To be 'sent away to quiver on the sea' (ψαίρειν ἐπὶ πελάγους)[12] seems to mean to be 'cast adrift', but the word ψαίρειν, 'to graze' (trans.) or 'flutter' (intrans.) seems very pointless. Perhaps we should read σπείρειν, as 'sowing on the waters' was a proverbial phrase for wasted labour, like our 'ploughing the sands'.[13] (3) Bohemund compares his repentant self to a ἁλιεὺς πληγεὶς καὶ ἀπενεγκάμενος νοῦν,[14] and this same proverb is quoted by the

---

[1] IV. 5, p. 114; V. 4, p. 134; VII. 3, p. 197. N. Polites (*B. Z.* VII, p. 155) gives parallels from Soph. *O. T.* 438; Michael Glycas (*Stichoi*, No. 292), the *Rime of Belisarius*; and a modern Greek proverb. [2] VIII. 5, p. 230.

[3] X. 8, p. 290; XIII. 6, p. 394. Cf. Attal. p. 14; Nic. Bry. II. 22, p. 60. Anna has a less picturesque form in IV. 2, p. 106, 'the very thing they fled from, into that did they fall'.

[4] XIV. 6, p. 443. In III. 6, p. 84, there is this neat sentence to express complete union of spirit and of goods: 'The mine or the thine, that frigid word, was not spoken.' [5] XIII. 8, p. 399; 9, p. 402.

[6] XII. 3, p. 351. Probably from Simonides, 3, line 15, in Bergk's *Anth. Lyr. Gr.* (Teubner 1897), p. 235.

[7] VII. 9, p. 212; XV. 11, p. 504; *Iliad* X. 173; Herod. VI. 11. In XII. 8, p. 368, ἐπὶ ξυροῦ means imminent. Cf. Nic. Bry. IV. 33, p. 104.

[8] VII. 6, p. 203.

[9] XI. 8, p. 331; XV. 6, p. 479. This was originally of taking oars when the wind fails.

[10] X. 11, p. 304. [11] *Ps.* vii. 16 (17 in LXX). [12] XII. 5, p. 360.

[13] So in *Barlaam und Joasaph*, ed. Boissonade, *Anecd. Gr.* IV, p. 183, and other references in K. Krumbacher's article on 'Mittelgriechische Sprichwörter, *Sitzungsber. zu München*, 1893, p. 243.

[14] XIII. 12, p. 406. In II. 6, p. 54, occur the words 'ὕστερον νοῦν οἴσαντες, according to the proverb'.

Scholiasts on Aristides¹ as the equivalent of Homer's phrase
ῥεχθὲν δέ τε νήπιος ἔγνω.² This phrase may be roughly rendered
by 'a burnt child fears the fire' or 'once bit twice shy'. But
why a fisherman should be specially chosen as an instance of
learning from experience is not clear. Aegean fishermen were
and are a resourceful, sharp-witted race, and that one of them
should be 'struck' and have to recover his senses may perhaps
give somewhat the idea of 'deceiving the very elect'. It is just
possible that Anna is using ἁλιεύς not for 'fisherman' but for
the crafty fish of that name, described by her favourite Plutarch³
as letting down a sort of fleshy line to draw small fish up to its
mouth. Then the picture would be of such a fish stunned by
the blow of a harpoon, and coming to its senses 'a sadder yet
a wiser fish'. But it is probably better to see merely a reference
to the fact that ἡ πληκτική was one of the two ways of fishing,
as minutely differentiated by Plato.⁴ He says that just as hunting is of land or water animals, so hunting of water-animals is
either by fowling or by fishing, fishing is by nets or by striking,
and striking is by spears or hooks. τὸ πληκτικόν is one-half of
fishing, and angling is one-half of τὸ πληκτικόν (or τῆς πληκτικῆς).
For a fisherman who is himself a 'striker' to be 'struck' would
be like being 'hoist with his own petard'.⁵

In conclusion we may mention Anna's characteristically
Byzantine sentiment that 'not even Heracles can fight against
two, as the proverbial phrase intimates'.⁶ This as Krumbacher
shows was such a favourite proverb as to be thought worthy
of a mystical explanation; Heracles meant Adam who 'was
deceived by two', the two being not the Devil and Eve (as we
might expect) but 'the soul and the body'.⁷

We may reckon it to Anna's credit as a woman of sense that
when she uses proverbs she never does so in this fantastical
way. Indeed our only criticism is that she uses them too

¹ ὑπὲρ τῶν τεττάρων, 235.
² Iliad XVII. 32; cf. Hesiod, Op. 218, παθὼν δέ τε νήπιος ἔγνω.
³ De Sollertia anim. 978 D.
⁴ Soph. 220 sqq.
⁵ Cedrenus (p. 755 D) has the proverb in full : οὕτω δὲ πληγεὶς οὐδὲ μετὰ
τὴν πληγὴν κατὰ τὸν ἐν παροιμίαις ἁλιέα νοῦν ἔσχεν. The proverb is not given by
Krumbacher in the article just quoted. We may mention here the suggestion
given above, p. 211, note 9, that in VIII. 3, p. 226, ὁπηνίκα τὰς κριθὰς καταλάβοι
is possibly a slang or proverbial phrase for 'when he got the swag' or (American)
'the beans'. But it may merely refer to getting in the crops of barley.
⁶ III. 11, p. 96; XIII. 7, p. 396. It occurs without Heracles in II. 9, p. 61;
VI. 1, p. 153; IX. 1, p. 246; XIII. 8, p. 399.
⁷ Loc. cit. p. 100, referring to a Vatican codex. In an earlier article in the same
journal (1888, p. 94) Krumbacher gives the modern Greek equivalent, 'Woe to the
brave man if two weaklings attack him', and in the second article (1893, p. 197)
the Turkish 'Two cats are enough for one lion.'

sensibly and prosaically to permit any inference as to her own views. As we said before of her metaphors and similes, so of her proverbs: any writer of any period might have employed the same.[1]

75. CONCLUSION

WE have now come back in a sort of circle to the point where we began. We have dealt with Anna as a princess, as an educated woman, as a historian, and as a writer, and because a writer must express ideas we stand once more at the very threshold of our inquiry. What were her moral and intellectual standards and how did she exhibit them?

We do not however propose to travel over the same road once more. Her ideas as such and their similarities to those of her contemporaries[2] have been set forth as far as possible under appropriate headings. In her generalizations and moralizings she either repeats the common platitudes of literature[3] or shows her personal bias as a Greek princess against common people and barbarians, and as an orthodox believer against heretics.[4] Approaching them from the side of style, we are constrained to say that only on a very few occasions do her maxims possess any individual flavour[5] or deserve notice from the literary point of view.[6] Indeed, the chief remark to be made

[1] It should be said that Oster (Pt. III, p. 67) considers these figures and proverbs in Anna's writing as 'ein unwiderlegliches Zeugniss von Anna's feiner Auffassungs- und Beobachtungsgabe und ihrer tiefen Menschenkenntniss', as well as 'einen untrüglichen Maasstab zur Beurtheilung der Bildungsfähigkeit der Sprache und des Volkscharakters', because so many of them were popular sayings.

[2] Especially Cecaumenus and Nicephorus Bryennius.

[3] e.g. that fortune is fickle (III. 1, p. 71; X. 2, p. 272; XII. 3, p. 353; cf. Zonaras, XVIII. 29); and youth more rash than age (III. 7, p. 86; VIII. 7, p. 237; 9, p. 241; IX. 4, p. 252; XV. 5, p. 475); that women are cowardly (XV. 2, p. 463) and weak characters unstable (II. 3, p. 48; 9, p. 61); that it is easy to criticize, hard to achieve (Pref. 2, p. 2; VI. 7, p. 166; XII. 3, p. 353); that a noble death is better than ignoble life (VII. 3, p. 197), &c.

[4] e.g. I. 2, p. 6; 3, p. 7; 7, p. 17 (cf. Nic. Bry., Pref., p. 2); II. 4, p. 49; III. 1, p. 72; 2, p. 74; VI. 8, p. 168; X. 9, p. 294; XIII. 1, p. 378; XIV. 7, p. 445. We have spoken at length of her attitude to the Crusaders and to the horrors of false doctrine. Her statement (XV. 10, p. 494) that 'the elements' attack the impious and spare the pious is translated in full a little later on.

[5] Thus her acceptance of the jealousy of kinsmen or fellow-soldiers as the usual thing seems to point to unfortunate incidents in her own experience (VIII. 3, p. 225; X. 6, p. 286).

[6] We may quote the passage in IX. 9, p. 264, as being finely worded: 'Such are the ways of men. For towards the man whom to-day they think worthy of blessings and furnish with an escort and hold in honour, when they see the die of life turned upside down for him, they have no shame in showing quite a different

about her generalizations is that their wordy elaborateness often makes translation very difficult. The sentence about Monomachatus and his double-dealing is a case in point,[1] so are two passages describing a virtuous man's agitation over his first fault,[2] and the fatal results of departing from 'the mean'.[3] One of the most stilted and cumbrous passages in the whole work is Anna's defence of her father for preferring strategy to fighting.[4] It is full of high-sounding theories and maxims, but her anxiety to deliver her father from the stigma of cowardice may well remind the reader of her own aphorism, δεινὸς ἔλεγχος ἡ συνείδησις.[5]

Where then in the final summing up does she stand as a writer? That must always remain largely a matter of individual judgement, but after admitting that she often gives us trite maxims, involved sentences, and long dull passages, we may still justly claim for her the 'verve' and 'chaleur' of which Chalandon speaks. She is enthusiastic about her main subject, which is a great thing; and she can present pictures vividly to her reader, which is an even greater.

Some have been translated in full in the course of this volume; to others we can only make reference. But it is safe to say that there is not one of the fifteen Books that has not one graphic scene or more. Book I has the night-attack of Basilacius on Alexius' camp and the parley between Robert Guiscard and his father-in-law;[6] Book II shows us the Palace at meal-times and the womenkind of the Comneni taking sanctuary in St. Sophia,[7] while John Ducas Caesar gets strange news at night and sits up in bed thoughtfully stroking his beard. Book III has lifelike portraits of the ex-Empress Maria and her son Constantine, and of the new sovereigns Alexius and Irene.[8] It also contains the great eulogy on Anna Dalassena and a wonderful picture of the storm which wrecks Robert's fleet.[9] Book IV has Anna's best battle-scenes, and especially Alexius' marvellous escape on horseback.[10] Book V gives us the very

face.' We may compare Keble's lines in the *Christian Year* (Advent Sunday, stanza 5):

> 'Hosanna' now, to-morrow 'Crucify',
> The changeless burden still of their rude, lawless cry.

[1] I. 16, p. 39 D.   [2] III. 5, p. 80 B and C.   [3] X. 11, p. 303 A.
[4] XV. 3. See p. 245 above, and a translation of the passage on p. 143 above.
[5] IX. 5, p. 255. This is roughly equivalent to 'qui s'excuse s'accuse', rather than to 'conscience doth make cowards of us all', unless we use 'conscience' for Anna's consciousness of her father's failings, which made her afraid of blame for him, and in that sense a 'coward'. Cf. 1 *John* iii. 20, 21.
[6] I. 7, 8, 11.   [7] II. 3, 5, 6.   [8] III. 1, 2, 3, 7, 8.
[9] III. 7, 8, 12.   [10] IV. 7.

realistic description of the philosopher Italus, and also shows
us Irene reading the Fathers at meals.[1] Book VI is on the whole
a dull one, but Alexius' treatment of the Manichaeans is put
well if unpleasantly before us,[2] and Anna's account of her own
birth is inimitable.[3] In Book VII we get her father's fighting with
the Patzinaks and his trick over the eclipse;[4] the adventures of
George Palaeologus[5] during his flight are graphically narrated,
as are the insolence of the deserter Neantzes,[6] and Alexius'
ingenious device in rolling wheels against the Scythian horses'
legs.[7] Book VIII gives us several fine passages, the picture of
the torchlight procession and service held in the camp on the
eve of battle, the thirst of the troops eagerly relieved by the
local peasants, and the curious story of the Emperor's suspected
nephew John Comnenus, with the intrusions and quarrels of
which the imperial tent is the scene.[8] Book IX has the really
thrilling account of Nicephorus Diogenes' rebellion: indeed the
episodes first of Alexius' narrow escape from being assassinated
at night, an escape due to the presence of a handmaid brushing
away the mosquitoes from the imperial pair as they sleep, then
of the audience in the great tent, where Alexius sits in irate
majesty on his throne and harangues the trembling malcontents, are among Anna's most successful pages.[9] Book X
has no less than six and a half chapters of sustained interest
about the coming of the Crusaders, of whom Bohemund is
portrayed with special care.[10] Book XI, though gory, is dull,
except for the description of the Greek fire-ships encountering
the Pisan fleet,[11] and for Bohemund's journey from Syria in
a coffin.[12] Book XII shows us the Empress in camp, and
also contains the vivid picture of the convicted Anemas
conspirators led with contumely through the town, while the
compassionate Anna hesitates to disturb on their behalf her
parents' prayers.[13] Book XIII is at first chiefly interesting as
showing Anna's own interest in Bohemund's siegecraft, of
which she gives three instances;[14] but then we get the amazingly
modern passage where minute points of 'protocole' almost bring
the whole peace-negotiations to grief,[15] and the great pen-picture
of the Norman prince.[16] Book XIV is raised from its low level of
long-windedness (with the Emperor's virtues and noble

[1] V. 8, 9.   [2] VI. 2.   [3] VI. 8.   [4] VII. 2.
[5] VII. 4.   [6] VII. 9.   [7] VII. 11.   [8] VIII. 5, 8.
[9] IX. 5–10, especially ch. 9.
[10] X. 5–11, especially 11, pp. 301–4. The story of the insolent Frankish Count
in ch. 10 is admirably told, as is also that of the fighting Latin priest hurling
stones and barley-loaves in ch. 8.
[11] XI. 10.   [12] XI. 12.   [13] XII. 3 and 6.   [14] XIII. 3.
[15] XIII. 9, 10.   [16] See pp. 473–4 above.

sentiments dwelt on *ad nauseam*) by the gem of the book, the account of Alexius sitting or standing all day and most of the night while the Crusaders talked and talked.[1] It seems worth while to give this passage in full:

'As soon as day came and directly the sun had leapt up over the Eastern horizon, he seated himself on the imperial throne, giving orders that all the Celts should come in each day unhindered, partly because he wanted them to set forth their demands, partly scheming to subdue them by all sorts of arguments. But the Celtic counts . . . did not make their approach to the Emperor in orderly fashion, but each of the counts came in bringing with him as many men as he wished, and the next came directly behind, and another after him again. And on coming in they did not make their discourse by the water-clock, as formerly was enjoined on orators, but however much time each one (whoever he was) desired for conversing with the Emperor, that he had . . . And when evening came [Alexius] who had remained without food all day stood up from his throne, turning to the imperial bed-chamber, but not even thus was he freed from the annoyance of the Celts. For while one hurried in before another, not only of those who had been left out of the day's interview but also of the others coming back and producing more and more verbal arguments, that man stood unmoved, enduring their immense loquacity, hemmed in by the Celts.'

After dwelling on his patience both in answering and in listening, while he stood like a statue often till the small hours, she points out:

'And they all when weary went often away and rested, and went in again reluctantly. Indeed after a while none of his own attendants were capable of such prolonged standing immovable, but all in turns shifted from one leg to the other; and one would sit down and another would bend his head and prop it up, and a third would lean against the wall. In face of this great fatigue the Emperor alone was staunch . . . For as the interview was with myriads of men, each one spoke much . . . and one departing handed on the talk to another and he passed it to a third and he again to a fourth. And for them the standing was at intervals, but he had limitless standing, up to the first or second cock-crowing. Then he rested a little, but when the sun rose again he seated himself on his throne and once more there were other labours and redoubled contests succeeding to those of the night.'

All this brought on the pain in his feet. 'But he was so patient that he never said a murmuring word . . . and if in any way a word of faint-heartedness escaped his lips, straightway he used the sign of the cross against the abominable demon, saving: "Avaunt from me, wicked one." '

[1] XIV. 4.

To set with this picture of passive endurance we get in the
next chapter a graphic description of the Emperor disabled
from riding by gout, but brave and active as ever:

'As if forgetting the pain that oppressed him he started on the road
leading to Nicaea in a covered chariot, holding on to the basket
frame (λύγον) with his right hand. Then the soldiers, taking up their
spears on their shoulders (reading ἐπ' ὤμων for τούτων), hastened in
companies after him, forming a row on each side. Some marched
alongside, some preceded him, some followed, rejoicing in his
expedition against the barbarians but sorrowing for the pain that
kept him from riding. He however spurred them all to courage
by signs and words, smiling and speaking to them with sweetness.'[1]

In Book XV, while the account of Alexius' Orphanage is
full of sound information uninterestingly stated,[2] the description of the execution of Basil the Bogomile is quite horribly
vivid.[3] After the heretic had been sentenced to death the
Emperor

'kindled an immense fire in the Hippodrome. Now an immense
trench had been dug and a mass of logs, all tall trees heaped up,
appeared a mountain in composition. Then when the pyre was
lighted the crowd came silently together in numbers on the floor
of the arena and on the steps, all waiting to see what was going to
happen. On the other side a cross had been erected and a choice
given to the impious man, if perchance fearing the fire and changing
his mind he should go to the cross, so that then he might become
free from the furnace. And the multitude of the heretics was present,
beholding their leader Basil. But he showed himself contemptuous
towards every punishment and threat, and when he was some way
off he laughed at the pyre and talked extravagantly, saying that
angels would snatch him from the midst of the fire, and he chanted
that word of David's: 'It shall not come nigh thee, only with thine
eyes shalt thou see.'   But when the crowd stood aside and allowed
him freely to see that terrible sight of the pyre (for from some
distance he perceived the fire and saw the flame rising and as it
were thundering, and sending out fiery fragments which rose to
the height of the stone pyramid standing in the middle of the
arena), then that bold man seemed to turn coward towards the
fire and to be troubled. For he rolled his eyes often and struck his
hands together and smote his thigh as though entirely confounded.
Yet even when he was in this state at the mere sight, he was as
though of adamant. For neither did the fire soften his iron soul nor
did the instructions of the Emperor transmitted to him charm him,
but either boundless folly seized him through his present need and
misfortunes, and he was thus astray in mind and could not take
any decision whatever about the best thing to do, or else, which

seems more probable, the devil that had seized his soul poured profound darkness on him. So that abominable Basil stood helpless against every threat and every fear, and now gaped towards the pyre, now towards the bystanders. And to all he truly appeared mad, neither hastening to the pyre nor turning altogether back, but he stuck fast and was immovable on the spot where he had first arrived. Now when much talk was going on and his extravagant discourses were borne about on every tongue, the executioners feared lest perhaps the demons round Basil might do some strange wonder by the permission of God, and this scoundrel might be seen coming into some very public place unharmed from the midst of so great a fire, and the last error might be worse than the first. So they resolved to make an experiment. For as he talked extravagantly and boasted that he would be seen unharmed in the midst of the fire, they took up his gown and said: 'Let us see if the fire will not catch thy clothes.' And straightway they threw it into the middle of the furnace. However Basil was so entirely buoyed up by the demon that was deceiving him as to say: 'See the gown flying up into the air.' They then understanding what the stuff was from its hem[1] lifted him and thrust him, clothes and shoes and all, into the midst of the furnace. And to such an extent did the flame (as though enraged against him) devour the impious man, that there was neither smell nor any other novel appearance in the smoke, except only a fine smoky line in the middle of the flame. For even the elements are roused up against the impious, but they truly spare those dear to God, as once they yielded and submitted to those God-beloved youths in Babylon, and the fire enclosed them like some golden bed. Therefore before those who had raised him had got this deceiver Basil in the right position, the flame seemed to leap forward to seize that ungodly man. As for the remaining number, all who shared in the corruption of Basil, the crowd standing by was panting and struggling to throw them also on the fire, but the Emperor did not allow it, and ordered them to be shut up in the porches and colonnades of the Great Palace. And when this was done the spectators dispersed.'

Finally in the same Book parts of Alexius' last illness are made to stand out before us as though they had happened yesterday.[2] 'Then at that time every doctor was summoned and the illness of the Emperor was laid before them as a subject of discussion. And they were parted and divided in opinions, and one diagnosed one thing and one another and each tried to adapt the treatment to the diagnosis.' The sick man's gasping for breath, with 'some pitying sleep' only serving to

[1] See p. 513 above.
[2] XV. 11. The vividness and the conviction it carries have been dwelt on already, but repetition must be pardoned on a point so vital to our whole estimate of the writer.

increase the choking, the failure of phlebotomy and cautery and drugs, even though the family for a time was wild with joy over the apparent success of a 'remedy with pepper' and consequently offered up a χαριστήριον to God, the restlessness that made him crave to be carried from room to room, what nurse or doctor is not alive to the modernness of it all? We can almost see the princess Anna, 'despising philosophy and learning', trying to get liquid down the patient's swollen throat, or feeling his pulse and watching his breathing in momentary expectation of the end. We have all been acquainted with doctors who 'dissembled over the crisis, and suggested hopes that did not appear sound' in order to prevent some devoted wife from breaking down. Even in the present age of trained nurses we can still parallel the loving daughter who holds up her dying father so that he may drink, sprinkles him in his faintness with rose water and tactfully stands between him and her anguished mother to screen her from the sight of the death agony. The picture has a poignant pathos which cannot be altogether destroyed even by the wretched state of the text, or still more by the rhetorical bombast of Anna's peroration, as of a dirge made to order. She was a princess and a scholar writing a language she did not speak, and bitter personal resentments cumber her style still further, but under it all any one not morally deaf can detect the cry of genuine grief. He that hath ears to hear, let him hear.

Such then is a catalogue of Anna Comnena's outstanding passages, and the number may be said to err greatly on the side of under-statement. Are they not enough to entitle any writer to rank among the great historians, among those who make the dry bones of past ages live?

Sir William Ramsay in one of his books[1] has a passage which may be justly applied to our authoress. He speaks of 'historical work of the highest order, in which a writer commands excellent means of knowledge either through personal acquaintance or through access to original authorities, and brings to the treatment of his subject genius, literary skill, and sympathetic historical insight into human character and the movement of events'. Anna Comnena certainly had excellent means of knowledge, she certainly had literary skill; her characters live for us, and she shows the 'infinite capacity for taking pains' with which genius has been identified. Surely no more is needed to give her forever on Parnassus the place which her own age awarded to her as the Tenth Muse.

[1] *St. Paul the Traveller*, p. 2.

BIBLIOGRAPHY

Académie roumaine—Bulletin. Tome XI. Bukharest, 1924.

ADAM, Paul: *Princesses byzantines.* Paris, 1893.

AESCHYLUS: *Plays,* in Dindorf, *Poetae Sc. Gr.,* 5th ed., 1869.

ANON.: *L'art de vérifier les dates,* 3rd ed. 1783.

Anonymi Barensis Chronicon in Muratori, *Scriptores Rerum Italicarum,* Vol. V.

Anonymi gesta Francorum, ed. (1) B. A. Lees, (2) L. Bréhier.

Anonymou Synopsis Chronike, ed. C. Sathas, in *Bibliotheca Graeca medii aevi,* Vol. VII, 1894.

Anthologia Palatina.

Archives de l'Orient latin, I, 1881 and II, 1884.

ARISTOPHANES: *Plays* in Dindorf, *Poetae Sc. Gr.,* 5th ed., 1869.

ARISTOTLE: *Works,* ed. Teubner.

ATTALIATES, Michael: *History,* ed. Bekker, 1853, in *C. S. H. B.*

BARKER, Ernest: *The Crusades,* 1923, in The World's Manuals.

BAYNES, N. H.: *The Byzantine Empire,* 1925. (Home University Library.)

BEZOBRAZOV, P.: Article on Psellus' Discourse (unpublished) on the Miracle of Blachernae, in *Journ. of Ministry of Publ. Instruction.* St. Petersburg, March, 1889.

Bibliotheca Graeca medii aevi = B. G. Med., ed. C. Sathas.

BIDEZ, J.: *Vie de Porphyre.* Univ. de Gand, Recueil de travaux, publ. par la Faculté de Philosophie et Lettres; Fasc. 43 (1913).

BOISSONADE, J. F.: *Anecdota Graeca.* Paris, 1829–33.

—— *Psellus de operatione daemonum, etc.* Nüremberg, 1838.

BOISSONNADE, P.: *Le travail dans l'Europe chrétienne au moyen âge.* Paris, 1921.

BOUILLET, M. N.: *Ennéades de Plotin.* Paris, 1857–61.

BRÉHIER, Louis: *Histoire anonyme de la première Croisade.* Paris, 1924.

—— *L'Église et l'Orient.* Paris, 1907.

BRIGHT, W.: *Canons of the first four General Councils.* 2nd ed., 1892.

BROWN, Horatio: *The Venetian Republic,* 1902. (Temple Primers.)

BRYENNIUS, Nicephorus: *Hyle,* ed. Meineke, 1836, in *C. S. H. B.*

Bulletin de l'inst. archéol. russe de C'ple, Vol. II, 1897, XIII, 1908.

BURKITT, F. C.: *Religion of the Manichees.* Cambridge, 1925.

BURY, J. B.: *Imperial administrative system in the Ninth Century.* (Brit. Acad. Suppl. Papers, 1911.)

—— Notes on Text of Anna Comnena (*B. Z.* II).

—— Notes on Gibbon's *Decline and Fall.* Latest ed., 1909–14.

—— in *The Hellenistic Age.* Cambridge, 1923.

Byzantinisches Archiv, Leipzig, 1898–

B. Z. = Byzantinische Zeitschrift, Leipzig, 1892–

CALLICLES, Nicolas: *Poems,* ed. by Leo Sternbach, q. v.

Cambridge Mediaeval History, Vols. IV, V.
CECAUMENUS: *Strategicon* and *Logos Nouthetetikos*, ed. B. Wassiliewsky. St. Petersburg, 1896.
CEDRENUS, Georgius: *Synopsis Historiarum*, ed. Bekker, 1838–9, in *C. S. H. B.*
CHALANDON, F.: *Histoire de la domination normande.* Paris, 1907.
—— *Essai sur le règne d'Alexis Ier Comnène.* Paris, 1900.
—— *Jean II Comnène et Manuel Ier Comnène.* Paris, 1912.
—— *Histoire de la première Croisade* (posthumous). Paris, 1925.
CHRIST and PARANIKAS: *Anth. Gr. carminum Christianorum.* Leipzig, 1871.
CINNAMUS, Ioannes: *History*, ed. Meineke, 1836, in *C. S. H. B.*
COMNENA, Anna: *Alexias.* 2 vols., ed. A. Reifferscheid, Leipzig, 1884. Also 2 vols. in *C. S. H. B.*, ed. Schopenus and Reifferscheid, 1839–78. Also in *P. G.* 131.
—— *Prologue* to her Will, ed. E. Kurtz. *B. Z.* XVI.
COMNENUS, Alexius: *Discourse against the Armenians*, in *Analecta Hierosol. Stach.*, I, ed. A. Papadopulos-Kerameus. St. Petersburg, 1891.
—— *Novels*, in *Jus Graeco-Romanum* of K. E. Zachariae von Lingenthal. Leipzig, 1856–84 and in *P. G.* 127.
—— *Mousai Alexiades Komneniades*, ed. P. Maas. *B. Z.* XXII.
CONSTANTINE PORPHYROGENITUS: *de Cerimoniis*; *de Thematibus*; *de Administrando imperio*, in *Works* (*C. S. H. B.*, 3 vols., 1829–40).
C. S. H. B. = *Corpus Scriptorum Historiae Byzantinae.* Bonn, 1828–97.
DALTON, O. M.: *East Christian Art.* Oxford, 1925.
DAMASCIUS: *Problèmes et solutions touchant les premiers principes*, trans. A. E. Chaignet, 1898.
DAWES, E. A. S.: *The Alexiad.* London 1928.
DIEHL, C.: *Byzance.* Paris, 1919.
—— in *Camb. Med. Hist.* IV.
—— *Études byzantines.* Paris, 1905.
—— *Figures byzantines*, 2 series, 1906–8.
—— *Histoire de l'empire byzantin.* Paris, 1919.
—— *Manuel d'art byzantin*, 2nd ed. Paris, 1925.
DIETER, K.: *Zur Glaubwürdigkeit der Anna Comnena* (*B. Z.* III).
DÖLGER, Fr.: *Beiträge zur Geschichte der byzantinischen Finanzenverwaltung besonders der 10. und 11. Jahrh.* (in *Byz. Arch.*, 1927).
—— *Regesten der Kaiserurkunden des oström. Reiches* von 565–1453. (Corpus der gr. Urkunden des Mittelalters, Reihe A, Abt. 1. Munich, 1924).
DU CANGE, C. du Fresne: *Constantinopolis Christiana* = Pt. II of his *Historia Byzantina.* Paris, 1680.
—— Notes on the *Alexias*, given in the *C. S. H. B.* edition.
DU SOMMERARD, Louis: *Anne Comnène.* Paris, 1907.
EBERSOLT, J.: *Sanctuaires de Byzance*, 1921.
EKKEHARDUS URAUGIENSIS: *Hierosolymita*, in *Hist. Occ. des croisades*, Vol. V. Paris, 1895.
Encyclopaedia Britannica, 11th ed.

EURIPIDES : *Plays*, and *Fragments*, in Dindorf, *Poetae Sc. Gr.*, 5th ed. 1869.

EUSTATHIUS of Thessalonica : Works in *P. G.* 135, 136, and in *Fontes Rer. Byz.*, q. v.

FABRICIUS : *Bibliotheca Graeca*, ed. G. C. Harles. Hamburg, 1790.

Fontes Rerum Byzantinarum, ed. W. Regel. St. Petersburg, 1892.

FUCHS, Fr. : *Die höheren Schulen von K'pel im Mittelalter* in *Byz. Arch.*, 1926.

FULCHERUS CARNOTENSIS : *Historia Hierosolymitana*, ed. H. Hagenmeyer, 1913.

GAY, Jules : *L'Italie méridionale et l'Empire byzantin.* Paris, 1904.

G. B. L., v. KRUMBACHER.

GIBBON, E. : *Decline and Fall of the Roman Empire*, ed. in 7 vols. by J. B. Bury, latest ed. 1909–14.

GLYCAS, Michael : *Biblos Chronike*, ed. Bekker, 1836, in *C. S. H. B.*

GRENIER, Pierre : *L'empire byzantin*, 1904.

GULIELMUS APULIENSIS : *De Rebus Normannorum* (in Muratori, *Scriptores Rerum Italicarum*, Vol. V.

HAGENMEYER, H. : *Kreuzzugsbriefe.* Innsbruck, 1901.

HART, G. : Suppl. Vol. XII (1881) of *Jahrb. für class. Philologie.*

HEUZEY, L. : *Mission archéologique de Macédoine*, 1876.

HOLMES, E. : *The Albigensian or Catharist Heresy.* London, 1925.

HOMER : *Iliad* and *Odyssey.*

IAMBLICHUS : *Works*, ed. N. Festa.

IRENE, Empress : *Typikon*, in *P. G.* 127.

JEANSELME, Dr. E. : *Les calendriers de régime à l'usage des Byzantins* (in *Mélanges offerts à M. Gustave Schlumberger*). Paris, 1924.

JOHN OF EPIPHANIA : *Fragment*, in *Hist. Gr. Min. I.*

KRUMBACHER, K. : *Geschichte der byzantinischen Litteratur*, 2nd ed. Munich, 1897, = *G. B. L.*

—— *Mittelgriechische Sprichwörter* in *Sitzungsberichte zu München*, 1888 and 1893.

KURTZ, E. : *Unedierte Texte* in *B. Z.* XVI.

LAURENT, J. : *Byzance et les Turcs seldjoucides* (in *Annales de l'Est.*) Nancy, 1913.

LE BARBIER, E. : *St. Christodule et la réforme des couvents grecs.* Paris, 1863.

LEES, B. A. : ed. *Anonymi gesta Francorum.* Oxford, 1924.

LEIB, Bernard : *Rome, Kiev et Byzance.* Paris, 1924.

LEO (III, the Isaurian) : *Tactica*, in Migne, *P. G.* 107.

MAAS, P. : *Mousai Alexiades Komneniades*, in *B. Z.* XXII.

MACARIUS MAGNES : *Works*, ed. C. Blondel. Paris, 1876.

MALATERRA, Gaufredus : *Historia Sicula* (in Muratori, *Scriptores Rerum Italicarum*, Vol. V).

McCABE, Joseph : *The Empresses of Constantinople.* London, 1913.

Mélanges offerts à M. Gustave Schlumberger. Paris, 1924.

MIGNE, J. P. : *Patrologia Graeca* = *P. G.*

—— *Patrologia latina* = *P. L.*

MILLER, William : *A Byzantine Blue-stocking, Anna Comnena*, in *Quarterly Review*, January 1920.

MITCHISON, N.: *Anna Comnena*. 1928. (Representative Women Series).

MORDTMANN, DR. A.: *Esquisse topographique de Constantinople*. Lille, 1892.

NEUMANN, C.: *Die Weltstellung des byzantinischen Reiches*. Leipzig, 1894.

—— *Griechische Geschichtschreiber des 12. Jahrhunderts*. Leipzig, 1888.

NICETAS (Acominatus or Choniates): *Lives of Emperors*, ed. Bekker, 1835, in *C. S. H. B.*

—— *Thesaurus orthodoxae fidei* and other theological works; in *P. G.* 139, 140.

Notices et extraits de la bibl. impériale, Vol. VIII. Paris, 1810.

OECONOMOS, L.: *La vie religieuse dans l'Empire byzantin*. Paris, 1918.

OMAN, Sir Charles: *The Art of War*, 2nd ed., 1924.

—— *The Byzantine Empire*, 1892. (Story of the Nations Series.)

ORDERICUS VITALIS: *Historia ecclesiastica*, in *P. L.* 188.

OSTER, E.: *Anna Komnena*. Rastatt, 1868–71.

OTTLEY, R. L.: *Doctrine of the Incarnation*, 2nd ed. 1902.

OUSPENSKY, Th.: *Synodikon for the 1st Sunday in Lent*, in *Journal of the Univ. of Odessa*, Vol. LIX, 1893.

—— *Trial of Italus*, in *Bull. de l'inst. archéol. russe de C'ple*. Vol. II, 1897.

PASPATES, A.: *Byzantinai Meletai*. Constantinople, 1877.

P. G. = (Migne's) *Patrologia Graeca*, in 166 vols.

PHOTIUS: *Opera*. *P. G.* 101.

PIRENNE, H.: *Apropos de la lettre d'Alexis Ier Comnène à Robert le Frison* (in *Revue de l'instruction publique en Belgique*, Vol. L, 1907).

P. L. = (Migne's) *Patrologia Latina*, in 221 vols.

PLATO: *Dialogues*, trans. B. Jowett. 2nd ed. 1875.

PLOTINUS: *Enneades*, ed. R. Volkmann (preceded by Porphyry's *Vita Plotini*). Leipzig, 1883. See also BOUILLET.

PLUTARCH: *Lives*, ed. Sintenis, and *Moralia*, ed. Bernardakis.

POLYBIUS: *History*, ed. L. Dinforf.

PORPHYRY: *Opuscula selecta*, ed. A. Nauck. (*See also* Plotinus *and* Macarius Magnes.)

PROCLUS: *In Platonis theologiam*, ed. Portus, 1618. Also *Works*, ed. G. Friedlein.

PRODROMUS, Theodore: Hitherto unpublished writings, ed. by E. Kurtz (*B. Z.* XVI).

—— *Works*, in Migne, *P. G.* 133.

—— *Works*, in *Notices et Extraits*, Vol. VIII.

—— *Poèmes Prodromiques en grec vulgaire*, ed. Hesseling and Perrot. Amsterdam, 1910.

PSELLUS, Michael: *Chronography* (or *History*), ed. C. Sathas, 1899 (in Byzantine Texts Series, ed. J. B. Bury).

—— *De operatione daemonum*, etc., ed. J. F. Boissonade. Nüremberg, 1838.

PSELLUS, Michael: *Works* (in *B. G. Med.* IV, V; *P. G.* 122).

PULLAN, L.: *The Church of the Fathers*, 5th ed., 1925.

RAIMUNDUS D'AGUILERS: *Historia Francorum qui ceperunt Hierusalem* (in *Historiens occidentaux des Croisades*, Vol. III).

RAMBAUD, A.: *Michel Psellos*, in *Revue Historique*, III, 1877.

RAMSAY, Sir William: *Historical Geography of Asia Minor* (Royal Geographical Society Supplementary Papers, Vol. IV). London, 1890.

REGEL, W.: *Fontes rerum Byzantinarum* (ed.). St. Petersburg, 1892.

RENAULD, E.: *Étude de la langue et du style de Michel Psellos*. Paris, 1920.

RIANT, le Comte P.: *Dépouilles religieuses enlevées à Constantinople*. Paris, 1875.

—— *Epistula spuria Alexii ad Robertum*. Paris, 1879.

—— *Expéditions et pélerinages des Scandinaves*. Paris, 1865.

—— *Inventaire des lettres historiques des Croisades* (*Archives de l'Orient latin, I*), 1881.

Russian Archaeological Institute in Constantinople.—See Bulletin.

SATHAS, C. N.: *Bibliotheca Graeca medii aevi* = *B. G. Med.*

SCHEMMEL, F.: *Die Hochschule von K'pel vom 5. bis 9. Jahrh.* Berlin, 1912.

—— *Die Schulen von K'pel im 12. bis 15. Jahrh.*, in *Philolog. Wochenschrift*, Feb. 21, 1925.

SCHILLER, F. von: *Allgemeine Sammlung historischer Mémoires vom 12ten Jahrhundert bis auf die neuesten Zeiten.*

SCHLUMBERGER, G.: *Monuments numismatiques et sphragistiques* (in *Revue archéologique*, Oct. 1880).

—— *Récits de Byzance et des Croisades*. 2 series. Paris, 1917–22.

—— *Sigillographie de l'empire byzantin*. Paris, 1884.

SCOTT, Sir Walter: *Count Robert of Paris.*

SCYLITZES, Johannes: *History*, in CEDRENUS (q. v.).

SEGER, J.: *Byzantinische Historiker der 10ten und 11ten Jahrh., I. Nikephoros Bryennios*. Munich, 1888.

SHAKESPEARE, William: *Plays* (Handy Volume ed.)

SOPHOCLES: *Plays*, in Dindorf, *Poetae Sc. Gr.* 5th ed. 1869.

SOPHOCLES, E. A.: *Greek Lexicon*. Cambridge, Mass., 1914.

STEMPLINGER, E.: *Das Plagiat in der griechischen Litteratur*. Leipzig, 1912.

STERNBACH, Leo: *Poems of Nicolas Callicles*. Rosprawy Akad. Umiejet. wydzial filol. (Krakow), Ser. II. XXI. 1903, p. 360.

Synodikon, v. OUSPENSKY.

THEOPHYLACT: *Works*, in *P. G.*, Vols. 123 and 126.

THUCYDIDES: *History*, trans. B. Jowett, 2nd ed., 1900.

TOUT, T. F.: *The Empire and the Papacy*. London, 1921.

Trial of Italus, v. OUSPENSKY.

ZACHARIAE VON LINGENTHAL, K. E.: *Geschichte des griechisch-römischen Rechts*. 3rd ed. Berlin, 1892.

—— *Jus Graeco-Romanum*, in 7 parts. Leipzig, 1856–84.

ZIGABENUS, Euthymius: *Confutatio; Expositio Symboli; Disputatio de Fide*: in *P. G.* 131.
—— *Panoplia*, in *P. G.* 130.
ZONARAS, Ioannes: *Epitome*, Vol. III, ed. Büttner-Wobst, 1897, in *C. S. H. B.*

NOTE: In citations from the *Alexias*, the Roman numerals denote the Book, the Arabic the chapter (as in *C. S. H. B.*, and in Reifferscheid's edition), while 'p.' refers to the page of the original Paris edition of 1651.

INDEX

INDEX TO GREEK WORDS

OTHER TITLES IN THIS HARDBACK REPRINT PROGRAMME FROM
SANDPIPER BOOKS LTD (LONDON) AND POWELLS BOOKS (CHICAGO)

ISBN 0–19–	Author	Title
8143567	ALFÖLDI A.	The Conversion of Constantine and Pagan Rome
9241775	ALLEN T.W	Homeri Ilias (3 volumes)
6286409	ANDERSON George K.	The Literature of the Anglo-Saxons
8219601	ARNOLD Benjamin	German Knighthood
8208618	ARNOLD T.W.	The Caliphate
8228813	BARTLETT & MacKAY	Medieval Frontier Societies
8219733	BARTLETT Robert	Trial by Fire and Water
8111010	BETHURUM Dorothy	Homilies of Wulfstan
8142765	BOLLING G. M.	External Evidence for Interpolation in Homer
814332X	BOLTON J.D.P.	Aristeas of Proconnesus
9240132	BOYLAN Patrick	Thoth, the Hermes of Egypt
8114222	BROOKS Kenneth R.	Andreas and the Fates of the Apostles
8214715	BUCKLER Georgina	Anna Comnena
8203543	BULL Marcus	Knightly Piety & Lay Response to the First Crusade
8216785	BUTLER Alfred J.	Arab Conquest of Egypt
8148046	CAMERON Alan	Circus Factions
8148054	CAMERON Alan	Porphyrius the Charioteer
8148348	CAMPBELL J.B.	The Emperor and the Roman Army 31 BC to 235
826643X	CHADWICK Henry	Priscillian of Avila
826447X	CHADWICK Henry	Boethius
8222025	COLGRAVE B. & MYNORS R.A.B.	Bede's Ecclesiastical History of the English People
8131658	COOK J.M.	The Troad
8219393	COWDREY H.E.J.	The Age of Abbot Desiderius
8644043	CRUM W.E.	Coptic Dictionary
8148992	DAVIES M.	Sophocles: Trachiniae
825301X	DOWNER L.	Leges Henrici Primi
814346X	DRONKE Peter	Medieval Latin and the Rise of European Love-Lyric
8142749	DUNBABIN T.J.	The Western Greeks
8154372	FAULKNER R.O.	The Ancient Egyptian Pyramid Texts
8221541	FLANAGAN Marie Therese	Irish Society, Anglo-Norman Settlers, Angevin Kingship
8143109	FRAENKEL Edward	Horace
8201540	GOLDBERG P.J.P.	Women, Work and Life Cycle in a Medieval Economy
8140215	GOTTSCHALK H.B.	Heraclides of Pontus
8266162	HANSON R.P.C.	Saint Patrick
8224354	HARRISS G.L.	King, Parliament and Public Finance in Medieval England to 1369
8581114	HEATH Sir Thomas	Aristarchus of Samos
8140444	HOLLIS A.S.	Callimachus: Hecale
8212968	HOLLISTER C. Warren	Anglo-Saxon Military Institutions
8226470	HOULDING J.A.	Fit for Service
2115480	HENRY Blanche	British Botanical and Horticultural Literature before 1800
8219523	HOUSLEY Norman	The Italian Crusades
8223129	HURNARD Naomi	The King's Pardon for Homicide – before AD 1307
9241783	HURRY Jamieson B.	Imhotep
8140401	HUTCHINSON G.O.	Hellenistic Poetry
9240140	JOACHIM H.H.	Aristotle: On Coming-to-be and Passing-away
9240094	JONES A.H.M	Cities of the Eastern Roman Provinces
8142560	JONES A.H.M.	The Greek City
8218354	JONES Michael	Ducal Brittany 1364–1399
8271484	KNOX & PELCZYNSKI	Hegel's Political Writings
8212755	LAWRENCE C.H.	St Edmund of Abingdon
8225253	LE PATOUREL John	The Norman Empire
8212720	LENNARD Reginald	Rural England 1086–1135
8212321	LEVISON W.	England and the Continent in the 8th century
8148224	LIEBESCHUETZ J.H.W.G.	Continuity and Change in Roman Religion
8143486	LINDSAY W.M.	Early Latin Verse
8141378	LOBEL Edgar & PAGE Sir Denys	Poetarum Lesbiorum Fragmenta
9240159	LOEW E.A.	The Beneventan Script
8241445	LUKASIEWICZ, Jan	Aristotle's Syllogistic
8152442	MAAS P. & TRYPANIS C.A .	Sancti Romani Melodi Cantica
8142684	MARSDEN E.W.	Greek and Roman Artillery—Historical
8142692	MARSDEN E.W.	Greek and Roman Artillery—Technical
8148178	MATTHEWS John	Western Aristocracies and Imperial Court AD 364–425
9240205	MAVROGORDATO John	Digenes Akrites
8223447	McFARLANE K.B.	Lancastrian Kings and Lollard Knights
8226578	McFARLANE K.B.	The Nobility of Later Medieval England
814296X	MEIGGS Russell	The Athenian Empire
8148100	MEIGGS Russell	Roman Ostia
8148402	MEIGGS Russell	Trees and Timber in the Ancient Mediterranean World

8141718	MERKELBACH R. & WEST M.L.	Fragmenta Hesiodea
8143362	MILLAR F.G.B.	Casssius Dio
8142641	MILLER J. Innes	The Spice Trade of the Roman Empire
8147813	MOORHEAD John	Theoderic in Italy
8264259	MOORMAN John	A History of the Franciscan Order
8181469	MORISON Stanley	Politics and Script
9240582	MUSURILLO H.	Acts of the Pagan Martyrs & Christian Martyrs (2 vols)
9240213	MYRES J.L.	Herodotus The Father of History
9241791	NEWMAN W.L.	The Politics of Aristotle (4 volumes)
8219512	OBOLENSKY Dimitri	Six Byzantine Portraits
8270259	O'DONNELL J.J.	Augustine: Confessions (3 vols)
263268X	OSLER Sir William	Bibliotheca Osleriana
8116020	OWEN A.L.	The Famous Druids
8131445	PALMER, L.R.	The Interpretation of Mycenaean Greek Texts
8143427	PFEIFFER R.	History of Classical Scholarship (vol 1)
8143648	PFEIFFER Rudolf	History of Classical Scholarship 1300–1850
8111649	PHEIFER J.D.	Old English Glosses in the Epinal-Erfurt Glossary
8142277	PICKARD–CAMBRIDGE A.W.	Dithyramb Tragedy and Comedy
8269765	PLATER & WHITE	Grammar of the Vulgate
8213891	PLUMMER Charles	Lives of Irish Saints (2 vols)
820695X	POWICKE Michael	Military Obligation in Medieval England
8269684	POWICKE Sir Maurice	Stephen Langton
821460X	POWICKE Sir Maurice	The Christian Life in the Middle Ages
8225369	PRAWER Joshua	Crusader Institutions
8225571	PRAWER Joshua	The History of The Jews in the Latin Kingdom of Jerusalem
8143249	RABY F.J.E.	A History of Christian Latin Poetry
8143257	RABY F.J.E.	A History of Secular Latin Poetry in the Middle Ages (2 vols)
8214316	RASHDALL & POWICKE	The Universities of Europe in the Middle Ages (3 vols)
8154488	REYMOND E.A.E & BARNS J.W.B.	Four Martyrdoms from the Pierpont Morgan Coptic Codices
8148380	RICKMAN Geoffrey	The Corn Supply of Ancient Rome
8141556	ROSS Sir David	Aristotle: De Anima
8141076	ROSS Sir David	Aristotle: Metaphysics (2 vols)
8141092	ROSS Sir David	Aristotle: Physics
8142307	ROSTOVTZEFF M.	Social and Economic History of the Hellenistic World, 3 vols.
8142315	ROSTOVTZEFF M.	Social and Economic History of the Roman Empire, 2 vols.
8264178	RUNCIMAN Sir Steven	The Eastern Schism
814833X	SALMON J.B.	Wealthy Corinth
8171587	SALZMAN L.F.	Building in England Down to 1540
8218362	SAYERS Jane E.	Papal Judges Delegate in the Province of Canterbury 1198–1254
8221657	SCHEIN Sylvia	Fideles Crucis
8148135	SHERWIN WHITE A.N.	The Roman Citizenship
825153X	SHERWIN WHITE A.N.	Roman Society and Roman Law in the New Testament
9240167	SINGER Charles	Galen: On Anatomical Procedures
8113927	SISAM, Kenneth	Studies in the History of Old English Literature
8642040	SOUTER Alexander	A Glossary of Later Latin to 600 AD
8270011	SOUTER Alexander	Earliest Latin Commentaries on the Epistles of St Paul
8222254	SOUTHERN R.W.	Eadmer: Life of St. Anselm
8251408	SQUIBB G.	The High Court of Chivalry
8212011	STEVENSON & WHITELOCK	Asser's Life of King Alfred
8212011	SWEET Henry	A Second Anglo-Saxon Reader—Archaic and Dialectical
8148259	SYME Sir Ronald	History in Ovid
8143273	SYME Sir Ronald	Tacitus (2 vols)
8142714	THOMPSON E.A.	The Goths in Spain
8200951	THOMPSON Sally	Women Religious
924023X	WALBANK F.W.	Historical Commentary on Polybius (3 vols)
8201745	WALKER Simon	The Lancastrian Affinity 1361–1399
8161115	WELLESZ Egon	A History of Byzantine Music and Hymnography
8140185	WEST M.L.	Greek Metre
8141696	WEST M.L.	Hesiod: Theogony
8148542	WEST M.L.	The Orphic Poems
8140053	WEST M.L.	Hesiod: Works & Days
8152663	WEST M.L.	Iambi et Elegi Graeci
9240221	WHEELWRIGHT Philip	Heraclitus
822799X	WHITBY M. & M.	The History of Theophylact Simocatta
8206186	WILLIAMSON, E.W.	Letters of Osbert of Clare
8208103	WILSON F.P.	Plague in Shakespeare's London
8247672	WOODHOUSE C.M.	Gemistos Plethon
8114877	WOOLF Rosemary	The English Religious Lyric in the Middle Ages
8119224	WRIGHT Joseph	Grammar of the Gothic Language